A-Z WARWICK

CONTENTS

Key to Map Pages	2-5
Map Pages	6-134
Large Scale Coventry Centre	135
Large Scale Stratford-upon-Avon Centre	136-137
Road Map Pa... (Reference - ...)	
Index to Stre...	
Index to Hospitals & Hospices	192

REFERENCE

Motorway	M6
Primary Route	A46
A Road	A5
Under Construction	
Proposed	
B Road	B4455
Dual Carriageway	
One-way Street Traffic flow on A Roads is also indicated by a heavy line on the driver's left	
City Centre Ring Road & Junction Numbers	1
Restricted Access	
Pedestrianized Road	
Track / Footpath	
Residential Walkway	
Cycleway (Selected)	
Railway	Station, Heritage Station, Level Crossing, Tunnel
Built-up Area	HOOPER STREET
Local Authority Boundary	
Posttown Boundary	
Postcode Boundary within Posttown	
Map Continuation	40; Large Scale City Centre 135; Road Map Pages 144

Airport	
Car Park (Selected)	P
Church or Chapel	†
Fire Station	
Hospital	H
House Numbers (A & B Roads only)	20 40
Information Centre	i
Junction Name (M6 Toll only)	DUNTON INTERCHANGE
National Grid Reference	430
Park & Ride	P+R
Police Station	▲
Post Box (Stratford-upon-Avon Large Scale only)	✉
Post Office	★
Public Telephone (Stratford-upon-Avon Large Scale only)	
Toilet: without facilities for the Disabled	▽
with facilities for the Disabled	▽
Viewpoint	
Educational Establishment	
Hospital or Hospice	
Industrial Building	
Leisure or Recreational Facility	
Place of Interest	
Public Building	
Shopping Centre or Market	
Other Selected Buildings	

SCALES

Map Pages 6-134	Coventry City Centre Page 135	Stratford-upon-Avon Town Centre Pages 136-137
1:16,896 3¾ inches (9.52cm) to 1mile	1:8,448 7½ inches (19cm) to 1mile	1:4,224 15 inches (38.1cm) to 1mile
5.9cm to 1km	11.8cm to 1km	23.6cm to 1km
0 – ¼ Mile	0 – 100 – 200 Yards	0 – 50 – 100 Yards
0 – 250 Metres	0 – 100 – 200 Metres	0 – 50 – 100 Metres

Copyright of Geographers' A-Z Map Company Ltd.

Fairfield Road, Borough Green, Sevenoaks, Kent TN15 8PP
Telephone: 01732 781000 (Enquiries & Trade Sales)
01732 783422 (Retail Sales)
www.a-zmaps.co.uk

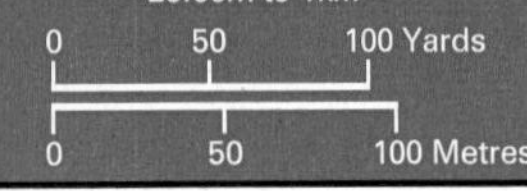

EDITION 1 2006

KEY TO MAP PAGES

North Section

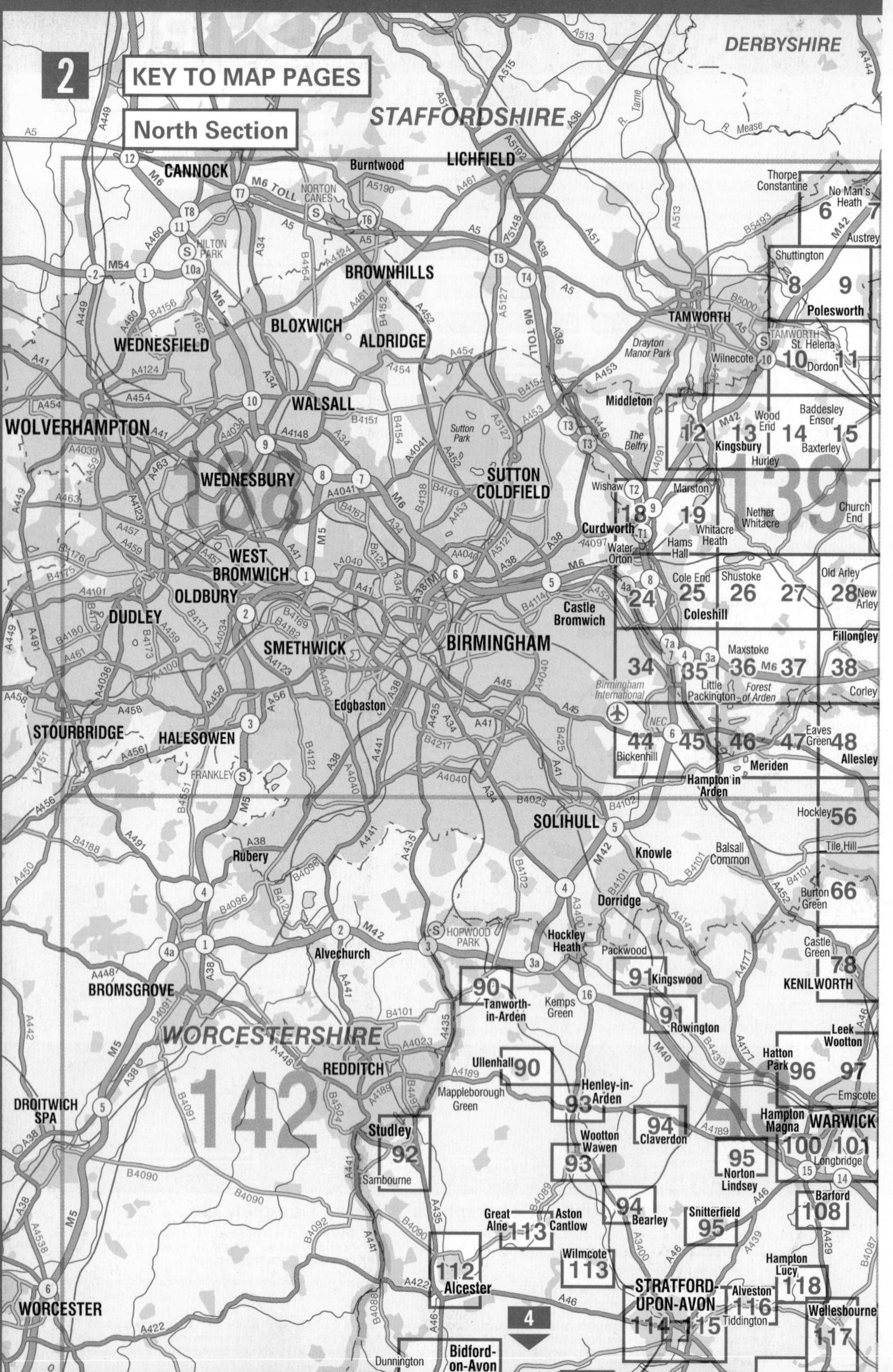

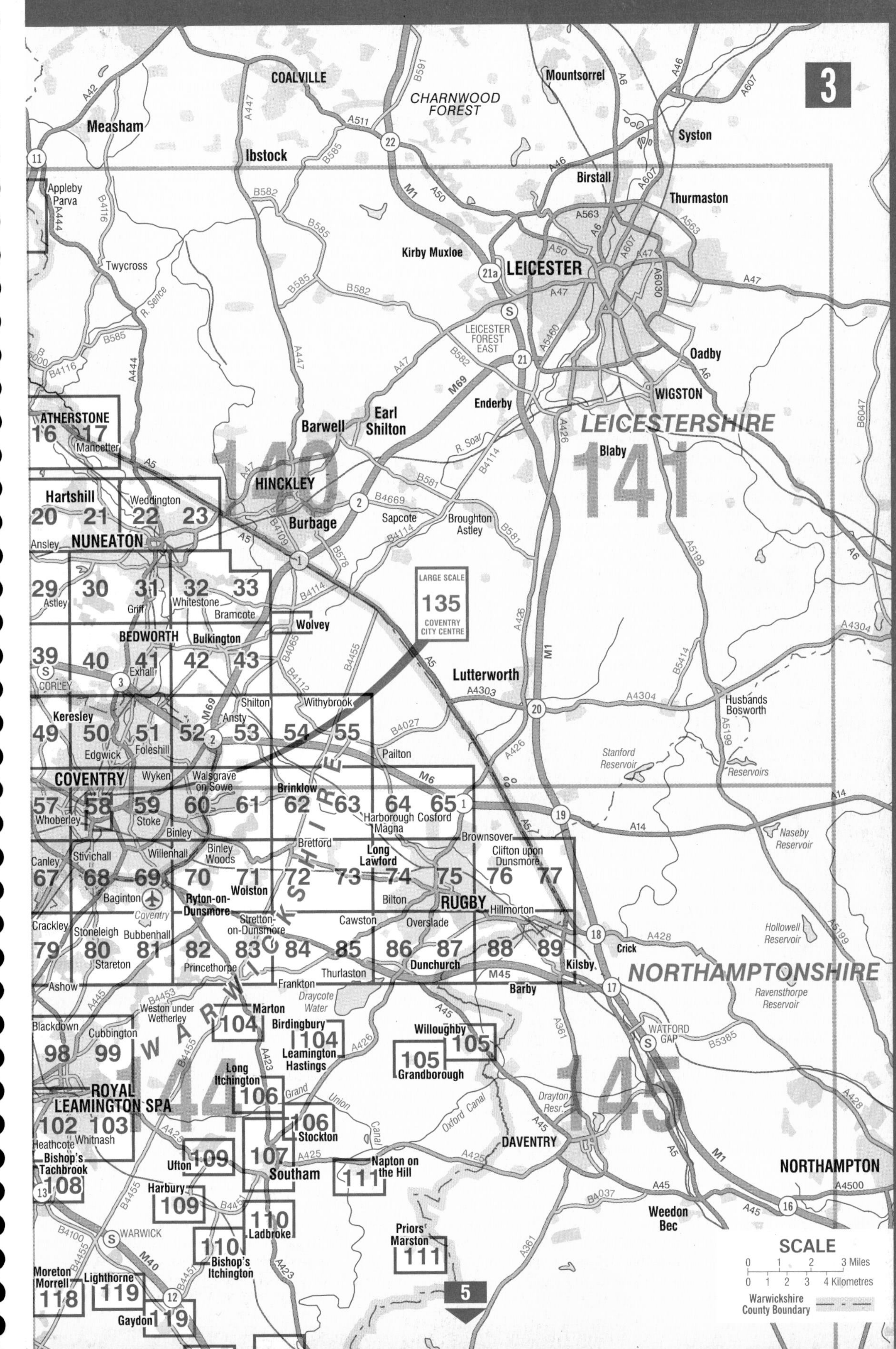
3
COALVILLE
Mountsorrel
CHARNWOOD FOREST
Measham
Ibstock
Syston
Birstall
Thurmaston
Appleby Parva
Twycross
Kirby Muxloe
LEICESTER
LEICESTER FOREST EAST
Oadby
WIGSTON
Enderby
LEICESTERSHIRE
Blaby
141
140
Barwell
Earl Shilton
HINCKLEY
Burbage
Sapcote
Broughton Astley
ATHERSTONE
Mancetter
Hartshill
Weddington
NUNEATON
Ansley
Astley
Griff
Whitestone
Bramcote
Wolvey
BEDWORTH
Bulkington
Exhall
CORLEY
LARGE SCALE
135
COVENTRY CITY CENTRE
Lutterworth
Husbands Bosworth
Keresley
Edgwick
Foleshill
Shilton
Ansty
Withybrook
Pailton
Stanford Reservoir
Reservoirs
COVENTRY
Wyken
Walsgrave on Sowe
Brinklow
Whoberley
Stoke
Binley
Harborough Magna
Cosford
Brownsover
Naseby Reservoir
Canley
Stivichall
Willenhall
Binley Woods
Bretford
Long Lawford
Clifton upon Dunsmore
Baginton
Coventry
Ryton-on-Dunsmore
Wolston
Bilton
RUGBY
Hillmorton
Crackley
Stoneleigh
Bubbenhall
Stretton-on-Dunsmore
Cawston
Overslade
Crick
Hollowell Reservoir
Stareton
Princethorpe
Thurlaston
Dunchurch
Kilsby
Ashow
Frankton
Draycote Water
Barby
NORTHAMPTONSHIRE
Ravensthorpe Reservoir
Weston under Wetherley
Marton
Birdingbury
Willoughby
WATFORD GAP
Blackdown
Cubbington
Leamington Hastings
Grandborough
WARWICKSHIRE
Long Itchington
ROYAL LEAMINGTON SPA
144
145
Drayton Resr.
Grand Union Canal
Oxford Canal
Heathcote
Whitnash
Stockton
DAVENTRY
Bishop's Tachbrook
Ufton
Southam
Napton on the Hill
NORTHAMPTON
Harbury
Weedon Bec
WARWICK
Ladbroke
Priors Marston
Bishop's Itchington
Moreton Morrell
Lighthorne
Gaydon
5
SCALE
0 1 2 3 Miles
0 1 2 3 4 Kilometres
Warwickshire County Boundary
16 17 20 21 22 23 29 30 31 32 33 39 40 41 42 43 49 50 51 52 53 54 55 57 58 59 60 61 62 63 64 65 67 68 69 70 71 72 73 74 75 76 77 79 80 81 82 83 84 85 86 87 88 89 98 99 102 103 104 105 106 107 108 109 110 111 118 119
M1 M6 M45 M69 M40 A5 A6 A14 A45 A46 A47 A50 A423 A425 A426 A428 A444 A447 A511 A563 A607 A4303 A4304 A4500 A5199 A6030 A5460 A361 B4114 B582 B585 B581 B4669 B578 B4109 B4065 B4112 B4455 B4027 B5414 B6047 B4453 B4451 B4100 B4037 B5385 B591 B4116 B5000
R. Sence
R. Soar

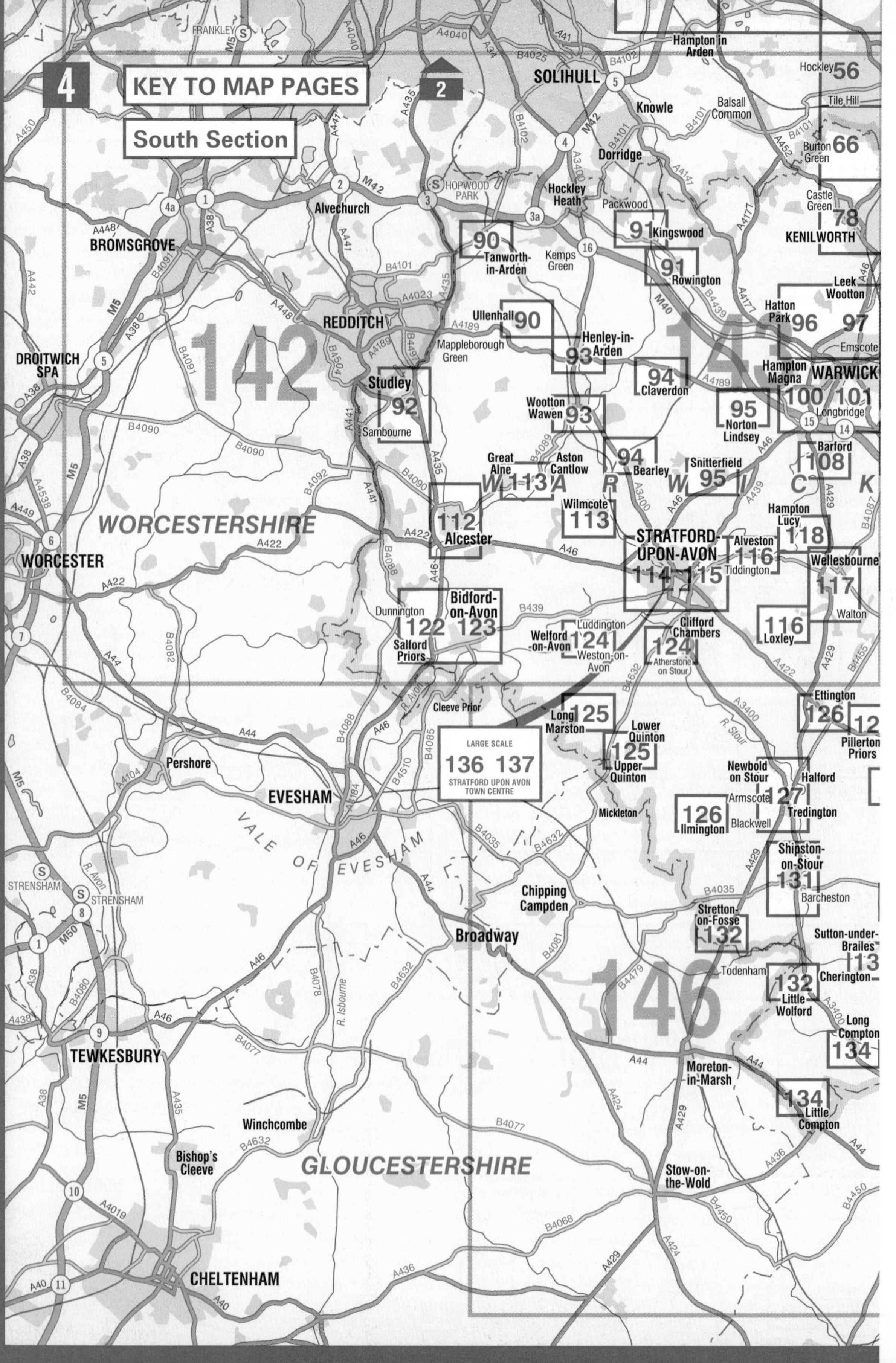

4
KEY TO MAP PAGES
South Section
2
FRANKLEY
SOLIHULL
Hampton in Arden
Hockley 56
Knowle
Balsall Common
Tile Hill
Burton Green 66
Dorridge
Castle Green 78
KENILWORTH
Hockley Heath
Packwood
HOPWOOD PARK
Alvechurch
BROMSGROVE
90 Tanworth-in-Arden
Kemps Green
91 Kingswood
91 Rowington
Leek Wootton
Hatton Park 96
97
REDDITCH
Ullenhall 90
Henley-in-Arden
93
Mappleborough Green
142
143
Emscote
DROITWICH SPA
Studley
92
Sambourne
94 Claverdon
Hampton Magna
WARWICK
100
101
Longbridge
95 Norton Lindsey
Wootton Wawen 93
Great Alne
Aston Cantlow
94 Bearley
Snitterfield 95
Barford 108
W 113 A R W I C K
WORCESTERSHIRE
112 Alcester
Wilmcote 113
STRATFORD-UPON-AVON
114 115
Alveston 116
Tiddington
Hampton Lucy 118
Wellesbourne
117
WORCESTER
Walton
116 Loxley
Dunnington
Bidford-on-Avon
122 123
Salford Priors
Luddington
Welford-on-Avon 124
Weston-on-Avon
Clifford Chambers
124
Atherstone on Stour
Ettington
126
Pillerton Priors
Cleeve Prior
Long Marston 125
Lower Quinton
125 Upper Quinton
LARGE SCALE
136 137
STRATFORD UPON AVON TOWN CENTRE
Pershore
EVESHAM
Newbold on Stour
Halford
Armscote 127
Tredington
Mickleton
126 Ilmington
Blackwell
VALE OF EVESHAM
Shipston-on-Stour
131
Barcheston
STRENSHAM
Chipping Campden
Stretton-on-Fosse 132
Broadway
Sutton-under-Brailes
Todenham
132 Little Wolford
Cherington
146
Long Compton
134
TEWKESBURY
Moreton-in-Marsh
134 Little Compton
Winchcombe
Bishop's Cleeve
GLOUCESTERSHIRE
Stow-on-the-Wold
CHELTENHAM

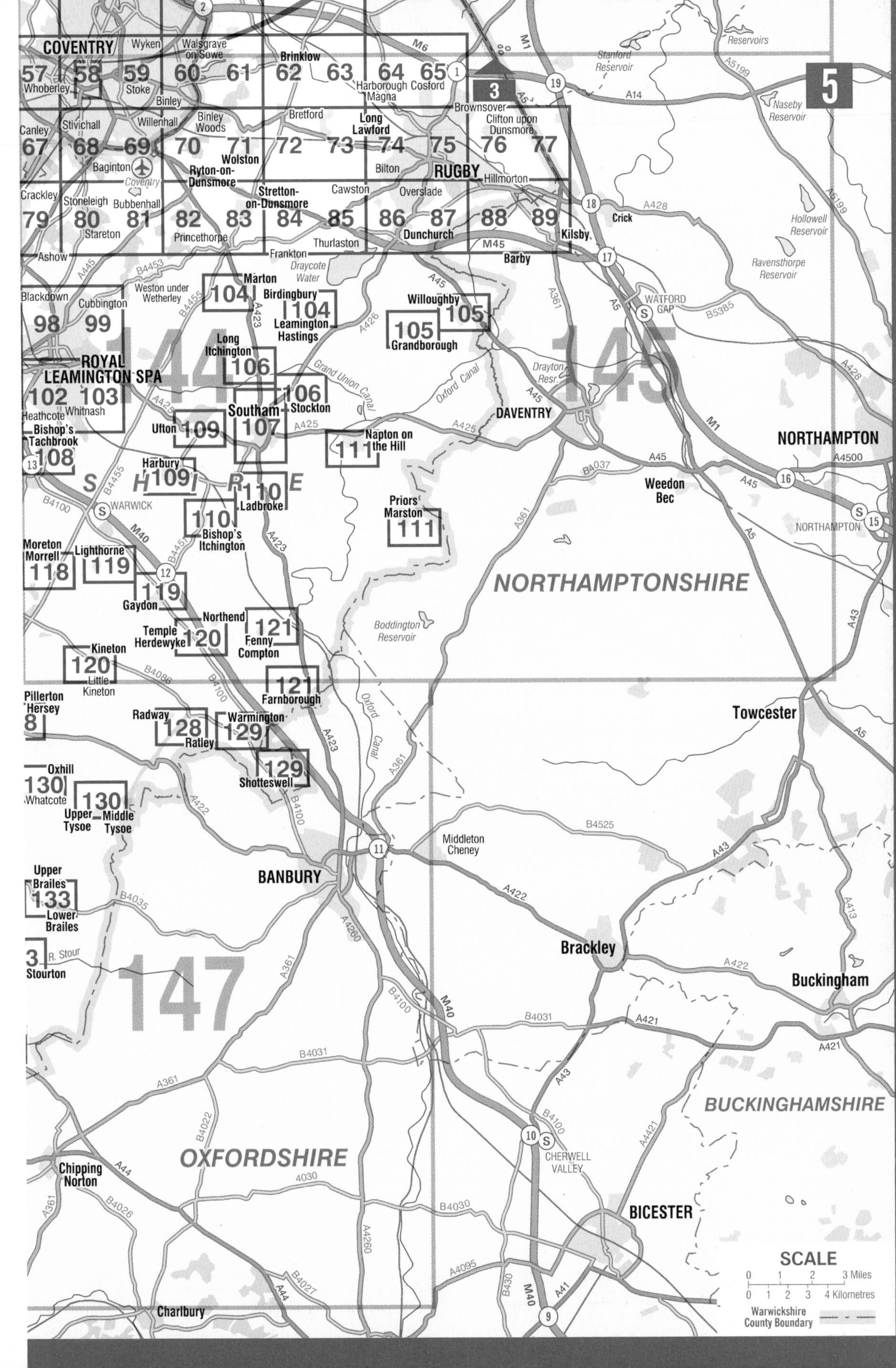

COVENTRY
Wyken
Walsgrave on Sowe
Brinklow
57
58
59
60
61
62
63
64
65
Whoberley
Stoke
Binley
Harborough Magna
Cosford
Brownsover
3
Canley
Stivichall
Willenhall
Binley Woods
Bretford
Long Lawford
Clifton upon Dunsmore
67
68
69
70
71
72
73
74
75
76
77
Baginton
Coventry
Wolston
Ryton-on-Dunsmore
Bilton
RUGBY
Hillmorton
Crackley
Stoneleigh
Bubbenhall
Stretton-on-Dunsmore
Cawston
Overslade
79
80
81
82
83
84
85
86
87
88
89
Stareton
Princethorpe
Thurlaston
Dunchurch
Kilsby
Crick
Ashow
Frankton
Barby
Draycote Water
Marton
104
Birdingbury
Willoughby
105
Blackdown
Cubbington
Weston under Wetherley
98
99
Leamington Hastings
Grandborough
Long Itchington
106
144
145
ROYAL LEAMINGTON SPA
Stockton
Grand Union Canal
Oxford Canal
Drayton Resr.
DAVENTRY
102
103
Heathcote
Whitnash
Southam
Bishop's Tachbrook
Ufton
109
107
Napton on the Hill
111
108
Harbury
110
Ladbroke
WARWICK
Priors Marston
Bishop's Itchington
Weedon Bec
NORTHAMPTON
NORTHAMPTONSHIRE
Moreton Morrell
Lighthorne
118
119
Gaydon
Northend
Temple Herdewyke
120
121
Fenny Compton
Boddington Reservoir
Kineton
Little Kineton
Farnborough
Pillerton Hersey
Towcester
Radway
128
Ratley
Warmington
129
Shotteswell
Oxhill
130
Whatcote
Upper Tysoe
Middle Tysoe
Middleton Cheney
BANBURY
Upper Brailes
133
Lower Brailes
Brackley
Buckingham
R. Stour
Stourton
147
BUCKINGHAMSHIRE
CHERWELL VALLEY
Chipping Norton
OXFORDSHIRE
BICESTER
Charlbury
Stanford Reservoir
Reservoirs
Naseby Reservoir
Hollowell Reservoir
Ravensthorpe Reservoir
WATFORD GAP
M1
M6
M45
M40
A5
A14
A45
A423
A425
A426
A428
A361
A422
A421
A43
A44
A41
A4260
A4095
A4421
A413
A5199
A4500
A445
B4453
B4455
B4100
B4037
B4086
B4035
B4031
B4030
B4022
B4026
B4027
B4525
B5385
B430
SCALE
0 1 2 3 Miles
0 1 2 3 4 Kilometres
Warwickshire County Boundary

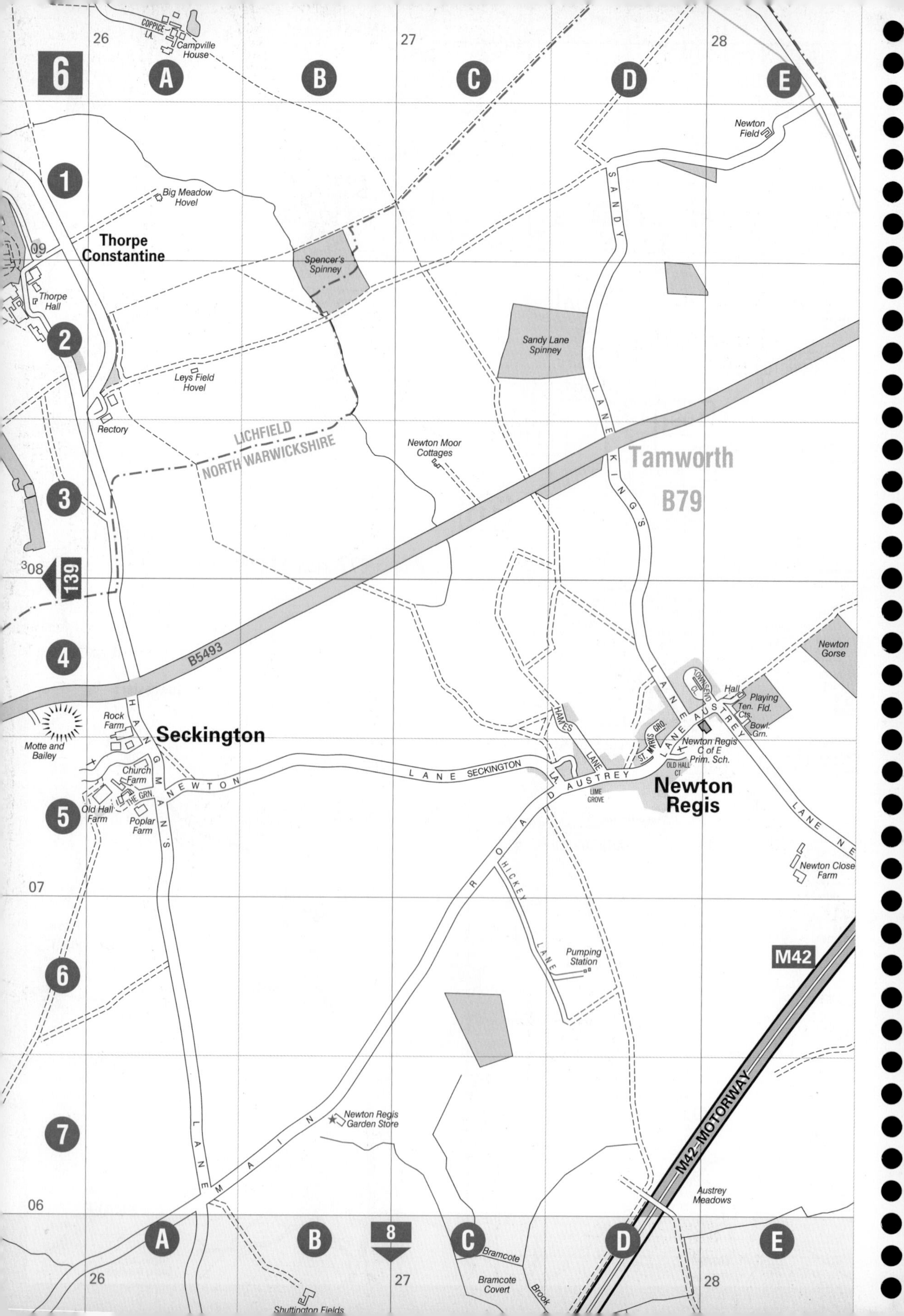
6
A
B
C
D
E
1
2
3
4
5
6
7
26
27
28
09
08
07
06
139
8
Coppice La.
Campville House
Newton Field
Big Meadow Hovel
Thorpe Constantine
Thorpe Hall
Spencer's Spinney
Sandy Lane
Sandy Lane Spinney
Leys Field Hovel
Rectory
Lichfield
North Warwickshire
Newton Moor Cottages
Tamworth
B79
King's Lane
B5493
Hames Lane
Townsend Cl.
Newton Gorse
Hall
Playing Fld.
Ten. Cts.
Bowl. Grn.
Rock Farm
Seckington
Motte and Bailey
Church Farm
The Grn.
Old Hall Farm
Poplar Farm
Hangman's Lane
Newton Lane
Seckington Lane
Austrey Road
Austrey Lane
St. Mark's Grd.
Lime Grove
Old Hall Ct.
Newton Regis C of E Prim. Sch.
Newton Regis
Newton Close Farm
Hickey Lane
Pumping Station
M42
M42 Motorway
Main Road
Newton Regis Garden Store
Austrey Meadows
Bramcote Brook
Bramcote Covert
Shuttington Fields

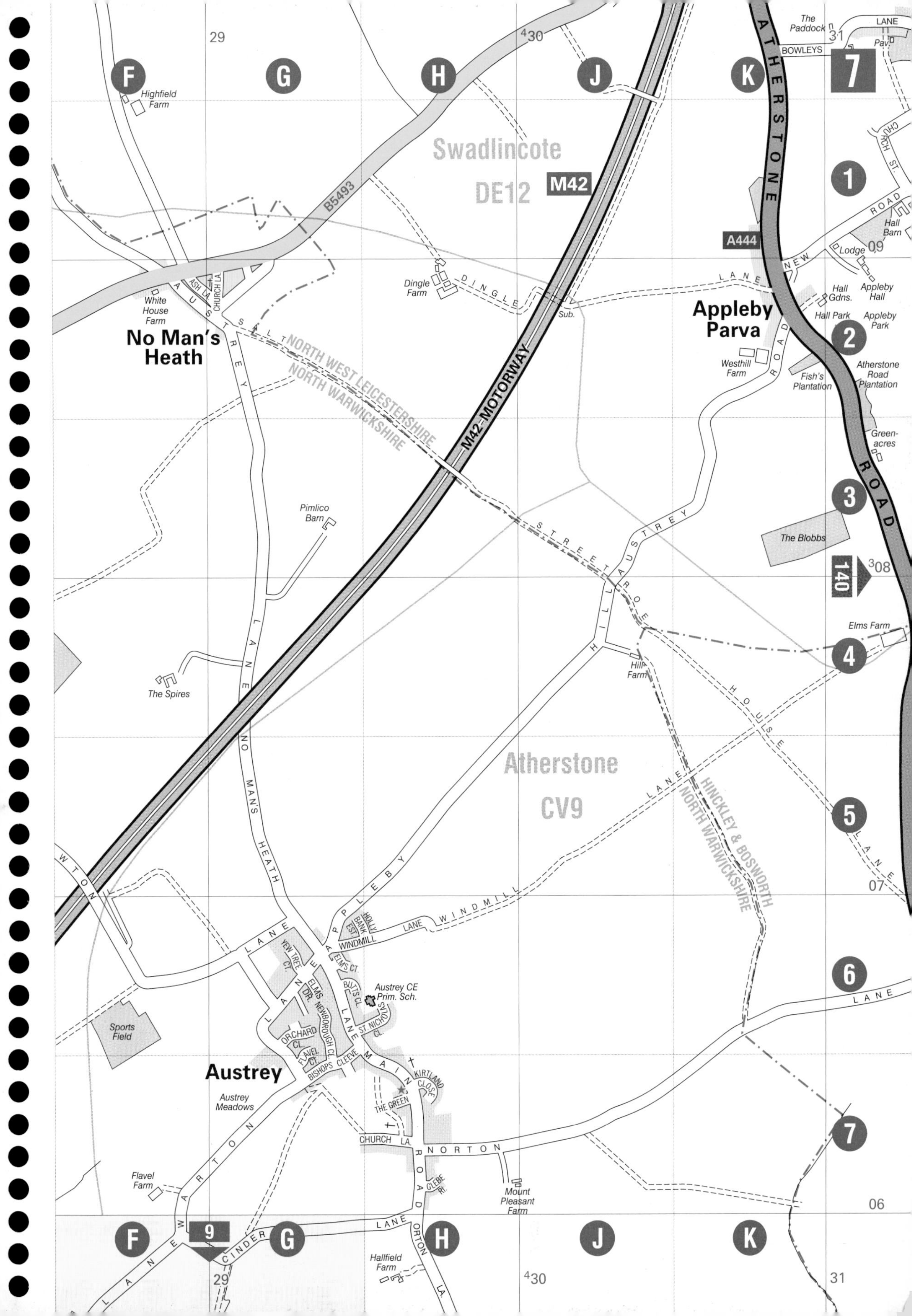

7
F
G
H
J
K
29
430
31
Highfield Farm
Swadlincote
DE12
M42
B5493
No Man's Heath
White House Farm
ASH LA.
CHURCH LA.
AUSTREY
SALT
STREET
NORTH WEST LEICESTERSHIRE
NORTH WARWICKSHIRE
Dingle Farm
DINGLE
LANE
Sub.
M42-MOTORWAY
ATHERSTONE ROAD
A444
The Paddock
BOWLEYS
LANE
Pav.
CHURCH ST.
NEW ROAD
Hall Barn
Lodge
09
Appleby Parva
Hall Gdns.
Appleby Hall
Hall Park
Appleby Park
Westhill Farm
Fish's Plantation
Atherstone Road Plantation
Green-acres
The Blobbs
140
308
Elms Farm
Pimlico Barn
The Spires
NO MAN'S HEATH LANE
HILL
Hill Farm
HOUSE LANE
Atherstone
CV9
HINCKLEY & BOSWORTH
NORTH WARWICKSHIRE
APPLEBY
HOLLY BANK EST.
WINDMILL
LANE
WINDMILL
07
YEW TREE CT.
ELMS CT.
ELMS DR.
NEWBOROUGH CL.
BUTTS CL.
Austrey CE Prim. Sch.
ST. NICHOLAS CL.
ORCHARD CL.
FLAVEL CT.
BISHOPS CLEEVE
MAIN
KIRTLAND CLOSE
Austrey
Austrey Meadows
Sports Field
THE GREEN
CHURCH LA.
NORTON
ROAD
GLEBE RI.
Mount Pleasant Farm
Flavel Farm
WARTON
LANE
06
9
CINDER LANE
ORTON LA.
Hallfield Farm
1
2
3
4
5
6
7

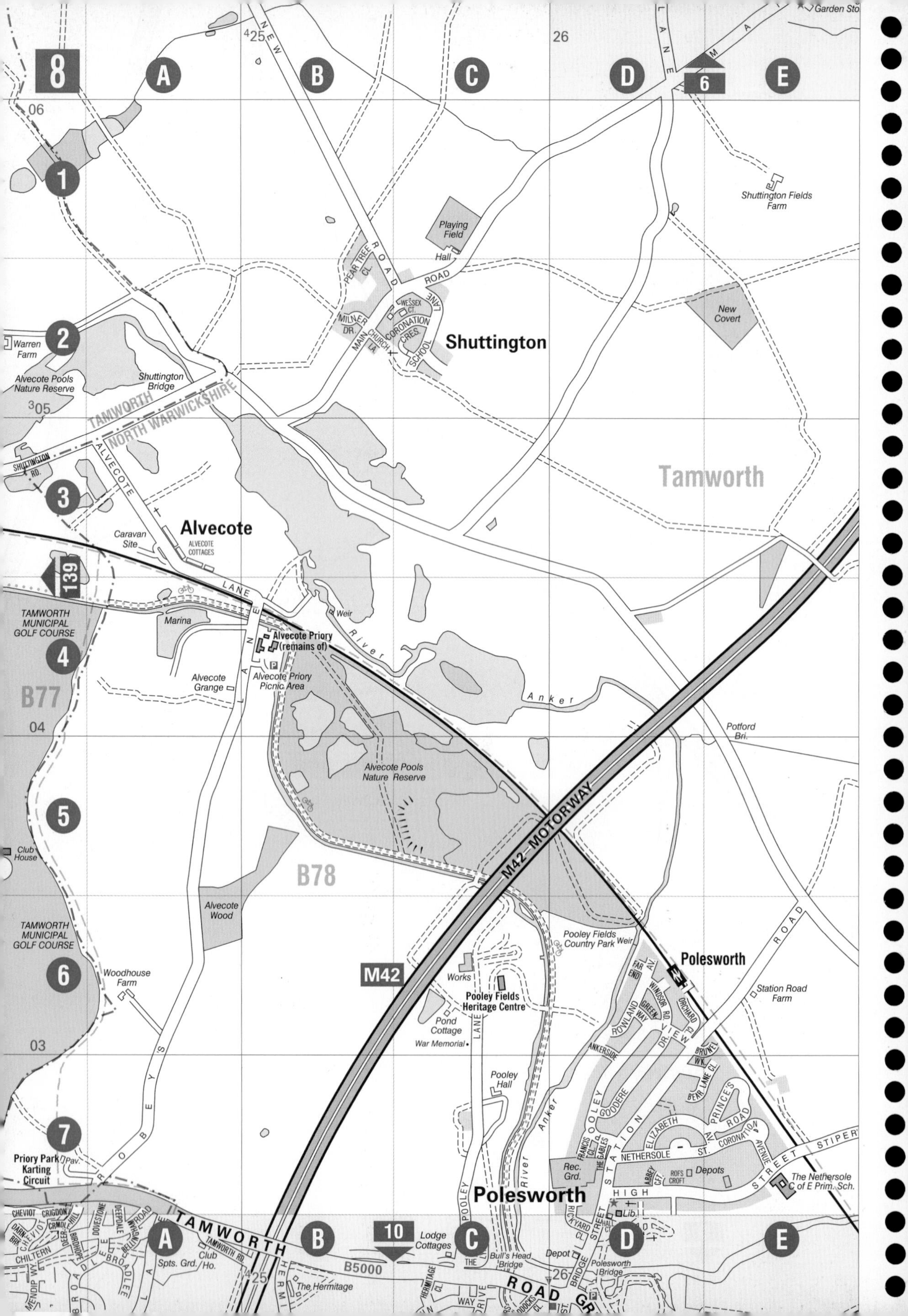

A
B
C
D
E
1
2
3
4
5
6
7
6
10
139
Shuttington
Alvecote
Polesworth
Tamworth
Warren Farm
Alvecote Pools Nature Reserve
Shuttington Bridge
TAMWORTH
NORTH WARWICKSHIRE
Playing Field
Hall
New Covert
Shuttington Fields Farm
Garden Sto
Caravan Site
ALVECOTE COTTAGES
TAMWORTH MUNICIPAL GOLF COURSE
Marina
Alvecote Priory (remains of)
Alvecote Priory Picnic Area
Alvecote Grange
Weir
River Anker
Potford Bri.
B77
B78
M42 MOTORWAY
M42
Club House
Alvecote Wood
Woodhouse Farm
Priory Park Karting Circuit
Pooley Fields Country Park
Weir
Works
Pooley Fields Heritage Centre
Pond Cottage
War Memorial
Pooley Hall
Station Road Farm
Rec. Grd.
Depots
The Nethersole C of E Prim. Sch.
Lib.
Depot
Polesworth Bridge
Bull's Head Bridge
Lodge Cottages
Spts. Grd.
Club Ho.
The Hermitage
B5000
TAMWORTH ROAD
ROBEYS LANE
NEW ROAD
MAIN ROAD
SCHOOL LANE
PEAR TREE CL.
WESSEX CT.
CORONATION CRES.
MILNER DR.
CHURCH LA.
ALVECOTE LANE
SHUTTINGTON RD.
STATION ROAD
HIGH STREET
NETHERSOLE ST.
CORONATION AVENUE
PRINCE'S ROAD
ELIZABETH AV.
GOODERE
ANKERSIDE
ROWLAND WAY
GREEN WAY
WINDSOR RD
ORCHARD
VIEW DR.
FAR END
FRANCIS CL.
THE GABLES
ABBEY CT.
ROFS CROFT
BRUNEL WK.
BEAR LANE CL.
POOLEY LANE
BRIDGE STREET
STIPERSTONES
CHEVIOT
CRIGDON
DOVESTONE
DEEPDALE
CHILTERN
BROADLEE
MENDIP WY.
TAMWORTH RD
HERMITAGE CL.
06
05
04
03
425
26

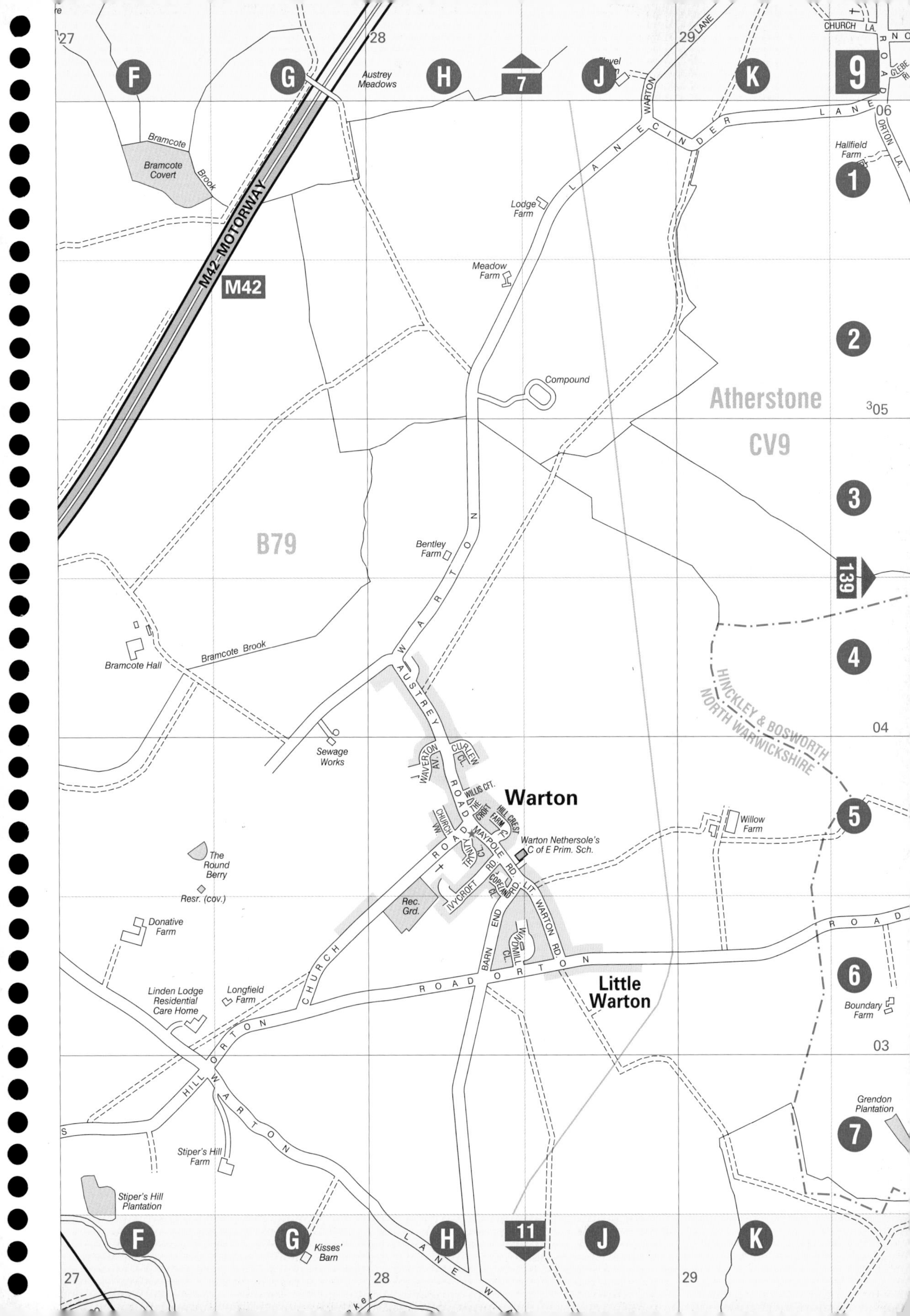
9
7
11
139
F
G
H
J
K
1
2
3
4
5
6
7
27
28
29
06
305
04
03
M42 MOTORWAY
M42
Austrey Meadows
Bramcote Covert
Bramcote Brook
Lodge Farm
Meadow Farm
Compound
Atherstone
CV9
B79
Bentley Farm
Hallfield Farm
CHURCH LA.
ORTON LA.
GLEBE RI.
WARTON LANE
CINDER LANE
WARTON
Bramcote Hall
Bramcote Brook
Sewage Works
AUSTREY ROAD
WAVERTON AV.
CURLEW CL.
WILLIS CFT.
THE CROFT
HILL CREST
FARM CL.
CHURCH WK.
MAYPOLE RD.
TRINITY CL.
IVYCROFT RD.
COPELAND CL.
LIT. WARTON RD.
BARN END
WINDMILL CL.
Warton
Warton Nethersole's C of E Prim. Sch.
Rec. Grd.
HINCKLEY & BOSWORTH
NORTH WARWICKSHIRE
Willow Farm
The Round Berry
Resr. (cov.)
Donative Farm
CHURCH ROAD
ORTON ROAD
Little Warton
Linden Lodge Residential Care Home
Longfield Farm
Boundary Farm
HILL
WARTON LANE
Stiper's Hill Farm
Stiper's Hill Plantation
Grendon Plantation
Kisses' Barn

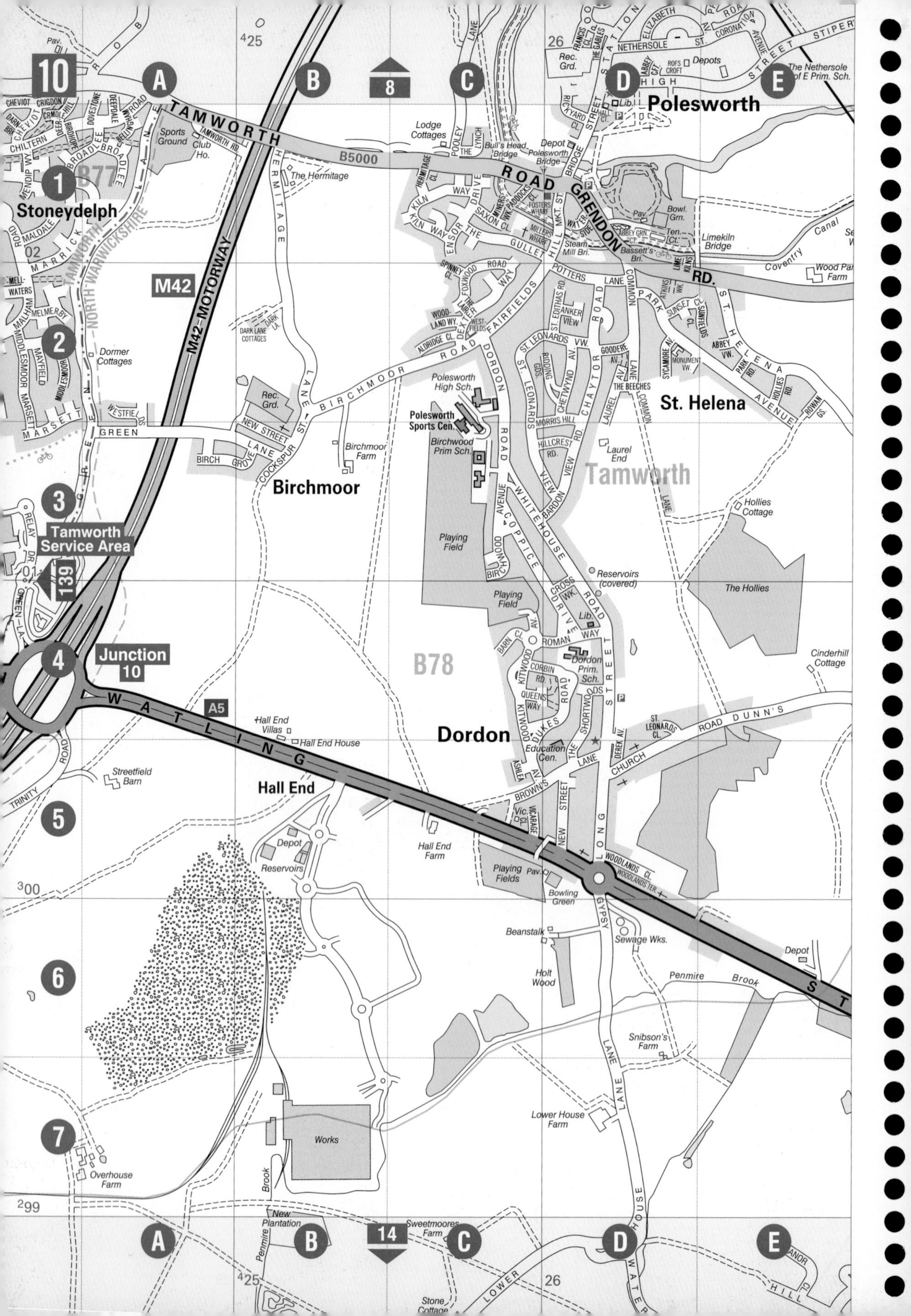
Polesworth
Stoneydelph
St. Helena
Tamworth
Birchmoor
Dordon
Hall End
B77
B78
M42
M42-MOTORWAY
A5
B5000
TAMWORTH ROAD
GRENDON RD.
WATLING ST
NORTH WARWICKSHIRE
TAMWORTH
Tamworth Service Area
Junction 10
Sports Ground
The Hermitage
Lodge Cottages
Bull's Head Bridge
Polesworth Bridge
Rec. Grd.
Depots
The Nethersole E Prim. Sch.
Limekiln Bridge
Coventry Canal
Wood Park Farm
Dormer Cottages
Dark Lane Cottages
Polesworth High Sch.
Polesworth Sports Cen.
Birchwood Prim Sch.
Birchmoor Farm
Laurel End
Hollies Cottage
The Hollies
Reservoirs (covered)
Playing Field
Cinderhill Cottage
Dordon Prim. Sch.
Education Cen.
Hall End Villas
Hall End House
Hall End Farm
Streetfield Barn
Depot
Reservoirs
Bowling Green
Beanstalk
Sewage Wks.
Holt Wood
Penmire Brook
Snibson's Farm
Lower House Farm
Works
Overhouse Farm
New Plantation
Sweetmoores Farm
Stone Cottage
Tamworth Club Ho.
Steam Mill Bri.
Bassett's Bri.
425
26
300
299
8
14
139

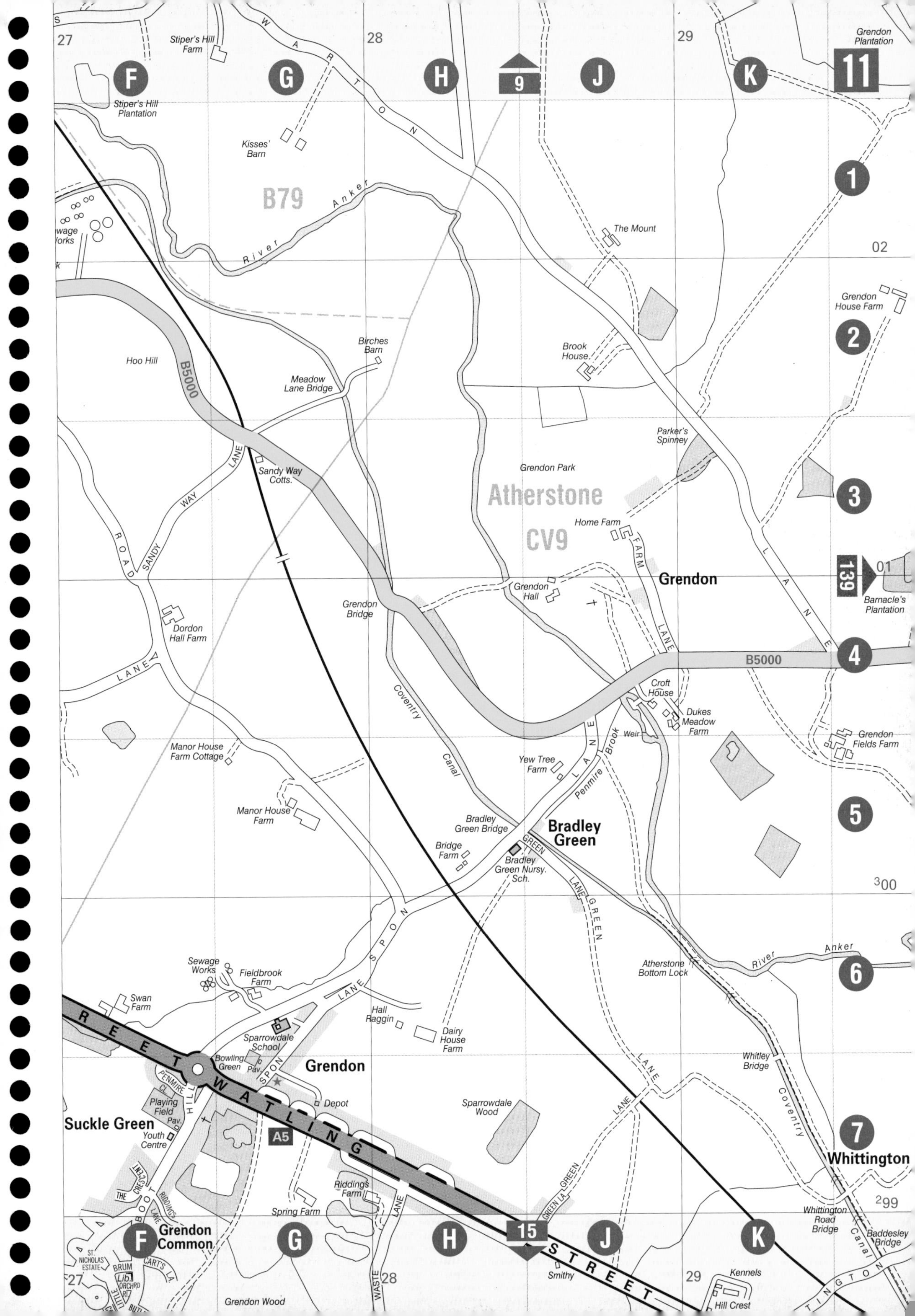

Stiper's Hill Farm
Stiper's Hill Plantation
Kisses' Barn
B79
River Anker
WARTON
9
11
Grendon Plantation
The Mount
Brook House
Birches Barn
Meadow Lane Bridge
Hoo Hill
B5000
Sandy Way Cotts.
SANDY WAY LANE
ROAD
Parker's Spinney
Grendon Park
Atherstone
CV9
Home Farm
Grendon
Grendon Hall
Grendon Bridge
FARM LANE
139
Barnacle's Plantation
Grendon House Farm
LANE
Dordon Hall Farm
LANE
Coventry Canal
Croft House
Dukes Meadow Farm
Weir
Grendon Fields Farm
Manor House Farm Cottage
Manor House Farm
Yew Tree Farm
Penmire Brook
Bradley Green Bridge
Bradley Green
Bridge Farm
Bradley Green Nursy. Sch.
LANE GREEN
SPON LANE
Sewage Works
Fieldbrook Farm
Swan Farm
Hall Raggin
Dairy House Farm
Atherstone Bottom Lock
River Anker
Whitley Bridge
Sparrowdale School
Bowling Green
Pav.
Grendon
Depot
WATLING STREET
A5
Suckle Green
Playing Field
Youth Centre
Sparrowdale Wood
Riddings Farm
Spring Farm
Grendon Common
Grendon Wood
Smithy
15
Kennels
Hill Crest
Whittington
Whittington Road Bridge
Baddesley Bridge
Coventry Canal
F G H J K
1 2 3 4 5 6 7
27 28 29
02 01 300 299

139
A
B
C
D
E
1
2
3
4
5
6
7
LICHFIELD
NORTH WARWICKSHIRE
TAMWORTH
Fisher's Mill Bridge
Ford
Mill Plantation
Langley Brook
Pool-tail Plantation
Newhouse Farm
Kennels Wood
Middleton Hall
Coneybury Farm
Coneybury Wood
Lower Farm
BODYMOOR
Stonehill Farm
The Folly
Old Marl Pit
TAMWORTH ROAD
A51
RUSH LANE
B77
Works
Tamworth
RIVER TAME
Cliff Farm
CLIFF HALL LA.
Cliff
Manor Farm
Thistlewood
Cliff Pool Nature Reserve
Cliff Pool
Canal Pool
KINGSBURY WATER PARK
Curdworth Bottom Lock
Kingsbury Swivel Bridge
Broomey Croft Pool
Broomey Croft Childrens Farm
Cliff Pool South
Grebe Pool
Heron Pool
Kingfisher Pool
Ash Pool
KINGSBURY WATER CAMPING & CARAVANING SITE
Gibsons Pool
Burdetts Pool
Alder Pool
Moorash Farm
Moorash Pool
Sandy Pool
Kingsbury Pool
Mitchell's Pool
M42 MOTORWAY
M42
Pumping Station
B78
Playing Field
Kingsbury Branch Sidings
Birmingham & Fazeley Canal
Bodymoor Heath Bri.
Sutton Coldfield
Cheatle's Farm Bridge
Double Bridge
B76
DOG LANE
Hotel
Play Area
KINGSBURY WATER PARK
Kingsbury Hall
The Mount
Hall
Ten. Cts.
Rec. Grd.
Kingsbury
Kingsbury Inf. & Jun. Schs.
Kingsbury Sch.
Lib.
CHURCH LA.
Works
Willows Pool
Visitors Cen.
HEATH
Bodymoor Heath Water
Tamworth Sailing Club
The Midlands Hydroplane Club
Bodymoor Heath
Theresa
Lake View
Hemlingford Water
Hemlingford Bridge
Kingsbury Mill
Hemlingford Green
COVENTRY ROAD
B4098
A4097
A4091
Causeway Pool
Mill Pool
Hemlingford House
Swann Pool
Marston Field Bridge
KINGSBURY ROAD
99
98
97
96
420
21

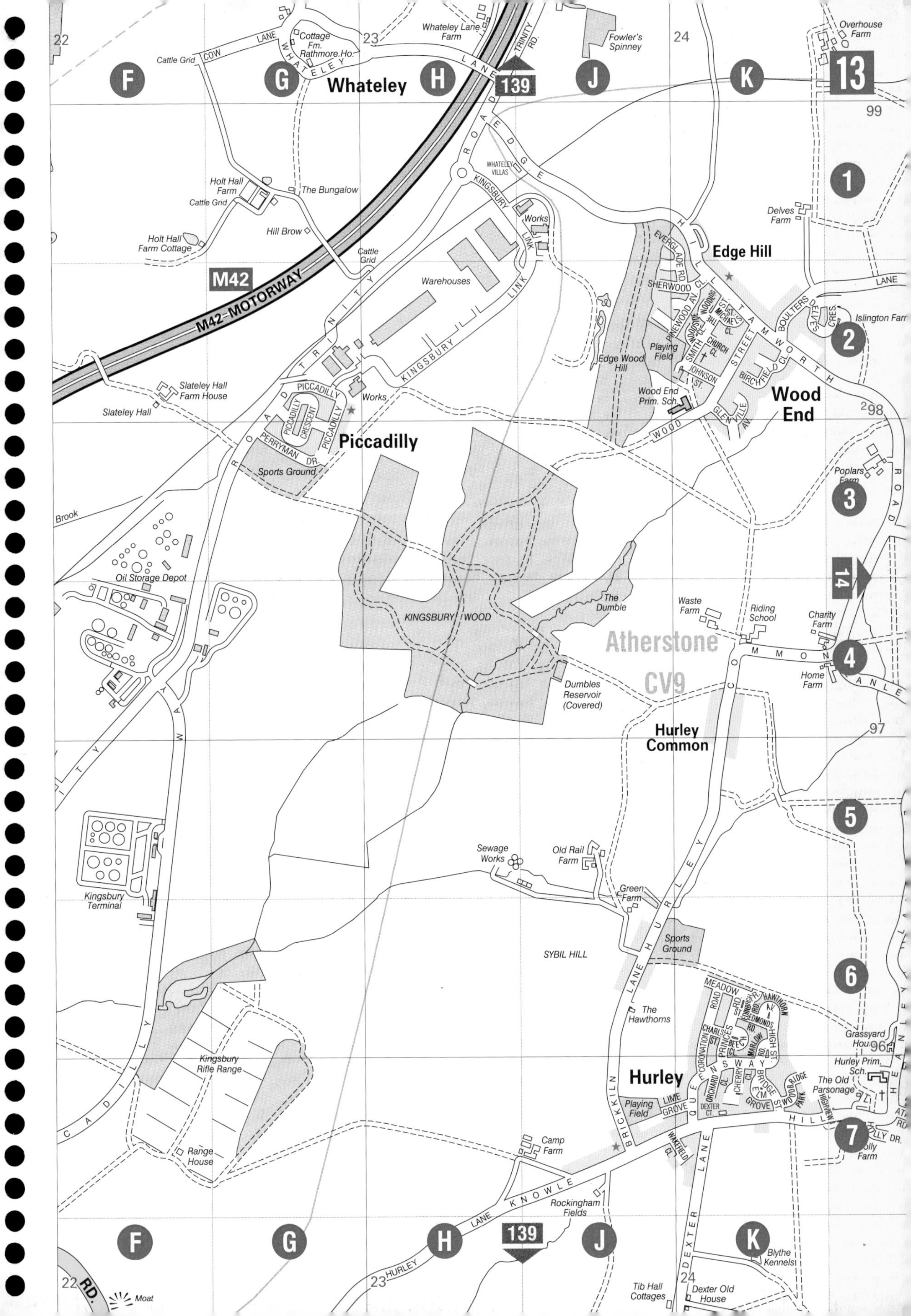

13
22
23
24
99
98
97
96
F
G
H
J
K
1
2
3
4
5
6
7
139
14
Whateley
Cottage Fm.
Rathmore Ho.
Whateley Lane Farm
Fowler's Spinney
Overhouse Farm
Cattle Grid
COW LANE
WHATELEY LANE
TRINITY RD.
ROAD
EDGE
WHATELEY VILLAS
KINGSBURY LINK
Works
Holt Hall Farm
The Bungalow
Hill Brow
Holt Hall Farm Cottage
Cattle Grid
Warehouses
M42
M42 MOTORWAY
Delves Farm
Edge Hill
EVERGLADE RD.
SHERWOOD CL.
PINEWOOD AV.
THE WOODLANDS
ST. MICHAEL'S CL.
WOODSIDE CL.
SMITH ST.
CHURCH CL.
JOHNSON ST.
STREET
TAMWORTH
BOULTERS LANE
DELVES CRES.
Islington Farm
BIRCHFIELD CL.
GLENVILLE AV.
Playing Field
Edge Wood Hill
Wood End Prim. Sch.
Wood End
WOOD
LANE
Slateley Hall Farm House
Slateley Hall
PICCADILLY
PICCADILLY CRESCENT
PERRYMAN DR.
Piccadilly
Sports Ground
Poplars Farm
ROAD
Brook
Oil Storage Depot
KINGSBURY WOOD
The Dumble
Waste Farm
Riding School
Charity Farm
Atherstone
CV9
COMMON
Home Farm
Dumbles Reservoir (Covered)
Hurley Common
TRINITY WAY
Sewage Works
Old Rail Farm
Kingsbury Terminal
Green Farm
Sports Ground
SYBIL HILL
HURLEY LANE
MEADOW ROAD
HAWTHORN
EDMONDS RD.
The Hawthorns
CHARLES ST.
PRINCES
BEECH
MARLOW
HIGH ST.
Grassyard House
Kingsbury Rifle Range
Hurley
QUEENSWAY
ORCHARD CL.
CHERRY
ELM GROVE
BRIDGE ST.
WOODRIDGE PARK
Hurley Prim. Sch.
The Old Parsonage
HIGHVIEW
Playing Field
LIME GROVE
DEXTER CT.
HILL
HOLLY DR.
Holly Farm
BRICKKILN
WAKEFIELD CL.
PICCADILLY
Camp Farm
Range House
KNOWLE LANE
Rockingham Fields
DEXTER LANE
HURLEY
RD.
Moat
Blythe Kennels
Tib Hall Cottages
Dexter Old House

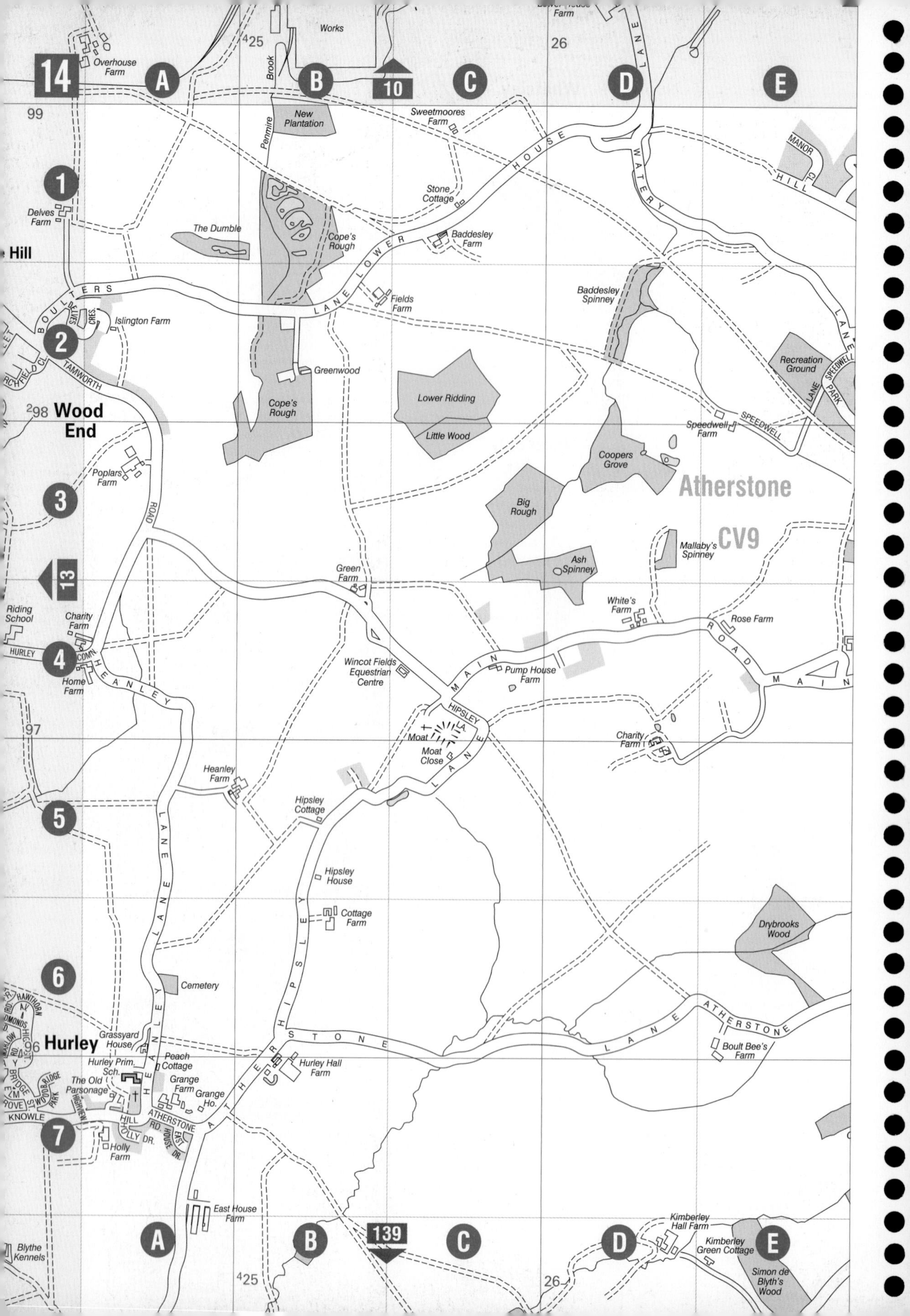
Works
425
26
Overhouse Farm
Brook
A
B
10
C
D
E
LANE
99
New Plantation
Sweetmoores Farm
Penmire
HOUSE
WATERY
MANOR
HILL
1
Stone Cottage
Delves Farm
The Dumble
Cope's Rough
Baddesley Farm
LOWER
Hill
BOULTERS
LANE
Fields Farm
Baddesley Spinney
DELVES CRES.
Islington Farm
2
FIELD CL.
TAMWORTH
Greenwood
Recreation Ground
SPEEDWELL
PARK
298
Wood End
Cope's Rough
Lower Ridding
Little Wood
Speedwell Farm
Poplars Farm
Coopers Grove
Atherstone
3
ROAD
Big Rough
CV9
Mallaby's Spinney
13
Ash Spinney
Green Farm
Riding School
Charity Farm
White's Farm
Rose Farm
HURLEY
4
COMN.
Wincot Fields Equestrian Centre
MAIN
Pump House Farm
ROAD
MAIN
Home Farm
HEANLEY
HIPSLEY LA.
Moat
Moat Close
97
Charity Farm
Heanley Farm
5
Hipsley Cottage
LANE
Hipsley House
Cottage Farm
HIPSLEY
Drybrooks Wood
6
Cemetery
HAWTHORN
ATHERSTONE
Grassyard House
Hurley
96
Peach Cottage
LANE
Boult Bee's Farm
Hurley Prim. Sch.
Hurley Hall Farm
The Old Parsonage
Grange Farm
Grange Ho.
HEANLEY
ATHERSTONE
KNOWLE
HILL
7
HOLLY DR.
HOUSE DR.
Holly Farm
East House Farm
139
Kimberley Hall Farm
Kimberley Green Cottage
Blythe Kennels
425
26
Simon de Blyth's Wood

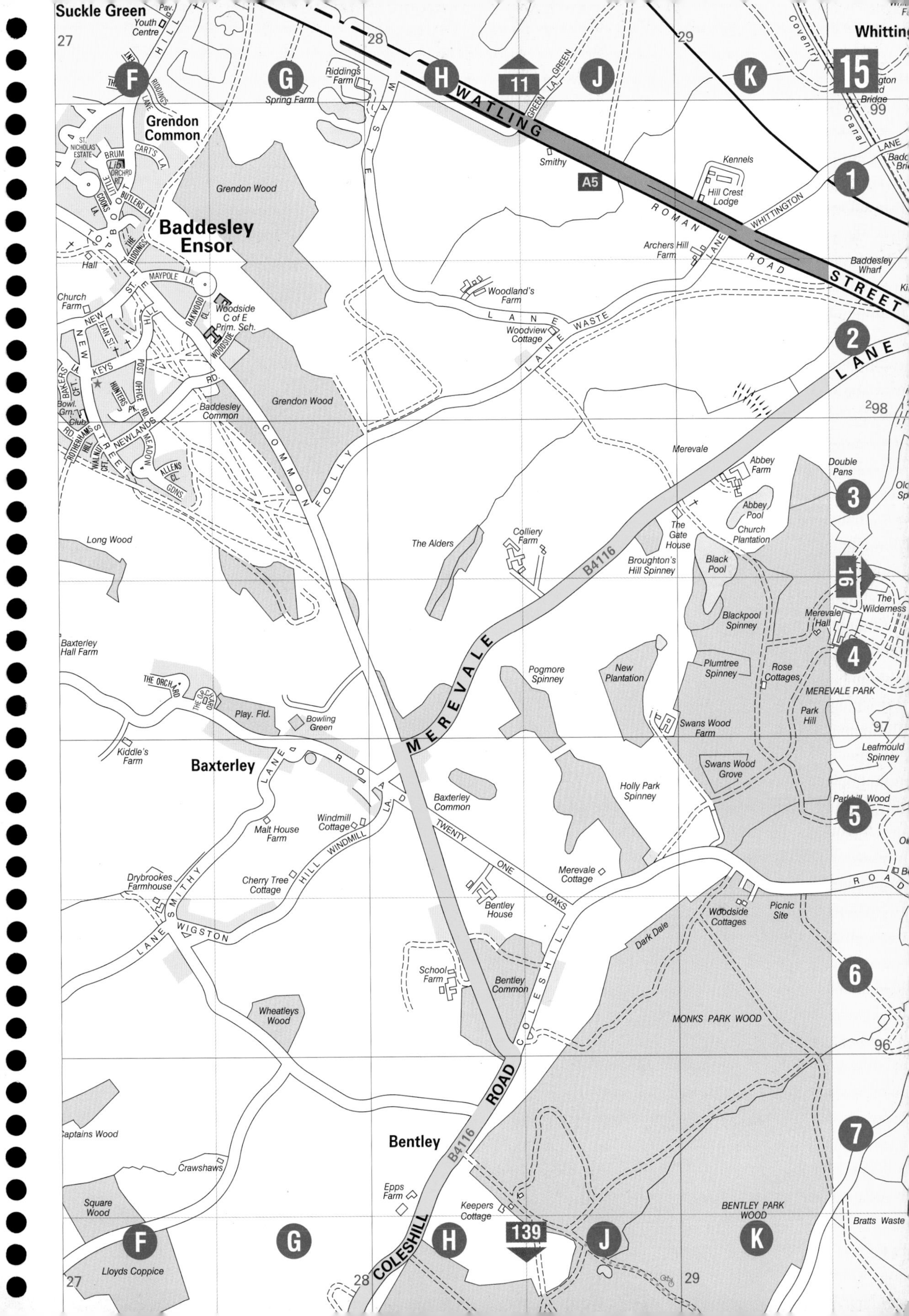

Suckle Green
Youth Centre
Whittington
15
11
WATLING STREET
A5
Grendon Common
Baddesley Ensor
Grendon Wood
Spring Farm
Riddings Farm
Smithy
Kennels
Hill Crest Lodge
ROMAN ROAD
WHITTINGTON LANE
Archers Hill Farm
Baddesley Wharf
Woodland's Farm
Woodview Cottage
WASTE LANE
Woodside C of E Prim. Sch.
Church Farm
Baddesley Common
COMMON FOLLY
MEREVALE LANE
B4116
Merevale
Abbey Farm
Abbey Pool
Double Pans
Church Plantation
The Gate House
Colliery Farm
The Alders
Broughton's Hill Spinney
Black Pool
Long Wood
16
The Wilderness
Merevale Hall
Blackpool Spinney
Baxterley Hall Farm
Pogmore Spinney
New Plantation
Plumtree Spinney
Rose Cottages
MEREVALE PARK
Park Hill
THE ORCHARD
Play. Fld.
Bowling Green
Swans Wood Farm
Leafmould Spinney
Kiddle's Farm
Baxterley
Swans Wood Grove
Holly Park Spinney
Baxterley Common
Parkhill Wood
Windmill Cottage
Malt House Farm
TWENTY ONE OAKS
Merevale Cottage
Drybrookes Farmhouse
Cherry Tree Cottage
WINDMILL HILL
SMITHY LANE
WIGSTON
Bentley House
Woodside Cottages
Picnic Site
Dark Dale
COLESHILL
School Farm
Bentley Common
Wheatleys Wood
MONKS PARK WOOD
Captains Wood
Bentley
COLESHILL ROAD
Crawshaws
Epps Farm
Keepers Cottage
BENTLEY PARK WOOD
Square Wood
139
Bratts Waste
Lloyds Coppice

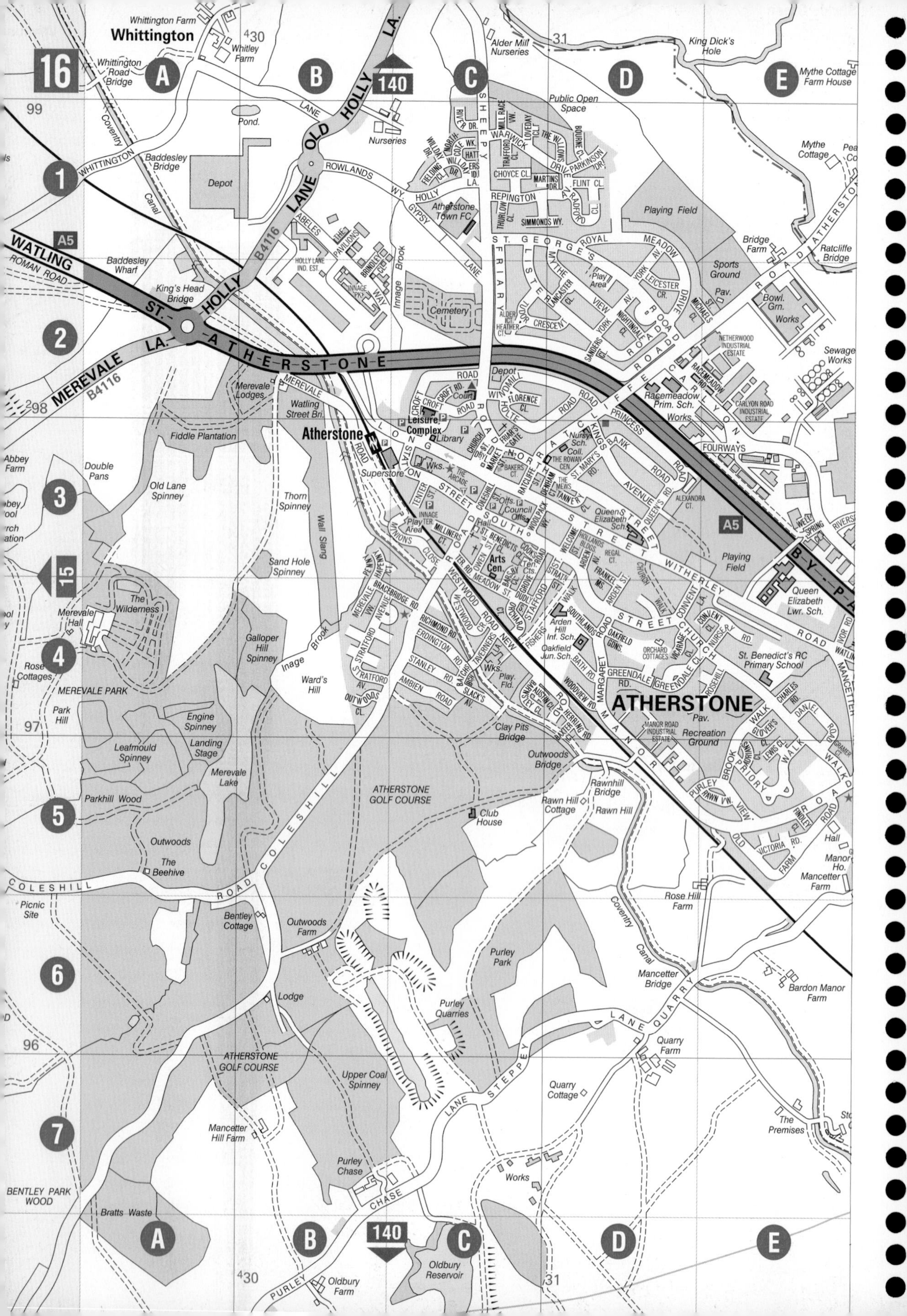

Whittington
Whittington Farm
Whitley Farm
Whittington Road Bridge
Alder Mill Nurseries
King Dick's Hole
Mythe Cottage Farm House
Mythe Cottage
Pond.
Nurseries
Public Open Space
Depot
Baddesley Bridge
Canal
Coventry
Atherstone Town FC
Playing Field
Bridge Farm
Ratcliffe Bridge
Sports Ground
Baddesley Wharf
King's Head Bridge
Holly Lane Ind. Est.
Cemetery
Bowl. Grn.
Works
Netherwood Industrial Estate
Sewage Works
WATLING ST.
ROMAN ROAD
MEREVALE LA.
B4116
ATHERSTONE
Merevale Lodges
Watling Street Bri.
Racemeadow Prim. Sch.
Carlyon Road Industrial Estate
Fourways
Fiddle Plantation
Atherstone
Leisure Complex
Library
Court
Superstore
Abbey Farm
Double Pans
Old Lane Spinney
Thorn Spinney
Wall Slang
Queen Elizabeth Sch.
Council Offs.
Arts Cen.
Playing Field
Queen Elizabeth Lwr. Sch.
Sand Hole Spinney
The Wilderness
Merevale Hall
Galloper Hill Spinney
Inage Brook
Ward's Hill
Arden Hill Inf. Sch.
Oakfield Jun. Sch.
St. Benedict's RC Primary School
Rose Cottages
MEREVALE PARK
Park Hill
Engine Spinney
Landing Stage
Leafmould Spinney
Merevale Lake
Clay Pits Bridge
Outwoods Bridge
ATHERSTONE
Manor Road Industrial Estate
Recreation Ground
Parkhill Wood
ATHERSTONE GOLF COURSE
Club House
Rawnhill Bridge
Rawn Hill Cottage
Rawn Hill
Outwoods
The Beehive
COLESHILL ROAD
Picnic Site
Bentley Cottage
Outwoods Farm
Rose Hill Farm
Mancetter Farm
Manor Ho.
Purley Park
Mancetter Bridge
Bardon Manor Farm
Lodge
Purley Quarries
QUARRY LANE
Quarry Farm
ATHERSTONE GOLF COURSE
Upper Coal Spinney
Quarry Cottage
STEPPEY LANE
The Premises
Mancetter Hill Farm
Purley Chase
Works
CHASE
BENTLEY PARK WOOD
Bratts Waste
Oldbury Reservoir
Oldbury Farm
PURLEY
140
15
A5

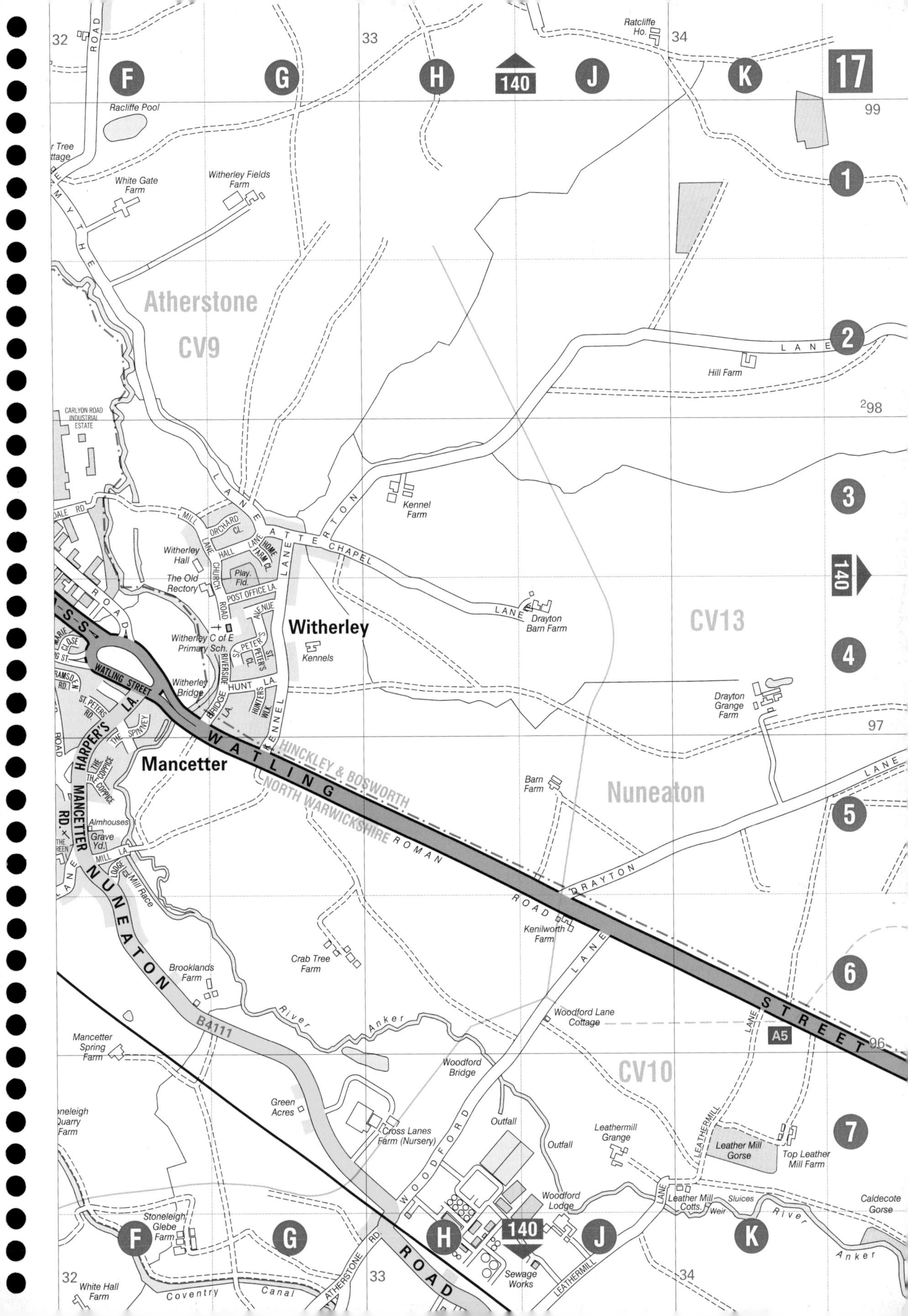

Ratcliffe Ho.
Racliffe Pool
White Gate Farm
Witherley Fields Farm
Atherstone
CV9
CARLYON ROAD INDUSTRIAL ESTATE
Hill Farm
Kennel Farm
Witherley Hall
The Old Rectory
Witherley C of E Primary Sch.
Witherley Bridge
Witherley
Kennels
Drayton Barn Farm
CV13
Drayton Grange Farm
Mancetter
HINCKLEY & BOSWORTH
NORTH WARWICKSHIRE
WATLING STREET
ROMAN
Barn Farm
Nuneaton
Almhouses
Grave Yd.
Mill Race
Kenilworth Farm
Brooklands Farm
Crab Tree Farm
River Anker
Woodford Lane Cottage
A5
Mancetter Spring Farm
B4111
Woodford Bridge
CV10
Green Acres
Cross Lanes Farm (Nursery)
Outfall
Leathermill Grange
Leather Mill Gorse
Top Leather Mill Farm
Woodford Lodge
Leather Mill Cotts.
Sluices
Weir
Caldecote Gorse
Stoneleigh Glebe Farm
Stoneleigh Quarry Farm
Sewage Works
White Hall Farm
Coventry Canal
NUNEATON ROAD
ATHERSTONE RD
WOODFORD LANE
LEATHERMILL LANE
DRAYTON LANE
ATTERTON LANE
CHAPEL LANE
KENNEL LANE
MANCETTER RD.
HARPER'S LA.

140
140
140

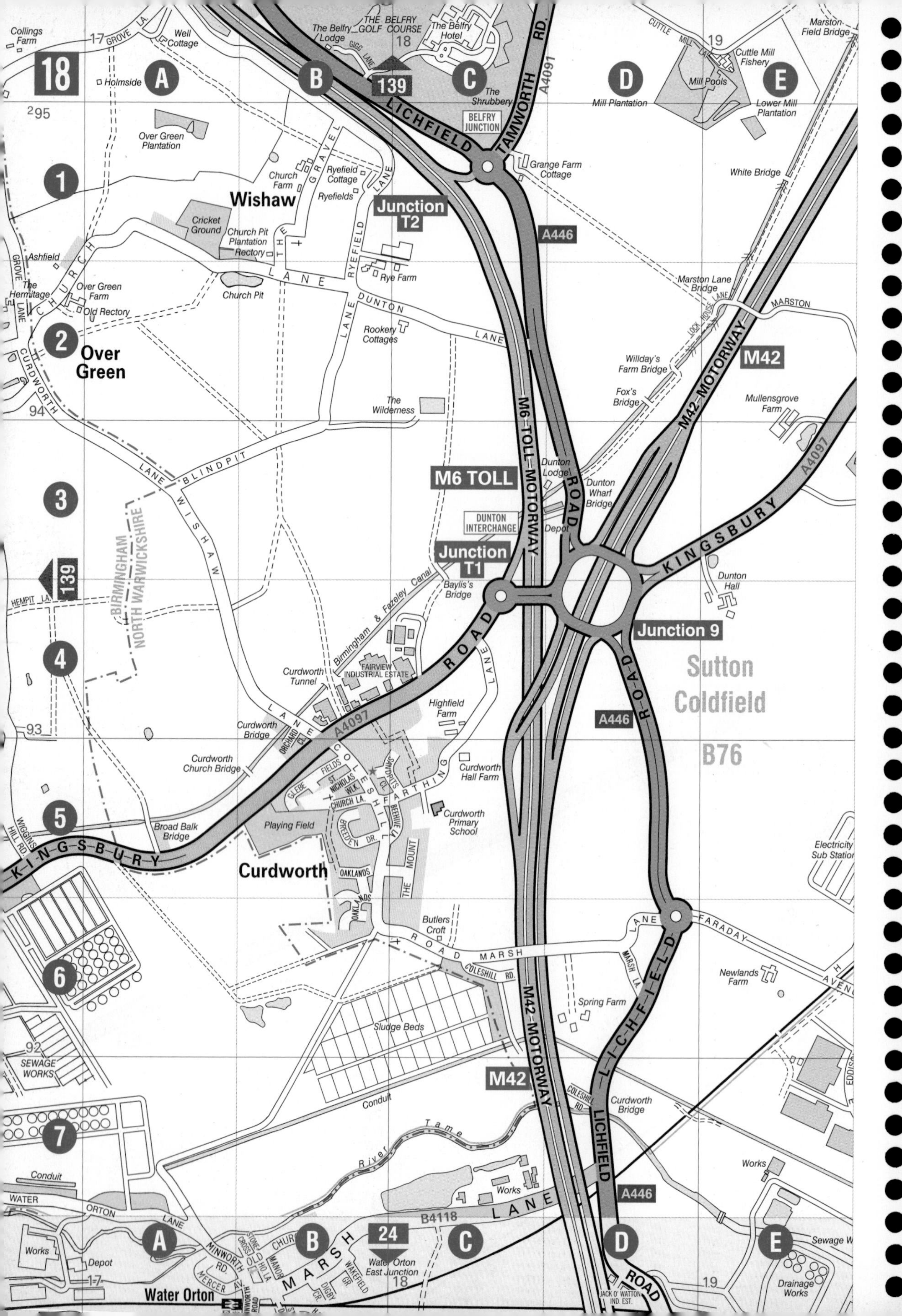

18
Wishaw
Over Green
Curdworth
Water Orton
Sutton Coldfield
B76
Junction T2
Junction T1
Junction 9
M6 TOLL
M42
BELFRY JUNCTION
DUNTON INTERCHANGE
LICHFIELD ROAD
KINGSBURY ROAD
M6 TOLL MOTORWAY
M42 MOTORWAY
A446
A4097
B4118
139
24
The Belfry Golf Course
The Belfry Hotel
Mill Pools
Cuttle Mill Fishery
Cricket Ground
Sludge Beds
Sewage Works
River Tame
BIRMINGHAM
NORTH WARWICKSHIRE

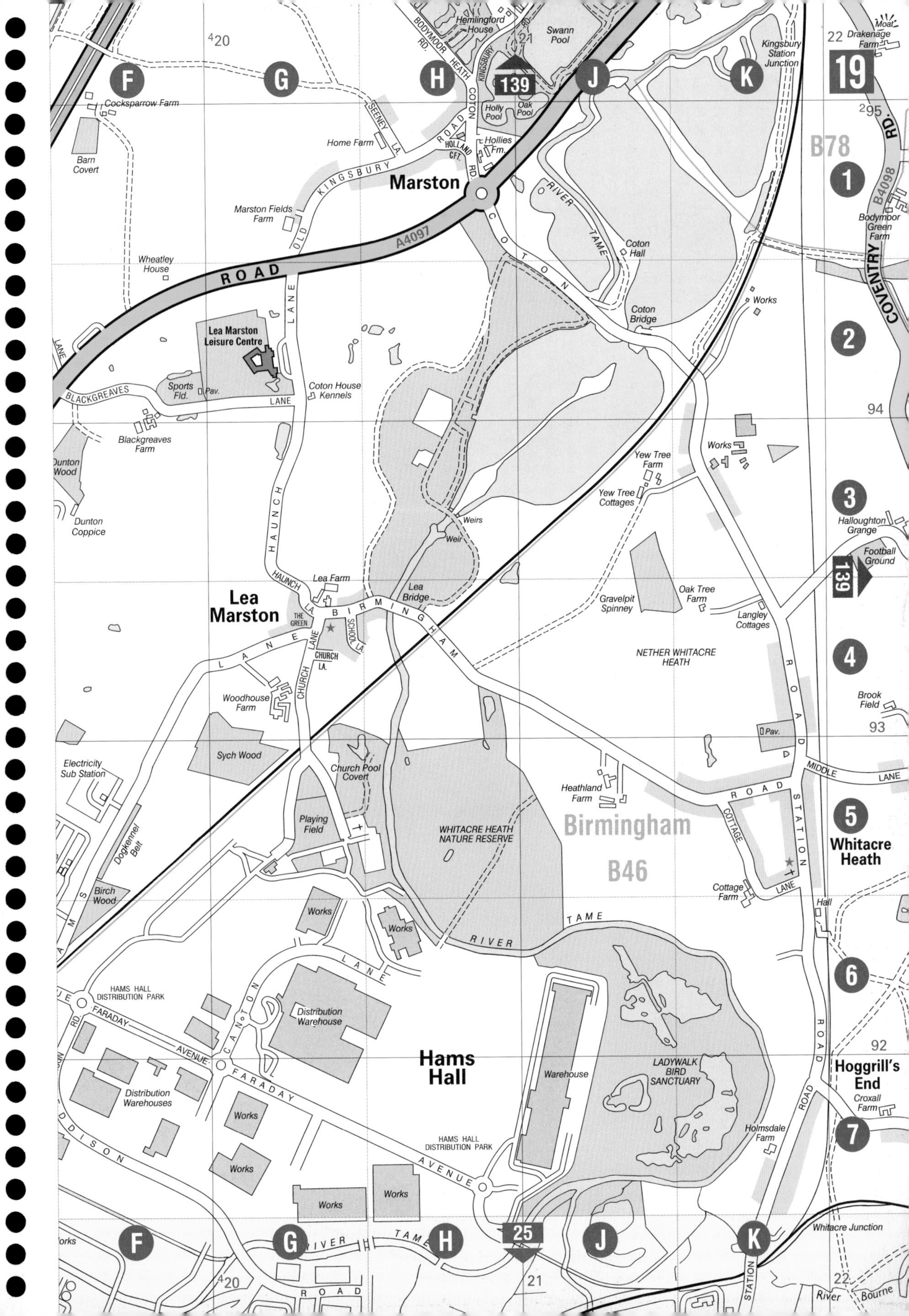
19
139
25
F
G
H
J
K
1
2
3
4
5
6
7
420
21
22
295
94
93
92
B78
B46
Marston
Lea Marston
Hams Hall
Whitacre Heath
Hoggrill's End
Birmingham
Hemlingford House
Swann Pool
Holly Pool
Oak Pool
Hollies Fm.
Kingsbury Station Junction
Drakenage Farm
Moat
Cocksparrow Farm
Barn Covert
Home Farm
Marston Fields Farm
Wheatley House
Lea Marston Leisure Centre
Sports Fld.
Pav.
Blackgreaves Farm
Dunton Wood
Dunton Coppice
Coton House Kennels
Coton Hall
Coton Bridge
Works
Bodymoor Green Farm
Yew Tree Farm
Yew Tree Cottages
Weirs
Weir
Lea Farm
Lea Bridge
Halloughton Grange
Football Ground
Gravelpit Spinney
Oak Tree Farm
Langley Cottages
NETHER WHITACRE HEATH
Brook Field
Woodhouse Farm
Sych Wood
Electricity Sub Station
Church Pool Covert
Playing Field
Heathland Farm
WHITACRE HEATH NATURE RESERVE
Dogkennel Belt
Birch Wood
Cottage Farm
Hall
HAMS HALL DISTRIBUTION PARK
Distribution Warehouse
Distribution Warehouses
Warehouse
LADYWALK BIRD SANCTUARY
Croxall Farm
Holmsdale Farm
Whitacre Junction
River Bourne
RIVER TAME
ROAD
A4097
B4098
COVENTRY RD.
KINGSBURY RD.
BODYMOOR HEATH RD.
COTON RD.
SEENEY LA.
HOLLAND CFT.
OLD KINGSBURY ROAD
HAUNCH LANE
BLACKGREAVES LANE
THE GREEN
BIRMINGHAM LANE
SCHOOL LA.
CHURCH LANE
CHURCH LA.
MIDDLE LANE
STATION ROAD
COTTAGE LANE
COTON LANE
CANTON LANE
FARADAY AVENUE
EDDISON ROAD

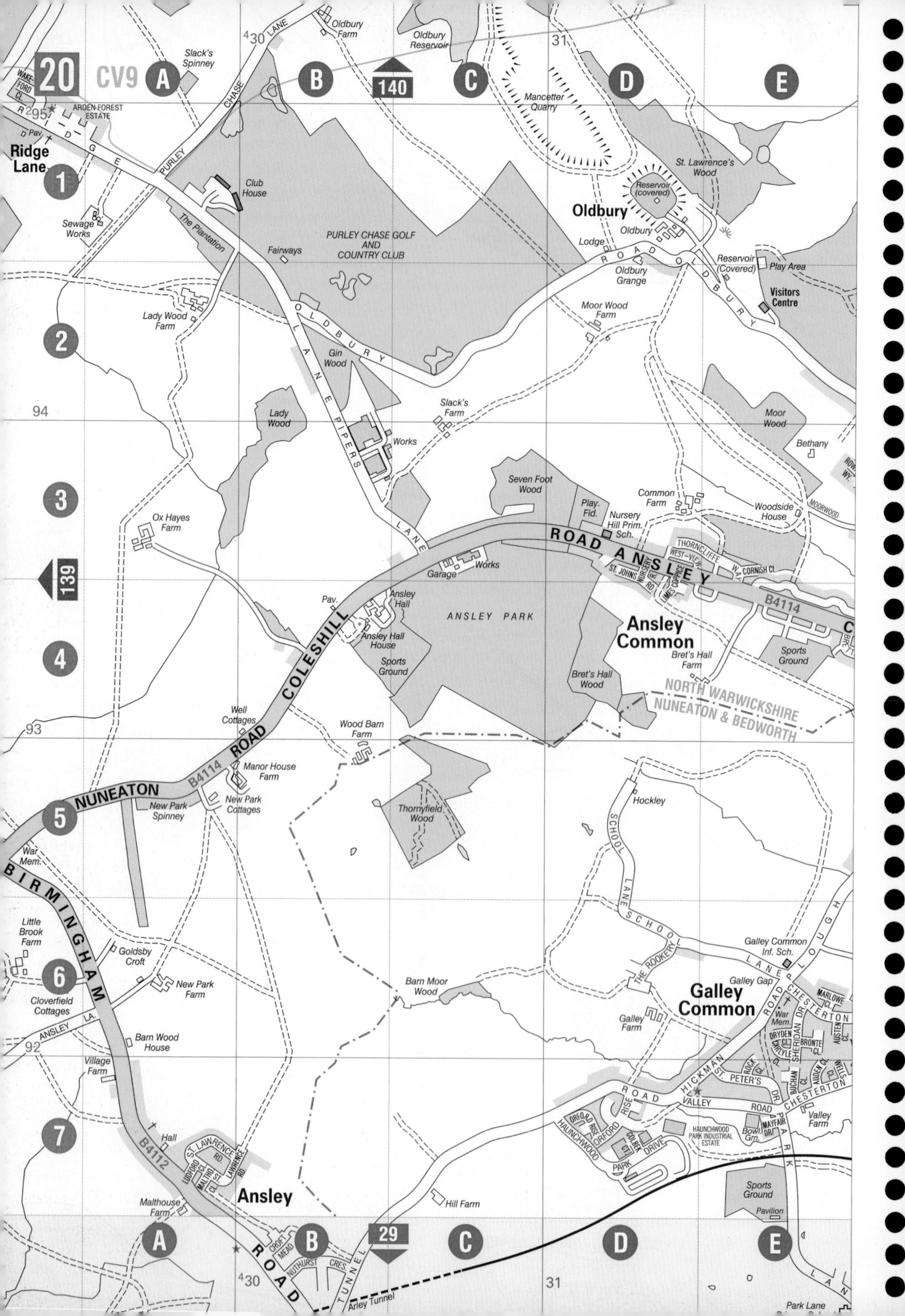

20
CV9
A
B
C
D
E
140
139
29
1
2
3
4
5
6
7
Slack's Spinney
Oldbury Farm
Oldbury Reservoir
Mancetter Quarry
ARDEN FOREST ESTATE
WAKEFORD CL.
RIDGE
Pav.
Ridge Lane
PURLEY CHASE LANE
Club House
The Plantation
Sewage Works
PURLEY CHASE GOLF AND COUNTRY CLUB
Fairways
St. Lawrence's Wood
Reservoir (covered)
Oldbury
Lodge
OLDBURY ROAD
Oldbury Grange
Reservoir (Covered)
Play Area
Visitors Centre
Lady Wood Farm
Moor Wood Farm
Gin Wood
PIPERS LANE
Slack's Farm
Lady Wood
Works
Moor Wood
Bethany
Seven Foot Wood
Play. Fld.
Common Farm
Woodside House
MOORWOOD
Ox Hayes Farm
Nursery Hill Prim. Sch.
ANSLEY ROAD
THORNCLIFFE WAY
WEST VIEW
ST. JOHNS
NURSERY RD.
LIMES COPPICE
CORNISH CL.
Garage
B4114
Pav.
Ansley Hall
ANSLEY PARK
Ansley Common
COLESHILL ROAD
Ansley Hall House
Sports Ground
Bret's Hall Farm
Bret's Hall Wood
NORTH WARWICKSHIRE
NUNEATON & BEDWORTH
Well Cottages
Wood Barn Farm
Manor House Farm
NUNEATON
New Park Cottages
New Park Spinney
Hockley
Thornyfield Wood
War Mem.
BIRMINGHAM ROAD
SCHOOL LANE
Little Brook Farm
Goldsby Croft
New Park Farm
Barn Moor Wood
THE ROOKERY
Galley Common Inf. Sch.
Galley Gap
Galley Common
Cloverfield Cottages
ANSLEY LA.
Barn Wood House
Galley Farm
CHESTERTON
MARLOWE CL.
DRYDEN CL.
CARLYLE CL.
BRONTE CL.
AUSTEN CL.
SHERIDAN DR.
BUCHAN CL.
AUDEN CL.
WELLS
ROCK CL.
ST. PETER'S
HICKMAN
Village Farm
VALLEY ROAD
RISE ROAD
ORFORD RISE
HAUNCHWOOD PARK DRIVE
COLBEK CT.
HAUNCHWOOD PARK INDUSTRIAL ESTATE
Bowl Grn.
MAYFAIR DR.
Valley Farm
PLOUGH
PARK LANE
Hall
B4112
ST. LAWRENCE RD.
LUDFORD CL.
MALTHOUSE CL.
Ansley
Malthouse Farm
Hill Farm
Sports Ground
Pavilion
CROFT MEAD
NUTHURST CRES.
TUNNEL ROAD
Arley Tunnel
Park Lane
430
31
95
94
93
92

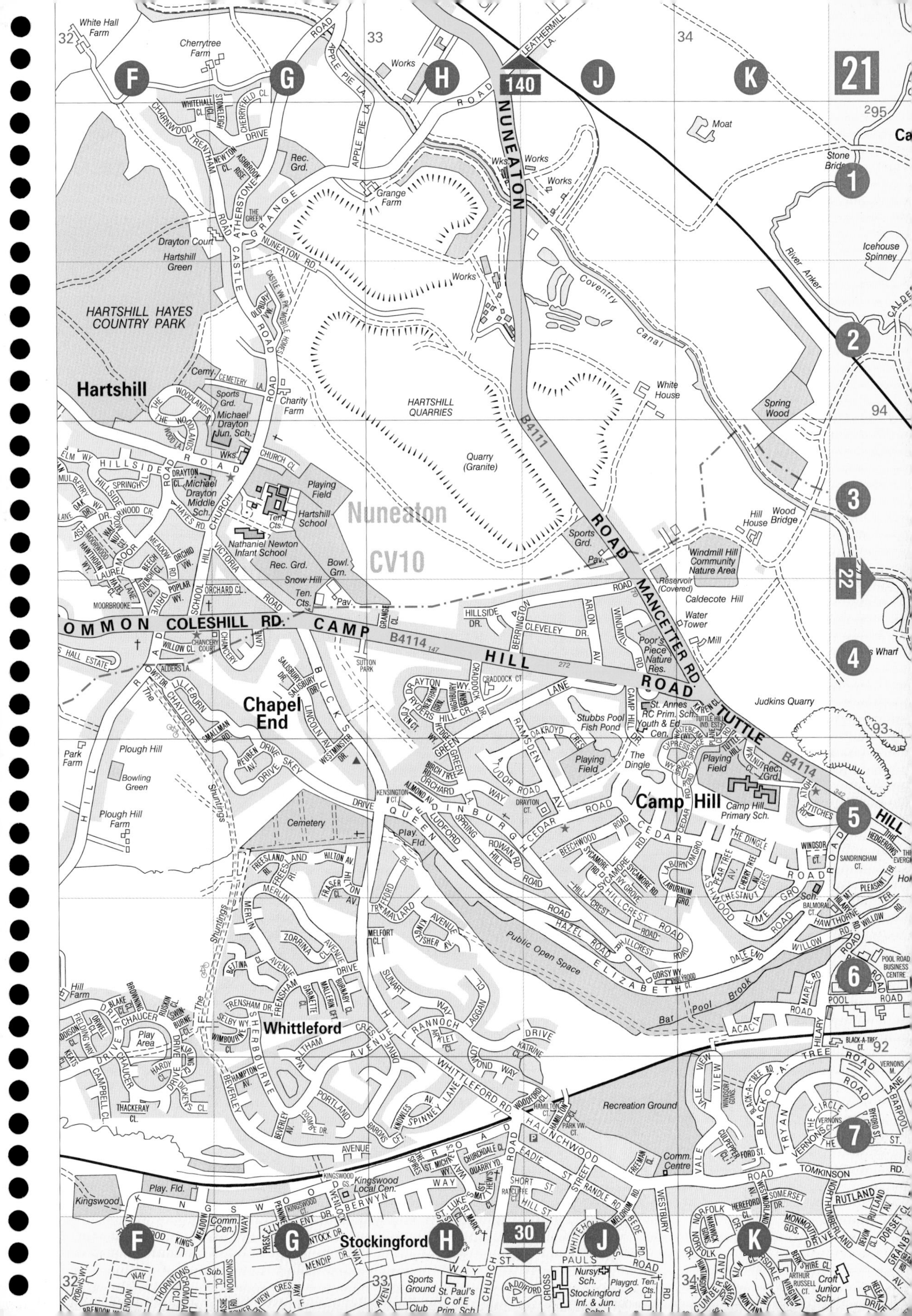
Hartshill
HARTSHILL HAYES COUNTRY PARK
HARTSHILL QUARRIES
Quarry (Granite)
Nuneaton
CV10
Chapel End
Camp Hill
Whittleford
Stockingford
Kingswood
NUNEATON
ROAD
MANCETTER RD.
CAMP HILL ROAD
COLESHILL RD.
TUTTLE HILL
B4111
B4114
Coventry Canal
River Anker
Windmill Hill Community Nature Area
Recreation Ground
Public Open Space
Cemetery
Judkins Quarry
Spring Wood
Icehouse Spinney
Moat
140
30
22
F
G
H
J
K
1
2
3
4
5
6
7

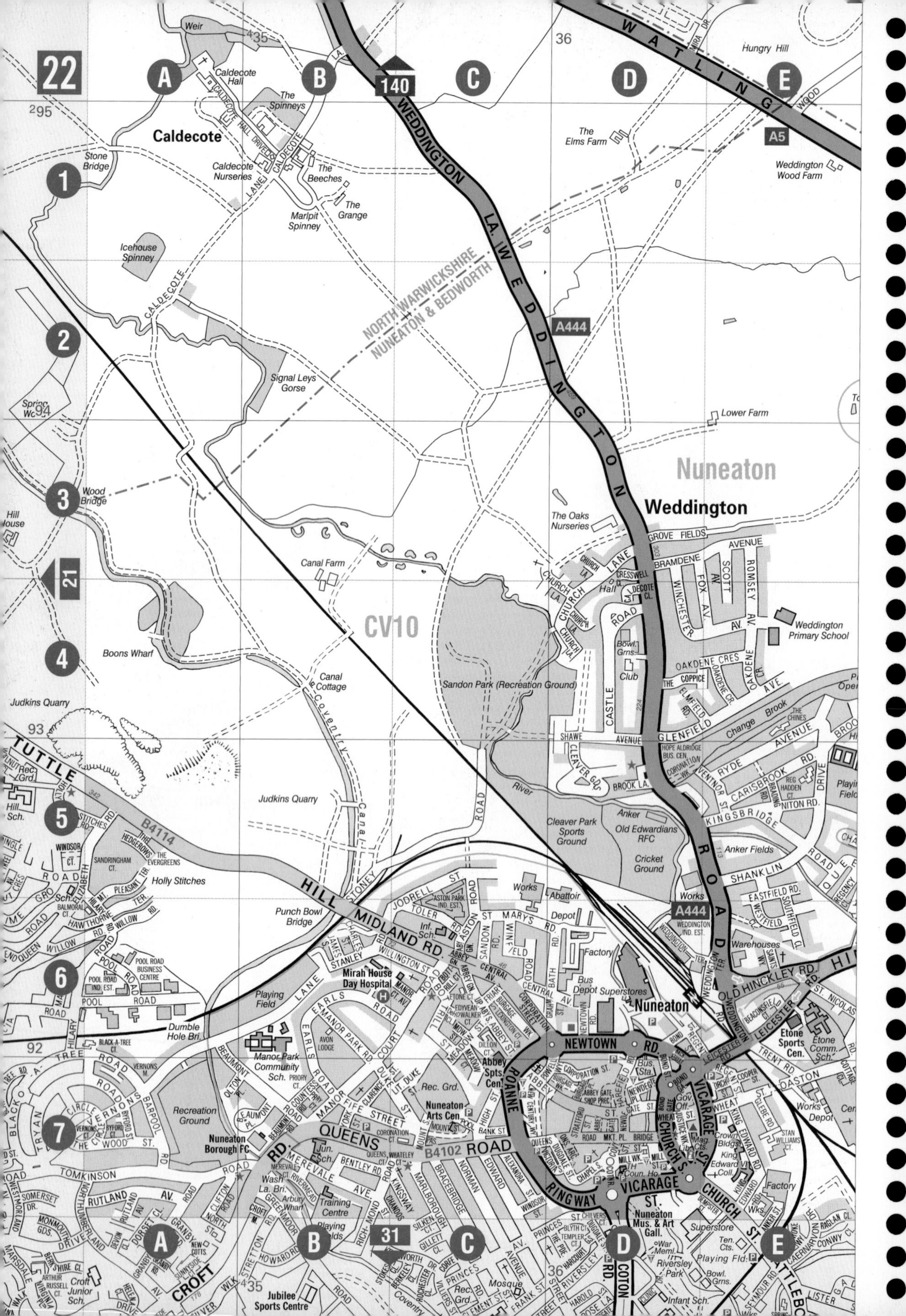

22
A
B
C
D
E
1
2
3
4
5
6
7
140
21
31
Weir
Caldecote Hall
The Spinneys
Caldecote
Stone Bridge
Caldecote Nurseries
The Beeches
The Grange
Marlpit Spinney
Icehouse Spinney
Hungry Hill
WATLING
WOOD
A5
The Elms Farm
Weddington Wood Farm
WEDDINGTON LA.
A444
NORTH WARWICKSHIRE
NUNEATON & BEDWORTH
Signal Leys Gorse
Lower Farm
Nuneaton
Weddington
Wood Bridge
The Oaks Nurseries
Canal Farm
CV10
Boons Wharf
Canal Cottage
Judkins Quarry
Sandon Park (Recreation Ground)
Weddington Primary School
GROVE FIELDS
AVENUE
BRAMDENE
SCOTT
ROMSEY AV.
FOX AV.
WINCHESTER AV.
OAKDENE CRES
CASTLE
GLENFIELD
SHAWE AVENUE
CLEAVER GDS.
BROOK LA.
HOPE ALDRIDGE BUS. CEN.
Change Brook
RYDE AVENUE
CARISBROOK RD.
KINGSBRIDGE RD.
River Anker
Cleaver Park Sports Ground
Old Edwardians RFC
Cricket Ground
Anker Fields
SHANKLIN
EASTFIELD RD.
WESTFIELD
SOUTHFIELD RD.
TUTTLE HILL
B4114
Holly Stitches
Punch Bowl Bridge
HILL MIDLAND RD
STONEY ROAD
Works
Abattoir
Depot
Factory
Bus Depot
Superstores
Warehouses
WEDDINGTON IND. EST.
OLD HINCKLEY RD.
LEICESTER RD.
Etone Sports Cen.
Etone Comm. Sch.
Mirah House Day Hospital
Playing Field
Dumble Hole Bri.
POOL ROAD
POOL ROAD BUSINESS CENTRE
POOL ROAD IND. EST.
Manor Park Community Sch.
Recreation Ground
Nuneaton Borough FC
QUEENS ROAD
B4102
Nuneaton Arts Cen.
Rec. Grd.
Abbey Spts. Cen.
NEWTOWN RD.
ROANNE RINGWAY
VICARAGE ST.
CHURCH ST.
Bus Sta.
Nuneaton Mus. & Art Gall.
War Meml.
Riversley Park
Superstore
Playing Fld.
Bowl. Grns.
Infant Sch.
Ten. Cts.
King Edward VI Coll.
Crown Bldgs.
Factory
Works Depot
TOMKINSON RD.
RUTLAND AV.
NORTHUMBERLAND
CROFT
Croft Junior Sch.
Jubilee Sports Centre
Training Centre
Arbury Wharf
Wash La. Bri.
Mosque
Coventry Canal
COTON RD.
ATTLEBOROUGH

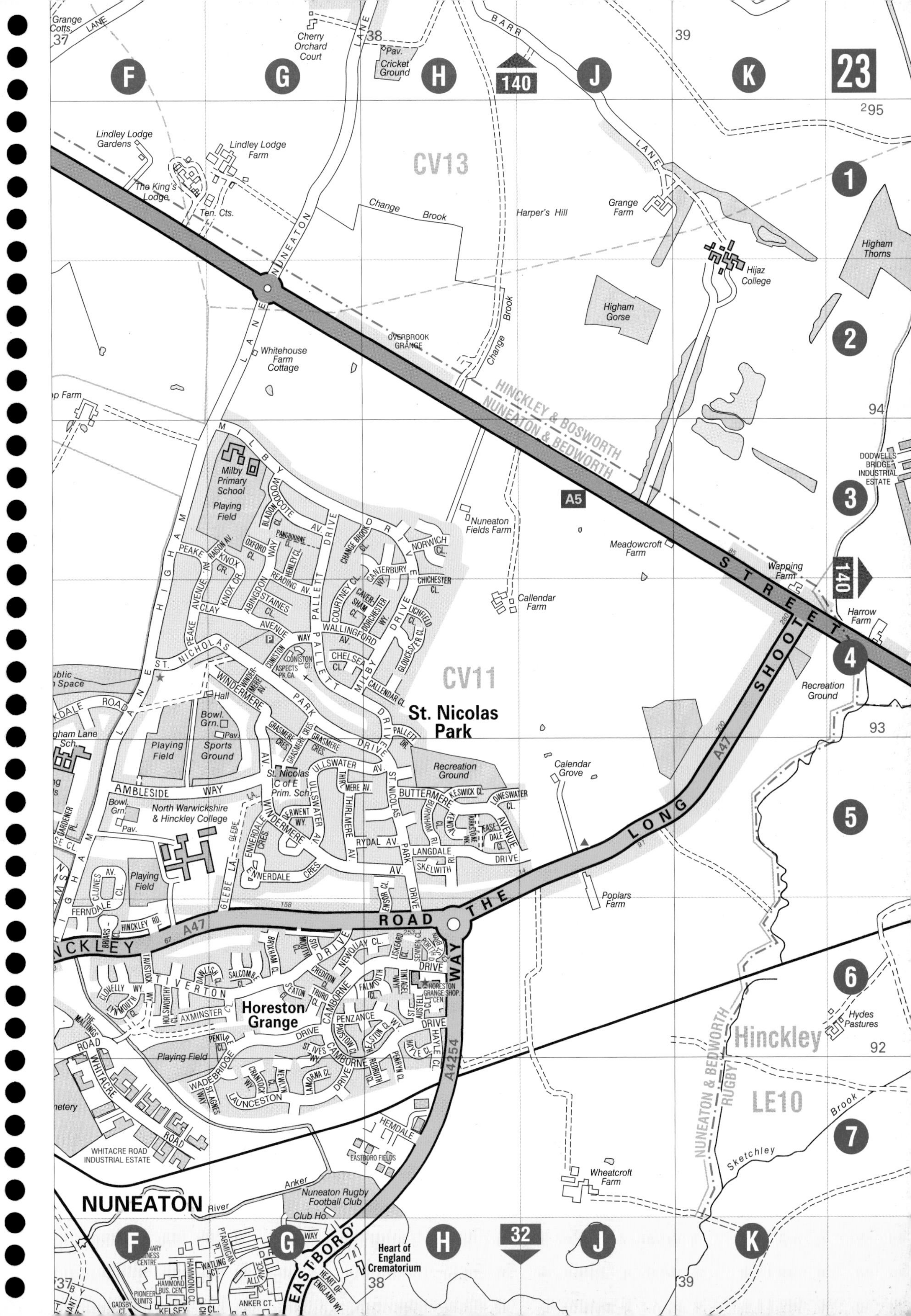

F
G
H
J
K
140
1
2
3
4
5
6
7
39
95
94
93
92
37
38
Grange Cotts.
Cherry Orchard Court
Pav.
Cricket Ground
BARR LANE
Lindley Lodge Gardens
Lindley Lodge Farm
The King's Lodge
Ten. Cts.
CV13
Change Brook
Harper's Hill
Grange Farm
Higham Thorns
Hijaz College
Higham Gorse
NUNEATON LANE
Whitehouse Farm Cottage
OVERBROOK GRANGE
HINCKLEY & BOSWORTH
NUNEATON & BEDWORTH
A5
Nuneaton Fields Farm
Meadowcroft Farm
Wapping Farm
Harrow Farm
DODWELLS BRIDGE INDUSTRIAL ESTATE
WATLING STREET
Callendar Farm
Milby Primary School
Playing Field
CV11
St. Nicolas Park
Recreation Ground
Calendar Grove
THE LONG SHOOT
A47
Sports Ground
Bowl. Grn.
St. Nicolas C of E Prim. Sch.
AMBLESIDE WAY
North Warwickshire & Hinckley College
Poplars Farm
HINCKLEY ROAD
A4254
Horeston Grange
Hinckley
LE10
NUNEATON & BEDWORTH
RUGBY
Hydes Pastures
Brook
Sketchley
Wheatcroft Farm
WHITACRE ROAD INDUSTRIAL ESTATE
NUNEATON
River Anker
Nuneaton Rugby Football Club
Club Ho.
EASTBORO' WAY
Heart of England Crematorium
32

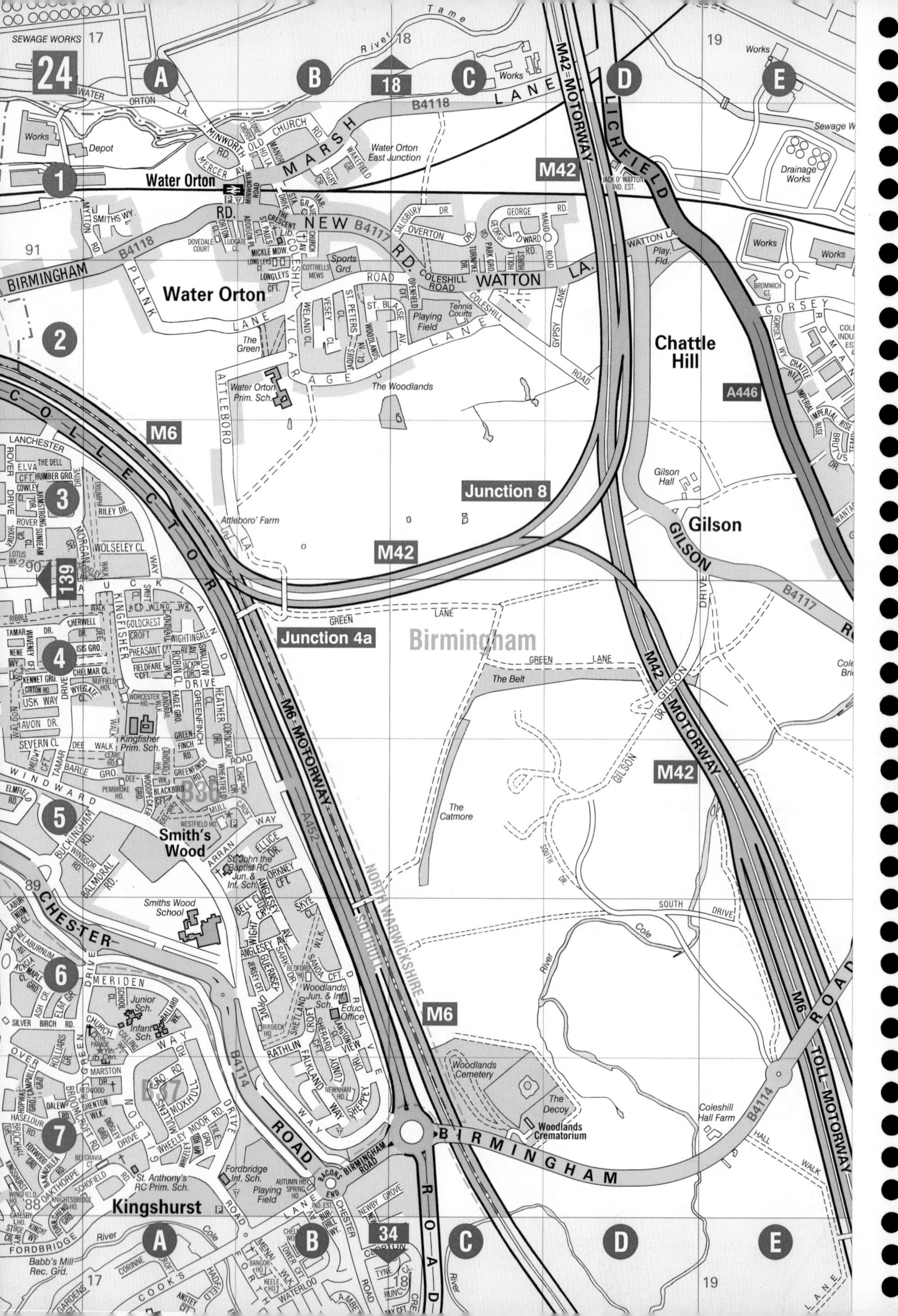

SEWAGE WORKS
Water Orton
Water Orton East Junction
Chattle Hill
Junction 8
Junction 4a
Birmingham
Gilson
Smith's Wood
Kingshurst
Water Orton Prim. Sch.
The Woodlands
Attleboro' Farm
Kingfisher Prim. Sch.
Smiths Wood School
Woodlands Cemetery
Woodlands Crematorium
The Decoy
The Catmore
The Belt
Gilson Hall
Coleshill Hall Farm
Drainage Works
M42 MOTORWAY
M6 MOTORWAY
M6 TOLL MOTORWAY
COLLECTOR ROAD
BIRMINGHAM ROAD
LICHFIELD ROAD
MARSH LANE
WATTON LA.
GILSON ROAD
CHESTER ROAD
River Tame
River Cole

18
139
34

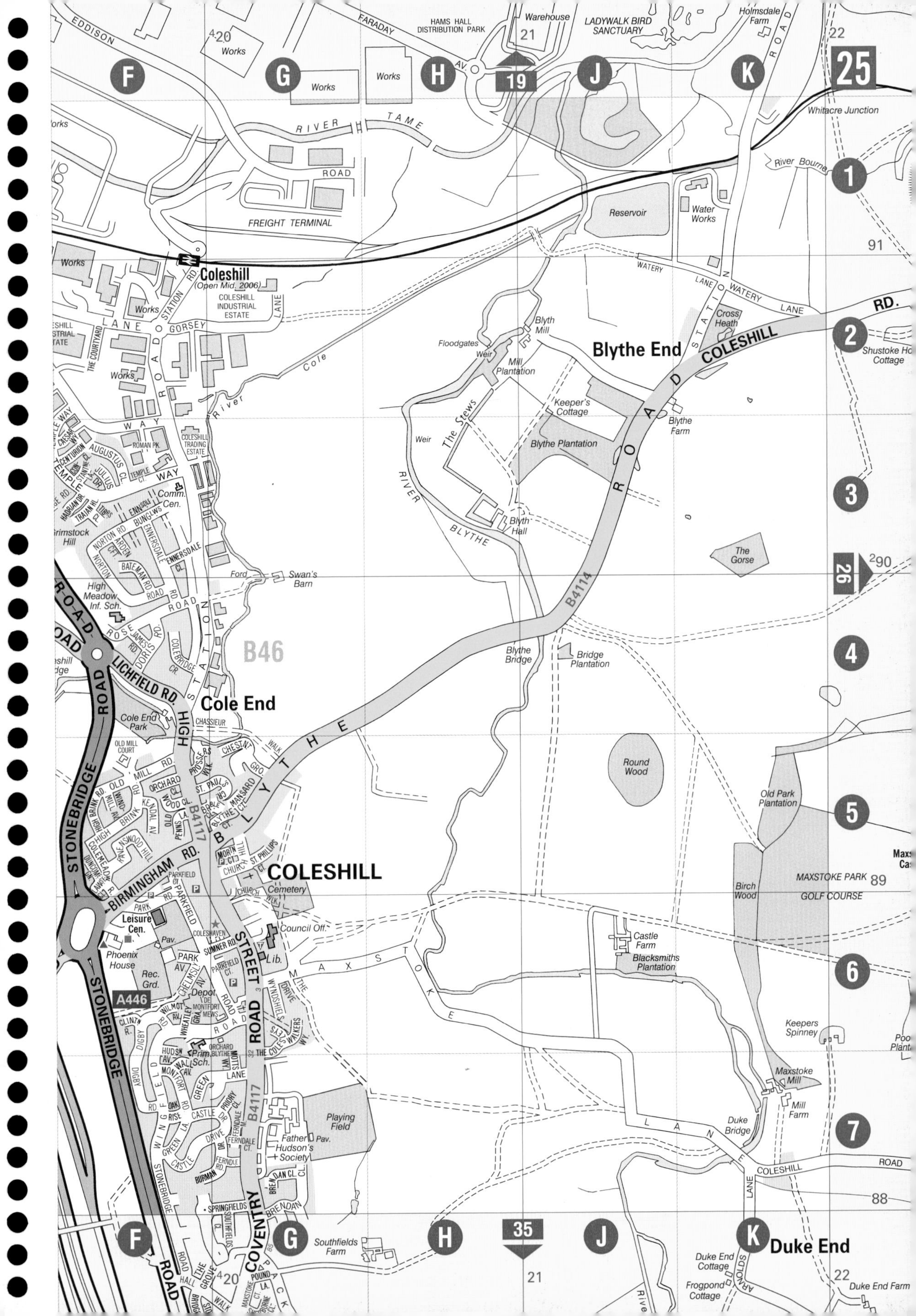

25
19
26
35
F
G
H
J
K
1
2
3
4
5
6
7
Coleshill
(Open Mid. 2006)
COLESHILL
Blythe End
Cole End
Duke End
LADYWALK BIRD SANCTUARY
HAMS HALL DISTRIBUTION PARK
FREIGHT TERMINAL
COLESHILL INDUSTRIAL ESTATE
COLESHILL TRADING ESTATE
Reservoir
Water Works
Whitacre Junction
River Bourne
Holmsdale Farm
Cross Heath
Shustoke House Cottage
Blyth Mill
Floodgates
Weir
Mill Plantation
The Stews
Keeper's Cottage
Blythe Farm
Blythe Plantation
Blyth Hall
RIVER BLYTHE
The Gorse
Swan's Barn
Ford
Blythe Bridge
Bridge Plantation
Round Wood
Old Park Plantation
Birch Wood
MAXSTOKE PARK GOLF COURSE
Castle Farm
Blacksmiths Plantation
Keepers Spinney
Maxstoke Mill
Mill Farm
Duke Bridge
Playing Field
Father Hudson's Society
Southfields Farm
Duke End Cottage
Frogpond Cottage
Duke End Farm
Cemetery
Council Off.
Lib.
Leisure Cen.
Phoenix House
Rec. Grd.
Depot
Prim. Sch.
Comm. Cen.
High Meadow Inf. Sch.
Cole End Park
Grimstock Hill
B4114
B4117
B46
A446
COLESHILL ROAD
BLYTHE ROAD
STONEBRIDGE ROAD
COVENTRY ROAD
HIGH STREET
STATION ROAD
LICHFIELD RD.
BIRMINGHAM RD.
MAXSTOKE LANE
WATERY LANE
RIVER TAME
River Cole
GORSEY LANE
FARADAY AV.
EDDISON ROAD
Works
Warehouse

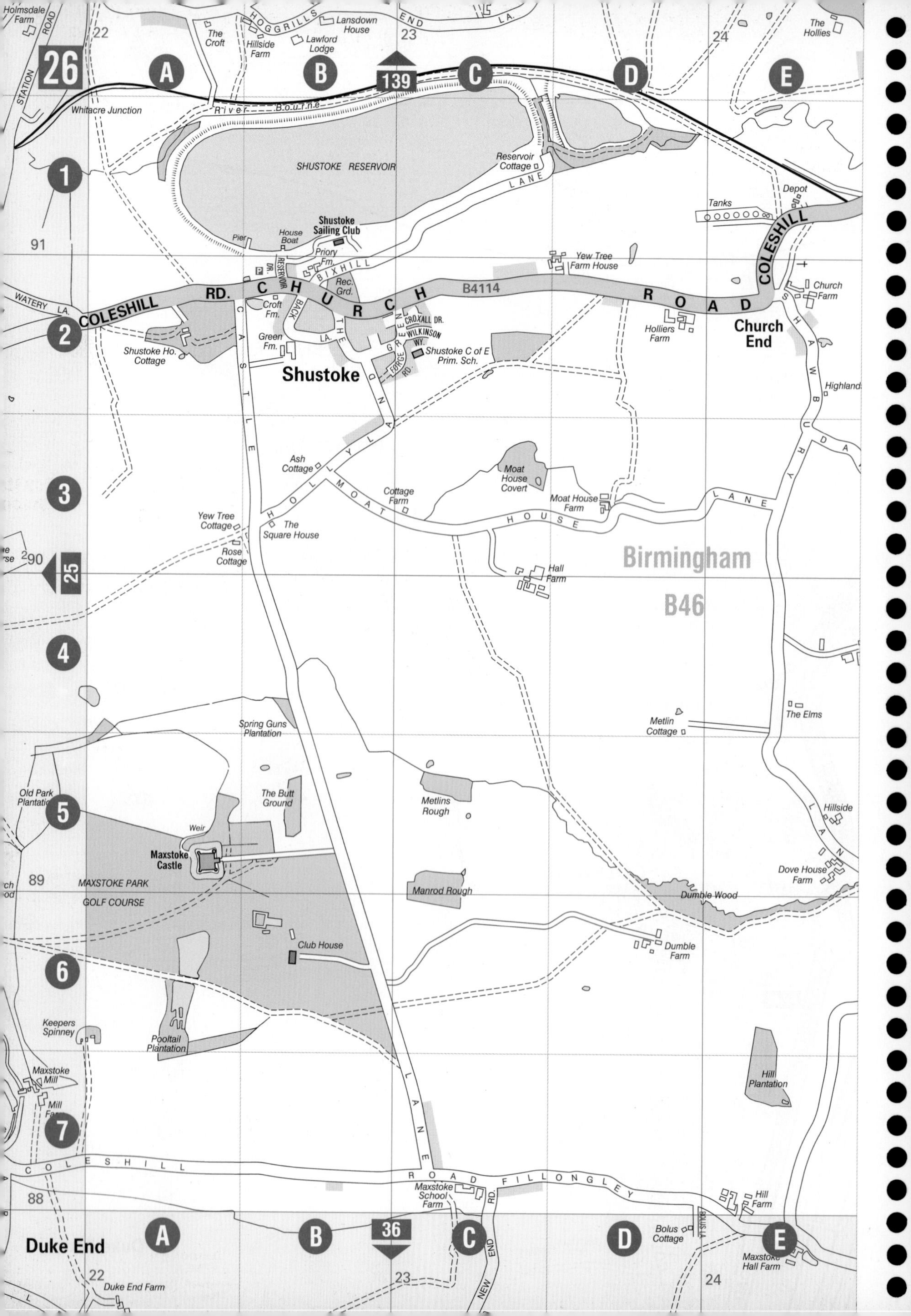

Holmsdale Farm
STATION ROAD
The Croft
Hillside Farm
HOGGRILLS END LA.
Lansdown House
Lawford Lodge
The Hollies
139
A
B
C
D
E
Whitacre Junction
River Bourne
SHUSTOKE RESERVOIR
Reservoir Cottage
LANE
Depot
Tanks
COLESHILL
Pier
House Boat
Shustoke Sailing Club
Priory Fm.
BIXHILL
Rec. Grd.
RESERVOIR DR.
Yew Tree Farm House
Church Farm
WATERY LA.
COLESHILL RD.
CHURCH
B4114
ROAD
Croft Fm.
BACK LA.
THE GREEN
CROXALL DR.
WILKINSON WY.
Shustoke C of E Prim. Sch.
FORGE RD.
Holliers Farm
Church End
Green Fm.
Shustoke Ho. Cottage
Shustoke
SHAWBURY LANE
Highlands
CASTLE LANE
HOLLY LANE
Ash Cottage
Moat House Covert
Cottage Farm
Moat House Farm
MOAT HOUSE LANE
Yew Tree Cottage
The Square House
Rose Cottage
Birmingham
B46
Hall Farm
25
1
2
3
4
5
6
7
91
90
89
88
22
23
24
The Elms
Metlin Cottage
Spring Guns Plantation
Old Park Plantation
The Butt Ground
Metlins Rough
Hillside
Weir
Maxstoke Castle
MAXSTOKE PARK GOLF COURSE
Manrod Rough
Dove House Farm
Dumble Wood
Club House
Dumble Farm
Keepers Spinney
Pooltail Plantation
Hill Plantation
Maxstoke Mill
Mill Farm
COLESHILL ROAD
FILLONGLEY
Maxstoke School Farm
NEW END RD.
Hill Farm
BOLUS LA.
Bolus Cottage
36
Duke End
Duke End Farm
Maxstoke Hall Farm

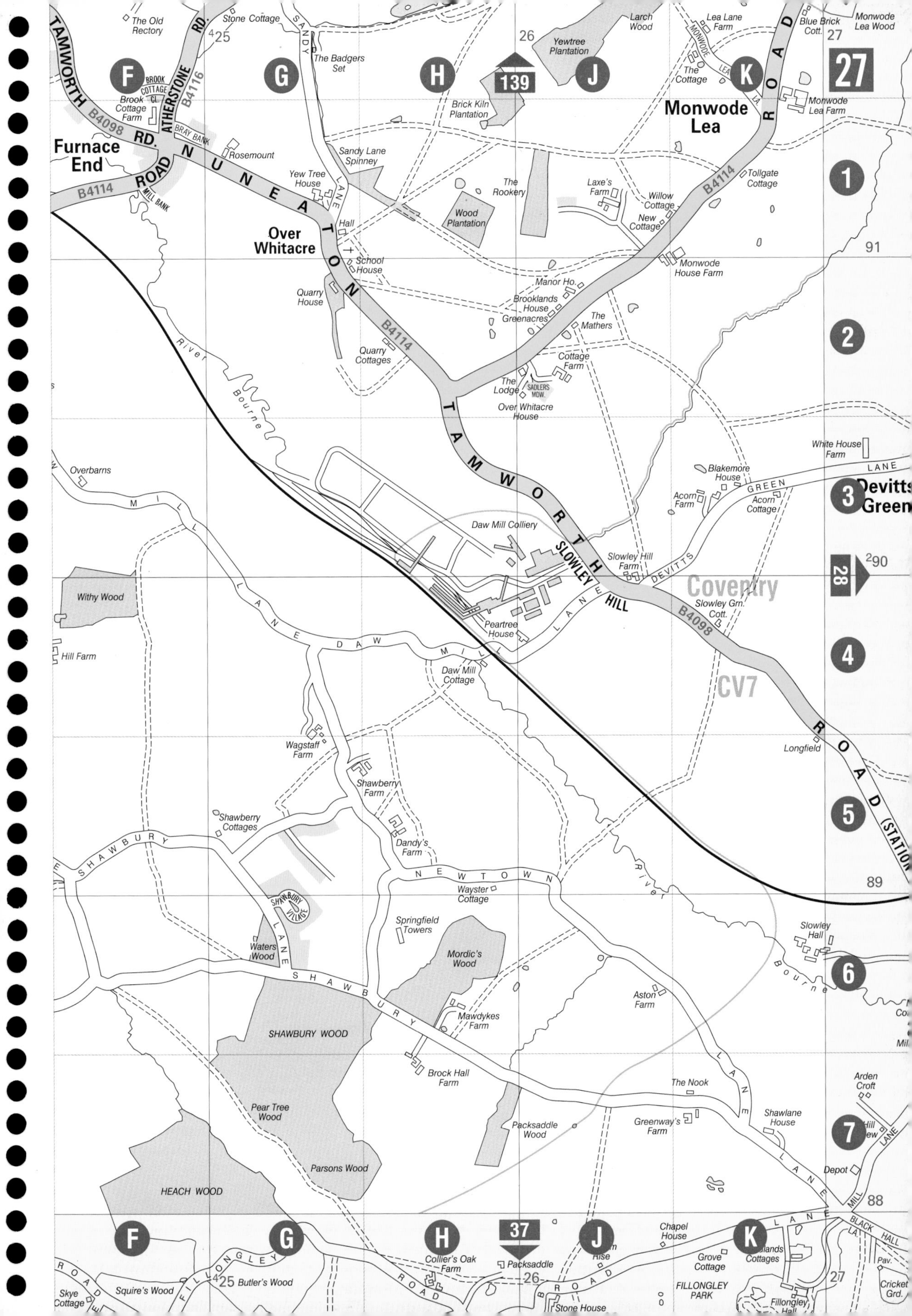

27
Furnace End
Over Whitacre
Monwode Lea
Devitts Green
Coventry
CV7
The Old Rectory
Stone Cottage
The Badgers Set
Larch Wood
Yewtree Plantation
Lea Lane Farm
Blue Brick Cott.
Monwode Lea Wood
Monwode Lea Farm
The Cottage
Brick Kiln Plantation
Brook Cottage Farm
Rosemount
Sandy Lane Spinney
Yew Tree House
The Rookery
Wood Plantation
Laxe's Farm
Willow Cottage
New Cottage
Tollgate Cottage
Hall
School House
Quarry House
Monwode House Farm
Manor Ho.
Brooklands House
Greenacres
The Mathers
Quarry Cottages
Cottage Farm
The Lodge
Over Whitacre House
White House Farm
Blakemore House
Acorn Farm
Acorn Cottage
Overbarns
Daw Mill Colliery
Slowley Hill Farm
Slowley Grn. Cott.
Withy Wood
Peartree House
Hill Farm
Daw Mill Cottage
Wagstaff Farm
Shawberry Farm
Longfield
Shawberry Cottages
Dandy's Farm
Wayster Cottage
Springfield Towers
Mordic's Wood
Waters Wood
Slowley Hall
Aston Farm
Mawdykes Farm
SHAWBURY WOOD
Brock Hall Farm
The Nook
Arden Croft
Pear Tree Wood
Packsaddle Wood
Greenway's Farm
Shawlane House
Parsons Wood
Depot
HEACH WOOD
Chapel House
Collier's Oak Farm
Packsaddle
Grove Cottage
Squire's Wood
Butler's Wood
Skye Cottage
FILLONGLEY PARK
Stone House
Cricket Grd.
Pav.
TAMWORTH ROAD
NUNEATON ROAD
ATHERSTONE RD.
BRAY BANK
BROOK COTTAGE CL.
MILL BANK
SANDY LANE
MONWODE LEA LA.
B4098
B4114
B4116
TAMWORTH ROAD
SLOWLEY HILL
DEVITTS GREEN LANE
MILL LANE
DAW MILL LANE
SHAWBURY LANE
NEWTOWN LANE
SHAWBURY VILLAGE
SADLERS MDW.
ROAD (STATION
SHAW LANE
BLACK HALL LA.
FILLONGLEY ROAD
BROAD ROAD
MILL LANE
River Bourne
139
28
37
F G H J K
1 2 3 4 5 6 7
425 26 27 88 89 90 91

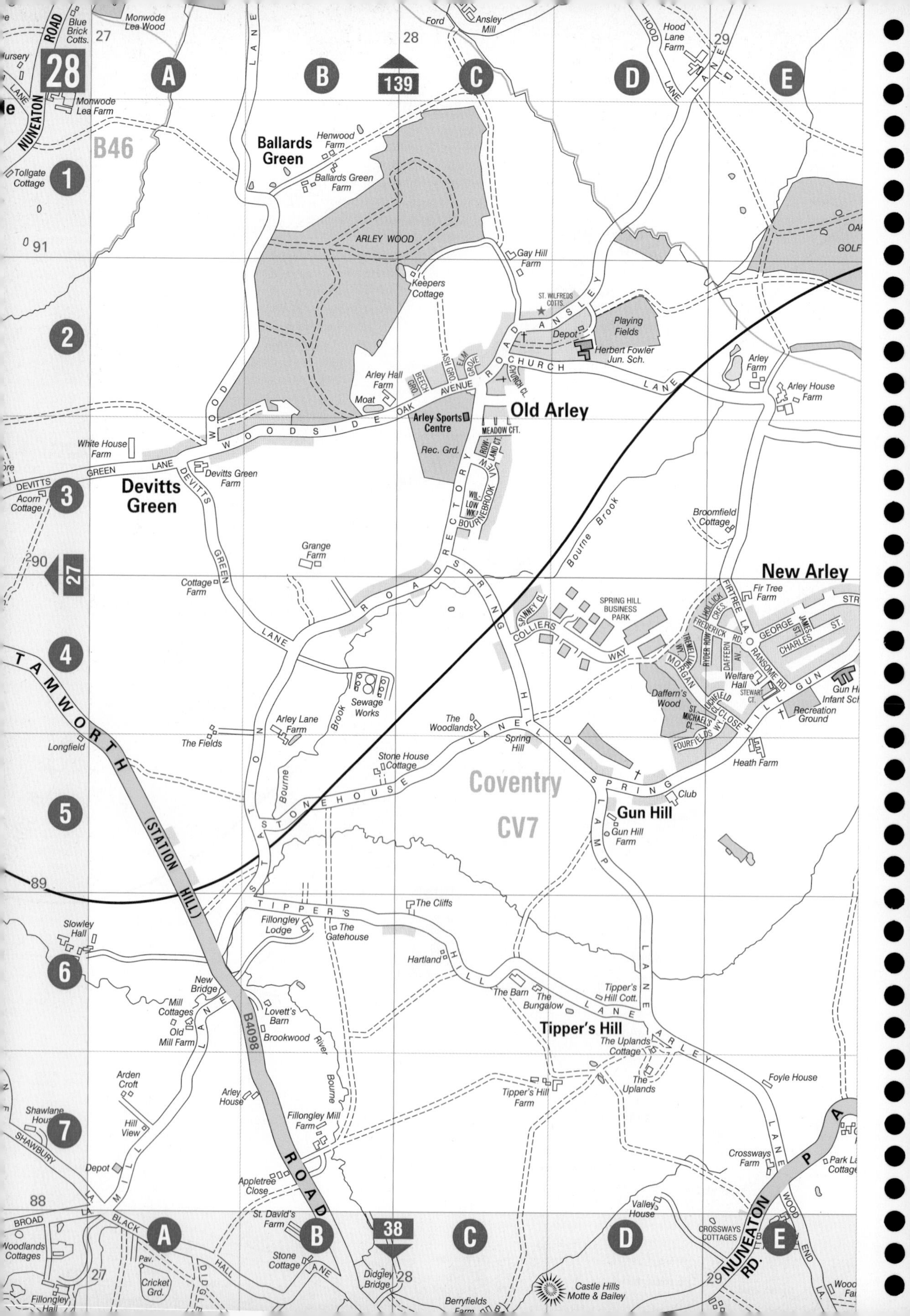

28
139
38
27
A
B
C
D
E
1
2
3
4
5
6
7
Monwode Lea Wood
Blue Brick Cotts.
Nursery
NUNEATON ROAD
LANE
Monwode Lea Farm
B46
Tollgate Cottage
91
90
89
88
Ford
Ansley Mill
Hood Lane Farm
HOOD LANE
Ballards Green
Henwood Farm
Ballards Green Farm
ARLEY WOOD
Gay Hill Farm
Keepers Cottage
ST. WILFREDS COTTS.
ANSLEY ROAD
Depot
Playing Fields
Herbert Fowler Jun. Sch.
CHURCH LANE
CHURCH CL.
ASH GRO.
ELM GROVE
BEECH GRO.
Arley Hall Farm
Moat
OAK AVENUE
WOODSIDE
WOOD
Old Arley
Arley Sports Centre
Rec. Grd.
MEADOW CFT.
ROW-LAND CT.
BOURNEBROOK VIEW
WIL-LOW WK.
RECTORY ROAD
Arley Farm
Arley House Farm
White House Farm
GREEN LANE
DEVITTS GREEN
Devitts Green Farm
Devitts Green
Acorn Cottage
Grange Farm
Bourne Brook
Broomfield Cottage
New Arley
Fir Tree Farm
Cottage Farm
SPRING HILL
SPINNEY CL.
SPRING HILL BUSINESS PARK
COLLIERS WAY
FIRTREE LA.
HOLLICK CRES.
FREDERICK RD.
GEORGE ST.
JAMES ST.
CHARLES ST.
TREMELLING WY.
RYDER ROW
DAFFERN AV.
MORGAN
RANSOME RD.
Welfare Hall
STEWART CT.
GUN HILL
Gun Hill Infant Sch.
Daffern's Wood
ST. MICHAELS CL.
LICHFIELD CLOSE
FOURFIELDS WY.
Recreation Ground
Heath Farm
TAMWORTH ROAD
(STATION HILL)
Sewage Works
Brook
Arley Lane Farm
STATION ROAD
The Fields
Longfield
The Woodlands
Spring Hill
STONEHOUSE LANE
Stone House Cottage
Coventry
CV7
Club
Gun Hill
Gun Hill Farm
LAMP LANE
The Cliffs
TIPPER'S HILL LANE
Fillongley Lodge
The Gatehouse
Slowley Hall
Hartland
The Barn
The Bungalow
Tipper's Hill Cott.
Tipper's Hill
New Bridge
Mill Cottages
Old Mill Farm
Lovett's Barn
B4098
Brookwood
River Bourne
The Uplands Cottage
ARLEY LANE
The Uplands
Tipper's Hill Farm
Foyle House
Arden Croft
Arley House
Fillongley Mill Farm
Hill View
Shawlane House
SHAWBURY
MILL LANE
Depot
Appletree Close
Crossways Farm
Park Lane Cottage
PARK LANE
NUNEATON RD.
WOOD END LA.
Valley House
CROSSWAYS COTTAGES
BROAD LA.
BLACK HALL LANE
Woodlands Cottages
St. David's Farm
Stone Cottage
Pav.
Cricket Grd.
DIDGLEY LANE
Didgley Bridge
Castle Hills Motte & Bailey
Berryfields Farm
Fillongley Hall
29

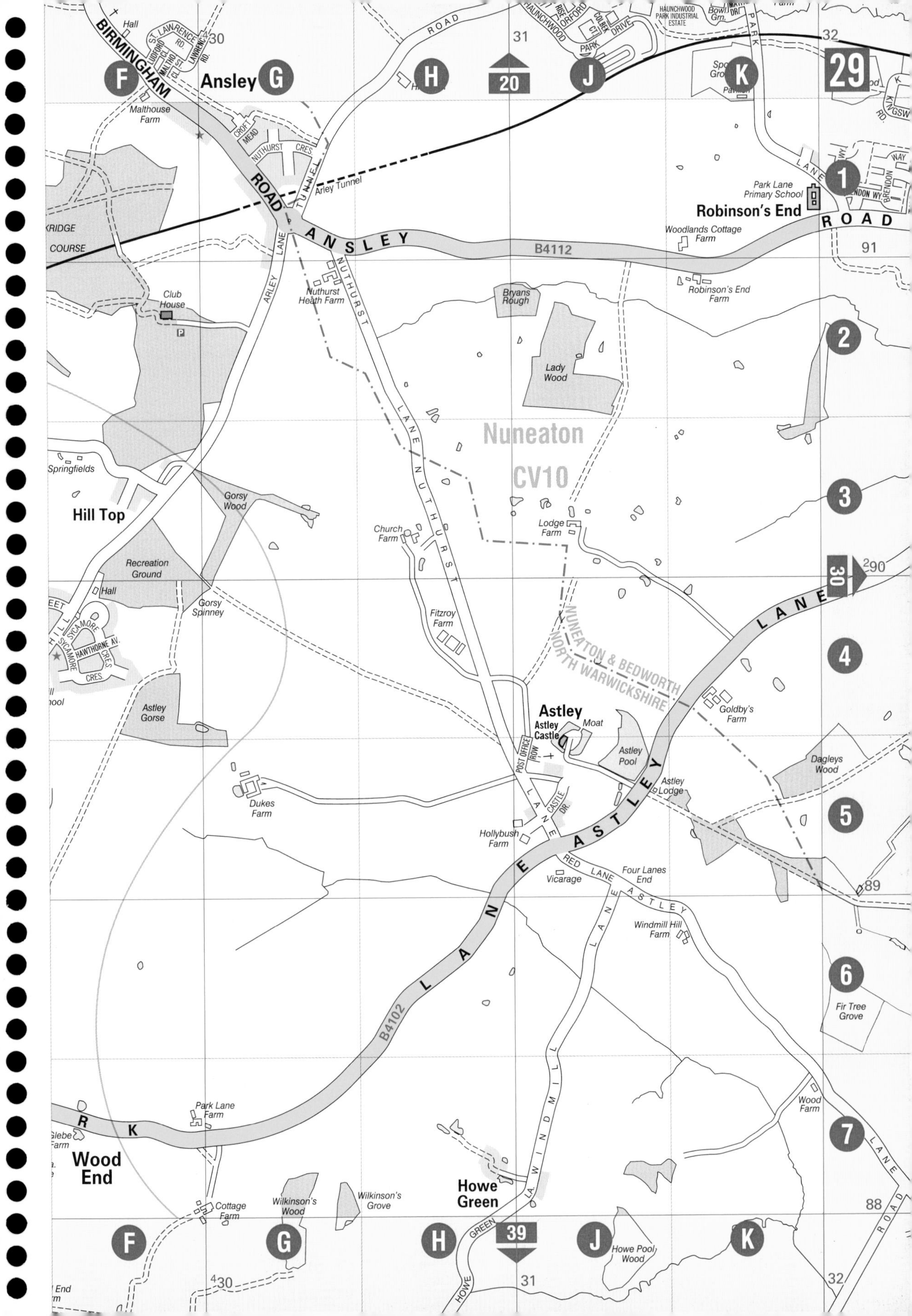

29
20
39
30
F
G
H
J
K
1
2
3
4
5
6
7
30
31
32
91
90
89
88
Ansley
Robinson's End
Hill Top
Astley
Wood End
Howe Green
Nuneaton
CV10
NUNEATON & BEDWORTH
NORTH WARWICKSHIRE
BIRMINGHAM ROAD
ANSLEY ROAD
B4112
B4102
ASTLEY LANE
NUTHURST LANE
ARLEY LANE
RED LANE
WINDMILL LA.
HOWE GREEN
Arley Tunnel
Malthouse Farm
Club House
Recreation Ground
Gorsy Wood
Gorsy Spinney
Astley Gorse
Springfields
Nuthurst Heath Farm
Bryans Rough
Lady Wood
Church Farm
Fitzroy Farm
Lodge Farm
Astley Castle
Moat
Astley Pool
Astley Lodge
Goldby's Farm
Dagleys Wood
Dukes Farm
Hollybush Farm
Vicarage
Four Lanes End
Windmill Hill Farm
Fir Tree Grove
Wood Farm
Park Lane Farm
Cottage Farm
Wilkinson's Wood
Wilkinson's Grove
Howe Pool Wood
Park Lane Primary School
Woodlands Cottage Farm
Robinson's End Farm
HAUNCHWOOD PARK INDUSTRIAL ESTATE
CROFT MEAD
NUTHURST CRES.
SYCAMORE CRES.
HAWTHORNE AV.
POST OFFICE ROW
CASTLE DR.

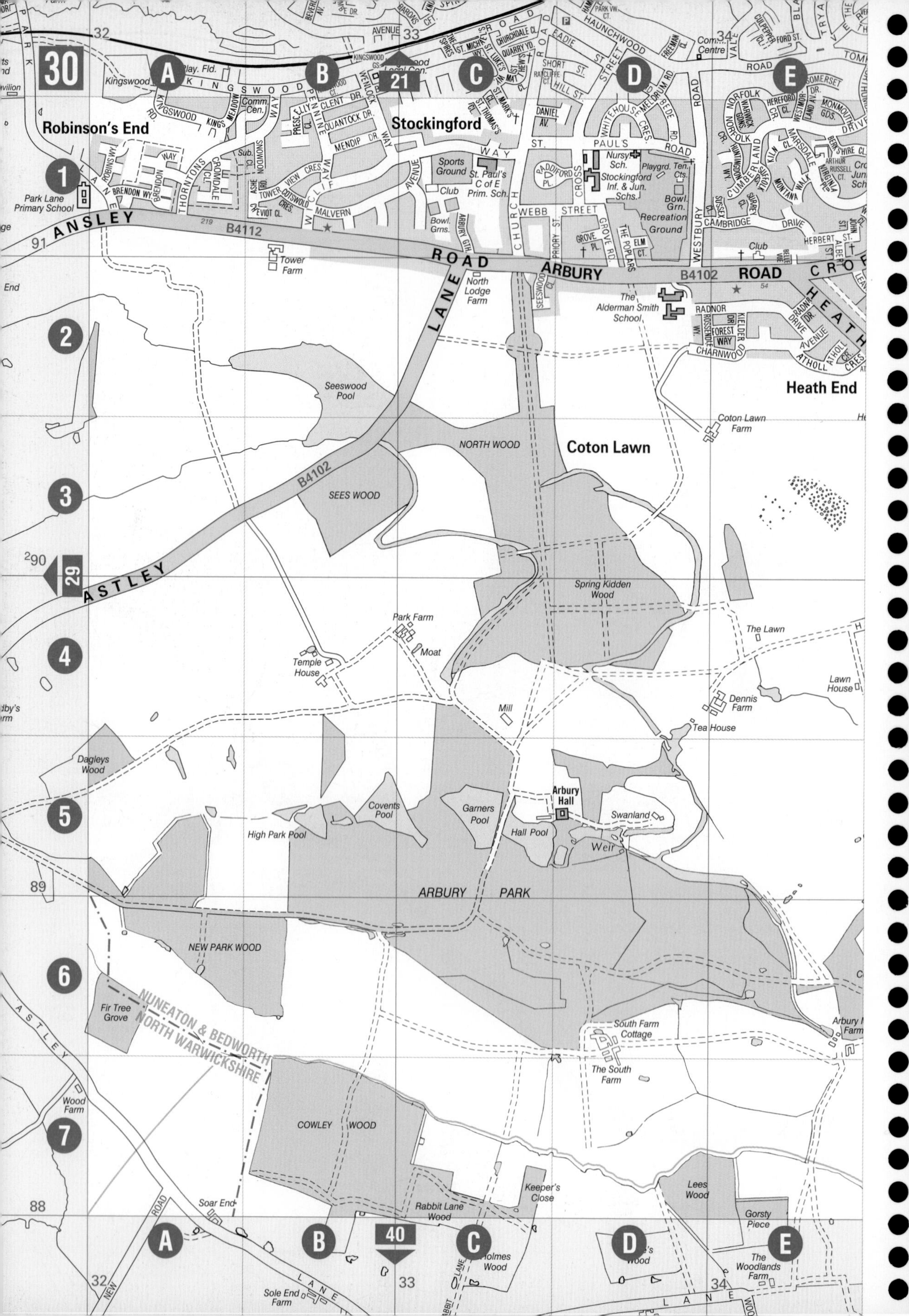

Robinson's End
Stockingford
Kingswood
Comm. Cen.
Park Lane Primary School
ANSLEY
B4112
ROAD
ARBURY
B4102
ROAD
Tower Farm
North Lodge Farm
LANE
The Alderman Smith School
Heath End
Seeswood Pool
NORTH WOOD
Coton Lawn
Coton Lawn Farm
SEES WOOD
B4102
ASTLEY
29
Spring Kidden Wood
Park Farm
Moat
Temple House
The Lawn
Lawn House
Dennis Farm
Mill
Tea House
Dagleys Wood
Arbury Hall
Covents Pool
Garners Pool
Swanland
Hall Pool
Weir
High Park Pool
ARBURY PARK
NEW PARK WOOD
NUNEATON & BEDWORTH
NORTH WARWICKSHIRE
Fir Tree Grove
South Farm Cottage
The South Farm
Wood Farm
COWLEY WOOD
Lees Wood
Keeper's Close
Rabbit Lane Wood
Soar End
Gorsty Piece
Holmes Wood
The Woodlands Farm
Sole End Farm
21
40
St. Paul's C of E Prim. Sch.
Sports Ground
Stockingford Inf. & Jun. Schs.
Recreation Ground

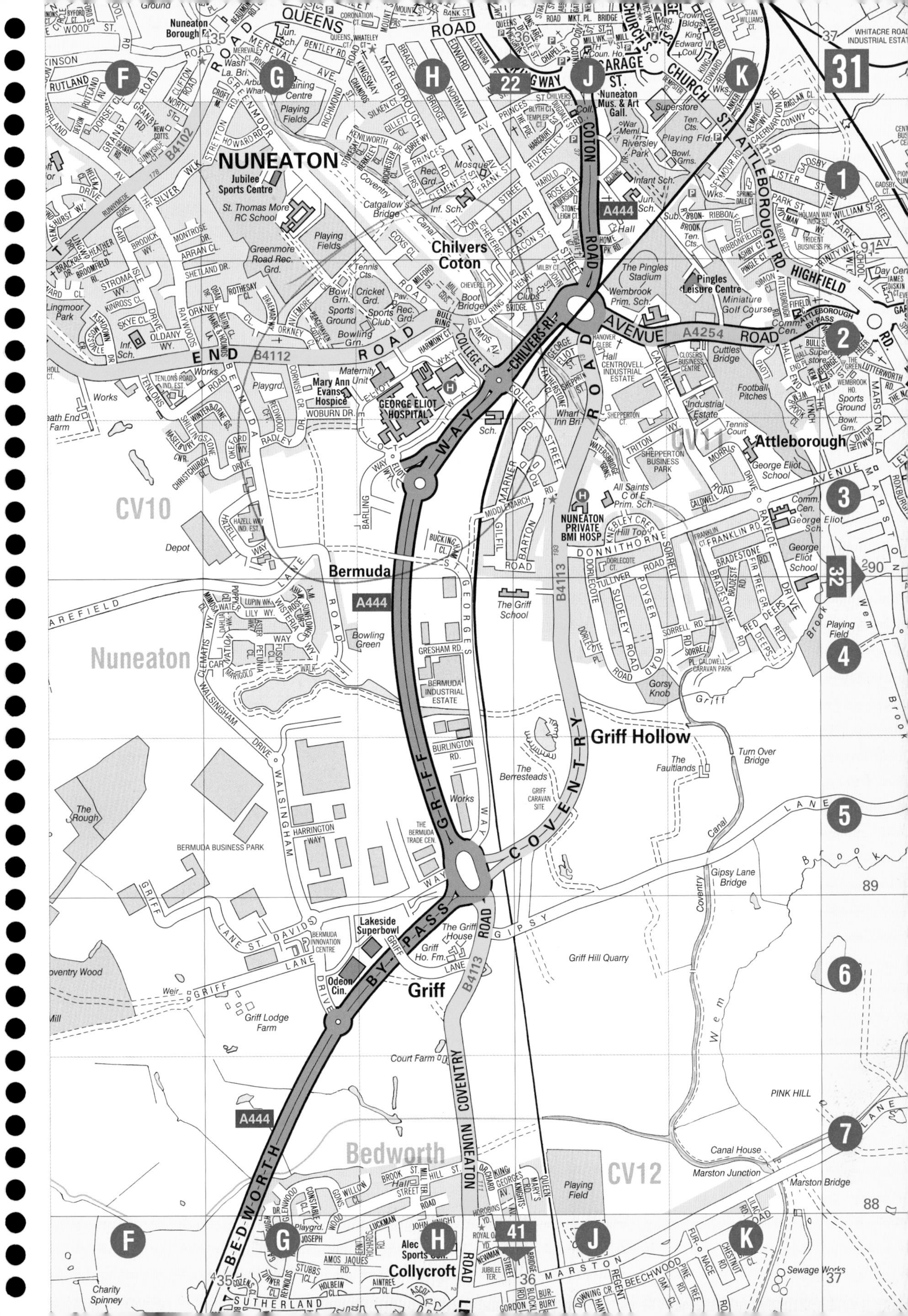

31
NUNEATON
Chilvers Coton
Bermuda
Griff Hollow
Griff
Attleborough
Collycroft
Bedworth
Nuneaton
CV10
CV11
CV12
22
32
41
QUEENS ROAD
ATTLEBOROUGH RD.
HIGHFIELD
AVENUE A4254 ROAD
END B4112 ROAD
A444
B4113
B4102
GRIFF WAY
BEDWORTH BY-PASS
COVENTRY ROAD
NUNEATON ROAD
COTON ROAD
BERMUDA ROAD
WALSINGHAM DRIVE
GRIFF LANE
MARSTON LANE
GIPSY LANE
Nuneaton Borough
Jubilee Sports Centre
St. Thomas More RC School
Greenmore Road Rec. Grd.
Nuneaton Mus. & Art Gall.
Riversley Park
The Pingles Stadium
Wembrook Prim. Sch.
Pingles Leisure Centre
Miniature Golf Course
Cuttles Bridge
Football Pitches
Maternity Unit
Mary Ann Evans Hospice
GEORGE ELIOT HOSPITAL
Bowling Grn.
Centrovell Industrial Estate
Shepperton Business Park
All Saints C of E Prim. Sch.
NUNEATON PRIVATE BMI HOSP.
George Eliot School
The Griff School
Bowling Green
Bermuda Industrial Estate
Gorsy Knob
Caldwell Caravan Park
The Faultlands
Turn Over Bridge
The Berresteads
Griff Caravan Site
The Rough
BERMUDA BUSINESS PARK
THE BERMUDA TRADE CEN.
Lakeside Superbowl
Odeon Cin.
BERMUDA INNOVATION CENTRE
The Griff House
Griff Ho. Fm.
Griff Hill Quarry
Gipsy Lane Bridge
Griff Lodge Farm
Court Farm
Coventry Wood
Charity Spinney
PINK HILL
Canal House
Marston Junction
Marston Bridge
Playing Field
Sewage Works
Alec Sports Cen.
Depot
Works
Lingmoor Park
Heath End Farm
F G H J K
1 2 3 4 5 6 7
35 36 37
88 89 90 91

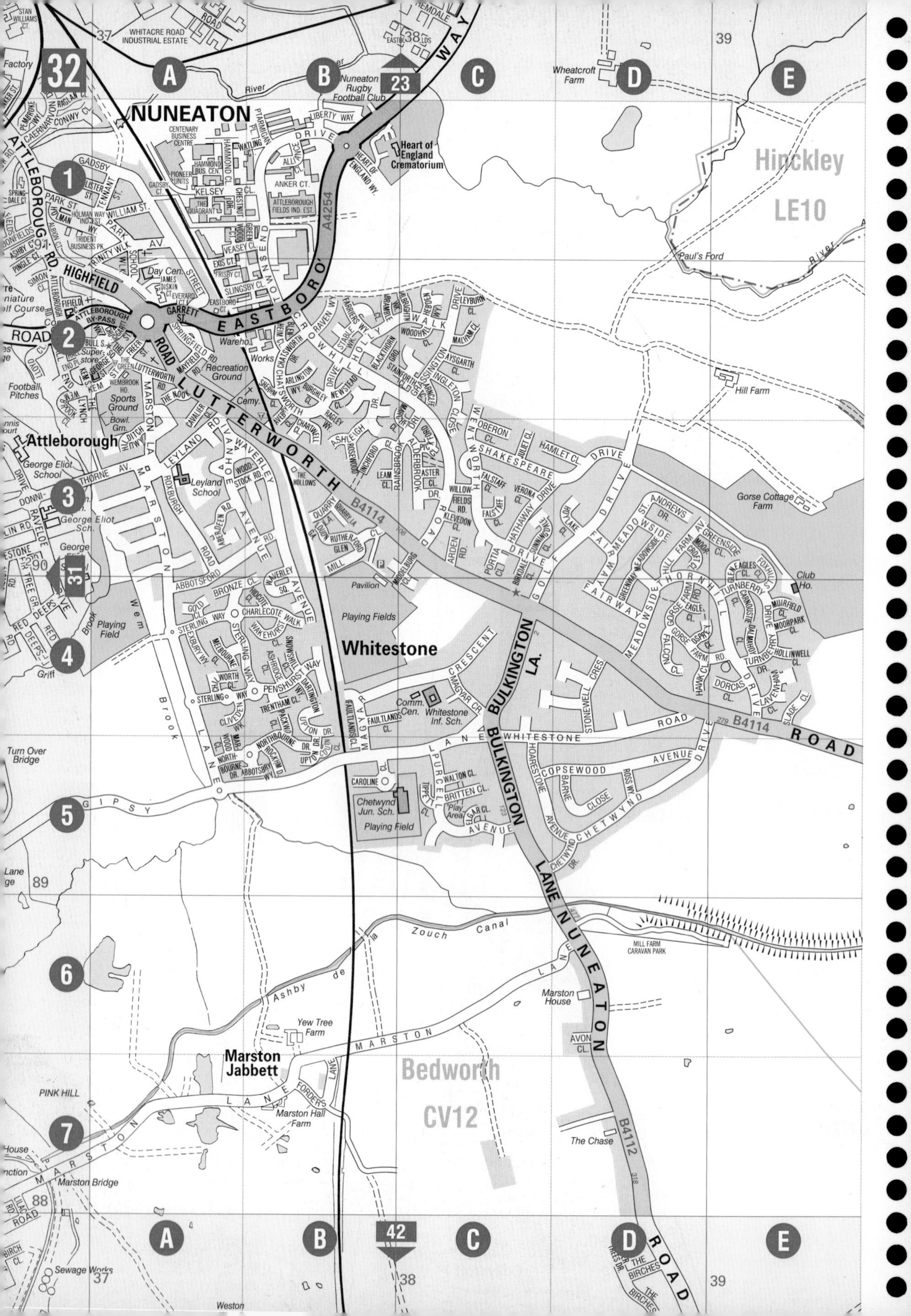
32
NUNEATON
Attleborough
Whitestone
Marston Jabbett
Hinckley
LE10
Bedworth
CV12
23
31
42
A
B
C
D
E
1
2
3
4
5
6
7
37
38
39
89
90
88
91
Nuneaton Rugby Football Club
Heart of England Crematorium
Whitacre Road Industrial Estate
Wheatcroft Farm
Hill Farm
Gorse Cottage Farm
Paul's Ford
River Anker
Attleborough Fields Ind. Est.
Centenary Business Centre
Trident Business Pk.
George Eliot School
Leyland School
George Eliot Sch.
Recreation Ground
Sports Ground
Playing Fields
Pavilion
Playing Field
Comm. Cen.
Whitestone Inf. Sch.
Chetwynd Jun. Sch.
Club Ho.
Turn Over Bridge
Ashby de la Zouch Canal
Mill Farm Caravan Park
Marston House
Yew Tree Farm
Marston Hall Farm
The Chase
Pink Hill
Marston Bridge
Sewage Works
Weston
Lutterworth Road
Eastboro' Way
Highfield Road
Attleborough Rd.
Bulkington La.
Nuneaton Lane
Whitestone Road
Marston Lane
Gipsy Lane
B4114
B4112
A4254

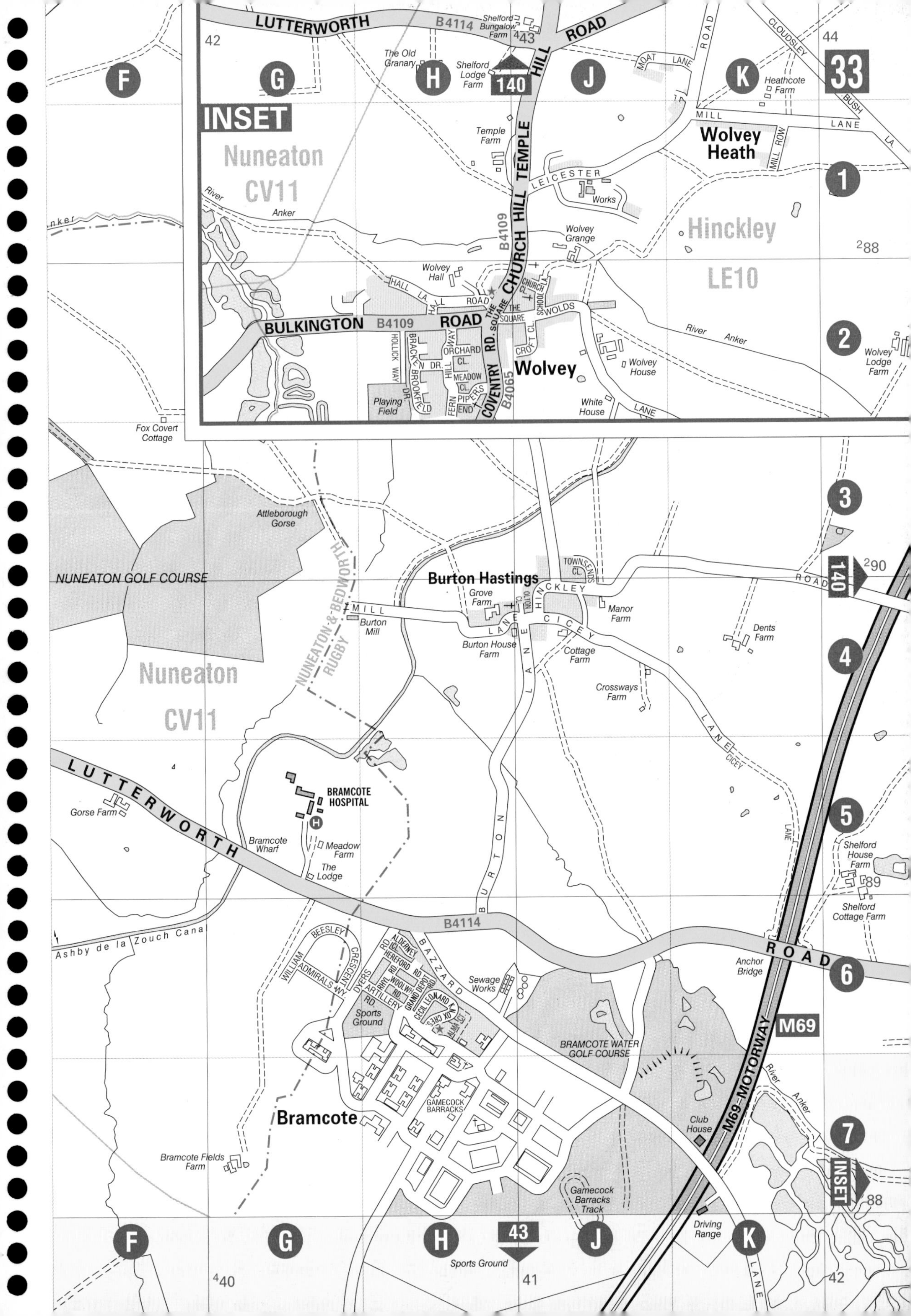
33
INSET
LUTTERWORTH
B4114
ROAD
Shelford Bungalow Farm
43
140
The Old Granary
Shelford Lodge Farm
HILL
MOAT LANE
ROAD
CLOUDSLEY
44
BUSH LA.
F
G
H
J
K
Heathcote Farm
MILL LANE
Wolvey Heath
MILL ROW
42
Temple Farm
TEMPLE
Nuneaton
CV11
LEICESTER
Works
River Anker
1
CHURCH HILL
B4109
Wolvey Grange
Hinckley
LE10
288
Wolvey Hall
HALL LA.
HALL ROAD
CHURCH CL.
SCHOOL LA.
THE SQUARE
WOLDS
BULKINGTON B4109 ROAD
HOLLICK WAY
BRACKEN DR.
HILL WAY
ORCHARD CL.
MEADOW CL.
COVENTRY RD.
CROFT CL.
Wolvey
Wolvey House
River Anker
2
Wolvey Lodge Farm
Playing Field
DR.
BROOKFIELD
FERN END
PIPERS
B4065
White House
LANE
Fox Covert Cottage
Attleborough Gorse
3
NUNEATON GOLF COURSE
NUNEATON & BEDWORTH
RUGBY
TOWNSENDS CL.
Burton Hastings
Grove Farm
HINCKLEY
ROAD
140
290
MILL
Burton Mill
LANE
Manor Farm
Dents Farm
Burton House Farm
CICEY
Cottage Farm
4
Crossways Farm
Nuneaton
CV11
CICEY LANE
BRAMCOTE HOSPITAL
LUTTERWORTH
Gorse Farm
5
Bramcote Wharf
Meadow Farm
The Lodge
BURTON
LANE
Shelford House Farm
89
Shelford Cottage Farm
B4114
Ashby de la Zouch Canal
BEESLEY
CRESCENT
WILLIAM
ADMIRALS WAY
DYERS
ALDERNEY CL.
HEREFORD RD.
RHYL RD.
WOOLWICH RD.
ARTILLERY RD.
GRAND DEPOT RD.
BAZZARD RD.
Sewage Works
ROAD
Anchor Bridge
6
Sports Ground
CECIL LEONARD
KNOX CRES.
ALMA CT.
M69
BRAMCOTE WATER GOLF COURSE
River Anker
M69 MOTORWAY
GAMECOCK BARRACKS
Bramcote
Club House
7
INSET
Bramcote Fields Farm
Gamecock Barracks Track
88
F
G
H
43
J
K
Driving Range
Sports Ground
440
41
LANE
42

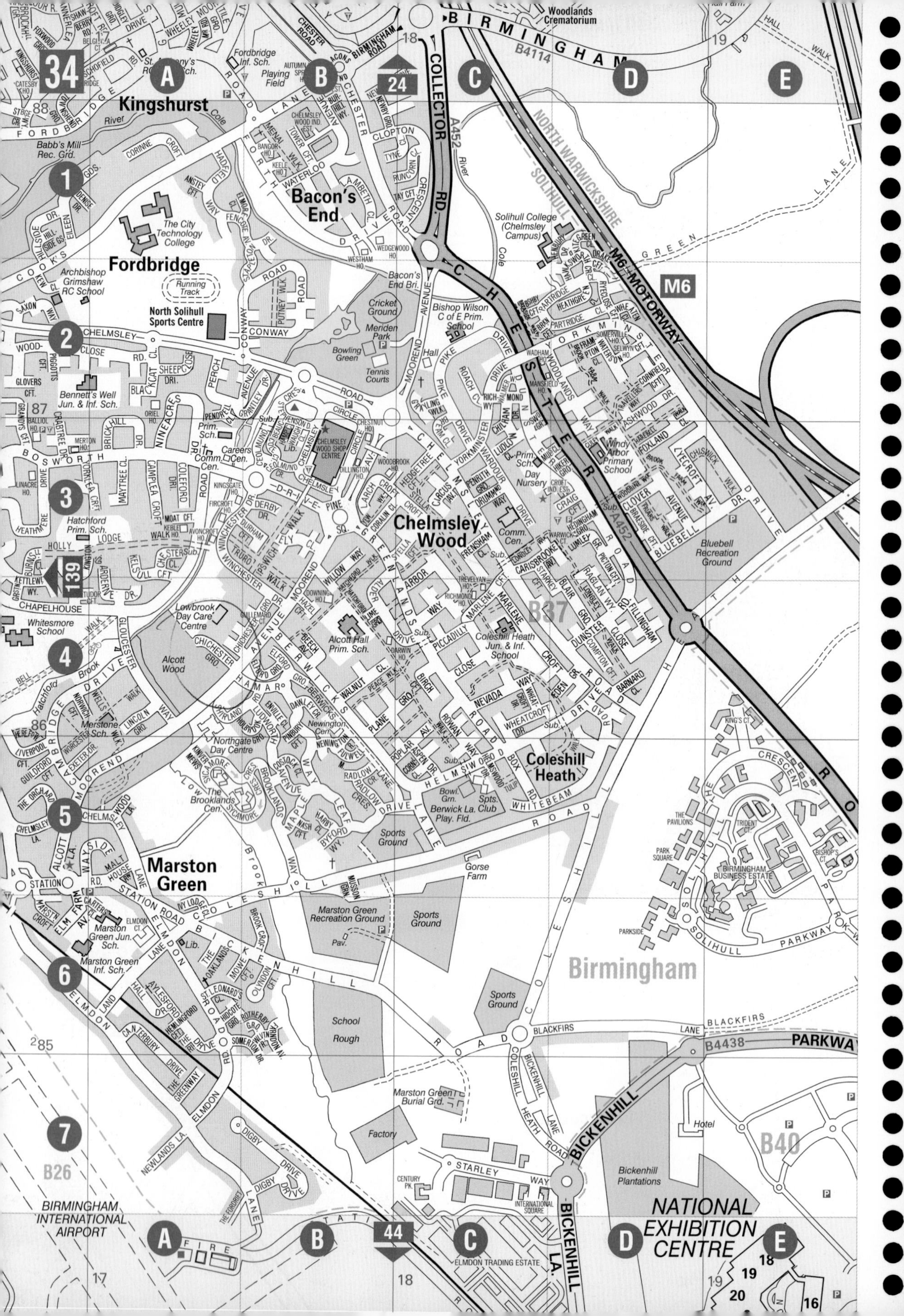

34
Kingshurst
Fordbridge
Bacon's End
Chelmsley Wood
Coleshill Heath
Marston Green
Birmingham
B37
B26
B40
M6
M6 MOTORWAY
24
139
44
BIRMINGHAM ROAD
B4114
COLLECTOR RD.
A452
NORTH WARWICKSHIRE
SOLIHULL
Woodlands Crematorium
St. Anthony's RC Sch.
Fordbridge Inf. Sch.
Playing Field
Babb's Mill Rec. Grd.
The City Technology College
Archbishop Grimshaw RC School
Running Track
North Solihull Sports Centre
Bennett's Well Jun. & Inf. Sch.
Hatchford Prim. Sch.
Whitesmore School
Lowbrook Day Care Centre
Alcott Wood
Merstone Sch.
Northgate Day Centre
The Brooklands Cen.
Cricket Ground
Meriden Park
Bowling Green
Tennis Courts
Bishop Wilson C of E Prim. School
Solihull College (Chelmsley Campus)
Chelmsley Wood Shop Centre
Careers Cen.
Comm. Cen.
Windy Arbor Primary School
Day Nursery
Bluebell Recreation Ground
Alcott Hall Prim. Sch.
Coleshill Heath Jun. & Inf. School
Newington Cen.
Berwick La. Play. Fld.
Bowl. Grn.
Spts. Club
Sports Ground
Gorse Farm
Marston Green Recreation Ground
Marston Green Jun. Sch.
Marston Green Inf. Sch.
School Rough
Marston Green Burial Grd.
Factory
Century Pk.
International Square
Bickenhill Plantations
Hotel
Birmingham Business Estate
The Pavilions
Park Square
Parkside
BIRMINGHAM INTERNATIONAL AIRPORT
NATIONAL EXHIBITION CENTRE
ELMDON TRADING ESTATE
COLESHILL ROAD
BICKENHILL LANE
BLACKFIRS LANE
B4438
PARKWAY
STARLEY WAY
SOLIHULL PARKWAY
STATION ROAD
CHELMSLEY ROAD
MOOREND AVENUE
BERWICKS LANE
WHITEBEAM ROAD

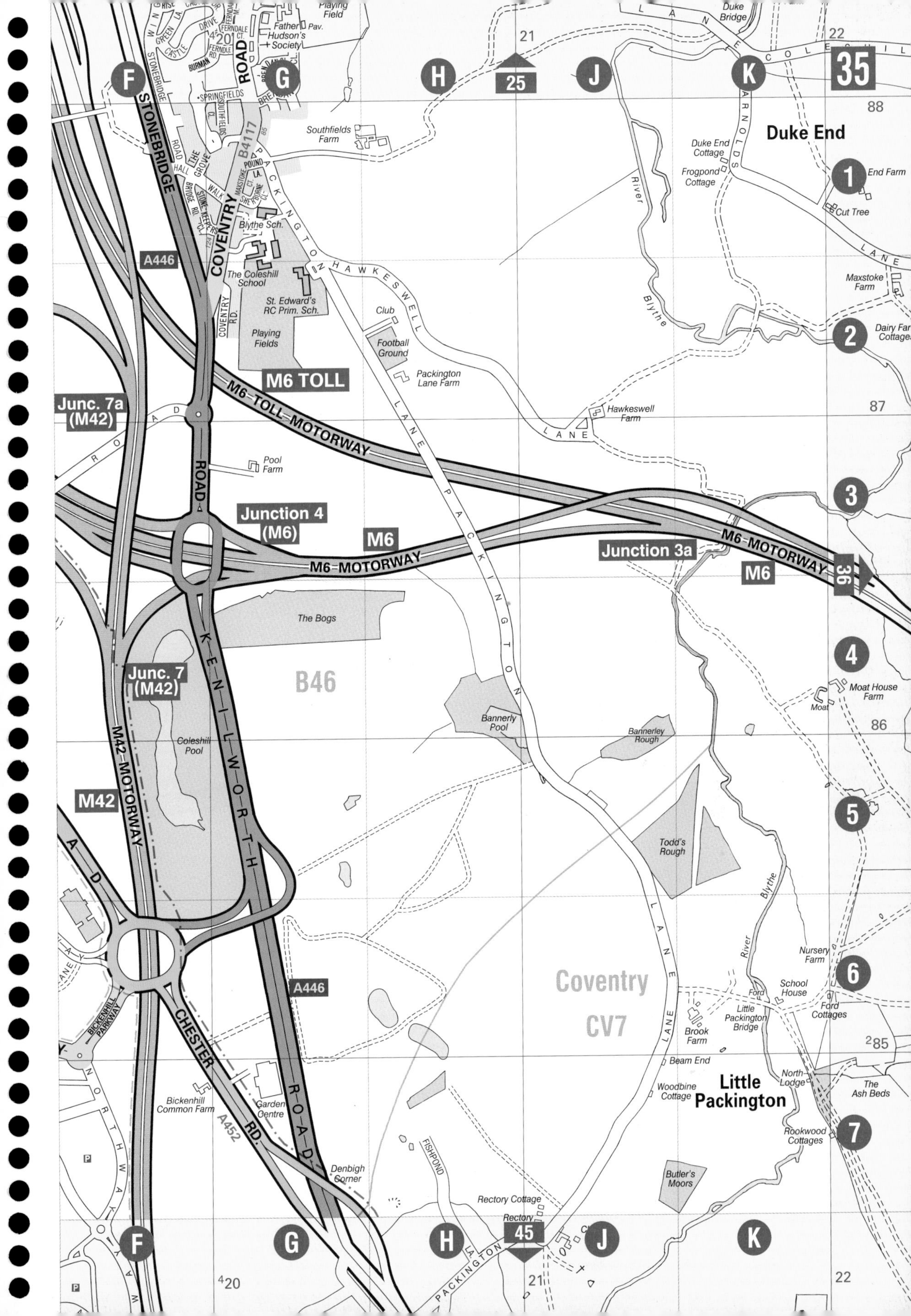
35
25
45
36
Duke End
Little Packington
Coventry CV7
B46
Duke Bridge
Southfields Farm
Duke End Cottage
Frogpond Cottage
End Farm
Cut Tree
Maxstoke Farm
Dairy Farm Cottages
Father Hudson's Society
Playing Field
Blythe Sch.
The Coleshill School
St. Edward's RC Prim. Sch.
Playing Fields
Club
Football Ground
Packington Lane Farm
Hawkeswell Farm
Pool Farm
M6 TOLL
M6 TOLL MOTORWAY
Junc. 7a (M42)
Junction 4 (M6)
M6
M6 MOTORWAY
Junction 3a
The Bogs
Junc. 7 (M42)
M42 MOTORWAY
M42
Coleshill Pool
Bannerly Pool
Bannerley Rough
Todd's Rough
Moat House Farm
Moat
Nursery Farm
School House
Ford
Ford Cottages
Little Packington Bridge
Brook Farm
Beam End
Woodbine Cottage
North Lodge
The Ash Beds
Rookwood Cottages
Butler's Moors
Rectory Cottage
Rectory
Denbigh Corner
Garden Centre
Bickenhill Common Farm
River Blythe
A446
A452
B4117
COVENTRY ROAD
STONEBRIDGE ROAD
KENILWORTH ROAD
CHESTER RD.
PACKINGTON LANE
HAWKESWELL LANE
ARNOLDS LANE
COLESHILL LANE
BICKENHILL PARKWAY
FISHPOND LA.
21
22
88
87
86
85
420

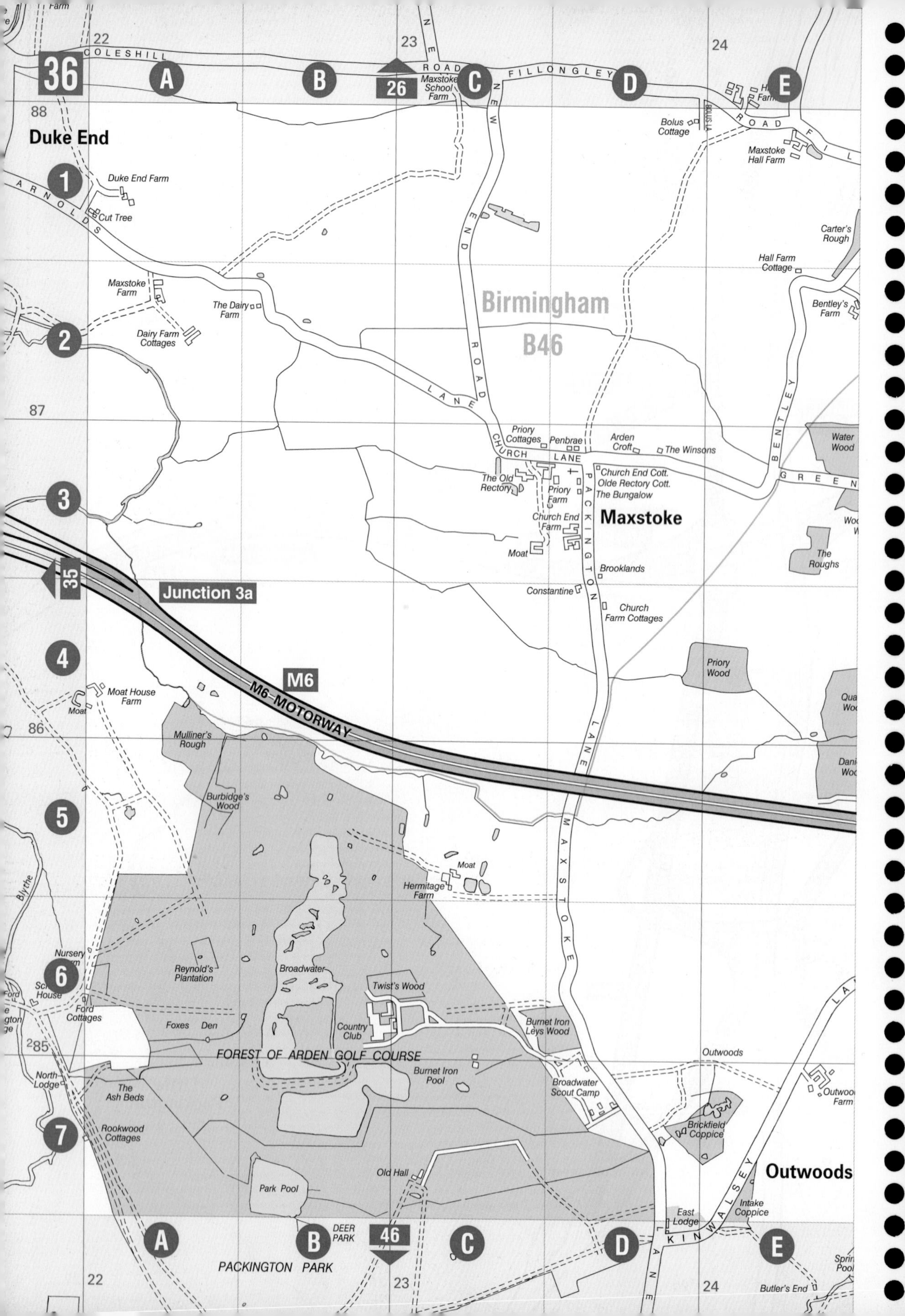

36
26
35
46
Junction 3a
M6
M6 MOTORWAY
Birmingham
B46
Duke End
Maxstoke
Outwoods
COLESHILL ROAD
FILLONGLEY ROAD
NEW END ROAD
ARNOLDS LANE
CHURCH LANE
PACKINGTON LANE
MAXSTOKE LANE
BENTLEY GREEN
KINWALSEY LANE
Maxstoke School Farm
Bolus Cottage
Maxstoke Hall Farm
Duke End Farm
Cut Tree
Carter's Rough
Hall Farm Cottage
Maxstoke Farm
The Dairy Farm
Dairy Farm Cottages
Bentley's Farm
Priory Cottages
Penbrae
Arden Croft
The Winsons
Water Wood
The Old Rectory
Priory Farm
Church End Cott.
Olde Rectory Cott.
The Bungalow
Church End Farm
Moat
Brooklands
Constantine
Church Farm Cottages
The Roughs
Priory Wood
Moat House Farm
Mulliner's Rough
Burbidge's Wood
Hermitage Farm
Blythe
Reynold's Plantation
Broadwater
Twist's Wood
Country Club
Burnet Iron Leys Wood
Foxes Den
FOREST OF ARDEN GOLF COURSE
Burnet Iron Pool
Broadwater Scout Camp
Outwoods
Brickfield Coppice
Ford Cottages
North Lodge
The Ash Beds
Rookwood Cottages
Old Hall
Park Pool
Intake Coppice
East Lodge
DEER PARK
PACKINGTON PARK
Butler's End
22
23
24
88
87
86
85
A
B
C
D
E
1
2
3
4
5
6
7

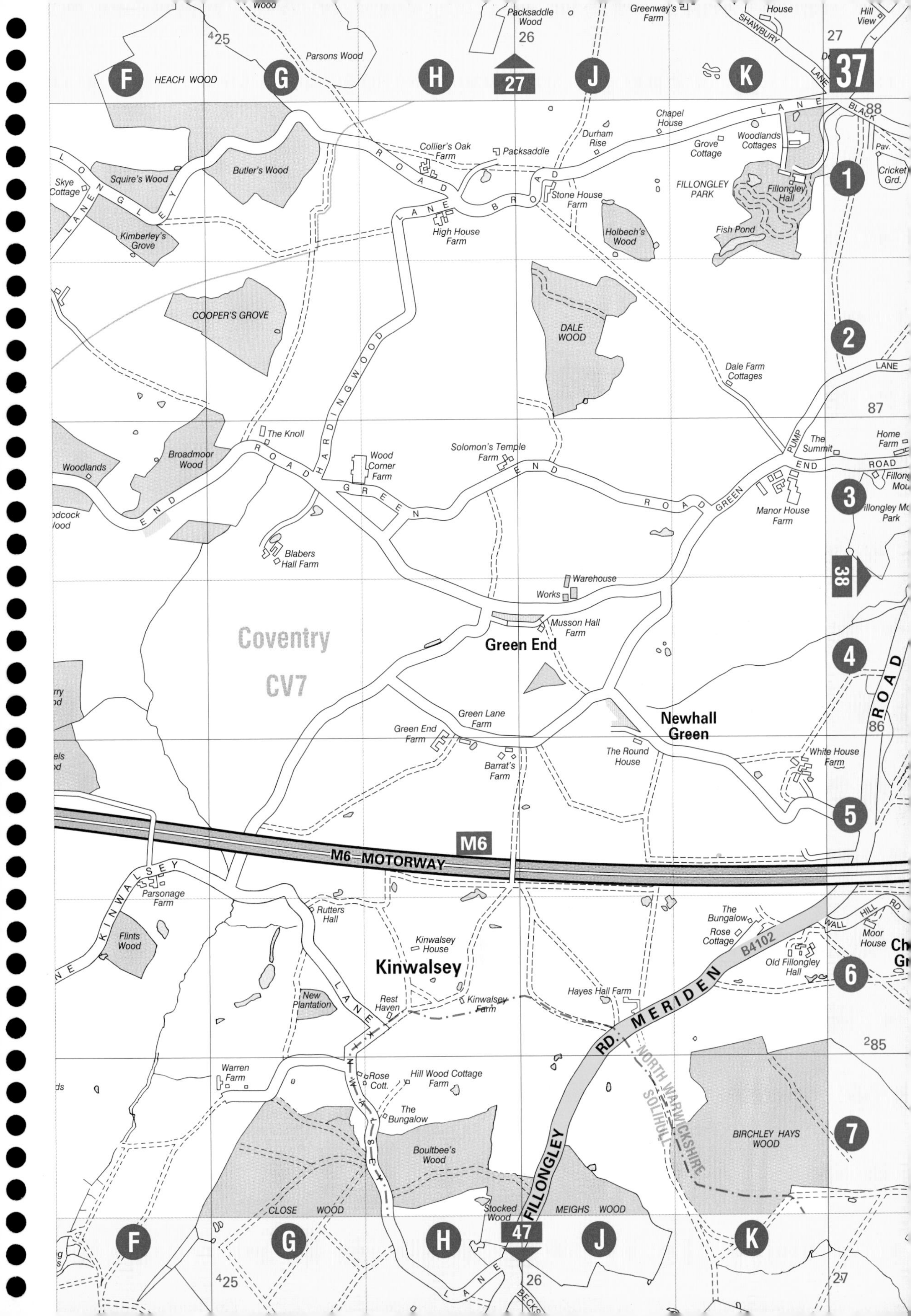

37
27
38
47
M6
M6 MOTORWAY
B4102
Coventry
CV7
Green End
Newhall Green
Kinwalsey
HEACH WOOD
Parsons Wood
Packsaddle Wood
Greenway's Farm
Chapel House
Durham Rise
Grove Cottage
Woodlands Cottages
Collier's Oak Farm
Packsaddle
Stone House Farm
High House Farm
Holbech's Wood
FILLONGLEY PARK
Fillongley Hall
Fish Pond
Cricket Grd.
Pav.
Squire's Wood
Butler's Wood
Skye Cottage
Kimberley's Grove
COOPER'S GROVE
DALE WOOD
Dale Farm Cottages
The Knoll
Broadmoor Wood
Woodlands
Wood Corner Farm
Solomon's Temple Farm
The Summit
Home Farm
Manor House Farm
Blabers Hall Farm
Warehouse
Works
Musson Hall Farm
Green Lane Farm
Green End Farm
Barrat's Farm
The Round House
White House Farm
Parsonage Farm
Flints Wood
Rutters Hall
Kinwalsey House
The Bungalow
Rose Cottage
Moor House
Old Fillongley Hall
Hayes Hall Farm
New Plantation
Rest Haven
Kinwalsey Farm
Warren Farm
Rose Cott.
Hill Wood Cottage Farm
The Bungalow
Boultbee's Wood
BIRCHLEY HAYS WOOD
NORTH WARWICKSHIRE
SOLIHULL
CLOSE WOOD
Stocked Wood
MEIGHS WOOD
LONGLEY LANE
BROAD LANE
HARDINGWOOD LANE
GREEN END ROAD
KINWALSEY LANE
MERIDEN RD.
FILLONGLEY RD.
SHAWBURY LANE
BLACK HILL ROAD
PUMP LANE

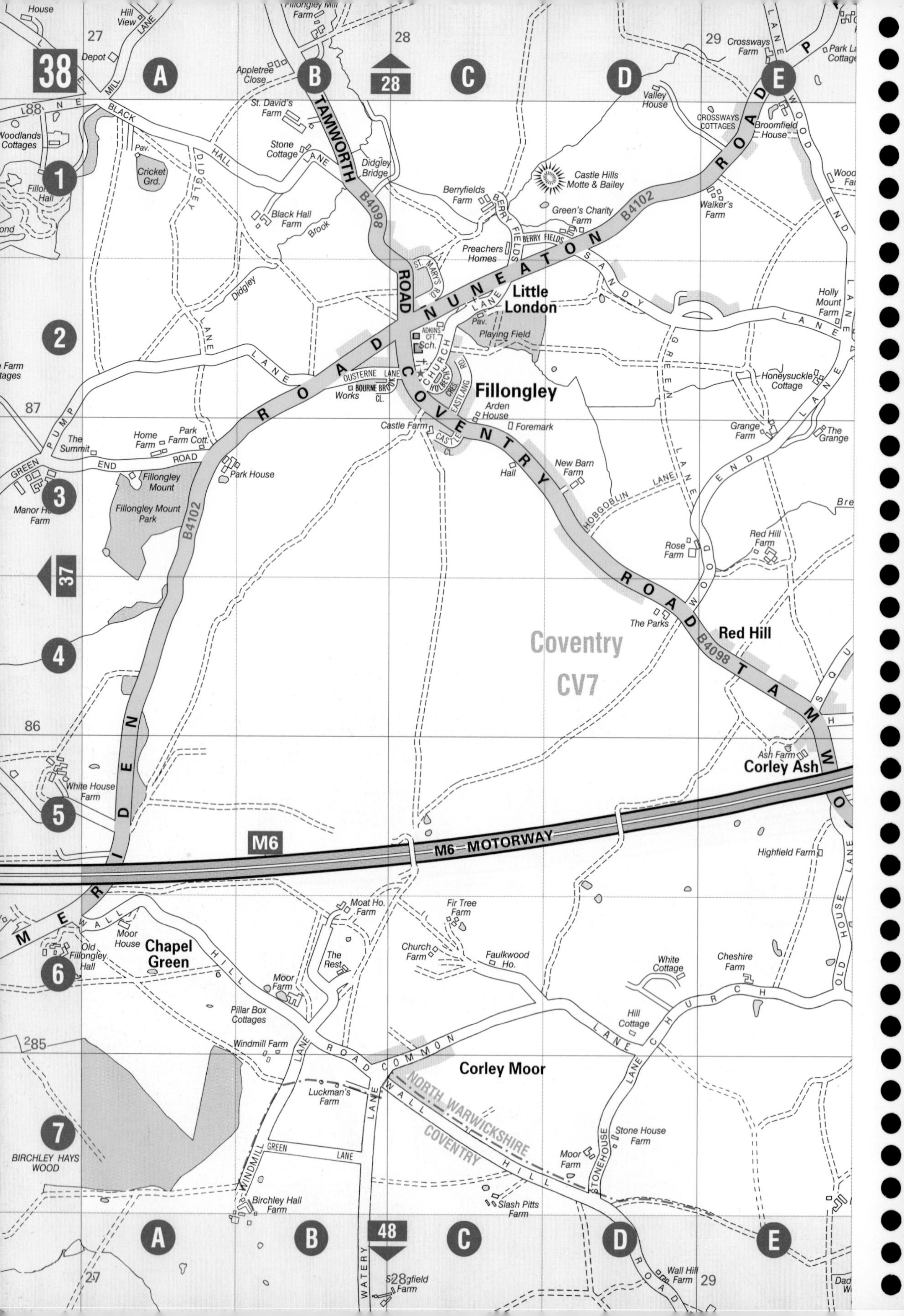

38
A
B
C
D
E
27
28
29
1
2
3
4
5
6
7
88
87
86
85
28
48
37
Fillongley
Little London
Corley Ash
Red Hill
Corley Moor
Chapel Green
Coventry
CV7
M6
M6 MOTORWAY
NUNEATON ROAD
COVENTRY ROAD
TAMWORTH ROAD
MERIDEN ROAD
B4102
B4098
BLACK HALL LANE
DIDGLEY LANE
PUMP LANE
GREEN END ROAD
SANDY LANE
GREEN LANE
WOOD END LANE
WOOD LANE
HOBGOBLIN LANE
WALL HILL
COMMON ROAD
WINDMILL LANE
GREEN LANE
WALL LANE
WALL HILL
COVENTRY
NORTH WARWICKSHIRE
CHURCH LANE
STONEHOUSE LANE
OLD HOUSE LANE
WATERY LANE
BERRY FIELDS
OUSTERNE LANE
BOURNE BROOK CL.
CHURCH LANE
HOLBECH CRES.
EASTLANG RD
ST. MARY'S RD.
ADKINS CFT.
CASTLE CL.
CROSSWAYS COTTAGES
Hill View
Depot
Appletree Close
St. David's Farm
Stone Cottage
Didgley Bridge
Black Hall Farm
Brook
Berryfields Farm
Castle Hills Motte & Bailey
Green's Charity Farm
Preachers Homes
Crossways Farm
Valley House
Broomfield House
Walker's Farm
Holly Mount Farm
Honeysuckle Cottage
Grange Farm
The Grange
Red Hill Farm
Rose Farm
The Parks
Woodlands Cottages
Pav.
Cricket Grd.
Didgley
Sch.
Playing Field
Works
Castle Farm
Arden House
Foremark
Hall
New Barn Farm
The Summit
Home Farm
Park Farm Cott.
Park House
Fillongley Mount
Fillongley Mount Park
White House Farm
Ash Farm
Highfield Farm
Moat Ho. Farm
Fir Tree Farm
Church Farm
Faulkwood Ho.
The Rest
Moor Farm
Moor House
Old Fillongley Hall
Pillar Box Cottages
Windmill Farm
Luckman's Farm
White Cottage
Cheshire Farm
Hill Cottage
Stone House Farm
Moor Farm
Slash Pitts Farm
Birchley Hall Farm
BIRCHLEY HAYS WOOD
Wall Hill Farm

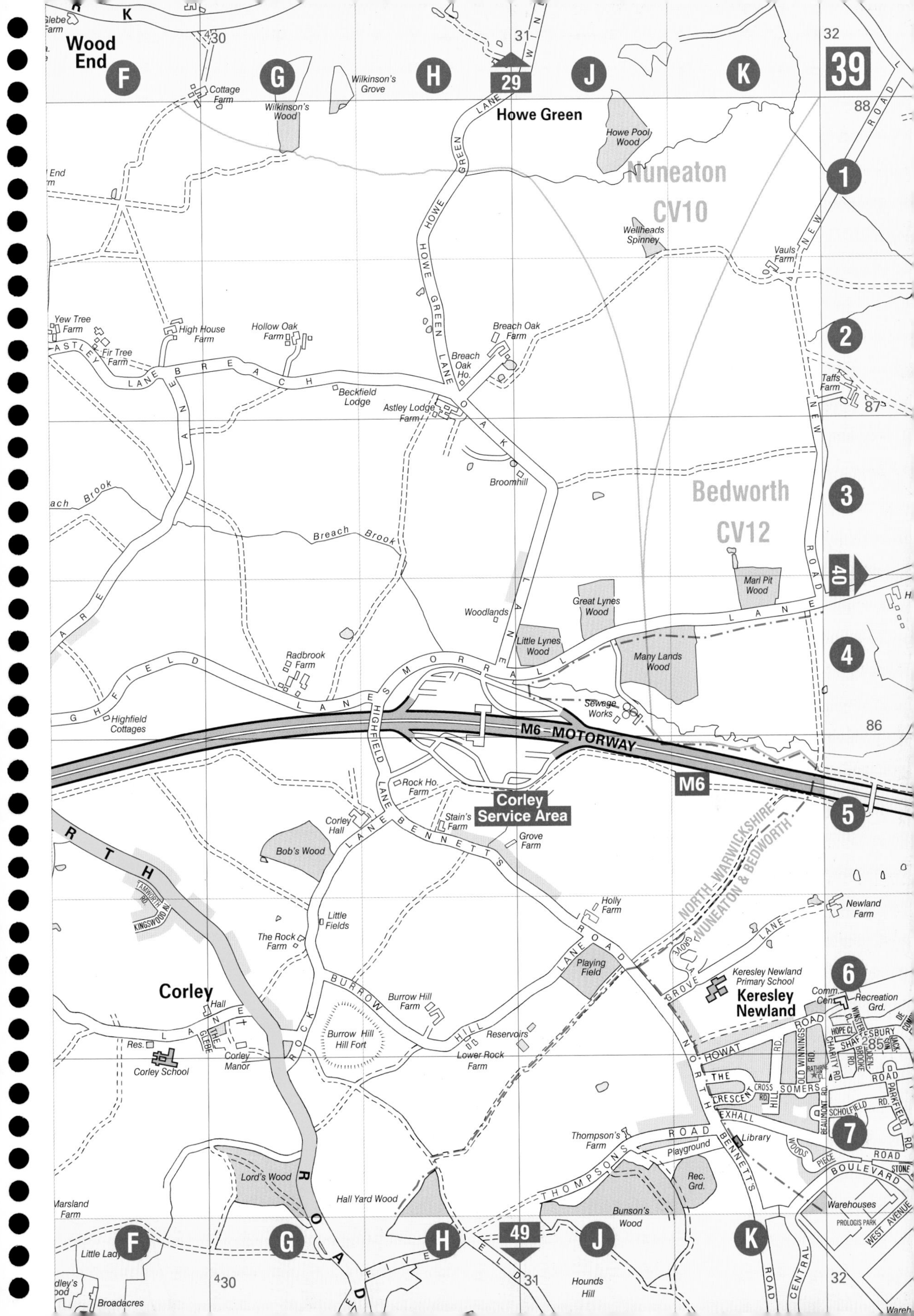

Wood End
Glebe Farm
Cottage Farm
Wilkinson's Wood
Wilkinson's Grove
29
Howe Green
Howe Pool Wood
Nuneaton CV10
Wellheads Spinney
Vauls Farm
Yew Tree Farm
Fir Tree Farm
High House Farm
Hollow Oak Farm
Breach Oak Farm
Breach Oak Ho.
Beckfield Lodge
Astley Lodge Farm
Broomhill
Taffs Farm
Bedworth CV12
Breach Brook
Marl Pit Wood
40
Great Lynes Wood
Woodlands
Little Lynes Wood
Many Lands Wood
Radbrook Farm
Highfield Cottages
Sewage Works
M6 MOTORWAY
M6
Rock Ho. Farm
Corley Service Area
Corley Hall
Stain's Farm
Grove Farm
Bob's Wood
NORTH WARWICKSHIRE
NUNEATON & BEDWORTH
Newland Farm
Holly Farm
Little Fields
The Rock Farm
Playing Field
Keresley Newland Primary School
Keresley Newland
Comm. Cen.
Recreation Grd.
Corley
Hall
Burrow Hill Farm
Burrow Hill Hill Fort
Reservoirs
Res.
Corley School
Corley Manor
Lower Rock Farm
Thompson's Farm
Library
Playground
Rec. Grd.
Lord's Wood
Hall Yard Wood
Bunson's Wood
Marsland Farm
Warehouses
PROLOGIS PARK
49
Little Lady
Broadacres
Hounds Hill

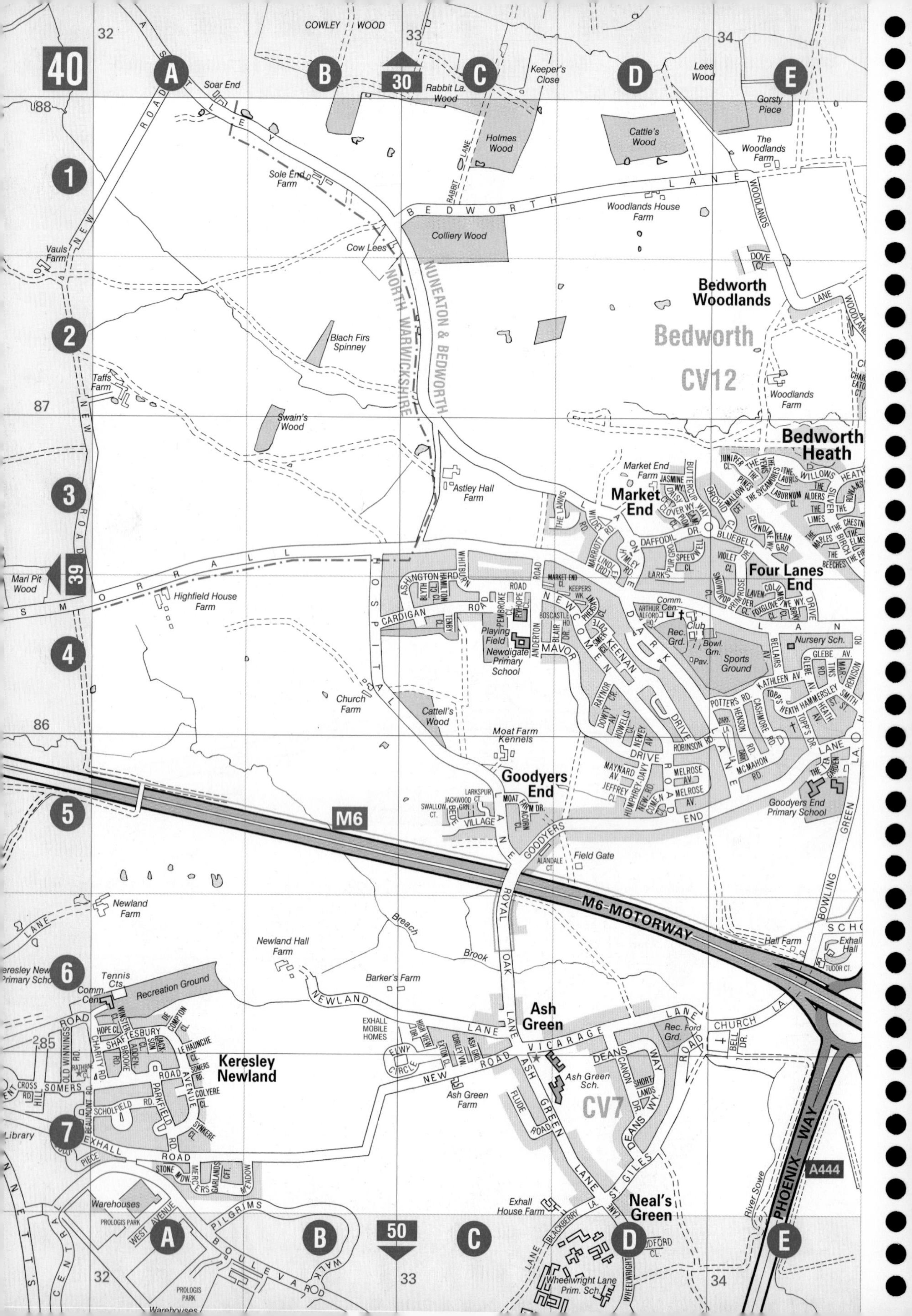

COWLEY WOOD
Soar End
30
Rabbit La. Wood
Keeper's Close
Lees Wood
Gorsty Piece
Holmes Wood
Cattle's Wood
The Woodlands Farm
Sole End Farm
BEDWORTH LANE
Woodlands House Farm
Colliery Wood
Vauls Farm
Cow Lees
NORTH WARWICKSHIRE
NUNEATON & BEDWORTH
Bedworth Woodlands
Bedworth
CV12
Blach Firs Spinney
Taffs Farm
Woodlands Farm
Swain's Wood
Bedworth Heath
Market End Farm
Astley Hall Farm
Market End
Four Lanes End
Marl Pit Wood
39
SMORRALL LANE
Highfield House Farm
CARDIGAN ROAD
Playing Field
Newdigate Primary School
Comm. Cen.
Club
Rec. Grd.
Bowl. Grn.
Sports Ground
Nursery Sch.
Church Farm
Cattell's Wood
Moat Farm Kennels
Goodyers End
Goodyers End Primary School
M6
Field Gate
M6-MOTORWAY
Newland Farm
Newland Hall Farm
Breach Brook
Barker's Farm
Hall Farm
Exhall Hall
Tennis Cts.
Recreation Ground
Comm. Cen.
Keresley Newland Primary School
Ash Green
EXHALL MOBILE HOMES
Keresley Newland
Ash Green Sch.
Ash Green Farm
CV7
Rec. Grd.
CHURCH LANE
Library
EXHALL ROAD
A444
PHOENIX WAY
River Sowe
Warehouses
PROLOGIS PARK
Exhall House Farm
Neal's Green
50
Wheelwright Lane Prim. Sch.
BOULEVARD

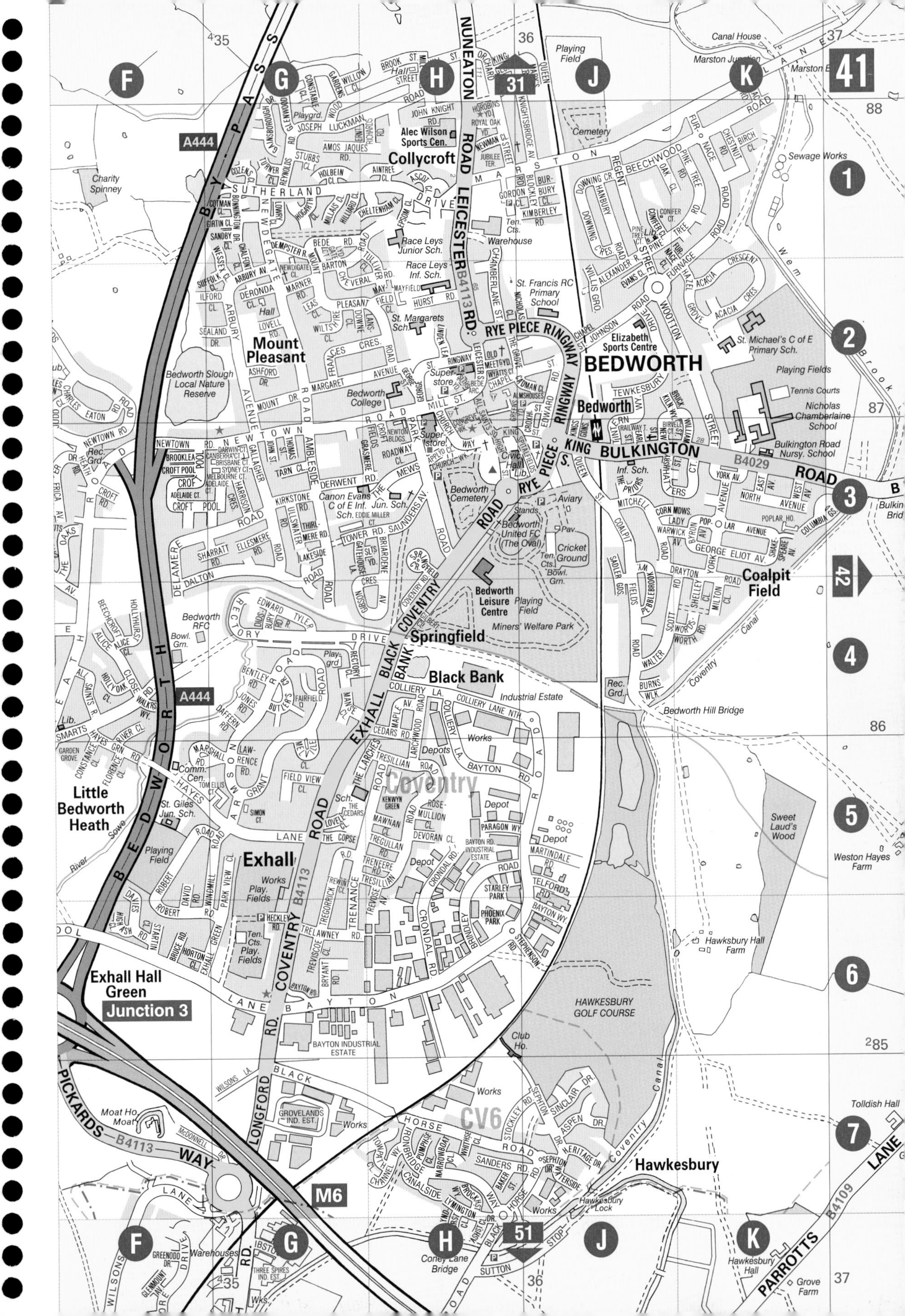

41
31
42
51
F
G
H
J
K
1
2
3
4
5
6
7
435
36
37
88
87
86
285
A444
B4113
B4029
B4109
M6
Junction 3
BEDWORTH
Collycroft
Mount Pleasant
Springfield
Black Bank
Exhall
Little Bedworth Heath
Exhall Hall Green
Coalpit Field
Hawkesbury
Coventry
CV6
BEDWORTH BY-PASS
NUNEATON ROAD
LEICESTER RD.
B4113 RD.
RYE PIECE RINGWAY
KING ST.
KING BULKINGTON ROAD
BULKINGTON ROAD
BLACK BANK
EXHALL
COVENTRY ROAD
LONGFORD RD.
BAYTON LANE
BAYTON RD.
COLLIERY LA.
COLLIERY LANE NTH.
PICKARDS WAY
HORSE ROAD
BLACK HORSE RD.
SUTTON STOP
PARROTTS LANE
RECTORY DRIVE
NEWTOWN RD.
MARSTON LANE
SUTHERLAND DRIVE
ARBURY AVENUE
MARGARET AVENUE
WOOTTON STREET
COALPIT FIELDS RD.
GEORGE ELIOT AV.
Alec Wilson Sports Cen.
Race Leys Junior Sch.
Race Leys Inf. Sch.
St. Margarets Sch.
St. Francis RC Primary School
Elizabeth Sports Centre
St. Michael's C of E Primary Sch.
Playing Fields
Tennis Courts
Nicholas Chamberlaine School
Bulkington Road Nursy. School
Bedworth College
Bedworth Slough Local Nature Reserve
Bedworth
Super-store
Civic Hall Lib.
Bedworth Cemetery
Canon Evans C of E Inf. Jun. Sch.
Bedworth United FC (The Oval)
Cricket Ground
Bedworth Leisure Centre
Playing Field
Miners' Welfare Park
Aviary
Stands
Pav.
Bedworth RFC
Bowl. Grn.
Industrial Estate
Depots
Works
Depot
Bedworth Hill Bridge
Coventry Canal
Sweet Laud's Wood
Weston Hayes Farm
Hawkesbury Hall Farm
HAWKESBURY GOLF COURSE
Club Ho.
Tolldish Hall
Hawkesbury Lock
Hawkesbury Hall
Grove Farm
Coney Lane Bridge
Moat Ho. Moat
GROVELANDS IND. EST.
BAYTON INDUSTRIAL ESTATE
BAYTON RD. INDUSTRIAL ESTATE
STARLEY PARK
PHOENIX PARK
THREE SPIRES IND. EST.
Warehouses
Charity Spinney
Canal House
Marston Junction
Sewage Works
Cemetery
Warehouse
Playing Field
Inf. Sch.
Rec. Grd.
Comm. Cen.
St. Giles Jun. Sch.
Play. Fields
River Sowe
Bulkington Bridge
Wem Brook

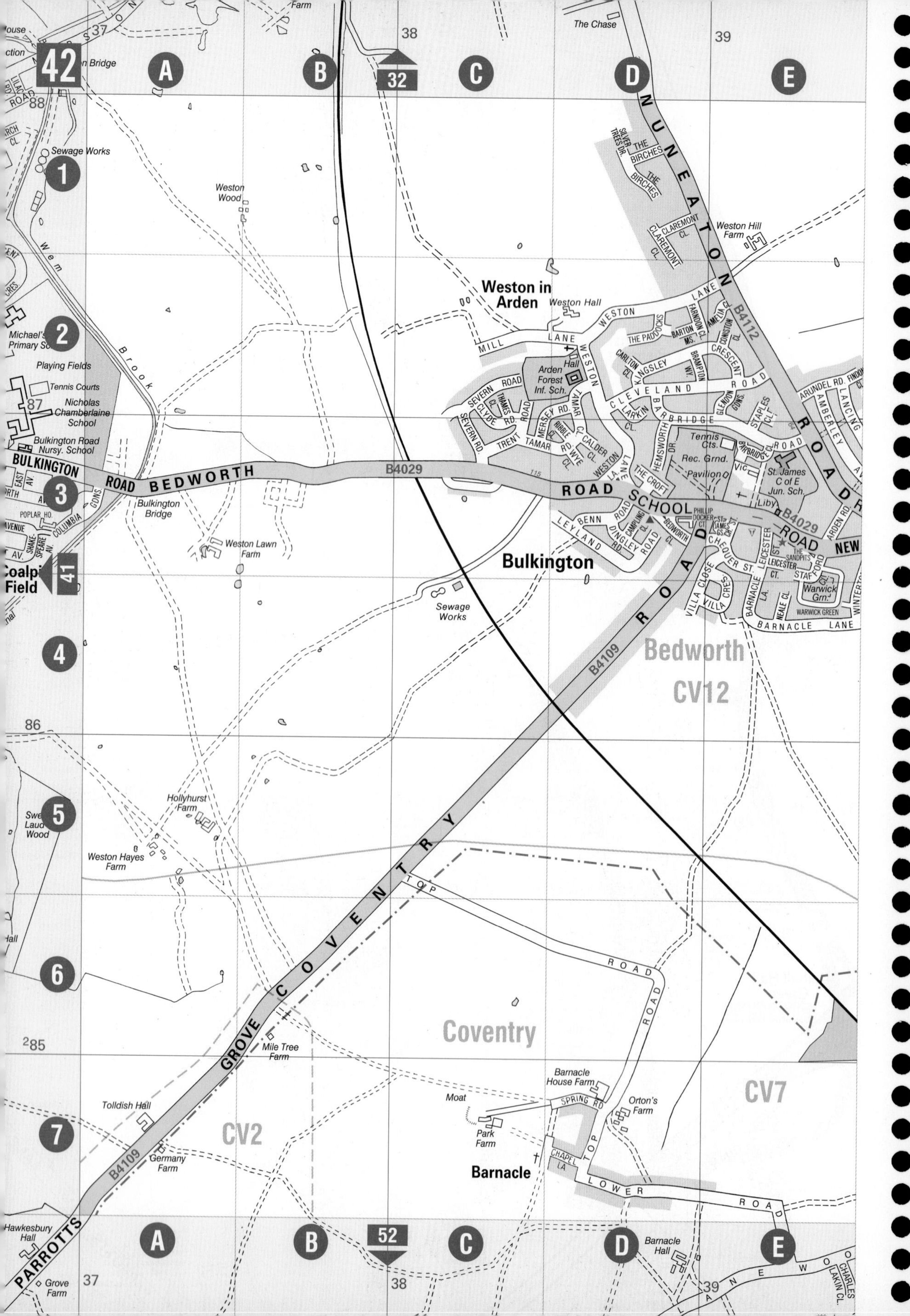

The Chase
Farm
38
39
37
A
B
C
D
E
32
n Bridge
Sewage Works
Weston Wood
NUNEATON ROAD
THE BIRCHES
SILVER TREES DR.
CLAREMONT CL.
Weston Hill Farm
B4112
Weston in Arden
Weston Hall
WESTON LANE
MILL LANE
WESTON
THE PADDOCKS
BARTON MS.
FARNDON CL.
AMELIA CL.
CONISTON CL.
CRESCENT
BRAMPTON WY.
KINGSLEY
CARLTON CL.
Hall
Arden Forest Inf. Sch.
CLEVELAND ROAD
SEVERN ROAD
THAMES RD.
CLYDE RD.
TAMAR CL.
MERSEY RD.
RIBBLE
CALDER CL.
TRENT
TAMAR
WYE CL.
SEVERN RD.
LARKIN CL.
BARBRIDGE
GLENDON GDNS.
STAPLES CL.
ARUNDEL RD.
FINDON
AMBERLEY
LANCING
Wem Brook
Michael's Primary Sc
Playing Fields
Tennis Courts
Nicholas Chamberlaine School
Bulkington Road Nursy. School
BULKINGTON ROAD
BEDWORTH ROAD
B4029
115
Bulkington Bridge
COLUMBIA GDNS.
POPLAR HO.
EAST AV.
SHAKESPEARE AV.
AVENUE
Coalpit Field
41
Weston Lawn Farm
HEMSWORTH DR.
Tennis Cts.
Rec. Grnd.
Pavilion
Vic
St. James C of E Jun. Sch.
Liby
THE CROFT
WESTON LANE
SCHOOL ROAD
NEW
PHILLIP DOCHER CT.
ST. JAMES GS.
BENN ROAD
LEYLAND RD.
DINGLEY ROAD
CAMPLING CL.
BEDWORTH CL.
CHEQUER ST.
LEICESTER ST.
LEICESTER CT.
STAFFORD CL.
THE SANDPITS
Warwick Grn.
WARWICK GREEN
WINTERTON
ARDEN RD.
Bulkington
VILLA CLOSE
VILLA CRES.
BARNACLE LA.
NEALE CL.
BARNACLE LANE
Sewage Works
B4109
Bedworth
CV12
86
Hollyhurst Farm
Weston Hayes Farm
Laud Wood
COVENTRY ROAD
TOP ROAD
ROAD
Coventry
GROVE
85
Mile Tree Farm
Barnacle House Farm
Moat
SPRING RD
Orton's Farm
Park Farm
TOP
CHAPEL LA
Barnacle
LOWER ROAD
CV7
CV2
Tolldish Hall
Germany Farm
Hawkesbury Hall
PARROTTS
Grove Farm
52
Barnacle Hall
NEW LANE
CHARLES LAKIN CL.
1
2
3
4
5
6
7
87
88

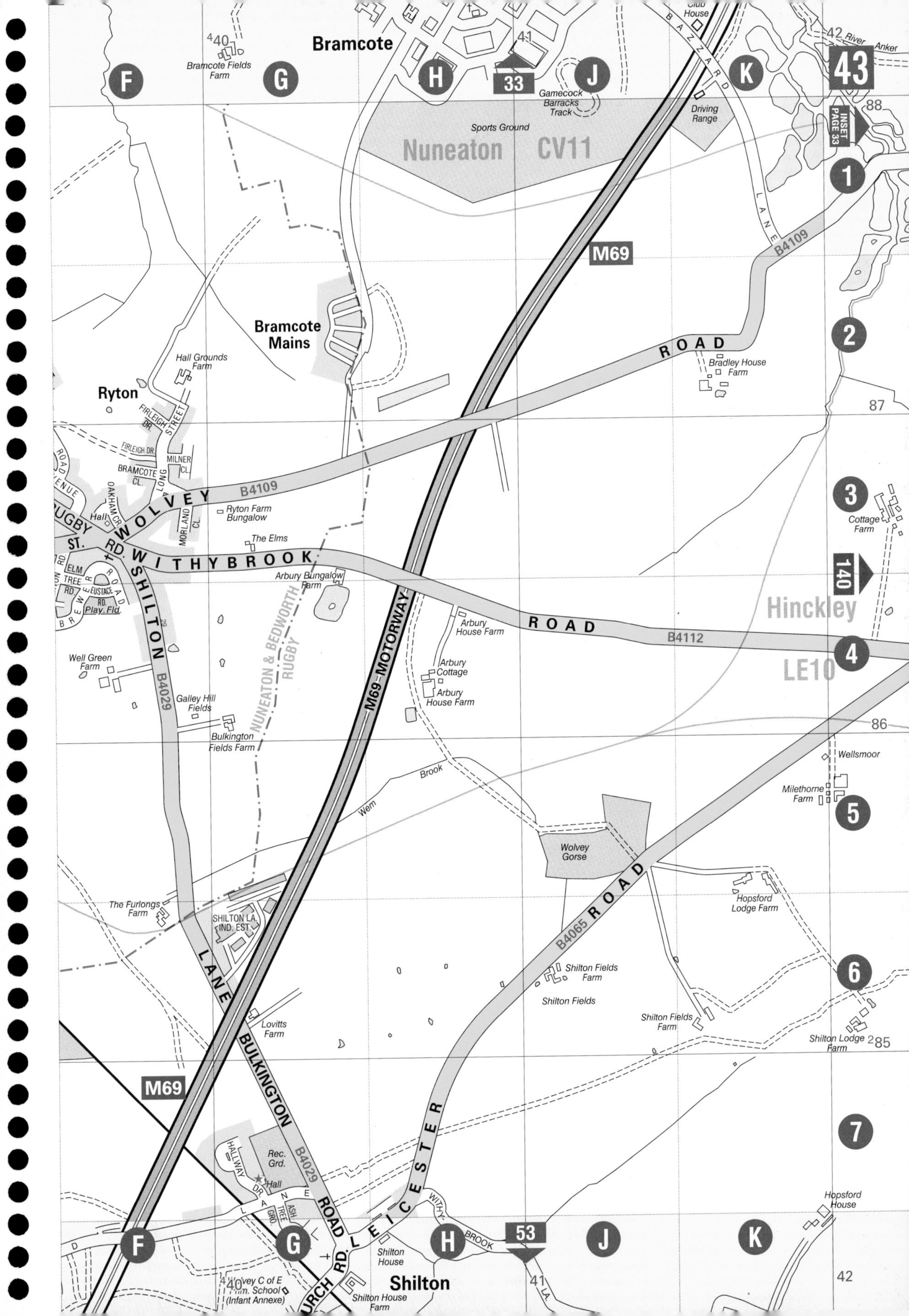

43
Bramcote
Bramcote Fields Farm
Club House
River Anker
BAZZARD LANE
33
Gamecock Barracks Track
Driving Range
Sports Ground
Nuneaton CV11
INSET PAGE 33
M69
B4109
Bramcote Mains
Hall Grounds Farm
Ryton
FIRLEIGH DR.
STREET
MILNER CL.
BRAMCOTE CL.
LONG
WOLVEY ROAD
B4109
Bradley House Farm
Ryton Farm Bungalow
OAKHAM CR.
MORLAND CL.
RUGBY RD.
ST.
WITHYBROOK ROAD
The Elms
Arbury Bungalow Farm
ELM TREE RD.
EUSTACE RD.
BREWER ROAD
Play. Fld.
Cottage Farm
140
Hinckley
LE10
Arbury House Farm
B4112
Arbury Cottage
Arbury House Farm
M69-MOTORWAY
NUNEATON & BEDWORTH
RUGBY
SHILTON
B4029
Well Green Farm
Galley Hill Fields
Bulkington Fields Farm
Wellsmoor
Milethorne Farm
Wem Brook
Wolvey Gorse
The Furlongs Farm
SHILTON LA. IND. EST.
B4065 ROAD
Hopsford Lodge Farm
Shilton Fields Farm
Shilton Fields
Shilton Fields Farm
Shilton Lodge Farm
Lovitts Farm
LANE
BULKINGTON ROAD
LEICESTER RD.
HALLWAY DR.
Rec. Grd.
Hall
LANE
ASH TREE GRO.
CHURCH RD.
WITHYBROOK
53
Shilton House
Shilton
Shilton House Farm
Wolvey C of E Prim. School (Infant Annexe)
Hopsford House
F
G
H
J
K
1
2
3
4
5
6
7
40
41
42
88
87
86
85

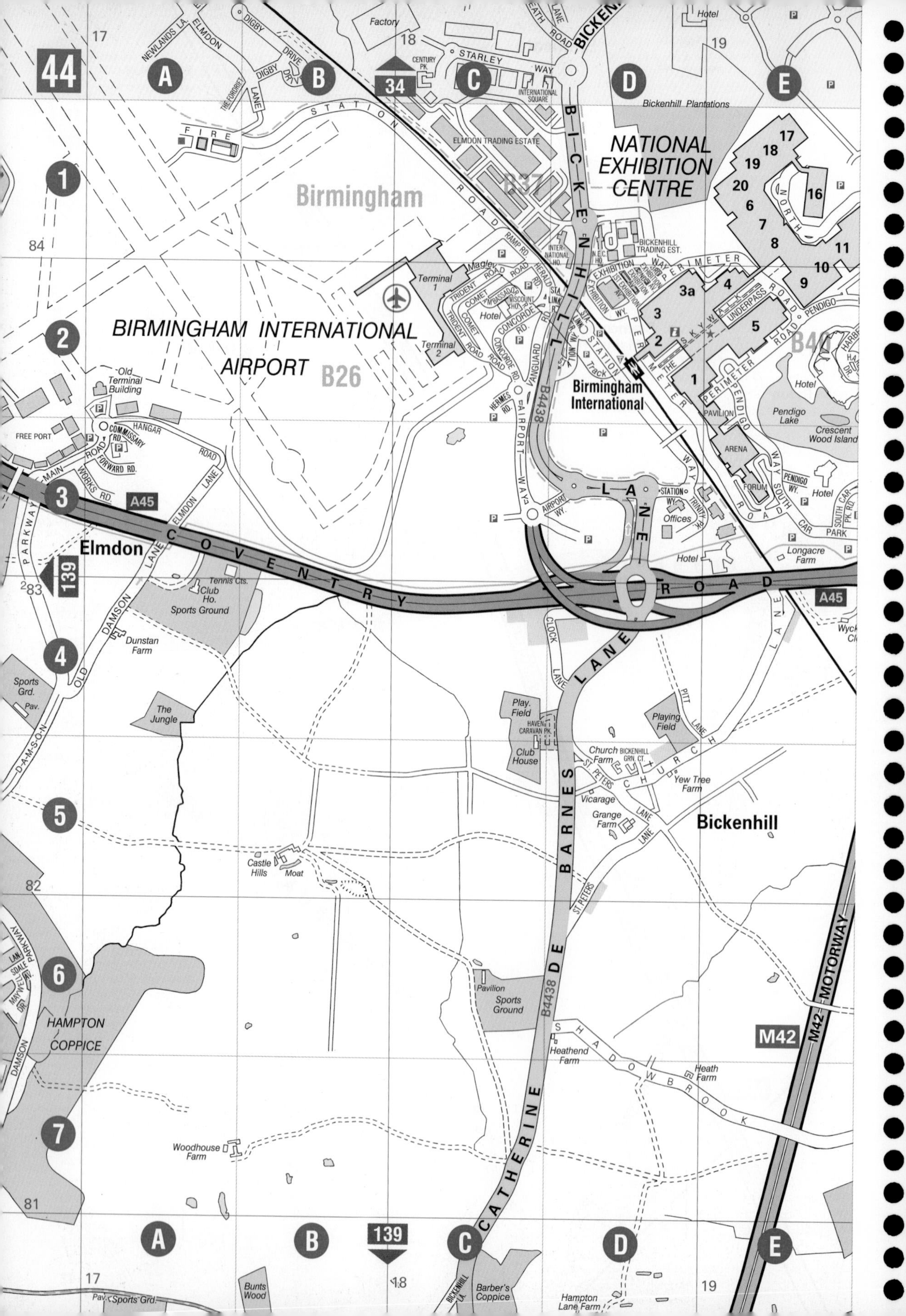

44
34
139
National Exhibition Centre
Birmingham International Airport
Birmingham
Birmingham International
Elmdon
Bickenhill
Coventry Road
A45
B4438
M42 Motorway
Catherine de Barnes Lane
Bickenhill Lane
Station Road
Elmdon Trading Estate
Bickenhill Plantations
Bickenhill Trading Est.
Terminal 1
Terminal 2
Old Terminal Building
Free Port
Pendigo Lake
Crescent Wood Island
Arena
Forum
Pavilion
Longacre Farm
Dunstan Farm
The Jungle
Castle Hills
Moat
Church Farm
Yew Tree Farm
Vicarage
Grange Farm
Heathend Farm
Heath Farm
Shadowbrook
Woodhouse Farm
Hampton Coppice
Barber's Coppice
Bunts Wood
Hampton Lane Farm
Sports Ground
Playing Field
Club House
Haven Caravan Pk.

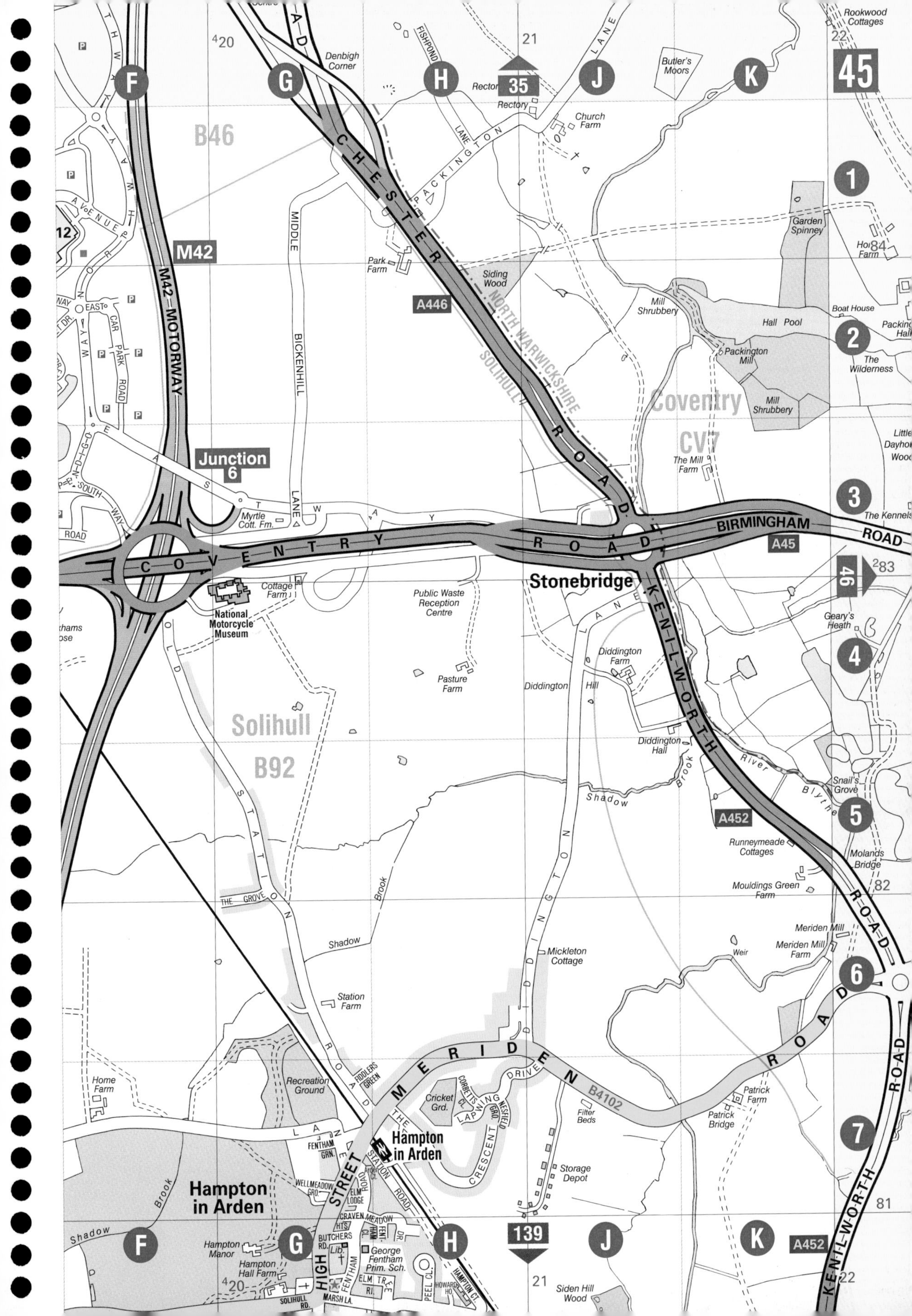

45
35
46
139
Denbigh Corner
Butler's Moors
Rookwood Cottages
Rectory
Church Farm
FISHPOND
LANE
PACKINGTON
CHESTER ROAD
A446
M42 MOTORWAY
M42
Junction 6
B46
Garden Spinney
Park Farm
Siding Wood
NORTH WARWICKSHIRE
SOLIHULL
MIDDLE BICKENHILL LANE
Mill Shrubbery
Hall Pool
Boat House
Packington Mill
The Wilderness
Coventry CV7
The Mill Farm
Little Dayhouse Wood
The Kennels
Myrtle Cott. Fm.
COVENTRY ROAD
BIRMINGHAM ROAD
A45
Stonebridge
National Motorcycle Museum
Cottage Farm
Public Waste Reception Centre
Pasture Farm
KENILWORTH ROAD
Geary's Heath
Diddington Farm
Diddington Hill
Diddington Hall
DIDDINGTON LANE
Solihull B92
STATION ROAD
River Blythe
Snail's Grove
Shadow Brook
A452
Runneymeade Cottages
Molands Bridge
Mouldings Green Farm
THE GROVE
Meriden Mill
Meriden Mill Farm
Weir
Mickleton Cottage
Station Farm
MERIDEN ROAD
B4102
Home Farm
Recreation Ground
FIDDLERS GREEN
Cricket Grd.
LAPWING GRO.
CORBETTS CL.
NESFIELD GRO.
CRESCENT
DRIVE
Patrick Farm
Patrick Bridge
Filter Beds
Storage Depot
Hampton in Arden
FENTHAM GRN.
WELLMEADOW GRO.
ELM LODGE
HIGH STREET
CRAVEN MEADOW
BUTCHERS RD.
Lib.
George Fentham Prim. Sch.
Hampton Manor
Hampton Hall Farm
ELM TREE RI.
PEEL CL.
HOWARDS HO.
HAMPTON CT.
SOLIHULL RD.
MARSH LA.
Siden Hill Wood
F G H J K
1 2 3 4 5 6 7
420 21 22
84 283 82 81

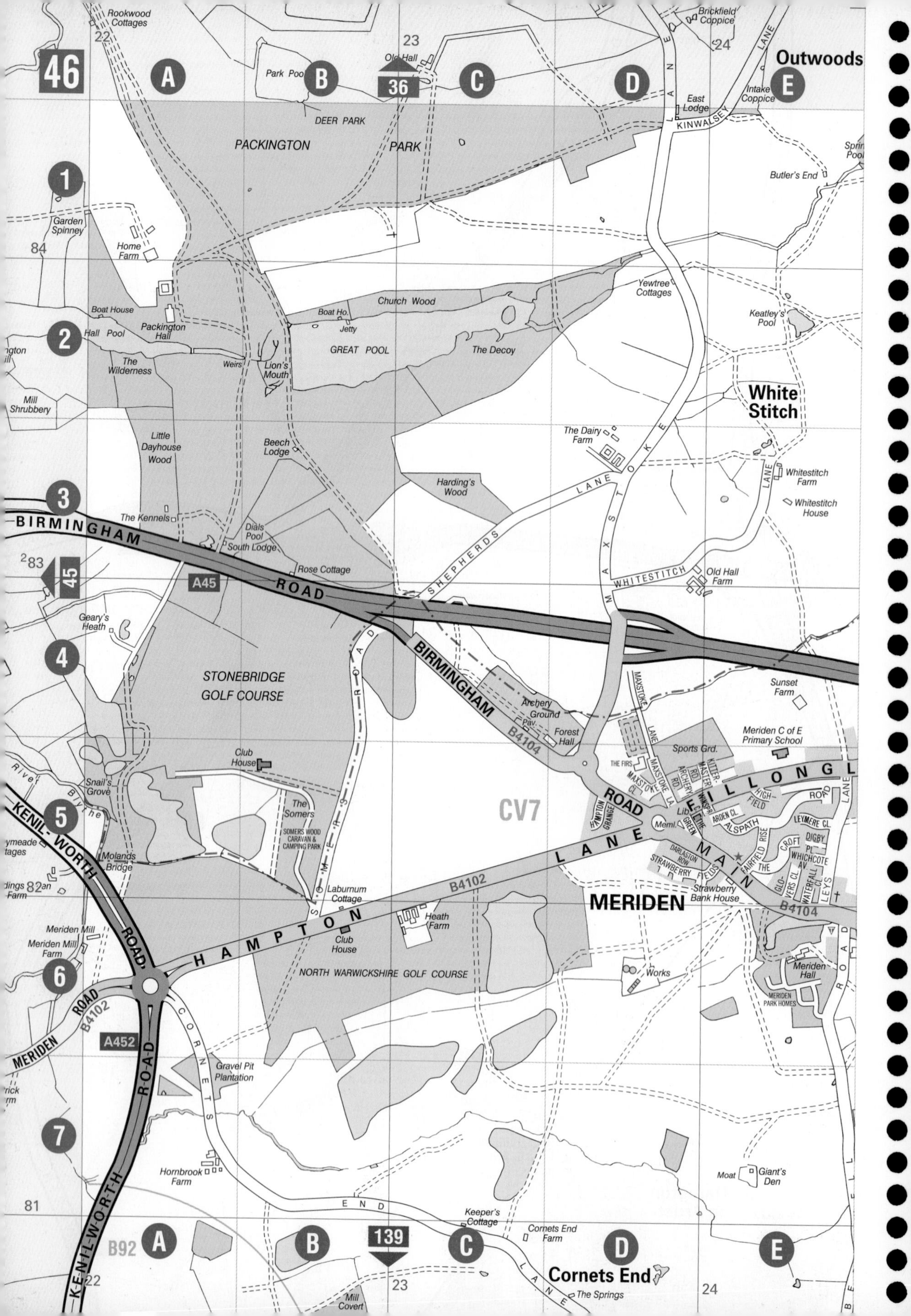

46
Outwoods
White Stitch
MERIDEN
Cornets End
CV7
PACKINGTON PARK
DEER PARK
GREAT POOL
Church Wood
The Decoy
Packington Hall
Boat House
Hall Pool
The Wilderness
Mill Shrubbery
Little Dayhouse Wood
Beech Lodge
Harding's Wood
The Dairy Farm
Yewtree Cottages
Keatley's Pool
Whitestitch Farm
Whitestitch House
Old Hall Farm
Butler's End
Intake Coppice
East Lodge
Brickfield Coppice
Rookwood Cottages
Park Pool
Old Hall
Garden Spinney
Home Farm
Lion's Mouth
Weirs
Jetty
Boat Ho.
The Kennels
Dials Pool
South Lodge
Rose Cottage
Geary's Heath
STONEBRIDGE GOLF COURSE
Club House
The Somers
SOMERS WOOD CARAVAN & CAMPING PARK
Snail's Grove
River Blythe
Molands Bridge
Meriden Mill
Meriden Mill Farm
Laburnum Cottage
Heath Farm
NORTH WARWICKSHIRE GOLF COURSE
Archery Ground
Forest Hall
Sports Grd.
Meriden C of E Primary School
Sunset Farm
Strawberry Bank House
Works
Meriden Hall
MERIDEN PARK HOMES
Gravel Pit Plantation
Hornbrook Farm
Keeper's Cottage
Cornets End Farm
Moat
Giant's Den
The Springs
Mill Covert
BIRMINGHAM ROAD
A45
B4104
HAMPTON LANE
B4102
KENILWORTH ROAD
A452
MERIDEN ROAD
CORNETS END LANE
SHEPHERDS LANE
MAXSTOKE LANE
WHITESTITCH LANE
KINWALSEY LANE
FILLONGLEY ROAD
MAIN ROAD
SOMERS ROAD
B92
36
45
139

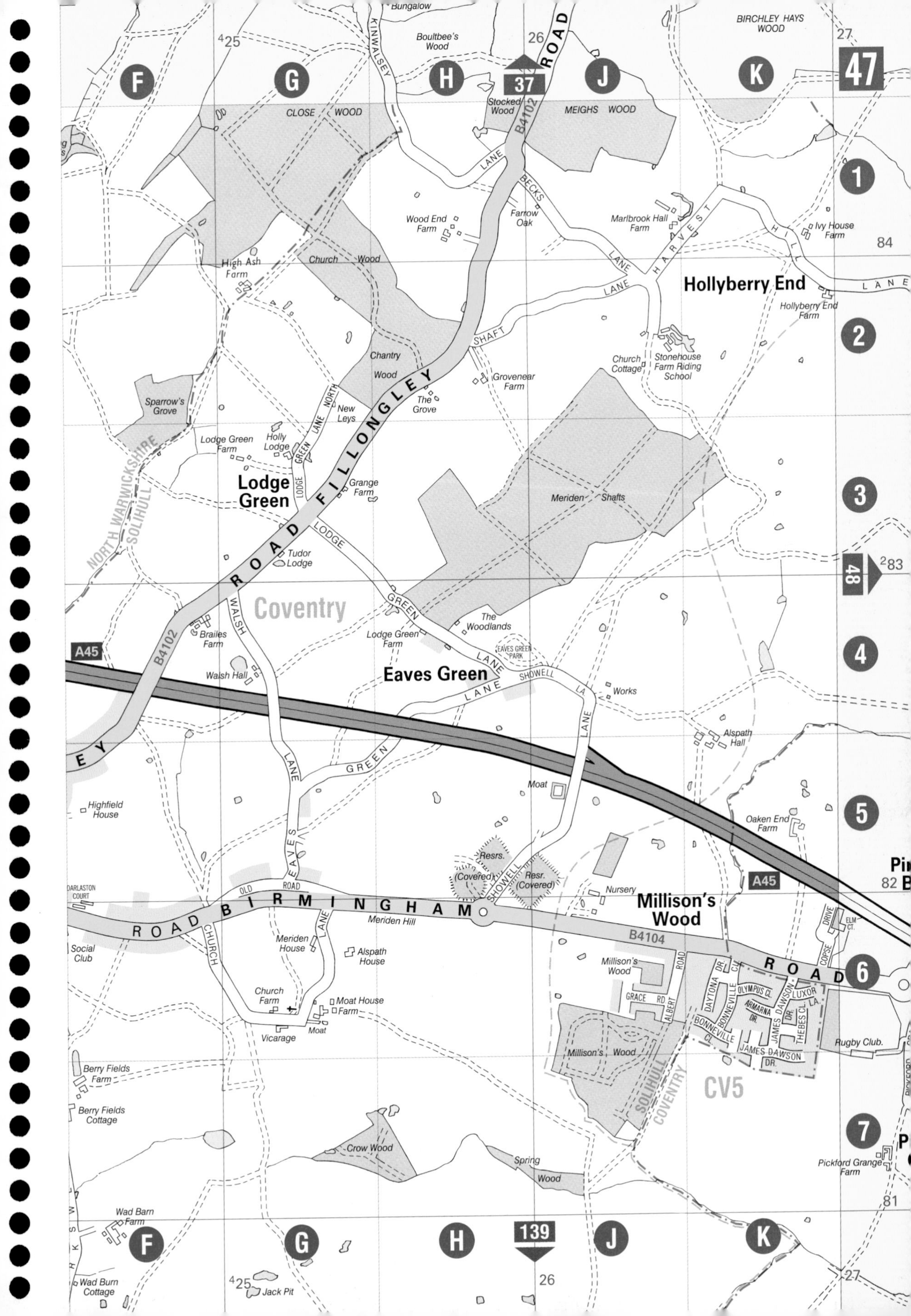
47
Hollyberry End
Lodge Green
Coventry
Eaves Green
Millison's Wood
CV5
FILLONGLEY ROAD
BIRMINGHAM ROAD
B4102
B4104
A45
Close Wood
Meighs Wood
Birchley Hays Wood
Boultbee's Wood
Stocked Wood
Church Wood
Chantry Wood
Sparrow's Grove
Meriden Shafts
Crow Wood
Spring Wood
Wood End Farm
Farrow Oak
Marlbrook Hall Farm
Ivy House Farm
Hollyberry End Farm
High Ash Farm
Grovenear Farm
Church Cottage
Stonehouse Farm Riding School
New Leys
The Grove
Lodge Green Farm
Holly Lodge
Grange Farm
Tudor Lodge
Brailes Farm
Walsh Hall
The Woodlands
Lodge Green Farm
Works
Alspath Hall
Moat
Oaken End Farm
Highfield House
Resrs. (Covered)
Resr. (Covered)
Nursery
Meriden Hill
Meriden House
Alspath House
Church Farm
Moat House Farm
Vicarage
Social Club
Rugby Club
Berry Fields Farm
Berry Fields Cottage
Wad Barn Farm
Wad Burn Cottage
Jack Pit
Pickford Grange Farm
Kinwalsey Lane
Becks Lane
Harvest Hill Lane
Shaft Lane
Lodge Green Lane
Lodge Green Lane
Walsh Lane
Showell Lane
Eaves Green Lane
Old Road
Church Lane
Albert Road
Grace Rd
Daytona Dr.
Bonneville Cl.
Olympus Cl.
Armarna Dr.
James Dawson Dr.
Luxor La.
Thebes Cl.
Copse Drive
Elm Ct.
North Warwickshire
Solihull
Coventry
Darlaston Court
Eaves Green Park
37
48
139
F G H J K
1 2 3 4 5 6 7
25 26 27
84 83 82 81

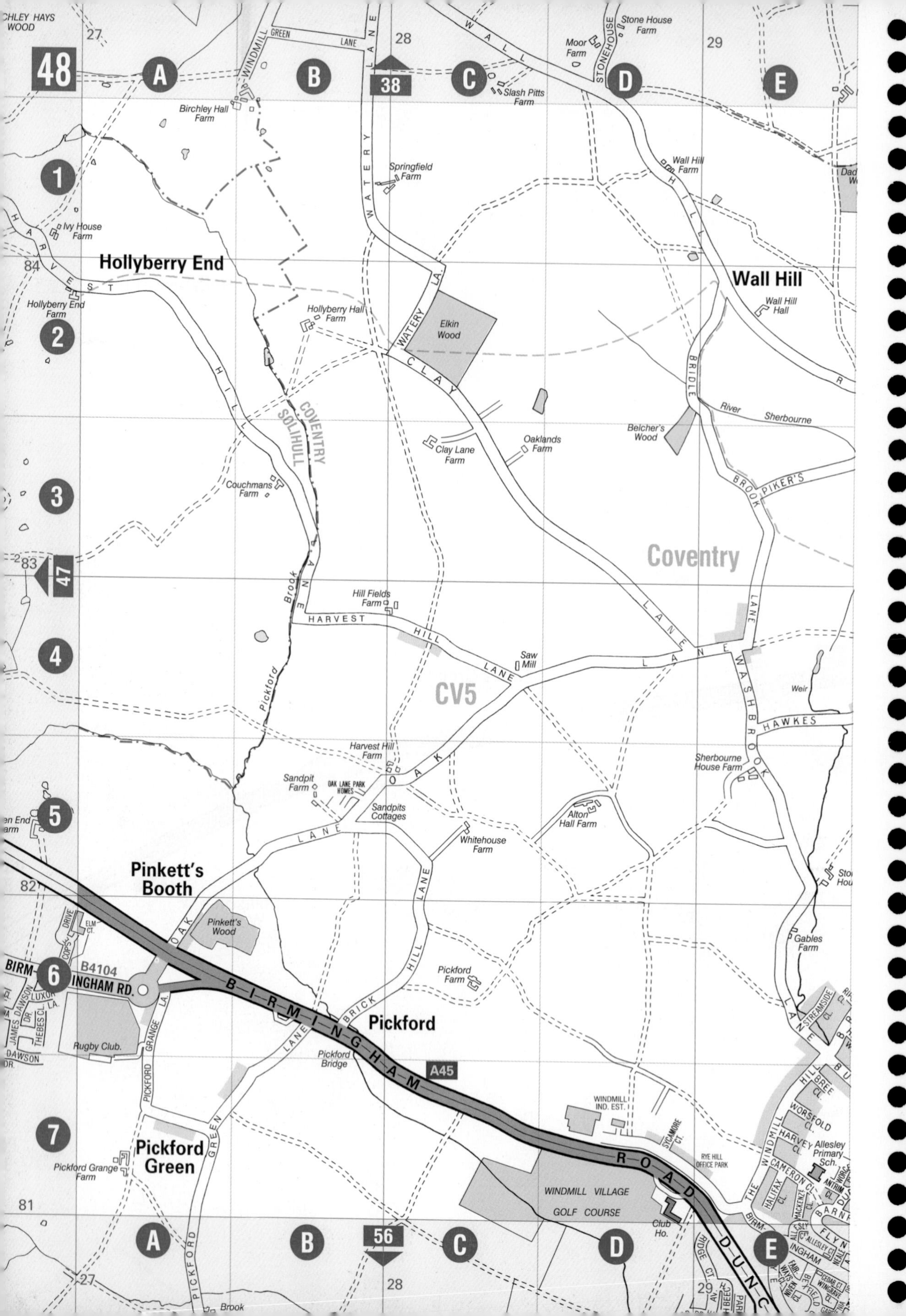

Hollyberry End
Wall Hill
Coventry
CV5
Pinkett's Booth
Pickford
Pickford Green
Birchley Hall Farm
Springfield Farm
Ivy House Farm
Hollyberry End Farm
Hollyberry Hall Farm
Elkin Wood
Wall Hill Farm
Wall Hill Hall
Stone House Farm
Moor Farm
Slash Pitts Farm
Belcher's Wood
River Sherbourne
Clay Lane Farm
Oaklands Farm
Couchmans Farm
Hill Fields Farm
Saw Mill
Harvest Hill Farm
Sandpit Farm
OAK LANE PARK HOMES
Sandpits Cottages
Whitehouse Farm
Alton Hall Farm
Sherbourne House Farm
Weir
Gables Farm
Pinkett's Wood
Pickford Farm
Rugby Club.
Pickford Bridge
Pickford Grange Farm
WINDMILL IND. EST.
RYE HILL OFFICE PARK
WINDMILL VILLAGE GOLF COURSE
Club Ho.
Allesley Primary Sch.
BIRMINGHAM ROAD
A45
B4104
WATERY LANE
CLAY LANE
HARVEST HILL LANE
OAK LANE
BRICK HILL LANE
WASHBROOK LANE
HAWKES
PIKER'S BROOK
BRIDLE
STONEHOUSE
WALL HILL
WINDMILL GREEN LANE
PICKFORD GRANGE LA.
PICKFORD GREEN
THE WINDMILL
SYCAMORE CT.
STREAMSIDE CL.
WORSFOLD CL.
HARVEY CL.
CAMERON CL.
HALIFAX CL.
COVENTRY
SOLIHULL
38
47
56
27
28
29
81
82
83
84

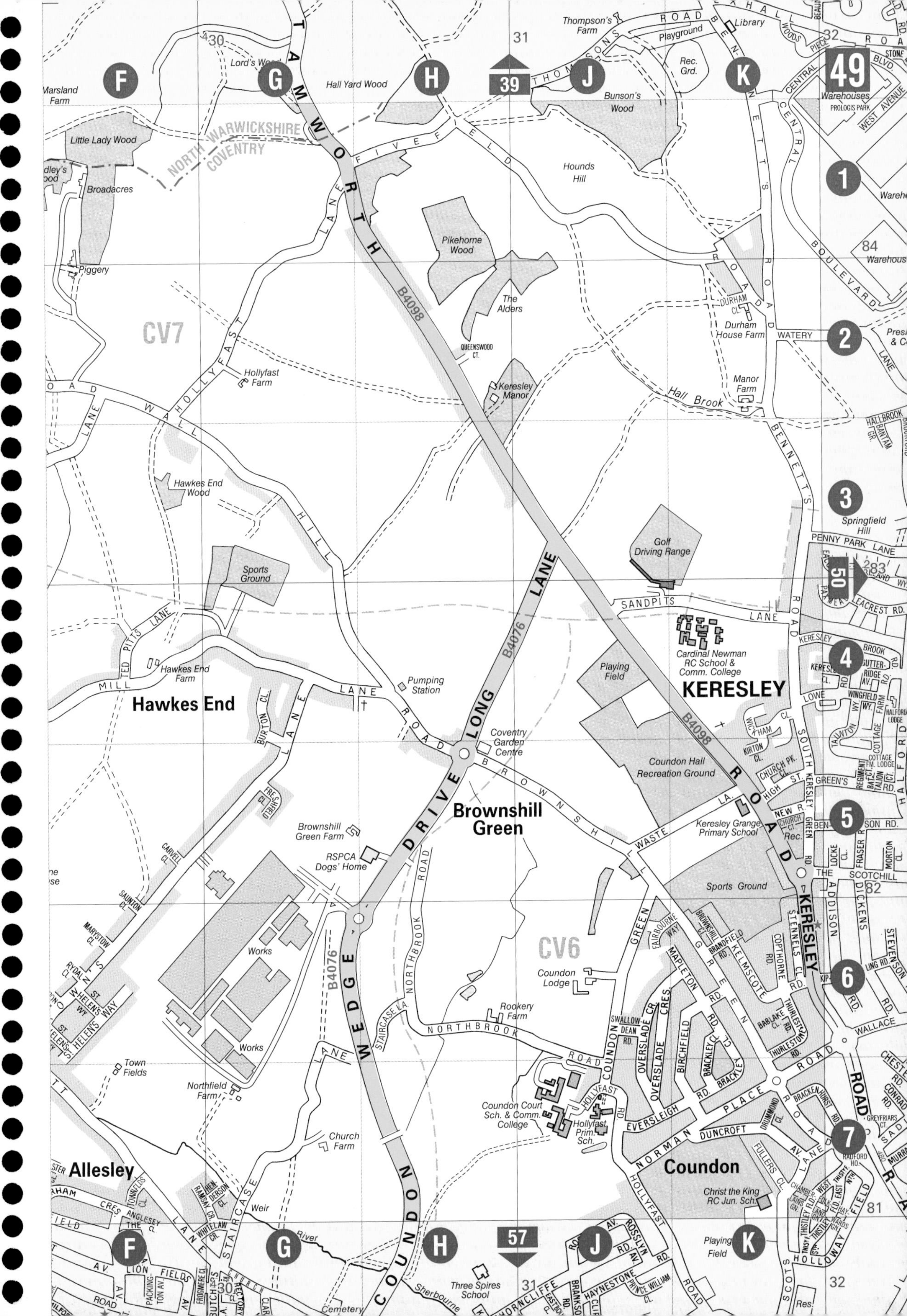

49
39
57
50
F
G
H
J
K
1
2
3
4
5
6
7
30
31
32
82
81
83
84
Marsland Farm
Lord's Wood
Hall Yard Wood
Thompson's Farm
THOMPSON'S ROAD
Library
Playground
Rec. Grd.
Bunson's Wood
Warehouses
PROLOGIS PARK
WEST AVENUE
CENTRAL BLVD
CENTRAL BOULEVARD
Little Lady Wood
NORTH WARWICKSHIRE
COVENTRY
FIVE FIELD
TAMWORTH
Broadacres
Piggery
Hounds Hill
Pikehorne Wood
The Alders
B4098
CV7
QUEENSWOOD CT.
Hollyfast Farm
Keresley Manor
Durham House Farm
DURHAM CL.
WATERY LANE
Manor Farm
Hall Brook
BENNETT'S ROAD
HOLLYFAST
WALL HILL ROAD
Hawkes End Wood
Springfield Hill
PENNY PARK LANE
Golf Driving Range
Sports Ground
SANDPITS LANE
LONG LANE
B4076
TED PITTS LANE
Hawkes End Farm
MILL LANE
Hawkes End
Pumping Station
Cardinal Newman RC School & Comm. College
Playing Field
KERESLEY
Coventry Garden Centre
Coundon Hall Recreation Ground
BROWNSHILL GREEN
Brownshill Green
Brownshill Green Farm
RSPCA Dogs' Home
DRIVE
WASTE LA.
Keresley Grange Primary School
HIGH ST.
GREEN'S
NEW R.
KERESLEY GREEN
Rec.
Sports Ground
THE SCOTCHILL
ADDISON
DICKENS
KERESLEY ROAD
CV6
Works
Coundon Lodge
Rookery Farm
NORTHBROOK ROAD
STAIRCASE LA.
WEDGE
COUNDON
Town Fields
Northfield Farm
Coundon Court Sch. & Comm. College
Hollyfast Prim. Sch.
EVERSLEIGH
NORMAN PLACE ROAD
DUNCROFT
Church Farm
Coundon
Christ the King RC Jun. Sch.
Playing Field
Allesley
Weir
River Sherbourne
Three Spires School
Cemetery
WALLACE ROAD
HOLLOWAY FIELD
RADFORD ROAD

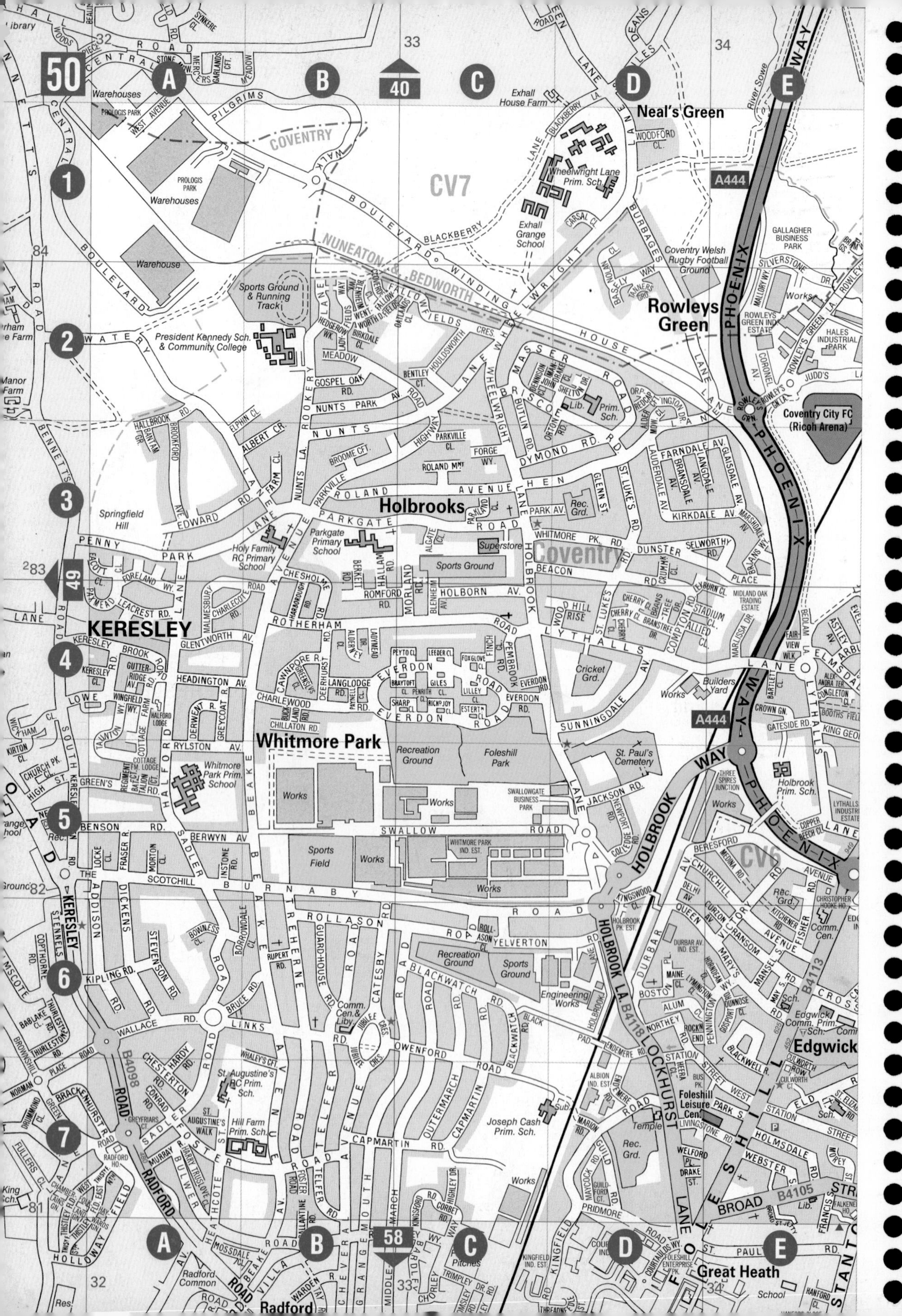

A
B
40
C
D
E
Neal's Green
Exhall House Farm
Warehouses
PROLOGIS PARK
COVENTRY
CV7
Wheelwright Lane Prim. Sch.
Exhall Grange School
A444
GALLAGHER BUSINESS PARK
Coventry Welsh Rugby Football Ground
Warehouse
Sports Ground & Running Track
NUNEATON & BEDWORTH
Rowleys Green
ROWLEYS GREEN IND. ESTATE
HALES INDUSTRIAL PARK
President Kennedy Sch. & Community College
Coventry City FC (Ricoh Arena)
Springfield Hill
Holbrooks
Parkgate Primary School
Holy Family RC Primary School
Superstore
Sports Ground
Coventry
MIDLAND OAK TRADING ESTATE
KERESLEY
Cricket Grd.
Builders Yard
Works
Whitmore Park
Recreation Ground
Foleshill Park
St. Paul's Cemetery
Whitmore Park Prim. School
SWALLOWGATE BUSINESS PARK
THREE SPIRES JUNCTION
Holbrook Prim. Sch.
Sports Field
WHITMORE PARK IND. EST.
CV6
HOLBROOK PK. EST.
DURBAR AV. IND. EST.
Comm. Cen.
Recreation Ground
Sports Ground
Engineering Works
Comm. Cen. & Liby.
Edgwick Comm. Prim. Sch.
Edgwick
St. Augustine's RC Prim. Sch.
Hill Farm Prim. Sch.
Joseph Cash Prim. Sch.
ALBION IND. EST.
Foleshill Leisure Cen.
Temple
Rec. Grd.
B4098
B4118
B4113
B4105
58
Radford Common
Radford
KINGFIELD IND. EST.
FOLESHILL ENTERPRISE PK.
Great Heath
School
Pitches
32
33
34
84
83
82
81
49

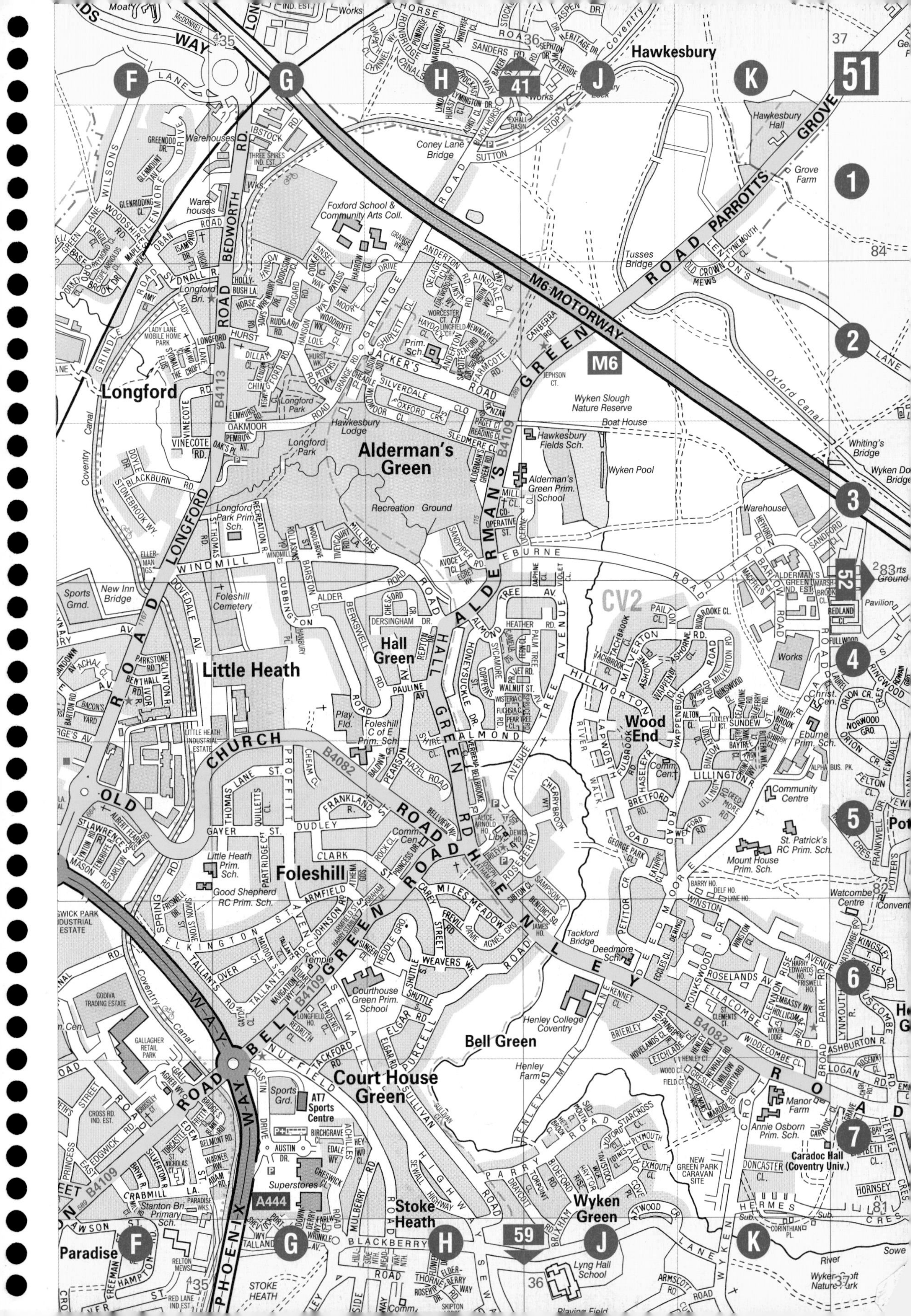

51
41
52
59
Hawkesbury
Hawkesbury Hall
Grove Farm
PARROTTS GROVE
M6 MOTORWAY
M6
Coney Lane Bridge
Tusses Bridge
Oxford Canal
Whiting's Bridge
Wyken Slough Nature Reserve
Boat House
Wyken Pool
Hawkesbury Fields Sch.
Alderman's Green Prim. School
Longford
Alderman's Green
Recreation Ground
Longford Park
Hawkesbury Lodge
Foxford School & Community Arts Coll.
Longford Park Prim. Sch.
Foleshill Cemetery
Sports Grnd.
New Inn Bridge
Little Heath
Little Heath Industrial Estate
Hall Green
Foleshill C of E Prim. Sch.
Little Heath Prim. Sch.
Good Shepherd RC Prim. Sch.
Foleshill
CV2
Wood End
Comm. Cen.
Community Centre
Eburne Prim. Sch.
St. Patrick's RC Prim. Sch.
Mount House Prim. Sch.
Watcombe Centre
Deedmore Sch.
Tackford Bridge
Henley College Coventry
Bell Green
Henley Farm
Courthouse Green Prim. School
Court House Green
AT7 Sports Centre
Superstores
A444
Stoke Heath
Wyken Green
Lyng Hall School
New Green Park Caravan Site
Manor Farm
Annie Osborn Prim. Sch.
Caradoc Hall (Coventry Univ.)
Godiva Trading Estate
Gallagher Retail Park
Cross Rd. Ind. Est.
Stanton Bri. Primary Sch.
Paradise
Stoke Heath
Wyken Croft Nature Park
Sowe River
PHOENIX WAY
BELL GREEN ROAD
OLD CHURCH ROAD
LONGFORD ROAD
BEDWORTH ROAD
ALDERMAN'S GREEN ROAD
HALL GREEN RD
HENLEY ROAD
B4113
B4109
B4082
Coventry Canal
F
G
H
J
K
1
2
3
4
5
6
7

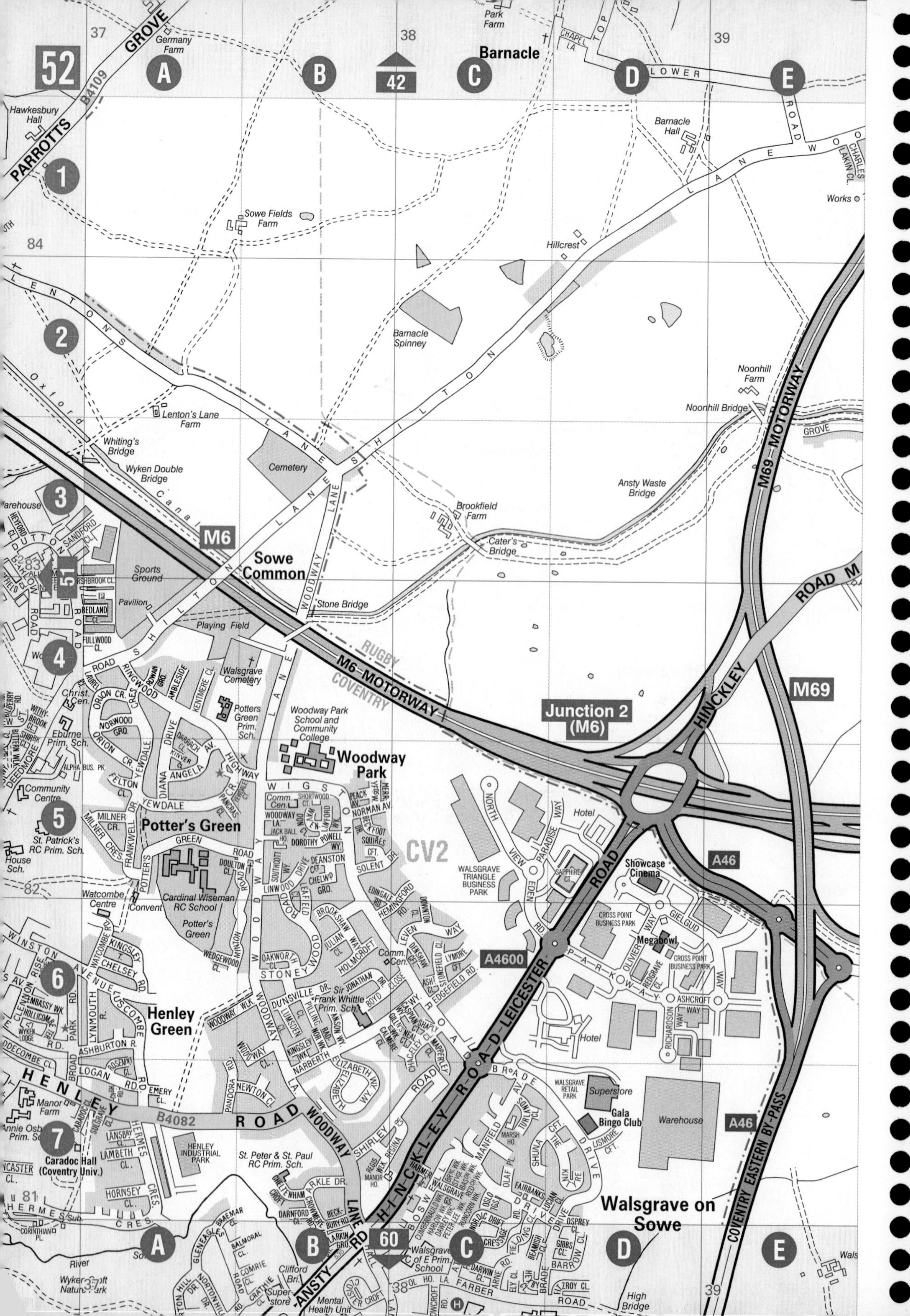

Barnacle
Sowe Common
Woodway Park
Potter's Green
Henley Green
Walsgrave on Sowe
CV2
Junction 2 (M6)
M6-MOTORWAY
M69-MOTORWAY
COVENTRY EASTERN BY-PASS
HINCKLEY ROAD
LEICESTER ROAD
HENLEY ROAD
SHILTON LANE
LENTON'S LANE
Barnacle Spinney
Sowe Fields Farm
Lenton's Lane Farm
Cemetery
Walsgrave Cemetery
Woodway Park School and Community College
Walsgrave Triangle Business Park
Cross Point Business Park
Showcase Cinema
Megabowl
Superstore
Gala Bingo Club
Warehouse
Henley Industrial Park
Cardinal Wiseman RC School
Noonhill Farm
Noonhill Bridge
Ansty Waste Bridge
Brookfield Farm
Cater's Bridge
Stone Bridge
Hawkesbury Hall
Germany Farm
Barnacle Hall
Hillcrest
Whiting's Bridge
Wyken Double Bridge
Sports Ground
Playing Field
Caradoc Hall (Coventry Univ.)
Wyken Croft Nature Park
Mental Health Unit
High Bridge

42 51 60

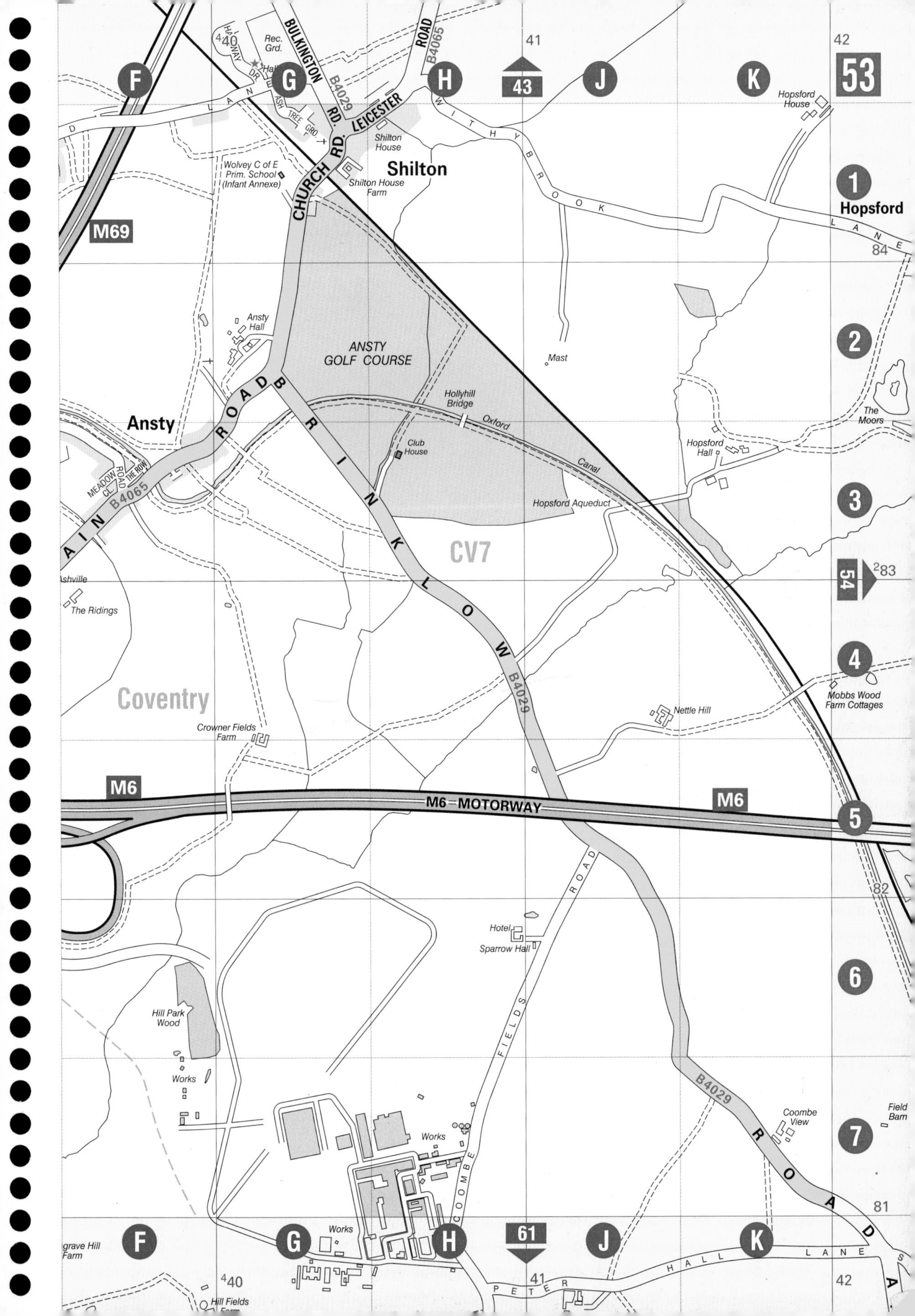

53
41
42
43
F
G
H
J
K
1
2
3
4
5
6
7
Hopsford
Hopsford House
84
83
82
81
54
Rec. Grd.
Hall
BULKINGTON
B4029
ROAD
B4065
LEICESTER
CHURCH RD.
ASH TREE GRO
WITHYBROOK LANE
Shilton House
Shilton
Shilton House Farm
Wolvey C of E Prim. School (Infant Annexe)
M69
ANSTY GOLF COURSE
Ansty Hall
Mast
The Moors
Hollyhill Bridge
Oxford Canal
Club House
Hopsford Hall
Ansty
ROAD
BRINKLOW
MEADOW CL.
ROAD
THE ROW
B4065
AIN
Hopsford Aqueduct
CV7
Ashville
The Ridings
Coventry
Mobbs Wood Farm Cottages
Nettle Hill
Crowner Fields Farm
M6
M6 MOTORWAY
Hotel
Sparrow Hall
FIELDS
COOMBE
Hill Park Wood
Works
Coombe View
Field Barn
B4029
ROAD
61
PETER HALL LANE
Hill Fields Farm
grave Hill Farm
440

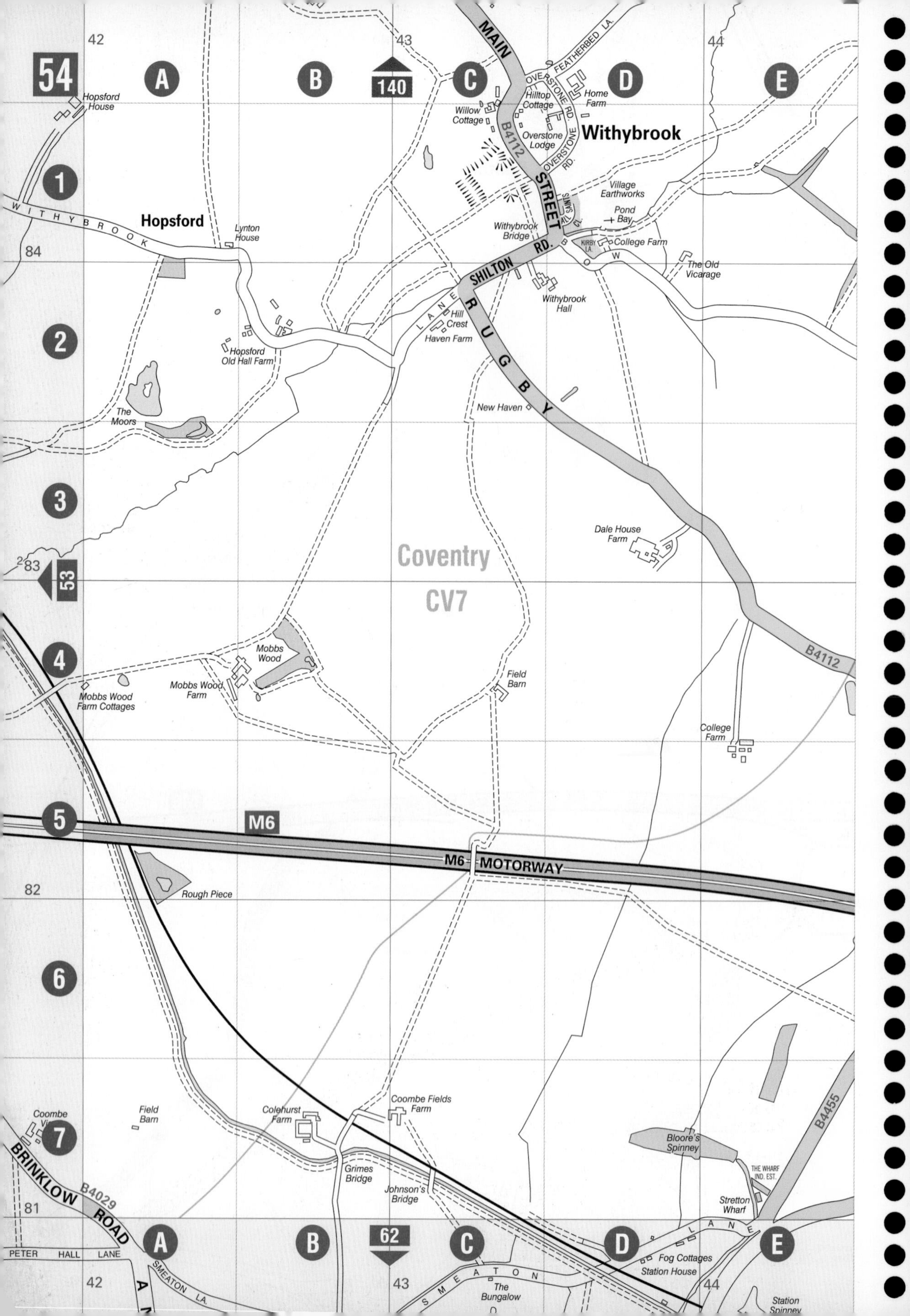

Withybrook
Hopsford
Hopsford House
Lynton House
Hopsford Old Hall Farm
The Moors
Willow Cottage
Hilltop Cottage
Overstone Lodge
Home Farm
Village Earthworks
Pond Bay
College Farm
The Old Vicarage
Withybrook Bridge
Withybrook Hall
Hill Crest
Haven Farm
New Haven
Dale House Farm
Coventry
CV7
Mobbs Wood
Mobbs Wood Farm
Mobbs Wood Farm Cottages
Field Barn
College Farm
M6
M6 MOTORWAY
Rough Piece
Field Barn
Colehurst Farm
Coombe Fields Farm
Grimes Bridge
Johnson's Bridge
Bloore's Spinney
THE WHARF IND. EST.
Stretton Wharf
Fog Cottages
Station House
The Bungalow
Station Spinney
MAIN STREET
B4112
OVERSTONE RD.
FEATHERBED LA.
ALL SAINTS
KIRBY LA.
SHILTON RD.
RUGBY LANE
BOW
WITHYBROOK
LANE
B4455
BRINKLOW ROAD
B4029
PETER HALL LANE
SMEATON LA.
SMEATON
LANE
140
53
62
A
B
C
D
E
1
2
3
4
5
6
7
42
43
44
84
83
82
81

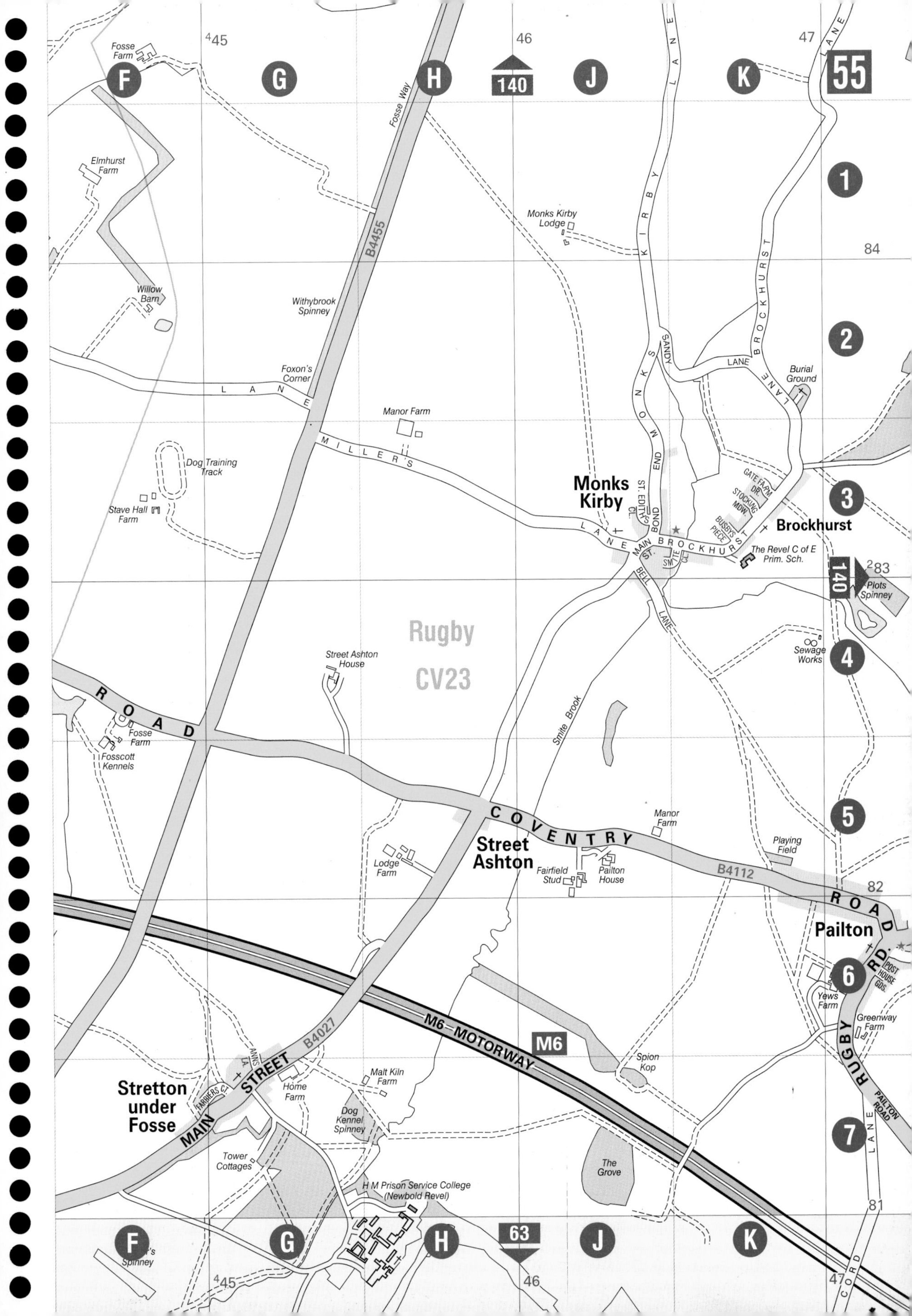
55
F
G
H
J
K
140
63
445
46
47
84
83
82
81
1
2
3
4
5
6
7
Fosse Farm
Elmhurst Farm
Willow Barn
Withybrook Spinney
Fosse Way
B4455
Monks Kirby Lodge
KIRBY LANE
LANE
Foxon's Corner
Manor Farm
MILLER'S LANE
Dog Training Track
Stave Hall Farm
Monks Kirby
Brockhurst
MONKS END
SANDY LANE
BROCKHURST LANE
Burial Ground
GATE FARM DR.
STOCKING MDW.
BUSBY'S PIECE
ST. EDITH'S CL.
BOND
MAIN ST.
BELL LANE
SMITE CL.
The Revel C of E Prim. Sch.
Plots Spinney
Sewage Works
Rugby
CV23
Street Ashton House
ROAD
Fosse Farm
Fosscott Kennels
Smite Brook
COVENTRY ROAD
B4112
Manor Farm
Street Ashton
Fairfield Stud
Pailton House
Lodge Farm
Playing Field
Pailton
RUGBY RD.
POST HOUSE GDS.
Yews Farm
Greenway Farm
PAILTON ROAD
M6 MOTORWAY
M6
Spion Kop
B4027
ANNS LA.
MAIN STREET
FARRIERS CT.
Stretton under Fosse
Home Farm
Malt Kiln Farm
Dog Kennel Spinney
Tower Cottages
The Grove
H M Prison Service College (Newbold Revel)
LANE
CORD
Spinney

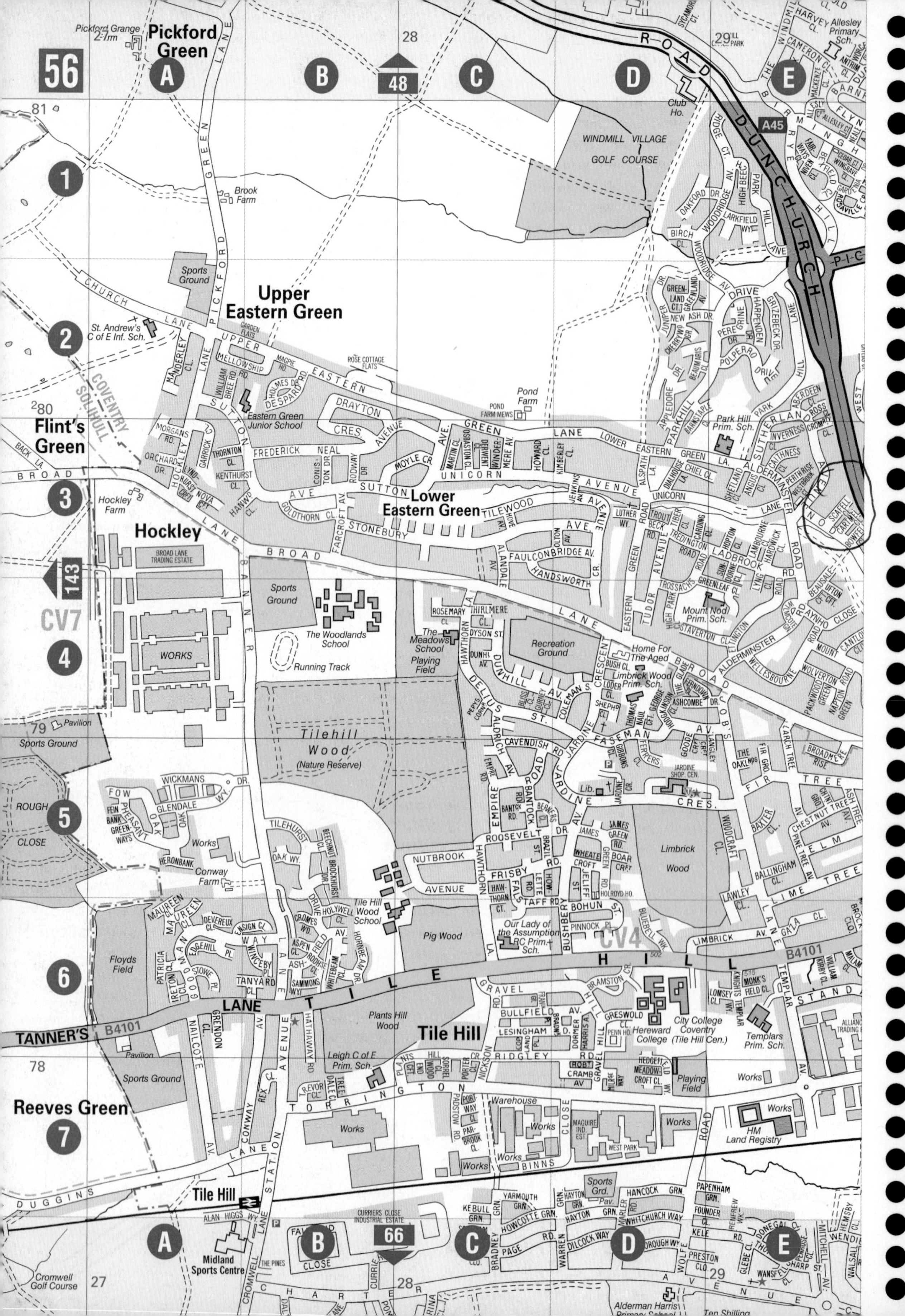
Pickford Green
Pickford Grange
Upper Eastern Green
Flint's Green
Hockley
Lower Eastern Green
Tile Hill
Reeves Green
CV7
CV4
Windmill Village Golf Course
Sports Ground
St. Andrew's C of E Inf. Sch.
Eastern Green Junior School
Brook Farm
Pond Farm
Hockley Farm
Broad Lane Trading Estate
Works
The Woodlands School
Running Track
Tilehill Wood (Nature Reserve)
The Meadows School Playing Field
Recreation Ground
Home For The Aged
Limbrick Wood Prim. Sch.
Limbrick Wood
Park Hill Prim. Sch.
Mount Nod Prim. Sch.
Tile Hill Wood School
Pig Wood
Our Lady of the Assumption RC Prim. Sch.
Plants Hill Wood
Leigh C of E Prim. Sch.
City College Coventry (Tile Hill Cen.)
Hereward College
Templars Prim. Sch.
HM Land Registry
Conway Farm
Floyds Field
Rough Close
Midland Sports Centre
Cromwell Golf Course
Alderman Harris Primary School
Allesley Primary Sch.
Church Lane
Pickford Green Lane
Broad Lane
Banner Lane
Tile Hill Lane
Tanner's Lane
B4101
A45
Dunchurch Road
Birmingham Road
Torrington Avenue
Station Avenue
Duggins Lane
Charter Avenue
Sutton Avenue
Unicorn Avenue
Lower Eastern Green Lane
Alderminster Road
Jardine Crescent
Fir Tree Avenue
Lime Tree Avenue
Limbrick Avenue
Standard Avenue
Templar Avenue
Coventry
Solihull
Tile Hill
143
48
66
A B C D E
1 2 3 4 5 6 7
27 28 29
78 79 80 81

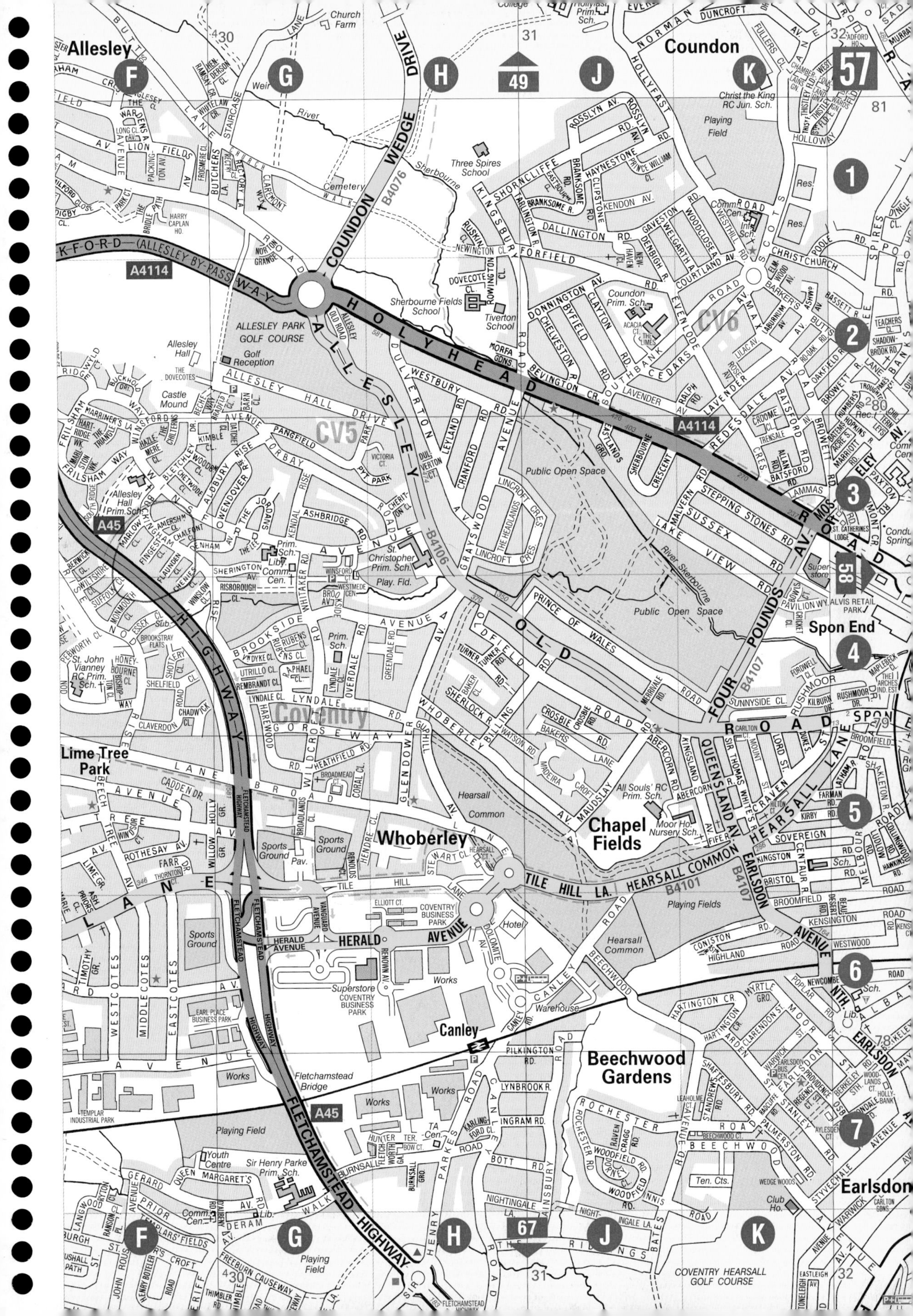
57
Allesley
Coundon
Coventry
CV5
CV6
Whoberley
Chapel Fields
Lime Tree Park
Spon End
Canley
Beechwood Gardens
Earlsdon
Allesley Park Golf Course
Public Open Space
Hearsall Common
Coventry Hearsall Golf Course
Three Spires School
Sherbourne Fields School
Tiverton School
Coundon Prim. Sch.
St. Christopher Prim. Sch.
Allesley Hall Prim. Sch.
Sir Henry Parke Prim. Sch.
All Souls' RC Prim. Sch.
St. John Vianney RC Prim. Sch.
Christ the King RC Jun. Sch.
Coventry Business Park
Templar Industrial Park
Fletchamstead Bridge
Holyhead Road
Allesley Old Road
Four Pounds Av.
Fletchamstead Highway
Tile Hill La.
Hearsall Common
Earlsdon Avenue
Coundon Wedge Drive
A4114
A45
B4076
B4106
B4107
B4101
49
58
67
F
G
H
J
K
1
2
3
4
5
6
7
430
31
32
81
80
79
78

58
50
57
135
68
A
B
C
D
E
1
2
3
4
5
6
7
COVENTRY
Radford
Radford Common
Gala Bingo Club
Great Heath
Broad Heath Community Prim. School
Courtaulds Ind. Est.
Football Pitches
Sports Ground
Newfield Lodge Day. Cen.
Recreation Ground
Brick Works
Temple
John Gulson Prim. Sch.
Bishopsgate Green
Draper's Field
Barr's Hill Sch. & Comm. Coll.
Naul's Mill Park
Bablake Sch.
Moseley Prim. Sch.
Conduit Springs Works
Coventry & Warwickshire Hosp.
Hillfields
Sidney Stringer Coll.
Spon End
Alvis Retail Park
Skydome
The Arena
Coventry RUFC (Butts Stadium)
City Coll. Coventry (Butts Cen.)
City Coll. Coventry (Maxwell Cen.)
Coventry Uni.
Gulson Hosp.
Spencer Park
King Henry VIII School
Coventry
Elm Bank Teachers Centre
Coventry Parkside
London Road Cemetery
Playing Field
Park Gardens
Earlsdon
Stivichall Common
War Memorial Park
Cheylesmore
Quinton Pool
CV5
CV6
A4114
A4053
A429
B4098
B4107
B4101
B4113
B4109
HOLYHEAD ROAD
FOLESHILL
STONEY STANTON
RADFORD ROAD
WARWICK ROAD
LONDON ROAD
KENILWORTH ROAD
EARLSDON AVENUE

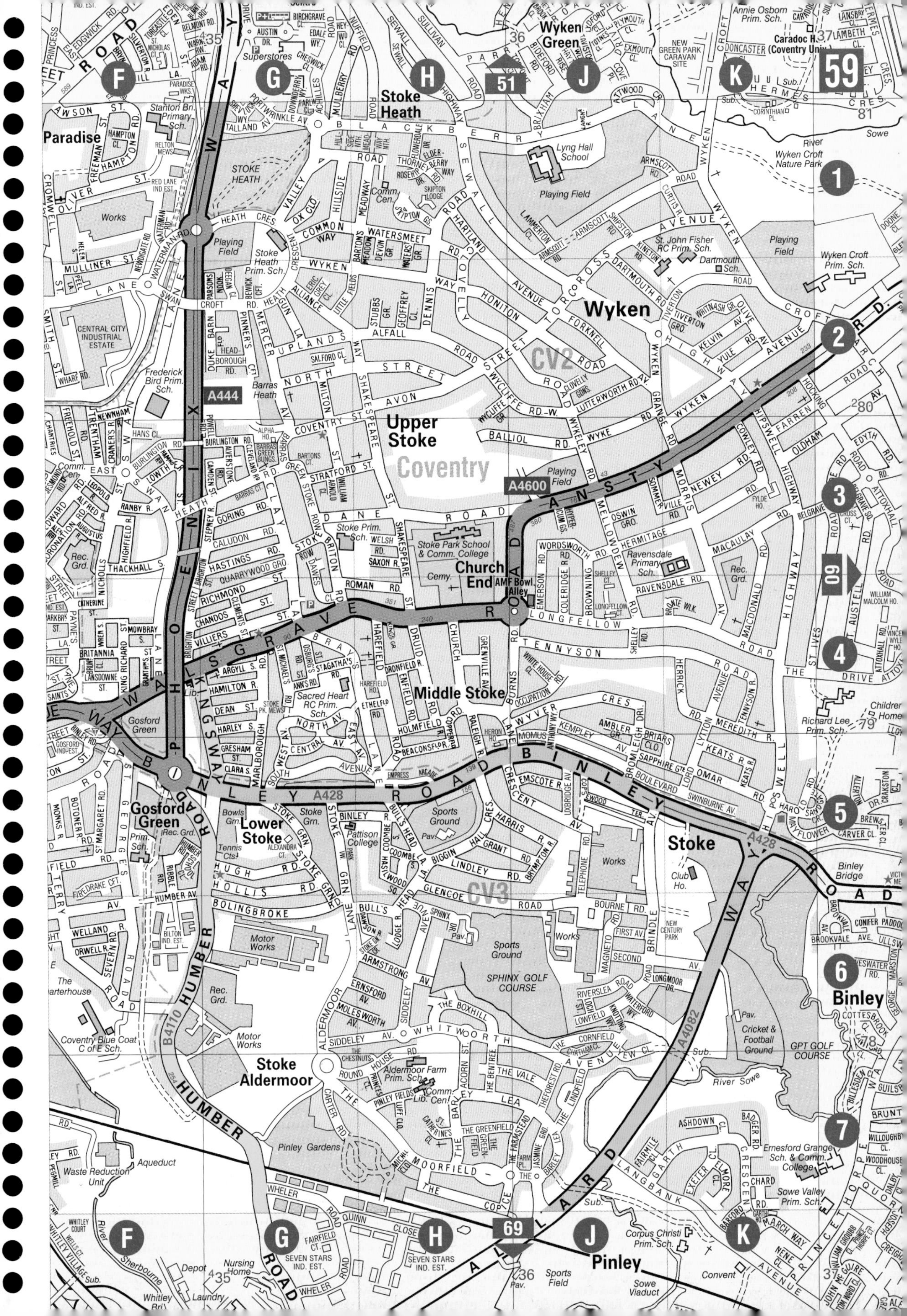
Stoke Heath
Wyken Green
Paradise
Wyken
Upper Stoke
Coventry
CV2
Church End
Middle Stoke
Gosford Green
Lower Stoke
Stoke
CV3
Binley
Stoke Aldermoor
Pinley
A444
A4600
A428
A4082
B4110
Lyng Hall School
Wyken Croft Nature Park
Sphinx Golf Course
GPT Golf Course
Pinley Gardens
River Sowe
51
60
69

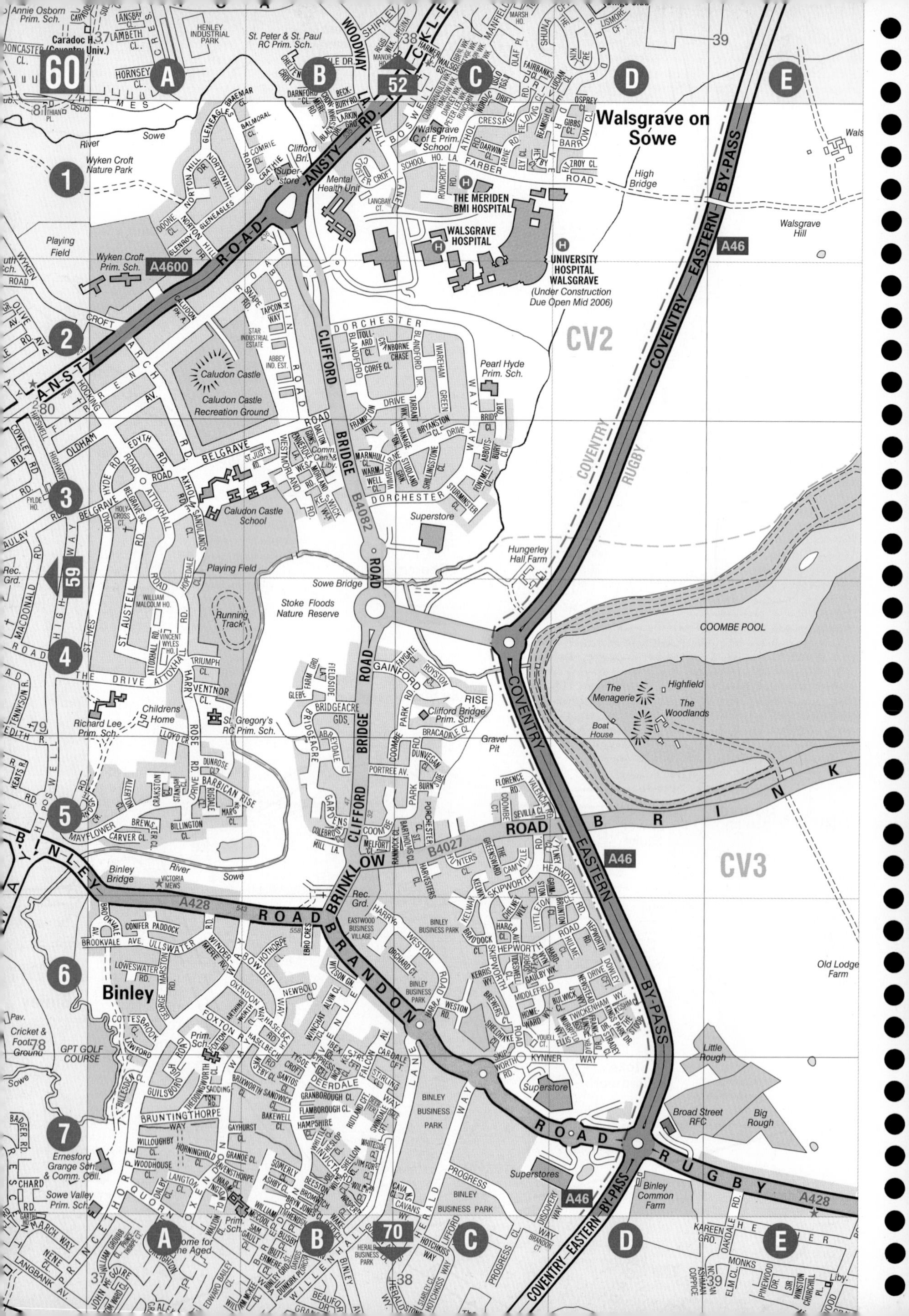

60
52
59
70
A
B
C
D
E
1
2
3
4
5
6
7
37
38
39
Walsgrave on Sowe
Binley
CV2
CV3
Annie Osborn Prim. Sch.
Caradoc H. (Coventry Univ.)
HENLEY INDUSTRIAL PARK
St. Peter & St. Paul RC Prim. Sch.
WOODWAY LA.
HERMES
River Sowe
Wyken Croft Nature Park
Playing Field
Wyken Croft Prim. Sch.
A4600
ANSTY ROAD
Clifford Bri.
Superstore
Mental Health Unit
Walsgrave C of E Prim. School
THE MERIDEN BMI HOSPITAL
WALSGRAVE HOSPITAL
UNIVERSITY HOSPITAL WALSGRAVE
(Under Construction Due Open Mid 2006)
FARBER ROAD
High Bridge
Walsgrave Hill
A46
COVENTRY EASTERN BY-PASS
STAR INDUSTRIAL ESTATE
ABBEY IND. EST.
Caludon Castle
Caludon Castle Recreation Ground
CLIFFORD BRIDGE ROAD
B4082
DORCHESTER WAY
Pearl Hyde Prim. Sch.
BELGRAVE ROAD
Caludon Castle School
Superstore
Hungerley Hall Farm
COVENTRY
RUGBY
Playing Field
Sowe Bridge
Stoke Floods Nature Reserve
Running Track
COOMBE POOL
The Menagerie
Highfield
The Woodlands
Boat House
Clifford Bridge Prim. Sch.
Gravel Pit
Childrens' Home
Richard Lee Prim. Sch.
St. Gregory's RC Prim. Sch.
BARBICAN RISE
BRINKLOW ROAD
B4027
BRINK
Binley Bridge
VICTORIA MEWS
A428
BRANDON ROAD
Rec. Grd.
EASTWOOD BUSINESS VILLAGE
BINLEY BUSINESS PARK
Old Lodge Farm
Little Rough
Big Rough
Broad Street RFC
Superstores
Binley Common Farm
RUGBY ROAD
Cricket & Foot. Ground
GPT GOLF COURSE
Ernesford Grange Sch. & Comm. Coll.
Sowe Valley Prim. Sch.
Home for the Aged
HERALD BUSINESS PARK

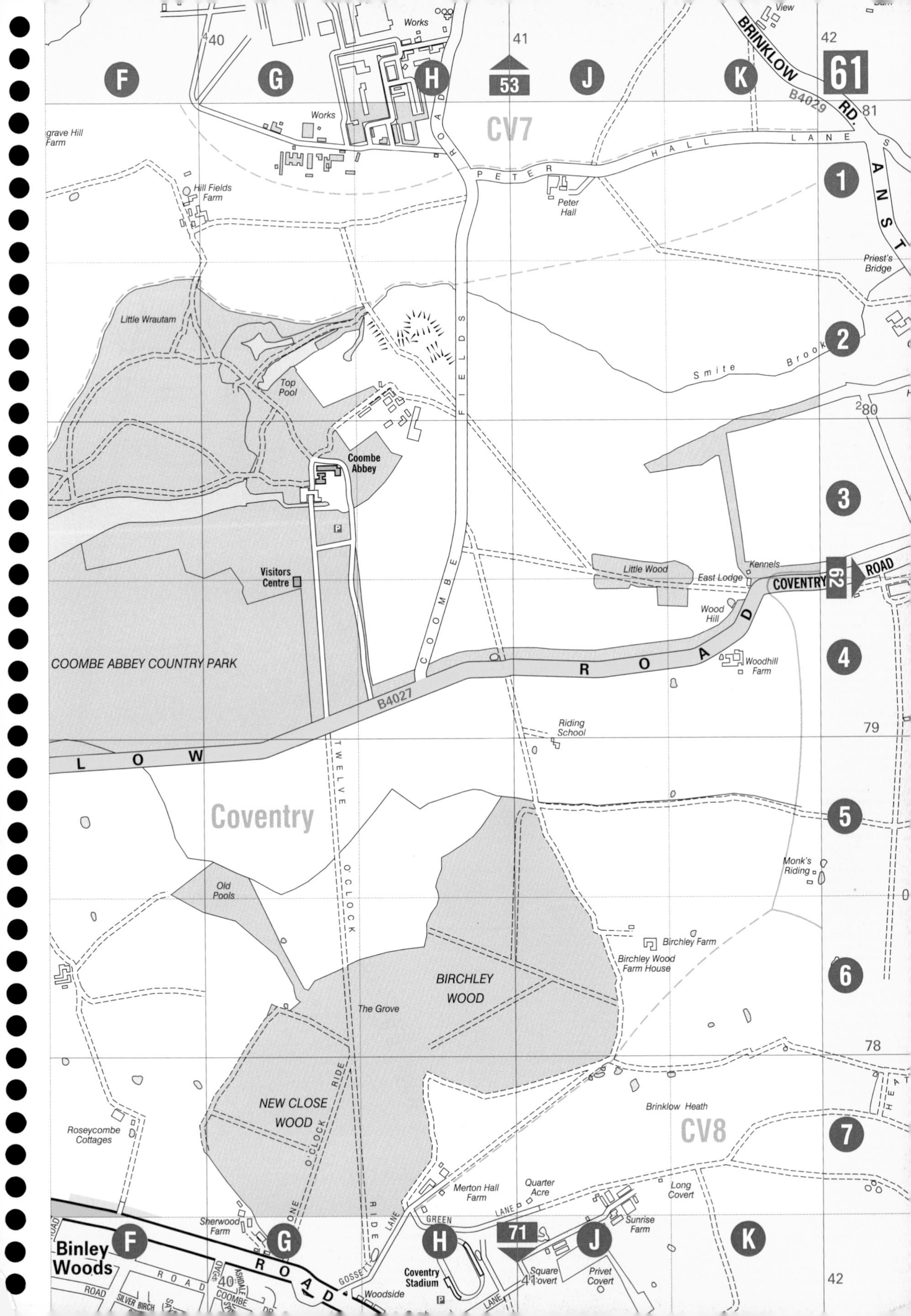

53
F
G
H
J
K
40
41
42
81
80
79
78
1
2
3
4
5
6
7
Works
View
BRINKLOW RD.
B4029
CV7
PETER HALL LANE
ANSTY
grave Hill Farm
Hill Fields Farm
Peter Hall
Priest's Bridge
Little Wrautam
Top Pool
Smite Brook
Coombe Abbey
Visitors Centre
COOMBE FIELDS ROAD
Little Wood
Kennels
East Lodge
COVENTRY ROAD
62
Wood Hill
Woodhill Farm
COOMBE ABBEY COUNTRY PARK
B4027
LOW ROAD
Riding School
Coventry
TWELVE O'CLOCK
Monk's Riding
Old Pools
Birchley Farm
Birchley Wood Farm House
BIRCHLEY WOOD
The Grove
NEW CLOSE WOOD
ONE O'CLOCK RIDE
Brinklow Heath
CV8
Roseycombe Cottages
Merton Hall Farm
Quarter Acre
Long Covert
GREEN LANE
71
Sunrise Farm
Sherwood Farm
Binley Woods
ROAD
GOSSETT LANE
Coventry Stadium
Woodside
Square Covert
Privet Covert
SILVER BIRCH
COOMBE
ASHDALE

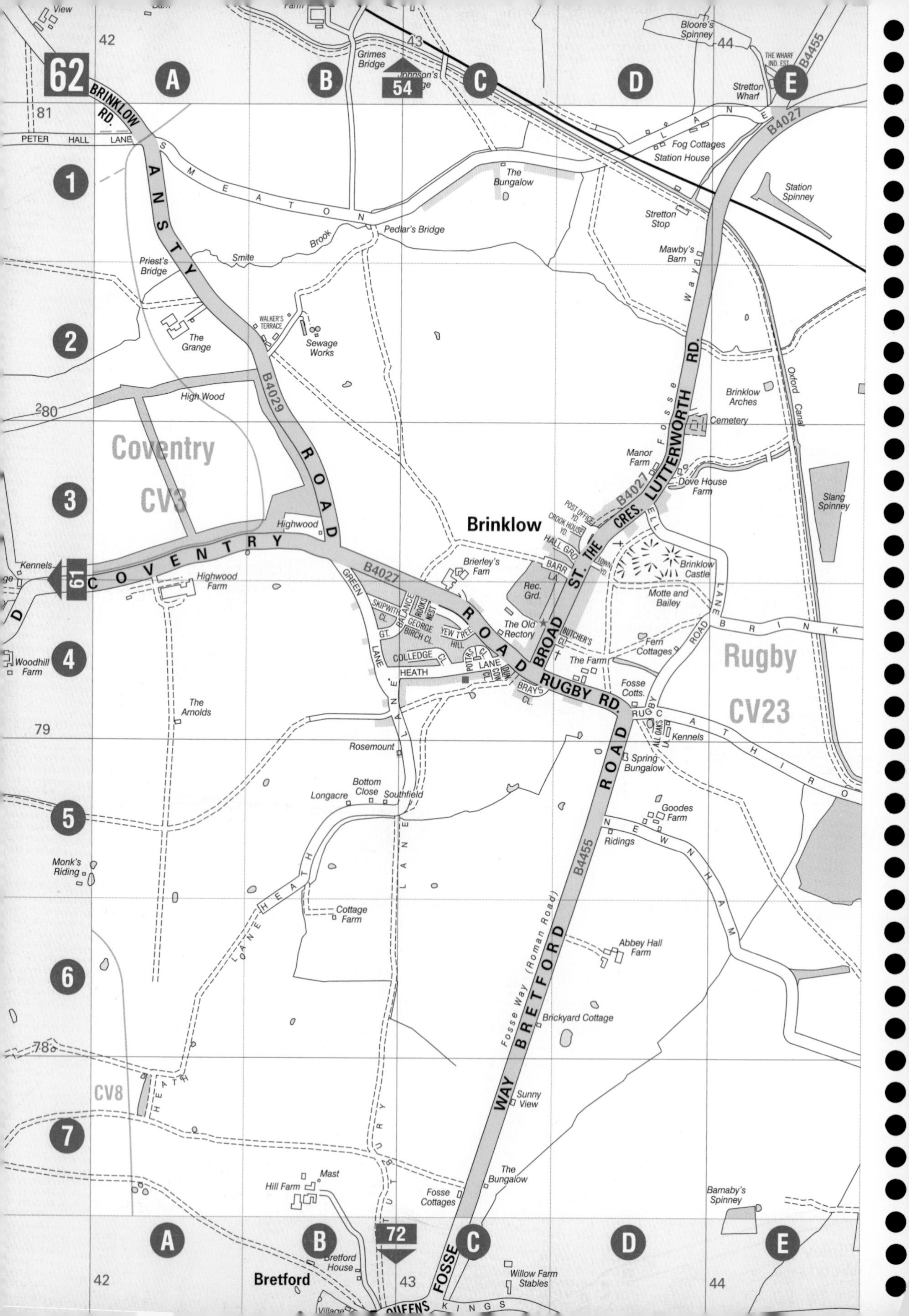
A
B
C
D
E
1
2
3
4
5
6
7
42
43
44
81
80
79
78
54
61
72
BRINKLOW RD.
PETER HALL LANE
SMEATON LANE
ANSTY ROAD
B4029
COVENTRY ROAD
B4027
ROAD
RUGBY RD.
ROAD
B4455
FOSSE WAY
BRETFORD ROAD
Fosse Way (Roman Road)
LUTTERWORTH RD.
Fosse Way
LANE
B4027
B4455
BROAD ST.
THE CRES.
BRINKLOW ROAD
RUGBY ROAD
CATHIRO
NEWNHAM
HEATH LANE
GREEN LANE
HEATH
LANE
BURY
QUEENS
KINGS
Coventry
CV3
Rugby
CV23
CV8
Brinklow
Bretford
Grimes Bridge
Johnson's Bridge
Bloore's Spinney
THE WHARF IND. EST.
Stretton Wharf
Fog Cottages
Station House
Station Spinney
Stretton Stop
The Bungalow
Pedlar's Bridge
Smite Brook
Priest's Bridge
Mawby's Barn
WALKER'S TERRACE
The Grange
Sewage Works
High Wood
Brinklow Arches
Cemetery
Oxford Canal
Manor Farm
Dove House Farm
Slang Spinney
Highwood
POST OFFICE YD.
CROOK HOUSE YD.
HALL GRO.
TOWN YD.
BARR LA.
Brinklow Castle
Motte and Bailey
Kennels
Highwood Farm
Brierley's Fm
Rec. Grd.
The Old Rectory
BUTCHER'S CL.
Fern Cottages
SKIPWITH CL.
BALANCE HILL
ROOKS NEST
GEORGE BIRCH CL.
YEW TREE HILL
GT.
COLLEDGE CL.
POTTERS CL.
HEATH LANE
DUN COW CL.
BRAYS CL.
The Farm
Fosse Cotts.
ALL OAKS LA.
Kennels
Woodhill Farm
The Arnolds
Rosemount
Spring Bungalow
Bottom Close
Longacre
Southfield
Goodes Farm
Ridings
Monk's Riding
Cottage Farm
Abbey Hall Farm
Brickyard Cottage
Sunny View
The Bungalow
Mast
Hill Farm
Fosse Cottages
Barnaby's Spinney
Bretford House
Willow Farm Stables
Village

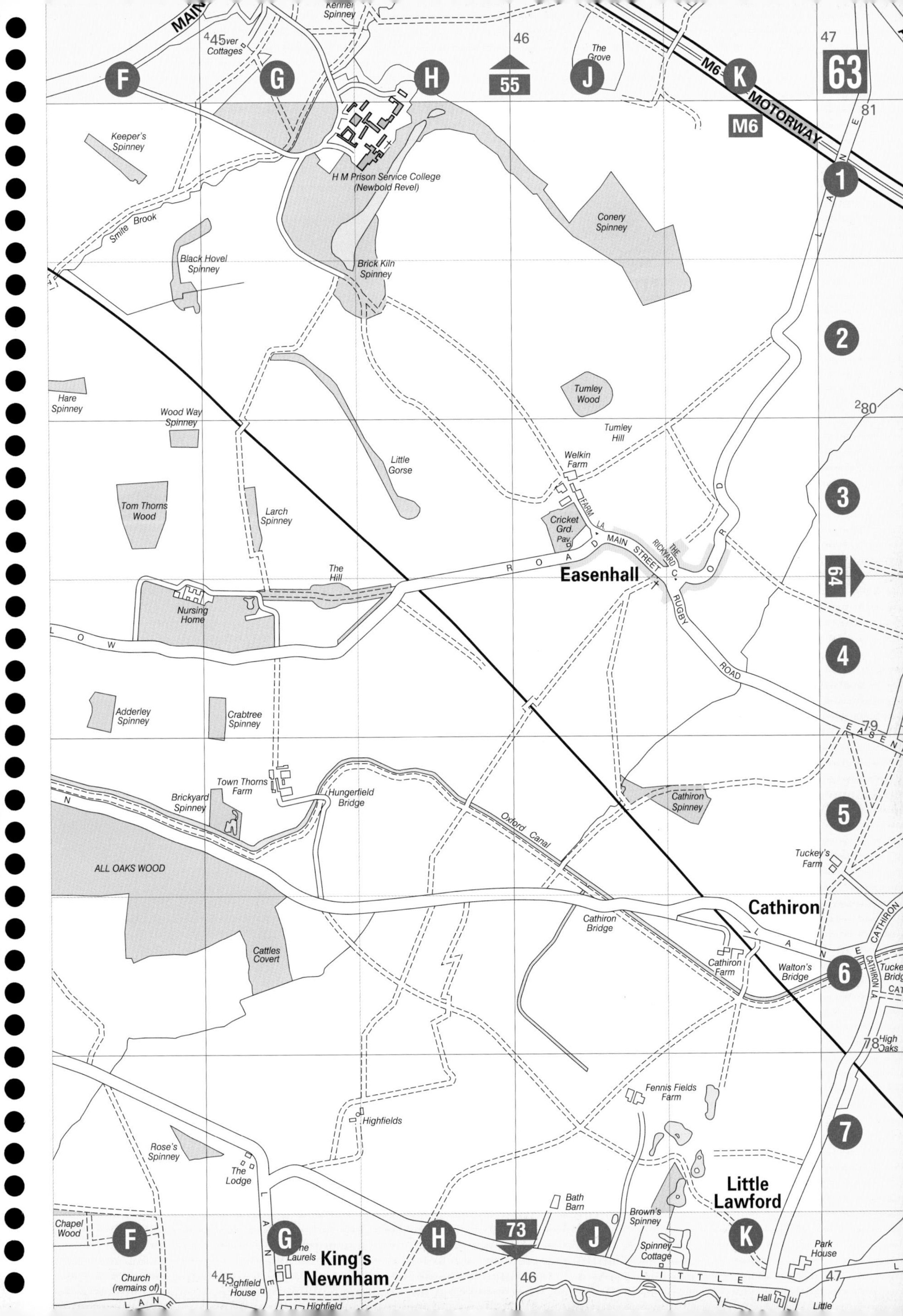
63
55
64
73
F
G
H
J
K
1
2
3
4
5
6
7
45
46
47
81
80
79
78
M6
MOTORWAY
Kennel Spinney
Cottages
The Grove
Keeper's Spinney
H M Prison Service College (Newbold Revel)
Smite Brook
Black Hovel Spinney
Brick Kiln Spinney
Conery Spinney
Hare Spinney
Wood Way Spinney
Tumley Wood
Tumley Hill
Little Gorse
Welkin Farm
Tom Thorns Wood
Larch Spinney
Cricket Grd. Pav.
FARM LA
MAIN STREET
THE RICKYARD
The Hill
ROAD
Easenhall
Nursing Home
RUGBY ROAD
Adderley Spinney
Crabtree Spinney
Town Thorns Farm
Brickyard Spinney
Hungerfield Bridge
Cathiron Spinney
Oxford Canal
ALL OAKS WOOD
Tuckey's Farm
Cathiron
Cathiron Bridge
Cattles Covert
Cathiron Farm
Walton's Bridge
CATHIRON LA
High Oaks
Fennis Fields Farm
Highfields
Rose's Spinney
The Lodge
Bath Barn
Little Lawford
Brown's Spinney
Chapel Wood
King's Newnham
Spinney Cottage
Park House
Church (remains of)
House
Highfield
LITTLE
Hall
Little

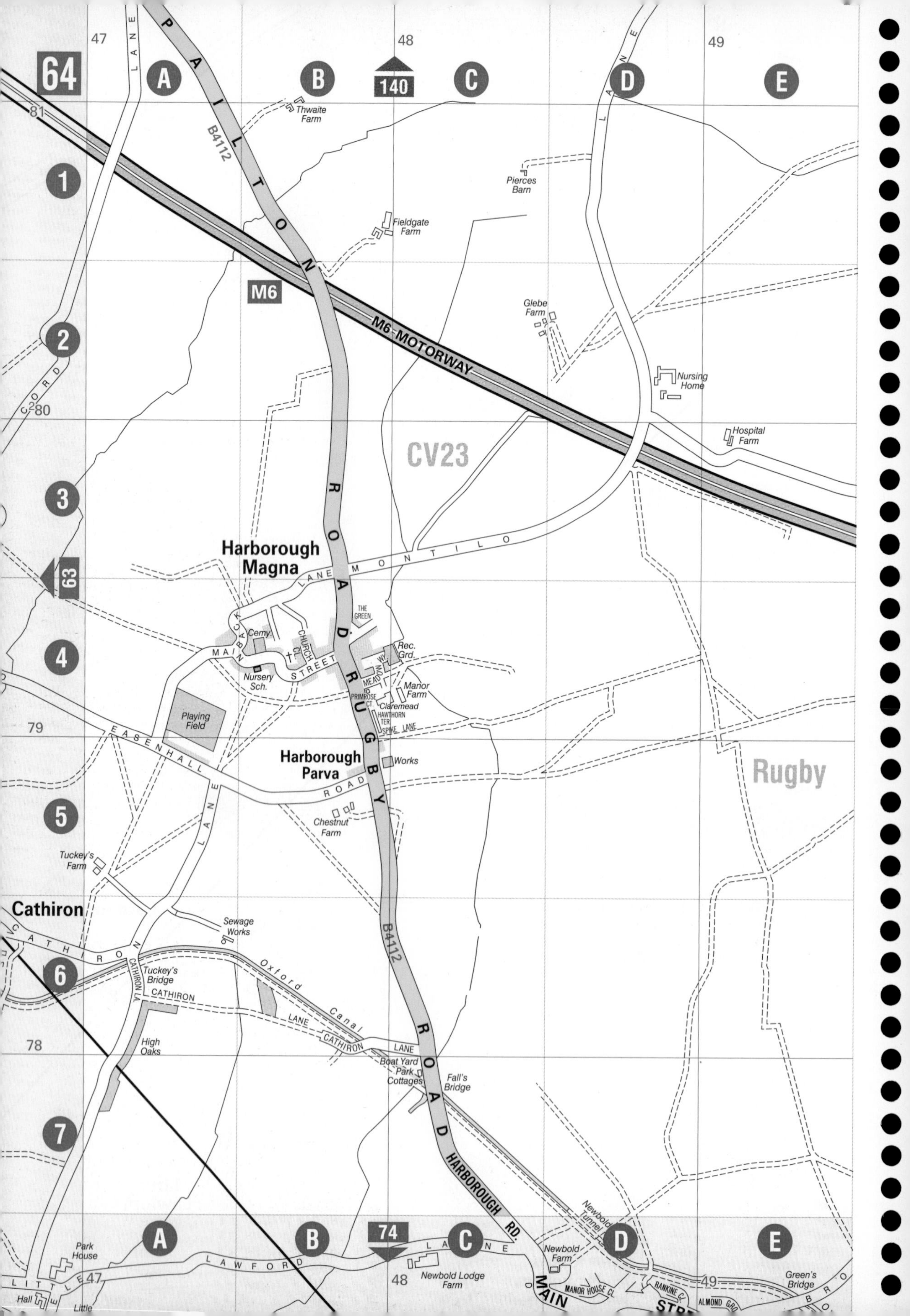
47
48
49
A
B
C
D
E
140
63
74
1
2
3
4
5
6
7
81
80
79
78
PAILTON
B4112
LANE
M6
M6 MOTORWAY
Thwaite Farm
Pierces Barn
Fieldgate Farm
Glebe Farm
Nursing Home
Hospital Farm
CV23
Harborough Magna
MONTILO LANE
THE GREEN
Cemy.
CHURCH CL.
MAIN STREET
BACK LANE
Nursery Sch.
Rec. Grd.
MEADOW WY.
Manor Farm
PRIMROSE CT.
Claremead
HAWTHORN TER.
SPIKE LANE
Playing Field
EASENHALL ROAD
Harborough Parva
Works
RUGBY ROAD
Rugby
LANE
Chestnut Farm
Tuckey's Farm
Cathiron
Sewage Works
CATHIRON LANE
CATHIRON LA.
Tuckey's Bridge
Oxford Canal
High Oaks
Boat Yard
Park Cottages
Fall's Bridge
HARBOROUGH RD.
Newbold Tunnel
Newbold Farm
LAWFORD LANE
Park House
Newbold Lodge Farm
LITTLE
Hall
Little
MAIN STREET
MANOR HOUSE CL.
RANKINE CL.
ALMOND GRO.
Green's Bridge
CORD

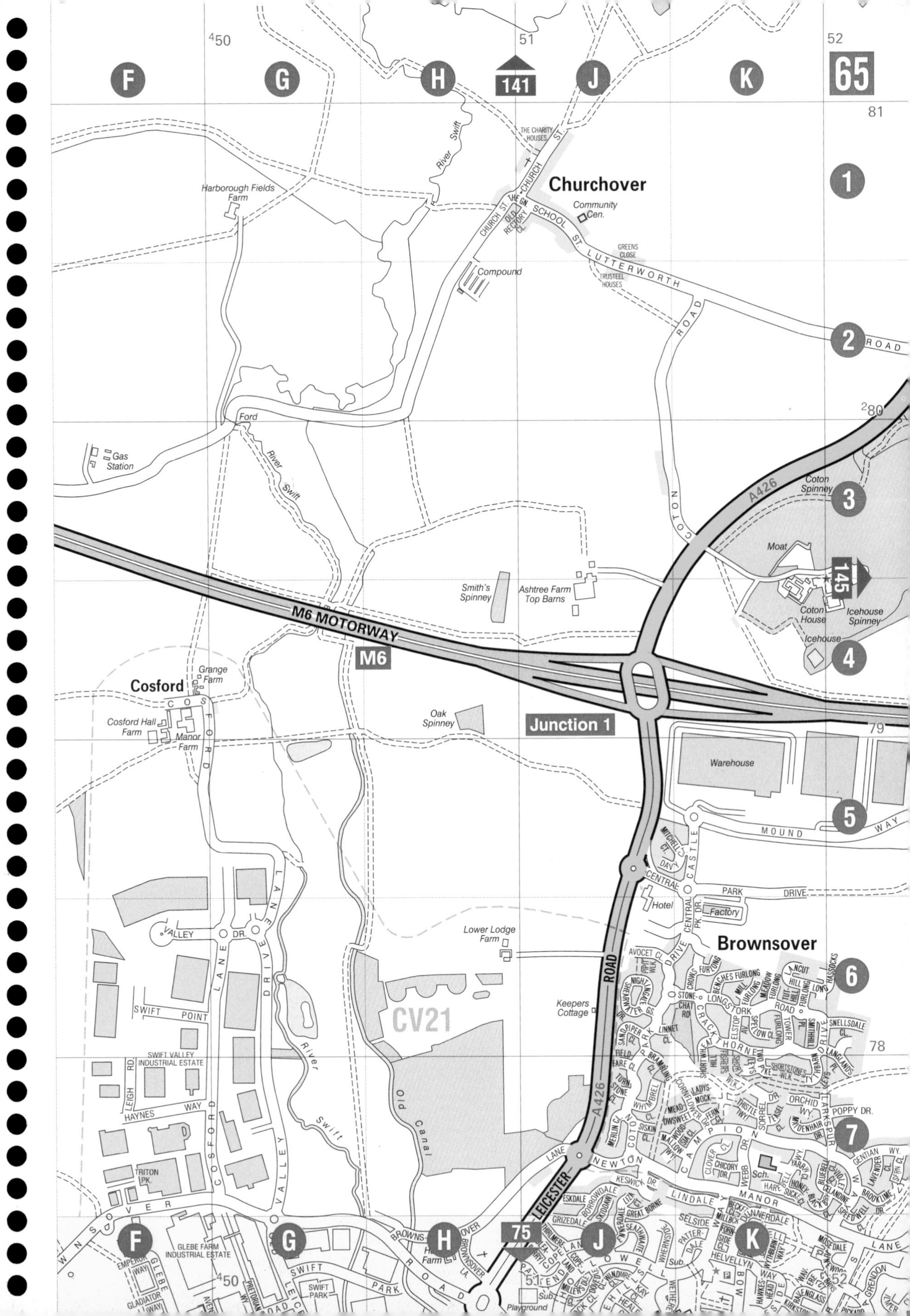

Churchover
Cosford
Brownsover
M6 MOTORWAY
M6
Junction 1
A426
CV21
141
145
75
Harborough Fields Farm
River Swift
THE CHARITY HOUSES
CHURCH ST.
SCHOOL ST.
OLD RECTORY CL.
THE GN.
Community Cen.
GREENS CLOSE
TRUSTEEL HOUSES
LUTTERWORTH ROAD
Compound
COTON ROAD
Ford
Gas Station
Coton Spinney
Moat
Coton House
Icehouse Spinney
Icehouse
Smith's Spinney
Ashtree Farm Top Barns
Grange Farm
Cosford Hall Farm
Manor Farm
COSFORD LANE
Oak Spinney
Warehouse
MOUND WAY
CASTLE
MITCHELL CL.
DAVY
CENTRAL PARK DRIVE
Hotel
Factory
Lower Lodge Farm
Keepers Cottage
LEICESTER ROAD
VALLEY DR.
VALLEY DRIVE
SWIFT POINT
SWIFT VALLEY INDUSTRIAL ESTATE
LEIGH RD.
HAYNES WAY
TRITON PK.
Old Canal
River Swift
NEWTON LANE
GLEBE FARM INDUSTRIAL ESTATE
EMPEROR WAY
GLADIATOR WAY
SWIFT PARK
BROWNSOVER ROAD
BROWNSOVER LA.
Playground
Sub.
AVOCET CL.
NIGHTINGALE GS.
CROWS
FURLONG
BENCHES FURLONG
HASSOCKS
LONGSTORK
STONECHAT RD.
CRACK
MEADOW FURLONG
TOWER
ROAD
SNELLSDALE CL.
LINNET CL.
SANDPIPER
HORNE
ELSTOP
SHORTSTONES WLK.
LANGLANDS
ORCHID WY.
POPPY DR.
LARKSPUR
CAMPION
SORREL
TEASEL
MAIDENHAIR
GENTIAN WY.
LAVENDER CL.
BROOKLIME
SPEEDWELL
BLUEBELL
CLOVER CL.
CHICORY DR.
WEBB DR.
Sch.
MANOR
LINDALE
KESWICK DR.
ESKDALE
BORROWDALE
GRIZEDALE
THIRLMERE
SKIDDAW
GREAT BORNE
ENNERDALE
SEATHWAITE
WHERNSIDE
SELSIDE
PATTERDALE
BECKFOOT
DUNNERDALE
HELVELLYN WAY
MOSEDALE
LOWE
COPELAND
GRENDON
TURNSTONE
MERLIN CL.
SISKIN
WHIMBREL
FIELDFARE CL.
COTON PARK
F G H J K
1 2 3 4 5 6 7
450 51 52
81 80 79 78

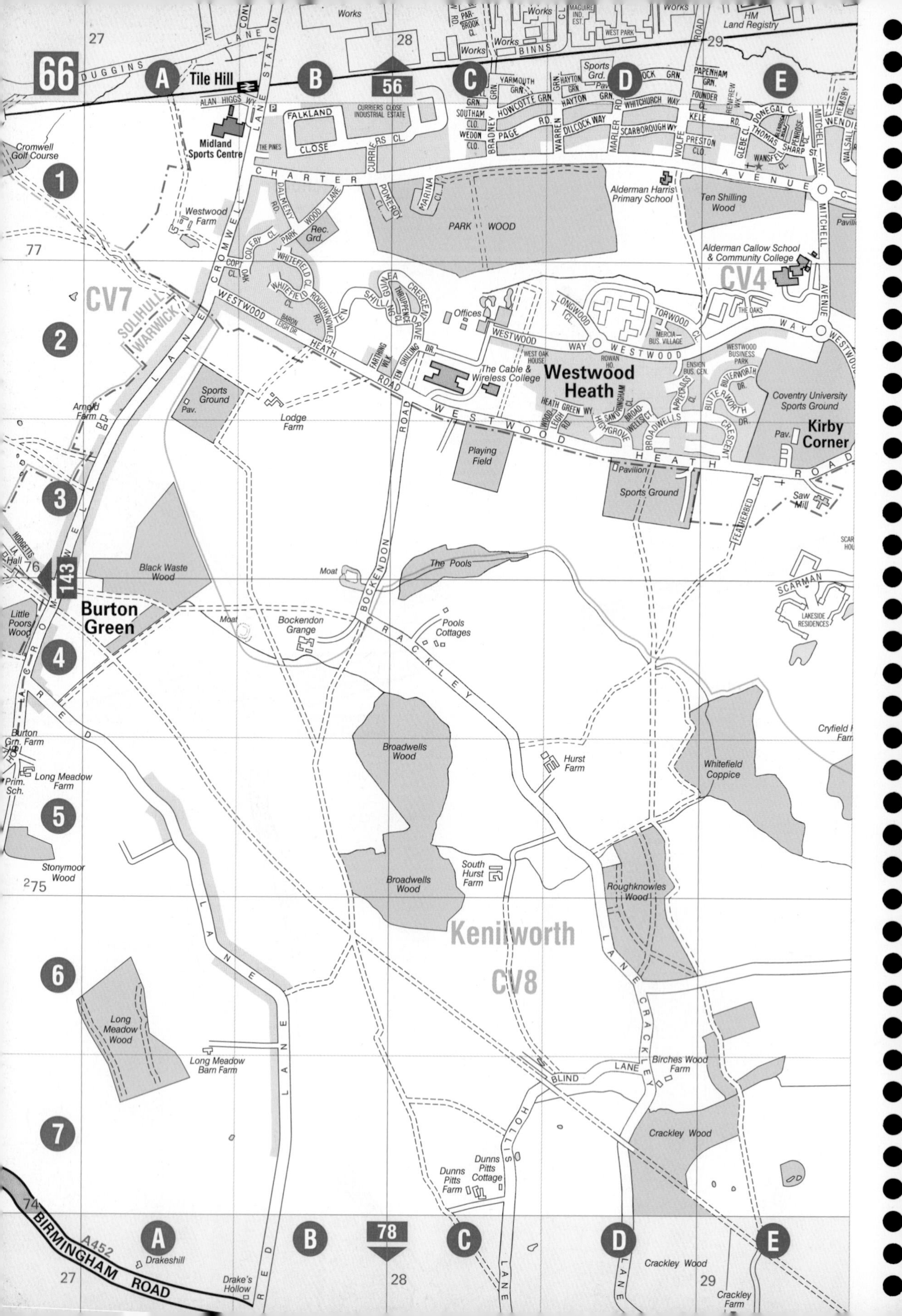

Tile Hill
Midland Sports Centre
Cromwell Golf Course
Westwood Farm
Falkland Close
Curriers Close Industrial Estate
Charter Avenue
Park Wood
Alderman Harris Primary School
Ten Shilling Wood
Alderman Callow School & Community College
CV4
CV7
Solihull
Warwick
Westwood Heath Road
Offices
The Cable & Wireless College
Westwood Heath
Westwood Way
Mercia Bus. Village
Westwood Business Park
Coventry University Sports Ground
Kirby Corner
Sports Ground
Lodge Farm
Arnold Farm
Playing Field
Pavilion
Saw Mill
Black Waste Wood
The Pools
Moat
Bockendon Road
Bockendon Grange
Pools Cottages
Crackley Lane
Burton Green
Little Poors Wood
Scarman
Lakeside Residences
Burton Grn. Farm
Long Meadow Farm
Prim. Sch.
Broadwells Wood
Hurst Farm
Whitefield Coppice
Cryfield Farm
Stonymoor Wood
South Hurst Farm
Roughknowles Wood
Kenilworth
CV8
Long Meadow Wood
Long Meadow Barn Farm
Red Lane
Blind Lane
Birches Wood Farm
Hollis Lane
Crackley Wood
Dunns Pitts Cottage
Dunns Pitts Farm
A452
Birmingham Road
Drakeshill
Drake's Hollow
Crackley Farm
56
143
78

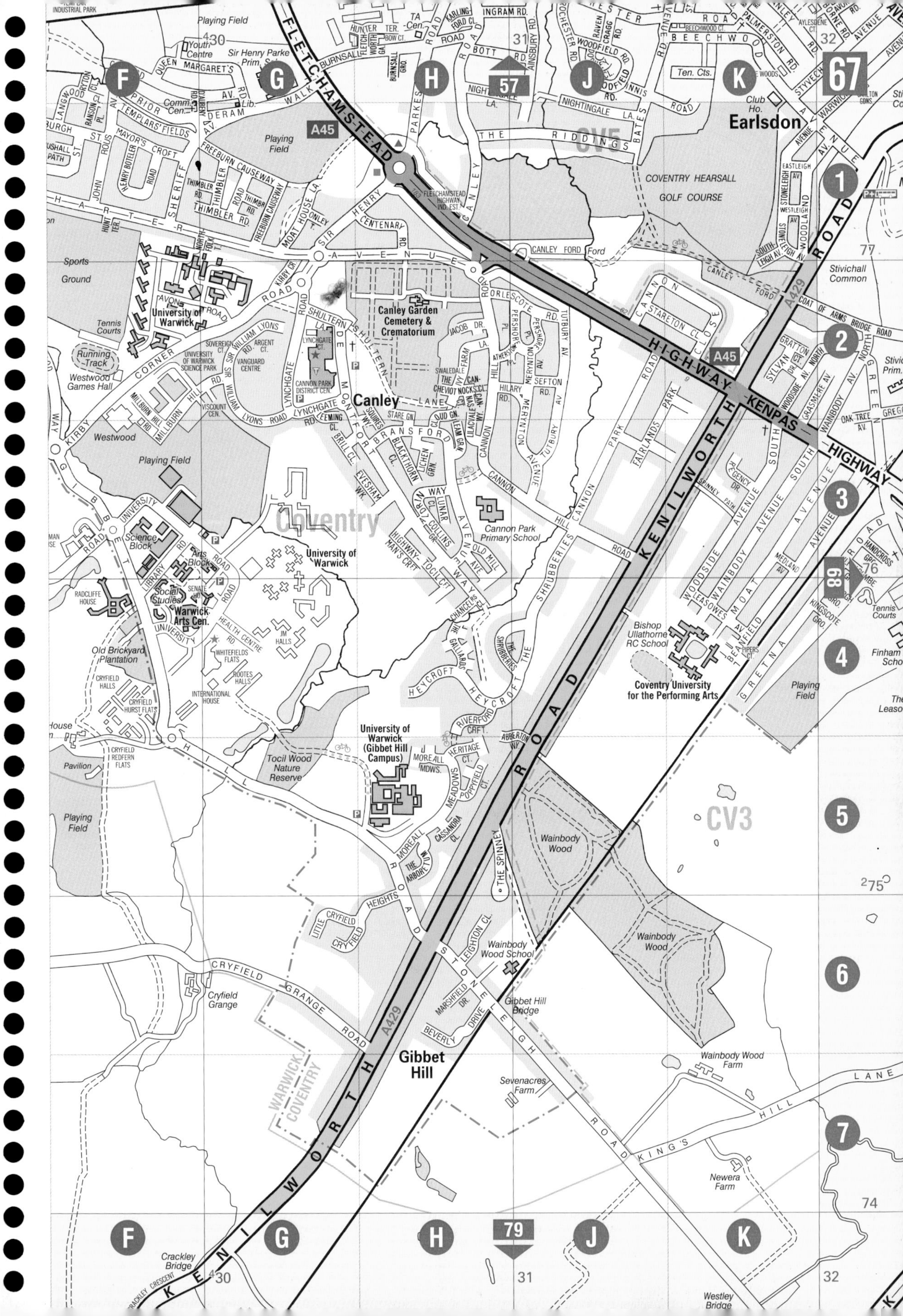

67
57
68
79
Earlsdon
Canley
Coventry
Gibbet Hill
CV3
CV5
FLETCHAMSTEAD HIGHWAY
KENILWORTH ROAD
KENPAS HIGHWAY
A45
A429
University of Warwick
Canley Garden Cemetery & Crematorium
Coventry Hearsall Golf Course
Stivichall Common
Cannon Park Primary School
Bishop Ullathorne RC School
Coventry University for the Performing Arts
University of Warwick (Gibbet Hill Campus)
Tocil Wood Nature Reserve
Wainbody Wood
Wainbody Wood School
Gibbet Hill Bridge
Sevenacres Farm
Wainbody Wood Farm
Newera Farm
Westley Bridge
Crackley Bridge
Cryfield Grange
Old Brickyard Plantation
Westwood Games Hall
Sports Ground
Tennis Courts
Running Track
Playing Field
Warwick Arts Cen.
Science Block
Arts Block
Social Studies
Sir Henry Parke Prim. Sch.
Youth Centre
KING'S HILL LANE
CRYFIELD GRANGE ROAD
GIBBET HILL ROAD
STONELEIGH ROAD
CANNON HILL ROAD
SIR HENRY PARKES ROAD
CHARTER AVENUE

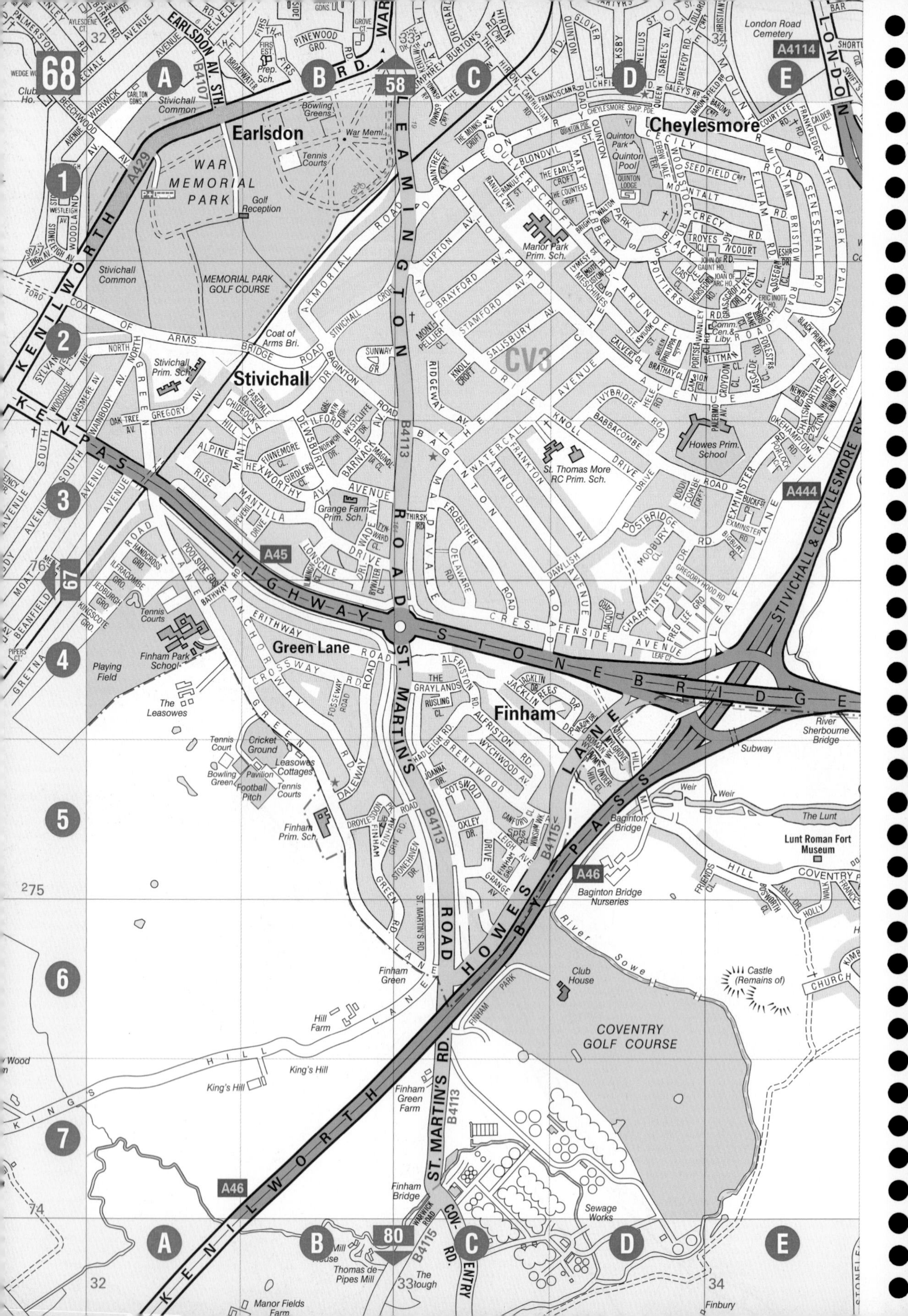
68
58
80
67
Earlsdon
Stivichall
Cheylesmore
Green Lane
Finham
WAR MEMORIAL PARK
MEMORIAL PARK GOLF COURSE
Stivichall Common
COVENTRY GOLF COURSE
London Road Cemetery
Lunt Roman Fort Museum
Castle (Remains of)
Sewage Works
Baginton Bridge Nurseries
River Sowe
The Lunt
Howes Prim. School
St. Thomas More RC Prim. Sch.
Manor Park Prim. Sch.
Grange Farm Prim. Sch.
Finham Park School
Finham Prim. Sch.
Stivichall Prim. Sch.
Coat of Arms Bri.
Finham Green
Finham Green Farm
Finham Bridge
King's Hill
Hill Farm
Thomas de Pipes Mill
Manor Fields Farm
The Leasowes
Leasowes Cottages
Cricket Ground
Football Pitch
Baginton Bridge
River Sherbourne Bridge
Subway
CV3
KENILWORTH ROAD
KENPAS HIGHWAY
STONEBRIDGE HIGHWAY
LEAMINGTON ROAD
ST. MARTIN'S ROAD
STIVICHALL & CHEYLESMORE BY-PASS
HOWES LANE
KENILWORTH BY-PASS
A429
A45
A46
A444
A4114
B4113
B4115
B4107
32
33
34
275
74
A
B
C
D
E
1
2
3
4
5
6
7

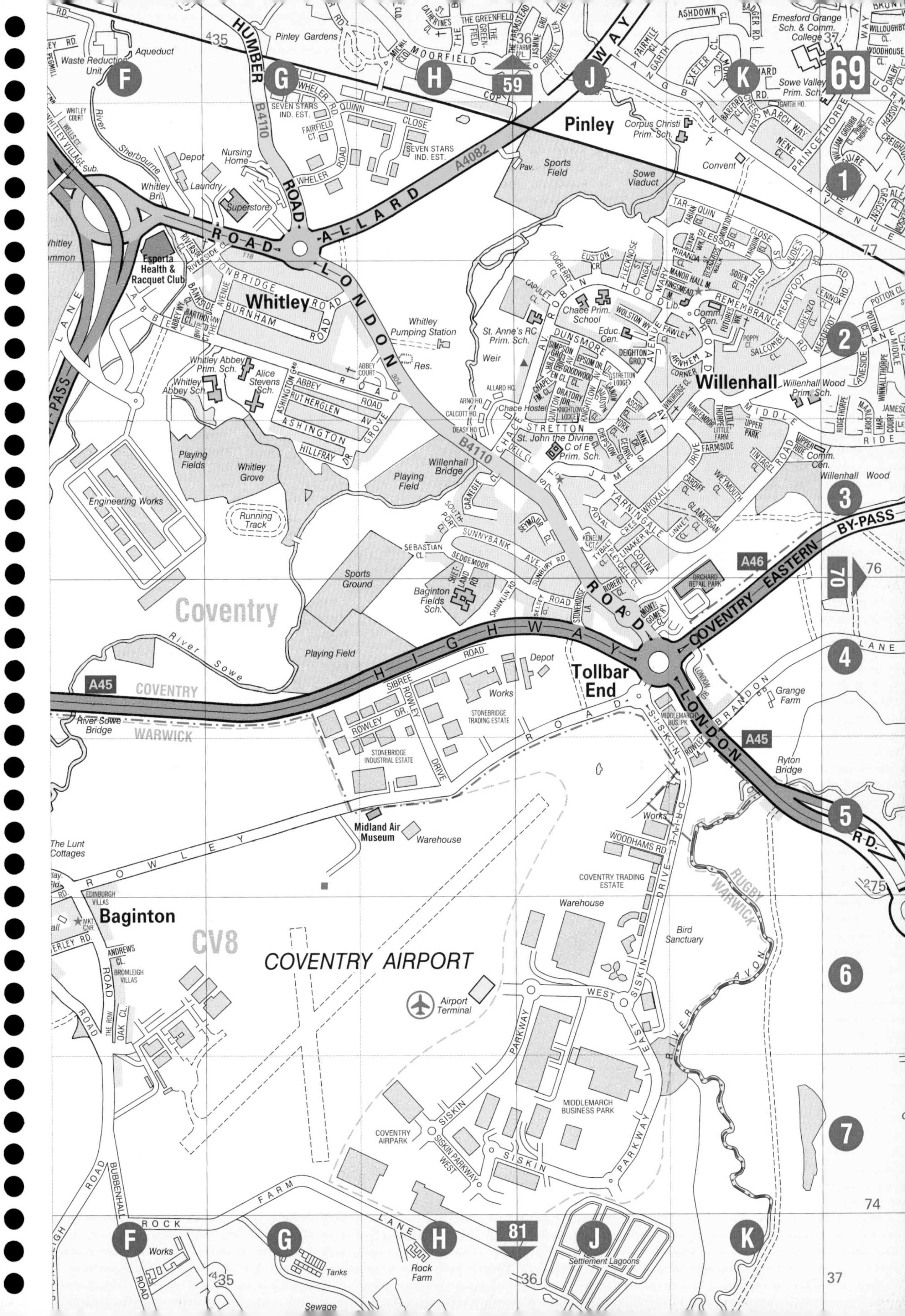

69
Pinley
Whitley
Willenhall
Tollbar End
Baginton
Coventry
CV8
COVENTRY AIRPORT
Airport Terminal
Midland Air Museum
Warehouse
Waste Reduction Unit
Aqueduct
Pinley Gardens
Seven Stars Ind. Est.
Nursing Home
Depot
Laundry
Superstore
Esporta Health & Racquet Club
Whitley Bri.
Whitley Common
River Sherbourne
Whitley Abbey Prim. Sch.
Alice Stevens Sch.
Whitley Abbey Sch.
Playing Fields
Whitley Grove
Engineering Works
Running Track
Whitley Pumping Station
Res.
Playing Field
Willenhall Bridge
Sports Ground
Sports Field
Pav.
Sowe Viaduct
Corpus Christi Prim. Sch.
Convent
Ernesford Grange Sch. & Comm. College
Sowe Valley Prim. Sch.
St. Anne's RC Prim. Sch.
Chace Prim. School
Educ. Cen.
Lib.
Comm. Cen.
Chace Hostel
St. John the Divine C of E Prim. Sch.
Willenhall Wood Prim. Sch.
Willenhall Wood
Comm. Cen.
Baginton Fields Sch.
Orchard Retail Park
Grange Farm
Ryton Bridge
River Sowe
River Sowe Bridge
Stonebridge Trading Estate
Stonebridge Industrial Estate
Works
Middlemarch Bus. Pk.
Coventry Trading Estate
Bird Sanctuary
River Avon
Middlemarch Business Park
Coventry Airpark
The Lunt Cottages
Rock Farm
Tanks
Settlement Lagoons
Sewage
HUMBER ROAD
ALLARD WAY
A4082
LONDON ROAD
B4110
A45
A46
COVENTRY EASTERN BY-PASS
HIGHWAY
COVENTRY
WARWICK
RUGBY
ROWLEY ROAD
SISKIN DRIVE
SISKIN PARKWAY
FARM LANE
ROCK LANE
BUBBENHALL ROAD
BRANDON ROAD
MIDDLE RIDE
STRETTON AVENUE
ST JAMES LANE
ABBEY ROAD
ASHINGTON GROVE
TONBRIDGE ROAD
BURNHAM ROAD
59
70
81
35
36
37
74
75
76
77

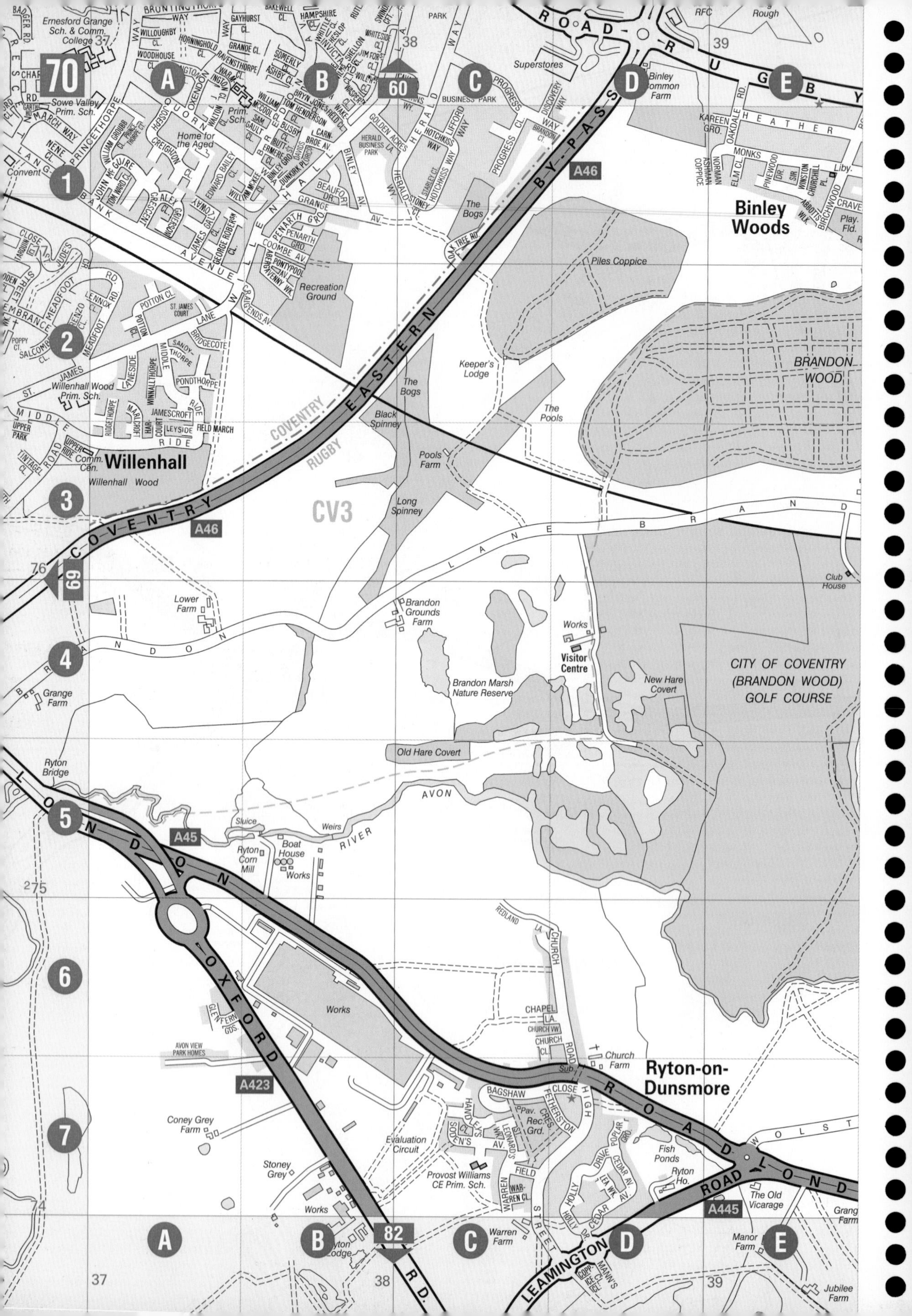

Willenhall
Binley Woods
Ryton-on-Dunsmore
CV3
BRANDON WOOD
CITY OF COVENTRY (BRANDON WOOD) GOLF COURSE
Brandon Marsh Nature Reserve
Visitor Centre
Piles Coppice
Keeper's Lodge
The Bogs
The Pools
Black Spinney
Pools Farm
Long Spinney
Recreation Ground
Old Hare Covert
New Hare Covert
Brandon Grounds Farm
Lower Farm
Grange Farm
Ryton Bridge
Ryton Corn Mill
Boat House
Sluice
Weirs
RIVER AVON
Works
Coney Grey Farm
Stoney Grey
Evaluation Circuit
Provost Williams CE Prim. Sch.
Warren Farm
Church Farm
Fish Ponds
Ryton Ho.
The Old Vicarage
Manor Farm
Jubilee Farm
Willenhall Wood Prim. Sch.
Willenhall Wood
Comm. Cen.
Home for the Aged
Sowe Valley Prim. Sch.
Ernesford Grange Sch. & Comm. College
Convent
Superstores
Binley Common Farm
Herald Business Park
Business Park
Club House
Play. Fld.
Liby.
COVENTRY EASTERN BY-PASS
COVENTRY RUGBY
RUGBY ROAD
BRANDON LANE
LONDON ROAD
OXFORD RD.
LEAMINGTON ROAD
HIGH STREET
CHURCH ROAD
A46
A45
A423
A445
60
69
82

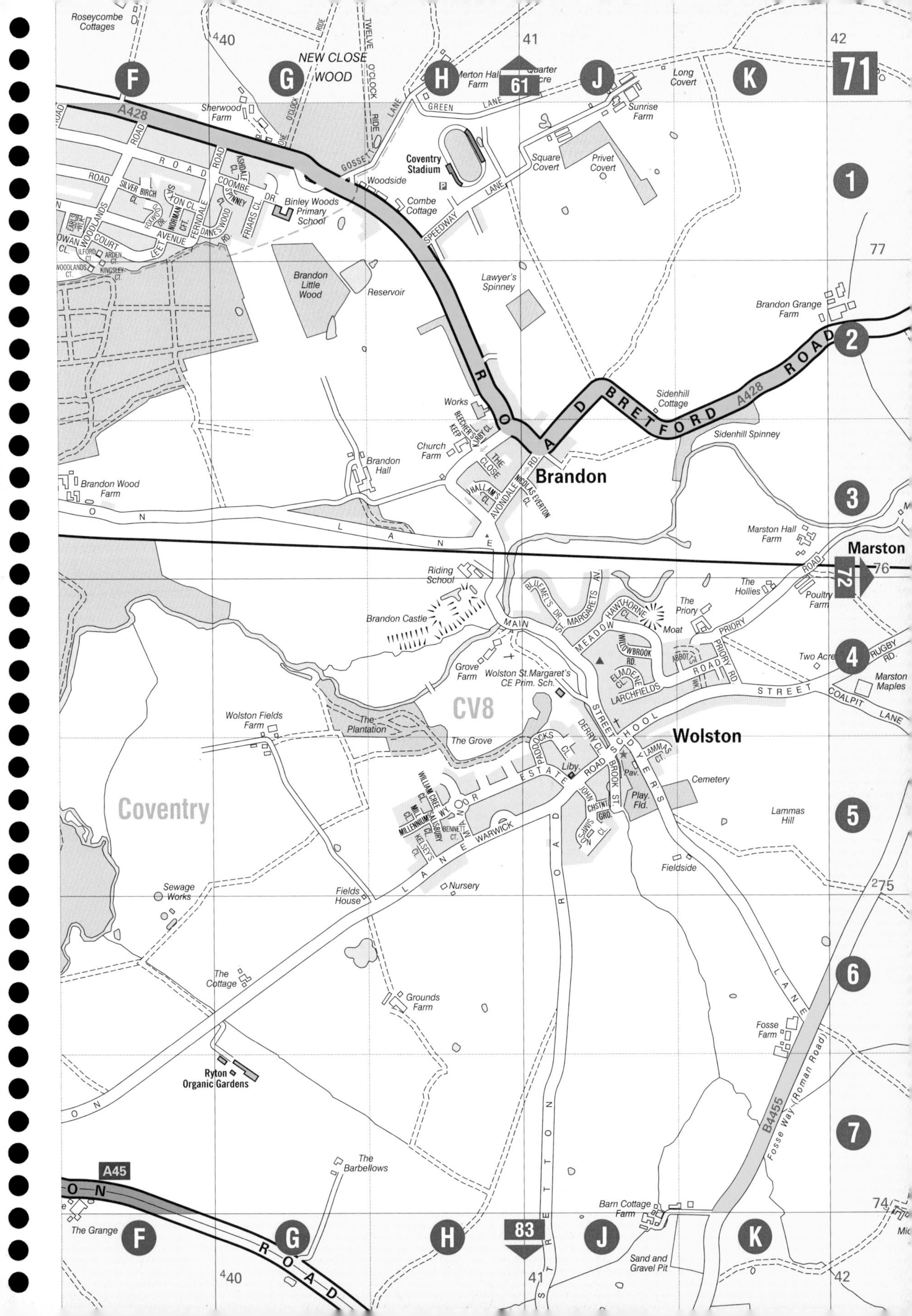

71
Roseycombe Cottages
NEW CLOSE WOOD
Merton Hall Farm
Quarter Acre
61
Long Covert
Sunrise Farm
Sherwood Farm
Coventry Stadium
Square Covert
Privet Covert
Woodside
Combe Cottage
Binley Woods Primary School
Brandon Little Wood
Reservoir
Lawyer's Spinney
Brandon Grange Farm
BRETFORD ROAD
A428
Sidenhill Cottage
Sidenhill Spinney
Works
Church Farm
Brandon Hall
Brandon
Brandon Wood Farm
Marston Hall Farm
Marston
72
Riding School
Brandon Castle
The Hollies
Poultry Farm
The Priory
Moat
Two Acre
Marston Maples
Grove Farm
Wolston St.Margaret's CE Prim. Sch.
CV8
Wolston Fields Farm
The Plantation
The Grove
Wolston
Cemetery
Liby.
Pav.
Play. Fld.
Lammas Hill
Coventry
Fieldside
Sewage Works
Fields House
Nursery
The Cottage
Grounds Farm
Fosse Farm
Ryton Organic Gardens
B4455
Fosse Way (Roman Road)
The Barbellows
A45
Barn Cottage Farm
The Grange
83
Sand and Gravel Pit

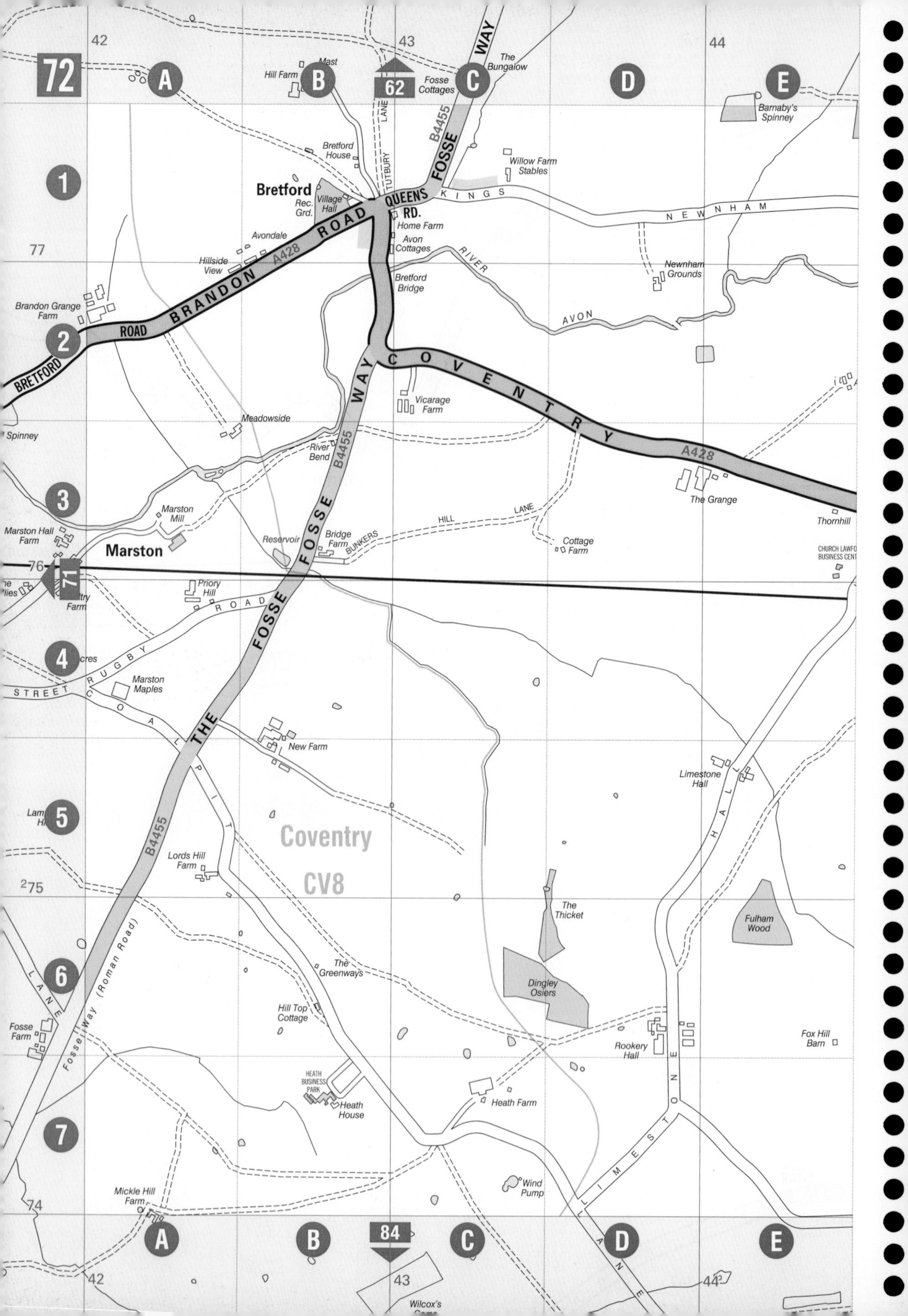
62
84
71
A
B
C
D
E
1
2
3
4
5
6
7
42
43
44
77
76
75
74
Bretford
Marston
Coventry
CV8
Hill Farm
Mast
Fosse Cottages
The Bungalow
Barnaby's Spinney
Bretford House
Willow Farm Stables
Rec. Grd.
Village Hall
Home Farm
Avon Cottages
Avondale
Hillside View
Brandon Grange Farm
Bretford Bridge
Newnham Grounds
Vicarage Farm
Meadowside
Spinney
River Bend
The Grange
Thornhill
Marston Mill
Marston Hall Farm
Reservoir
Bridge Farm
Cottage Farm
CHURCH LAWFO BUSINESS CENT
Priory Hill
Marston Maples
New Farm
Limestone Hall
Lords Hill Farm
The Thicket
Fulham Wood
The Greenways
Dingley Osiers
Hill Top Cottage
Fosse Farm
Rookery Hall
Fox Hill Barn
HEATH BUSINESS PARK
Heath House
Heath Farm
Wind Pump
Mickle Hill Farm
Wilcox's
BRETFORD
BRANDON ROAD
ROAD
A428
QUEENS RD.
KINGS
NEWNHAM
TUTBURY LANE
FOSSE WAY
B4455
RIVER AVON
COVENTRY
BUNKERS HILL LANE
THE FOSSE FOSSE WAY
RUGBY ROAD
STREET
COALPIT
LANE
Fosse Way (Roman Road)
LIMESTONE HALL LANE

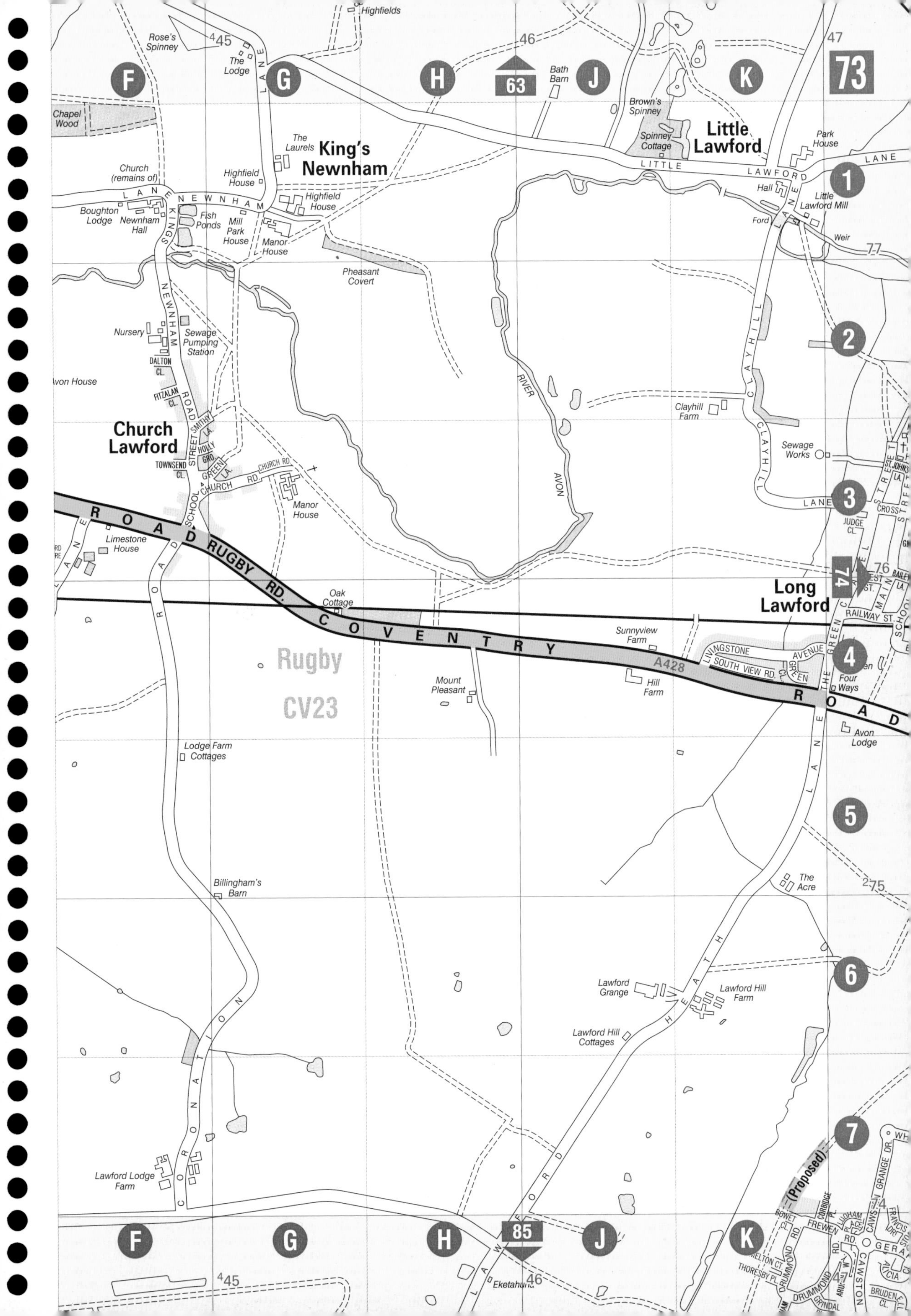
73
Highfields
Rose's Spinney
The Lodge
Bath Barn
Brown's Spinney
Spinney Cottage
Little Lawford
Park House
Chapel Wood
The Laurels
King's Newnham
Church (remains of)
Highfield House
Boughton Lodge
Newnham Hall
Fish Ponds
Mill Park House
Manor House
Highfield House
Pheasant Covert
Little Lawford Mill
Hall
Ford
Weir
Nursery
Sewage Pumping Station
Avon House
Church Lawford
Clayhill Farm
Sewage Works
River Avon
Manor House
Limestone House
Oak Cottage
Long Lawford
Sunnyview Farm
Rugby
CV23
Mount Pleasant
Hill Farm
Four Ways
Avon Lodge
Lodge Farm Cottages
Billingham's Barn
The Acre
Lawford Grange
Lawford Hill Farm
Lawford Hill Cottages
Lawford Lodge Farm
Eketahurst
KING'S NEWNHAM LANE
LITTLE LAWFORD LANE
CLAYHILL LANE
NEWNHAM ROAD
SCHOOL STREET
CHURCH RD.
CHURCH LA.
COVENTRY ROAD
RUGBY RD.
A428
CORONATION ROAD
HEATH LANE
LAWFORD ROAD
LIVINGSTONE AVENUE
SOUTH VIEW RD.
THE GREEN
RAILWAY ST.
MAIN STREET
(Proposed)
GRANGE DR.
FREWEN
DRUMMOND RD.
CAWSTON
BRUDENELL CL.
THORESBY PL.
63
74
85
F G H J K
1 2 3 4 5 6 7
45 46 47
77 76 75 74

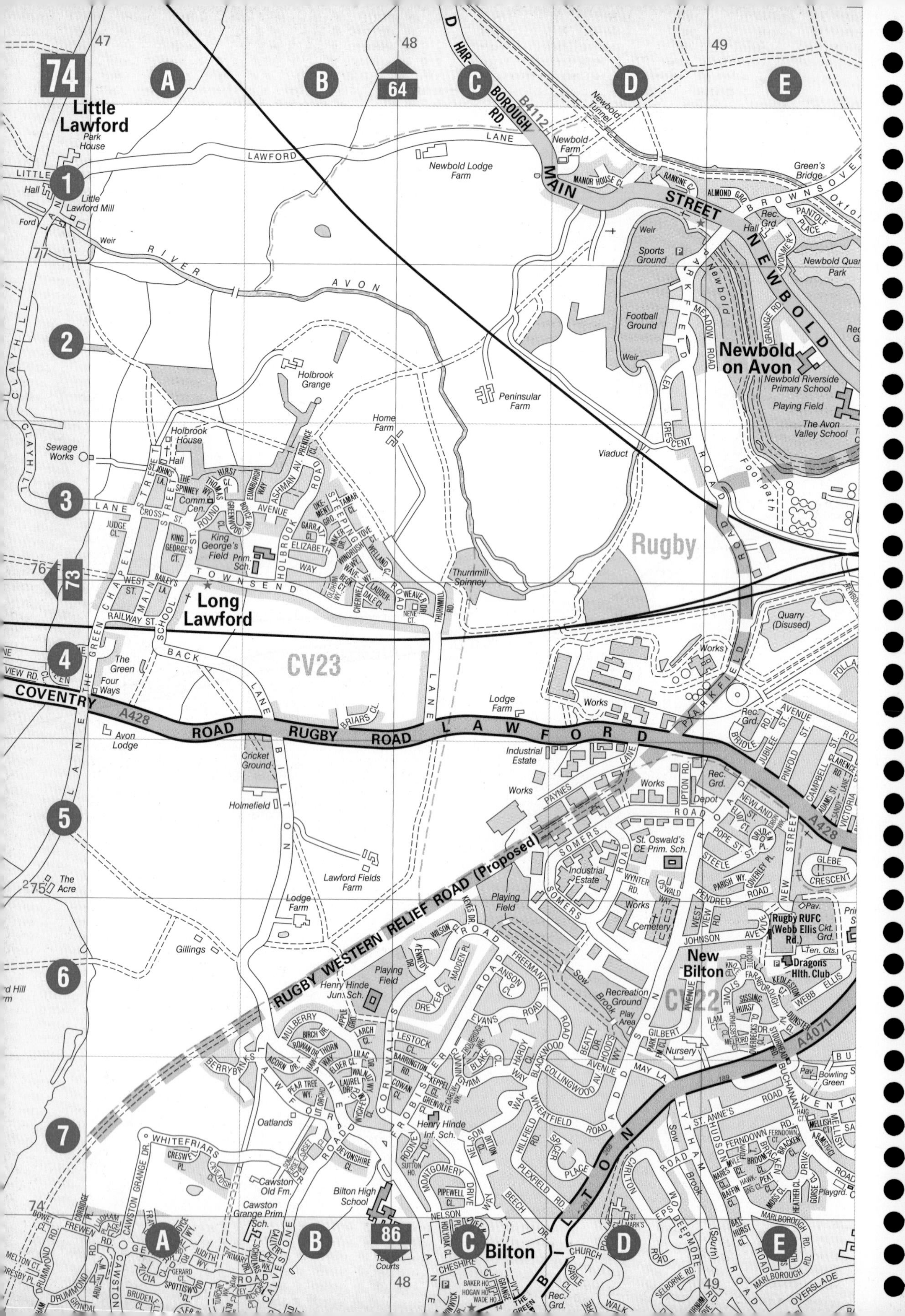
A
B
C
D
E
47
48
49
64
73
86
Little Lawford
Park House
Little Lawford Mill
Lawford Lane
Newbold Lodge Farm
Newbold Farm
Newbold Tunnel
Harborough Rd.
B4112
Main Street
Manor House Cl.
Rankine Cl.
Almond Gro.
Brownsover
Green's Bridge
Pantolf Place
Rec. Grd.
Hall
Sports Ground
Weir
Football Ground
Parkfield Road
Meadow Road
Lea Crescent
Newbold on Avon
Newbold Riverside Primary School
Playing Field
The Avon Valley School
Newbold Quarry Park
River Avon
Ford
Clayhill Lane
Holbrook Grange
Holbrook House
Sewage Works
Peninsular Farm
Home Farm
Viaduct
Footpath
Rugby
Thurnmill Spinney
Thurnmill Rd.
King George's Field
Prim. Sch.
Comm. Cen.
Townsend Lane
Long Lawford
Railway St.
School St.
Main St.
Chapel St.
Back Lane
CV23
The Green
Four Ways
Coventry Road
A428
Rugby Road
Lawford Road
Avon Lodge
Lodge Farm
Industrial Estate
Works
Quarry (Disused)
Cricket Ground
Holmefield
Bilton Lane
Rugby Western Relief Road (Proposed)
St. Oswald's CE Prim. Sch.
Somers Road
Cemetery
Playing Field
Lawford Fields Farm
The Acre
Gillings
Henry Hinde Jun. Sch.
Recreation Ground
Sow Brook
Play Area
CV22
New Bilton
Rugby RUFC (Webb Ellis Rd.)
Ckt. Grd.
Ten. Cts.
Dragons Hlth. Club
Webb Ellis
A4071
Bowling Green
Nursery
Oatlands
Henry Hinde Inf. Sch.
Cawston Old Fm.
Cawston Grange Prim. Sch.
Bilton High School
Bilton
Whitefriars
Cawston Grange Dr.
Montgomery Drive
Church Walk
Marlborough Road
Overslade
Playgrd.

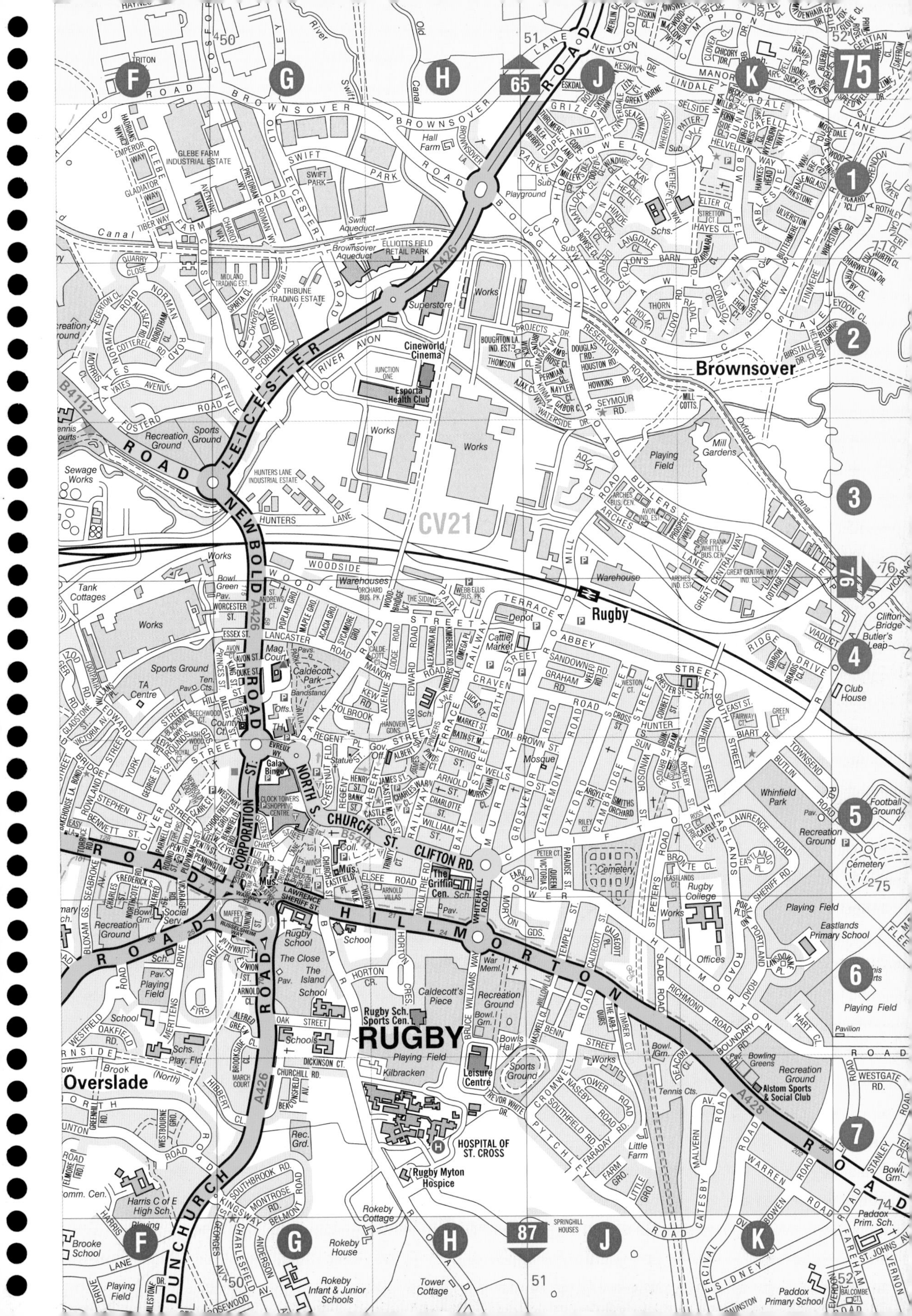

75
65
F
G
H
J
K
1
2
3
4
5
6
7
Brownsover
BROWNSOVER ROAD
LEICESTER ROAD
NEWBOLD ROAD
A426
B4112
GLEBE FARM INDUSTRIAL ESTATE
Canal
Swift Aqueduct
Brownsover Aqueduct
ELLIOTTS FIELD RETAIL PARK
Superstore
MIDLAND TRADING EST.
TRIBUNE TRADING ESTATE
Cineworld Cinema
JUNCTION ONE
Esporta Health Club
Works
HUNTERS LANE INDUSTRIAL ESTATE
HUNTERS LANE
CV21
Playing Field
Mill Gardens
Playground
Schs.
Sewage Works
Recreation Ground
Sports Ground
Tank Cottages
WOODSIDE
Warehouses
Warehouse
Rugby
Cattle Market
Caldecott Park
Gala Bingo
CLOCK TOWERS SHOPPING CENTRE
NORTH ST.
CHURCH ST.
CLIFTON RD.
B5414
The Griffin Cen.
HILLMORTON ROAD
A428
Mosque
Cemetery
Rugby College
Whinfield Park
Recreation Ground
Football Ground
Eastlands Primary School
Playing Field
Rugby School
The Close
The Island School
Caldecott's Piece
Rugby Sch. Sports Cen.
RUGBY
Kilbracken
Leisure Centre
Sports Ground
HOSPITAL OF ST. CROSS
Rugby Myton Hospice
Alstom Sports & Social Club
Bowling Greens
Overslade
Harris C of E High Sch.
Brooke School
DUNCHURCH ROAD
Rokeby Cottage
Rokeby House
Rokeby Infant & Junior Schools
Tower Cottage
Paddox Prim. Sch.
Paddox Primary School
87
76
Clifton Bridge
Butler's Leap
Club House
50
51
52

76
145
75
88
Brownsover
Clifton upon Dunsmore
Hillmorton
Rugby
Newton Manor
Manor Lane
Newton Road
River Avon
Clifton Mill Farm
Cemetery
Avondale
Station Road
Clifton-upon-Dunsmore C of E Prim. School
Sunnycroft Farm
Main St.
South Road
Playing Field
Tennis Cts.
Pav.
Shuttleworth Rd.
Church St.
Manor Road
Manor La.
Clifton Manor
The Old Hall
Buckwell Lane
Field View
Manor Farm
Lilbourne Road
Twiggetts Lodge
Dunsmore Hall Farm
Clifton Hall Farm
Dunsmore Lodge
Clifton Court Farm
Dunsmore Home Farm
Clifton Hall
Oakridge Farm
Rugby Road
Vicarage Hill
Clifton Bridge
Butler's Leap
Oxford Canal
Clifton Brook
Club House
RUGBY GOLF COURSE
Home Farm House
Grange Farm House
Home Farm
Hillmorton Road
Double Bridge
Whinfield Park
Football Ground
Recreation Ground
Cemetery
Nursery
Playing Field
Eastlands Primary School
Tennis Courts
Pavilion
CV21
CV22
Sewage Tanks
Infant Sch.
Junior Sch.
Depot
Hillmorton Locks
Alstom Sports & Social Club
Bowl. Grn.
Tennis Cts.
Normandy Farm
Paddox Prim. Sch.
Paddox Primary School
Comm. Cen.
Hillmorton Prim. Sch.
Rec. Grd.
A428
Moors Street
Oxford

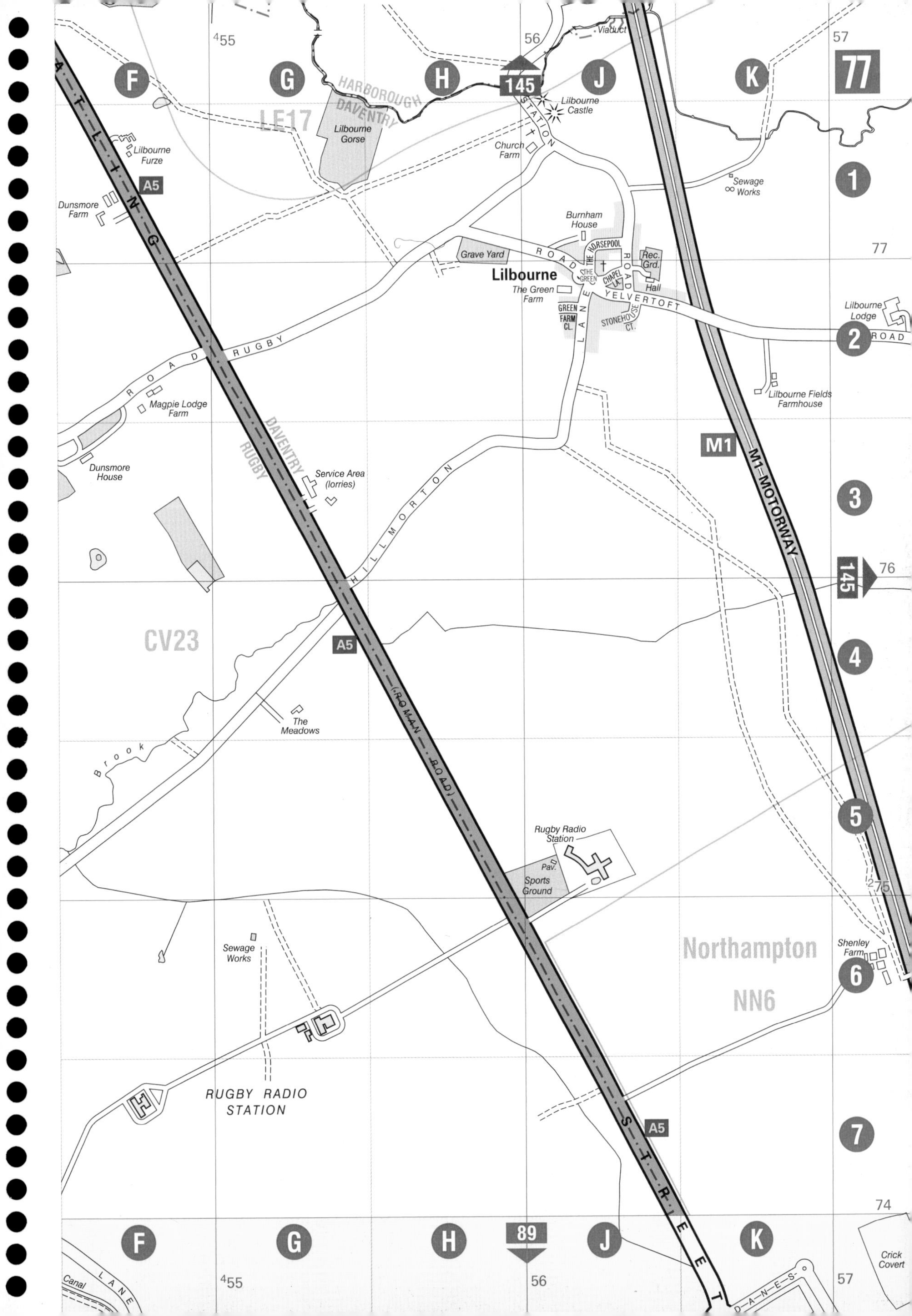

77
145
89
F
G
H
J
K
1
2
3
4
5
6
7
455
56
57
77
76
75
74
Viaduct
HARBOROUGH
DAVENTRY
LE17
Lilbourne Gorse
Lilbourne Castle
STATION
Church Farm
Lilbourne Furze
A5
Dunsmore Farm
Sewage Works
Burnham House
Grave Yard
ROAD
THE HORSEPOOL
Rec. Grd.
Lilbourne
THE GREEN
CHAPEL LA.
Hall
The Green Farm
YELVERTOFT
GREEN FARM CL.
LANE
STONEHOUSE CT.
Lilbourne Lodge
ROAD
RUGBY ROAD
Magpie Lodge Farm
Lilbourne Fields Farmhouse
M1
M1 MOTORWAY
DAVENTRY
RUGBY
Dunsmore House
Service Area (lorries)
HILLMORTON
CV23
A5
The Meadows
Brook
(ROMAN ROAD)
Rugby Radio Station
Pav.
Sports Ground
Northampton
NN6
Shenley Farm
Sewage Works
RUGBY RADIO STATION
A5
STREET
Crick Covert
Canal
LANE
DANES

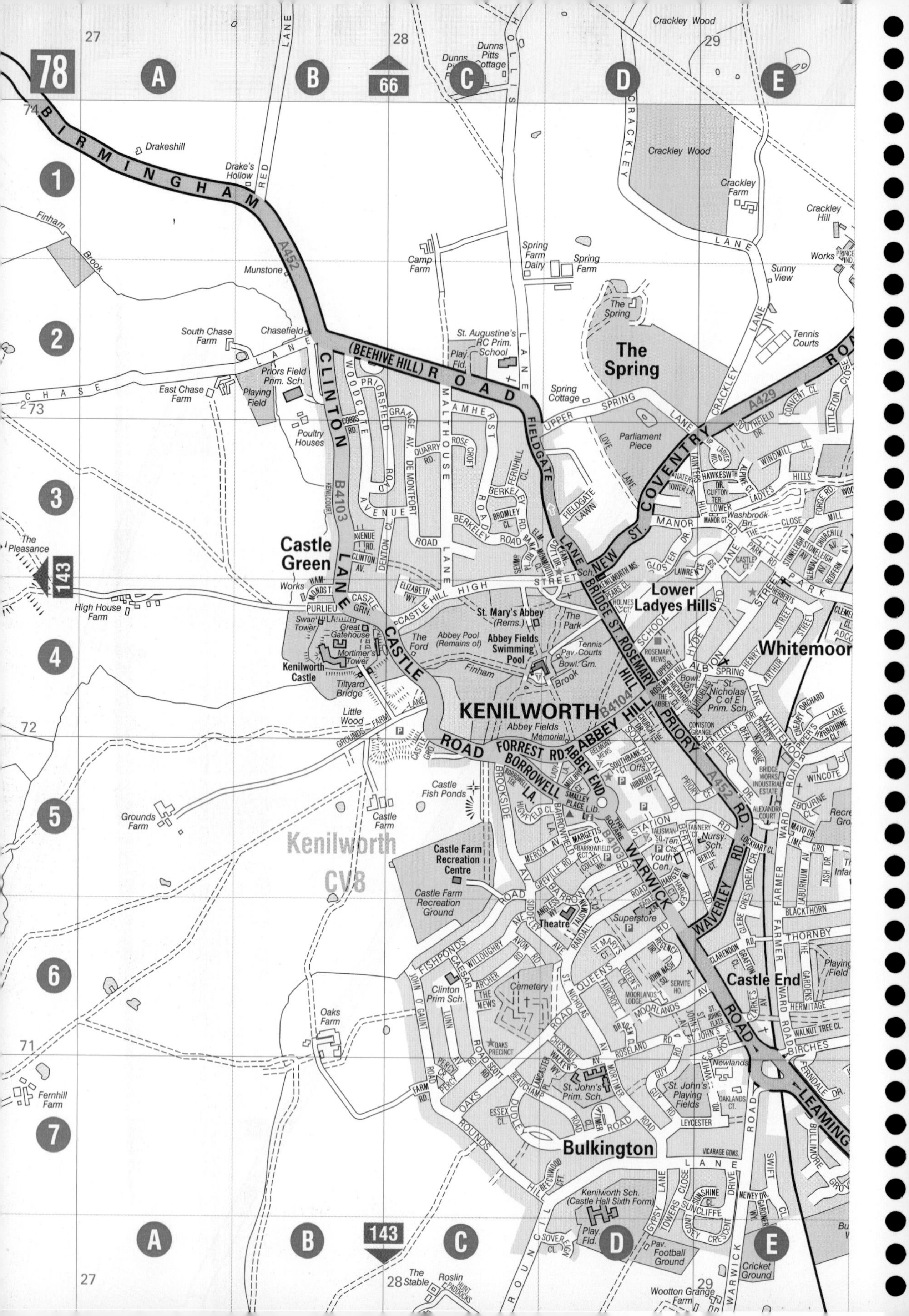
78
66
143
143
A
B
C
D
E
1
2
3
4
5
6
7
27
28
29
74
73
72
71
BIRMINGHAM ROAD
A452
Drakeshill
Drake's Hollow
RED LANE
Finham Brook
Munstone
South Chase Farm
Chasefield
CHASE LANE
East Chase Farm
Priors Field Prim. Sch.
Playing Field
Poultry Houses
Crackley Wood
CRACKLEY LANE
Crackley Farm
Crackley Hill
Works
Sunny View
Tennis Courts
Dunns Pitts Cottage
HOLLIS LANE
Camp Farm
Spring Farm Dairy
Spring Farm
The Spring
St. Augustine's RC Prim. School
Play. Fld.
(BEEHIVE HILL) ROAD
Spring Cottage
UPPER SPRING LANE
Parliament Piece
LOVE LANE
COVENTRY ROAD
A429
CLINTON LANE
B4103
FIELDGATE LANE
MALTHOUSE LANE
DE MONTFORT AVENUE
BERKELEY ROAD
FIELDGATE LAWN
NEW ST.
MANOR RD.
Castle Green
The Pleasance
High House Farm
Works
HIGH STREET
CASTLE HILL
PURLIEU LA.
Swan Tower
Great Gatehouse
Mortimer's Tower
Kenilworth Castle
Tiltyard Bridge
The Ford
Abbey Pool (Remains of)
St. Mary's Abbey (Rems.)
Abbey Fields Swimming Pool
The Park
Tennis Courts
Bowl. Grn.
Finham Brook
Lower Ladyes Hills
Whitemoor
KENILWORTH
B4104
ABBEY HILL
BRIDGE ST.
ROSEMARY HILL
PRIORY RD.
St. Nicholas' C of E Prim. Sch.
Little Wood
GROUNDS FARM LANE
CASTLE ROAD
FORREST RD.
Abbey Fields Memorial
BORROWELL LA.
ABBEY END
SMALLEY PLACE
Lib.
Castle Fish Ponds
Castle Farm
Grounds Farm
Kenilworth CV8
Castle Farm Recreation Centre
Castle Farm Recreation Ground
WARWICK ROAD
STATION RD.
Youth Cen.
Nursy. Sch.
WAVERLEY RD.
Theatre
Superstore
Castle End
FARMER WARD ROAD
Playing Field
Clinton Prim Sch.
Cemetery
OAKS PRECINCT
Oaks Farm
Fernhill Farm
St. John's Prim. Sch.
St. John's Playing Fields
Newlands
LEAMINGTON
Bulkington
VICARAGE GDNS.
LANE
Kenilworth Sch. (Castle Hall Sixth Form)
Play. Fld.
Pav.
Football Ground
Cricket Ground
Wootton Grange Farm
The Stable
Roslin
ROUNCIL LANE
WARWICK ROAD

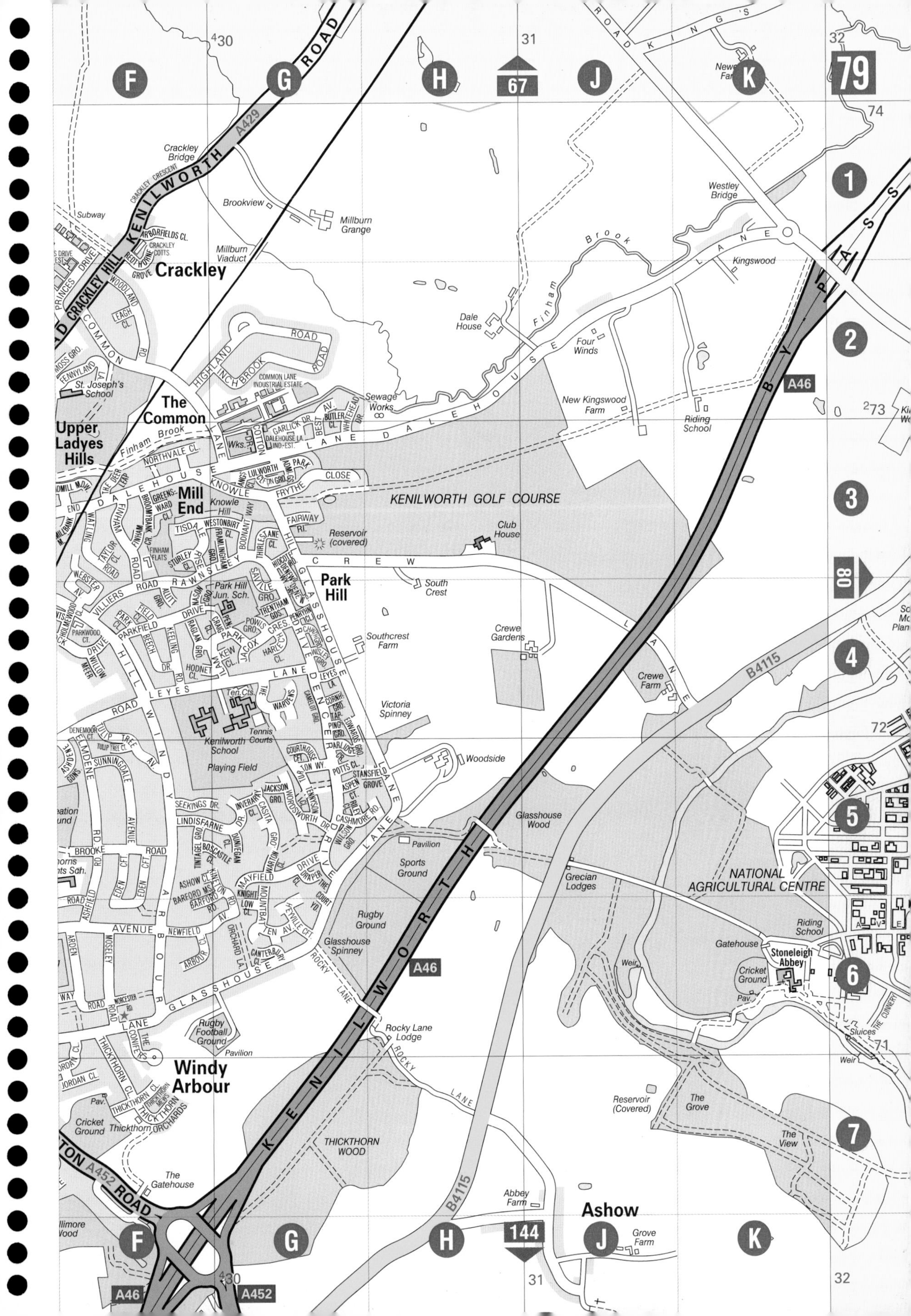
79
67
80
144
Crackley
Crackley Bridge
KENILWORTH ROAD
A429
Millburn Grange
Millburn Viaduct
Brookview
The Common
Upper Ladyes Hills
Mill End
Park Hill
Windy Arbour
KENILWORTH GOLF COURSE
Club House
Kenilworth School
Playing Field
Park Hill Jun. Sch.
St. Joseph's School
Common Lane Industrial Estate
Sewage Works
Dale House
Four Winds
New Kingswood Farm
Riding School
Kingswood
Westley Bridge
Finham Brook
DALEHOUSE LANE
CREWE LANE
GLASSHOUSE LANE
Southcrest Farm
South Crest
Crewe Gardens
Crewe Farm
Victoria Spinney
Woodside
Glasshouse Wood
Sports Ground
Rugby Ground
Glasshouse Spinney
Grecian Lodges
NATIONAL AGRICULTURAL CENTRE
Stoneleigh Abbey
Gatehouse
Cricket Ground
Rocky Lane Lodge
ROCKY LANE
THICKTHORN WOOD
Rugby Football Ground
Pavilion
Cricket Ground
The Gatehouse
Reservoir (Covered)
The Grove
The View
Abbey Farm
Ashow
Grove Farm
A46
A452
B4115
BYPASS

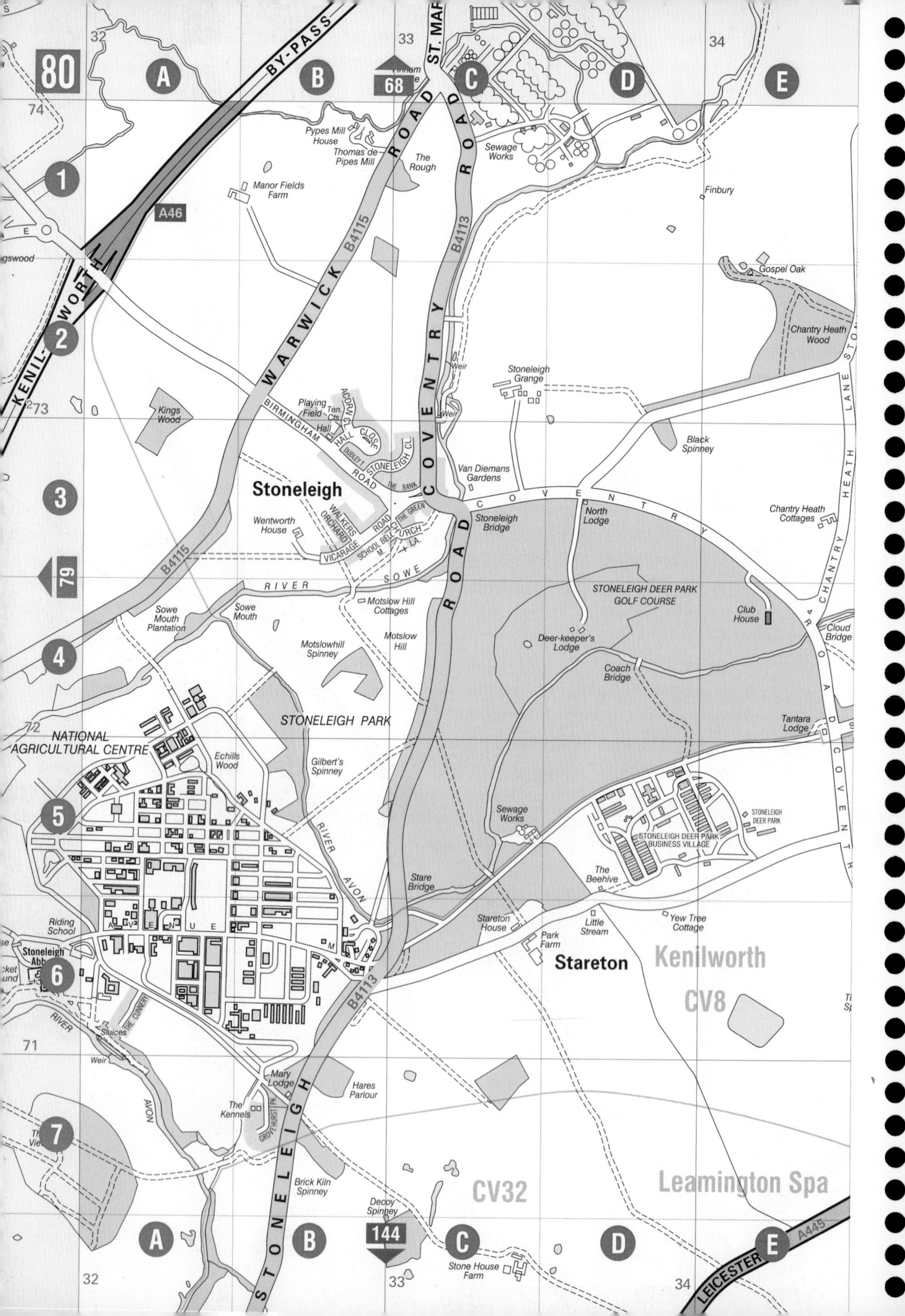

80
BY-PASS
ST. MARY'S
68
A46
KENILWORTH
WARWICK ROAD
B4115
COVENTRY ROAD
B4113
Pypes Mill House
Thomas de Pipes Mill
The Rough
Sewage Works
Manor Fields Farm
Finbury
Gospel Oak
Chantry Heath Wood
Stoneleigh Grange
Weir
Kings Wood
Playing Field
Ten. Cts.
Hall
BIRMINGHAM ROAD
ACORN CL.
HALL CLOSE
STONELEIGH CL.
DUDLEY T.
THE BANK
Black Spinney
Van Diemans Gardens
Stoneleigh
Stoneleigh Bridge
North Lodge
COVENTRY
Chantry Heath Cottages
HEATH LANE
CHANTRY
Wentworth House
WALKERS ORCHARD
VICARAGE ROAD
SCHOOL BELL M.
CHURCH LA.
THE GREEN
79
RIVER SOWE
STONELEIGH DEER PARK GOLF COURSE
Club House
Cloud Bridge
Sowe Mouth Plantation
Sowe Mouth
Motslow Hill Cottages
Motslow Hill
Motslowhill Spinney
Deer-keeper's Lodge
Coach Bridge
STONELEIGH PARK
Tantara Lodge
NATIONAL AGRICULTURAL CENTRE
Echills Wood
Gilbert's Spinney
Sewage Works
STONELEIGH DEER PARK
STONELEIGH DEER PARK BUSINESS VILLAGE
RIVER AVON
Stare Bridge
The Beehive
Riding School
AVENUE
Stareton House
Park Farm
Little Stream
Yew Tree Cottage
Stoneleigh Abbey
Stareton
Kenilworth
CV8
B4113
THE COPPICE
RIVER
Sluices
Weir
Mary Lodge
Hares Parlour
The Kennels
GROVEHURST PK.
AVON
STONELEIGH
Brick Kiln Spinney
Decoy Spinney
CV32
Leamington Spa
144
Stone House Farm
LEICESTER
A445
32
33
34
74
73
72
71
A B C D E
1 2 3 4 5 6 7

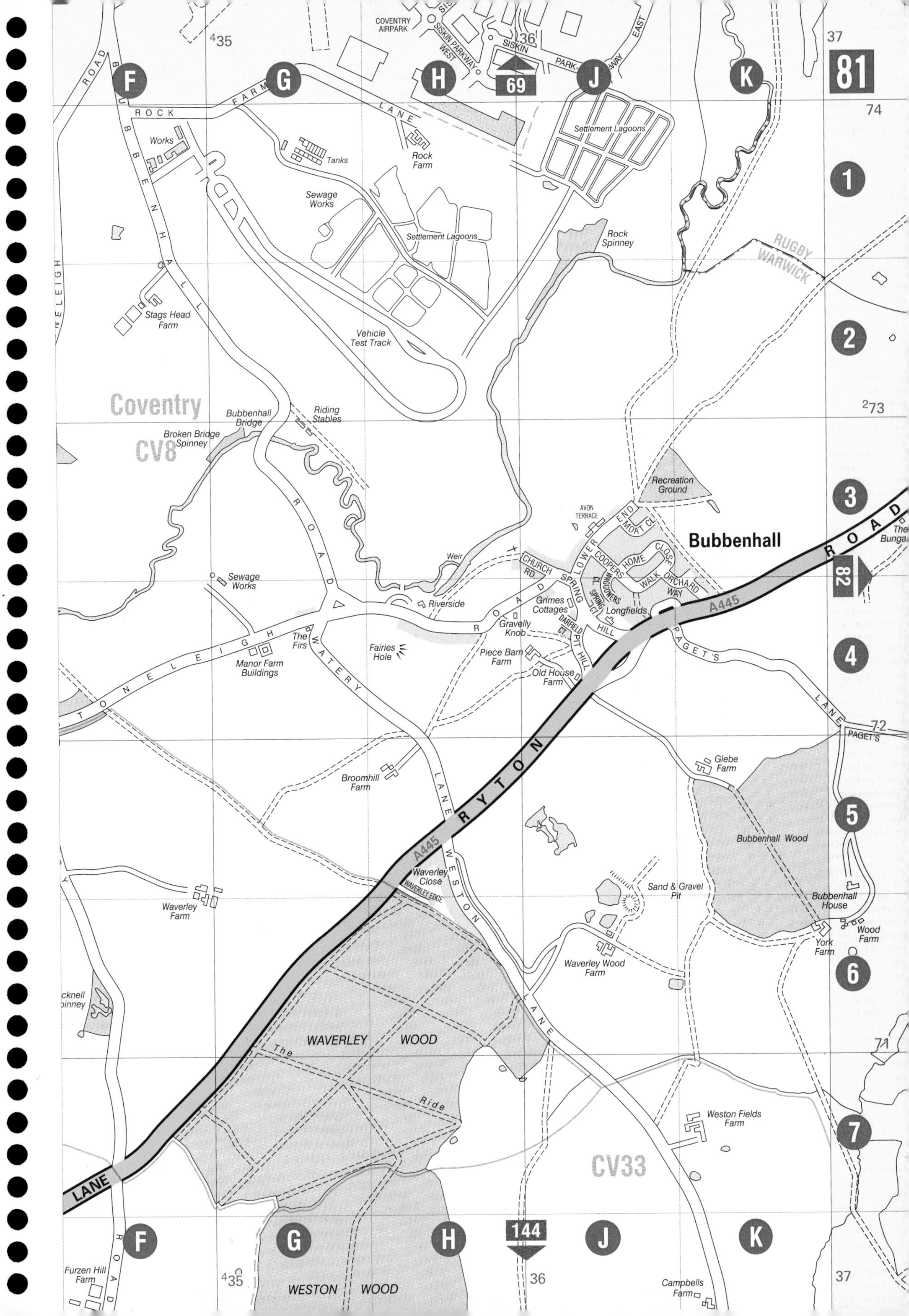
81
COVENTRY AIRPARK
SISKIN PARKWAY WEST
SISKIN PARKWAY EAST
69
ROCK FARM LANE
BUBBENHALL ROAD
Works
Tanks
Rock Farm
Settlement Lagoons
Sewage Works
Settlement Lagoons
Rock Spinney
RUGBY
WARWICK
Stags Head Farm
Vehicle Test Track
Coventry
CV8
Bubbenhall Bridge
Riding Stables
Broken Bridge Spinney
Recreation Ground
AVON TERRACE
END
MOAT CL
Bubbenhall
LOWER
COOPERS
HOME
CLOSE
WALK
ORCHARD WAY
SPRING CL
WAGGONERS
SPRING CT
DARFIELD CT
CHURCH RD
Weir
Sewage Works
Riverside
Grimes Cottages
Longfields
Gravelly Knob
SPRING HILL
PIT HILL
ROAD
A445
82
The Bungalow
The Firs
Fairies Hole
Piece Barn Farm
Old House Farm
PAGET'S LANE
Manor Farm Buildings
STONELEIGH ROAD
WATERY LANE
Glebe Farm
PAGET'S
Broomhill Farm
RYTON ROAD
Bubbenhall Wood
Waverley Close
WAVERLEY EDGE
Sand & Gravel Pit
Bubbenhall House
Waverley Farm
WESTON LANE
Wood Farm
York Farm
Waverley Wood Farm
WAVERLEY WOOD
The Ride
Weston Fields Farm
CV33
LANE
144
Furzen Hill Farm
WESTON WOOD
Campbells Farm
F G H J K
1 2 3 4 5 6 7
35 36 37
74 73 72 71

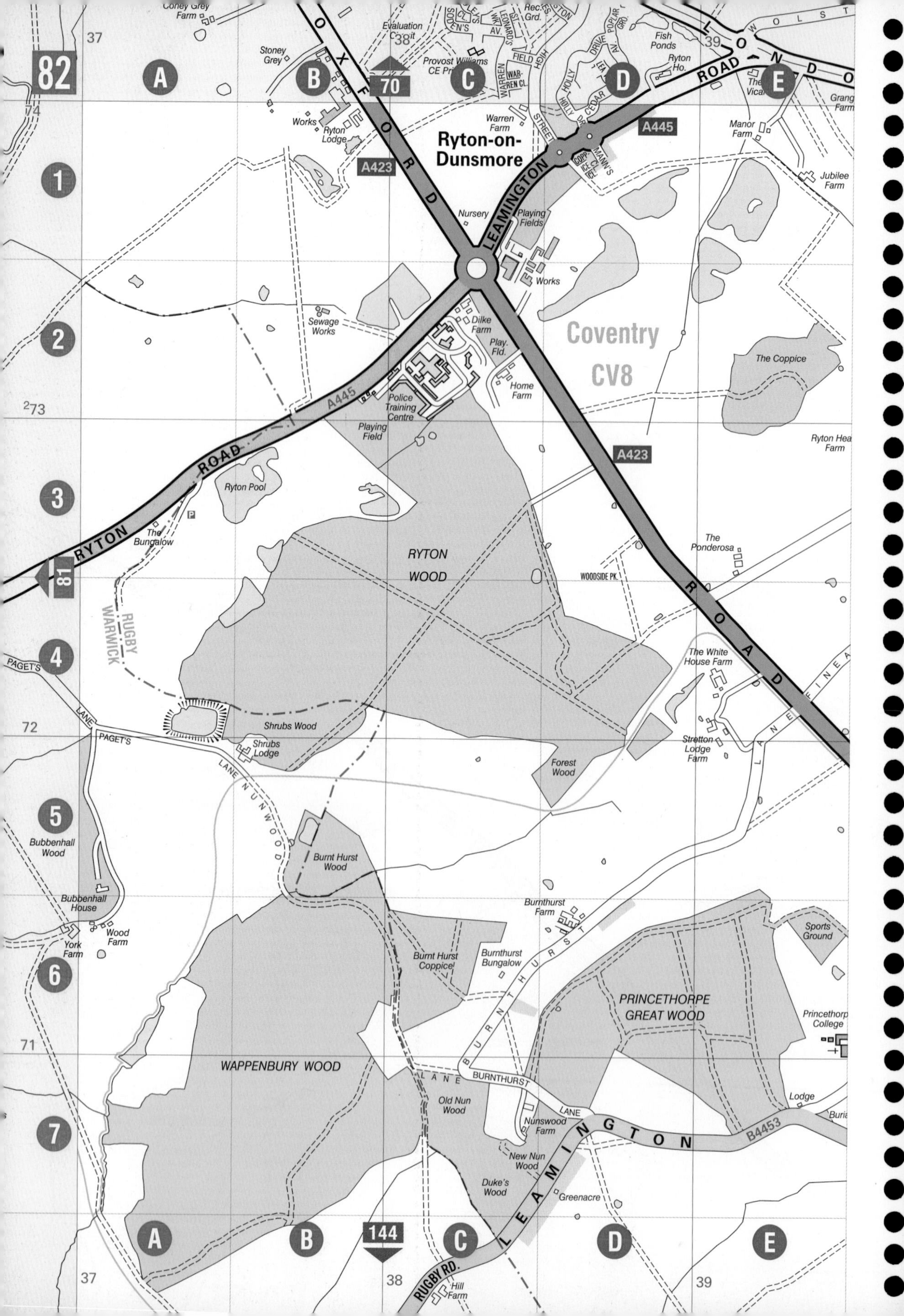
Ryton-on-Dunsmore
Coventry
CV8
OXFORD ROAD
LEAMINGTON ROAD
LONDON ROAD
RYTON ROAD
A423
A445
B4453
RYTON WOOD
WAPPENBURY WOOD
PRINCETHORPE GREAT WOOD
Ryton Pool
Police Training Centre
Playing Field
Playing Fields
Dilke Farm
Play. Fld.
Home Farm
Sewage Works
Works
Ryton Lodge
Stoney Grey
Coney Grey Farm
Evaluation Circuit
Provost Williams CE Pri.
Warren Farm
Nursery
Fish Ponds
Ryton Ho.
The Vicarage
Grange Farm
Manor Farm
Jubilee Farm
The Coppice
Ryton Heath Farm
The Ponderosa
WOODSIDE PK.
The White House Farm
Stretton Lodge Farm
Forest Wood
Shrubs Wood
Shrubs Lodge
PAGET'S LANE
NUNWOOD LANE
Burnt Hurst Wood
Burnt Hurst Coppice
Burnthurst Farm
Burnthurst Bungalow
BURNTHURST LANE
Old Nun Wood
Nunswood Farm
New Nun Wood
Duke's Wood
Greenacre
Bubbenhall Wood
Bubbenhall House
York Farm
Wood Farm
Sports Ground
Princethorpe College
Lodge
The Bungalow
RUGBY
WARWICK
RUGBY RD.
Hill Farm
FINE A LANE
HIGH STREET
HOLLY DRIVE
CEDAR
POPLAR GRO.
FIELD
WARREN
WAR-REN CL.
SODEN'S AV.
ST. LEONARD'S WK.
Rec. Grd.
COPPICE CL.
MANN'S CL.
A B C D E
1 2 3 4 5 6 7
37 38 39
74 73 72 71
70
81
144

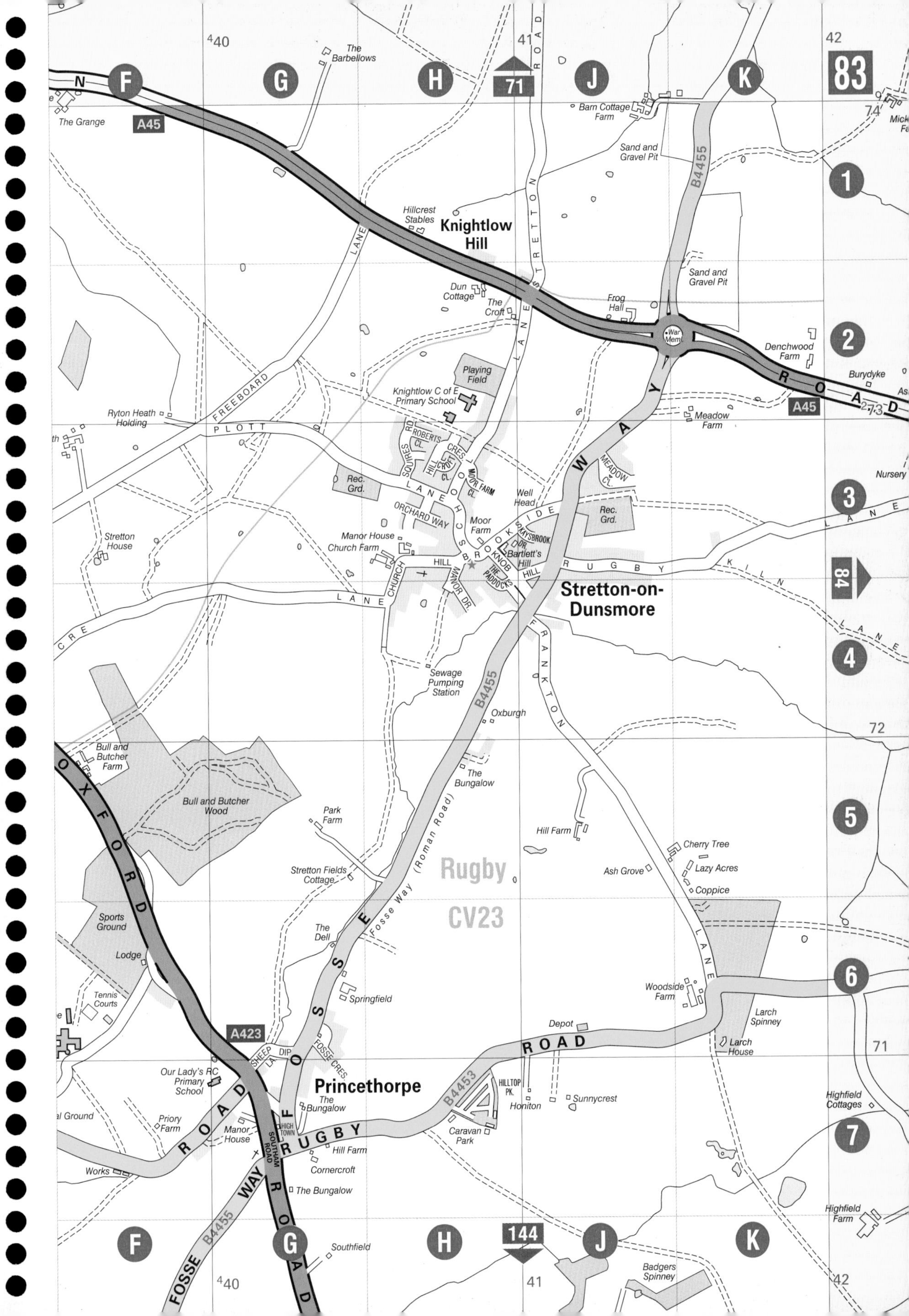

The Barbellows
The Grange
A45
Hillcrest Stables
Knightlow Hill
Barn Cottage Farm
Sand and Gravel Pit
B4455
Dun Cottage
The Croft
Frog Hall
War Meml.
Sand and Gravel Pit
Denchwood Farm
Burydyke
Playing Field
Knightlow C of E Primary School
Meadow Farm
Ryton Heath Holding
FREEBOARD
PLOTT LANE
ROBERTS CL.
SQUIRES RD.
HILL CROFT
MOOR FARM CL.
Rec. Grd.
ORCHARD WAY
Well Head
MEADOW CL.
Rec. Grd.
Nursery
Stretton House
Manor House
Church Farm
Moor Farm
BROOKSIDE
KNOB HILL
Bartlett's Hill
RUGBY LANE
KILN LANE
CHURCH HILL
MANOR DR.
THE PADDOCKS
Stretton-on-Dunsmore
FRANKTON LANE
Sewage Pumping Station
Oxburgh
Bull and Butcher Farm
Bull and Butcher Wood
OXFORD ROAD
The Bungalow
Park Farm
Fosse Way (Roman Road)
Hill Farm
Cherry Tree
Lazy Acres
Ash Grove
Coppice
Stretton Fields Cottage
Rugby
CV23
Sports Ground
The Dell
FOSSE WAY
Lodge
Springfield
Tennis Courts
Woodside Farm
Larch Spinney
A423
Depot
Larch House
SHEEP DIP LA.
FOSSE CRES.
ROAD
Our Lady's RC Primary School
Princethorpe
The Bungalow
HILLTOP PK.
Honiton
Sunnycrest
B4453
Highfield Cottages
Priory Farm
Manor House
HIGH TOWN
SOUTHAM ROAD
RUGBY ROAD
Caravan Park
Hill Farm
Cornercroft
Works
The Bungalow
Highfield Farm
Southfield
Badgers Spinney
71
84
144
440
41
42
74
73
72
71

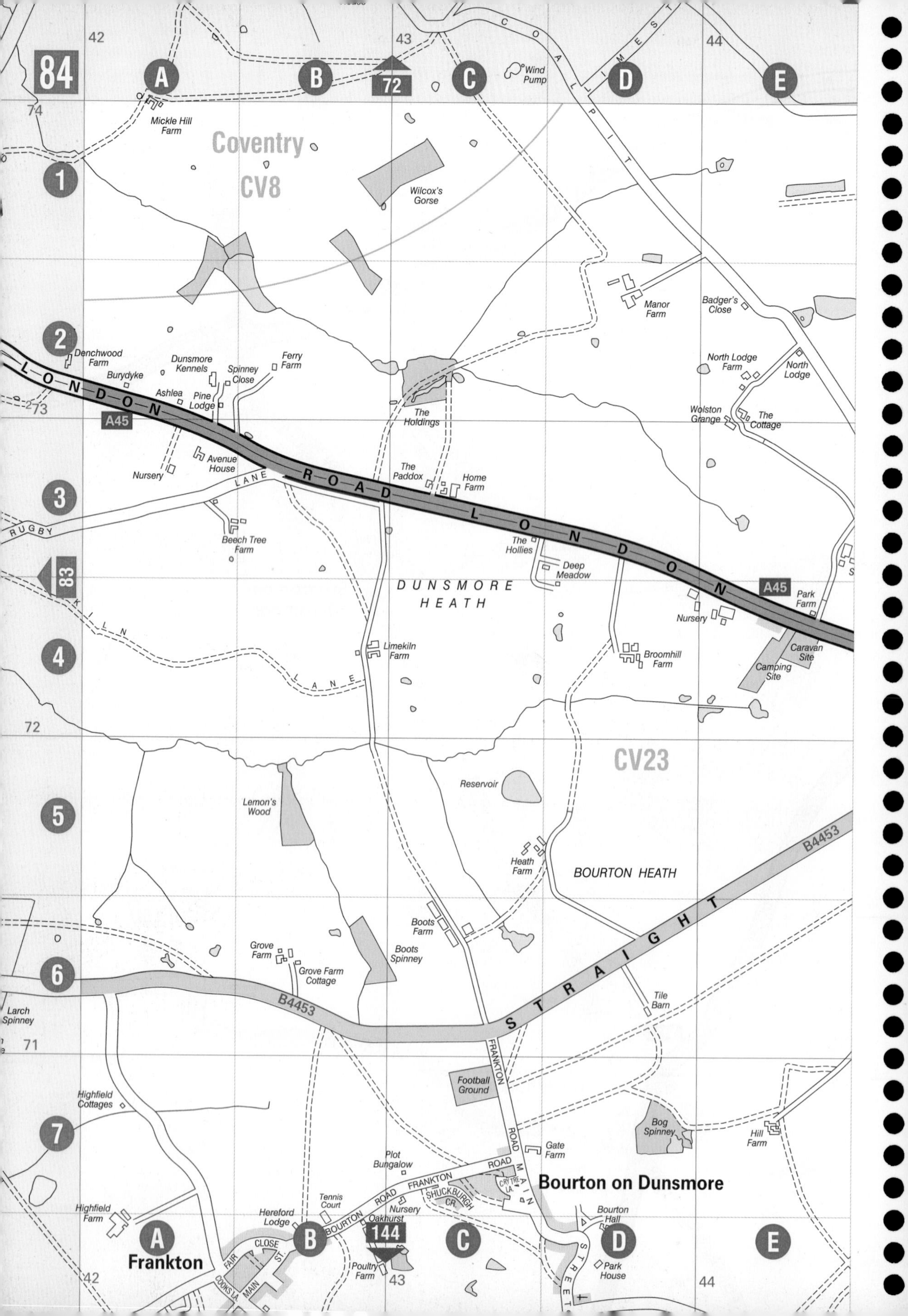

84
72
83
144
42
43
44
74
73
72
71
A
B
C
D
E
1
2
3
4
5
6
7
Coventry
CV8
CV23
Mickle Hill Farm
Wind Pump
Wilcox's Gorse
COAL PIT
LIMEST
Manor Farm
Badger's Close
North Lodge Farm
North Lodge
Wolston Grange
The Cottage
Denchwood Farm
Dunsmore Kennels
Spinney Close
Ferry Farm
Burydyke
Ashlea
Pine Lodge
LONDON ROAD
A45
The Holdings
Avenue House
Nursery
RUGBY LANE
The Paddox
Home Farm
Beech Tree Farm
The Hollies
Deep Meadow
DUNSMORE HEATH
Park Farm
Nursery
Caravan Site
Camping Site
KILN LANE
Limekiln Farm
Broomhill Farm
Reservoir
Lemon's Wood
Heath Farm
BOURTON HEATH
B4453
Boots Farm
Boots Spinney
Grove Farm
Grove Farm Cottage
STRAIGHT
Larch Spinney
Tile Barn
FRANKTON ROAD
Football Ground
Highfield Cottages
Bog Spinney
Hill Farm
Gate Farm
Plot Bungalow
MAIN ROAD
Bourton on Dunsmore
FRANKTON ROAD
BOURTON ROAD
Tennis Court
Hereford Lodge
Oakhurst
Nursery
SHUCKBURGH CR.
CRYTREE LA.
Bourton Hall
Highfield Farm
Frankton
FAIR CLOSE
ST.
COOKS LA.
MAIN
Poultry Farm
STREET
Park House

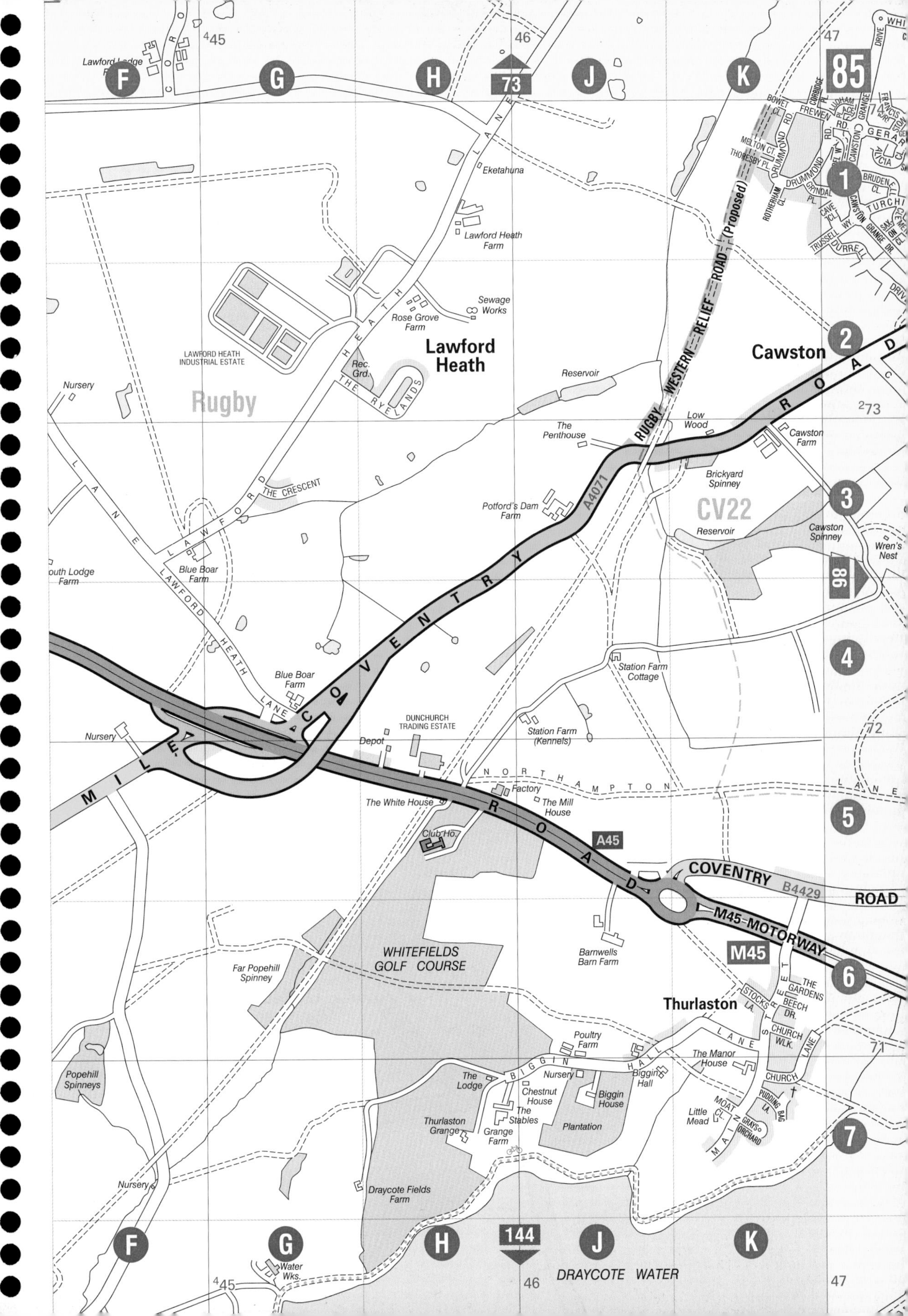

85
Lawford Heath
Cawston
Rugby
CV22
Thurlaston
LAWFORD HEATH INDUSTRIAL ESTATE
DUNCHURCH TRADING ESTATE
WHITEFIELDS GOLF COURSE
DRAYCOTE WATER
COVENTRY ROAD
A4071
A45
B4429
M45 MOTORWAY
M45
RUGBY WESTERN RELIEF ROAD (Proposed)
NORTHAMPTON LANE
LAWFORD HEATH LANE
THE CRESCENT
THE RYELANDS
MILE LANE
BIGGIN HALL LANE
MAIN STREET
CHURCH LANE
Eketahuna
Lawford Heath Farm
Sewage Works
Rose Grove Farm
Rec. Grd.
Reservoir
The Penthouse
Low Wood
Cawston Farm
Brickyard Spinney
Potford's Dam Farm
Cawston Spinney
Wren's Nest
Blue Boar Farm
Nursery
Station Farm Cottage
Station Farm (Kennels)
Depot
Factory
The White House
The Mill House
Club Ho.
Barnwells Barn Farm
Far Popehill Spinney
Popehill Spinneys
Poultry Farm
The Lodge
Chestnut House
The Stables
Thurlaston Grange
Grange Farm
Biggin House
Biggin Hall
Plantation
The Manor House
Little Mead
Draycote Fields Farm
Water Wks.
73
98
144

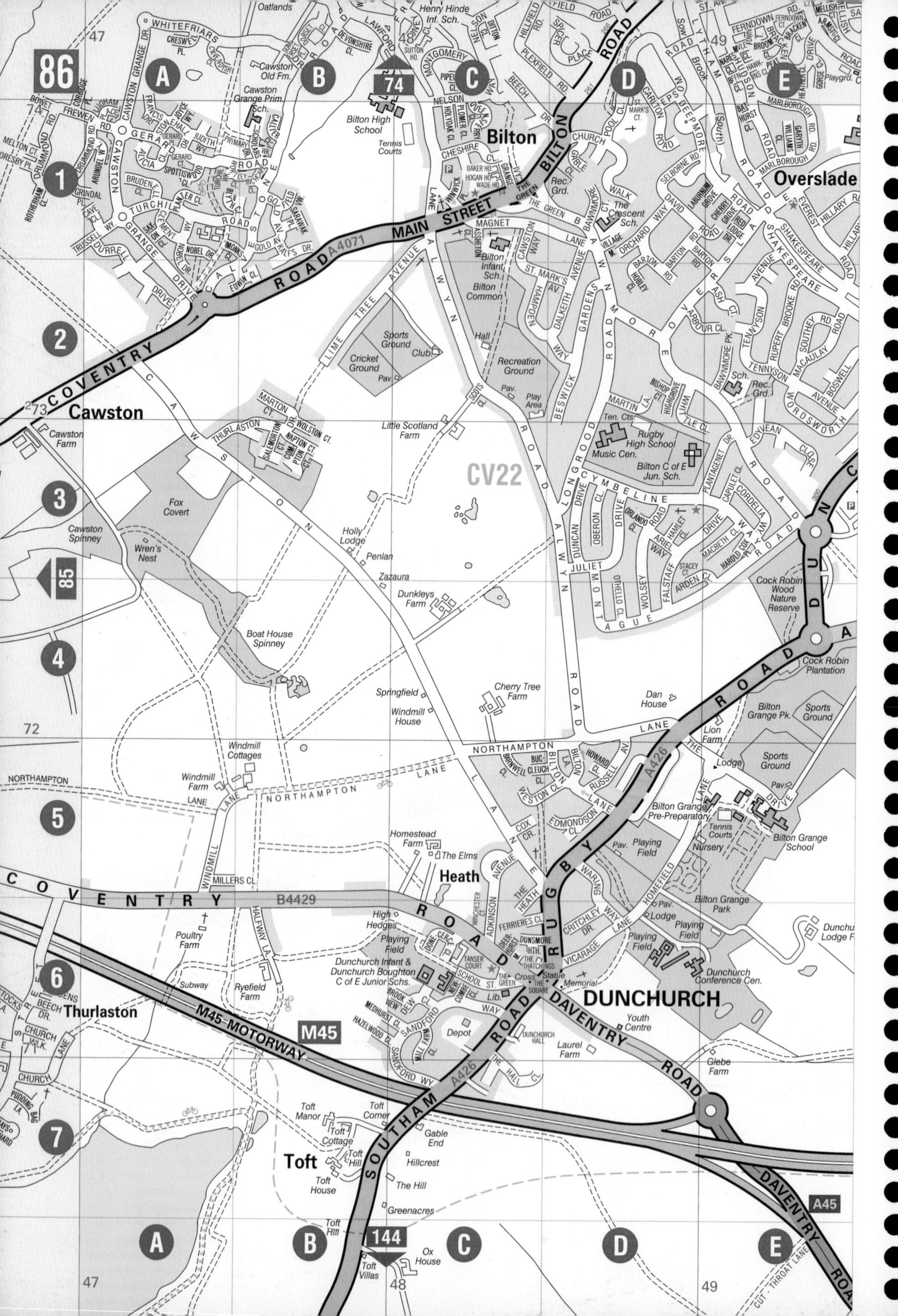
74
85
144
Bilton
Overslade
Cawston
CV22
Heath
DUNCHURCH
Thurlaston
Toft
COVENTRY ROAD
A4071
MAIN STREET
BILTON ROAD
COVENTRY ROAD
B4429
M45 MOTORWAY
M45
SOUTHAM ROAD
A426
DAVENTRY ROAD
A45
RUGBY ROAD
DUNCHURCH ROAD
NORTHAMPTON LANE
ALWYN ROAD
LONGROOD ROAD
BAWNMORE ROAD
LIME TREE AVENUE
CAWSTON LANE
WINDMILL LANE
HALFWAY LA.
CUT THROAT LANE
Oatlands
Henry Hinde Inf. Sch.
Cawston Old Fm.
Cawston Grange Prim. Sch.
Bilton High School
Tennis Courts
Rec. Grd.
The Crescent Sch.
Bilton Infant Sch.
Bilton Common
Hall
Recreation Ground
Play Area
Sports Ground
Cricket Ground
Club
Pav.
Little Scotland Farm
Rugby High School
Music Cen.
Bilton C of E Jun. Sch.
Ten. Cts.
Cawston Farm
Cawston Spinney
Fox Covert
Wren's Nest
Holly Lodge
Penlan
Zazaura
Dunkleys Farm
Boat House Spinney
Springfield
Windmill House
Cherry Tree Farm
Dan House
Cock Robin Wood Nature Reserve
Cock Robin Plantation
Bilton Grange Pk.
Sports Ground
Lion Farm
Lodge
Windmill Cottages
Windmill Farm
Homestead Farm
The Elms
Bilton Grange Pre-Preparatory
Tennis Courts
Nursery
Bilton Grange School
Playing Field
Bilton Grange Park
Poultry Farm
Ryefield Farm
Subway
High Hedges
Dunchurch Infant & Dunchurch Boughton C of E Junior Schs.
Cross
Statue
Memorial
Lib.
Depot
Dunchurch Conference Cen.
Youth Centre
Laurel Farm
Glebe Farm
Dunchurch Lodge F
Toft Manor
Toft Corner
Toft Cottage
Toft Hill
Toft House
Gable End
Hillcrest
The Hill
Greenacres
Ox House
Toft Villas
47
48
49
72
73
74
A
B
C
D
E
1
2
3
4
5
6
7

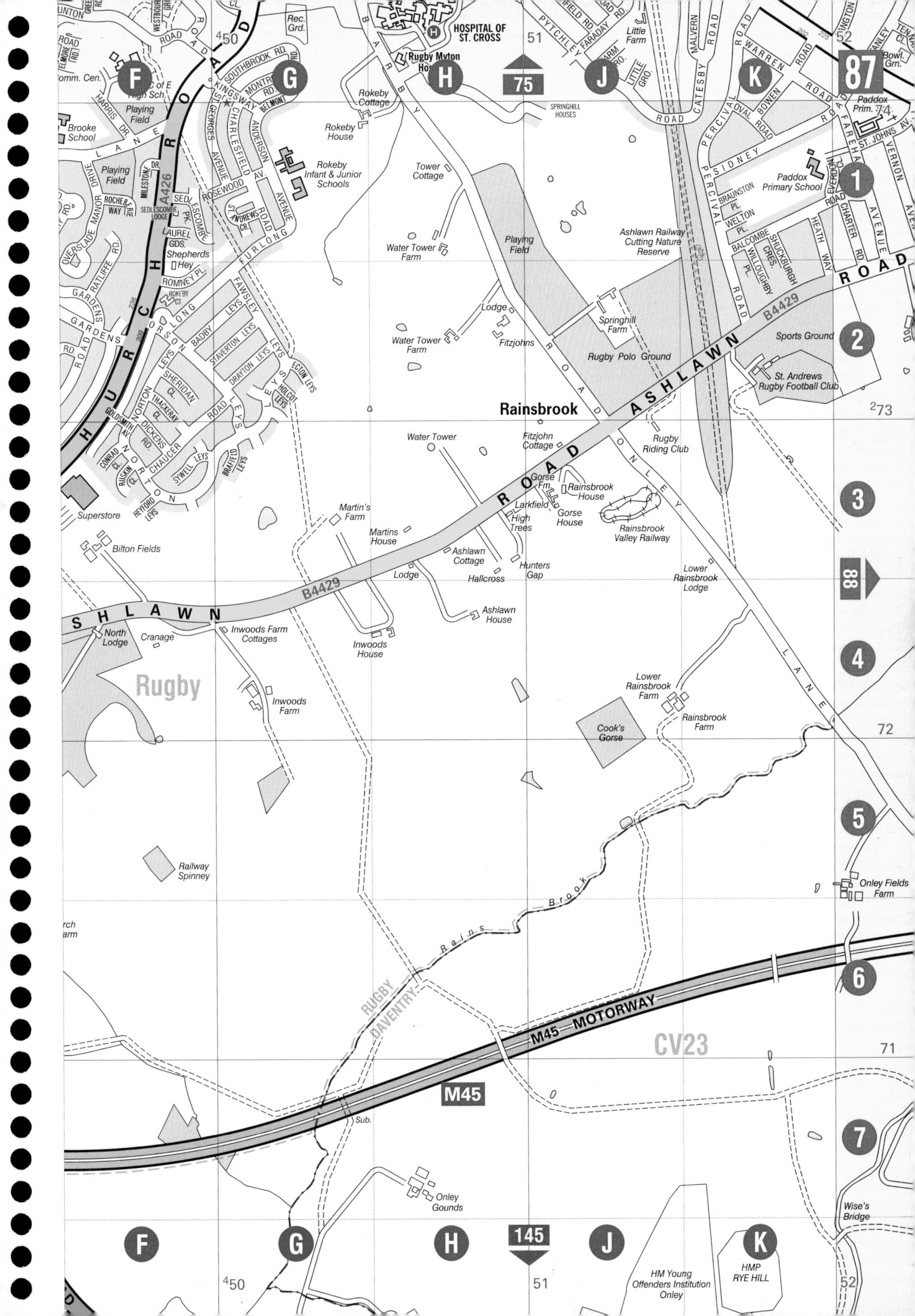

HOSPITAL OF ST. CROSS
Rugby Myton Hos
Rec. Grd.
75
SPRINGHILL HOUSES
Little Farm
Paddox Prim.
Playing Field
Brooke School
Rokeby Cottage
Rokeby House
Rokeby Infant & Junior Schools
Tower Cottage
Paddox Primary School
Ashlawn Railway Cutting Nature Reserve
Water Tower Farm
Playing Field
Springhill Farm
Rugby Polo Ground
Sports Ground
St. Andrews Rugby Football Club
Lodge
Fitzjohns
Rainsbrook
Water Tower
Fitzjohn Cottage
Rugby Riding Club
Gorse Fm.
Rainsbrook House
Larkfield
High Trees
Gorse House
Rainsbrook Valley Railway
Superstore
Martin's Farm
Martins House
Bilton Fields
Ashlawn Cottage
Hallcross
Hunters Gap
Lower Rainsbrook Lodge
Lodge
Ashlawn House
North Lodge
Cranage
Inwoods Farm Cottages
Inwoods House
Rugby
Inwoods Farm
Lower Rainsbrook Farm
Rainsbrook Farm
Cook's Gorse
Railway Spinney
Onley Fields Farm
Rains Brook
RUGBY DAVENTRY
M45 MOTORWAY
CV23
M45
Sub.
Onley Gounds
Wise's Bridge
145
HM Young Offenders Institution Onley
HMP RYE HILL
B4429
ASHLAWN ROAD
CHURCH ROAD
A426

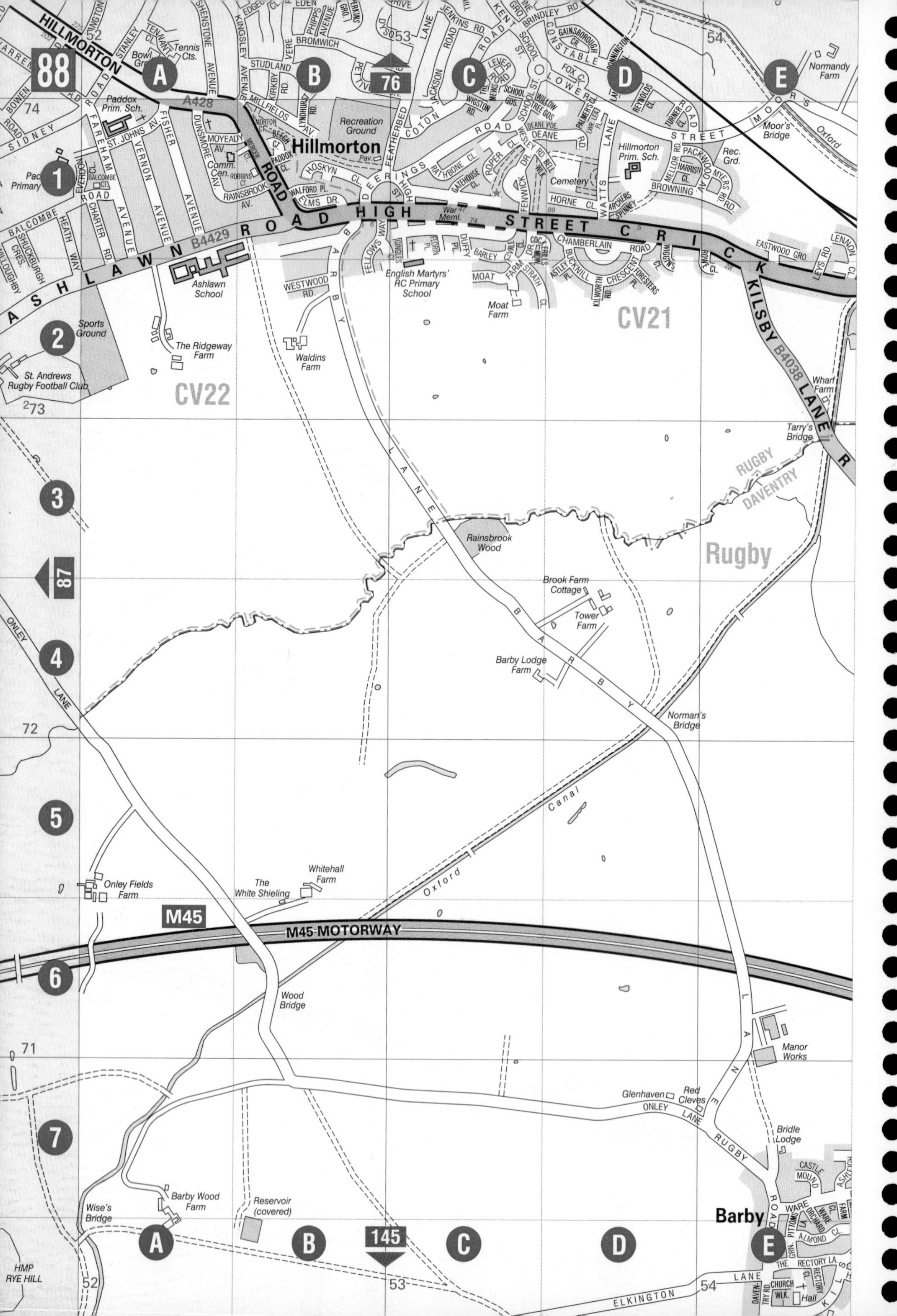
Hillmorton
Recreation Ground
Paddox Prim. Sch.
Tennis Cts.
Bowl Grn.
Comm. Cen.
Pav.
Hillmorton Prim. Sch.
Cemetery
Rec. Grd.
Moor's Bridge
Normandy Farm
War Meml.
English Martyrs' RC Primary School
Ashlawn School
Moat Farm
CV21
CV22
Sports Ground
St. Andrews Rugby Football Club
The Ridgeway Farm
Waldins Farm
Wharf Farm
Tarry's Bridge
RUGBY
DAVENTRY
Rugby
Rainsbrook Wood
Brook Farm Cottage
Tower Farm
Barby Lodge Farm
Norman's Bridge
Canal
Oxford
Whitehall Farm
The White Shieling
Onley Fields Farm
M45
M45 MOTORWAY
Wood Bridge
Manor Works
Glenhaven
Red Cleves
Bridle Lodge
Barby Wood Farm
Wise's Bridge
Reservoir (covered)
HMP RYE HILL
Barby
Hall
A428
B4429
B4038
HILLMORTON ROAD
ASHLAWN ROAD
HIGH STREET
CRICK ROAD
KILSBY LANE
BARBY LANE
ONLEY LANE
RUGBY ROAD
ELKINGTON LANE
76
87
145
52
53
54
74
73
72
71

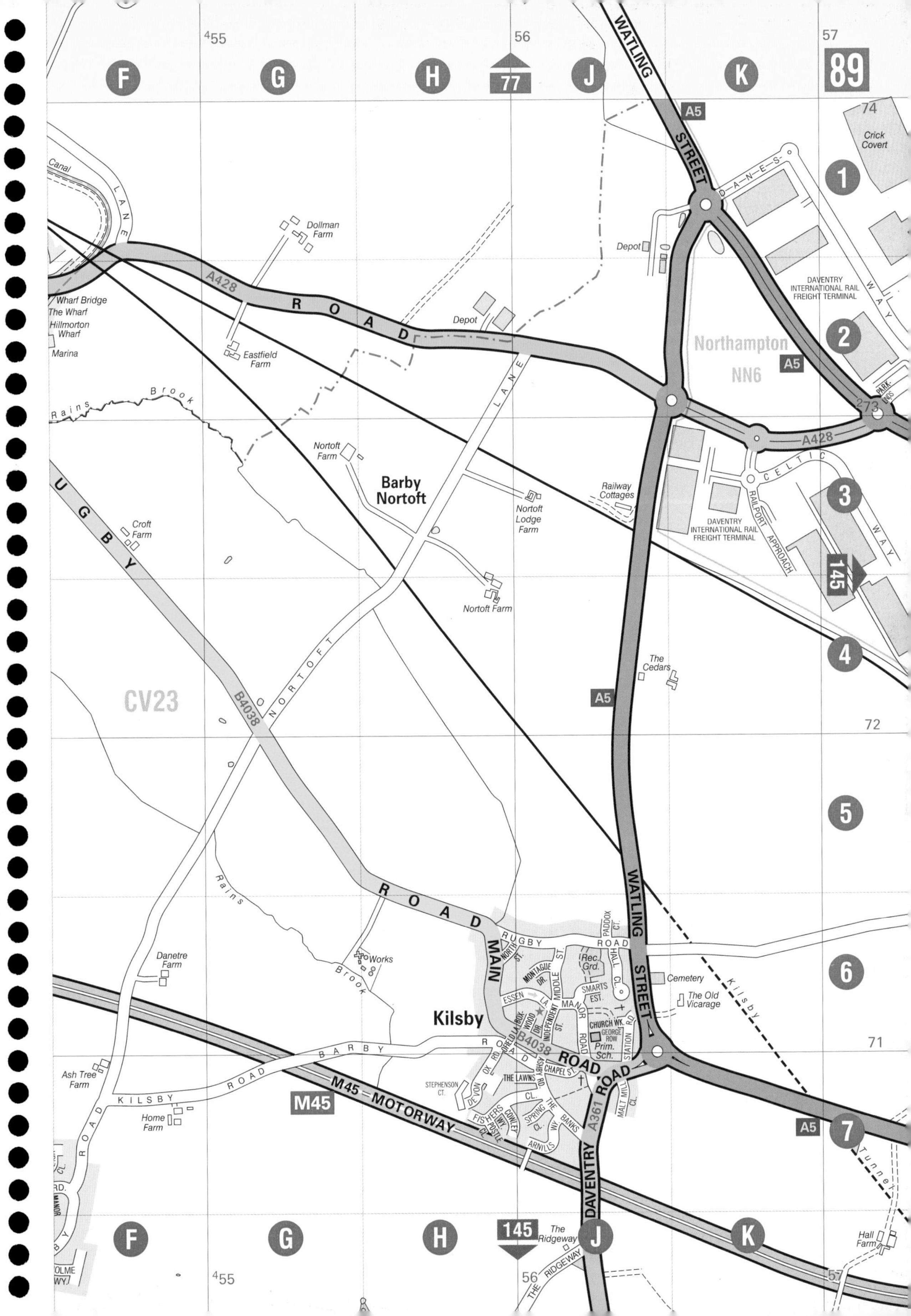
F
G
H
J
K
455
56
57
77
74
73
72
71
1
2
3
4
5
6
7
145
WATLING STREET
A5
Crick Covert
DANES WAY
Canal
LANE
Dollman Farm
Depot
DAVENTRY INTERNATIONAL RAIL FREIGHT TERMINAL
A428 ROAD
Wharf Bridge
The Wharf
Hillmorton Wharf
Marina
Eastfield Farm
Northampton
NN6
PARK-WAY
Rains Brook
Nortoft Farm
Barby Nortoft
CELTIC WAY
Railway Cottages
Nortoft Lodge Farm
RAILPORT APPROACH
RUGBY
Croft Farm
Nortoft Farm
The Cedars
CV23
B4038
NORTOFT LANE
ROAD
Kilsby
RUGBY ROAD
MAIN ROAD
PADDOX CT.
Rec. Grd.
HALL CL.
NORTH ST.
MONTAGUE DR.
MIDDLE ST.
SMARTS EST.
ESSEN LA.
MANOR ST.
Danetre Farm
Works
Cemetery
The Old Vicarage
Kilsby
CHURCH WK.
GEORGE ROW
Prim. Sch.
STATION RD.
INDEPENDENT DR.
BOX WOOD DR.
HEDLA
B4038
ROAD
BARBY ROAD
Ash Tree Farm
KILSBY ROAD
M45
M45 MOTORWAY
STEPHENSON CT.
DEVON OX RD.
ASHBY RD.
THE LAWNS
CHAPEL ST.
A361 ROAD
MALT MILL CL.
Home Farm
FISHERS CL.
POSTLE WY.
COWLEY
SPRING CL.
THE BANKS WY.
ARNILLS
DAVENTRY
Tunnel
Hall Farm
The Ridgeway
THE RIDGEWAY
MANOR RD.
HOLME WY.

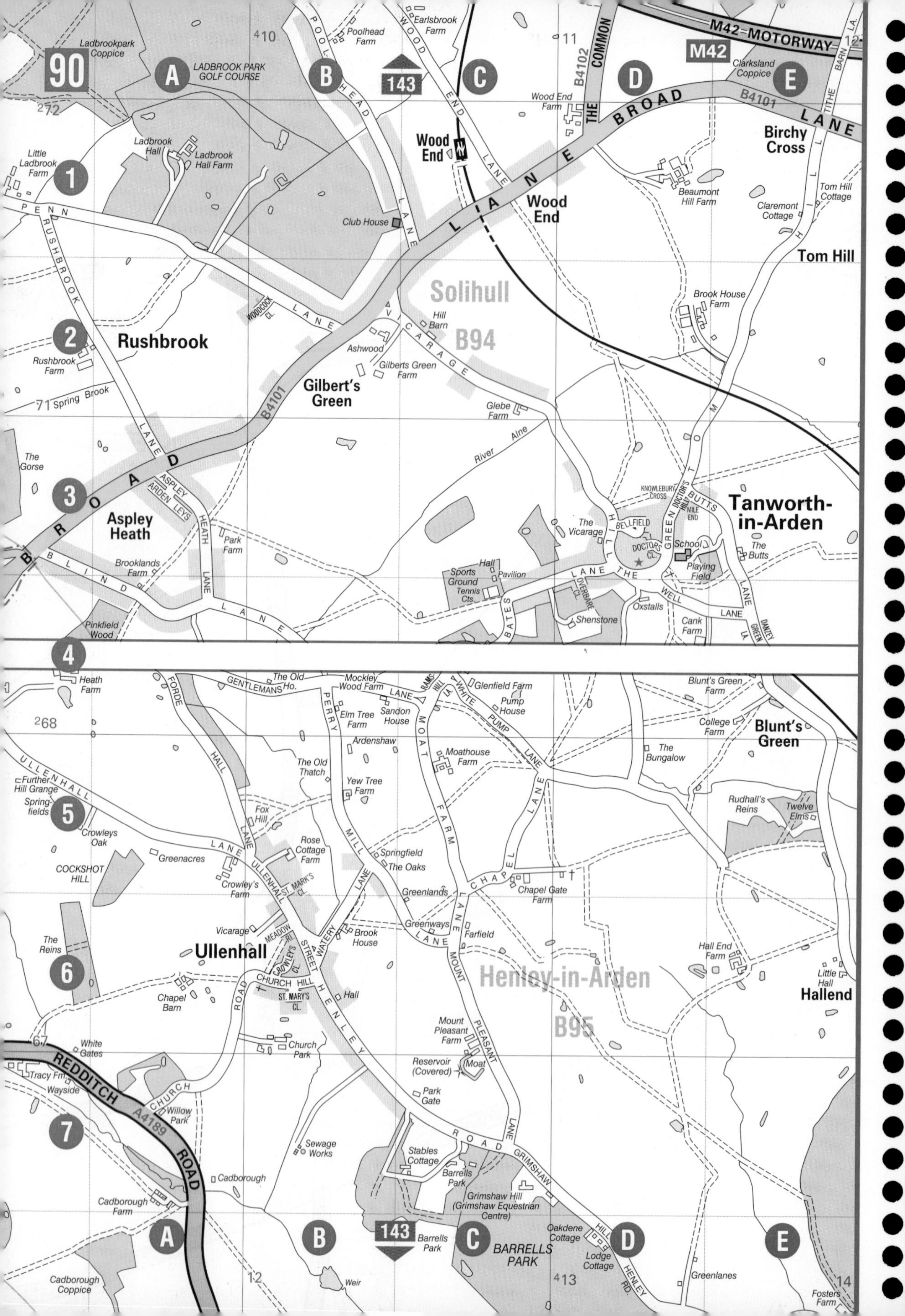
90
Ladbrookpark Coppice
LADBROOK PARK GOLF COURSE
Poolhead Farm
Earlsbrook Farm
143
M42 MOTORWAY
M42
Clarksland Coppice
Wood End Farm
B4102
THE COMMON
BROAD LANE
B4101
Birchy Cross
Wood End
Ladbrook Hall
Ladbrook Hall Farm
Little Ladbrook Farm
PENN LANE
RUSHBROOK LANE
POOLHEAD LANE
WOOD END LANE
Beaumont Hill Farm
Tom Hill Cottage
Claremont Cottage
Club House
Tom Hill
Solihull
Brook House Farm
Hill Barn
VICARAGE LANE
B94
WOODCOCK CL.
Rushbrook
Rushbrook Farm
Ashwood
Gilberts Green Farm
Gilbert's Green
Spring Brook
Glebe Farm
River Alne
The Gorse
BROAD LANE
Aspley Heath
ASPLEY HEATH LANE
ARDEN LEYS
KNOWLEBURY CROSS
DOCTOR'S HILL
BUTTS
Tanworth-in-Arden
MILE END
The Vicarage
BELLFIELD
DOCTORS CL.
School
The Butts
Park Farm
Brooklands Farm
Hall
Sports Ground
Tennis Cts.
Pavilion
Playing Field
BLIND LANE
OVERBARE CL.
Shenstone
Oxstalls
WELL LANE
Cank Farm
DANZEY GREEN LA.
BATES
Pinkfield Wood
Heath Farm
The Old Ho.
GENTLEMANS LANE
Mockley Wood Farm
RAMS HILL
Glenfield Farm
Pump House
WHITE PUMP LANE
Blunt's Green Farm
College Farm
Blunt's Green
FORDE HALL
PERRY MILL LANE
Elm Tree Farm
Sandon House
Ardenshaw
MOAT FARM LANE
Moathouse Farm
The Bungalow
ULLENHALL LANE
Further Hill Grange
Spring-fields
The Old Thatch
Yew Tree Farm
Fox Hill
Rudhall's Reins
Twelve Elms
Crowleys Oak
Greenacres
COCKSHOT HILL
Rose Cottage Farm
Springfield
The Oaks
CHAPEL LANE
Chapel Gate Farm
Crowley's Farm
ST. MARK'S CL.
Greenlands
Greenways
MEADOW RI.
Vicarage
Brook House
Farfield
The Reins
Ullenhall
CROWLEY'S CL.
WATERY LANE
Hall End Farm
Henley-in-Arden
Little Hall Farm
Hallend
CHURCH HILL
ST. MARY'S CL.
Hall
Chapel Barn
STREET HENLEY
Mount Pleasant Farm
MOUNT PLEASANT LANE
B95
White Gates
Church Park
Reservoir (Covered)
Moat
Tracy Fm.
Wayside
REDDITCH ROAD
A4189
CHURCH ROAD
Willow Park
Park Gate
Sewage Works
Stables Cottage
Barrells Park
GRIMSHAW LANE
Cadborough
Grimshaw Hill (Grimshaw Equestrian Centre)
Cadborough Farm
143
Barrells Park
BARRELLS PARK
Oakdene Cottage
Lodge Cottage
HENLEY RD.
Cadborough Coppice
Weir
Greenlanes
Fosters Farm

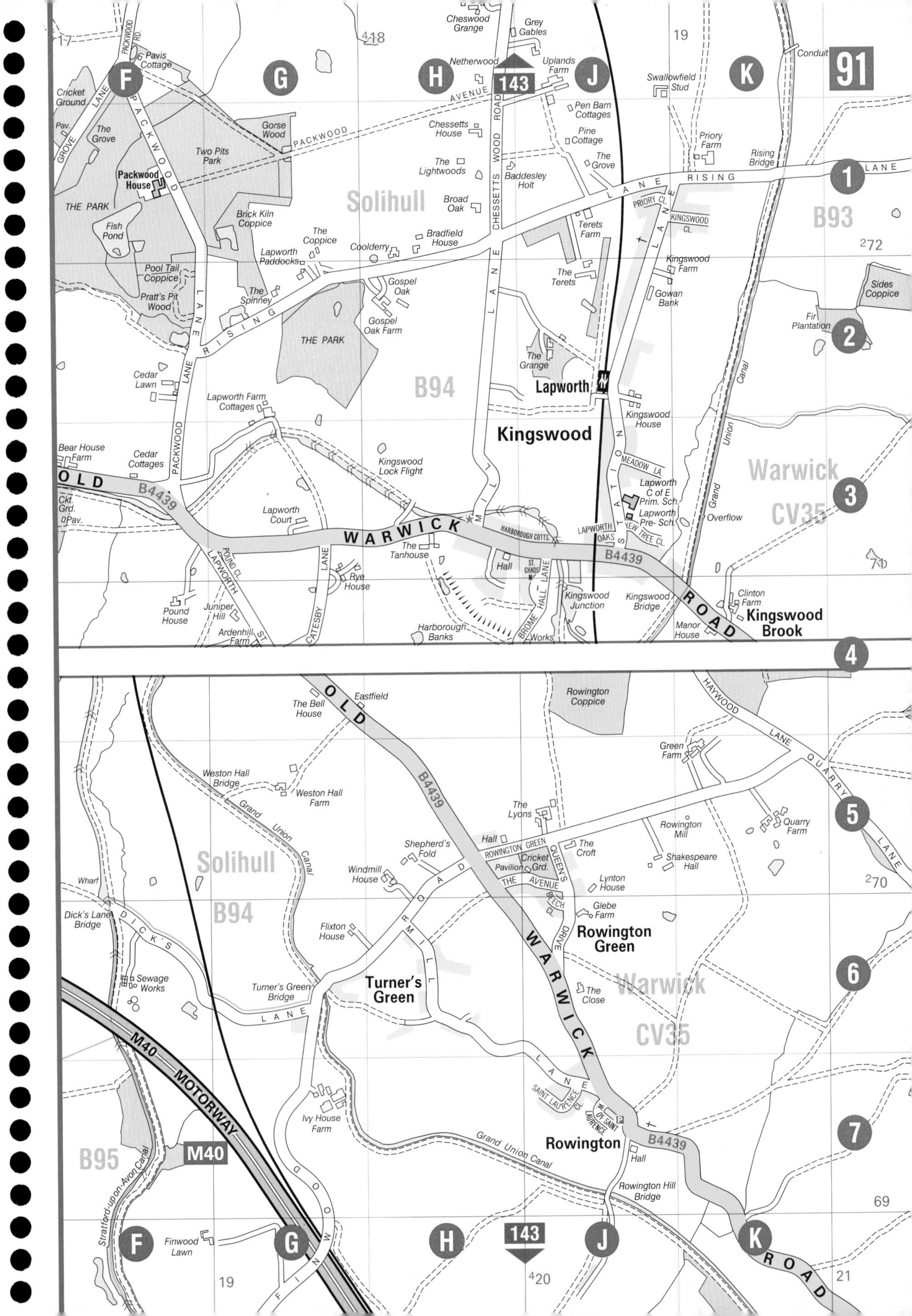
91
143
F
G
H
J
K
1
2
3
4
5
6
7
Packwood House
THE PARK
Fish Pond
Two Pits Park
Gorse Wood
Brick Kiln Coppice
Pool Tail Coppice
Pratt's Pit Wood
Cricket Ground
The Grove
Pavis Cottage
Cheswood Grange
Grey Gables
Netherwood
Uplands Farm
Swallowfield Stud
Conduit
Pen Barn Cottages
Pine Cottage
The Grove
Priory Farm
Rising Bridge
Chessetts House
The Lightwoods
Baddesley Holt
Broad Oak
Bradfield House
Coolderry
The Coppice
Lapworth Paddocks
The Spinney
Gospel Oak
Gospel Oak Farm
THE PARK
Terets Farm
The Terets
Kingswood Farm
Gowan Bank
Sides Coppice
Fir Plantation
Solihull
B93
B94
The Grange
Lapworth
Kingswood
Kingswood House
Lapworth C of E Prim. Sch.
Lapworth Pre- Sch.
Cedar Lawn
Lapworth Farm Cottages
Bear House Farm
Cedar Cottages
Kingswood Lock Flight
Lapworth Court
Overflow
Warwick
CV35
OLD WARWICK ROAD
B4439
The Tanhouse
Hall
Rye House
Pound House
Juniper Hill
Ardenhill Farm
Harborough Banks
Kingswood Junction
Kingswood Bridge
Manor House
Clinton Farm
Kingswood Brook
Works
Grand Union Canal
PACKWOOD LANE
RISING LANE
CHESSETTS WOOD ROAD
MILL LANE
STATION LANE
HAYWOOD LANE
QUARRY LANE
Rowington Coppice
The Bell House
Eastfield
Green Farm
Weston Hall Bridge
Weston Hall Farm
The Lyons
Rowington Mill
Quarry Farm
Shepherd's Fold
Hall
The Croft
Shakespeare Hall
Windmill House
Cricket Grd.
Pavilion
Lynton House
Glebe Farm
Rowington Green
Flixton House
Turner's Green
Turner's Green Bridge
The Close
Wharf
Dick's Lane Bridge
Sewage Works
Solihull
B94
Warwick
CV35
M40 MOTORWAY
M40
B95
Stratford-upon-Avon Canal
Ivy House Farm
Rowington
Hall
Rowington Hill Bridge
Finwood Lawn
FINWOOD ROAD
MILL LANE
19
418
420
21
272
71
270
69

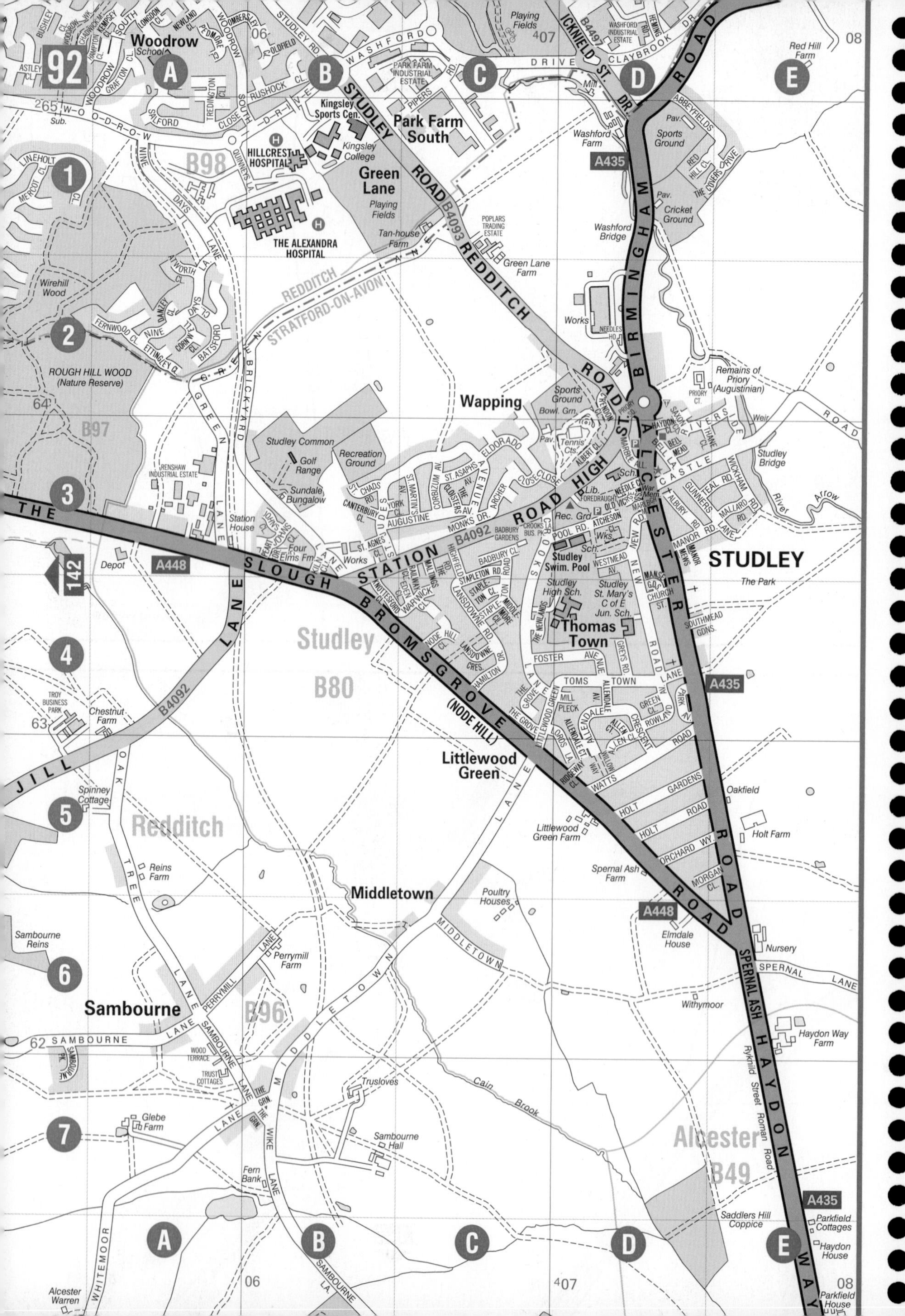

Woodrow
Park Farm South
Green Lane
Kingsley Sports Cen.
Kingsley College
HILLCREST HOSPITAL
THE ALEXANDRA HOSPITAL
Playing Fields
Wirehill Wood
ROUGH HILL WOOD (Nature Reserve)
Wapping
Studley Common
Golf Range
Recreation Ground
Sundale Bungalow
Station House
Four Elms Fm
Depot
STUDLEY
Thomas Town
Studley Swim. Pool
Studley High Sch.
Studley St. Mary's C of E Jun. Sch.
Littlewood Green
Littlewood Green Farm
Middletown
Sambourne
Perrymill Farm
Reins Farm
Sambourne Reins
Glebe Farm
Trusloves
Sambourne Hall
Fern Bank
Alcester Warren
Spinney Cottage
Chestnut Farm
TROY BUSINESS PARK
RENSHAW INDUSTRIAL ESTATE
POPLARS TRADING ESTATE
Green Lane Farm
Tan-house Farm
Washford Farm
Washford Bridge
Sports Ground
Cricket Ground
Works
Remains of Priory (Augustinian)
Studley Bridge
River Arrow
The Park
Oakfield
Holt Farm
Sperncal Ash Farm
Poultry Houses
Elmdale House
Nursery
Withymoor
Haydon Way Farm
Saddlers Hill Coppice
Parkfield Cottages
Haydon House
Parkfield House
Red Hill Farm
PARK FARM INDUSTRIAL ESTATE
WASHFORD INDUSTRIAL ESTATE
Cain Brook
Rykniid Street Roman Road
A435
A448
B4092
B4093
B4497
B98
B97
B80
B96
B49
Studley
Redditch
Alcester
142

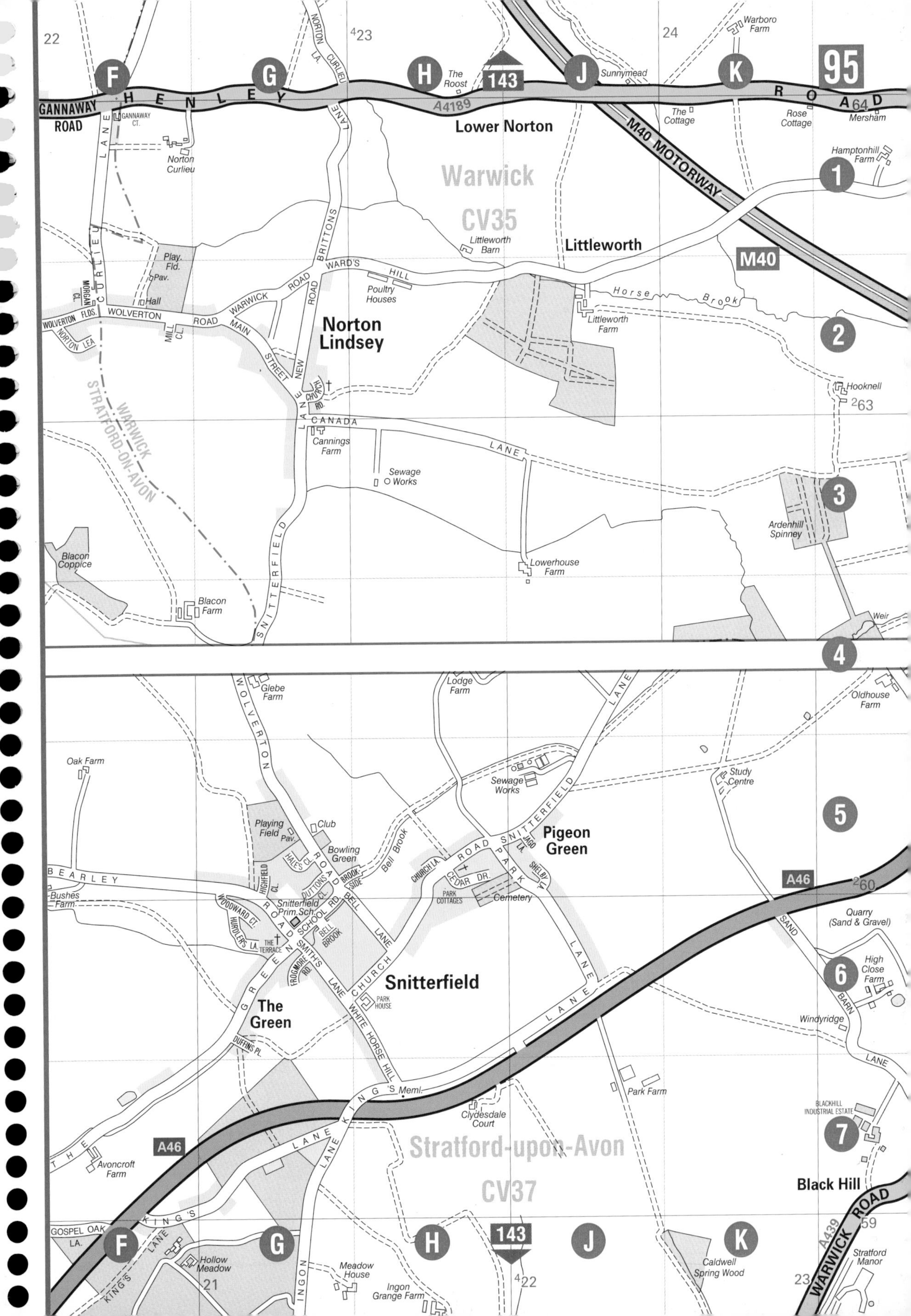

22
423
24
F
G
H
J
K
The Roost
143
Sunnymead
Warboro Farm
GANNAWAY ROAD
HENLEY ROAD
A4189
Lower Norton
The Cottage
Rose Cottage
Mersham
464
NORTON CURLIEU LA.
Norton Curlieu
GANNAWAY CT.
M40 MOTORWAY
Hamptonhill Farm
1
Warwick
CV35
Littleworth Barn
Littleworth
M40
Play. Fld.
Pav.
Hall
BRITTONS LANE
WARD'S HILL
Poultry Houses
Horse Brook
Littleworth Farm
2
MORGAN CL.
CURLIEU LANE
WOLVERTON FLDS.
WOLVERTON ROAD
WARWICK ROAD
MILL CL.
NORTON LEA
MAIN STREET
NEW ROAD
Norton Lindsey
CHURCH RD.
Hooknell
263
CANADA LANE
Cannings Farm
Sewage Works
WARWICK
STRATFORD-ON-AVON
3
Ardenhill Spinney
Blacon Coppice
SNITTERFIELD LANE
Lowerhouse Farm
Blacon Farm
Weir
4
Glebe Farm
WOLVERTON ROAD
Lodge Farm
Oldhouse Farm
Oak Farm
Study Centre
Sewage Works
SNITTERFIELD ROAD
5
Playing Field
Pav.
Club
Bowling Green
Bell Brook
Pigeon Green
BEARLEY ROAD
HALE'S CL.
HIGHFIELD CL.
DUTTONS CL.
BROOKSIDE
CHURCH LA.
CEDAR DR.
JAGO LA.
PARK
SHELBY LA.
A46
260
Bushes Farm
WOODWARD CT.
Snitterfield Prim. Sch.
SCHOOL RD.
BELL LANE
PARK COTTAGES
Cemetery
SAND
Quarry (Sand & Gravel)
HURDLERS LA.
THE TERRACE
BELL BROOK
SMITH'S LANE
CHURCH
Snitterfield
6
High Close Farm
FROGMORE RD.
GREEN
The Green
PARK HOUSE
WHITE HORSE HILL
LANE
BARN LANE
Windyridge
DUFFINS PL.
KING'S Meml.
Park Farm
BLACKHILL INDUSTRIAL ESTATE
Clydesdale Court
7
A46
Stratford-upon-Avon
CV37
THE
Avoncroft Farm
KING'S LANE
Black Hill
GOSPEL OAK LA.
KING'S LANE
INGON LANE
143
A439 WARWICK ROAD
259
Hollow Meadow
Meadow House
Caldwell Spring Wood
Stratford Manor
21
Ingon Grange Farm
422
23

96
143
100
A
B
C
D
E
1
2
3
4
5
6
7
Kite's Nest Farm
DANGER AREA
Bulloak Farm
Deer Park Farm
Goodrest Lodge (site of)
Inchford Brook Farm
Inchford
Brook
WEDGNOCK
Old Park Cottages
Kenilworth
CV8
Kingstanding Farm
Larch Covert
DANGER AREA
Range Plantation
Deer Park Wood
The Close
Brownlow Green Fm.
Brownlow Green
DEER PARK
Keepers Cottages
Woodbine Cottages
Prospect Farm
Turkey Farm
WEDGNOCK OLD PARK
Wedgnock Rifle Range
Blackbrake Plantation
Warwick
Community Centre
Hatton Park
Smith's Covert
CV35
Wedgnock Park Farm
Middle Lock Bridge
Lock House
BIRMINGHAM ROAD
A4177
A46
Ugly Bridge
Brookside
Oaklands Farm
Grand Union Canal
Great Western Cottages
Warehouse
WEDGNOCK INDUSTRIAL ESTATE
BROXELL CLOSE INDUSTRIAL EST.
Budbrooke Farm
Warwick Cemetery
Oldence
Grange Farm
Gog Brook
Zaragoza
Birmingham Road Bri.
Saltisford Common
A425
Church Farm
Budbrooke
Warwick Parkway
Holes Wood
Stanks Farm
BUDBROOKE IND. EST.
LYSTER CRESCENT
WOODWAY

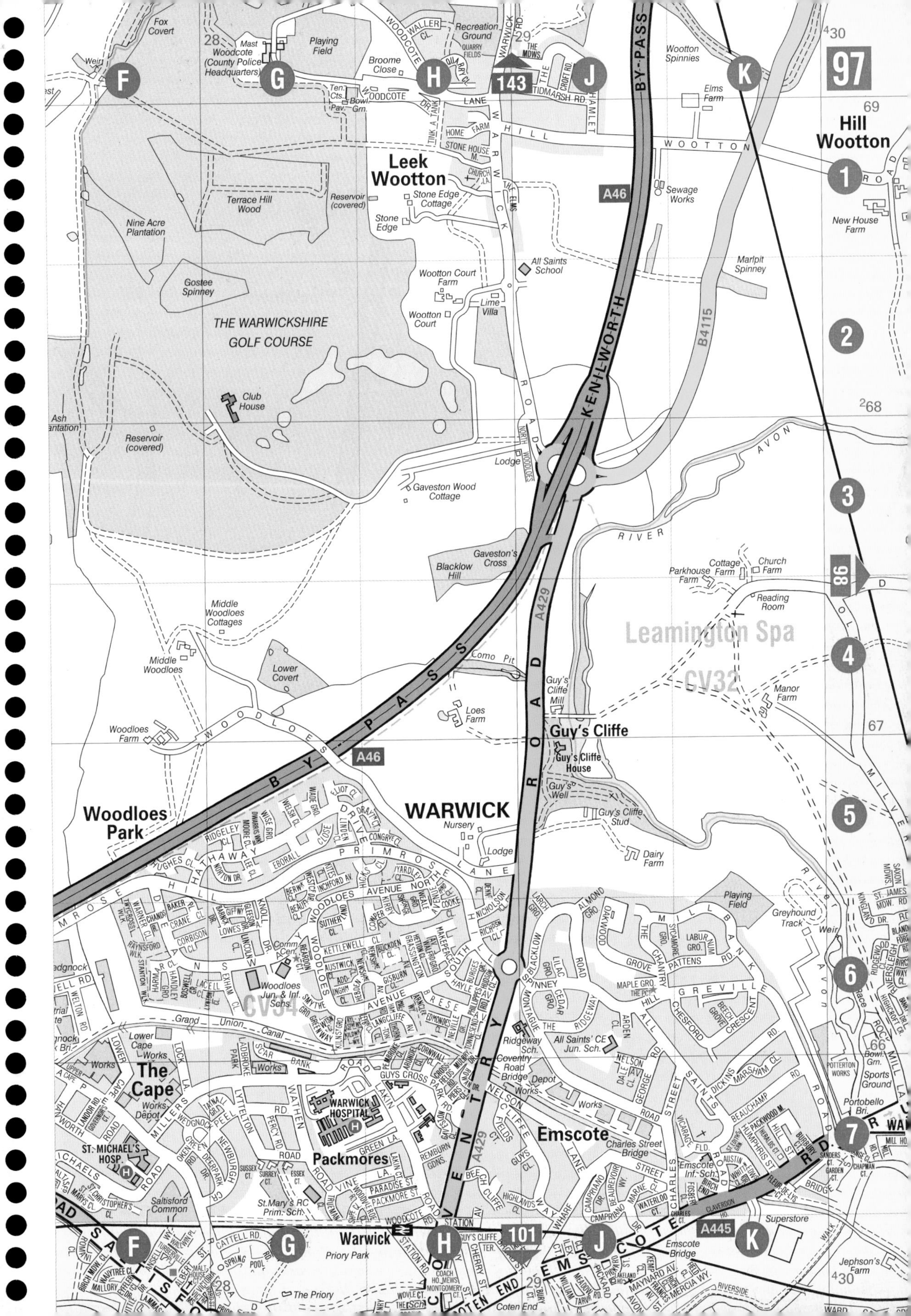

97
Hill Wootton
Leek Wootton
Woodcote (County Police Headquarters)
Playing Field
Recreation Ground
Broome Close
Fox Covert
Wootton Spinnies
Elms Farm
Sewage Works
New House Farm
Terrace Hill Wood
Nine Acre Plantation
Reservoir (covered)
Stone Edge Cottage
Stone Edge
All Saints School
Wootton Court Farm
Lime Villa
Wootton Court
Marlpit Spinney
Gostee Spinney
THE WARWICKSHIRE GOLF COURSE
Club House
KENILWORTH BY-PASS
A46
B4115
Gaveston Wood Cottage
Lodge
RIVER AVON
Blacklow Hill
Gaveston's Cross
Parkhouse Farm
Cottage Farm
Church Farm
Reading Room
Leamington Spa
CV32
Middle Woodloes Cottages
Middle Woodloes
Lower Covert
Como Pit
Guy's Cliffe Mill
Loes Farm
Manor Farm
Woodloes Farm
Guy's Cliffe
Guy's Cliffe House
Guy's Well
Guy's Cliffe Stud
Dairy Farm
Woodloes Park
WARWICK
Nursery
A429
COVENTRY ROAD
Playing Field
Greyhound Track
Weir
Woodloes Jun. & Inf. Schs.
CV34
Grand Union Canal
Lower Cape
Works
The Cape
Ridgeway Sch.
All Saints' CE Jun. Sch.
Coventry Road Bridge
Depot
WARWICK HOSPITAL
ST. MICHAEL'S HOSP.
Packmores
Emscote
Charles Street Bridge
Emscote Inf. Sch.
Sports Ground
Portobello Bri.
Saltisford Common
St.Mary's RC Prim. Sch.
Warwick
Priory Park
The Priory
Coten End
Emscote Bridge
Superstore
Jephson's Farm
A445
143
101
98

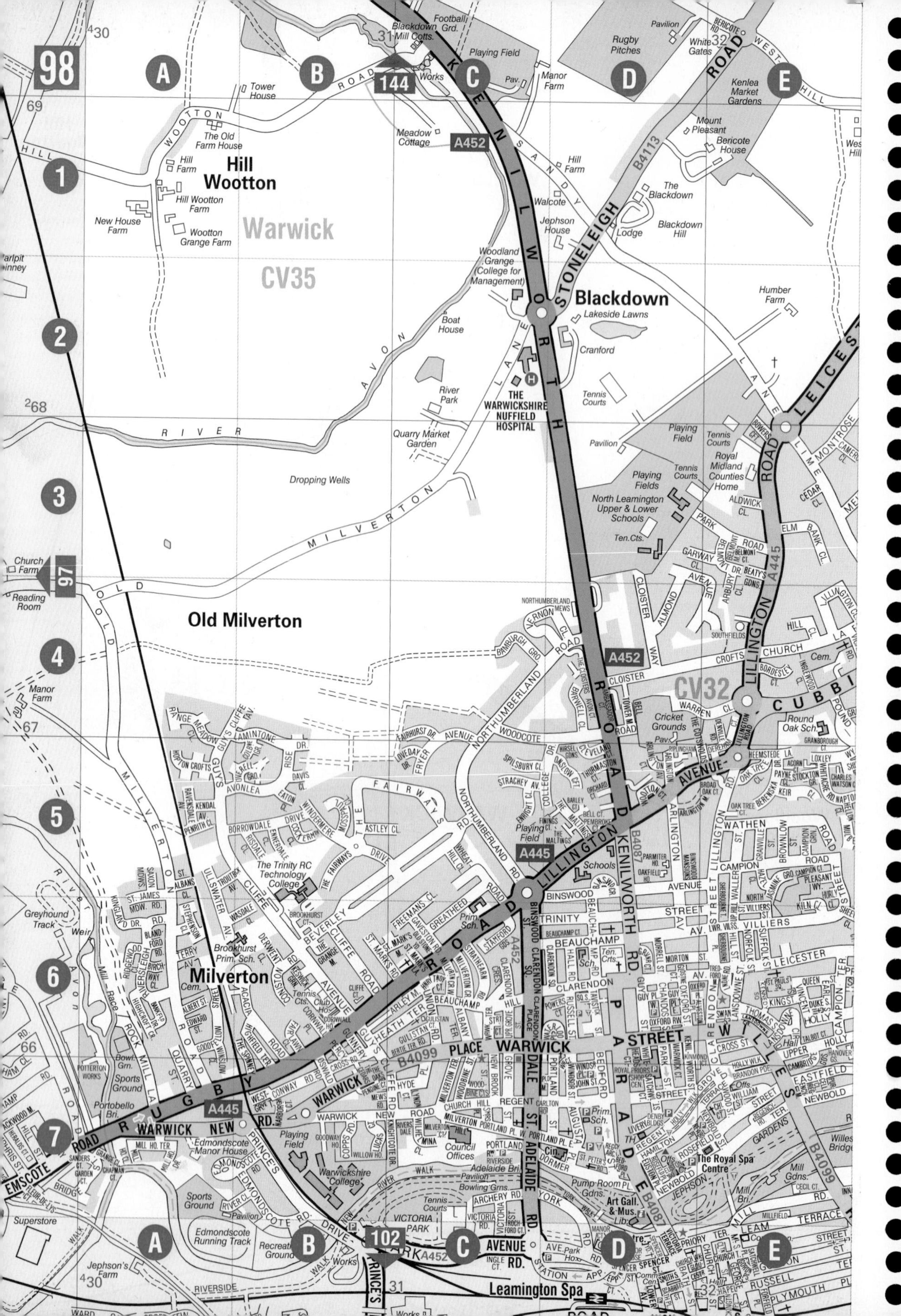

Hill Wootton
Warwick
CV35
Blackdown
Old Milverton
Milverton
CV32
THE WARWICKSHIRE NUFFIELD HOSPITAL
Leamington Spa
The Trinity RC Technology College
The Royal Spa Centre
Warwickshire College
KENILWORTH ROAD
STONELEIGH ROAD
LILLINGTON ROAD
RUGBY ROAD
LILLINGTON AVENUE
WARWICK STREET
PARADE
A452
A445
B4113
B4087
B4099
144
97
102

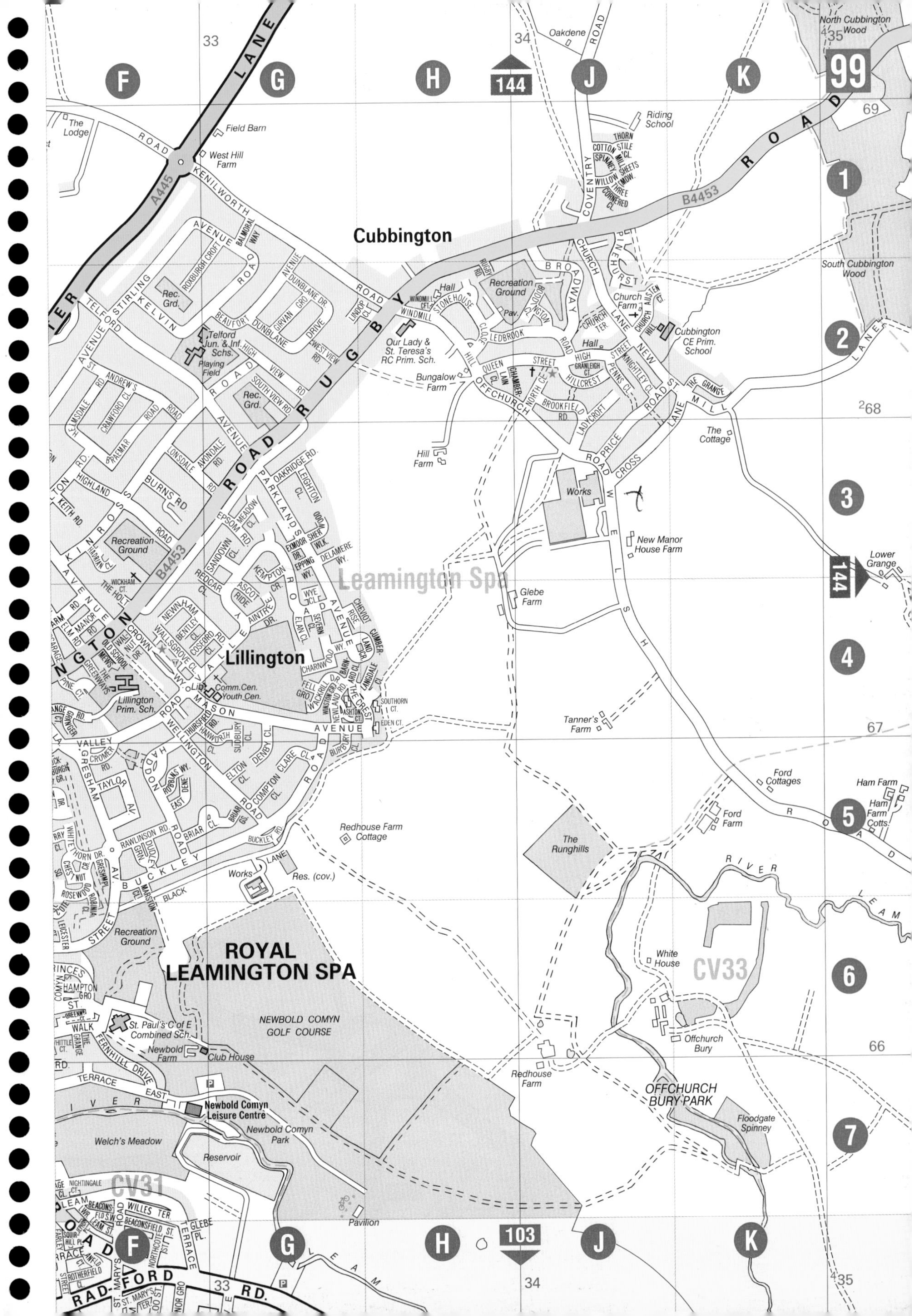

99
F
G
H
J
K
144
103
33
34
35
69
68
67
66
1
2
3
4
5
6
7
Cubbington
Lillington
Leamington Spa
ROYAL LEAMINGTON SPA
CV33
CV31
North Cubbington Wood
South Cubbington Wood
Oakdene
Riding School
Field Barn
West Hill Farm
The Lodge
KENILWORTH ROAD
A445
LANE
RUGBY ROAD
B4453
COVENTRY ROAD
Recreation Ground
Rec. Grd.
Telford Jun. & Inf. Schs.
Playing Field
Our Lady & St. Teresa's RC Prim. Sch.
Hall
Church Farm
Cubbington CE Prim. School
Bungalow Farm
Hill Farm
The Cottage
Works
New Manor House Farm
Lower Grange
Glebe Farm
Lillington Prim. Sch.
Comm.Cen. Youth Cen.
Tanner's Farm
Ford Cottages
Ham Farm
Ham Farm Cotts.
Ford Farm
The Runghills
Redhouse Farm Cottage
Res. (cov.)
RIVER LEAM
White House
Offchurch Bury
OFFCHURCH BURY PARK
Floodgate Spinney
Redhouse Farm
NEWBOLD COMYN GOLF COURSE
St. Paul's C of E Combined Sch.
Newbold Farm
Club House
Newbold Comyn Leisure Centre
Newbold Comyn Park
Welch's Meadow
Reservoir
Pavilion
MILL LANE
WELSH ROAD
CROSS ROAD
OFFCHURCH LANE
BUCKLEY ROAD
BLACK LANE
MASON AVENUE
WELLINGTON ROAD
VALLEY ROAD
CHURCH LANE
NEW STREET
PRICE ROAD
HIGH STREET
BROADWAY
WINDMILL ROAD
PARKLAND ROAD
STIRLING AVENUE
KELVIN ROAD
TELFORD AVENUE
HIGHLAND ROAD
BURNS RD.
RADFORD RD.
TERRACE EAST
FERNHILL DRIVE

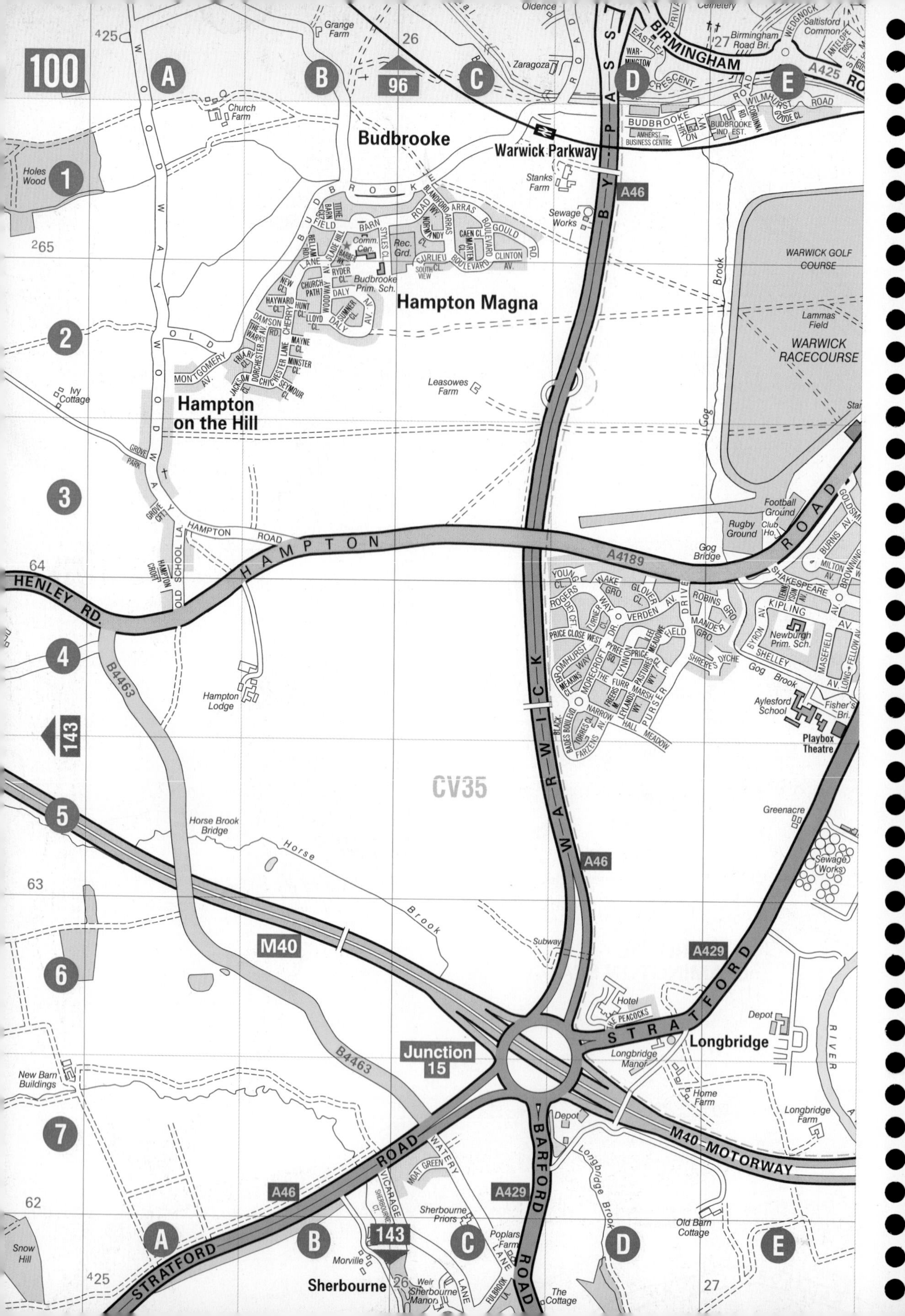
96
143
Budbrooke
Hampton Magna
Hampton on the Hill
Warwick Parkway
Longbridge
Sherbourne
Holes Wood
Church Farm
Grange Farm
Ivy Cottage
Stanks Farm
Sewage Works
Leasowes Farm
WARWICK GOLF COURSE
Lammas Field
WARWICK RACECOURSE
Football Ground
Rugby Ground
Club Ho.
Gog Bridge
Gog Brook
Newburgh Prim. Sch.
Aylesford School
Fisher's Bri.
Playbox Theatre
Hampton Lodge
Horse Brook Bridge
Horse Brook
CV35
Greenacre
Sewage Works
Subway
Hotel
THE PEACOCKS
Depot
Longbridge Manor
Home Farm
Longbridge Farm
Old Barn Cottage
New Barn Buildings
Snow Hill
Sherbourne Priors
Poplars Farm
Morville
Weir
Sherbourne Manor
The Cottage
Longbridge Brook
Junction 15
M40
M40 MOTORWAY
A46
A429
A4189
A425
B4463
WARWICK BY-PASS
HAMPTON ROAD
HENLEY RD.
STRATFORD ROAD
BARFORD ROAD
BIRMINGHAM ROAD
WOODWAY
OLD WOODWAY
BUDBROOKE ROAD
Zaragoza
Oldence
Cemetery
Birmingham Road Bri.
Saltisford Common
BUDBROOKE IND. EST.
AMHERST BUSINESS CENTRE
Comm. Cen.
Rec. Grd.
Budbrooke Prim. Sch.
RIVER AVON
425
26
27
265
64
63
62

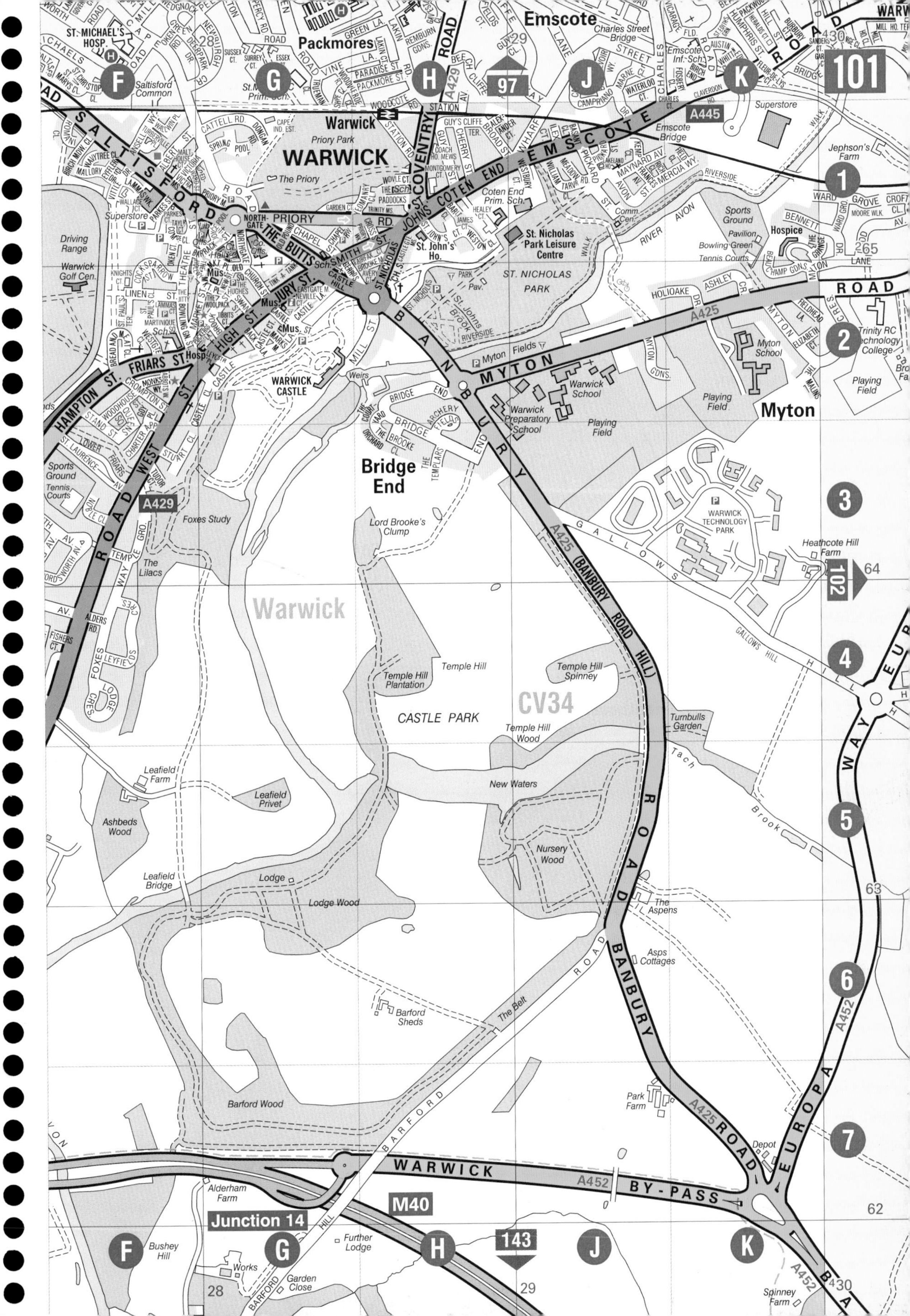
101
Emscote
Packmores
WARWICK
Warwick
Priory Park
The Priory
Saltisford Common
ST. MICHAEL'S HOSP.
Superstore
Driving Range
Warwick Golf Cen.
SALTISFORD
PRIORY RD.
EMSCOTE
COTEN END
ST. JOHNS
COVENTRY RD.
A429
A445
97
Emscote Bridge
Charles Street Bridge
Jephson's Farm
Superstore
St. Nicholas Park Leisure Centre
ST. NICHOLAS PARK
RIVER AVON
Sports Ground
Hospice
Bowling Green
Tennis Courts
MYTON ROAD
A425
Myton School
Trinity RC Technology College
Playing Field
Myton
Warwick School
Warwick Preparatory School
WARWICK CASTLE
Bridge End
BANBURY
HIGH ST.
JURY ST.
SMITH ST.
FRIARS ST.
HAMPTON ST.
ROAD WEST
A429
Sports Ground
Tennis Courts
Foxes Study
The Lilacs
Lord Brooke's Clump
WARWICK TECHNOLOGY PARK
GALLOWS HILL
Heathcote Hill Farm
102
64
Warwick
A425 (BANBURY ROAD HILL)
Temple Hill
Temple Hill Plantation
Temple Hill Spinney
CV34
CASTLE PARK
Temple Hill Wood
Turnbulls Garden
Tach Brook
New Waters
Leafield Farm
Leafield Privet
Ashbeds Wood
Nursery Wood
Leafield Bridge
Lodge
Lodge Wood
The Aspens
63
Asps Cottages
BANBURY ROAD
The Belt
Barford Sheds
EUROPA WAY
A452
Barford Wood
Park Farm
A425 ROAD
Depot
WARWICK BY-PASS
A452
Alderham Farm
M40
Junction 14
BARFORD HILL
Further Lodge
143
62
Bushey Hill
Works
Garden Close
28
29
30
Spinney Farm
F
G
H
J
K
1
2
3
4
5
6
7

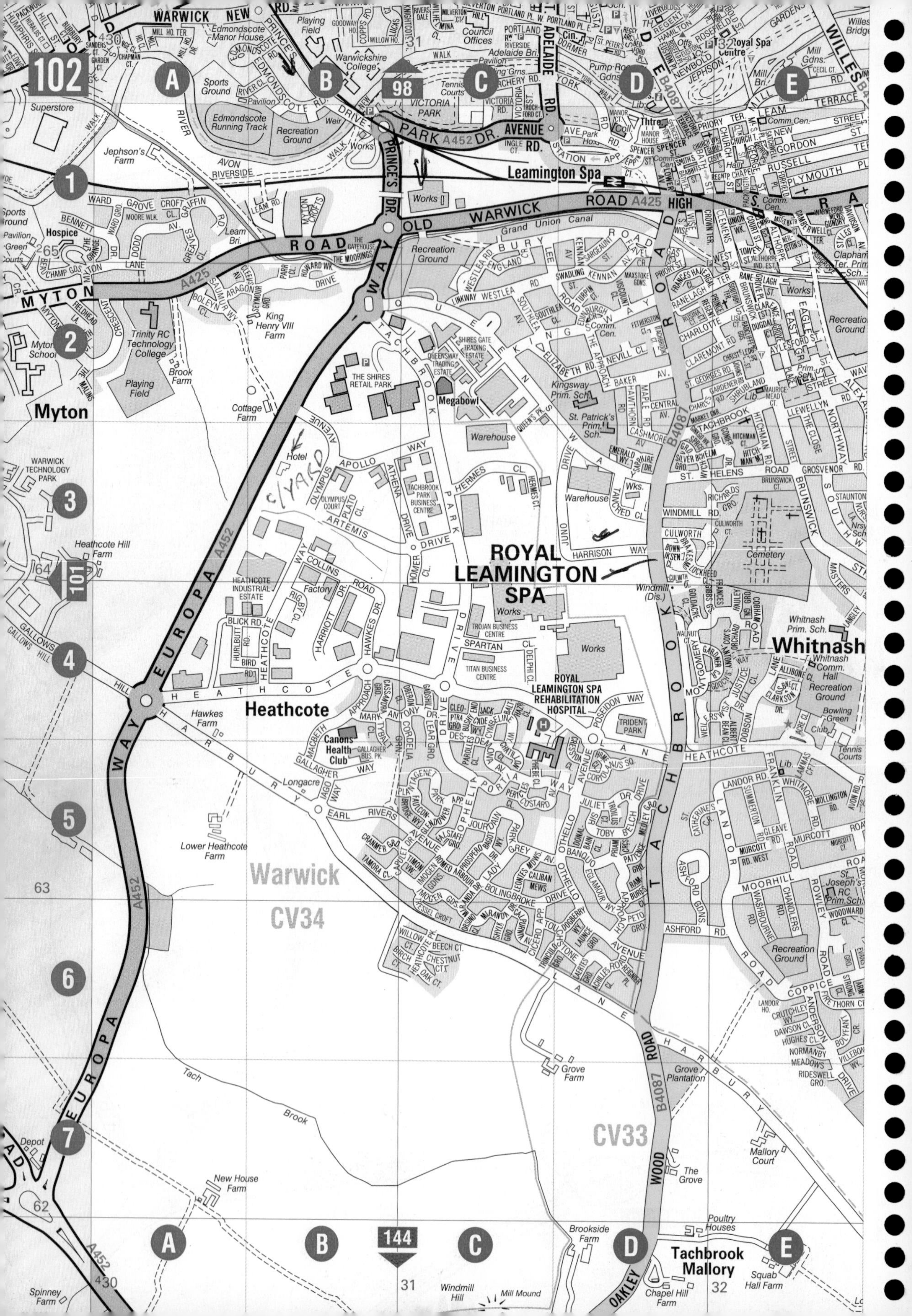
102
98
101
144
ROYAL LEAMINGTON SPA
Leamington Spa
Myton
Heathcote
Whitnash
Warwick
CV34
CV33
Tachbrook Mallory
EUROPA WAY
A452
A425
B4087
OLD WARWICK ROAD
MYTON ROAD
PRINCE'S DR.
TACHBROOK ROAD
HEATHCOTE LANE
HARBURY LANE
OAKLEY WOOD ROAD
Grand Union Canal
Victoria Park
Edmondscote Running Track
Recreation Ground
Warwickshire College
Trinity RC Technology College
Myton School
Hospice
The Shires Retail Park
Megabowl
Tachbrook Park Business Centre
Heathcote Industrial Estate
Trojan Business Centre
Titan Business Centre
Royal Leamington Spa Rehabilitation Hospital
Canons Health Club
Trident Park
Cemetery
Kingsway Prim. Sch.
St. Patrick's Prim. Sch.
Whitnash Prim. Sch.
Whitnash Comm. Hall
St. Joseph's RC Prim. Sch.
King Henry VIII Farm
Jephson's Farm
Brook Farm
Cottage Farm
Hawkes Farm
Lower Heathcote Farm
Heathcote Hill Farm
Warwick Technology Park
Longacre
Grove Farm
Grove Plantation
Mallory Court
The Grove
New House Farm
Brookside Farm
Poultry Houses
Squab Hall Farm
Chapel Hill Farm
Windmill Hill
Mill Mound
Spinney Farm
Depot
Tach Brook
A
B
C
D
E
1
2
3
4
5
6
7
62
63
64
265
31
32
430

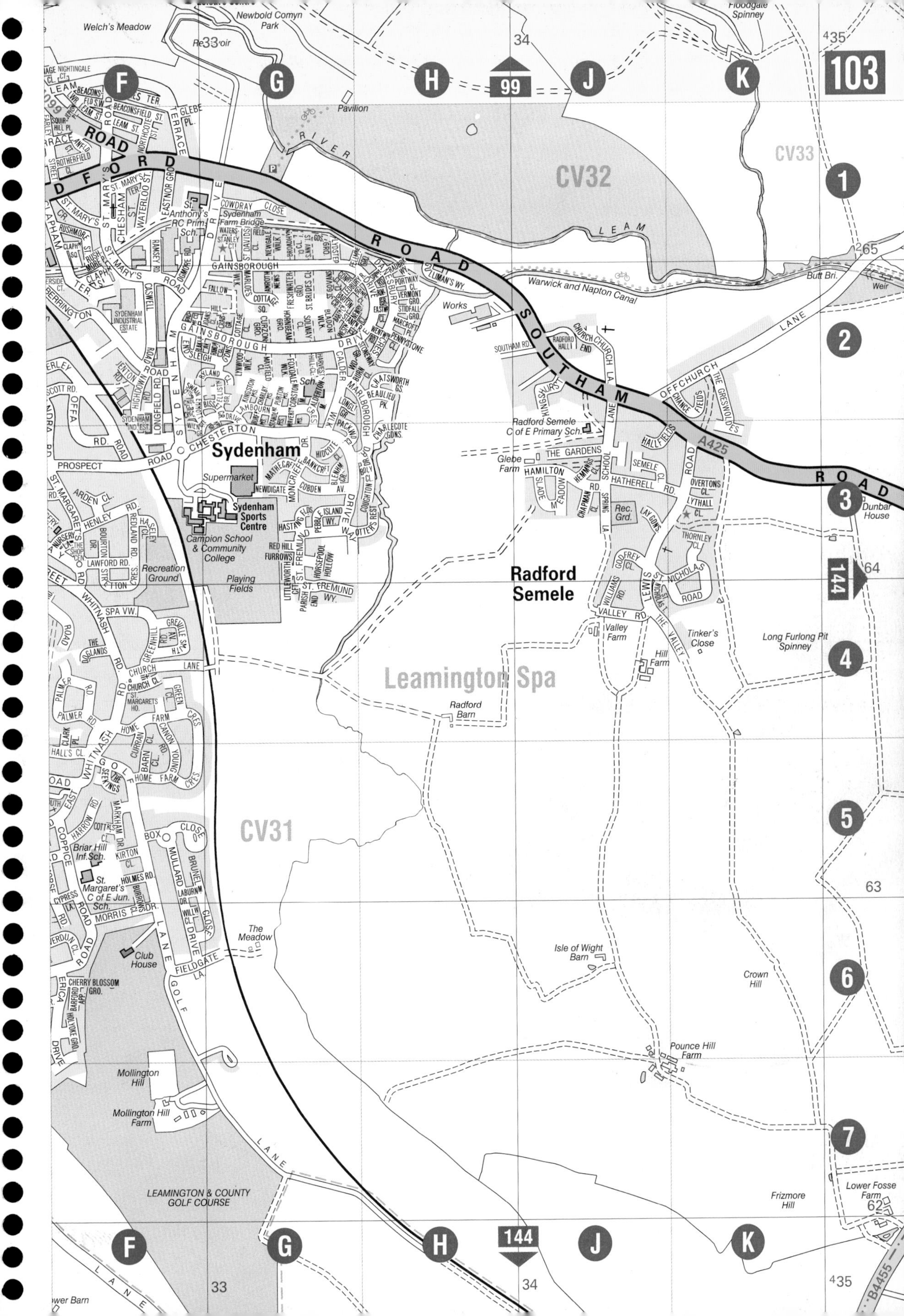

103
F
G
H
J
K
99
144
1
2
3
4
5
6
7
33
34
435
65
64
63
62
CV32
CV33
CV31
Sydenham
Radford Semele
Leamington Spa
Welch's Meadow
Newbold Comyn Park
Floodgate Spinney
Pavilion
RIVER LEAM
Warwick and Napton Canal
Butt Bri.
Weir
SOUTHAM ROAD
A425
OFFCHURCH LANE
CHESTERTON ROAD
PROSPECT
GAINSBOROUGH DRIVE
SYDENHAM DRIVE
St. Anthony's RC Prim. Sch.
Sydenham Farm Bridge
Sydenham Industrial Estate
Sydenham Ind. Est.
Supermarket
Sydenham Sports Centre
Campion School & Community College
Recreation Ground
Playing Fields
Works
Radford Semele C of E Primary Sch.
Glebe Farm
Rec. Grd.
Dunbar House
Valley Farm
Hill Farm
Tinker's Close
Long Furlong Pit Spinney
Radford Barn
The Meadow
Isle of Wight Barn
Crown Hill
Pounce Hill Farm
Frizmore Hill
Lower Fosse Farm
Club House
Mollington Hill
Mollington Hill Farm
LEAMINGTON & COUNTY GOLF COURSE
Briar Hill Inf.Sch.
St. Margaret's C of E Jun. Sch.
WHITNASH ROAD
CHURCH LANE
GOLF LANE
FIELDGATE LA.
B4455

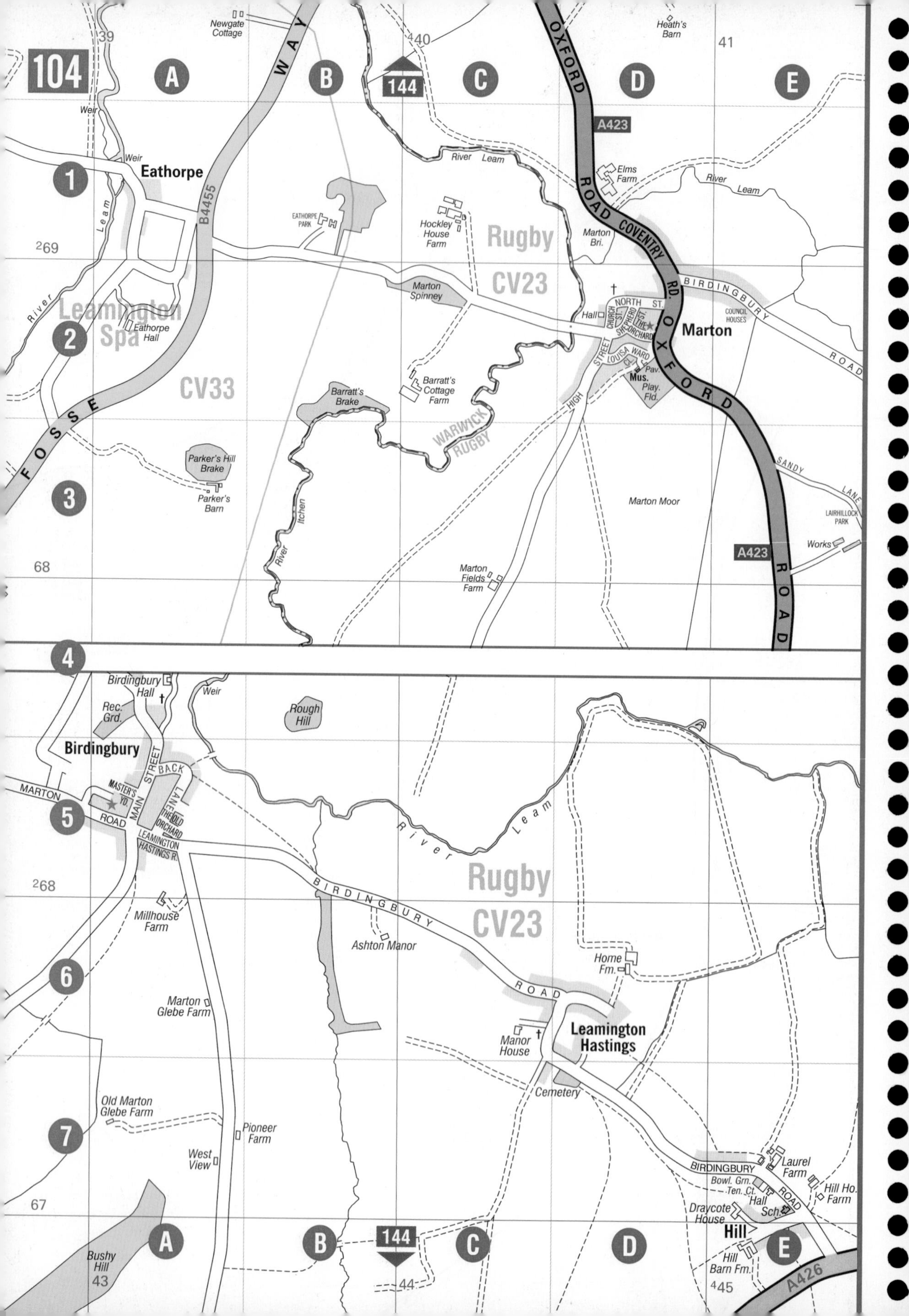
A
B
C
D
E
1
2
3
4
5
6
7
144
Eathorpe
Leamington Spa
CV33
Rugby
CV23
Marton
Birdingbury
Leamington Hastings
Hill
Newgate Cottage
Heath's Barn
Weir
River Leam
Eathorpe Park
Hockley House Farm
Elms Farm
Marton Bri.
Marton Spinney
Eathorpe Hall
Barratt's Cottage Farm
Barratt's Brake
Parker's Hill Brake
Parker's Barn
River Itchen
Warwick
Rugby
Marton Moor
Marton Fields Farm
Lairhillock Park
Works
Council Houses
Hall
Mus.
Pav.
Play. Fld.
North St.
Church St.
Shepherd St.
The Orchard
Louisa Ward Cl.
High Street
Fosse Way
B4455
A423
Oxford Road
Coventry Road
Birdingbury Road
Sandy Lane
Birdingbury Hall
Rec. Grd.
Rough Hill
Back Lane
Main Street
Master's Yd.
The Old Orchard
Marton Road
Leamington Hastings R.
Millhouse Farm
Ashton Manor
Home Fm.
Manor House
Cemetery
Marton Glebe Farm
Old Marton Glebe Farm
Pioneer Farm
West View
Laurel Farm
Hill Ho. Farm
Bowl. Grn.
Ten. Ct.
Sch.
Draycote House
Hill Barn Fm.
Bushy Hill
A426
39
440
41
269
68
268
67
43
44
445

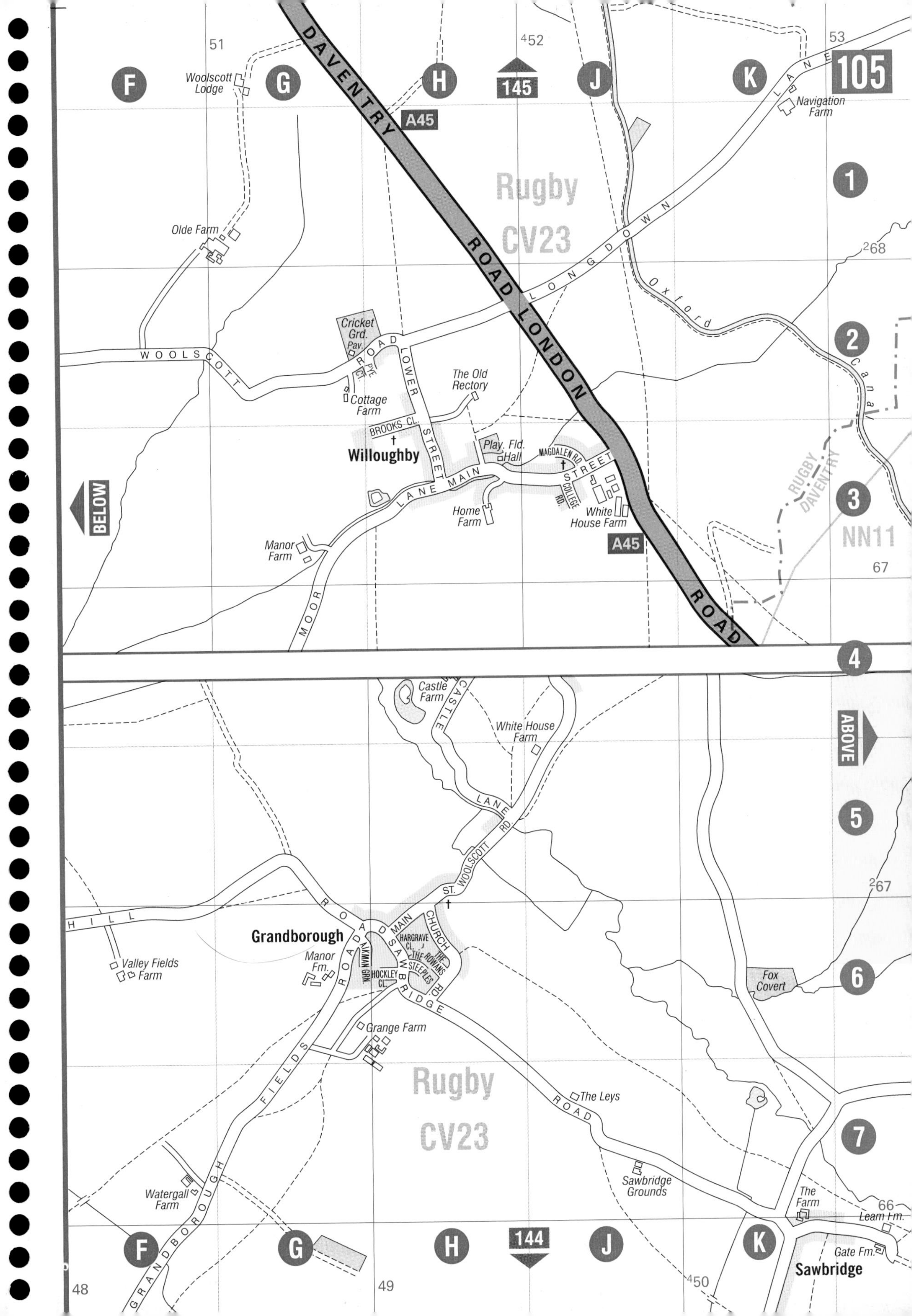

51
452
53
F
G
H
J
K
145
Woolscott Lodge
DAVENTRY ROAD LONDON ROAD
A45
LANE
Navigation Farm
Rugby
CV23
1
Olde Farm
LONGDOWN
268
Oxford Canal
2
Cricket Grd. Pav.
WOOLSCOTT ROAD
PYE CT.
LOWER STREET
The Old Rectory
Cottage Farm
BROOKS CL.
Willoughby
Play. Fld. Hall
MAGDALEN RD.
STREET
MAIN LANE
COLLEGE RD.
RUGBY DAVENTRY
3
NN11
BELOW
Home Farm
White House Farm
Manor Farm
67
MOOR
4
Castle Farm
CASTLE
White House Farm
ABOVE
LANE
WOOLSCOTT RD.
5
ST.
267
HILL ROAD
MAIN
CHURCH
Grandborough
HARGRAVE CL.
THE ROWANS
THE STEEPLES
AIKMAN GRN.
HOCKLEY CL.
SAWBRIDGE RD.
Manor Fm.
Valley Fields Farm
Fox Covert
6
Grange Farm
FIELDS
Rugby
CV23
The Leys
ROAD
7
GRANDBOROUGH
Watergall Farm
Sawbridge Grounds
The Farm
66
Leam Fm.
F
G
H
144
J
K
Gate Fm.
Sawbridge
48
49
450

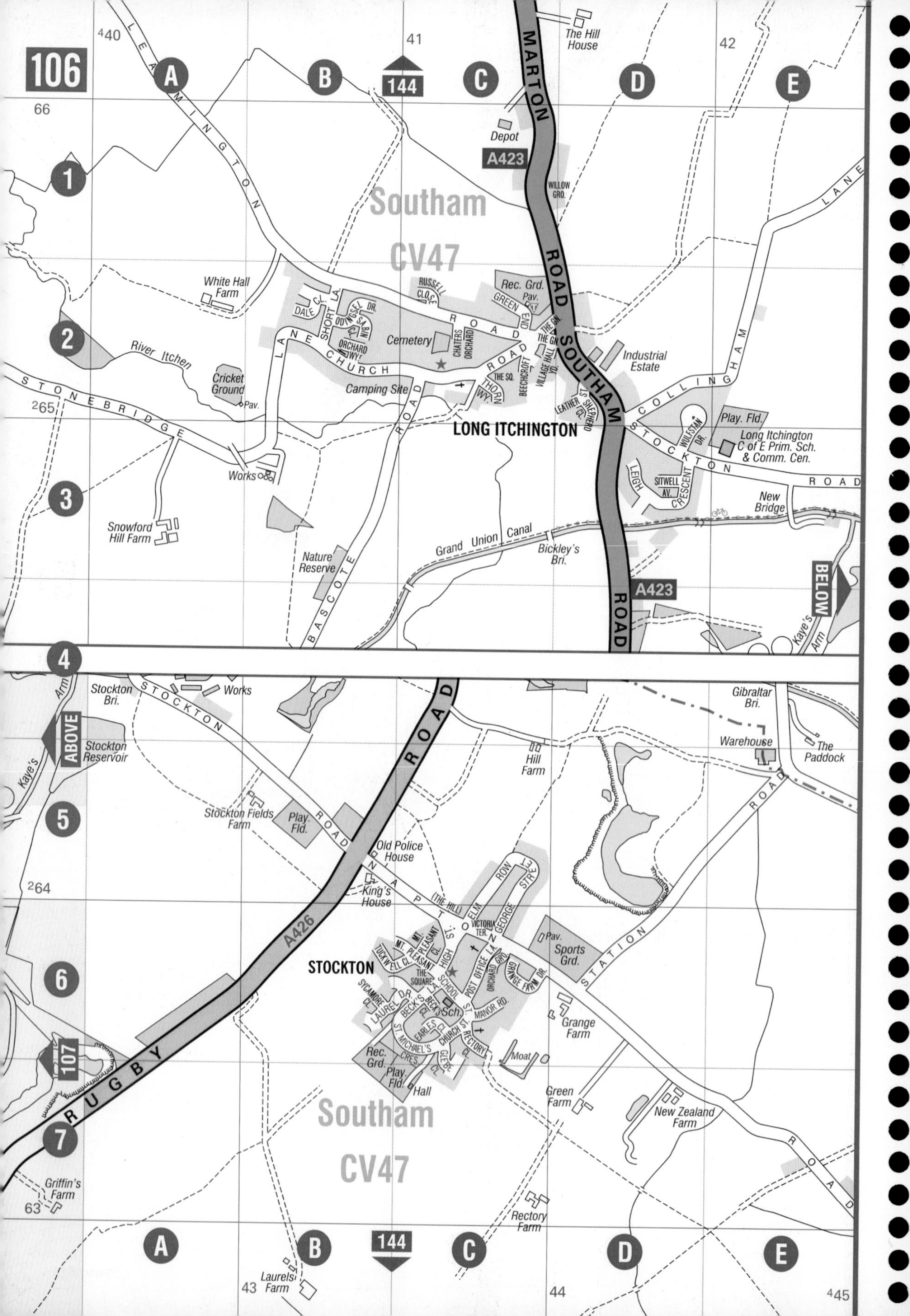

144
The Hill House
MARTON ROAD
LEAMINGTON
Depot
A423
Southam
CV47
WILLOW GRO.
White Hall Farm
RUSSELL CLOSE
Rec. Grd.
Pav.
GREEN END
DALE CL.
SHORT LA.
DOWNSEL DR.
SABIN CL.
ORCHARD WY.
Cemetery
CHATERS ORCHARD
ROAD
THE GN.
SOUTHAM ROAD
VILLAGE HALL YD.
Industrial Estate
River Itchen
Cricket Ground
Pav.
CHURCH LANE
THE SQ.
BEECHCROFT
THORN WY.
Camping Site
STONEBRIDGE
COLLINGHAM LANE
LEATHER CL.
ST. SHEPHERD
WILLSTAN DR.
Play. Fld.
Long Itchington C of E Prim. Sch. & Comm. Cen.
LONG ITCHINGTON
STOCKTON ROAD
Works
LEIGH
SITWELL AV.
CRESCENT
Snowford Hill Farm
New Bridge
Grand Union Canal
Bickley's Bri.
Nature Reserve
BASCOTE ROAD
BELOW
Kaye's Arm
Stockton Bri.
STOCKTON ROAD
Works
ABOVE
Stockton Reservoir
Gibraltar Bri.
Warehouse
The Paddock
Hill Farm
Stockton Fields Farm
Play. Fld.
Old Police House
NAPTON (THE HILL)
King's House
ROW
ELM
GEORGE STREET
VICTORIA TER.
A426
HIGH ST.
MT. PLEASANT CL.
TUCKWELL CL.
THE SQUARE
SCHOOL LA.
POST OFFICE LA.
ORCHARD GRO.
GRANGE FARM DR.
Pav.
Sports Grd.
STATION ROAD
STOCKTON
SYCAMORE CL.
LAUREL DR.
BECK'S CL.
Sch.
CHURCH ST.
MANOR RD.
ST. MICHAEL'S CRES.
EARLES CL.
RECTORY CL.
Grange Farm
GLEBE CL.
Rec. Grd.
Play. Fld.
Hall
Moat
107
RUGBY ROAD
Green Farm
New Zealand Farm
Southam
CV47
Griffin's Farm
Rectory Farm
Laurels Farm
A
B
C
D
E
1
2
3
4
5
6
7
440
41
42
66
265
264
63
43
44
445

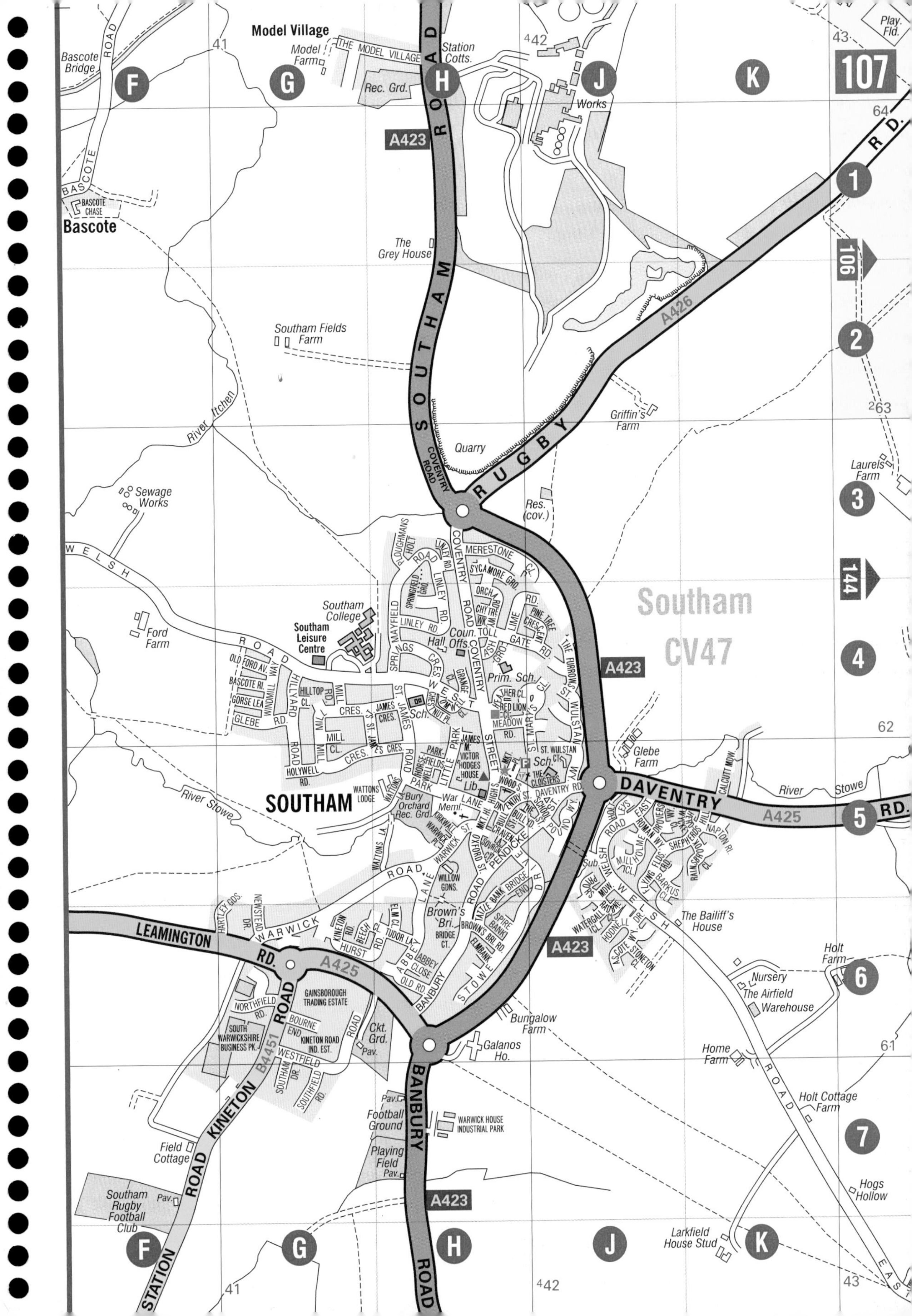

107
106
144
Southam
CV47
SOUTHAM
Model Village
Model Farm
THE MODEL VILLAGE
Station Cotts.
Rec. Grd.
Works
Bascote Bridge
BASCOTE ROAD
BASCOTE CHASE
Bascote
The Grey House
Southam Fields Farm
River Itchen
Quarry
Griffin's Farm
Laurels Farm
Sewage Works
Res. (cov.)
SOUTHAM ROAD
RUGBY RD.
COVENTRY ROAD
WELSH ROAD
Ford Farm
Southam College
Southam Leisure Centre
Glebe Farm
River Stowe
DAVENTRY RD.
The Bailiff's House
Holt Farm
Nursery
The Airfield
Warehouse
Bungalow Farm
Galanos Ho.
Home Farm
Holt Cottage Farm
LEAMINGTON RD.
WARWICK ROAD
GAINSBOROUGH TRADING ESTATE
SOUTH WARWICKSHIRE BUSINESS PK.
KINETON ROAD IND. EST.
KINETON ROAD
BANBURY ROAD
Ckt. Grd.
Football Ground
WARWICK HOUSE INDUSTRIAL PARK
Playing Field
Field Cottage
Southam Rugby Football Club
STATION ROAD
Hogs Hollow
Larkfield House Stud
A423
A426
A425
B4451

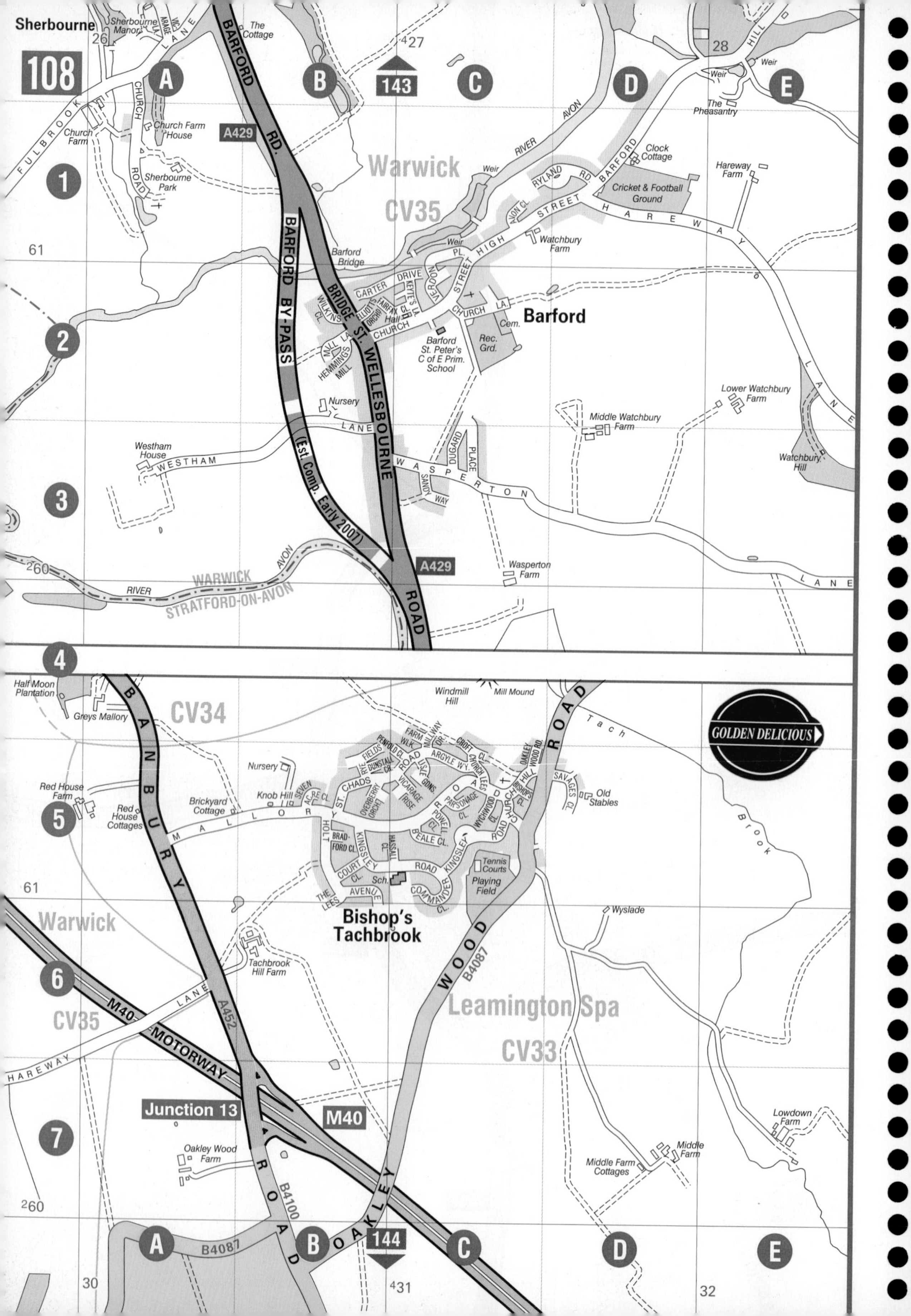
Sherbourne
Sherbourne Manor
The Cottage
Church Farm
Church Farm House
Sherbourne Park
BARFORD RD.
A429
Warwick
CV35
RIVER AVON
Clock Cottage
Cricket & Football Ground
Hareway Farm
The Pheasantry
Weir
Watchbury Farm
Barford Bridge
BARFORD BY-PASS
BRIDGE ST.
WELLESBOURNE ROAD
Barford
Cem.
Rec. Grd.
Barford St. Peter's C of E Prim. School
Hall
Nursery
Lower Watchbury Farm
Middle Watchbury Farm
Watchbury Hill
Westham House
WESTHAM LANE
WASPERTON LANE
(Est. Comp. Early 2007)
Wasperton Farm
WARWICK
STRATFORD-ON-AVON
RIVER AVON
Half Moon Plantation
Greys Mallory
CV34
Windmill Hill
Mill Mound
GOLDEN DELICIOUS
BANBURY ROAD
MALLORY ROAD
Nursery
Red House Farm
Red House Cottages
Brickyard Cottage
Knob Hill
Old Stables
Tach Brook
Tennis Courts
Playing Field
Sch.
Bishop's Tachbrook
Wyslade
Warwick
Tachbrook Hill Farm
CV35
M40 MOTORWAY
A452
WOOD ROAD
B4087
Leamington Spa
CV33
HAREWAY LANE
Junction 13
M40
Oakley Wood Farm
OAKLEY ROAD
B4100
B4087
Middle Farm
Middle Farm Cottages
Lowdown Farm
143
144

144
Wood Farm
Long Itchington Wood
WELSH ROAD
Fox Farm
Bascote Heath
FEATHERBED LANE
Southam
CV47
Thorpe Rough
War Memorial
Ufton Wood
Ashgrove Farm
LEAMINGTON (UFTON HILL) ROAD
Leamington Spa
CV33
Home Farm
WHITE HART LA.
Old Rectory
SOUTHAM RD.
A425
Greystone Kennels
Stoney Thorpe Home Farm
Dallas Burston Polo Grounds
Club House
Stand
REEDS PK.
ST. MICHAEL'S CL.
Ufton
FIELDS
BROAD CL.
Town Farm
FIELD CL.
B4452
Ufton Fields (Nature Reserve)
Monkey Barn Farm
UFTON
Bull Ring Farm
B4452
Churchland Farm
CHURCHLANDS BUS. PK.
Harbury Spoilbank Nature Reserve
MIDDLE
BULL RING FARM RD.
Northfields
Harbury Hall
Station Road Farm
HILLSIDE
LEYCESTER CL.
ROAD BINSWOOD END MILL
HALL LANE
STATION
B4452 ROAD
WOODFORD M.
MILL LA.
Lib.
CHURCH TER.
CROWN ST.
THE POUND
HOUSE LA.
NEALE'S CL.
PIRIE CL.
BUTT LANE
Springfields Farm
THE BEECHES
FARM
STREET HIGH ST.
CHURCH ST.
DOV FRANCES
SUTCLIFFE DR.
FARLEY
DICKENS R.
MACKLEY W.
FARM CL.
ORCHARD
HEBER DR.
KNIGHTLOW WY.
FOX CL.
IVY LANE
THE BULL RING
VICARAGE
DRINKWATER CL.
QUEENS CL.
HONIWELL CL.
AVENUE
WAGSTAFFE CL.
Prim. Sch.
CHAPEL ST.
PARK LA. TER.
SOUTH PARADE
LANE
ROAD TEMPLE
STREET
MANOR
END PARK LANE
Cemetery
Hall
PINEHAM AV.
PERCIVAL DR.
ROAD
CHESTERTON
Whitegates Farm
BUSH
MANOR RD
PENELOPE CL.
CONSTANCE DR.
MARGARET CL.
Meadow Farm
Model Farm
Harbury
Play. Fld.
Leamington Spa
CV33
Southam
CV47
Henrys
HEATH
Pineham Farm
HEATH
BUSH
Roseleigh
Bishops Bowl Lakes
LANE
144
Harbury Heath House
F G H J K
1 2 3 4 5 6 7
36 437 38 38 39 440
263 262 260 259

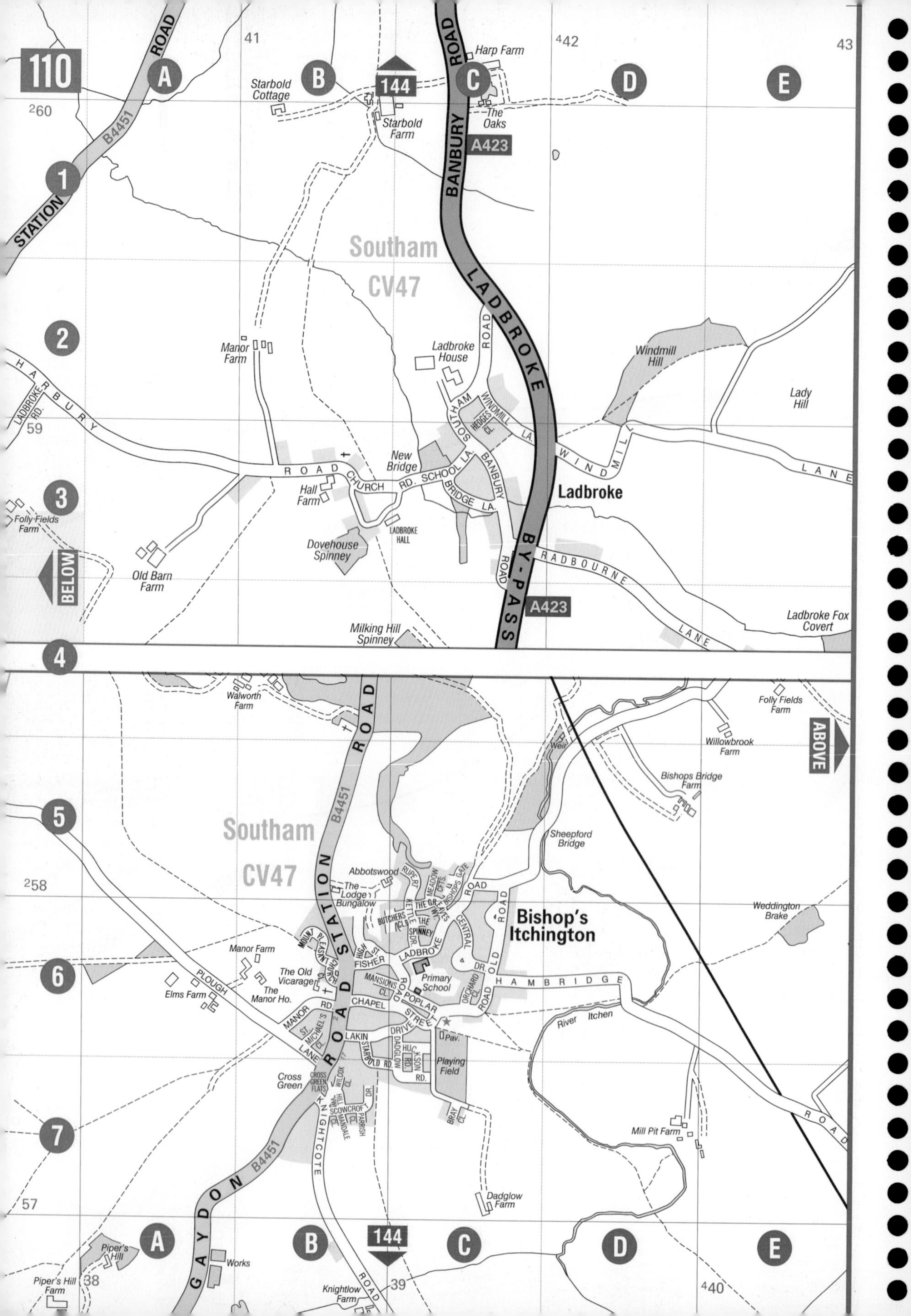

144
Harp Farm
Starbold Cottage
Starbold Farm
The Oaks
BANBURY ROAD
A423
STATION ROAD
B4451
Southam CV47
LADBROKE BY-PASS
Manor Farm
Ladbroke House
Windmill Hill
Lady Hill
HARBURY
LADBROKE RD.
SOUTHAM ROAD
WINDMILL LA.
HEDGES CL.
WINDMILL LANE
New Bridge
CHURCH RD.
SCHOOL LA.
BANBURY
BRIDGE LA.
Ladbroke
Hall Farm
Folly Fields Farm
LADBROKE HALL
Dovehouse Spinney
RADBOURNE LANE
Old Barn Farm
Ladbroke Fox Covert
Milking Hill Spinney
BELOW
Walworth Farm
Folly Fields Farm
ABOVE
Willowbrook Farm
Weir
Bishops Bridge Farm
Sheepford Bridge
Southam CV47
Abbotswood
The Lodge Bungalow
RUPERT
MEADOW
BISHOPS GATE
OLD ROAD
Bishop's Itchington
BUTCHERS CL.
THE SPINNEY
CENTRAL
Weddington Brake
MOUNT PLEASANT
HIGH ST.
FISHER
LADBROKE
Manor Farm
The Old Vicarage
Primary School
ORCHARD CL.
HAMBRIDGE ROAD
PLOUGH
Elms Farm
The Manor Ho.
MANSIONS CL.
CHAPEL
POPLAR
STREET
River Itchen
MANOR RD
ST. MICHAEL'S CL.
LANE
LAKIN DRIVE
Pav.
STARBOLD RD.
DADGLOW RD.
HUCKSON RD.
Playing Field
Cross Green
CROSS GREEN FLATS
KNIGHTCOTE
SCOWCROFT CL.
PARRISH DR.
BRAY CL.
Mill Pit Farm
GAYDON ROAD
Dadglow Farm
Piper's Hill
Piper's Hill Farm
Works
Knightlow Farm

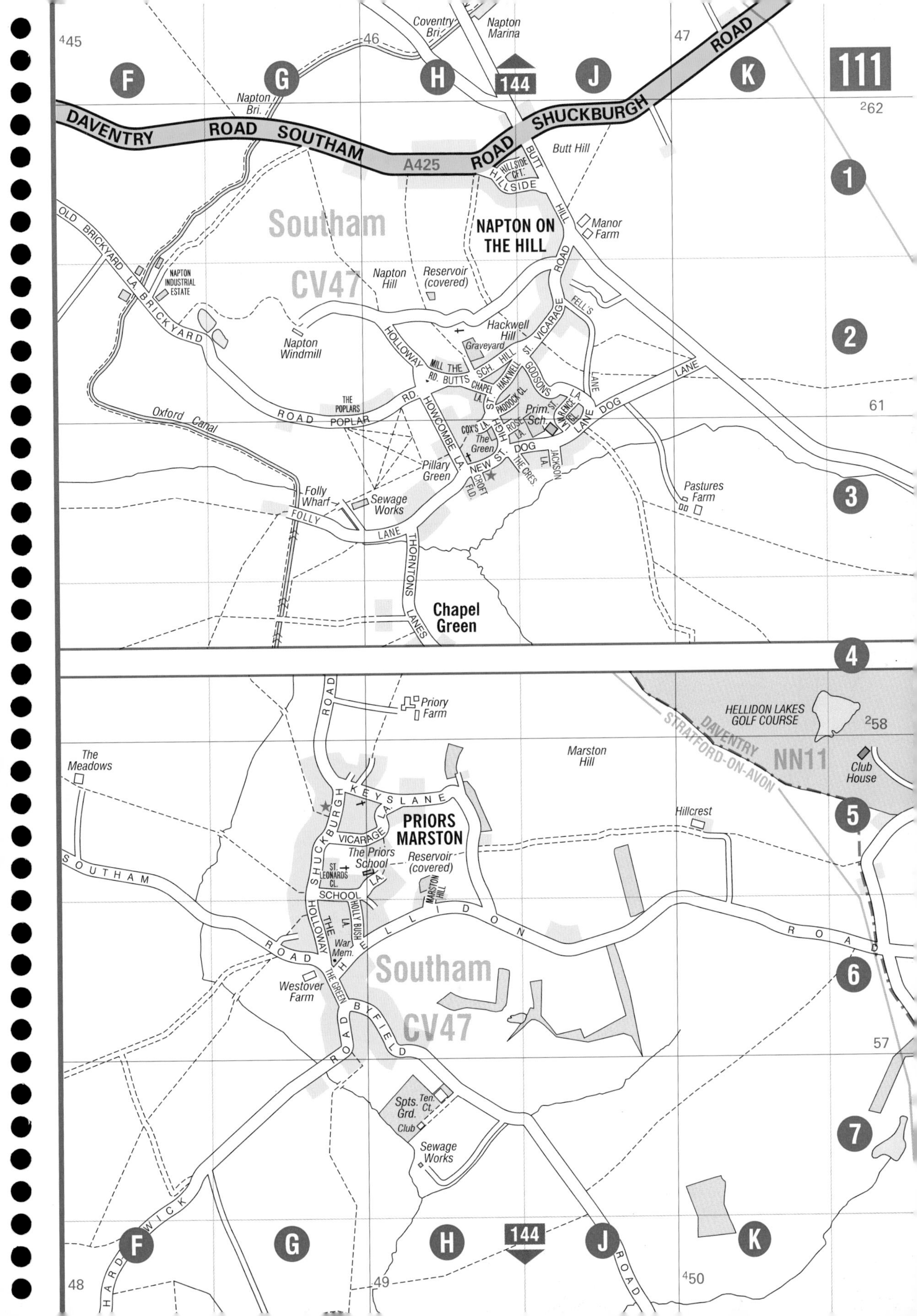

F
G
H
J
K
144
Coventry Bri.
Napton Marina
Napton Bri.
DAVENTRY ROAD SOUTHAM ROAD SHUCKBURGH ROAD
A425
Butt Hill
Manor Farm
Southam
CV47
NAPTON ON THE HILL
Napton Hill
Reservoir (covered)
NAPTON INDUSTRIAL ESTATE
OLD BRICKYARD LA.
BRICKYARD RD.
Napton Windmill
Hackwell Hill
Graveyard
HOLLOWAY
VICARAGE
FELL'S LANE
DOG LANE
THE POPLARS
POPLAR ROAD
Oxford Canal
HOWCOMBE LA.
Prim. Sch.
The Green
NEW ST.
THE CRES.
JACKSON
Pillary Green
Folly Wharf
Sewage Works
FOLLY LANE
THORNTONS LANES
Chapel Green
Pastures Farm
Priory Farm
The Meadows
HELLIDON LAKES GOLF COURSE
DAVENTRY
STRATFORD-ON-AVON
NN11
Club House
Marston Hill
Hillcrest
PRIORS MARSTON
KEYS LANE
SHUCKBURGH ROAD
VICARAGE LA.
The Priors School
Reservoir (covered)
ST. LEONARDS CL.
SCHOOL
MARSTON HILL
SOUTHAM ROAD
HOLLOWAY
THE LA.
HOLLY BUSH
HELLIDON ROAD
War Mem.
Westover Farm
THE GREEN
BYFIELD ROAD
Spts. Grd.
Ten. Ct.
Club
Sewage Works
HARDWICK
ROAD

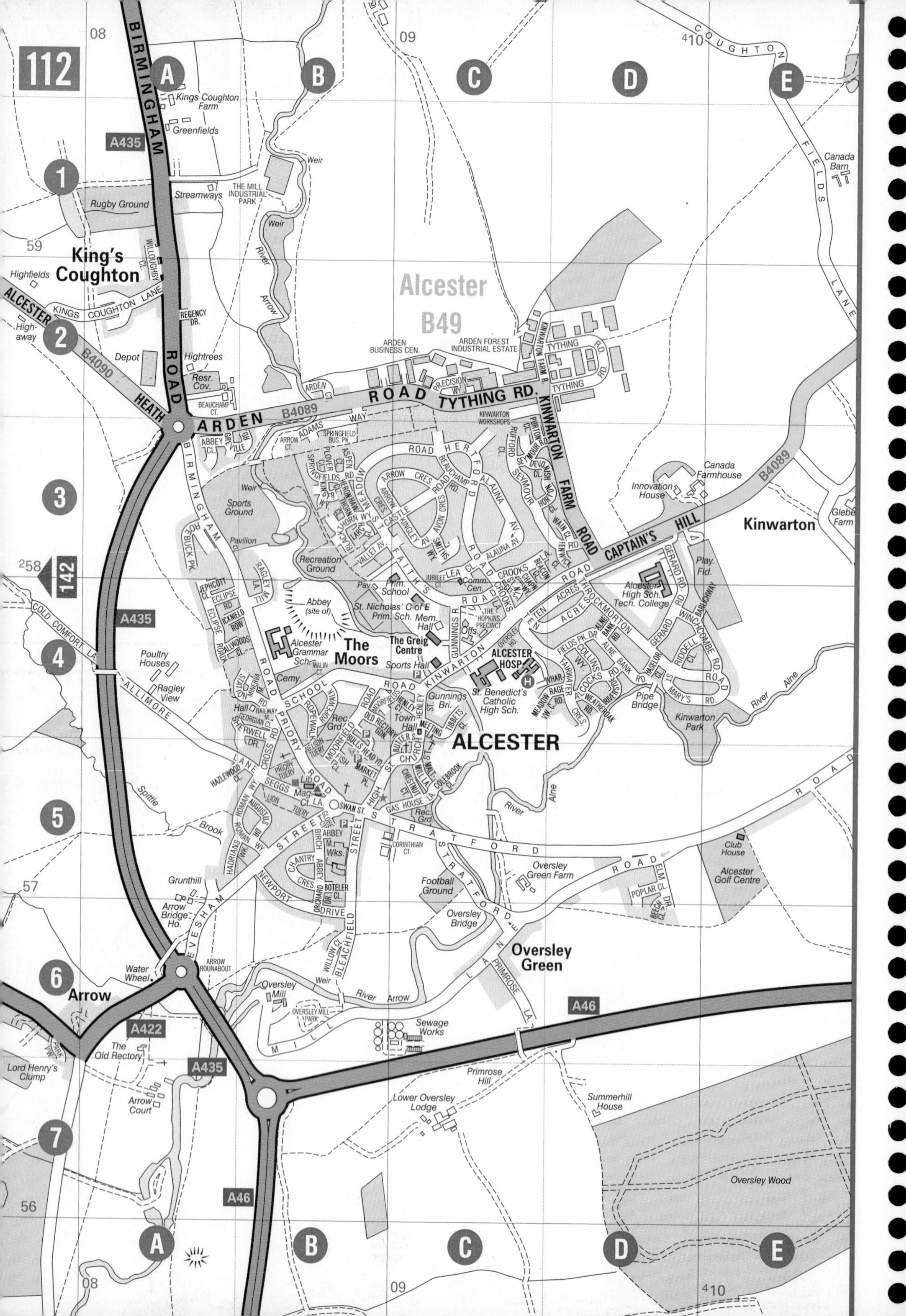
08
09
410
A
B
C
D
E
1
2
3
4
5
6
7
59
258
57
56
142
BIRMINGHAM ROAD
A435
Kings Coughton Farm
Greenfields
Rugby Ground
Streamways
THE MILL INDUSTRIAL PARK
Weir
River Arrow
King's Coughton
Highfields
KINGS COUGHTON LANE
WILLOUGHBY CL.
ALCESTER HEATH
High-away
REGENCY DR.
B4090
Depot
Hightrees
Resr. Cov.
BEAUCHAMP CT.
Alcester B49
ARDEN BUSINESS CEN.
ARDEN FOREST INDUSTRIAL ESTATE
KINWARTON FARM R.
TYTHING RD.
PRECISION WY.
ARDEN ROAD
B4089
KINWARTON WORKSHOPS
KINWARTON FARM ROAD
ABBEY CL.
ADAMS WAY
ARROW CT.
SPRINGFIELD BUS. PK.
HERTFORD ROAD
ARROW CRES.
BEAUCHAMP RD.
ALAUNA AV.
RUFFORD CL.
SEYMOUR RD.
Sports Ground
Pavilion
ROEBUCK PK.
Recreation Ground
CASTLE
FAITHS ROAD
JUBILEE CT.
LEA CL.
Comm. Cen.
CROOKS LA.
Prim. School
St. Nicholas' C of E Prim. Sch. Mem. Hall
Abbey (site of)
Alcester Grammar Sch.
The Moors
The Greig Centre
Sports Hall
GUNNINGS R.
THE HOPKINS PRECINCT
Offs.
ALCESTER HOSP.
St. Benedict's Catholic High Sch.
KINWARTON ROAD
CAPTAIN'S HILL
Kinwarton
Innovation House
Canada Farmhouse
Glebe Farm
Canada Barn
COUGHTON FIELDS LANE
Play. Fld.
Alcester High Sch. Tech. College
TEN ACRES
THROCKMORTON ROAD
GERARD RD.
WINCHCOMBE ROAD
RIDDELL CL.
ST. MARY'S RD.
Pipe Bridge
River Alne
Kinwarton Park
COLD COMFORT LA.
Poultry Houses
Ragley View
ALLIMORE LA.
JEPHCOTT CL.
ECLIPSE RD.
ECLIPSE ROAD
ICKNIELD ROW
RAGLEY MILL LA.
Cemy.
SCHOOL ROAD
PRIORY ROAD
ROPEWALK
Rec. Grd.
MOORFIELD RD.
HENLEY ST.
Town Hall
Gunnings Bri.
TIBBETS
ALCESTER
SHERWELL DR.
HAZLEWOOD CL.
SEGGS LANE
Mag. Ct.
SWAN ST.
GAS HOUSE LA.
COLEBROOK CL.
CHURCH ST.
BUTTER ST.
River Alne
Spittle Brook
ROMAN WY.
HADRIANS WK.
EVESHAM STREET
ABBEY
BIRCH
M. Wks.
CHANTRY CRES.
BOTELER CL.
NEWPORT DRIVE
ORCHARD DR.
CORINTHIAN CT.
STRATFORD ROAD
Football Ground
Oversley Green Farm
Oversley Bridge
Club House
Alcester Golf Centre
ELM DR.
POPLAR CL.
BEECH CL.
Oversley Green
PRIMROSE LA.
Grunthill
Arrow Bridge Ho.
ARROW ROUNABOUT
Water Wheel
Arrow
WILLOW CL.
BLEACHFIELD
Oversley Mill
OVERSLEY MILL PARK
MILL LANE
River Arrow
A46
A422
Sewage Works
The Old Rectory
Lord Henry's Clump
Arrow Court
Primrose Hill
Lower Oversley Lodge
Summerhill House
Oversley Wood

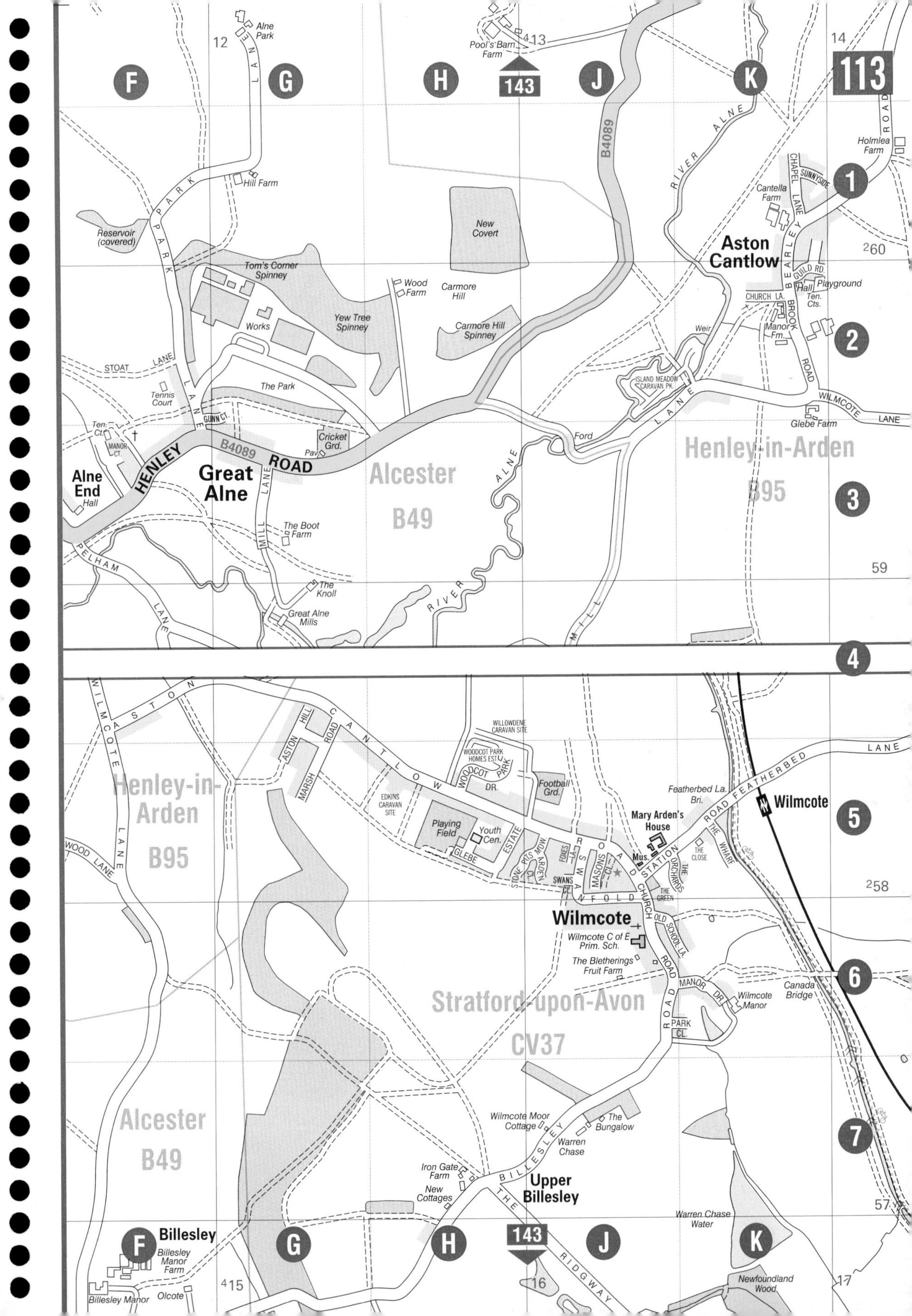

Alne Park
Pool's Barn Farm
143
Hill Farm
Reservoir (covered)
New Covert
Tom's Corner Spinney
Works
Yew Tree Spinney
Wood Farm
Carmore Hill
Carmore Hill Spinney
Aston Cantlow
Cantella Farm
Holmlea Farm
Playground
Hall
Ten. Cts.
Manor Fm.
Weir
ISLAND MEADOW CARAVAN PK.
STOAT LANE
Tennis Court
The Park
GUNN CT.
Cricket Grd.
Pav.
Ford
Glebe Farm
Henley-in-Arden B95
Alne End
Hall
HENLEY ROAD
B4089
Great Alne
Alcester B49
MILL LANE
The Boot Farm
The Knoll
Great Alne Mills
PELHAM LANE
RIVER ALNE
ASTON CANTLOW ROAD
WILMCOTE LANE
WILLOWDENE CARAVAN SITE
WOODCOT PARK HOMES EST.
Football Grd.
EDKINS CARAVAN SITE
Playing Field
Youth Cen.
Featherbed La. Bri.
FEATHERBED LANE
Wilmcote
Mary Arden's House
Mus.
THE CLOSE
THE WHARF
THE ORCHARDS
THE GREEN
WOOD LANE
Wilmcote C of E Prim. Sch.
The Bletherings Fruit Farm
MANOR DR.
Wilmcote Manor
Canada Bridge
PARK CL.
Stratford-upon-Avon CV37
Wilmcote Moor Cottage
The Bungalow
Warren Chase
Iron Gate Farm
New Cottages
BILLESLEY
Upper Billesley
THE RIDGWAY
Warren Chase Water
Billesley
Billesley Manor Farm
Billesley Manor
Olcote
Newfoundland Wood

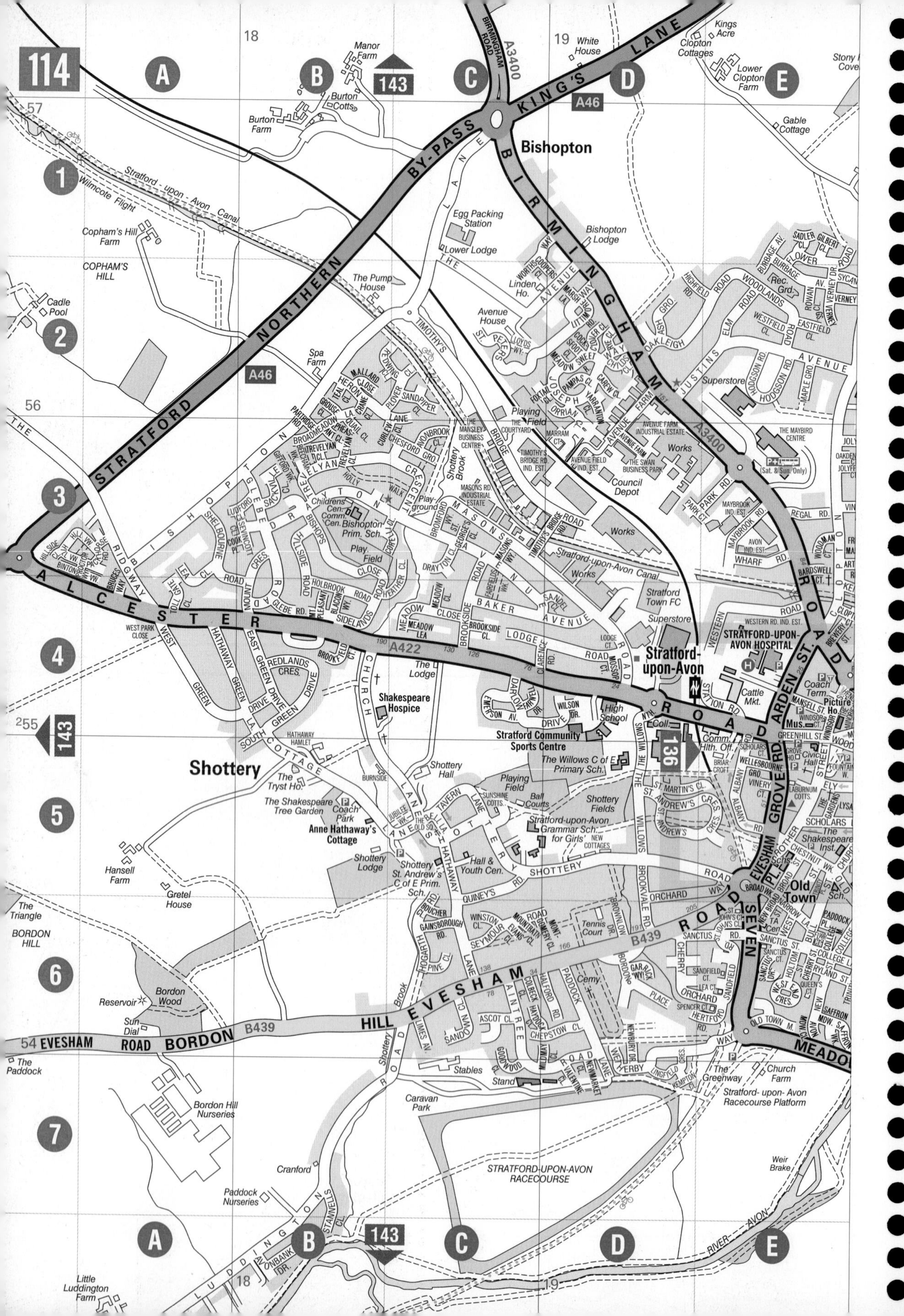
143
136
Bishopton
Shottery
Stratford-upon-Avon
Old Town
STRATFORD-UPON-AVON HOSPITAL
STRATFORD-UPON-AVON RACECOURSE
Stratford- upon- Avon Racecourse Platform
Stratford - upon - Avon Canal
Wilmcote Flight
STRATFORD NORTHERN BY-PASS
KING'S LANE
BIRMINGHAM ROAD
ALCESTER ROAD
EVESHAM ROAD
BORDON HILL
A46
A3400
A422
B439
Manor Farm
Burton Cotts.
Burton Farm
White House
Kings Acre
Clopton Cottages
Lower Clopton Farm
Gable Cottage
Copham's Hill Farm
COPHAM'S HILL
Cadle Pool
Egg Packing Station
Lower Lodge
The Pump House
Spa Farm
Bishopton Lodge
Linden Ho.
Avenue House
Superstore
THE MAYBIRD CENTRE
Council Depot
Works
Stratford Town FC
Shakespeare Hospice
The Lodge
Stratford Community Sports Centre
High School
Anne Hathaway's Cottage
The Shakespeare Tree Garden
Shottery Hall
Playing Field
Shottery Fields
Stratford-upon-Avon Grammar Sch. for Girls'
Hansell Farm
Gretel House
The Triangle
Bordon Wood
Reservoir
Sun Dial
The Paddock
Bordon Hill Nurseries
Caravan Park
Cranford
Paddock Nurseries
Little Luddington Farm
Church Farm
The Greenway
Weir Brake
RIVER AVON
LUDDINGTON

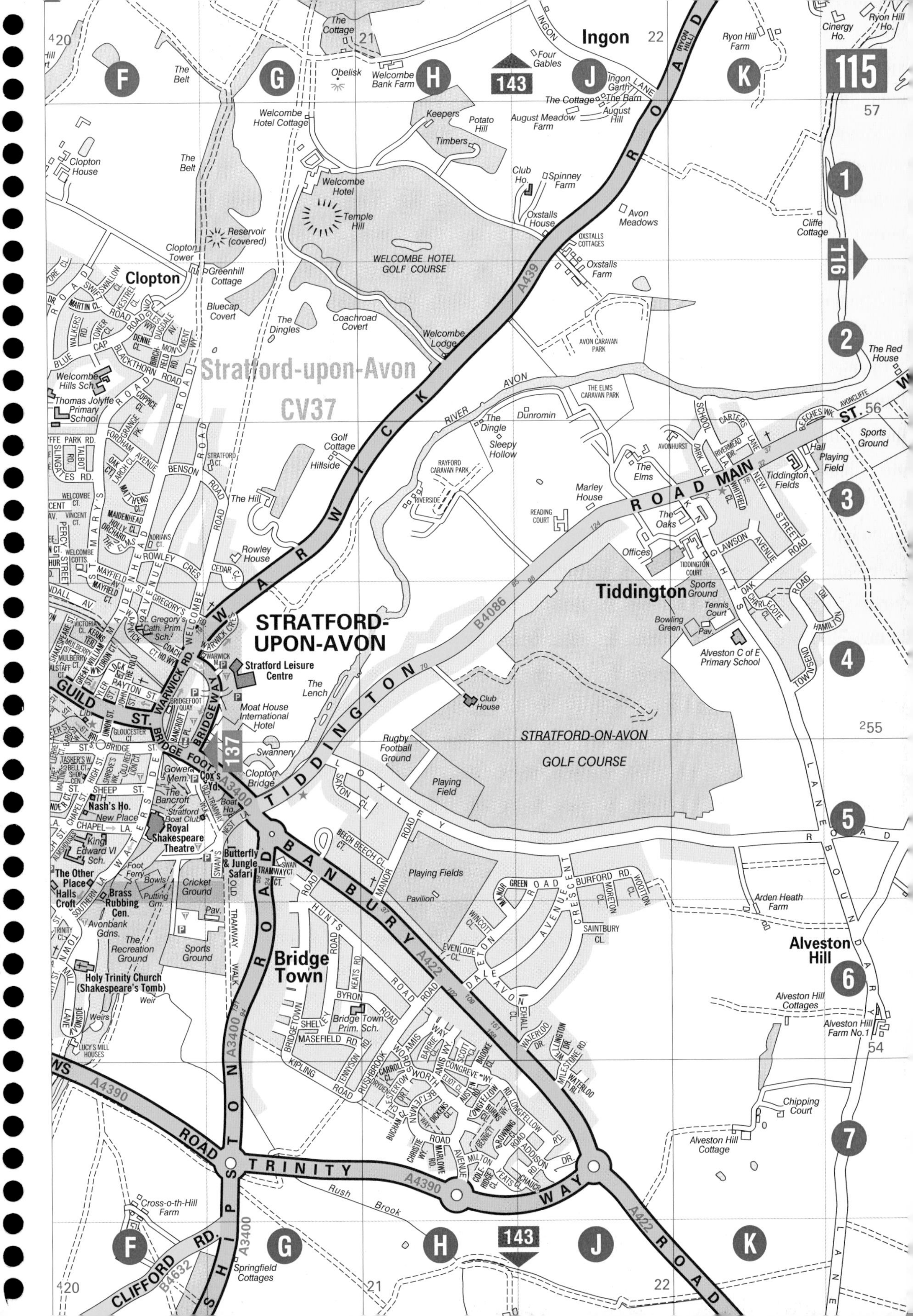

115
143
116
137
Ingon
Four Gables
Ingon Garth
The Cottage
The Barn
August Hill
August Meadow Farm
Ryon Hill Farm
Cinergy Ho.
Ryon Hill Ho.
The Cottage
Obelisk
Welcombe Bank Farm
Keepers
Potato Hill
Timbers
The Belt
Clopton House
Welcombe Hotel Cottage
Welcombe Hotel
Temple Hill
Reservoir (covered)
Clopton Tower
Greenhill Cottage
WELCOMBE HOTEL GOLF COURSE
Club Ho.
Spinney Farm
Oxstalls House
OXSTALLS COTTAGES
Oxstalls Farm
Avon Meadows
Cliffe Cottage
Clopton
Bluecap Covert
The Dingles
Coachroad Covert
Welcombe Lodge
AVON CARAVAN PARK
The Red House
Stratford-upon-Avon
CV37
Welcombe Hills Sch.
Thomas Jolyffe Primary School
RIVER AVON
THE ELMS CARAVAN PARK
The Dingle
Dunromin
Sleepy Hollow
RAYFORD CARAVAN PARK
RIVERSIDE
Golf Cottage
Hillside
The Hill
Rowley House
The Elms
Marley House
READING COURT
The Oaks
Offices
TIDDINGTON COURT
Tiddington
Sports Ground
Tennis Court
Bowling Green
Pav.
Alveston C of E Primary School
Hall
Playing Field
Tiddington Fields
Sports Ground
STRATFORD-UPON-AVON
St. Gregory's Cath. Prim. Sch.
Stratford Leisure Centre
Moat House International Hotel
The Lench
Club House
STRATFORD-ON-AVON GOLF COURSE
Rugby Football Ground
Playing Field
Swannery
Clopton Bridge
Gower Mem.
Cox's Yds.
The Bancroft
Stratford Boat Club
Boat Ho.
Nash's Ho.
New Place
King Edward VI Sch.
Royal Shakespeare Theatre
Butterfly & Jungle Safari
The Other Place
Halls Croft
Brass Rubbing Cen.
Foot Ferry
Bowls
Putting Grn.
Cricket Ground
Avonbank Gdns.
The Recreation Ground
Sports Ground
Holy Trinity Church (Shakespeare's Tomb)
Weir
Weirs
LUCY'S MILL HOUSES
Playing Fields
Pavilion
Bridge Town
Bridge Town Prim. Sch.
Arden Heath Farm
Alveston Hill
Alveston Hill Cottages
Alveston Hill Farm No.1
Chipping Court
Alveston Hill Cottage
Cross-o-th-Hill Farm
Springfield Cottages
Rush Brook
WARWICK ROAD
A439
TIDDINGTON ROAD
B4086
MAIN ROAD
MAIN ST.
BANBURY ROAD
A422
TRINITY WAY
A4390
SHIPSTON ROAD
A3400
CLIFFORD RD.
B4632
LOXLEY ROAD
BOUNDARY LANE
GUILD ST.
BRIDGE ST.
BRIDGEWAY
BRIDGEFOOT
WATERSIDE
SOUTHERN LA.
TRAMWAY WALK
F
G
H
J
K
1
2
3
4
5
6
7
420
21
22
57
56
255
54

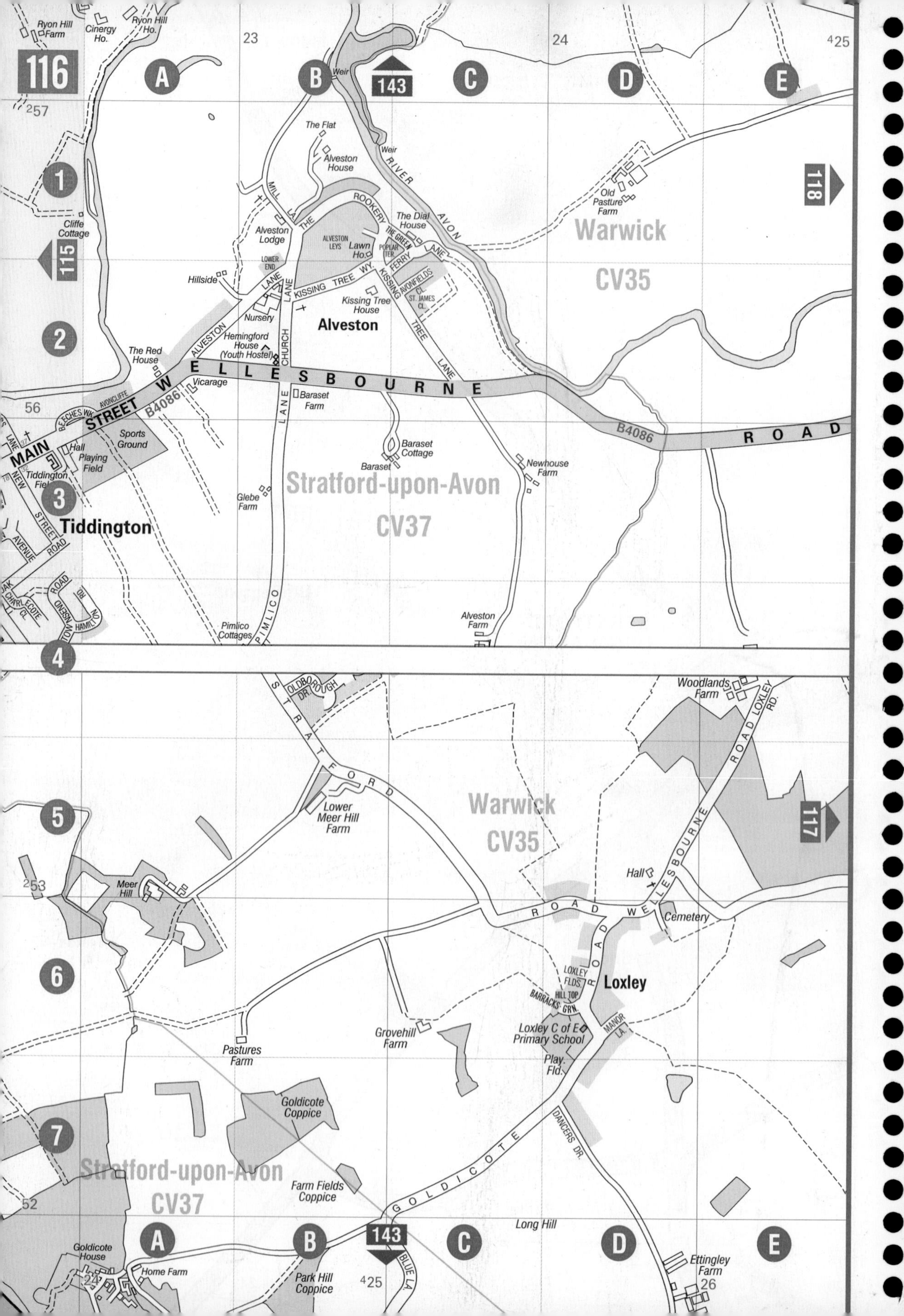

Ryon Hill Farm
Cinergy Ho.
Ryon Hill Ho.
143
Weir
The Flat
Alveston House
RIVER AVON
118
Old Pasture Farm
Warwick CV35
Cliffe Cottage
115
Alveston Lodge
THE ROOKERY
The Dial House
ALVESTON LEYS
Lawn Ho.
POPLAR TER.
THE GREEN
FERRY LANE
LOWER END
Hillside
KISSING TREE WY.
AVONFIELDS CL.
ST. JAMES CL.
Kissing Tree House
Nursery
Alveston
Hemingford House (Youth Hostel)
The Red House
ALVESTON
CHURCH LANE
KISSING TREE LANE
WELLESBOURNE
Vicarage
B4086
ROAD
Baraset Farm
AVONCLIFFE
BEECHES WK.
STREET
MAIN
Sports Ground
Hall
Playing Field
Baraset Cottage
Baraset
Newhouse Farm
Tiddington Fields
Stratford-upon-Avon CV37
Glebe Farm
Tiddington
NEW STREET
AVENUE
ROAD
CHARLECOTE CL.
TOWNSEND RD.
HAMILTON
PIMLICO LANE
Pimlico Cottages
Alveston Farm
OLDBOROUGH DR.
STRATFORD ROAD
Woodlands Farm
LOXLEY RD.
Lower Meer Hill Farm
Warwick CV35
117
Meer Hill
Hall
WELLESBOURNE ROAD
Cemetery
LOXLEY FLDS.
HILL TOP
BARRACKS GRN.
Loxley
Loxley C of E Primary School
Play. Fld.
MANOR LA.
Pastures Farm
Grovehill Farm
Goldicote Coppice
DANCERS DR.
Stratford-upon-Avon CV37
Farm Fields Coppice
GOLDICOTE
Long Hill
Goldicote House
Home Farm
Park Hill Coppice
BLUE LA.
Ettingley Farm
143
23
24
25
257
56
253
52
26
A B C D E
1 2 3 4 5 6 7

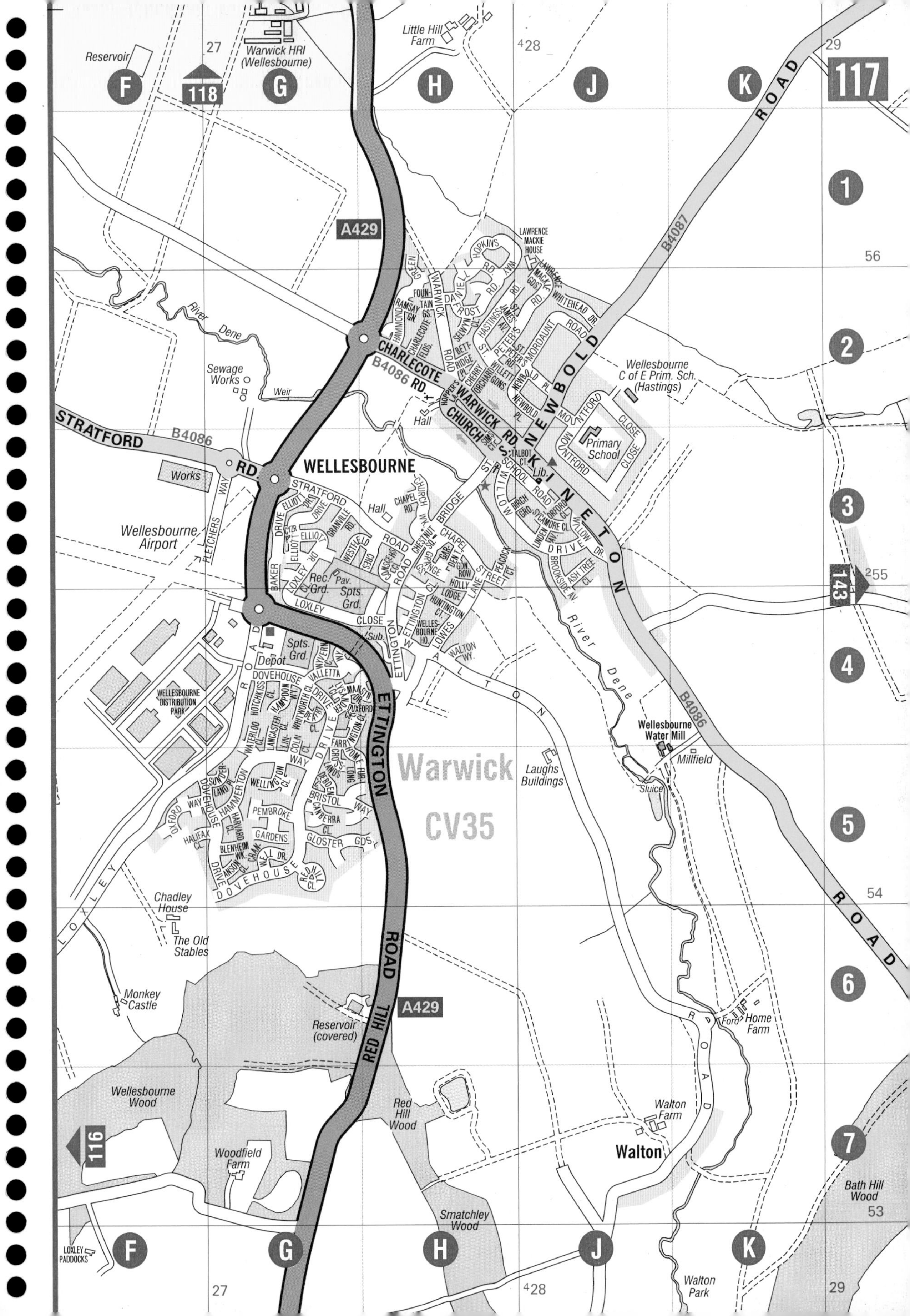
Reservoir
Warwick HRI (Wellesbourne)
Little Hill Farm
118
A429
B4087
ROAD
LAWRENCE MACKIE HOUSE
WHITEHEAD DR.
River Dene
Sewage Works
Weir
STRATFORD
B4086
RD.
Works
WELLESBOURNE
CHARLECOTE
B4086 RD.
WARWICK RD.
CHURCH
NEWBOLD
KINETON
Wellesbourne C of E Prim. Sch. (Hastings)
Primary School
Lib.
Hall
Wellesbourne Airport
FLETCHERS WAY
Rec. Grd.
Pav.
Spts. Grd.
Depot
WELLESBOURNE DISTRIBUTION PARK
ETTINGTON
WALTON
Warwick
CV35
Laughs Buildings
Wellesbourne Water Mill
Millfield
Sluice
B4086
143
LOXLEY
Chadley House
The Old Stables
Monkey Castle
Reservoir (covered)
RED HILL ROAD
A429
Wellesbourne Wood
116
Red Hill Wood
Woodfield Farm
Smatchley Wood
Walton Farm
Walton
Ford
Home Farm
Bath Hill Wood
LOXLEY PADDOCKS
Walton Park
F
G
H
J
K
1
2
3
4
5
6
7
27
428
29
56
55
54
53

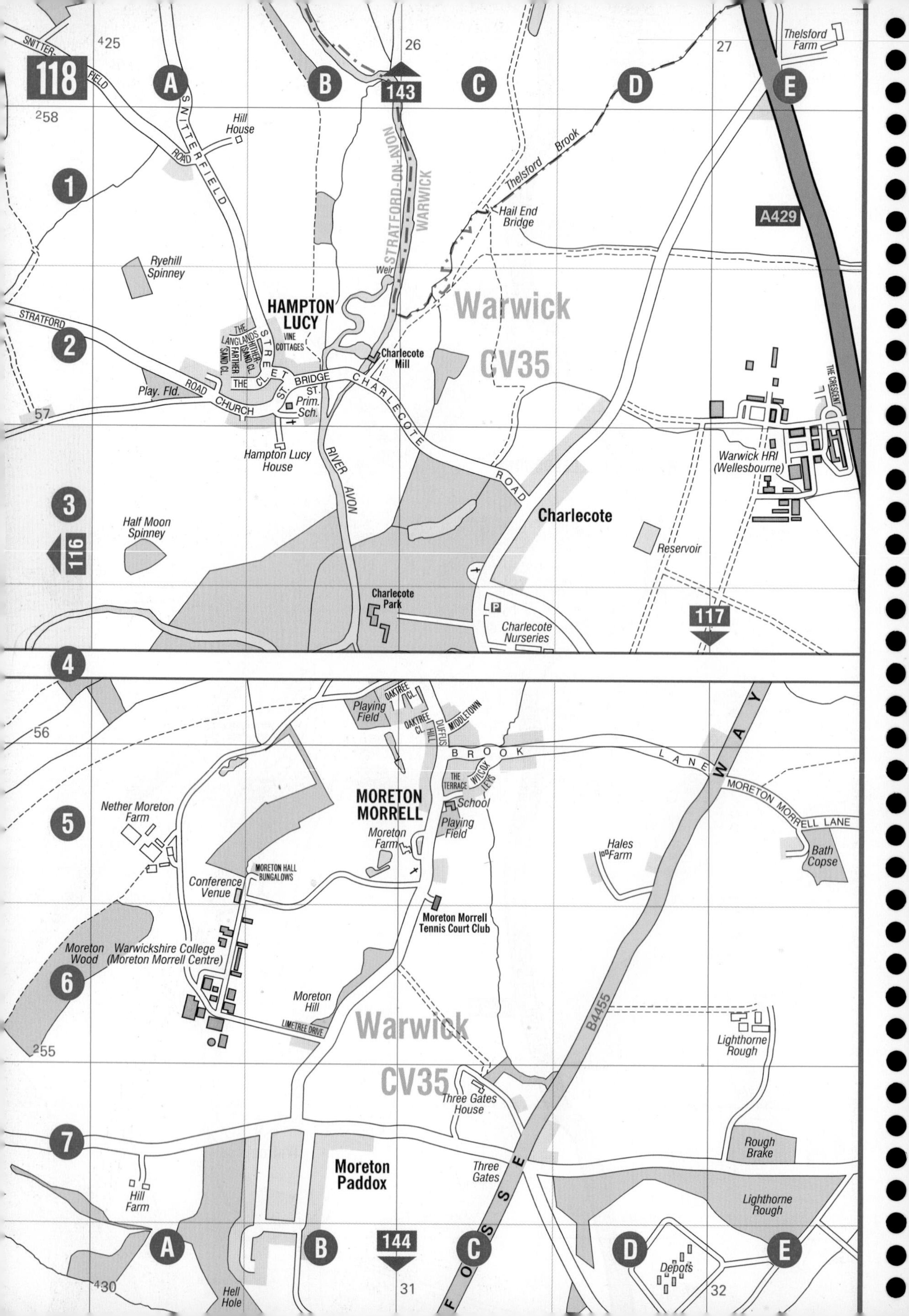

118
A
B
C
D
E
143
116
117
144
425
26
27
258
57
56
255
430
31
32
1
2
3
4
5
6
7
SNITTERFIELD ROAD
Hill House
Thelsford Farm
Thelsford Brook
Hail End Bridge
STRATFORD-ON-AVON
WARWICK
A429
Ryehill Spinney
Weir
HAMPTON LUCY
VINE COTTAGES
Warwick
CV35
STRATFORD ROAD
THE LANGLANDS
CHURCH ST.
Charlecote Mill
BRIDGE ST.
CHARLECOTE ROAD
Play. Fld.
Prim. Sch.
THE CRESCENT
Hampton Lucy House
RIVER AVON
Warwick HRI (Wellesbourne)
Half Moon Spinney
Charlecote
Reservoir
Charlecote Park
Charlecote Nurseries
Playing Field
OAKTREE CL.
MIDDLETOWN
DUFFUS HILL
BROOK LANE
FOSSE WAY
MORETON MORRELL LANE
THE TERRACE
WILCOX LEYS
School
Nether Moreton Farm
MORETON MORRELL
Playing Field
Moreton Farm
Hales Farm
Bath Copse
MORETON HALL BUNGALOWS
Conference Venue
Moreton Morrell Tennis Court Club
Moreton Wood
Warwickshire College (Moreton Morrell Centre)
Moreton Hill
LIMETREE DRIVE
B4455
Lighthorne Rough
Three Gates House
Rough Brake
Moreton Paddox
Three Gates
Hill Farm
Lighthorne Rough
Depots
Hell Hole

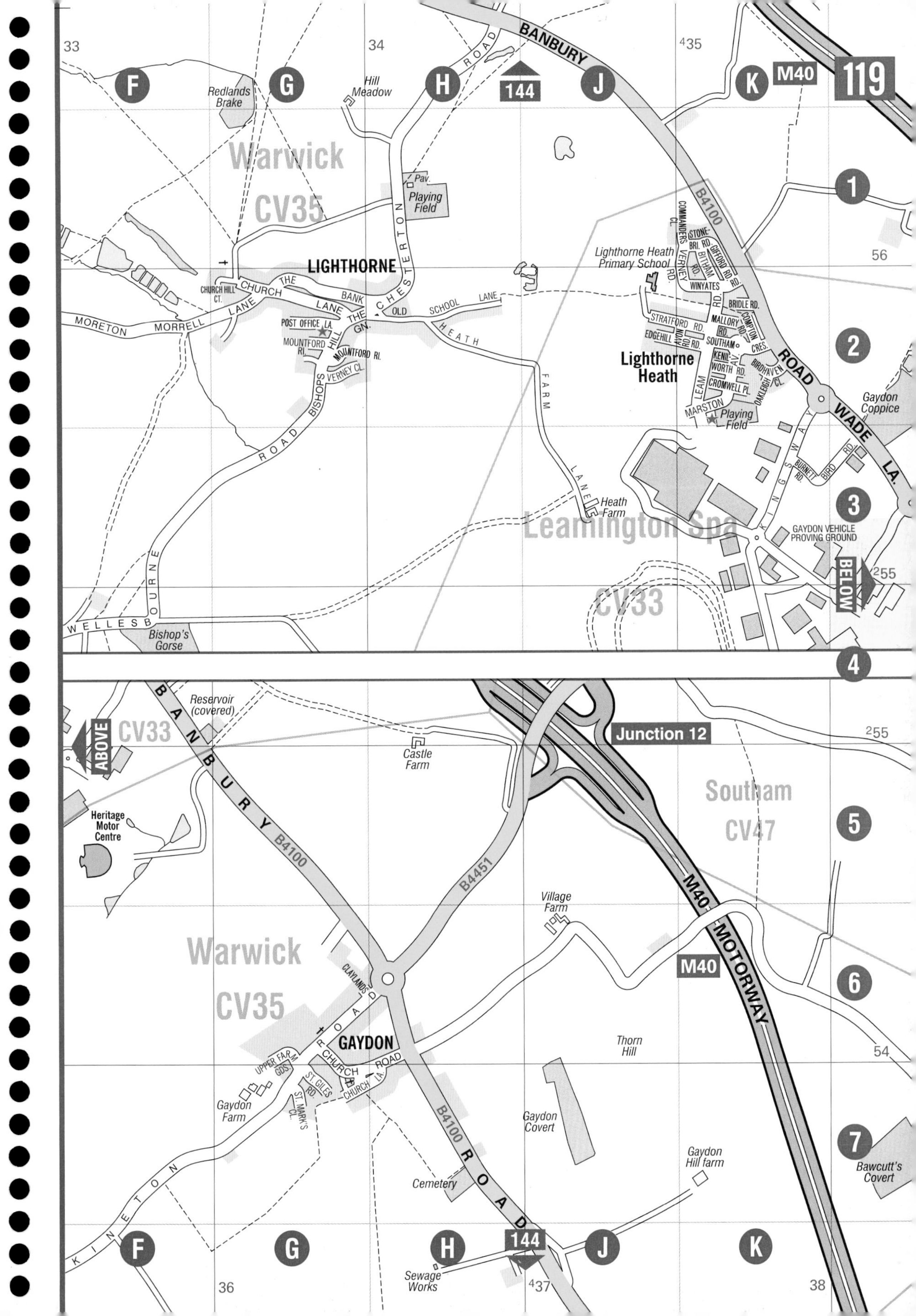

M40
144
BANBURY ROAD
Redlands Brake
Hill Meadow
Warwick CV35
Playing Field
LIGHTHORNE
CHURCH HILL CT.
CHURCH LANE
THE BANK
CHESTERTON
MORETON MORRELL LANE
POST OFFICE LA.
THE GN.
OLD SCHOOL LANE
HEATH FARM LANE
MOUNTFORD RI.
VERNEY CL.
BISHOPS HILL
BISHOPS ROAD
Lighthorne Heath Primary School
B4100
COMMANDERS CL.
VERNEY RD.
STONE-BRI. RD.
GIFFORD RD.
BITHAM RD.
WINYATES RD.
BRIDLE RD.
STRATFORD RD.
EDGEHILL RD.
AVON RD.
MALLORY RD.
COMPTON CRES.
SOUTHAM
KENILWORTH RD.
BIRDHAVEN CL.
CROMWELL PL.
OAKLEIGH
LEAM AV.
MARSTON
Lighthorne Heath
Playing Field
Gaydon Coppice
WADE LA.
KINGSWAY
BURNETT RD.
BIRD RD.
Heath Farm
Leamington Spa
GAYDON VEHICLE PROVING GROUND
CV33
WELLESBOURNE ROAD
Bishop's Gorse
BELOW
ABOVE
Reservoir (covered)
Junction 12
Castle Farm
Heritage Motor Centre
Southam CV47
B4451
Village Farm
M40 MOTORWAY
CLAYLANDS RD.
GAYDON
UPPER FARM GDS.
CHURCH RD.
CHURCH LA.
ST. GILES RD.
ST. MARK'S CL.
Gaydon Farm
Thorn Hill
Gaydon Covert
Gaydon Hill farm
Bawcutt's Covert
Cemetery
KINETON ROAD
Sewage Works

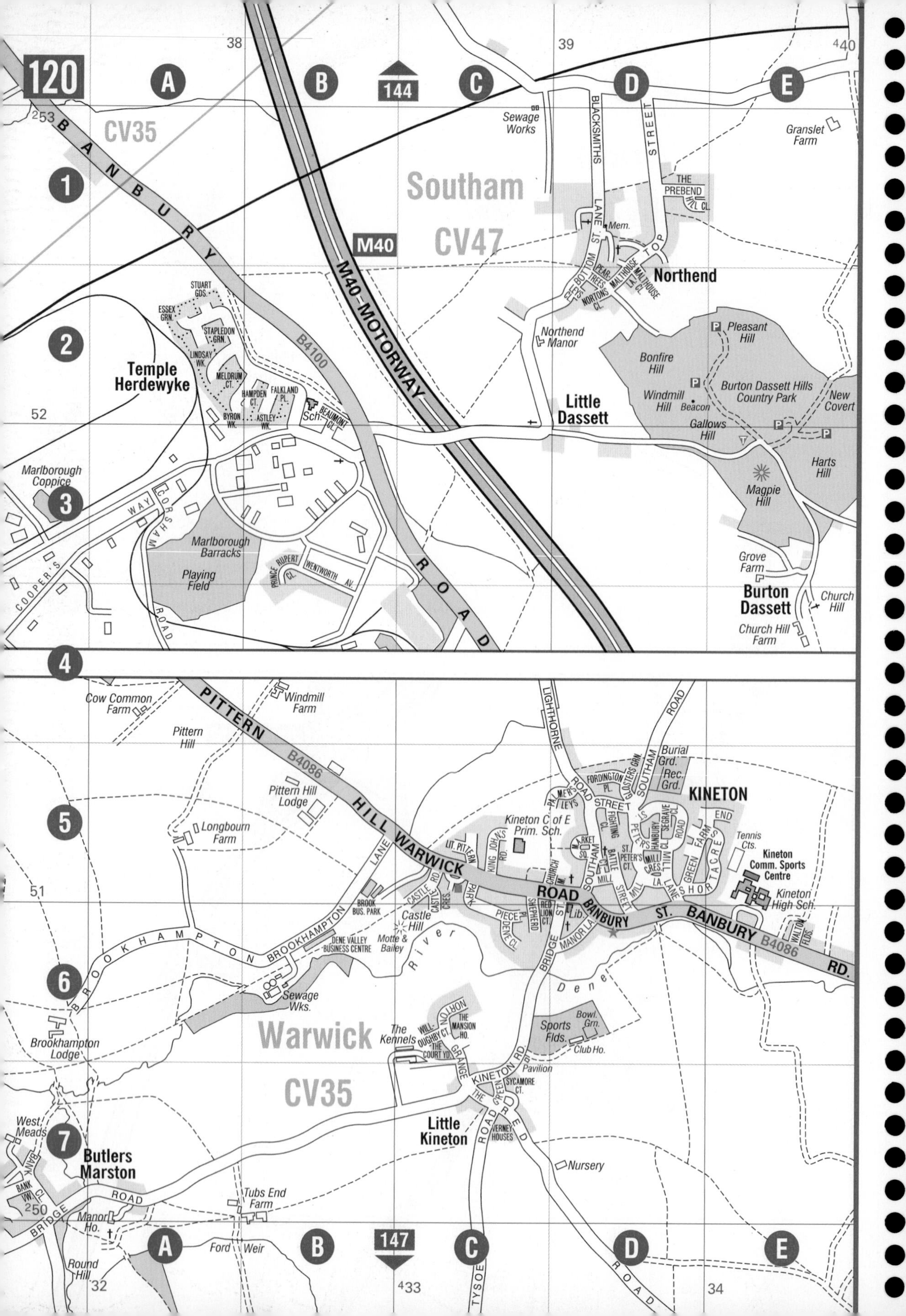

144
147
Southam CV47
Warwick CV35
CV35
Temple Herdewyke
Northend
Little Dassett
Burton Dassett
KINETON
Little Kineton
Butlers Marston
M40 MOTORWAY
BANBURY ROAD
B4100
PITTERN HILL
B4086
WARWICK ROAD
BANBURY ST.
BANBURY RD.
Sewage Works
Granslet Farm
Northend Manor
Pleasant Hill
Bonfire Hill
Windmill Hill
Beacon
Burton Dassett Hills Country Park
New Covert
Gallows Hill
Harts Hill
Magpie Hill
Grove Farm
Church Hill
Church Hill Farm
Marlborough Coppice
Marlborough Barracks
Playing Field
Cow Common Farm
Windmill Farm
Pittern Hill
Pittern Hill Lodge
Longbourn Farm
Kineton C of E Prim. Sch.
Kineton Comm. Sports Centre
Kineton High Sch.
Tennis Cts.
Burial Grd.
Rec. Grd.
Castle Hill
Motte & Bailey
River Dene
Brookhampton Lodge
Sewage Wks.
The Kennels
Sports Flds.
Bowl. Grn.
Club Ho.
Pavilion
Nursery
Tubs End Farm
Manor Ho.
Ford
Weir
Round Hill
West Meads
BROOKHAMPTON LANE
BROOK BUS. PARK
DENE VALLEY BUSINESS CENTRE
LIGHTHORNE ROAD
SOUTHAM ROAD
SOUTHAM STREET
BRIDGE STREET
KINETON RD.
TYSOE ROAD

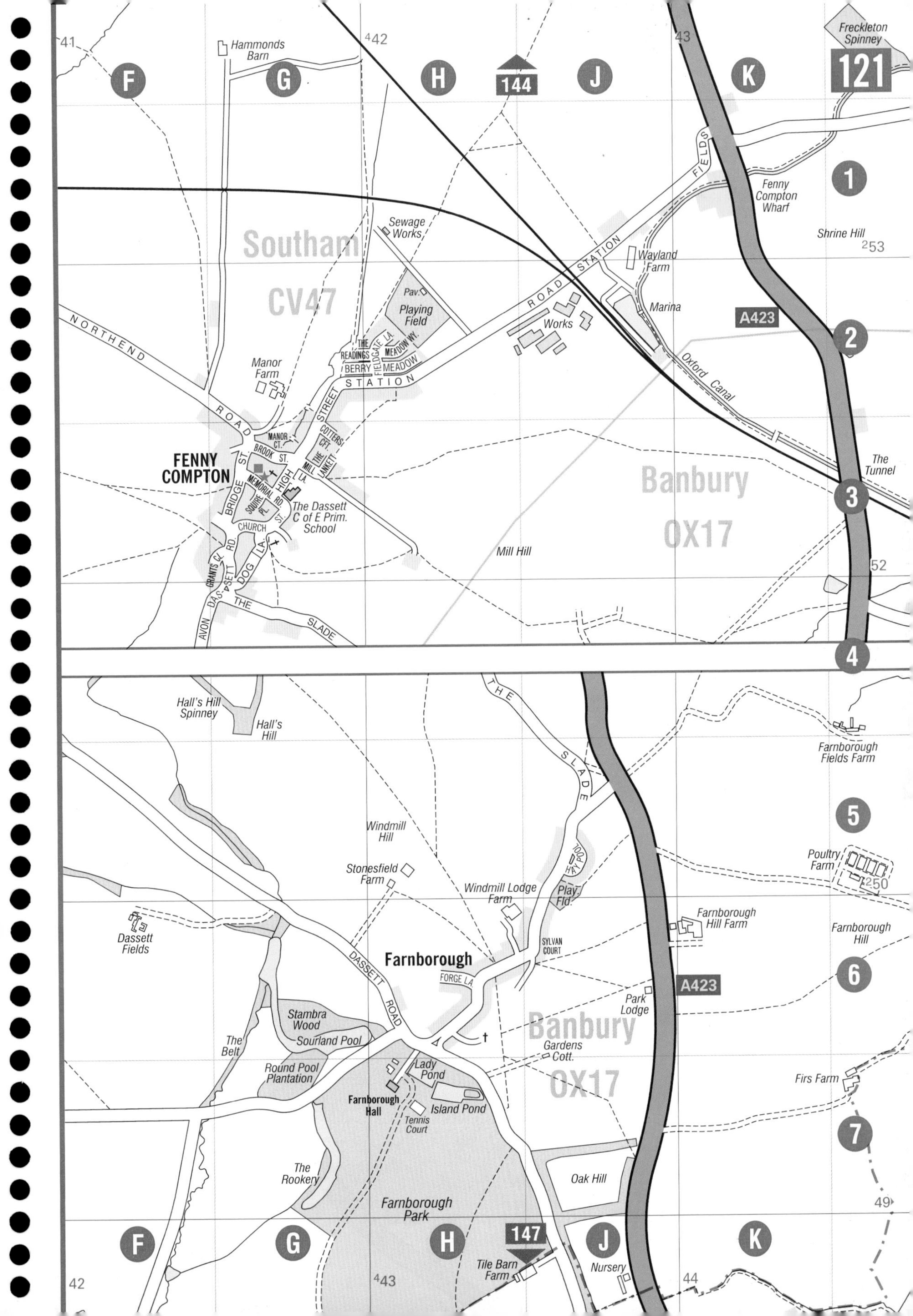

121
144
147
Freckleton Spinney
Hammonds Barn
Southam CV47
Banbury OX17
Sewage Works
Playing Field
Pav.
Wayland Farm
Marina
Works
Fenny Compton Wharf
Shrine Hill
A423
Oxford Canal
The Tunnel
Manor Farm
FENNY COMPTON
The Dassett C of E Prim. School
Mill Hill
NORTHEND ROAD
STATION ROAD
FIELDS
STATION
BERRY
MEADOW
THE READINGS
FIELDGATE LA.
MEADOW WY.
STREET
MANOR CT.
BROOK ST.
COTTERS CFT.
THE LINKETT
MILL LA.
HIGH
MEMORIAL RD
SQUIRE PL.
BRIDGE ST.
CHURCH ST.
DOG LA.
GRANTS CL.
DASSETT RD.
AVON
THE SLADE
Hall's Hill Spinney
Hall's Hill
Farnborough Fields Farm
Windmill Hill
Stonesfield Farm
Windmill Lodge Farm
HAY POOL
Play. Fld.
Poultry Farm
Farnborough Hill Farm
Farnborough Hill
Dassett Fields
Farnborough
FORGE LA.
SYLVAN COURT
DASSETT ROAD
Park Lodge
Stambra Wood
Sourland Pool
The Belt
Round Pool Plantation
Lady Pond
Gardens Cott.
Farnborough Hall
Island Pond
Tennis Court
Firs Farm
The Rookery
Oak Hill
Farnborough Park
Tile Barn Farm
Nursery

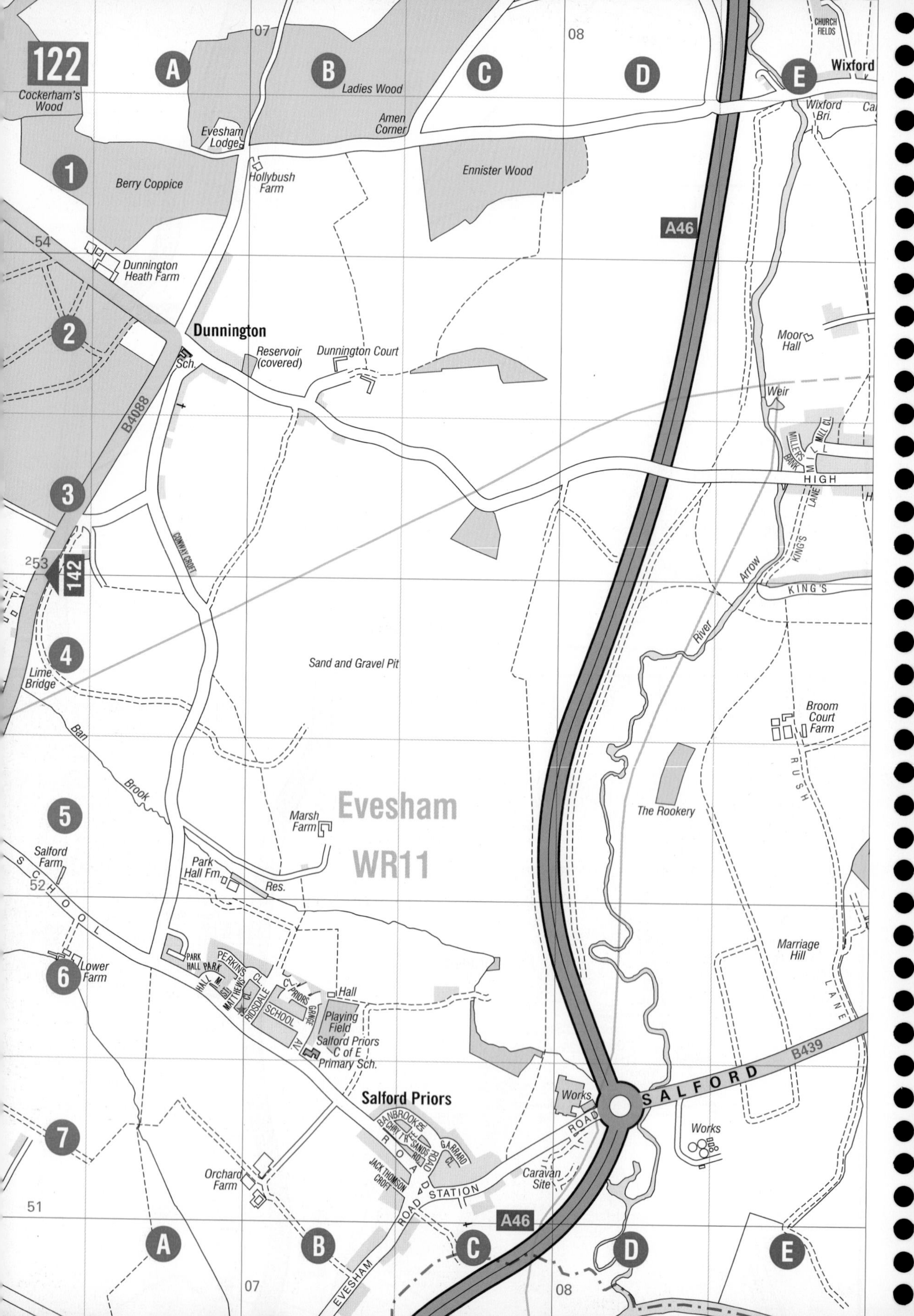
A
B
C
D
E
07
08
Cockerham's Wood
Ladies Wood
Amen Corner
Evesham Lodge
Wixford
Wixford Bri.
1
Berry Coppice
Hollybush Farm
Ennister Wood
A46
54
Dunnington Heath Farm
2
Dunnington
Sch.
Reservoir (covered)
Dunnington Court
Moor Hall
Weir
B4088
HIGH
3
CONWAY CROFT
KING'S
LANE
53
142
Arrow
River
4
Lime Bridge
Sand and Gravel Pit
Broom Court Farm
Bar Brook
RUSH
The Rookery
5
Evesham
WR11
Marsh Farm
Salford Farm
Park Hall Fm.
Res.
52
SCHOOL
Marriage Hill
6
Lower Farm
PARK HALL
PERKINS CL.
Hall
Playing Field
Salford Priors C of E Primary Sch.
RIDSDALE
SCHOOL AV.
LANE
B439
SALFORD
Salford Priors
Works
ROAD
7
BANBROOK
GARRARD CL.
Orchard Farm
JACK THOMSON CROFT
Caravan Site
STATION
51
A46
EVESHAM
A
B
C
D
E
07
08

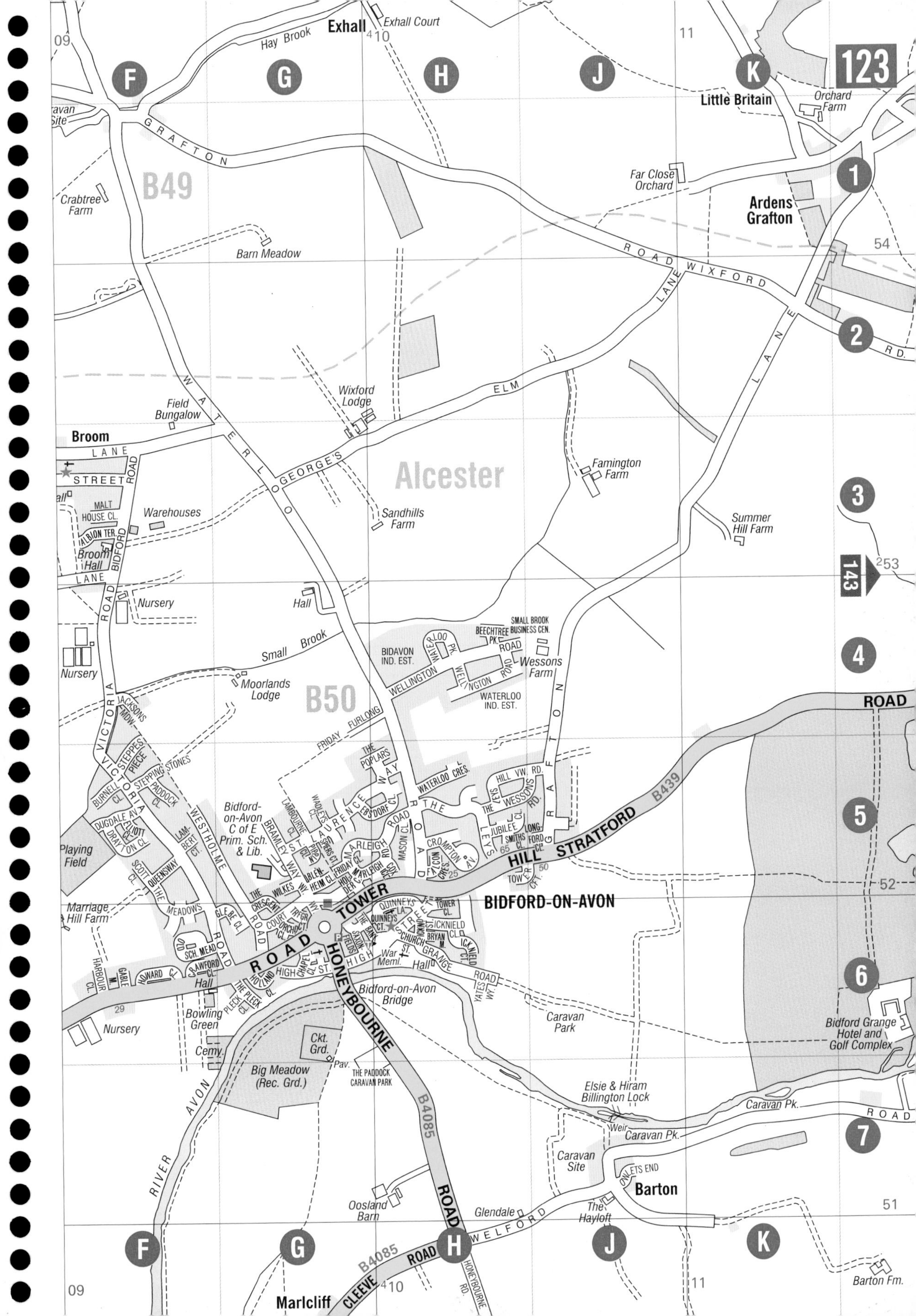
123
Exhall
Exhall Court
Hay Brook
Little Britain
Orchard Farm
Caravan Site
GRAFTON
B49
Crabtree Farm
Far Close Orchard
Ardens Grafton
Barn Meadow
ROAD WIXFORD
LANE
RD.
ELM
Wixford Lodge
Field Bungalow
Broom
WATERLOO
GEORGE'S
Alcester
Famington Farm
Sandhills Farm
Warehouses
Summer Hill Farm
143
Broom Hall
Nursery
Hall
SMALL BROOK BUSINESS CEN.
BEECHTREE PK.
BIDAVON IND. EST.
Small Brook
Wessons Farm
WATERLOO IND. EST.
Moorlands Lodge
B50
WELLINGTON
FRIDAY FURLONG
GRAFTON
ROAD
B439
STRATFORD
HILL
Bidford-on-Avon C of E Prim. Sch. & Lib.
Playing Field
Marriage Hill Farm
BIDFORD-ON-AVON
TOWER
ROAD
HONEYBOURNE
Bidford-on-Avon Bridge
Bowling Green
Nursery
Cemy.
Ckt. Grd.
Big Meadow (Rec. Grd.)
THE PADDOCK CARAVAN PARK
Caravan Park
Bidford Grange Hotel and Golf Complex
Elsie & Hiram Billington Lock
Weir
Caravan Pk.
Caravan Site
Barton
RIVER AVON
B4085
Oosland Barn
Glendale
The Hayloft
WELFORD
CLEEVE
Marlcliff
Barton Fm.

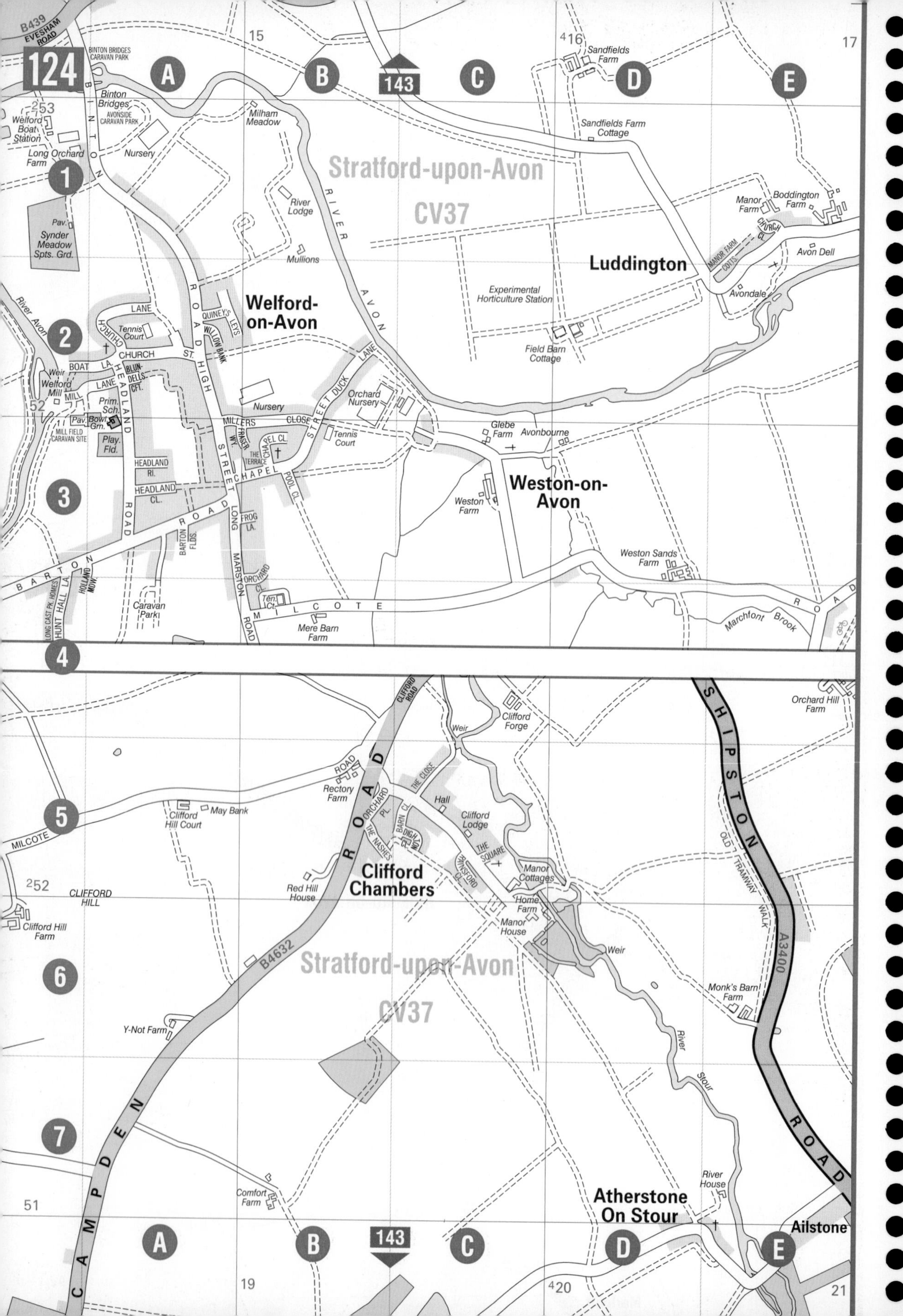
124
143
B439
EVESHAM ROAD
BINTON BRIDGES CARAVAN PARK
Binton Bridges
AVONSIDE CARAVAN PARK
Welford Boat Station
Long Orchard Farm
Nursery
Milham Meadow
Sandfields Farm
Sandfields Farm Cottage
Stratford-upon-Avon
CV37
Synder Meadow Spts. Grd.
Pav.
River Lodge
Mullions
RIVER AVON
Manor Farm
Boddington Farm
CHURCH CL.
MANOR FARM COTTS.
Avon Dell
Luddington
Avondale
Experimental Horticulture Station
Field Barn Cottage
Welford-on-Avon
River Avon
LANE
CHURCH
Tennis Court
QUINEY'S LEYS
WILLOW BANK
HIGH ROAD
CHURCH ST.
BOAT LA.
Weir
Welford Mill
MILL LANE
HEADLAND
BLUNDELLS CFT.
Prim. Sch.
Bowl Grn.
MILL FIELD CARAVAN SITE
Play. Fld.
Nursery
Orchard Nursery
DUCK LANE
STREET
MILLERS CLOSE
FRASER WY.
CHAPEL CL.
THE TERRACE
Tennis Court
Glebe Farm
Avonbourne
HEADLAND RI.
HEADLAND CL.
CHAPEL STREET
POOL CL.
Weston-on-Avon
Weston Farm
BARTON ROAD
LONG MARSTON ROAD
FROG LA.
BARTON FLDS.
HOLLAND MDW.
HUNT HALL LA.
LONG CAST PK. HOMES
Caravan Park
ORCHARD CL.
Ten. Ct.
MILCOTE ROAD
Mere Barn Farm
Weston Sands Farm
Marchfont Brook
CLIFFORD ROAD
Clifford Forge
Weir
Orchard Hill Farm
SHIPSTON ROAD
A3400
ROAD
Rectory Farm
THE CLOSE
Hall
ORCHARD PL.
BARN CL.
DIGHTON CL.
THE NASHES
Clifford Lodge
THE SQUARE
RAINSFORD CL.
Clifford Hill Court
May Bank
MILCOTE
Red Hill House
Clifford Chambers
Manor Cottages
Home Farm
Manor House
OLD TRAMWAY WALK
CLIFFORD HILL
Clifford Hill Farm
B4632
Weir
Stratford-upon-Avon
CV37
Monk's Barn Farm
Y-Not Farm
River Stour
CAMPDEN ROAD
Comfort Farm
River House
Atherstone On Stour
Ailstone
15
416
17
253
52
252
51
19
420
21
A
B
C
D
E
1
2
3
4
5
6
7

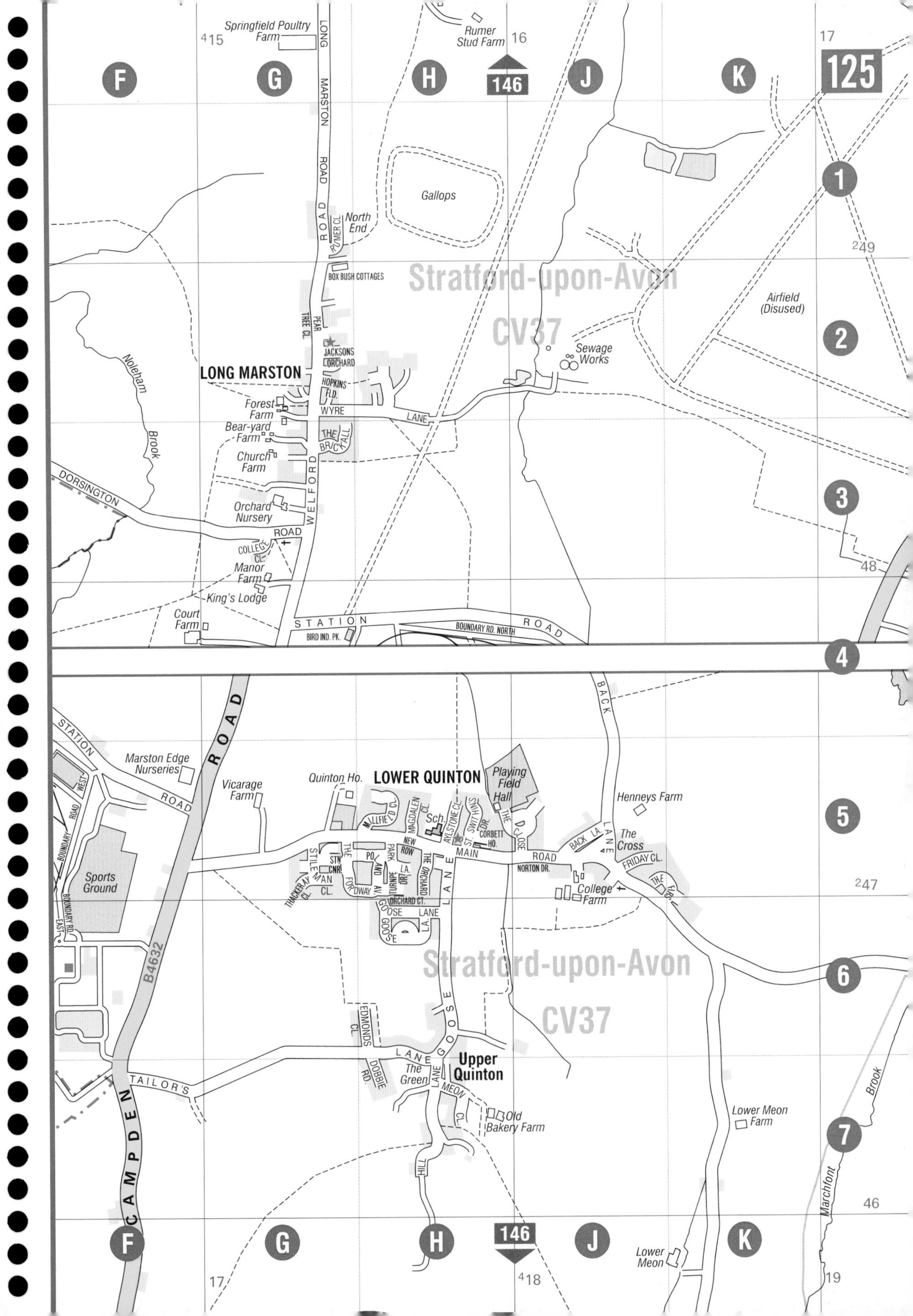
125
146
F
G
H
J
K
1
2
3
4
5
6
7
415
16
17
249
48
247
46
17
418
19
Springfield Poultry Farm
Rumer Stud Farm
LONG MARSTON ROAD
Gallops
North End
RUMER CL.
BOX BUSH COTTAGES
Stratford-upon-Avon
CV37
PEAR TREE CL.
JACKSONS ORCHARD
HOPKINS FLD.
LONG MARSTON
Sewage Works
Airfield (Disused)
Noleham Brook
Forest Farm
Bear-yard Farm
WYRE LANE
THE BRICKALL
Church Farm
DORSINGTON ROAD
Orchard Nursery
WELFORD ROAD
COLLEGE CL.
Manor Farm
King's Lodge
Court Farm
STATION ROAD
BIRD IND. PK.
BOUNDARY RD. NORTH
BACK LANE
STATION ROAD
Marston Edge Nurseries
WEST ROAD
BOUNDARY ROAD
Sports Ground
BOUNDARY RD. EAST
Vicarage Farm
Quinton Ho.
LOWER QUINTON
Playing Field
Hall
MILLFIELD CL.
MAGDALEN CL.
Sch.
AYLSTONE CL.
ST. SWITHIN'S DR.
THE CLOSE
CORBETT HO.
BACK LA.
Henneys Farm
The Cross
FRIDAY CL.
MAIN ROAD
NORTON DR.
NEW ROW
THE STN CNR.
STILEMAN CL.
THACKERAY CL.
POLAND AV.
PARK DR.
TURNPIKE LA.
THE ORCHARD
FORDWAY AV.
ORCHARD CT.
GOOSE LANE
GOOSE LA.
College Farm
THE FURLONG
B4632
CAMPDEN ROAD
EDMONDS CL.
LANE
DOBBIE RD.
The Green
Upper Quinton
TAILOR'S LANE
MEON CL.
Old Bakery Farm
HILL
Lower Meon Farm
Brook
Marchfont
Lower Meon

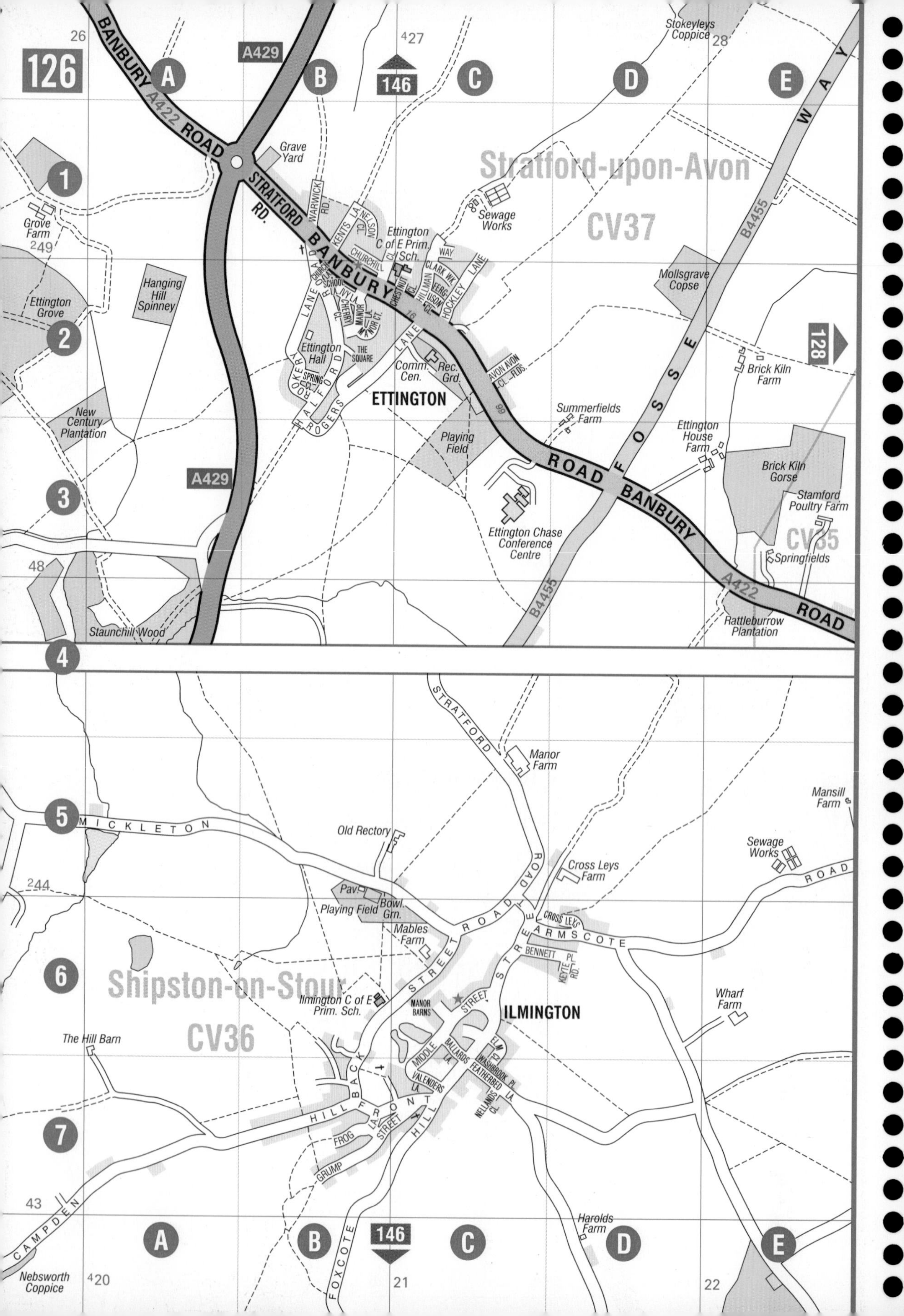

126
146
128
A429
BANBURY ROAD
A422
STRATFORD RD.
Grave Yard
Grove Farm
Ettington Grove
Hanging Hill Spinney
New Century Plantation
Staunchill Wood
Stratford-upon-Avon
CV37
Sewage Works
Ettington C of E Prim. Sch.
ETTINGTON
Ettington Hall
THE SQUARE
Comm. Cen.
Rec. Grd.
Playing Field
Summerfields Farm
Ettington Chase Conference Centre
Stokeyleys Coppice
Mollsgrave Copse
FOSSE WAY
B4455
Brick Kiln Farm
Ettington House Farm
Brick Kiln Gorse
Stamford Poultry Farm
CV35
Springfields
Rattleburrow Plantation
Manor Farm
Mansill Farm
MICKLETON
Old Rectory
Cross Leys Farm
Sewage Works
Pav.
Bowl. Grn.
Playing Field
Mables Farm
ARMSCOTE ROAD
Shipston-on-Stour
CV36
Ilmington C of E Prim. Sch.
ILMINGTON
Wharf Farm
The Hill Barn
CAMPDEN
FOXCOTE
Harolds Farm
Nebsworth Coppice

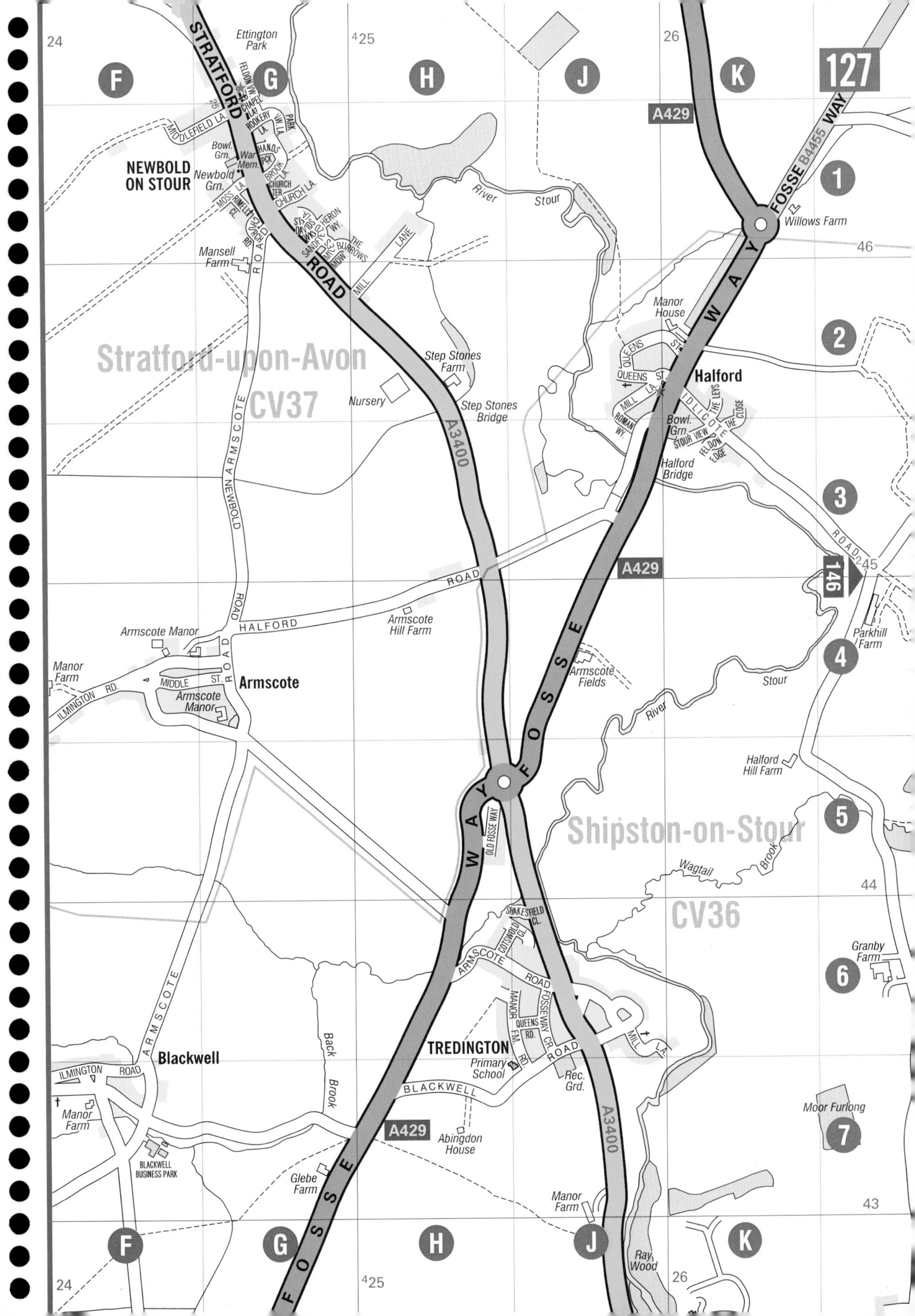

127
146
24
425
26
46
45
44
43
F
G
H
J
K
1
2
3
4
5
6
7
A429
A3400
B4455
STRATFORD ROAD
FOSSE WAY
Ettington Park
NEWBOLD ON STOUR
MIDDLEFIELD LA.
Bowl. Grn.
War Mem.
Newbold Grn.
MOSS LA.
RIMELL CL.
CHURCH LA.
CHURCH TER.
BROOK LA.
ROOKERY LA.
PARK VW. LA.
FELDON VW.
CHAPEL LA.
HANDS PCK
HERON WY.
ST. DAVIDS WY.
SANDPIT LA.
THE BURROWS
MILL LANE
Mansell Farm
River Stour
Willows Farm
Manor House
QUEENS ST.
Halford
MILL LA.
ROMAN WY.
IDLICOTE ROAD
THE LEYS
THE CLOSE
Bowl. Grn.
STOUR VIEW
FELDON EDGE
Halford Bridge
Stratford-upon-Avon
CV37
Step Stones Farm
Nursery
Step Stones Bridge
ARMSCOTE NEWBOLD ROAD
HALFORD ROAD
Armscote Manor
Armscote Hill Farm
Manor Farm
ILMINGTON RD.
MIDDLE ST.
Armscote Manor
Armscote
Armscote Fields
Parkhill Farm
Halford Hill Farm
OLD FOSSE WAY
Shipston-on-Stour
Wagtail Brook
CV36
SHAKESFIELD CL.
COTSWOLD CL.
ARMSCOTE ROAD
MANOR FM. RD.
QUEENS RD.
FOSSEWAY CR.
MILL LA.
TREDINGTON
Primary School
Rec. Grd.
Granby Farm
ARMSCOTE
Blackwell
ILMINGTON ROAD
Manor Farm
Back Brook
BLACKWELL ROAD
BLACKWELL BUSINESS PARK
Abingdon House
Glebe Farm
Moor Furlong
Manor Farm
Ray Wood

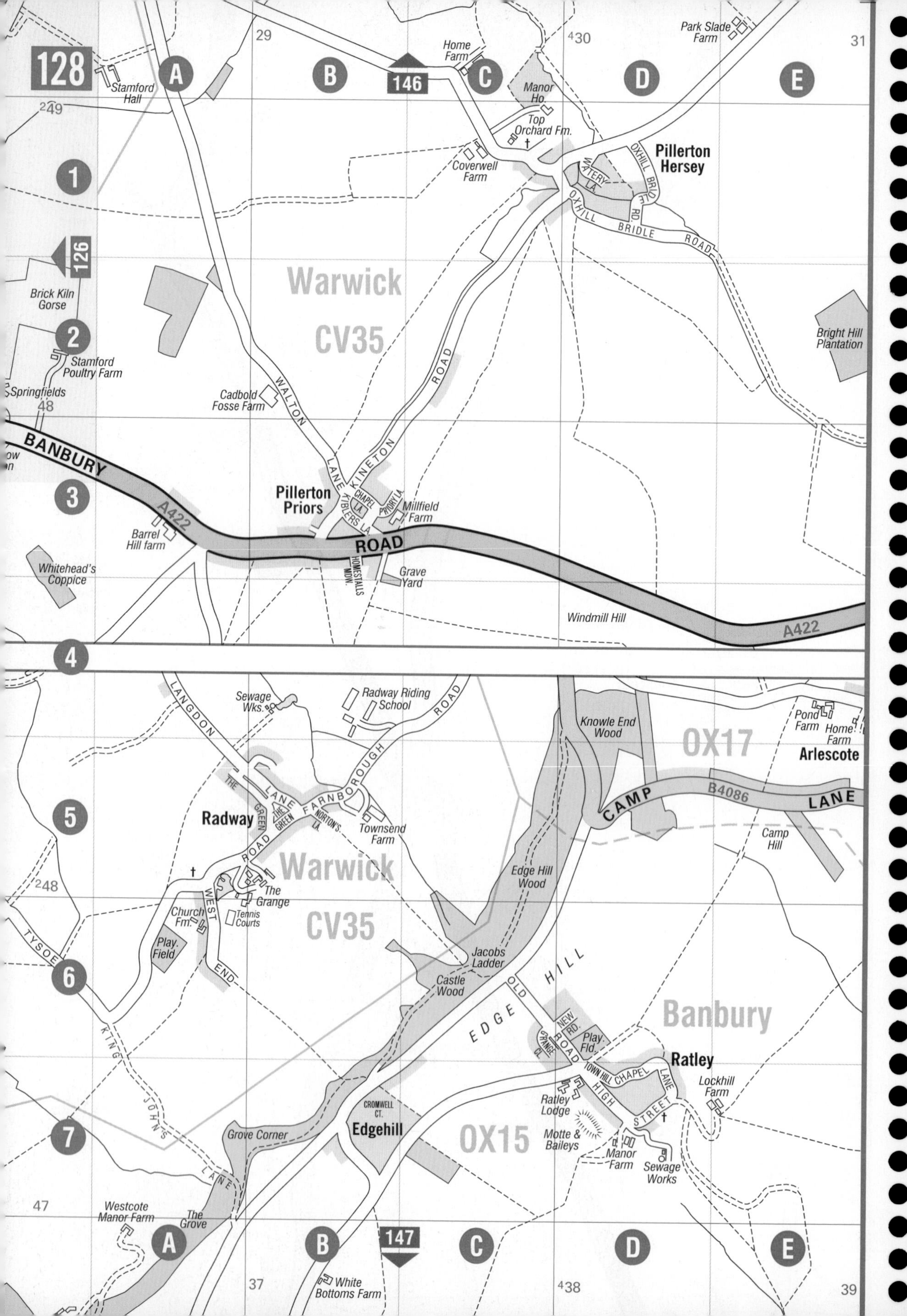
146
Stamford Hall
Home Farm
Park Slade Farm
Manor Ho.
Top Orchard Fm.
Coverwell Farm
Pillerton Hersey
WATERY LA
OXHILL BRIDLE ROAD
126
Brick Kiln Gorse
Warwick
CV35
Bright Hill Plantation
Stamford Poultry Farm
Springfields
Cadbold Fosse Farm
WALTON LANE
KINETON ROAD
BANBURY ROAD
A422
Pillerton Priors
CHAPEL LA
PRIORY LA
KIBLERS LA
Millfield Farm
Barrel Hill farm
HOMESTALLS MDW.
Grave Yard
Whitehead's Coppice
Windmill Hill
LANGDON
Sewage Wks.
Radway Riding School
FARNBOROUGH ROAD
Knowle End Wood
OX17
Pond Farm
Home Farm
Arlescote
CAMP LANE
B4086
Camp Hill
THE GREEN
Radway
NORTON'S LA.
Townsend Farm
Warwick
WEST END
The Grange
Church Fm.
Tennis Courts
Edge Hill Wood
CV35
Play. Field
TYSOE
Jacobs Ladder
Castle Wood
EDGE HILL
OLD HILL
NEW RD.
Banbury
GRANGE CL.
Play. Fld.
Ratley
TOWN HILL
CHAPEL LANE
HIGH STREET
Lockhill Farm
Ratley Lodge
KING JOHN'S LANE
CROMWELL CT.
Edgehill
OX15
Motte & Baileys
Grove Corner
Manor Farm
Sewage Works
Westcote Manor Farm
The Grove
147
White Bottoms Farm
29
430
31
249
48
248
47
37
438
39
A
B
C
D
E
1
2
3
4
5
6
7

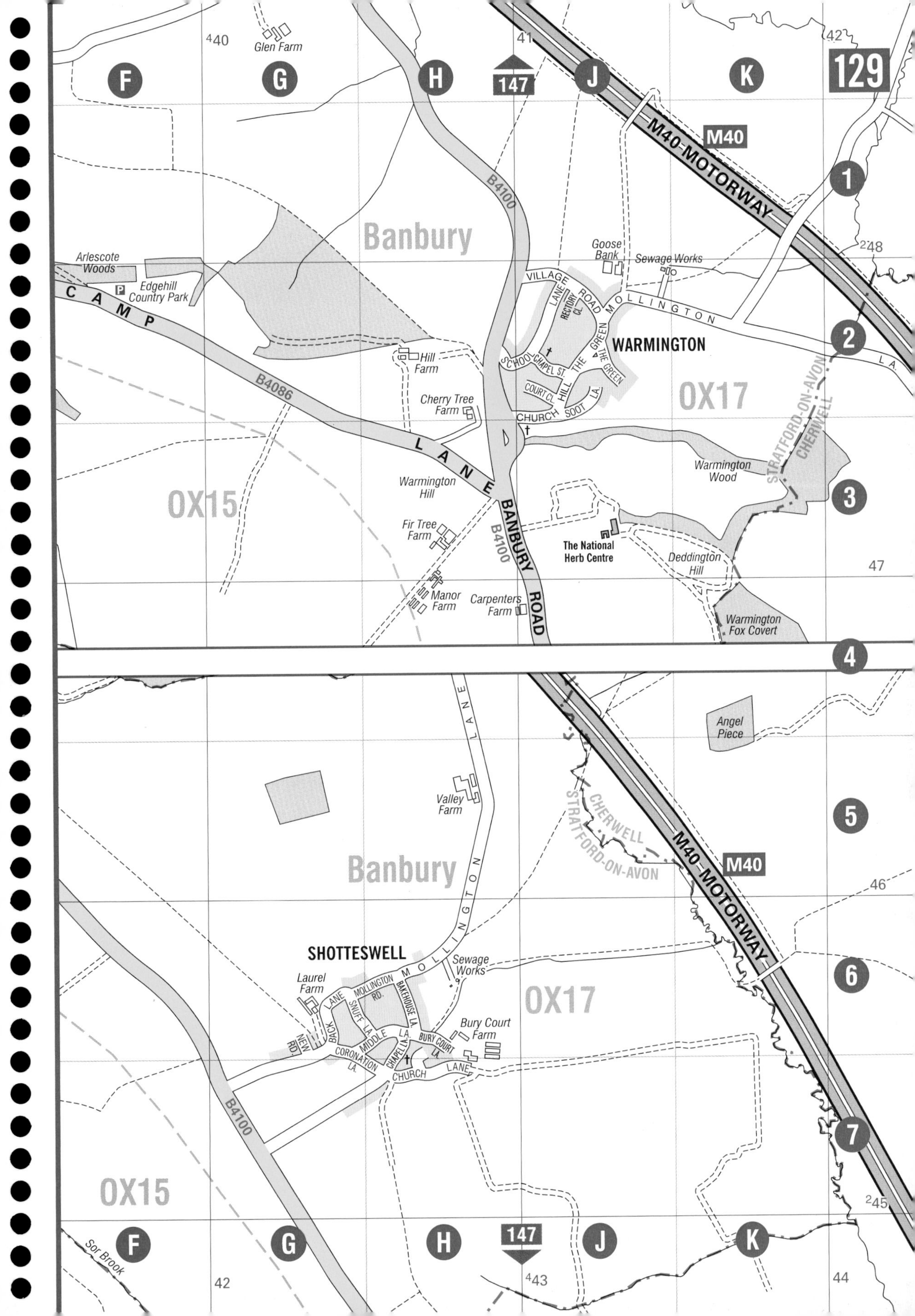
440
Glen Farm
41
147
42
F
G
H
J
K
M40
M40-MOTORWAY
B4100
Banbury
Goose Bank
Sewage Works
Arlescote Woods
Edgehill Country Park
CAMP
VILLAGE
LANE
ROAD
RECTORY CL.
MOLLINGTON
WARMINGTON
SCHOOL
CHAPEL ST.
THE GREEN
HILL
COURT CL.
SOOT LA.
CHURCH
LA.
Hill Farm
Cherry Tree Farm
B4086
LANE
OX17
OX15
STRATFORD-ON-AVON
CHERWELL
Warmington Wood
Warmington Hill
BANBURY ROAD
Fir Tree Farm
The National Herb Centre
Deddington Hill
Manor Farm
Carpenters Farm
Warmington Fox Covert
248
47
1
2
3
4
Angel Piece
Valley Farm
Banbury
MOLLINGTON LANE
CHERWELL
STRATFORD-ON-AVON
M40-MOTORWAY
M40
46
5
6
7
SHOTTESWELL
Sewage Works
Laurel Farm
MOLLINGTON RD.
BAKEHOUSE LA.
BACK LANE
SNUFF LA.
NEW RD.
MIDDLE LA.
CORONATION LA.
CHAPEL LA.
BURY COURT LA.
CHURCH LANE
Bury Court Farm
OX17
B4100
OX15
245
Sor Brook
147
443
42
44

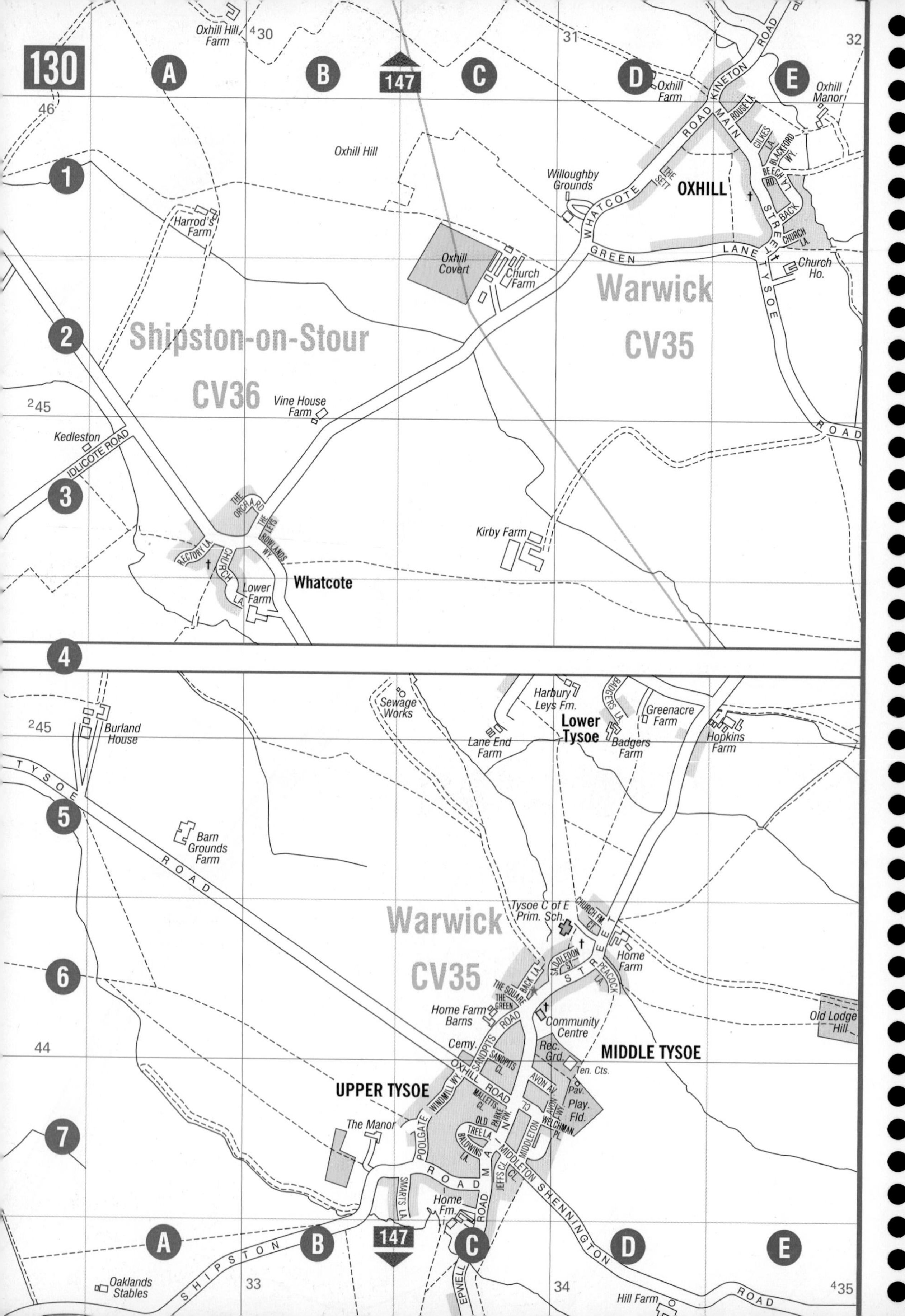

147
Oxhill Hill Farm
Oxhill Farm
Oxhill Manor
Oxhill Hill
Willoughby Grounds
OXHILL
KINETON ROAD
MAIN
ROUSE LA.
GILKES LA.
BLACKFORD WY.
BEECH LA.
RD.
BACK
STREET
CHURCH LA.
THE SETT
WHATCOTE ROAD
GREEN LANE
TYSOE ROAD
Church Ho.
Harrod's Farm
Oxhill Covert
Church Farm
Warwick
CV35
Shipston-on-Stour
CV36
Vine House Farm
Kedleston
IDLICOTE ROAD
THE ORCHARD
THE LEYS
ROWLANDS WY.
RECTORY LA.
CHURCH LA.
Lower Farm
Whatcote
Kirby Farm
Sewage Works
Harbury Leys Fm.
BADGERS LA.
Greenacre Farm
Lower Tysoe
Badgers Farm
Lane End Farm
Hopkins Farm
Burland House
TYSOE ROAD
Barn Grounds Farm
Warwick
CV35
Tysoe C of E Prim. Sch.
CHURCH FM CT.
SADDLEDON ST.
STREET
PEACOCK LA.
Home Farm
BACK LA.
THE SQUARE
THE GREEN
Home Farm Barns
ROAD
Community Centre
Old Lodge Hill
Cemy.
SANDPITS ROAD
SANDPITS CL.
Rec. Grd.
Ten. Cts.
MIDDLE TYSOE
OXHILL ROAD
AVON AV.
AVON WY.
Pav.
Play. Fld.
UPPER TYSOE
WINDMILL WY.
MALLETTS CL.
OLD PARK NR. RW.
OLD TREE LA.
MAIN
WELCHMAN PL.
MIDDLETON CL.
The Manor
POOLGATE
BALDWINS LA.
JEFFS CL.
ROAD
SMARTS LA.
Home Fm.
MIDDLETON CL.
SHENNINGTON ROAD
SHIPSTON
EPWELL ROAD
Oaklands Stables
Hill Farm
147

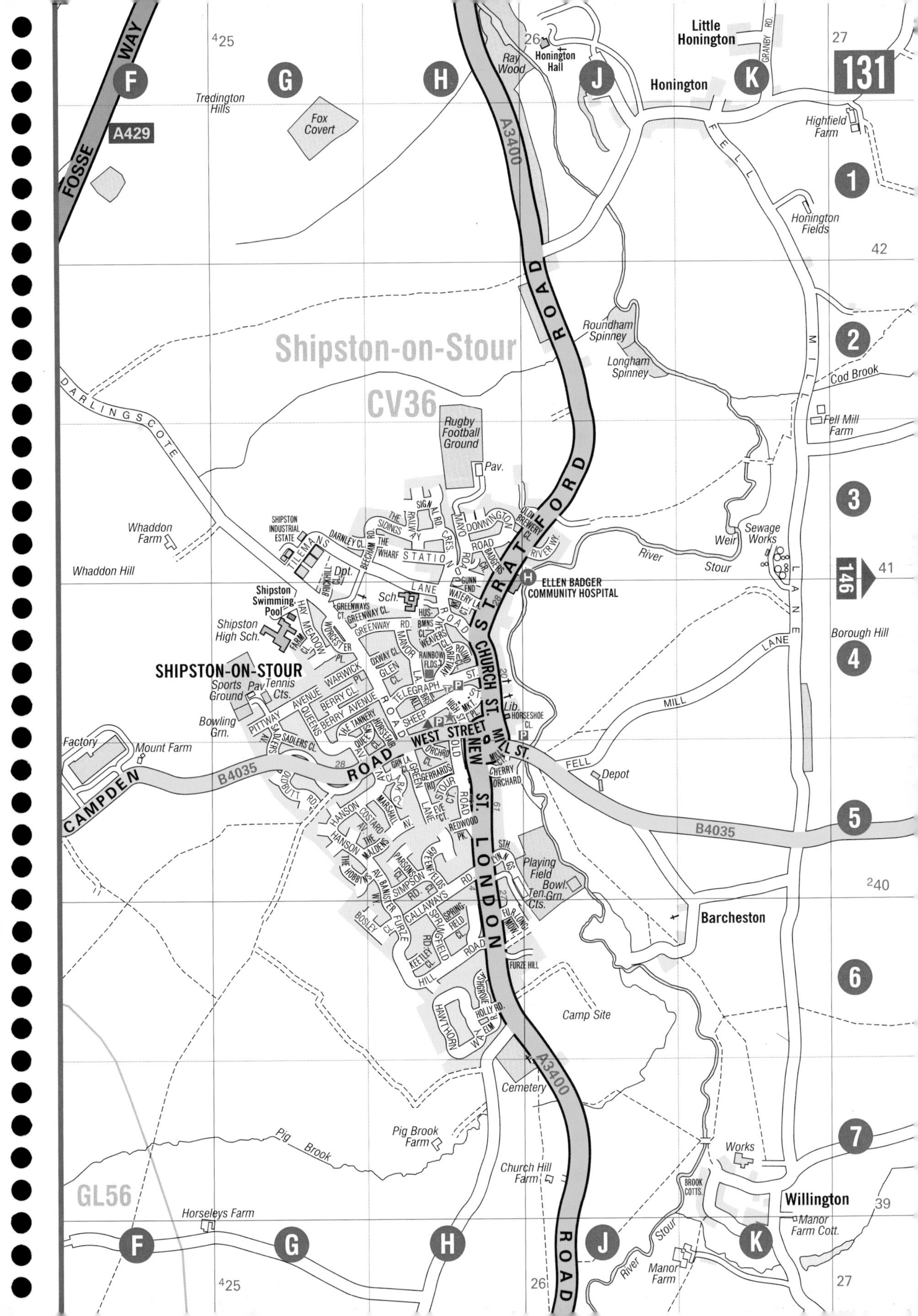

131
146
Shipston-on-Stour
CV36
GL56
SHIPSTON-ON-STOUR
Little Honington
Honington
Honington Hall
Ray Wood
Tredington Hills
Fox Covert
FOSSE WAY
A429
A3400
STRATFORD ROAD
LONDON ROAD
Highfield Farm
Honington Fields
FELL MILL LANE
Roundham Spinney
Longham Spinney
Cod Brook
Fell Mill Farm
Rugby Football Ground
Pav.
DARLINGSCOTE
Whaddon Farm
Whaddon Hill
Sewage Works
Weir
River Stour
ELLEN BADGER COMMUNITY HOSPITAL
Shipston Swimming Pool
Shipston High Sch.
Sports Ground
Tennis Cts.
Bowling Grn.
Factory
Mount Farm
CAMPDEN ROAD
B4035
WEST STREET
CHURCH ST.
NEW ST.
MILL ST.
HIGH ST.
STATION ROAD
TELEGRAPH ST.
SHEEP ST.
Lib.
Borough Hill
MILL LANE
Depot
Barcheston
Playing Field
Bowl.
Ten.Crts.
Camp Site
Cemetery
Pig Brook Farm
Pig Brook
Church Hill Farm
Works
Willington
BROOK COTTS.
Manor Farm Cott.
Manor Farm
River Stour
Horseleys Farm
FURZE HILL
HAWTHORN WAY
HOLLY RD.

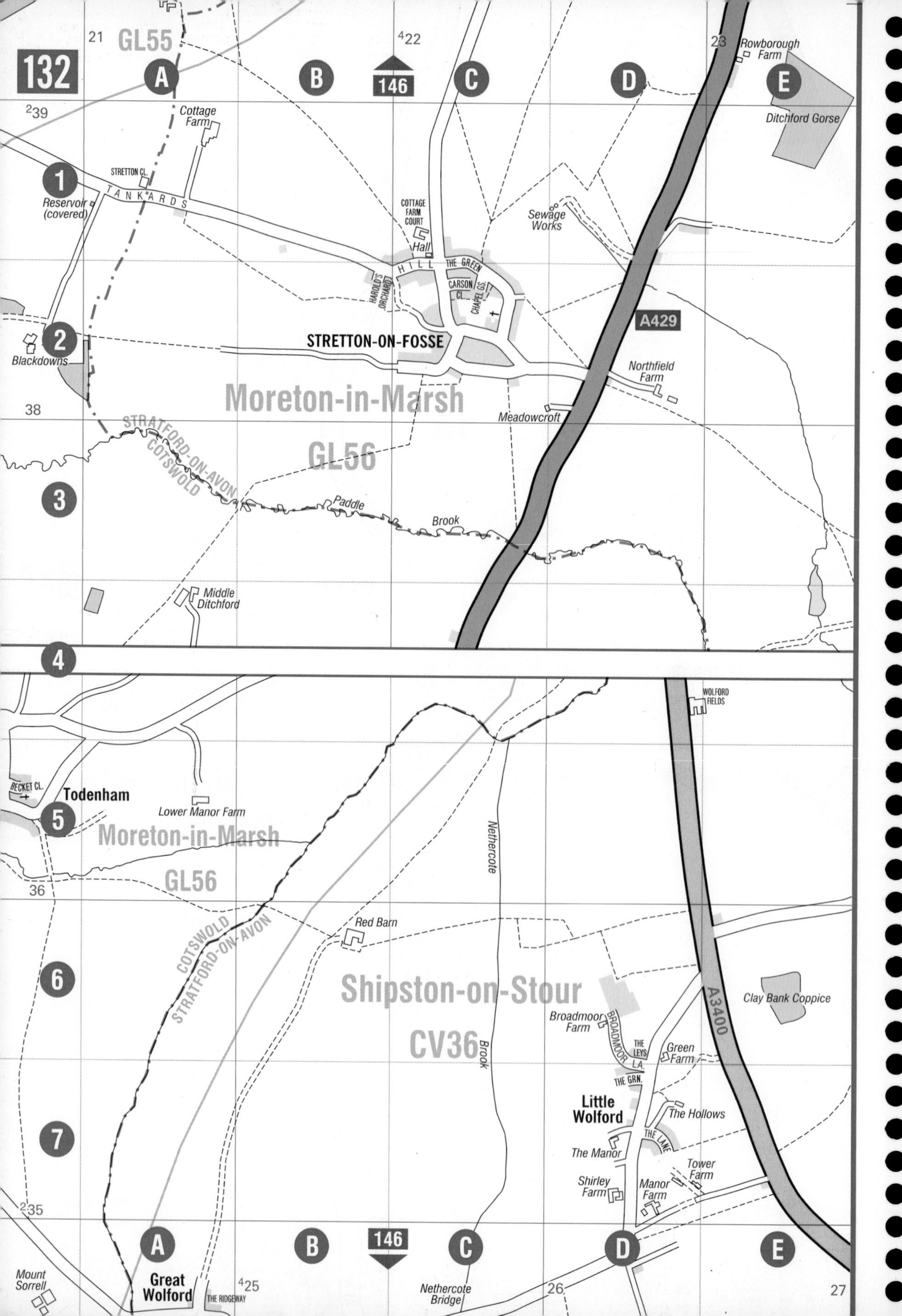

GL55
146
Rowborough Farm
Ditchford Gorse
Cottage Farm
STRETTON CL.
TANKARDS
Reservoir (covered)
COTTAGE FARM COURT
Hall
HILL
THE GREEN
Sewage Works
HAROLD'S ORCHARD
CARSON CL.
CHAPEL SQ.
A429
STRETTON-ON-FOSSE
Blackdowns
Northfield Farm
Moreton-in-Marsh
Meadowcroft
STRATFORD-ON-AVON
COTSWOLD
GL56
Paddle
Brook
Middle Ditchford
WOLFORD FIELDS
BECKET CL.
Todenham
Lower Manor Farm
Moreton-in-Marsh
GL56
Nethercote
Red Barn
COTSWOLD
STRATFORD-ON-AVON
Shipston-on-Stour
CV36
Brook
Clay Bank Coppice
A3400
Broadmoor Farm
BROADMOOR LA.
THE LEYS
Green Farm
THE GRN.
Little Wolford
The Hollows
THE LANE
The Manor
Tower Farm
Shirley Farm
Manor Farm
146
Mount Sorrell
Great Wolford
THE RIDGEWAY
Nethercote Bridge

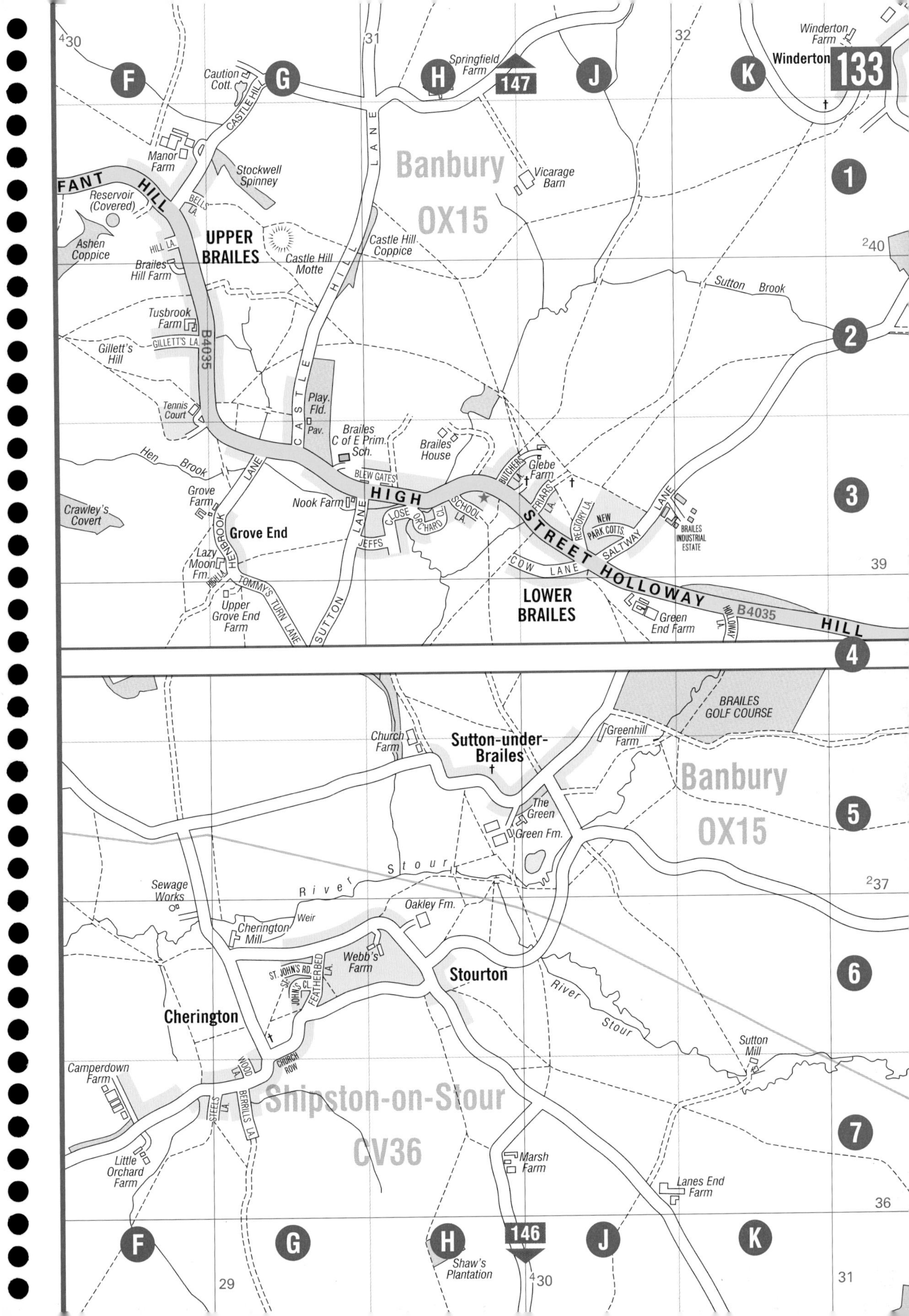

133
147
146
Winderton Farm
Winderton
Springfield Farm
Caution Cott.
CASTLE HILL
Manor Farm
Stockwell Spinney
Banbury
OX15
Vicarage Barn
FANT HILL
Reservoir (Covered)
BELLS LA.
Ashen Coppice
UPPER BRAILES
HILL LA.
Brailes Hill Farm
Castle Hill Motte
Castle Hill Coppice
CASTLE HILL LANE
Sutton Brook
Tusbrook Farm
B4035
Gillett's Hill
GILLETT'S LA.
Tennis Court
Play. Fld.
Pav.
Brailes C of E Prim. Sch.
Brailes House
Hen Brook
BLEW GATES
HIGH STREET HOLLOWAY HILL
Glebe Farm
BUTCHERS LA.
FRIARS LA.
Grove Farm
Crawley's Covert
Nook Farm
CLOSE
ORCHARD CL.
SCHOOL LA.
RECTORY LA.
NEW PARK COTTS.
SALTWAY LANE
BRAILES INDUSTRIAL ESTATE
HENBROOK LANE
Grove End
JEFFS
Lazy Moon Fm.
TOMMY'S TURN LANE
Upper Grove End Farm
SUTTON LANE
COW LANE
LOWER BRAILES
Green End Farm
HOLLOWAY LA.
B4035
BRAILES GOLF COURSE
Church Farm
Sutton-under-Brailes
Greenhill Farm
Banbury
OX15
The Green
Green Fm.
River Stour
Sewage Works
Oakley Fm.
Weir
Cherington Mill
Webb's Farm
ST. JOHN'S RD
ST. JOHN'S CL
FEATHERBED LA.
Stourton
River Stour
Cherington
Sutton Mill
WOOD LA.
CHURCH ROW
Camperdown Farm
STEELS LA.
BERRILLS LA.
Shipston-on-Stour
CV36
Little Orchard Farm
Marsh Farm
Lanes End Farm
Shaw's Plantation
F
G
H
J
K
1
2
3
4
5
6
7
430
31
32
240
39
237
36
29
31

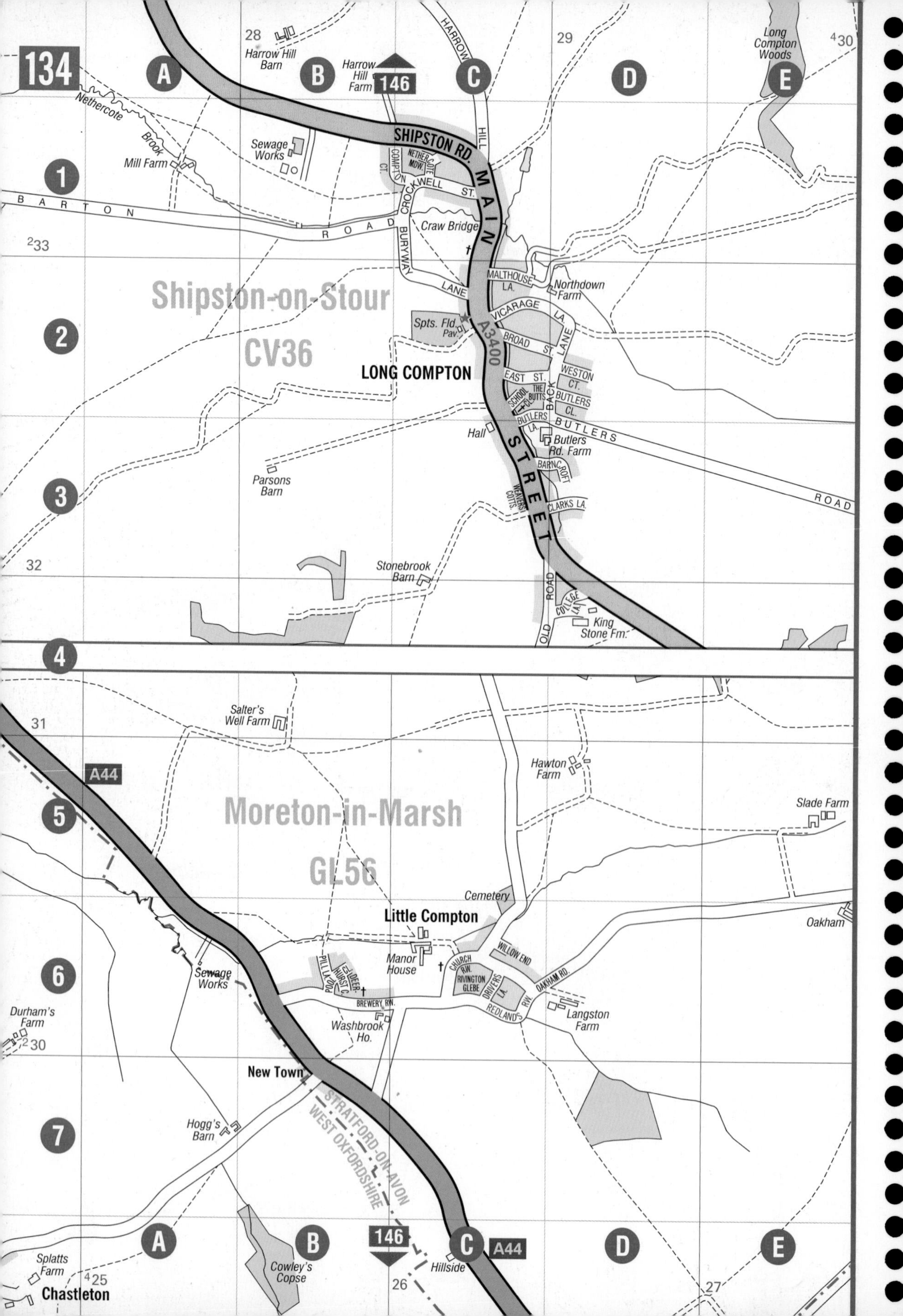

Harrow Hill Barn
Harrow Hill Farm
146
Long Compton Woods
Nethercote Brook
Mill Farm
Sewage Works
SHIPSTON RD.
HARROW HILL
MAIN STREET
A3400
BARTON ROAD
CROCKWELL ST.
COMPTON CT.
NETHERCOTE MDW.
BURYWAY LANE
Craw Bridge
MALTHOUSE LA.
Northdown Farm
VICARAGE LA.
BROAD ST.
BACK LANE
EAST ST.
WESTON CT.
BUTLERS CL.
SCHOOL CL.
THE BUTTS
BUTLERS LA.
BUTLERS ROAD
Butlers Rd. Farm
BARN CROFT
WEAVERS COTTS.
CLARKS LA.
Shipston-on-Stour
CV36
LONG COMPTON
Spts. Fld. Pav.
Hall
Parsons Barn
Stonebrook Barn
OLD ROAD
COLLEGE LA.
King Stone Fm.
Salter's Well Farm
Hawton Farm
A44
Moreton-in-Marsh
GL56
Slade Farm
Cemetery
Little Compton
Oakham
Manor House
WILLOW END
CHURCH RW.
RIVINGTON GLEBE
DRIVERS LA.
OAKHAM RD.
REDLANDS RW.
Langston Farm
POOL LA.
PILL
DEERHURST CL.
BREWERY RW.
Sewage Works
Durham's Farm
Washbrook Ho.
New Town
Hogg's Barn
STRATFORD-ON-AVON
WEST OXFORDSHIRE
146
A44
Hillside
Splatts Farm
Cowley's Copse
Chastleton
28
29
430
233
32
31
230
425
26
27
A B C D E
1 2 3 4 5 6 7

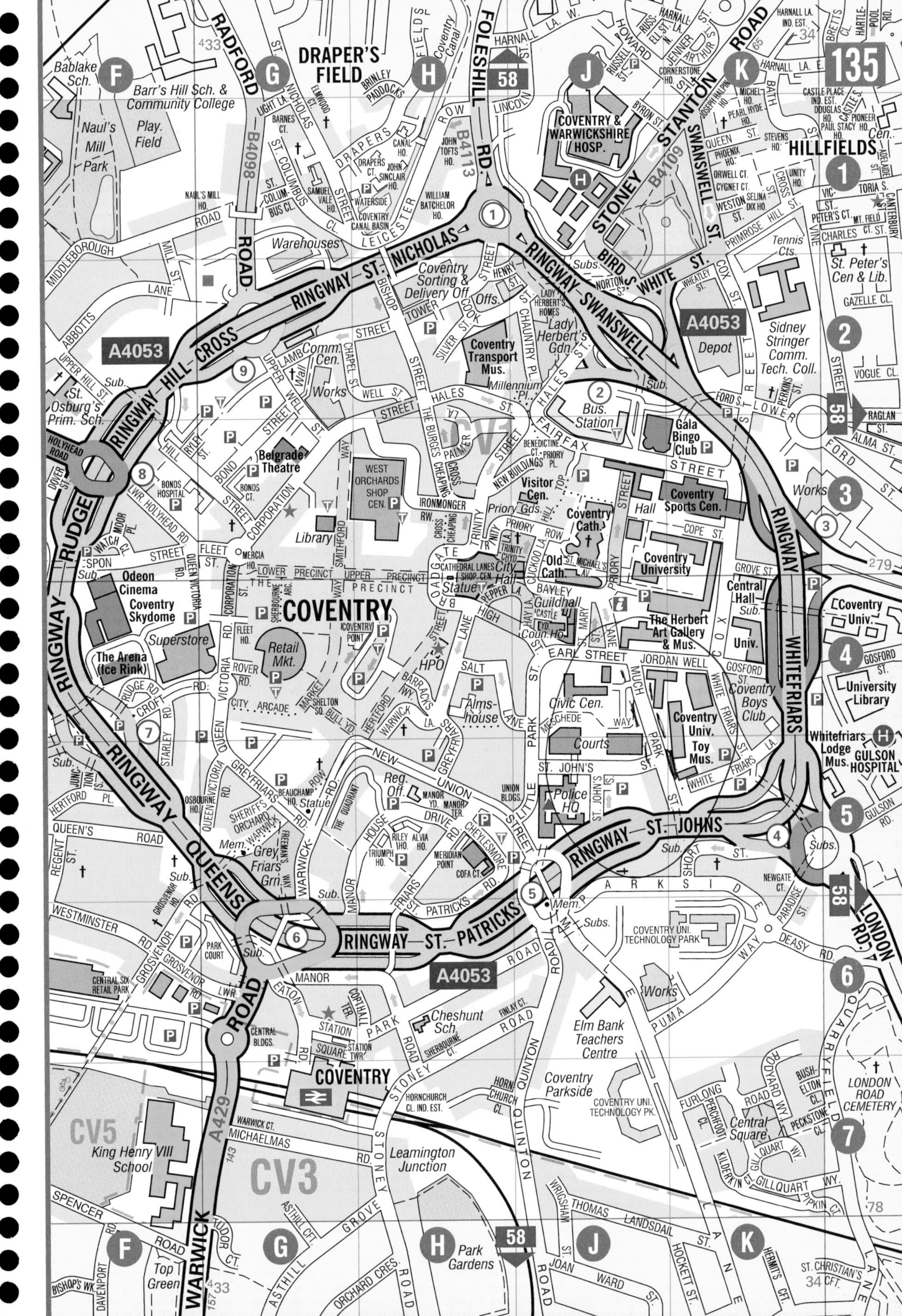
135
COVENTRY
DRAPER'S FIELD
HILLFIELDS
CV1
CV3
CV5
RINGWAY ST. NICHOLAS
RINGWAY HILL CROSS
RINGWAY RUDGE
RINGWAY QUEENS
RINGWAY ST. PATRICKS
RINGWAY ST. JOHNS
RINGWAY WHITEFRIARS
RINGWAY SWANSWELL
A4053
A429
B4098
B4113
B4109
FOLESHILL RD.
RADFORD ROAD
STONEY STANTON ROAD
WARWICK ROAD
LONDON RD.
QUINTON ROAD
STONEY ROAD
Coventry & Warwickshire Hosp.
Coventry Transport Mus.
Belgrade Theatre
West Orchards Shop Cen.
Coventry Cath.
Coventry University
Coventry Sports Cen.
The Herbert Art Gallery & Mus.
Gala Bingo Club
Bus Station
Odeon Cinema
Coventry Skydome
The Arena (Ice Rink)
Retail Mkt.
Civic Cen.
Courts
Police HQ
Toy Mus.
Whitefriars Lodge Mus.
Gulson Hospital
University Library
King Henry VIII School
Leamington Junction
Coventry Parkside
Elm Bank Teachers Centre
Central Six Retail Park
Coventry Uni. Technology Park
London Road Cemetery
Sidney Stringer Comm. Tech. Coll.
St. Peter's Cen & Lib.
Barr's Hill Sch. & Community College
Naul's Mill Park
Bablake Sch.
Park Gardens
Top Green
58
F G H J K
1 2 3 4 5 6 7
433
279
78
34

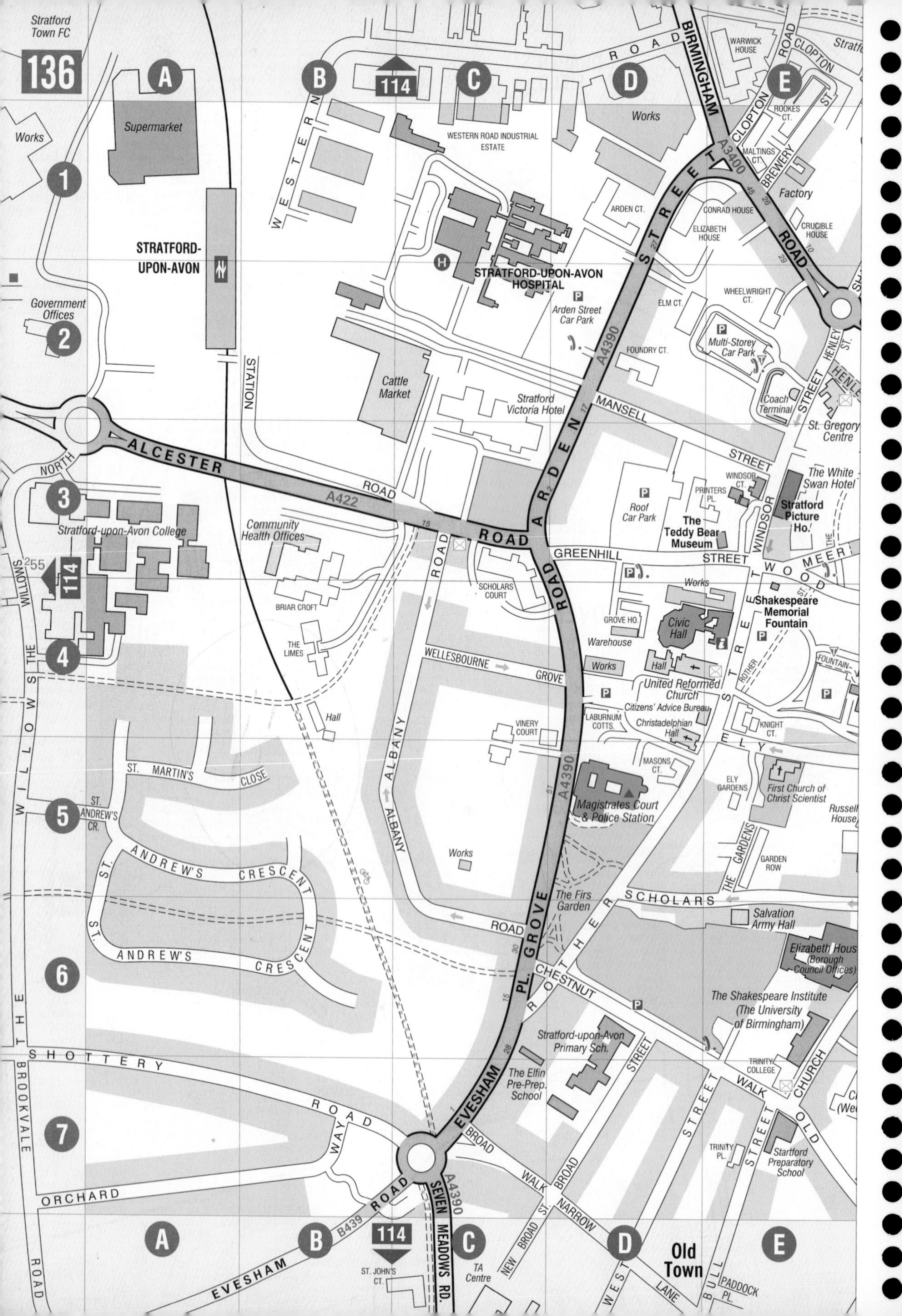

Stratford Town FC
Works
Supermarket
STRATFORD-UPON-AVON
Government Offices
STATION
ALCESTER ROAD
A422
NORTH
Stratford-upon-Avon College
WILLOWS
THE WILLOWS
114
WESTERN ROAD
WESTERN ROAD INDUSTRIAL ESTATE
STRATFORD-UPON-AVON HOSPITAL
Arden Street Car Park
Cattle Market
Stratford Victoria Hotel
Community Health Offices
BRIAR CROFT
THE LIMES
Hall
SCHOLARS COURT
ALBANY ROAD
WELLESBOURNE GROVE
VINERY COURT
Works
ST. MARTIN'S CLOSE
ST. ANDREW'S CR.
ST. ANDREW'S CRESCENT
SHOTTERY ROAD
BROOKVALE ROAD
ORCHARD WAY
EVESHAM ROAD
B439
EVESHAM PL.
GROVE ROAD
A4390
SEVEN MEADOWS RD.
ST. JOHN'S CT.
TA Centre
BIRMINGHAM ROAD
ARDEN STREET
A3400
WARWICK HOUSE
CLOPTON ROAD
ROOKES CT.
MALTINGS CT.
BREWERY ST.
Factory
ARDEN CT.
CONRAD HOUSE
ELIZABETH HOUSE
CRUCIBLE HOUSE
WHEELWRIGHT CT.
ELM CT.
Multi-Storey Car Park
FOUNDRY CT.
Coach Terminal
HENLEY STREET
St. Gregory Centre
MANSELL STREET
WINDSOR CT.
PRINTERS PL.
Roof Car Park
The Teddy Bear Museum
The White Swan Hotel
Stratford Picture Ho.
GREENHILL STREET
WOOD STREET
MEER
ROTHER STREET
Shakespeare Memorial Fountain
GROVE HO.
Civic Hall
Warehouse
Works
United Reformed Church
Citizens' Advice Bureau
LABURNUM COTTS.
Christadelphian Hall
KNIGHT CT.
ELY STREET
MASONS CT.
ELY GARDENS
First Church of Christ Scientist
Russell House
Magistrates Court & Police Station
THE GARDENS
GARDEN ROW
The Firs Garden
SCHOLARS LANE
Salvation Army Hall
Elizabeth House (Borough Council Offices)
CHESTNUT WALK
The Shakespeare Institute (The University of Birmingham)
Stratford-upon-Avon Primary Sch.
The Elfin Pre-Prep. School
TRINITY COLLEGE
CHURCH STREET
OLD TOWN
BROAD STREET
BROAD WALK
TRINITY PL.
Stratford Preparatory School
NEW BROAD ST.
NARROW LANE
WEST STREET
Old Town
BULL STREET
PADDOCK PL.

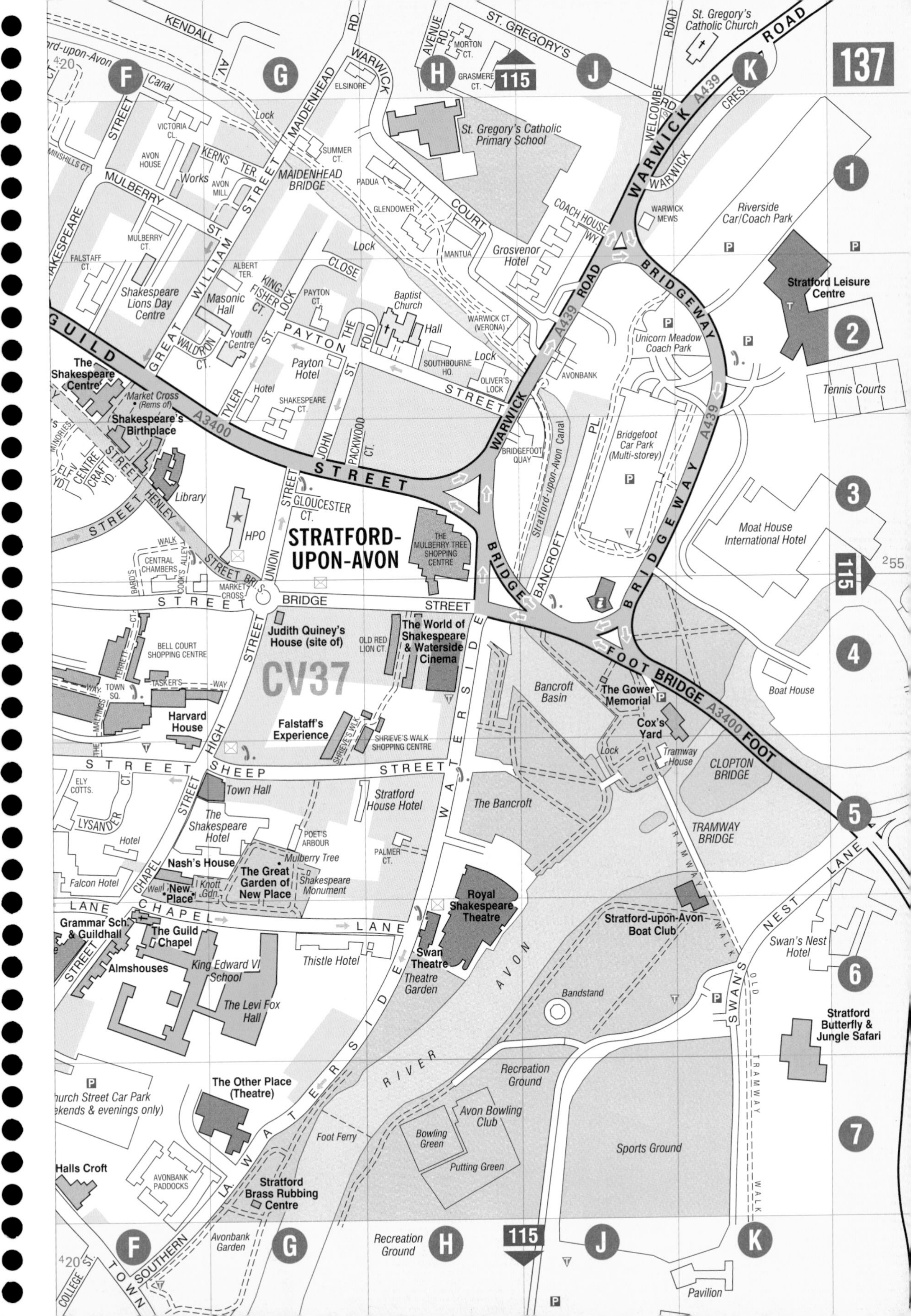
137
STRATFORD-UPON-AVON
CV37
115
KENDALL AV.
ST. GREGORY'S ROAD
St. Gregory's Catholic Church
MORTON CT.
GRASMERE CT.
ELSINORE
WARWICK RD.
MAIDENHEAD RD.
Canal
Lock
VICTORIA CL.
St. Gregory's Catholic Primary School
SUMMER CT.
WELCOMBE RD.
WARWICK CRES.
AVON HOUSE
KERNS TER.
Works
AVON MILL
MAIDENHEAD BRIDGE
PADUA
MULBERRY ST.
GLENDOWER
WARWICK MEWS
Riverside Car/Coach Park
COACH HOUSE WY.
COURT
MULBERRY CT.
MANTUA
Grosvenor Hotel
Stratford Leisure Centre
FALSTAFF CT.
ALBERT TER.
CLOSE
Shakespeare Lions Day Centre
Masonic Hall
KINGFISHER CT.
LOCK
PAYTON CT.
Baptist Church
Hall
BRIDGEWAY
Unicorn Meadow Coach Park
GREAT WILLIAM STREET
Youth Centre
WALDRON CT.
PAYTON STREET
THE FOLD
WARWICK CT. (VERONA)
SOUTHBOURNE HO.
OLIVER'S LOCK
AVONBANK
Tennis Courts
GUILD STREET
The Shakespeare Centre
Market Cross (Rems of)
TYLER ST.
Hotel
Payton Hotel
SHAKESPEARE CT.
JOHN ST.
PACKWOOD CT.
Shakespeare's Birthplace
A3400
WARWICK ROAD
A439
BRIDGEFOOT QUAY
Stratford-upon-Avon Canal
PL.
Bridgefoot Car Park (Multi-storey)
MINORIES
ELM CT.
CENTRE CRAFT YD.
HENLEY STREET
Library
GLOUCESTER CT.
HPO
UNION STREET
THE MULBERRY TREE SHOPPING CENTRE
BRIDGE
BANCROFT
Moat House International Hotel
WALK
CENTRAL CHAMBERS
BARD'S WALK
COOK'S ALLEY
MARKET CROSS
BRIDGE STREET
255
Judith Quiney's House (site of)
OLD RED LION CT.
The World of Shakespeare & Waterside Cinema
BELL COURT SHOPPING CENTRE
TERRETT CT.
TASKER'S WAY
TOWN SQ.
THE MALTINGS
FOOT BRIDGE
Bancroft Basin
The Gower Memorial
Boat House
Harvard House
HIGH STREET
Falstaff's Experience
SHRIEVE'S WLK.
SHRIEVE'S WALK SHOPPING CENTRE
Cox's Yard
Tramway House
CLOPTON BRIDGE
SHEEP STREET
ELY COTTS.
Town Hall
Stratford House Hotel
WATERSIDE
The Bancroft
TRAMWAY BRIDGE
LYSANDER CT.
The Shakespeare Hotel
POET'S ARBOUR
PALMER CT.
Nash's House
Mulberry Tree
Falcon Hotel
CHAPEL STREET
Well
New Place
Knott Gdn.
The Great Garden of New Place
Shakespeare Monument
Royal Shakespeare Theatre
SWAN'S NEST LANE
CHAPEL LANE
Grammar Sch. & Guildhall
The Guild Chapel
Stratford-upon-Avon Boat Club
Swan's Nest Hotel
TRAMWAY WALK
CHURCH STREET
Almshouses
King Edward VI School
Thistle Hotel
Swan Theatre
Theatre Garden
AVON
Bandstand
OLD TRAMWAY WALK
Stratford Butterfly & Jungle Safari
The Levi Fox Hall
RIVER
Recreation Ground
Church Street Car Park (weekends & evenings only)
The Other Place (Theatre)
Avon Bowling Club
Foot Ferry
Bowling Green
Putting Green
Sports Ground
Halls Croft
AVONBANK PADDOCKS
SOUTHERN LANE
Stratford Brass Rubbing Centre
Avonbank Garden
COLLEGE ST.
TOWN
Pavilion
420
F
G
H
J
K
1
2
3
4
5
6
7

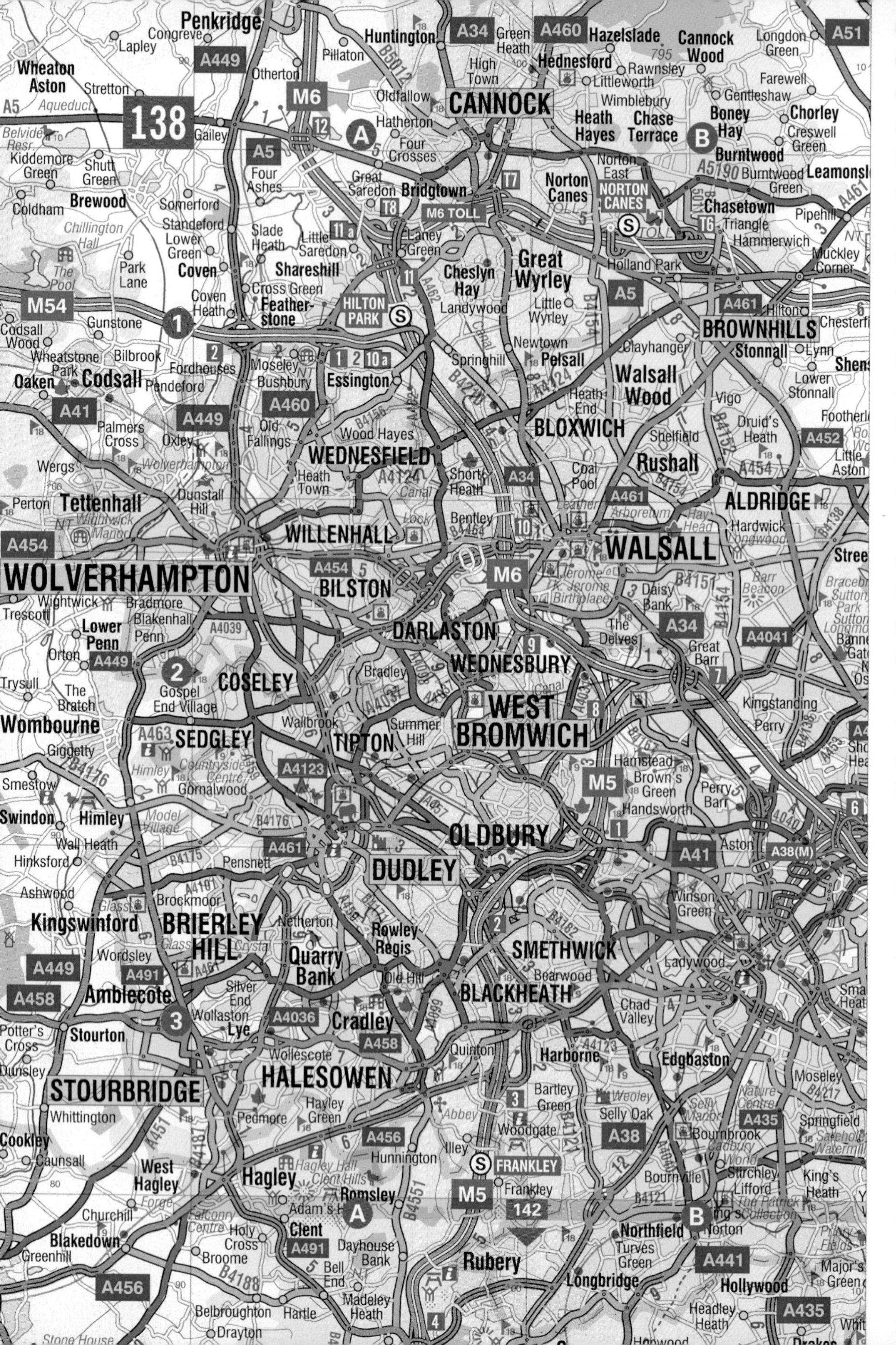

138
142
Penkridge
CANNOCK
Hednesford
Huntington
Cannock Wood
Brewood
Codsall
Great Wyrley
Cheslyn Hay
Norton Canes
Burntwood
Chasetown
BROWNHILLS
Walsall Wood
BLOXWICH
WEDNESFIELD
WILLENHALL
WOLVERHAMPTON
Tettenhall
BILSTON
DARLASTON
WALSALL
ALDRIDGE
WEDNESBURY
WEST BROMWICH
COSELEY
SEDGLEY
TIPTON
Wombourne
OLDBURY
DUDLEY
Kingswinford
BRIERLEY HILL
SMETHWICK
Quarry Bank
Rowley Regis
BLACKHEATH
Amblecote
Cradley
Stourton
STOURBRIDGE
HALESOWEN
Harborne
Edgbaston
Hagley
Clent
Romsley
Rubery
Northfield
Longbridge
Hollywood
FRANKLEY
M6
M5
M54
M6 TOLL
A449
A5
A460
A34
A41
A454
A461
A4123
A491
A458
A456
A38
A435
A441

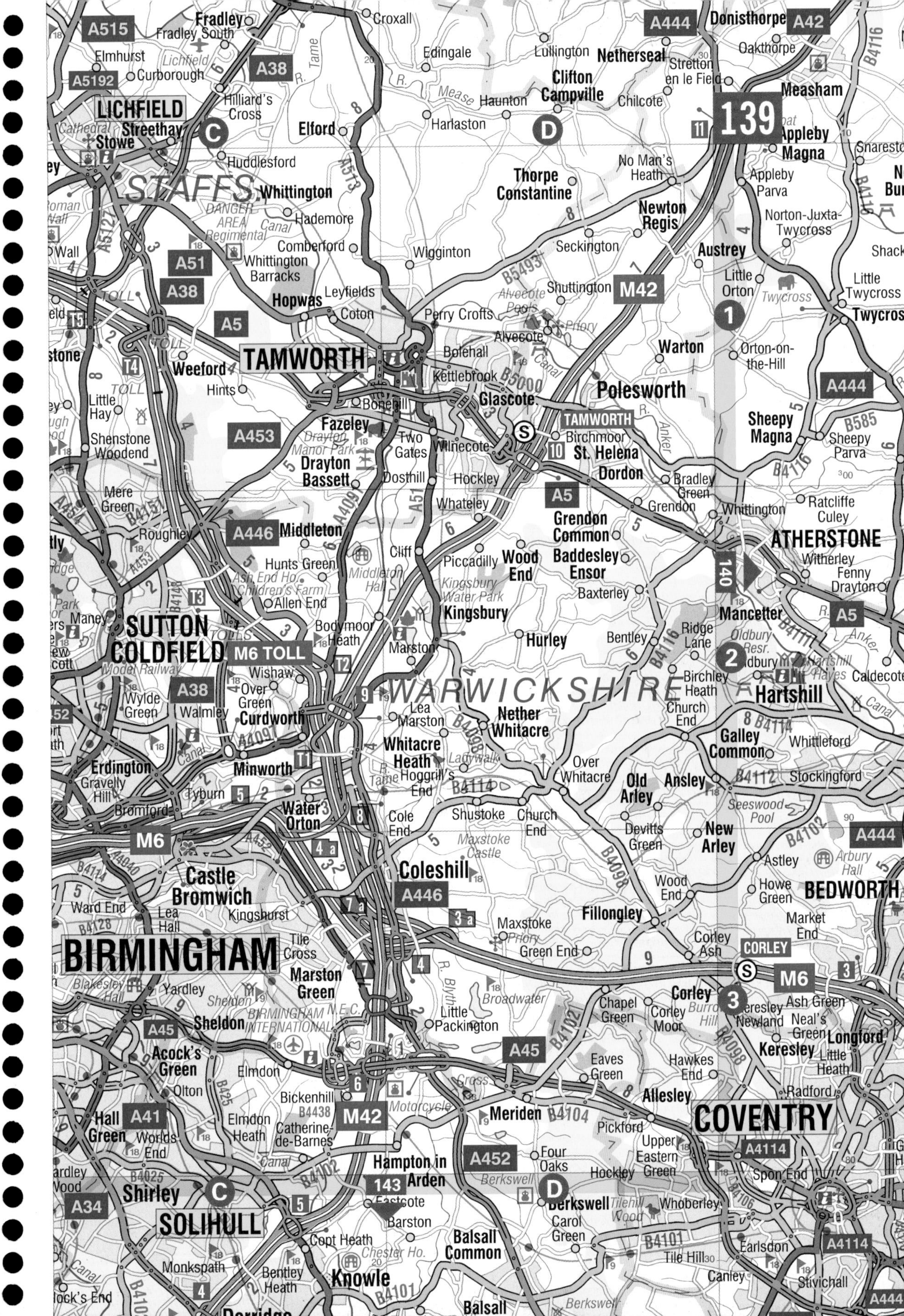

139
LICHFIELD
Fradley
Fradley South
Elmhurst
Curborough
Streethay
Stowe
Hilliard's Cross
Huddlesford
STAFFS
Whittington
Hademore
Comberford
Whittington Barracks
Hopwas
Leyfields
Coton
Croxall
Edingale
Elford
Harlaston
Haunton
Lullington
Clifton Campville
Netherseal
Stretton en le Field
Chilcote
Donisthorpe
Oakthorpe
Measham
Appleby Magna
Appleby Parva
Snarestone
No Man's Heath
Thorpe Constantine
Newton Regis
Norton-Juxta-Twycross
Seckington
Austrey
Wigginton
Shuttington
Alvecote
Little Orton
Twycross
Little Twycross
Perry Crofts
Warton
Orton-on-the-Hill
TAMWORTH
Weeford
Hints
Bolehall
Kettlebrook
Glascote
Polesworth
Little Hay
Shenstone Woodend
Fazeley
Bonehill
Drayton Bassett
Two Gates
Wilnecote
Birchmoor
St. Helena
Dordon
Sheepy Magna
Sheepy Parva
Dosthill
Hockley
Bradley Green
Grendon
Whateley
Whittington
Ratcliffe Culey
Mere Green
Roughley
Middleton
Grendon Common
ATHERSTONE
Hunts Green
Cliff
Piccadilly
Wood End
Baddesley Ensor
Witherley
Fenny Drayton
Middleton Hall
Kingsbury Water Park
Baxterley
Allen End
Kingsbury
Mancetter
Maney
SUTTON COLDFIELD
Bodymoor Heath
Marston
Hurley
Bentley
Ridge Lane
Oldbury Resr.
Hartshill Hayes
Caldecote
Wishaw
Birchley Heath
Hartshill
WARWICKSHIRE
Over Green
Wylde Green
Walmley
Curdworth
Lea Marston
Nether Whitacre
Church End
Galley Common
Whittleford
Erdington
Gravelly Hill
Minworth
Whitacre Heath
Hoggrill's End
Over Whitacre
Old Arley
Ansley
Stockingford
Tyburn
Bromford
Water Orton
Cole End
Shustoke
Church End
Devitts Green
New Arley
Seeswood Pool
M6
Castle Bromwich
Maxstoke Castle
Astley
Arbury Hall
Coleshill
Wood End
Howe Green
BEDWORTH
Ward End
Lea Hall
Kingshurst
Fillongley
Market End
BIRMINGHAM
Tile Cross
Maxstoke Priory
Green End
Corley Ash
CORLEY
Marston Green
Yardley
Blakesley Hall
Sheldon
BIRMINGHAM INTERNATIONAL
Little Packington
Broadwater
Chapel Green
Corley
Corley Moor
Keresley Newland
Ash Green
Neal's Green
Longford
Keresley
Acock's Green
Olton
Elmdon
Eaves Green
Hawkes End
Little Heath
Bickenhill
Meriden
Allesley
Radford
Hall Green
Worlds End
Elmdon Heath
Catherine-de-Barnes
Motorcycle
Pickford
COVENTRY
Hampton in Arden
143
Four Oaks
Upper Eastern Green
Hockley
Spon End
Shirley
SOLIHULL
Eastcote
Barston
Berkswell
Tilehill Wood
Whoberley
Carol Green
Copt Heath
Balsall Common
Chester Ho.
Tile Hill
Earlsdon
Monkspath
Bentley Heath
Knowle
Canley
Stivichall
Balsall
Dorridge

A444
Donisthorpe
A42
Ravenstone
Snibston
COALVILLE
M1
Lullington
Netherseal
Stretton en le Field
Oakthorpe
Normanton le Heath
Bardon
Hugglescote
A511
Donington le Heath
Measham
140
Clifton Campville
Chilcote
The Moat Ho.
Heather
Ellistown
Appleby Magna
Swepstone
Snarestone
Ibstock
B585
Stanton under Bardon
Field Head
Thorpe Constantine
No Man's Heath
Appleby Parva
Newton Burgoland
B582
Herb
Bagworth
Thornton Resr.
Newton Regis
Norton-Juxta-Twycross
Odstone
A447
Thornton
Seckington
Austrey
Barton in the Beans
Shackerstone
Nailstone
Merry Lees
Shuttington
M42
Little Orton
Twycross
Little Twycross
Battlefield Line
Congerstone
Barlestone
Priory
Bilstone
Carlton
Osbaston
Botcheston
Warton
Orton-on-the-Hill
A444
Gibbet Post
Market Bosworth
B582
Bird Garden
Water Trust
R. Sence
Newbold Verdon
Desford
Polesworth
Cadeby
Cadeby Light Railway
TAMWORTH
Wellsborough
Sheepy Magna
B585
Sheepy Parva
Birchmoor
St. Helena
Dordon
Bosworth Battlefield Visitor Centre
Peckleton
Sibson
Kirkby Mallory
A5
Bradley Green
B4116
Shenton
Sutton Cheney
Mallory Park
Grendon
Upton
Ratcliffe Culey
Bosworth Field
Canal
Ashby-de-la-Zouch
Thurlaston
Grendon Common
Whittington
ATHERSTONE
Stapleton
A47
Baddesley Ensor
139
Witherley
Dadlington
Earl Shilton
Baxterley
Fenny Drayton
Stoke Golding
Barwell
Mancetter
Elmesthorpe
Hurley
Bentley
Ridge Lane
Oldbury Resr.
R. Anker
B4111
Higham on the Hill
Wykin
LEICE
B4116
Birchley Heath
Oldbury
Hartshill Hayes
Caldecote
A5
HINCKLEY
B4668
Stoney Stanton
Hartshill
Weddington
B4666
B4669
Church End
Canal
Burbage
Sapcote
Galley Common
B4114
Whittleford
A47
Sketchley
Aston Flamville
Over Whitacre
Old Arley
Ansley
B4112
Stockingford
NUNEATON
B4109
B578
Sharnford
Seeswood Pool
Fosse Meadows
Church End
Devitts Green
New Arley
A444
Attleborough
Burton Hastings
Smockington
Claybrooke Magna
B4102
Shelford
B4098
Astley
Arbury Hall
Marston Jabbett
B4114
Wood End
Howe Green
BEDWORTH
Griff
Marston Junction
Bramcote
Wolvey Heath
Copston Magna
Bedworth Sloughs
Weston in Arden
Ryton
B4109
Fillongley
Market End
Wolvey
Wibtoft
Ullesthorpe
Corley Ash
CORLEY
Bulkington
Green End
M6
M69
B4455
B4113
B4109
B4065
B4112
Chapel Green
Corley
Corley Moor
Burrow Hill
Keresley Newland
Ash Green
Neal's Green
Barnacle
WARWICKSHIRE
Willey
B4102
B4098
Longford
Shilton
Withybrook
A45
Eaves Green
Hawkes End
Keresley
Little Heath
Ansty
Oxford
Monks Kirby
B4027
Allesley
Radford
Foleshill
B4082
B4104
COVENTRY
Pailton
Pickford
Upper Eastern Green
Wyken
B4029
A4114
Caludon
Walsgrave on Sowe
Canal
Stretton under Fosse
Four Oaks
Hockley
Spon End
Great Heath
Coombe Abbey
M6
Easenhall
144
A4600
Berkswell
Tilehill Wood
Whoberley
A428
Brinklow
Harborough Magna
Carol Green
B4106
Stoke
B4027
Coombe Abbey
B4112
B4101
A4114
Binley
A428
King's Newnham
Little Lawford
Newbold on Avon
Tile Hill
Earlsdon
Bretford
R. Avon
Canley
Stivichall
Pinley
Church Lawford
Long Lawford
Berkswell
A444
Willenhall
Brandon
Brandon Marsh

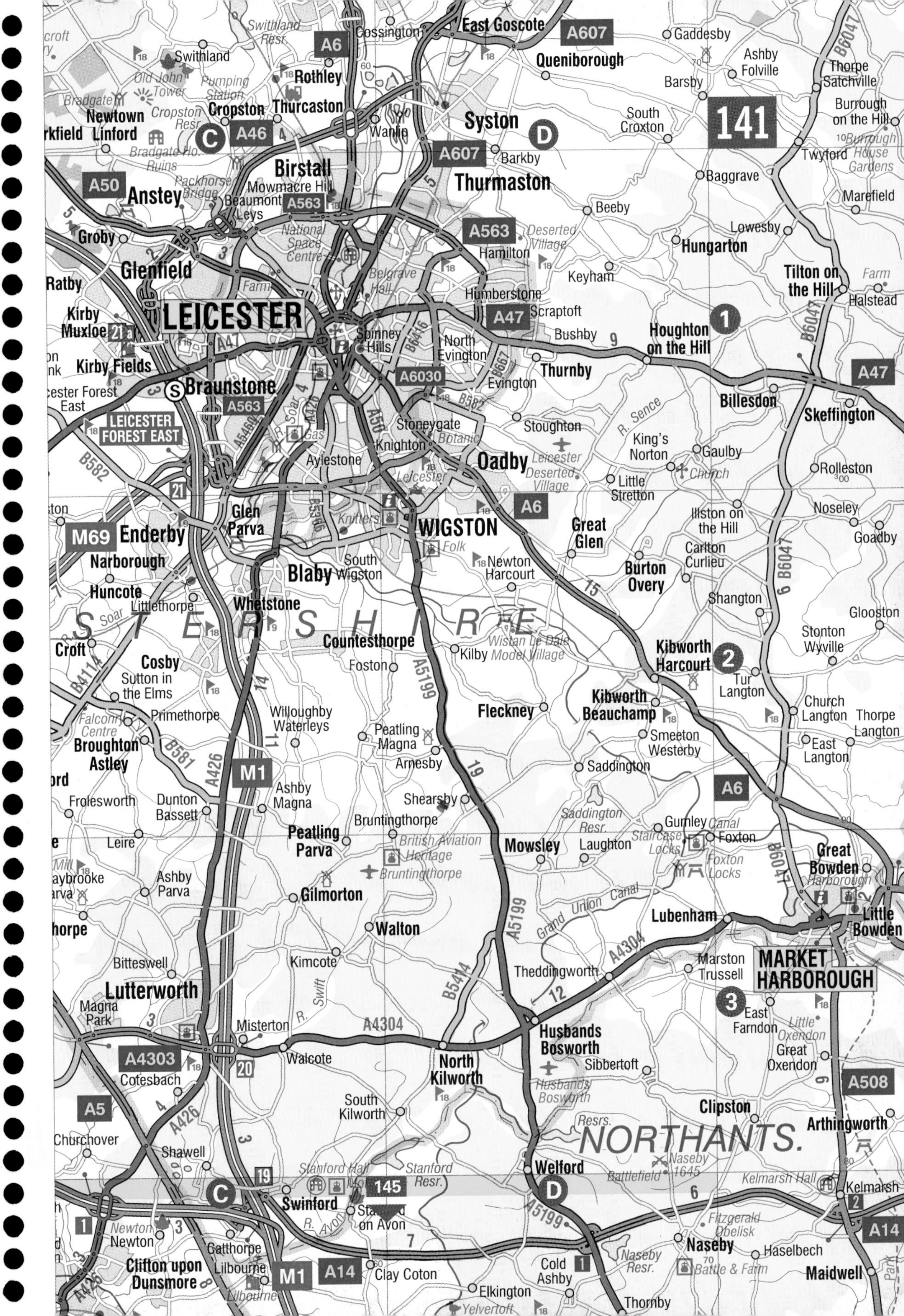
Swithland Resr.
Cossington
East Goscote
A607
Gaddesby
A6
Swithland
Queniborough
Ashby Folville
Old John Tower
Pumping Station
Rothley
Barsby
Thorpe Satchville
Bradgate
Newtown Linford
Cropston Resr.
Cropston
Thurcaston
141
Burrough on the Hill
Syston
South Croxton
Burrough House Gardens
C
A46
Wanlip
D
Twyford
Bradgate Ho. Ruins
A607
Barkby
Birstall
Baggrave
A50
Packhorse Bridge
Thurmaston
Marefield
Anstey
Mowmacre Hill
Beaumont Leys
A563
Beeby
Lowesby
Groby
National Space Centre
A563
Deserted Village
Hungarton
Hamilton
Glenfield
Keyham
Tilton on the Hill
Farm
Ratby
Belgrave Hall
Farm
Humberstone
Halstead
Kirby Muxloe
LEICESTER
A47
Scraptoft
Spinney Hills
Bushby
Houghton on the Hill
1
A47
North Evington
Kirby Fields
B6416
B667
Thurnby
A47
Braunstone
A6030
Evington
Leicester Forest East
A563
B582
Billesdon
Skeffington
R. Soar
LEICESTER FOREST EAST
A426
A5460
A50
R. Sence
Stoneygate
Stoughton
Gas
Botanic
King's Norton
B582
Knighton
Gaulby
Aylestone
Oadby
Leicester Deserted Village
Leicester
Church
Rolleston
Little Stretton
21
Glen Parva
B5366
A6
Noseley
Knitters
WIGSTON
Ilston on the Hill
M69
Enderby
Great Glen
Goadby
Folk
Carlton Curlieu
Narborough
South Wigston
Newton Harcourt
Burton Overy
Blaby
B6047
Huncote
Whetstone
Littlethorpe
Shangton
Soar
Glooston
LEICESTERSHIRE
Stonton Wyville
Croft
Countesthorpe
Wistan Le Dale Model Village
Kilby
Kibworth Harcourt
2
Cosby
Foston
B4114
Tur Langton
Sutton in the Elms
A5199
Kibworth Beauchamp
Fleckney
Church Langton
Thorpe Langton
Falconry Centre
Primethorpe
Willoughby Waterleys
Peatling Magna
Broughton Astley
Smeeton Westerby
East Langton
B581
A426
M1
Arnesby
Saddington
A6
Frolesworth
Dunton Bassett
Ashby Magna
Shearsby
Saddington Resr.
Gumley
Canal
Bruntingthorpe
Peatling Parva
Staircase Locks
Foxton
Leire
British Aviation Heritage
Mowsley
Laughton
Great Bowden
Mill
Claybrooke
Ashby Parva
Foxton Locks
B6047
Bruntingthorpe
Harborough
Gilmorton
Grand Union Canal
Lubenham
Little Bowden
A5199
Walton
A4304
MARKET HARBOROUGH
Marston Trussell
Bitteswell
Kimcote
Theddingworth
Lutterworth
B5414
R. Swift
3
Magna Park
East Farndon
Misterton
A4304
Little Oxendon
Husbands Bosworth
A4303
Walcote
North Kilworth
Sibbertoft
Great Oxendon
Cotesbach
20
Husbands Bosworth
A508
A5
South Kilworth
Clipston
Arthingworth
A426
Resrs.
NORTHANTS.
Churchover
Shawell
Naseby 1645
Stanford Hall
Stanford Resr.
Welford
Battlefield
19
Kelmarsh Hall
C
145
D
Kelmarsh
Swinford
Stanford on Avon
A5199
A14
R. Avon
Newton
Fitzgerald Obelisk
Gatthorpe
Naseby
Haselbech
Clifton upon Dunsmore
Lilbourne
Naseby Resr.
M1
A14
Clay Coton
Cold Ashby
Battle & Farm
Maidwell
Lilbourne
Elkington
Thornby
Yelvertoft

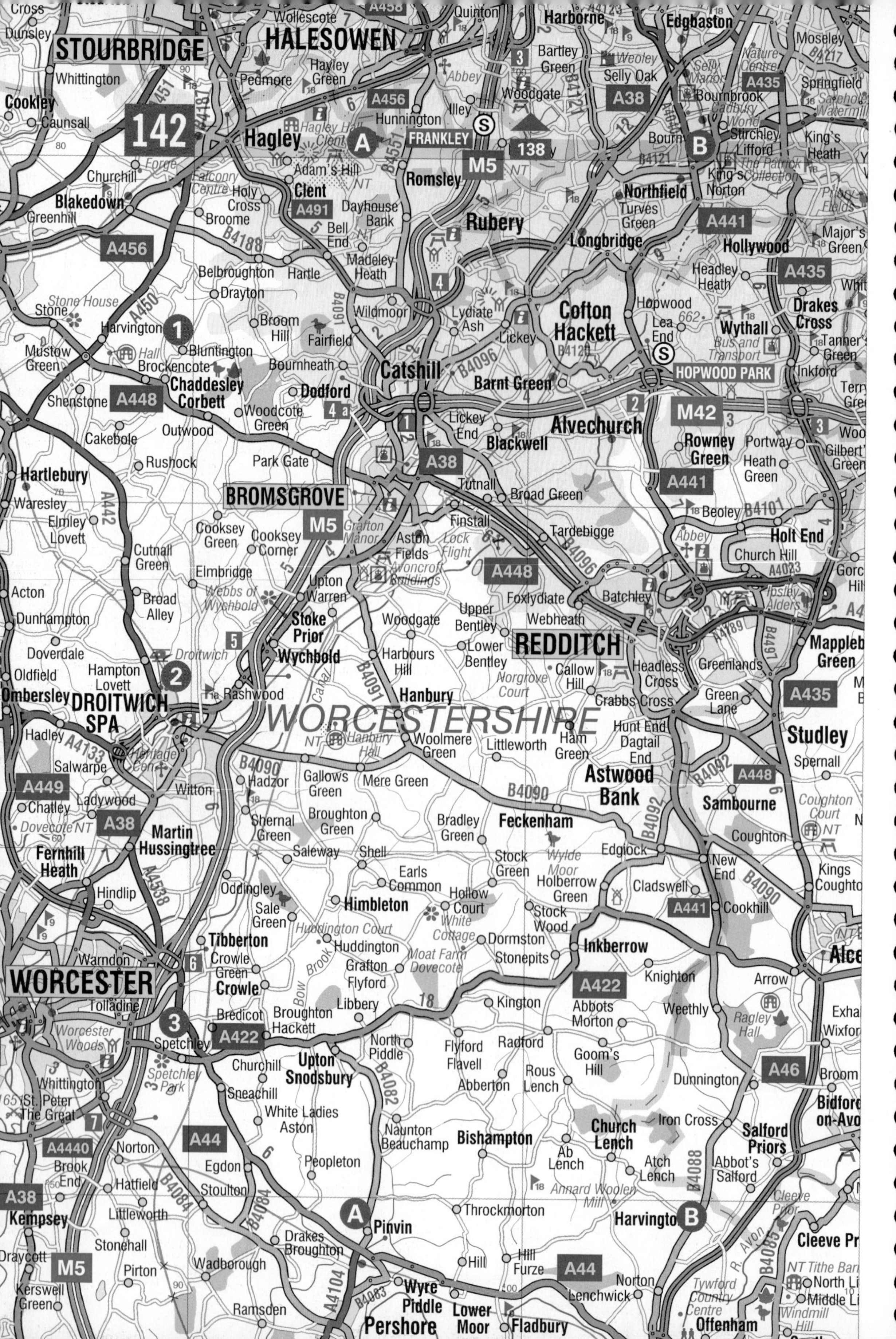

142
STOURBRIDGE
HALESOWEN
Wollescote
Quinton
Harborne
Edgbaston
Moseley
Dunsley
Cross
Whittington
Pedmore
Hayley Green
Abbey
Bartley Green
Weoley
Selly Oak
Selly Manor
Nature Centre
Springfield
Sarehole Watermill
Cookley
Caunsall
Hagley
Hagley Hall
Clent
A456
Hunnington
Illey
Woodgate
A38
Bournbrook
Cadbury World
Stirchley
Lifford
King's Heath
FRANKLEY
138
M5
Bourn
Churchill
Forge
Falconry Centre
Adam's Hill
NT
Romsley
The Patrick Collection
King's Norton
Blakedown
Greenhill
Holy Cross
Broome
A491
Dayhouse Bank
Bell End
Rubery
Northfield
Turves Green
A441
Major's Green
A456
B4188
Madeley Heath
Longbridge
Hollywood
Belbroughton
Hartle
Headley Heath
A435
Drayton
Wildmoor
Lydiate Ash
Cofton Hackett
Hopwood
Drakes Cross
Stone House
Stone
Harvington
A450
Broom Hill
Fairfield
Lickey
Lea End
Wythall
Bus and Transport
Tanner's Green
Mustow Green
Hall
Bluntington
Brockencote
Chaddesley Corbett
Bournheath
Catshill
B4096
Barnt Green
HOPWOOD PARK
Inkford
Shenstone
A448
Dodford
M42
Woodcote Green
Outwood
Lickey End
Blackwell
Alvechurch
Rowney Green
Portway
Heath Green
Cakebole
Rushock
Park Gate
Hartlebury
A442
Waresley
Elmley Lovett
BROMSGROVE
Tutnall
Broad Green
A441
Beoley
B4101
Finstall
Grafton Manor
Aston Fields
Lock Flight
Tardebigge
Holt End
Church Hill
Cooksey Green
Cooksey Corner
Cutnall Green
Elmbridge
Upton Warren
Avoncroft Buildings
A448
B4096
A4023
Acton
Broad Alley
Webbs of Wychbold
Foxlydiate
Batchley
Ipsley Alders
Dunhampton
Stoke Prior
Woodgate
Upper Bentley
Webheath
A4189
B4497
Mappleborough Green
Doverdale
Wychbold
Harbours Hill
Lower Bentley
REDDITCH
Droitwich
Oldfield
Hampton Lovett
B4091
Canal
Callow Hill
Headless Cross
Greenlands
Rashwood
Norgrove Court
Ombersley
DROITWICH SPA
Hanbury
Crabbs Cross
Green Lane
A435
WORCESTERSHIRE
Hunt End
Hadley
A4133
NT
Hanbury Hall
Woolmere Green
Littleworth
Ham Green
Dagtail End
Studley
Heritage Centre
Salwarpe
B4090
Gallows Green
Mere Green
Astwood Bank
B4092
A448
Spernall
A449
Hadzor
Witton
B4090
Chatley
Ladywood
Shernal Green
Broughton Green
Sambourne
Coughton Court
Dovecote NT
A38
Martin Hussingtree
Bradley Green
Feckenham
Coughton
Fernhill Heath
A4538
Saleway
Shell
Stock Green
Wylde Moor
Edgiock
New End
Kings Coughton
Earls Common
Holberrow Green
B4090
Cladswell
Hindlip
Oddingley
Himbleton
Hollow Court
White Cottage
Stock Wood
A441
Cookhill
Sale Green
Huddington Court
Huddington
Tibberton
Dormston
Inkberrow
Alcester
Warndon
Crowle Green
Brook
Moat Farm Dovecote
Stonepits
Knighton
Grafton Flyford
Bow Brook
A422
Arrow
WORCESTER
Crowle
Tolladine
Libbery
Kington
Abbots Morton
Weethly
Exhall
Wixford
Ragley Hall
Bredicot
Broughton Hackett
A422
Worcester Woods
Spetchley
North Piddle
Flyford Flavell
Radford
Goom's Hill
Churchill
Upton Snodsbury
Rous Lench
Dunnington
A46
Broom
Spetchley Park
Whittington
Abberton
Sneachill
B4082
St. Peter
The Great
White Ladies Aston
Church Lench
Iron Cross
Bidford-on-Avon
Salford Priors
Naunton Beauchamp
Bishampton
A4440
Norton
A44
Ab Lench
B4088
Brook End
Egdon
Peopleton
Atch Lench
Abbot's Salford
Hatfield
B4084
Annard Woolen Mill
Cleeve Prior
A38
Stoulton
Throckmorton
Kempsey
Littleworth
Pinvin
Harvington
R. Avon
Cleeve Prior
Draycott
Stonehall
Drakes Broughton
M5
Pirton
Wadborough
Hill
Hill Furze
A44
NT Tithe Barn
North Littleton
Middle Littleton
B4085
A4104
Kerswell Green
Wyre Piddle
Lenchwick
Norton
Tyford Country Centre
Windmill Hill
Ramsden
B4083
Lower Moor
Fladbury
Pershore
Offenham

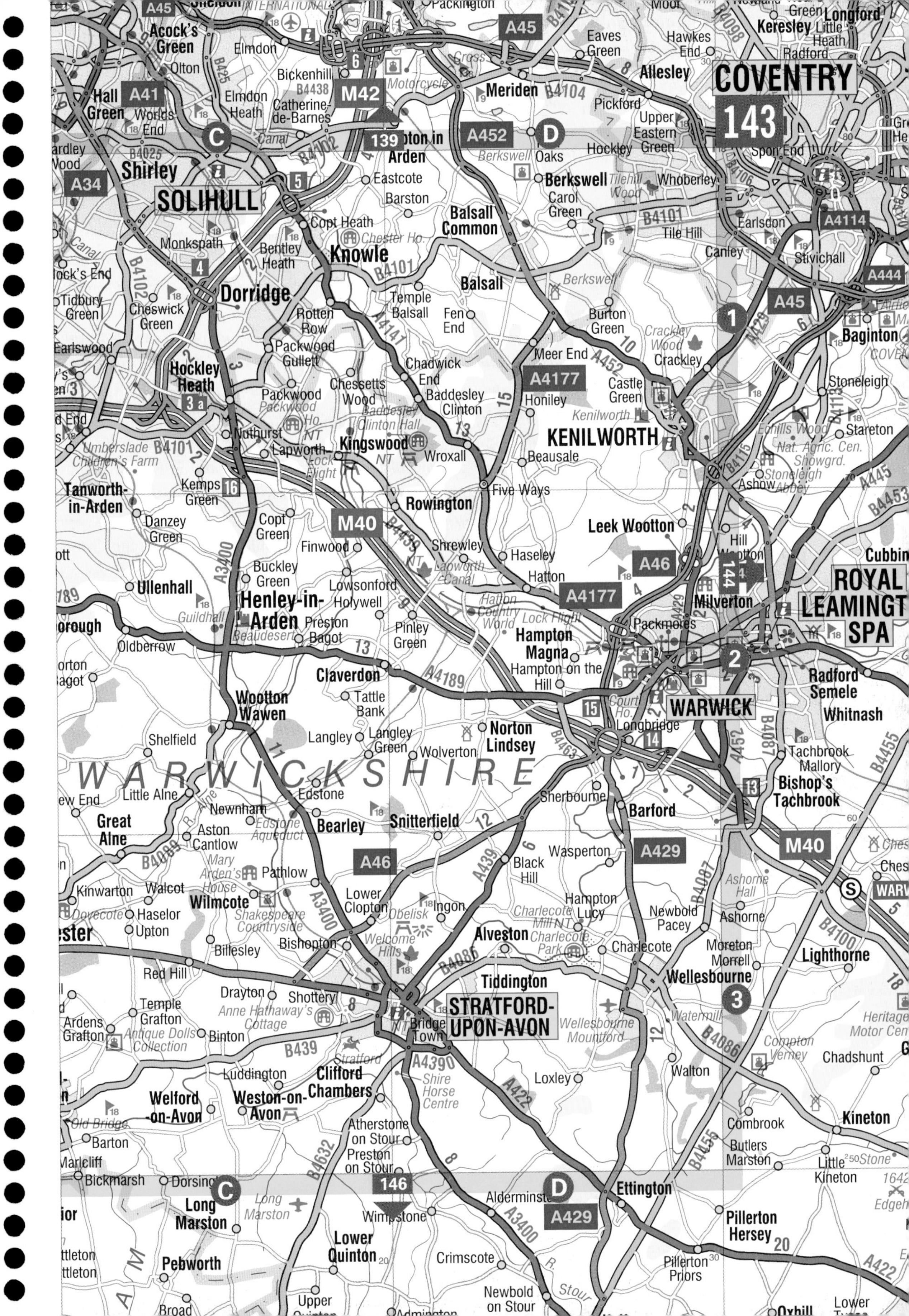

COVENTRY
143
139
144
146
ROYAL LEAMINGTON SPA
WARWICK
KENILWORTH
SOLIHULL
STRATFORD-UPON-AVON
WARWICKSHIRE
Acock's Green
Olton
Elmdon
Bickenhill
Hall Green
Worlds End
Elmdon Heath
Catherine-de-Barnes
Meriden
Eaves Green
Hawkes End
Allesley
Keresley
Longford
Radford
Pickford
Upper Eastern Green
Hockley
Berkswell
Oaks
Whoberley
Spon End
Shirley
Eastcote
Barston
Balsall Common
Carol Green
Tile Hill
Earlsdon
Canley
Stivichall
Copt Heath
Knowle
Monkspath
Bentley Heath
Dorridge
Tidbury Green
Cheswick Green
Temple Balsall
Balsall
Burton Green
Crackley
Baginton
Earlswood
Rotten Row
Packwood Gullett
Fen End
Chadwick End
Meer End
Hockley Heath
Packwood
Chessetts Wood
Baddesley Clinton
Honiley
Castle Green
Stoneleigh
Stareton
Nuthurst
Lapworth
Kingswood
Wroxall
Beausale
Umberslade Children's Farm
Kemps Green
Tanworth-in-Arden
Five Ways
Rowington
Ashow
Danzey Green
Copt Green
Leek Wootton
Hill Wootton
Finwood
Shrewley
Haseley
Ullenhall
Buckley Green
Lowsonford
Hatton
Henley-in-Arden
Holywell
Preston Bagot
Pinley Green
Hampton Magna
Hampton on the Hill
Packmores
Milverton
Oldberrow
Claverdon
Tattle Bank
Radford Semele
Whitnash
Wootton Wawen
Langley
Langley Green
Wolverton
Norton Lindsey
Longbridge
Shelfield
Tachbrook Mallory
Bishop's Tachbrook
Little Alne
Edstone
Newnham
Sherbourne
Barford
Great Alne
Aston Cantlow
Bearley
Snitterfield
Wasperton
Pathlow
Black Hill
Kinwarton
Walcot
Wilmcote
Lower Clopton
Ingon
Hampton Lucy
Newbold Pacey
Ashorne
Haselor
Upton
Alveston
Charlecote
Moreton Morrell
Lighthorne
Billesley
Bishopton
Wellesbourne
Red Hill
Tiddington
Drayton
Shottery
Temple Grafton
Ardens Grafton
Binton
Bridge Town
Wellesbourne Mountford
Walton
Chadshunt
Luddington
Clifford Chambers
Loxley
Welford-on-Avon
Weston-on-Avon
Atherstone on Stour
Combrook
Kineton
Barton
Preston on Stour
Butlers Marston
Little Kineton
Marlcliff
Bickmarsh
Dorsington
Ettington
Alderminster
Long Marston
Wimpstone
Pillerton Hersey
Lower Quinton
Pebworth
Crimscote
Pillerton Priors
Newbold on Stour
Upper Quinton
Broad
Admington
Oxhill
Lower
M42
M40
A45
A41
A34
A452
A4177
A46
A429
A4114
A444
A3400
A4189
A439
A422
A4390
A445
B4101
B4104
B4102
B4438
B4025
B4115
B4113
B4453
B4087
B4100
B4455
B4086
B4089
B4439
B4463
B439
B4632
B4632
B4456

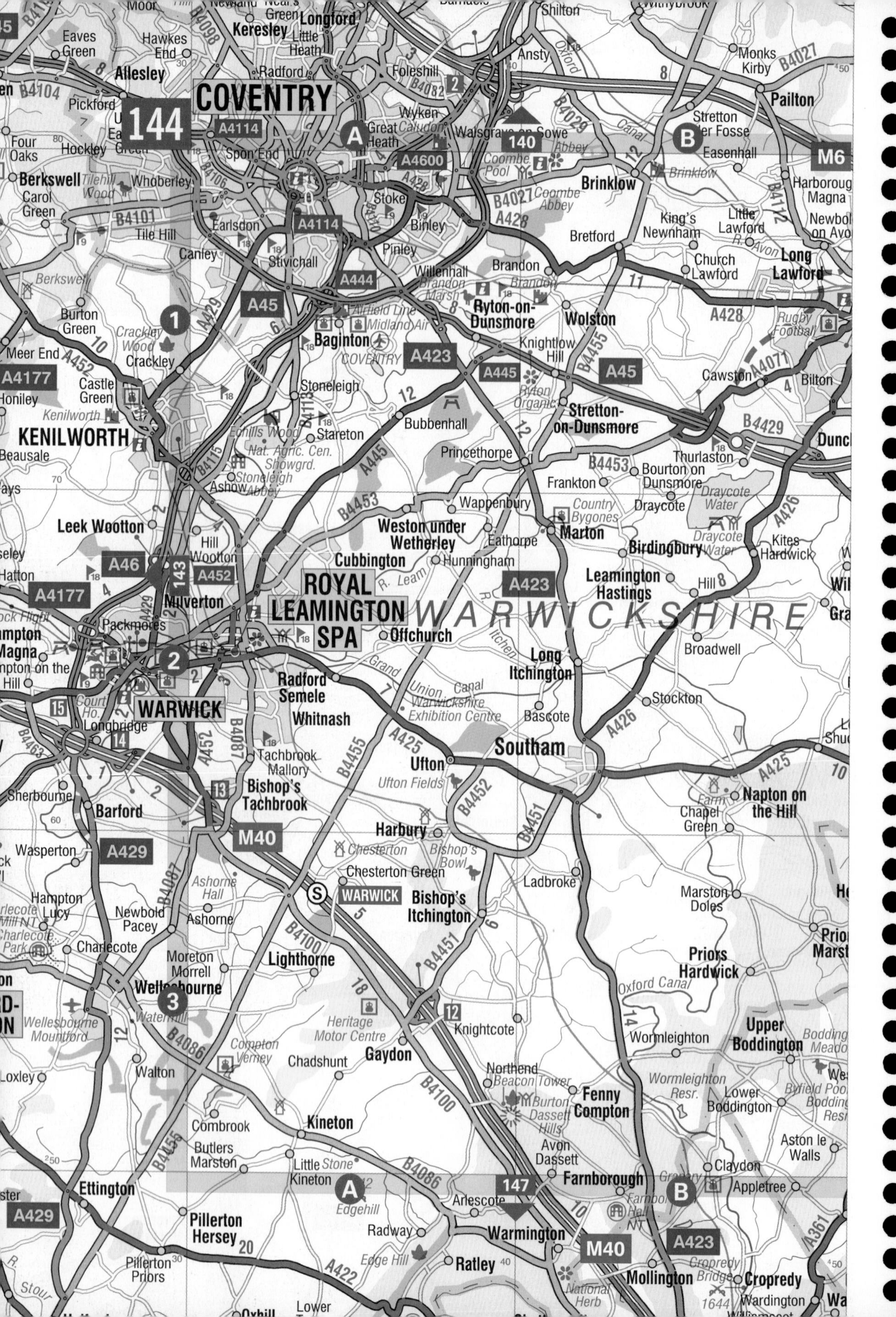
144
COVENTRY
Keresley
Longford
Little Heath
Eaves Green
Hawkes End
Allesley
Radford
Foleshill
Shilton
Ansty
Monks Kirby
Pailton
Pickford
Wyken
Great Heath
Caludon
Walsgrave on Sowe
140
Coombe Pool
Coombe Abbey
Stretton under Fosse
Easenhall
M6
Four Oaks
Hockley
Spon End
A4114
A4600
Brinklow
Berkswell
Tilehill Wood
Whoberley
Carol Green
Stoke
Binley
Harborough Magna
B4101
Tile Hill
Earlsdon
Canley
Stivichall
Pinley
Bretford
King's Newnham
Little Lawford
Church Lawford
Long Lawford
Newbold on Avon
Willenhall
Brandon
Brandon Marsh
A444
A45
Berkswell
Burton Green
Crackley Wood
Crackley
Meer End
Airfield Line
Midland Air
Baginton
COVENTRY
Ryton-on-Dunsmore
Wolston
A428
Rugby Football
A423
A445
Knightlow Hill
Cawston
Bilton
A4177
Honiley
Castle Green
Kenilworth
KENILWORTH
Beausale
Stoneleigh
Bubbenhall
Ryton Organic
Stretton-on-Dunsmore
Thurlaston
B4429
Stareton
Nat. Agric. Cen.
Showgrd.
Stoneleigh Abbey
Ashow
Princethorpe
B4453
Bourton on Dunsmore
Frankton
Draycote Water
Draycote
Wappenbury
Country Bygones
Leek Wootton
Weston under Wetherley
Eathorpe
Marton
Birdingbury
Kites Hardwick
Hill Wootton
Cubbington
Hunningham
A46
143
A452
Hatton
A4177
Milverton
R. Leam
ROYAL LEAMINGTON SPA
Leamington Hastings
Hill
WARWICKSHIRE
Packmores
Offchurch
Hampton Magna
Hampton on the Hill
Broadwell
Long Itchington
Grand Union Canal
Radford Semele
WARWICK
Court Ho.
Longbridge
Whitnash
Warwickshire Exhibition Centre
Bascote
Stockton
A426
Southam
Ufton
Tachbrook Mallory
A425
Sherbourne
Bishop's Tachbrook
Ufton Fields
B4452
Napton on the Hill
Barford
Chapel Green
Harbury
M40
A429
Wasperton
Chesterton
Bishop's Bowl
Chesterton Green
Ladbroke
WARWICK
Bishop's Itchington
Marston Doles
Hampton Lucy
Charlecote Mill NT
Charlecote Park
Newbold Pacey
Ashorne Hall
Ashorne
Charlecote
Moreton Morrell
Lighthorne
B4100
B4451
Priors Hardwick
Priors Marston
Wellesbourne
Watermill
Oxford Canal
Wellesbourne Mountford
Heritage Motor Centre
Knightcote
Upper Boddington
Wormleighton
Compton Verney
Chadshunt
Gaydon
Loxley
Walton
B4086
Northend
Beacon Tower
Fenny Compton
Burton Dassett Hills
Wormleighton Resr.
Lower Boddington
Combrook
Kineton
Avon Dassett
Aston le Walls
Butlers Marston
Little Kineton
Farnborough
Claydon
147
Ettington
Edgehill
Arlescote
Appletree
A429
Pillerton Hersey
Radway
Warmington
A423
M40
Edge Hill
Ratley
A422
Pillerton Priors
Mollington
Cropredy
National Herb
Wardington
R. Stour
Lower
Oxhill

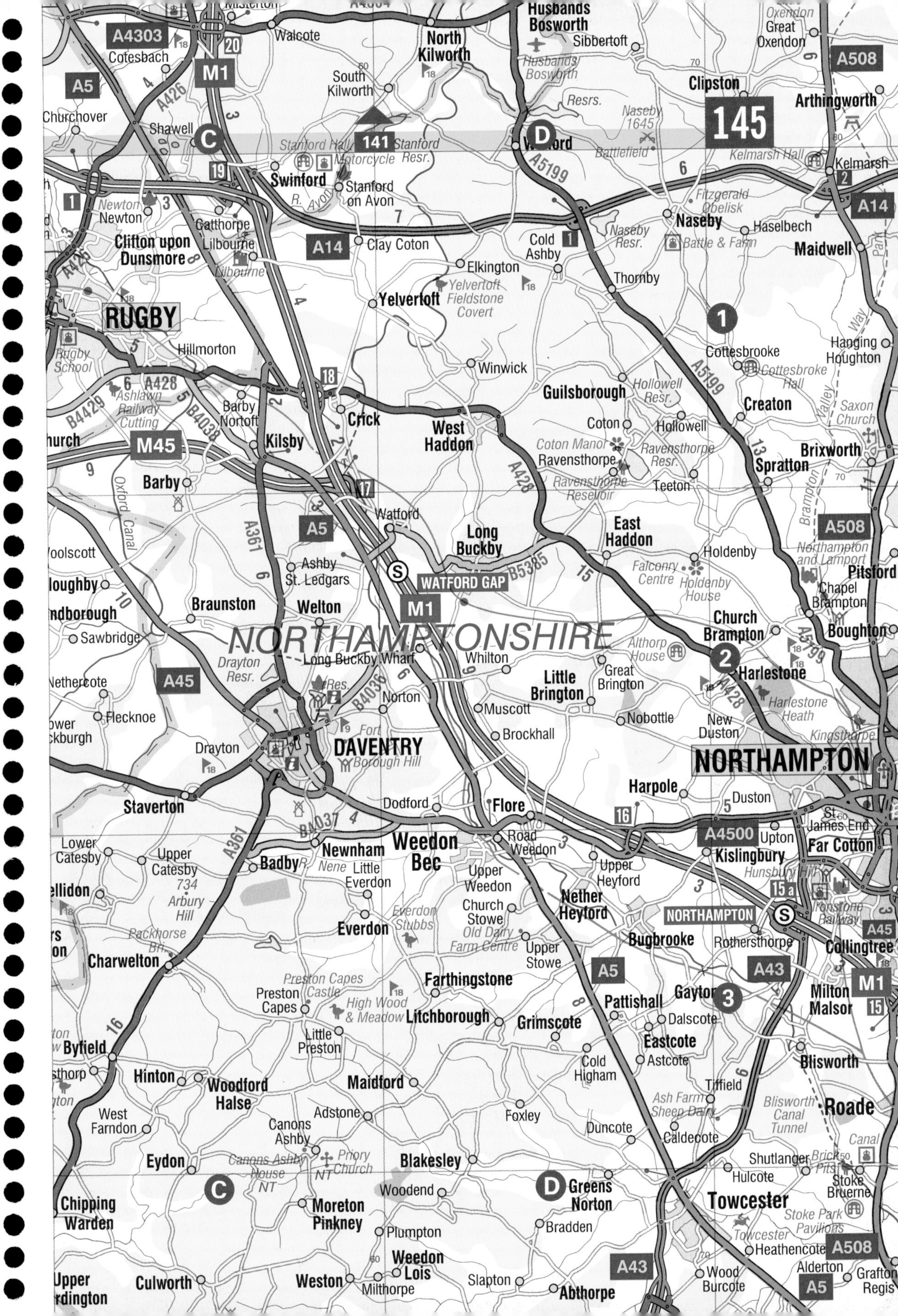

145
NORTHAMPTONSHIRE
RUGBY
DAVENTRY
NORTHAMPTON
Husbands Bosworth
North Kilworth
South Kilworth
Walcote
Cotesbach
Churchover
Shawell
Swinford
Stanford on Avon
Clifton upon Dunsmore
Newton
Catthorpe
Lilbourne
Clay Coton
Elkington
Yelvertoft
Cold Ashby
Thornby
Welford
Sibbertoft
Clipston
Great Oxendon
Arthingworth
Kelmarsh
Naseby
Haselbech
Maidwell
Cottesbrooke
Hanging Houghton
Creaton
Brixworth
Spratton
Teeton
Hollowell
Coton
Ravensthorpe
Guilsborough
Winwick
Hillmorton
Barby Nortoft
Crick
West Haddon
Kilsby
Barby
Watford
Long Buckby
East Haddon
Holdenby
Pitsford
Chapel Brampton
Church Brampton
Boughton
Harlestone
Ashby St. Ledgars
Welton
Braunston
Sawbridge
Long Buckby Wharf
Whilton
Great Brington
Little Brington
Muscott
Nobottle
New Duston
Norton
Brockhall
Flecknoe
Drayton
Staverton
Dodford
Flore
Harpole
Duston
St. James End
Upton
Far Cotton
Kislingbury
Weedon Bec
Newnham
Badby
Little Everdon
Everdon
Upper Weedon
Church Stowe
Upper Stowe
Upper Heyford
Nether Heyford
Bugbrooke
Rothersthorpe
Collingtree
Lower Catesby
Upper Catesby
Charwelton
Preston Capes
Farthingstone
Litchborough
Grimscote
Pattishall
Gayton
Dalscote
Eastcote
Astcote
Cold Higham
Milton Malsor
Blisworth
Little Preston
Byfield
Hinton
Woodford Halse
Maidford
Tiffield
Roade
West Farndon
Adstone
Canons Ashby
Foxley
Duncote
Caldecote
Eydon
Blakesley
Shutlanger
Hulcote
Stoke Bruerne
Chipping Warden
Moreton Pinkney
Woodend
Greens Norton
Towcester
Bradden
Plumpton
Weedon Lois
Heathencote
Culworth
Weston
Milthorpe
Slapton
Abthorpe
Wood Burcote
Alderton
Grafton Regis
WATFORD GAP
NORTHAMPTON
M1
M45
A5
A14
A45
A43
A361
A428
A508
A5199
A4303
A4500
B4036
B4037
B5385
B4038
B4429
Stanford Hall
Motorcycle
Stanford Resr.
Naseby 1645
Battlefield
Kelmarsh Hall
Fitzgerald Obelisk
Naseby Resr.
Battle & Farm
Yelvertoft Fieldstone Covert
Rugby School
Ashlawn Railway Cutting
Oxford Canal
Cottesbroke Hall
Hollowell Resr.
Coton Manor
Ravensthorpe Resr.
Ravensthorpe Reservoir
Saxon Church
Brampton Valley Way
Northampton and Lamport
Falconry Centre
Holdenby House
Althorp House
Harlestone Heath
Kingsthorpe
Drayton Resr.
Borough Hill
Fort
Hunsbury Hill
Ironstone Railway
Arbury Hill
Packhorse Bri.
Everdon Stubbs
Old Dairy Farm Centre
Preston Capes Castle
High Wood & Meadow
Ash Farm Sheep Dairy
Blisworth Canal Tunnel
Canons Ashby House NT
Priory Church NT
Stoke Park Pavilions
Towcester

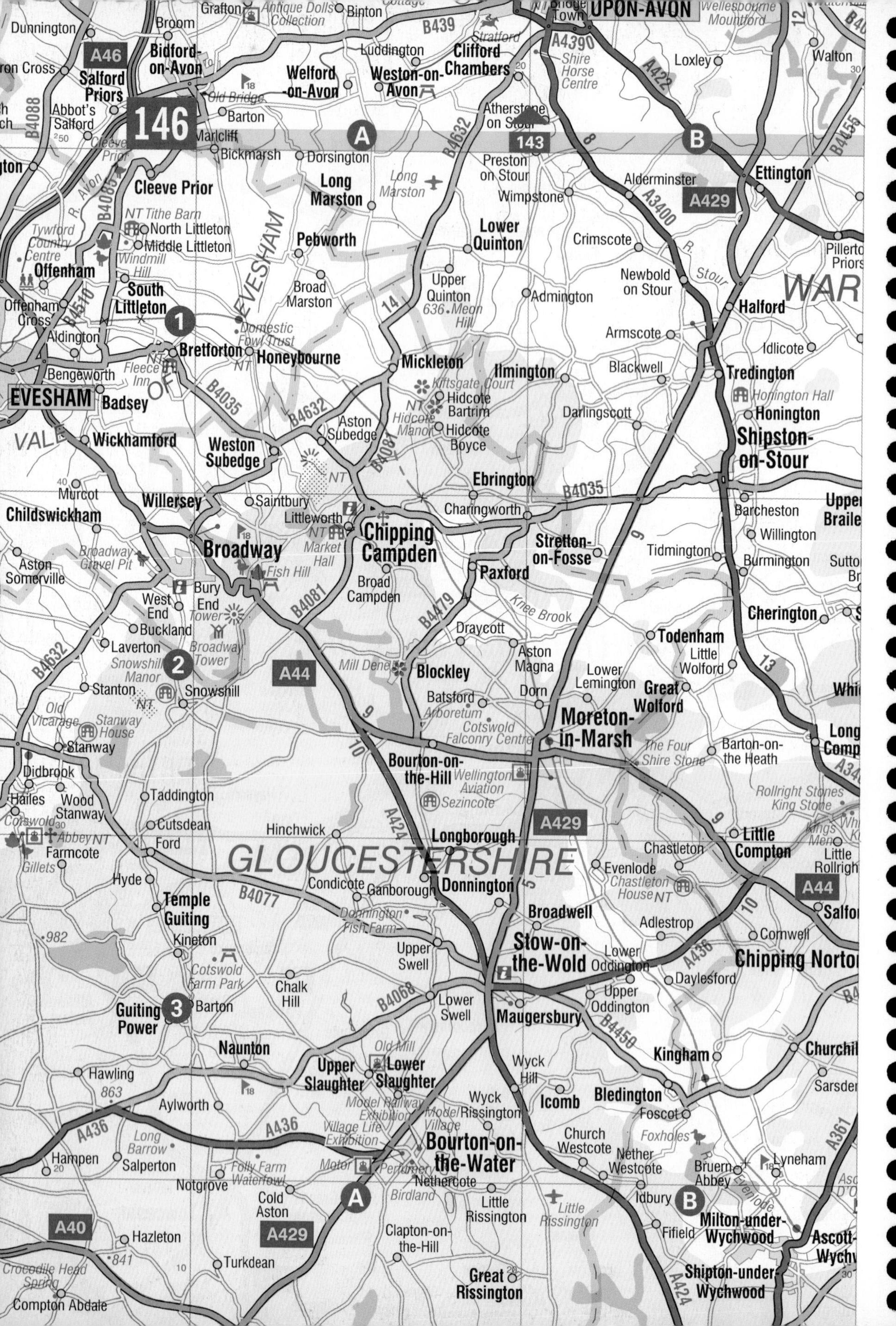

Dunnington
Broom
Grafton
Antique Dolls Collection
Binton
UPON-AVON
Bridge Town
Wellesbourne Mountford
A46
Iron Cross
Salford Priors
Bidford-on-Avon
B439
Stratford
Luddington
Clifford Chambers
Welford-on-Avon
Weston-on-Avon
A4390
Shire Horse Centre
Loxley
A422
Walton
Abbot's Salford
146
Old Bridge
Barton
Atherstone on Stour
B4088
Cleeve Prior
Marlcliff
A
B4632
143
B
Bickmarsh
Dorsington
Preston on Stour
Ettington
Cleeve Prior
Long Marston
Long Marston
Alderminster
A3400
A429
B4085
NT Tithe Barn
North Littleton
Middle Littleton
Wimpstone
Tywford Country Centre
Windmill Hill
Pebworth
Lower Quinton
Crimscote
Pillerton Priors
Offenham
EVESHAM
Broad Marston
Upper Quinton
Newbold on Stour
R. Stour
WAR
Offenham Cross
B4510
South Littleton
636 Meon Hill
Admington
Halford
1
Aldington
Domestic Fowl Trust
14
Armscote
Idlicote
Bretforton
Honeybourne
Mickleton
Ilmington
Blackwell
Tredington
Bengeworth
Fleece Inn
Kiftsgate Court
Hidcote Bartrim
Honington Hall
EVESHAM
Badsey
OF
B4035
B4632
Hidcote Manor
Hidcote Boyce
Darlingscott
Honington
VALE
Wickhamford
Weston Subedge
Aston Subedge
B4081
Shipston-on-Stour
Murcot
Ebrington
B4035
Childswickham
Willersey
Saintbury
Littleworth
Charingworth
Barcheston
Upper Brailes
Market Hall
Chipping Campden
Willington
Broadway
Broadway Gravel Pit
Stretton-on-Fosse
Tidmington
Aston Somerville
Fish Hill
Broad Campden
Paxford
Burmington
West End
Bury End
Tower
B4081
B4479
Knee Brook
Cherington
Buckland
Laverton
Broadway Tower
Draycott
Todenham
B4632
Snowshill Manor
2
A44
Mill Dene
Blockley
Aston Magna
Little Wolford
13
Stanton
Snowshill
Batsford Arboretum
Lower Lemington
Dorn
Great Wolford
Old Vicarage
Stanway House
9
Cotswold Falconry Centre
Moreton-in-Marsh
Long Compton
Stanway
10
Bourton-on-the-Hill
The Four Shire Stone
Barton-on-the-Heath
Didbrook
Wellington Aviation
Hailes
Wood Stanway
Taddington
Sezincote
Rollright Stones King Stone
Cotswold Abbey
Cutsdean
A424
A429
Hinchwick
Longborough
Little Compton
Farmcote
Ford
GLOUCESTERSHIRE
Chastleton
Little Rollright
Gillets
Evenlode
Hyde
Condicote
Ganborough
Donnington
Chastleton House
A44
Temple Guiting
B4077
Broadwell
Salford
Adlestrop
Donnington Fish Farm
Cornwell
982
Kineton
Stow-on-the-Wold
Upper Swell
Lower Oddington
A436
Chipping Norton
Cotswold Farm Park
Chalk Hill
Daylesford
B4068
Upper Oddington
Guiting Power
3
Barton
Lower Swell
Maugersbury
B4450
Naunton
Old Mill
Kingham
Churchill
Hawling
Upper Slaughter
Lower Slaughter
Wyck Hill
863
Aylworth
Wyck Rissington
Icomb
Bledington
Sarsden
Model Railway Exhibition
Model Village
A436
Village Life Exhibition
Foscot
A436
Long Barrow
Bourton-on-the-Water
Church Westcote
Foxholes
A361
Hampen
Salperton
Folly Farm Waterfowl
Motor
Perfumery
Nether Westcote
Lyneham
Notgrove
Nethercote
Bruern Abbey
Cold Aston
Birdland
Little Rissington
Little Rissington
Idbury
B
A
Evenlode
A40
Hazleton
A429
Clapton-on-the-Hill
Fifield
Milton-under-Wychwood
Ascott-under-Wychwood
Crocodile Head Spring
841
Turkdean
Great Rissington
A424
Shipton-under-Wychwood
Compton Abdale

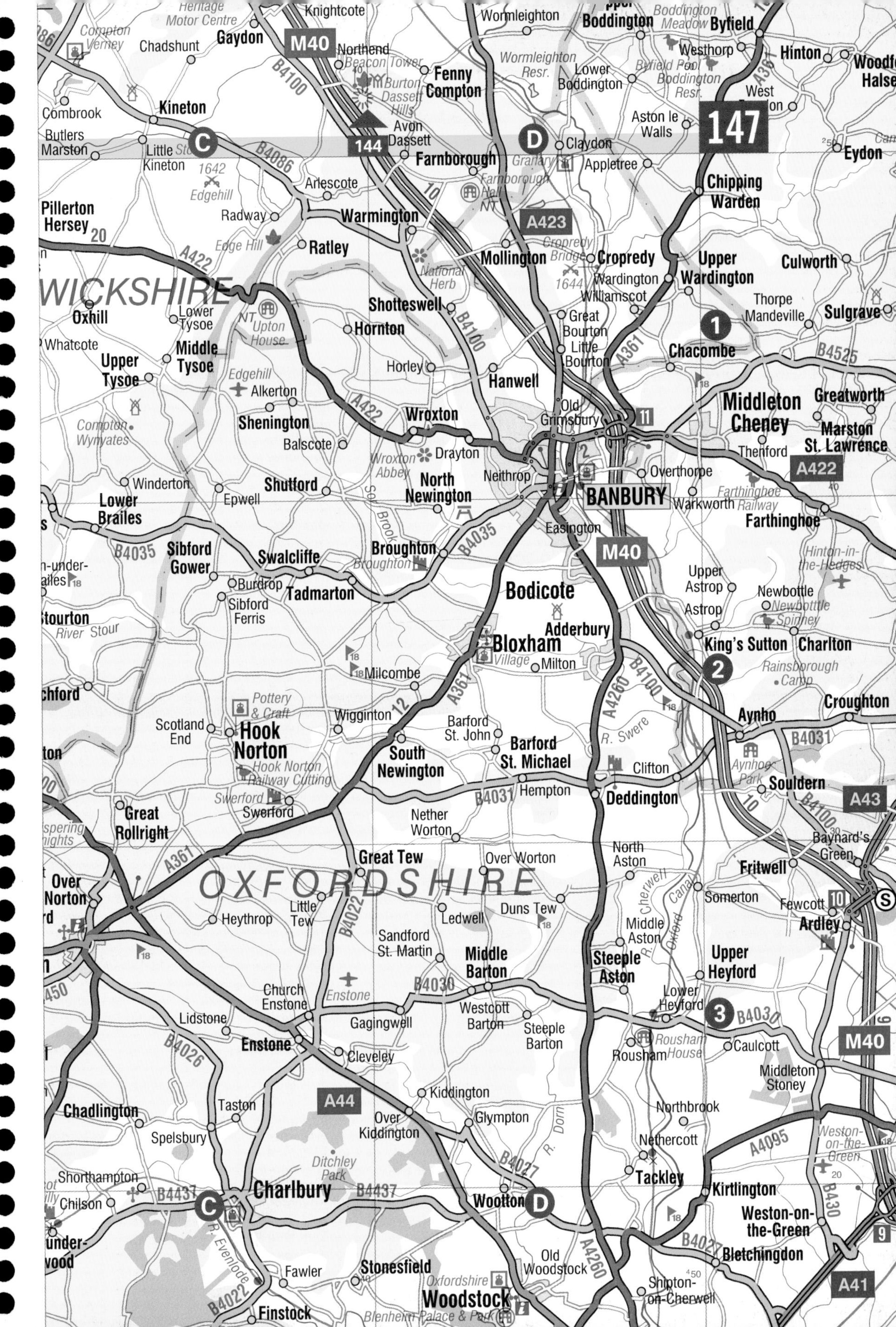

Heritage Motor Centre
Compton Verney
Chadshunt
Gaydon
Knightcote
M40
Northend
Beacon Tower
Burton Dassett Hills
Fenny Compton
B4100
Wormleighton
Wormleighton Resr.
Boddington
Boddington Meadow
Byfield
Westhorp
Byfield Pool
Boddington Resr.
Lower Boddington
Hinton
West
Aston le Walls
147
Combrook
Kineton
Butlers Marston
Little Kineton
C
B4086
1642
Edgehill
144
Avon Dassett
Farnborough
D
Claydon
Granary
Appletree
Farnborough Hall NT
Eydon
Chipping Warden
Arlescote
Pillerton Hersey
20
Radway
Warmington
A423
Edge Hill
Ratley
A422
Mollington
Cropredy Bridge
Cropredy
National Herb
1644
Wardington
Upper Wardington
Culworth
WICKSHIRE
Oxhill
Lower Tysoe
NT Upton House
Shotteswell
B4100
Williamscot
Thorpe Mandeville
Sulgrave
1
Whatcote
Middle Tysoe
Upper Tysoe
Hornton
Great Bourton
Little Bourton
A361
Chacombe
B4525
Edgehill
Alkerton
Horley
Hanwell
18
Greatworth
Middleton Cheney
Compton Wynyates
Shenington
Wroxton
Old Grimsbury
11
Marston St. Lawrence
Balscote
Drayton
Wroxton Abbey
Thenford
A422
Winderton
Lower Brailes
Epwell
Shutford
North Newington
Neithrop
Overthorpe
BANBURY
Farthinghoe Railway
Warkworth
Farthinghoe
Sor Brook
Easington
B4035
Sibford Gower
Swalcliffe
Broughton
M40
Hinton-in-the-Hedges
Burdrop
Tadmarton
Bodicote
Upper Astrop
Newbottle
Newbottle Spinney
Sibford Ferris
Adderbury
Astrop
River Stour
Bloxham
Bloxham Village
King's Sutton
Charlton
Milton
Milcombe
2
Rainsborough Camp
B4100
Pottery & Craft
Wigginton
12
A4260
R. Swere
Croughton
Scotland End
Hook Norton
Barford St. John
Barford St. Michael
Aynho
B4031
South Newington
Hook Norton Railway Cutting
Clifton
Aynhoe Park
Souldern
Swerford
Hempton
B4031
Deddington
A43
Great Rollright
Nether Worton
B4100
Baynard's Green
Over Worton
North Aston
Great Tew
A361
Fritwell
OXFORDSHIRE
Over Norton
Cherwell
Oxford Canal
Somerton
Fewcott
10
Little Tew
Heythrop
Ledwell
Duns Tew
Ardley
B4022
Middle Aston
Sandford St. Martin
Middle Barton
Steeple Aston
Upper Heyford
B4030
Church Enstone
Enstone
Lower Heyford
Westcott Barton
3
B4030
Lidstone
Gagingwell
Steeple Barton
Rousham House
Rousham
Caulcott
M40
B4026
Enstone
Cleveley
Middleton Stoney
Kiddington
A44
Taston
Northbrook
Chadlington
Over Kiddington
Glympton
R. Dorn
Spelsbury
Nethercott
A4095
Weston-on-the-Green
Ditchley Park
B4027
Shorthampton
Tackley
Kirtlington
B4437
Charlbury
B4437
Chilson
C
Wootton
D
Weston-on-the-Green
B430
R. Evenlode
A4260
B4027
Bletchingdon
9
Old Woodstock
Fawler
Stonesfield
Oxfordshire
Shipton-on-Cherwell
A41
B4022
Finstock
Woodstock
Blenheim Palace & Park

INDEX

Including Streets, Places & Areas, Industrial Estates, Flats & Walkways, Stations and Places of Interest.

HOW TO USE THIS INDEX

1. Each street name is followed by its Postcode District and then by its Locality abbreviation(s) and then by its map reference; e.g. **Abberton Way** CV4: Canly . . . .5H **67** is in the CV4 Postcode District and the Canley Locality and is to be found in square 5H on page **67**. The page number is shown in bold type.
2. A strict alphabetical order is followed in which Av., Rd., St., etc. (though abbreviated) are read in full and as part of the street name; e.g. **Abbey End** appears after **Abbeydale Cl.** but before **Abbeyfields Dr.**
3. Streets and a selection of flats and walkways too small to be shown on street map pages **6-137**, appear in the index with the thoroughfare to which it is connected shown in brackets; e.g. **Albion Ter.** *B46: Wat O . . . . 1B **24** (off St Pauls Ct.)*
4. Addresses that are in more than one part are referred to as not continuous.
5. Places and areas are shown in the index in BLUE TYPE and the map reference is to the actual map square in which the town centre or area is located and not to the place name shown on the map. Map references for entries that appear on street map pages **6-134** are shown first, with references to road map pages **138-147** shown in brackets; e.g. ALCESTER 5B 112 (3B 142)
6. An example of a selected place of interest is Anne Hathaway's Cottage 5B 114
7. An example of a station is Atherstone Station (Rail) . . . . 3B 16. Included are Rail (Rail) and Park & Ride (Park & Ride)
8. Map references for entries that appear on large scale pages **135-137** are shown first, with small scale map references shown in brackets; e.g. **Abbotts La.** CV1: Cov 2F **135** (4B **58**)

GENERAL ABBREVIATIONS

- **All.** : Alley
- **App.** : Approach
- **Arc.** : Arcade
- **Av.** : Avenue
- **Blvd.** : Boulevard
- **Bri.** : Bridge
- **Bldgs.** : Buildings
- **Bungs.** : Bungalows
- **Bus.** : Business
- **Cvn.** : Caravan
- **C'way.** : Causeway
- **Cen.** : Centre
- **Chu.** : Church
- **Chyd.** : Churchyard
- **Circ.** : Circle
- **Cir.** : Circus
- **Cl.** : Close
- **Coll.** : College
- **Comn.** : Common
- **Cnr.** : Corner
- **Cott.** : Cottage
- **Cotts.** : Cottages
- **Ct.** : Court
- **Cres.** : Crescent
- **Cft.** : Croft
- **Dpt.** : Depot
- **Dr.** : Drive
- **E.** : East
- **Ent.** : Enterprise
- **Est.** : Estate
- **Fld.** : Field
- **Flds.** : Fields
- **Gdn.** : Garden
- **Gdns.** : Gardens
- **Gth.** : Garth
- **Ga.** : Gate
- **Gt.** : Great
- **Grn.** : Green
- **Gro.** : Grove
- **Hgts.** : Heights
- **Ho.** : House
- **Ho's.** : Houses
- **Ind.** : Industrial
- **Info.** : Information
- **Intl.** : International
- **Junc.** : Junction
- **La.** : Lane
- **Lit.** : Little
- **Lwr.** : Lower
- **Mnr.** : Manor
- **Mans.** : Mansions
- **Mkt.** : Market
- **Mdw.** : Meadow
- **Mdws.** : Meadows
- **M.** : Mews
- **Mt.** : Mount
- **Mus.** : Museum
- **Nth.** : North
- **Pde.** : Parade
- **Pk.** : Park
- **Pas.** : Passage
- **Pl.** : Place
- **Pct.** : Precinct
- **Ri.** : Rise
- **Rd.** : Road
- **Rdbt.** : Roundabout
- **Shop.** : Shopping
- **Sth.** : South
- **Sq.** : Square
- **Sta.** : Station
- **St.** : Street
- **Ter.** : Terrace
- **Twr.** : Tower
- **Trad.** : Trading
- **Up.** : Upper
- **Va.** : Vale
- **Vw.** : View
- **Vs.** : Villas
- **Vis.** : Visitors
- **Wlk.** : Walk
- **W.** : West
- **Yd.** : Yard

LOCALITY ABBREVIATIONS

- A'ton : **Admington**
- Alc : **Alcester**
- Ald G : **Alderman's Green**
- Alle : **Allesley**
- A'cte : **Alvecote**
- A'ton : **Alveston**
- Ansl : **Ansley**
- Ans C : **Ansley Common**
- Ansty : **Ansty**
- App M : **Appleby Magna**
- Arb : **Arbury**
- Ard G : **Ardens Grafton**
- Arms : **Armscote**
- Arr : **Arrow**
- Ash G : **Ash Green**
- Asty : **Astley**
- Aston C : **Aston Cantlow**
- Ath : **Atherstone**
- Ath S : **Atherstone on Stour**
- Att : **Atterton**
- Aus : **Austrey**
- Bad C : **Baddesley Clinton**
- Bad E : **Baddesley Ensor**
- Bag : **Baginton**
- Barby : **Barby**
- Barf : **Barford**
- Barn : **Barnacle**
- Bart : **Barton**
- Bas : **Bascote**
- Bas H : **Bascote Heath**
- Bax : **Baxterley**
- Bear : **Bearley**
- Beau : **Beausale**
- Bed : **Bedworth**
- Bntly : **Bentley**
- Berk : **Berkswell**
- Bick : **Bickenhill**
- Bickm : **Bickmarsh**
- Bidf A : **Bidford-on-Avon**
- Bil : **Bilton**
- Bin : **Binley**
- Bin W : **Binley Woods**
- Bint : **Binton**
- B'moor : **Birchmoor**
- Bird : **Birdingbury**
- Birm A : **Birmingham Int. Airport**
- Bis I : **Bishop's Itchington**
- Bis T : **Bishop's Tachbrook**
- B'ton : **Bishopton**
- B'dwn : **Blackdown**
- B Hill : **Black Hill**
- Bod H : **Bodymoor Heath**
- Bour D : **Bourton on Dunsmore**
- Bram : **Bramcote**
- Bran : **Brandon**
- Bret : **Bretford**
- Brin : **Brinklow**
- Broom : **Broom**
- Brow : **Brownsover**
- Bubb : **Bubbenhall**
- Bud : **Budbrooke**
- Bulk : **Bulkington**
- Burt G : **Burton Green**
- Burt H : **Burton Hastings**
- But M : **Butlers Marston**
- Cald : **Caldecote**
- Canly : **Canley**
- Cas B : **Castle Bromwich**
- Cath B : **Catherine-de-Barnes**
- Cath : **Cathiron**
- Caw : **Cawston**
- Char : **Charlecote**
- Chel W : **Chelmsley Wood**
- Cher : **Cherington**
- Ches : **Chesterton**
- Chu L : **Church Lawford**
- C'over : **Churchover**
- Clav : **Claverdon**
- Cliff : **Cliff**
- Cliff C : **Clifford Chambers**
- Clift C : **Clifton Campville**
- Clift D : **Clifton upon Dusmore**
- Col : **Coleshill**
- C'brk : **Combrook**
- Cor : **Corley**
- Cosf : **Cosford**
- Cou : **Coughton**
- Cov : **Coventry**
- Crick : **Crick**
- Cubb : **Cubbington**
- Curd : **Curdworth**
- Dep B : **Deppers Bridge**
- D'wll : **Dodwell**
- Dord : **Dordon**
- Dost : **Dosthill**
- Dray : **Drayton**
- Dunc : **Dunchurch**
- Dunn : **Dunnington**
- Earls : **Earlswood**
- Eas : **Easenhall**
- E Grn : **Eastern Green**
- Eat : **Eathorpe**
- E'hill : **Edgehill**
- Ett : **Ettington**
- Exh : **Exhall**
- Farn : **Farnborough**
- Fen C : **Fenny Compton**
- Fen D : **Fenny Drayton**
- Fill : **Fillongley**
- Finh : **Finham**
- F'bri : **Fordbridge**
- F'ton : **Frankton**
- Frly : **Freasley**
- Gall C : **Galley Common**
- Gay : **Gaydon**
- Gold : **Goldicote**
- Gran : **Grandborough**
- Gran F : **Grandborough Fields**
- Gt Alne : **Great Alne**
- Gt Wol : **Great Wolford**
- Gren : **Grendon**
- Griff : **Griff**
- Gun H : **Gun Hill**
- Guys C : **Guy's Cliffe**
- Half : **Halford**
- H Ard : **Hampton in Arden**
- H Lucy : **Hampton Lucy**
- H Mag : **Hampton Magna**
- H Hill : **Hampton on the Hill**
- Harb M : **Harborough Magna**
- Har : **Harbury**
- Harts : **Hartshill**
- Hatt : **Hatton**
- H'cte : **Heathcote**
- Hen A : **Henley-in-Arden**
- High H : **Higham-on-the-Hill**
- Hill : **Hill**
- Hillm : **Hillmorton**
- Hill W : **Hill Wootton**
- Hinc : **Hinckley**
- H'ley H : **Hockley Heath**
- H'ton : **Honington**
- Hurl : **Hurley**
- Ilm : **Ilmington**
- Ing : **Ingon**
- Ken : **Kenilworth**
- Ker E : **Keresley End**
- Kils : **Kilsby**
- Kine : **Kineton**
- K'bry : **Kingsbury**
- K Cou : **King's Coughton**
- K'hrst : **Kingshurst**
- K New : **King's Newnham**
- Kinw : **Kinwarton**
- Ladb : **Ladbroke**
- Lapw : **Lapworth**

Law H : **Lawford Heath**
Lea M : **Lea Marston**
Lea H : **Leamington Hastings**
Lea S : **Leamington Spa**
Leek W : **Leek Wootton**
Light : **Lighthorne**
L Hth : **Lighthorne Heath**
Lilb : **Lilbourne**
Lill : **Lillington**
Lit Al : **Little Alne**
Lit C : **Little Compton**
Lit D : **Little Dassett**
Lit K : **Little Kineton**
Lit L : **Little Lawford**
Lit P : **Little Packington**
Lit Wol : **Little Wolford**
Long C : **Long Compton**
Longf : **Longford**
Long I : **Long Itchington**
Long L : **Long Lawford**
Long M : **Long Marston**
Lwr Bra : **Lower Brailes**
Lwr Clop : **Lower Clopton**
Lwr F : **Lower Fulbrook**
Lwr Q : **Lower Quinton**
Lwr T : **Lower Tysoe**
Lox : **Loxley**
Ludd : **Luddington**
Man : **Mancetter**
Map G : **Mappleborough Green**
Marlc : **Marlcliff**
Mars : **Marston**
Mars G : **Marston Green**
Mart : **Marton**
Max : **Maxstoke**
Mer : **Meriden**
Midd : **Middleton**
Mid T : **Middle Tysoe**
Milc : **Milcote**
Mil W : **Millison's Wood**
Min : **Minworth**
M Kirby : **Monks Kirby**
More M : **Moreton Morrell**
Nap : **Napton**
Nat E C : **National Exhibition Centre**
Neth W : **Nether Whitacre**
New A : **New Arley**
N'bld A : **Newbold on Avon**
N'bld S : **Newbold-on-Stour**
Newt : **Newton**
Newt R : **Newton Regis**
No Hth : **No Man's Heath**
N'end : **Northend**
N Lin : **Norton Lindsey**
Nun : **Nuneaton**
Off : **Offchurch**
Old A : **Old Arley**
Oldb : **Oldberrow**
Old M : **Old Milverton**
Ort H : **Orton-on-the-Hill**
Ove G : **Oversley Green**
Over W : **Over Whitacre**
Oxh : **Oxhill**
Pail : **Pailton**
Path : **Pathlow**
Peb : **Pebworth**
Picc : **Piccadilly**
Pill H : **Pillerton Hersey**
Pill P : **Pillerton Priors**
Pole : **Polesworth**
Pres B : **Preston Bagot**
Prin : **Princethorpe**
P Mars : **Priors Marston**
Rad S : **Radford Semele**
Rad : **Radway**
Ratl : **Ratley**
Redd : **Redditch**
Ridge L : **Ridge Lane**
Row : **Rowington**
Rugby : **Rugby**
Rytn D : **Ryton-on-Dunsmore**
Salf P : **Salford Priors**
Sam : **Sambourne**
Seck : **Seckington**
Sher : **Sherbourne**
Shil : **Shilton**
Ship S : **Shipston-on-Stour**
Shot : **Shottery**
Shotte : **Shotteswell**
Shu : **Shustoke**
Shut : **Shuttington**
Snitt : **Snitterfield**
Sol : **Solihull**
Sou : **Southam**
Sper : **Spernal**
Stare : **Stareton**
S'ton : **Stockton**
S'lgh : **Stoneleigh**
S'lgh P : **Stoneleigh Park**
S Avon : **Stratford-upon-Avon**
S Ash : **Street Ashton**
Stret D : **Stretton-on-Dunsmore**
Stret O : **Stretton-on-Fosse**
Stret U : **Stretton under Fosse**
Stud : **Studley**
Tan A : **Tanworth-in-Arden**
Temp H : **Temple Herdewyke**
Thurl : **Thurlaston**
Tidd : **Tiddington**
Tile H : **Tile Hill**
Tod : **Todenham**
Tred : **Tredington**
Ufton : **Ufton**
Ullen : **Ullenhall**
Up Bil : **Upper Billesley**
Up Bra : **Upper Brailes**
Up Qui : **Upper Quinton**
Up Tys : **Upper Tysoe**
W'grve S : **Walsgrave on Sowe**
W'ton : **Walton**
Wapp : **Wappenbury**
Warm : **Warmington**
Wart : **Warton**
Warw : **Warwick**
Wat O : **Water Orton**
Welf A : **Welford-on-Avon**
Welle : **Wellesbourne**
W Avon : **Weston-on-Avon**
W Weth : **Weston under Wetherley**
W'wd H : **Westwood Heath**
Whatc : **Whatcote**
What : **Whateley**
W'nsh : **Whitnash**
Whitt : **Whittington**
W'hall : **Willenhall**
W'ton : **Willington**
W'hby : **Willoughby**
Wilm : **Wilmcote**
Wiln : **Wilnecote**
Wind : **Winderton**
Wis : **Wishaw**
With : **Witherley**
Withy : **Withybrook**
Wix : **Wixford**
Wols : **Wolston**
Wlvy : **Wolvey**
Wood E : **Wood End**
Wool : **Woolscott**
Woot W : **Wootton Wawen**
Wrox : **Wroxall**
Yarn C : **Yarningale Common**

A

ABBERTON 3A 142
Abberton Way CV4: Canly 5H 67
Abbey, The CV8: Ken 4D 78
Abbey Cl. B49: Alc 3A 112
CV47: Sou 6H 107
Abbey Ct. CV3: Cov 2H 69
Abbey Cft. B78: Pole 7D 8
Abbeydale Cl. CV3: Bin 4B 60
Abbey End CV8: Ken 5D 78
Abbeyfields Dr. B80: Stud 1D 92
Abbey Fields Swimming Pool 4C 78
Abbey Ga. CV11: Nun 7D 22
Abbey Ga. Shop. Pct. CV11: Nun 7D 22
Abbey Grn. CV11: Nun 6C 22
Abbey Grn. Ct. B78: Pole 1D 10
Abbey Hill CV8: Ken 4D 78
Abbey Ind. Est. CV2: Cov 2B 60
Abbey La. CV47: Sou 6H 107
Abbey M. B49: Alc 5B 112
Abbey Rd. CV3: Cov 2F 69
(not continuous)
Abbey Sports Cen. 7C 22
Abbey St. CV11: Nun 6C 22
(not continuous)
CV21: Rugby 4J 75
Abbey Vw. B78: Pole 2E 10
Abbey Way CV3: Cov 2F 69
Abbotsbury Cl. CV2: W'grve S 3C 60
Abbotsbury Way CV11: Nun 5B 32
Abbotsford Rd. CV11: Nun 4A 32
ABBOTS MORTON 3B 142
ABBOT'S SALFORD 3B 142
Abbots Way CV34: Warw 2F 101
Abbotts La. CV1: Cov 2F 135 (4B 58)
Abbotts St. CV31: Lea S 1D 102
Abbotts Wlk. CV3: Bin W 1E 70
CV8: Wols 4K 71
Abbotts Way CV21: Hillm 7B 76
Abeles Way CV9: Ath 1B 16
Abercorn Rd. CV5: Cov 5J 57
Aberdeen Cl. CV5: E Grn 2E 56
Aberdeen Rd. CV11: Nun 3A 32
Abergavenny Wlk. CV3: Bin 1B 70
Abingdon Way CV11: Nun 4G 23
AB LENCH 3B 142
ABTHORPE 3D 145
Acacia Av. B37: K'hrst 6A 24
CV1: Cov 6E 58
Acacia Cl. B37: K'hrst 6A 24
Acacia Ct. CV6: Cov 2J 57
Acacia Cres. CV12: Bed 2K 41
Acacia Gro. CV21: Rugby 4G 75
Acacia Rd. CV10: Nun 6K 21
CV32: Lea S 6B 98
Achal Cl. CV6: Cov 4F 51
Achilles Cl. CV34: H'cte 6D 102
Achilles Rd. CV6: Cov 7G 51
Acklam Gdns. B95: Woot W 5H 93
ACOCK'S GREEN 3C 139
Acorn Cl. CV8: S'lgh 2B 80
CV12: Bed 5C 40
Acorn Ct. CV32: Lea S 5E 98
Acorn Dr. CV22: Bil 7B 74
Acorn St. CV3: Cov 7H 59
Acre Cl. CV31: W'nsh 4E 102
ACTON 2A 142
Adam Rd. CV6: Cov 7G 51
ADAM'S HILL 1A 142
Adams St. CV21: Rugby 5E 74
Adams Way B49: Alc 3B 112
Adare Dr. CV3: Cov 7C 58
Adcock Dr. CV8: Ken 4E 78
Addenbrooke Rd. CV7: Ker E 6A 40
ADDERBURY 2D 147
Adderley St. CV1: Cov 3E 58
Addingham Cl. CV34: Warw 6G 97
Addison Cl. CV10: Gall C 6F 21
Addison Dr. CV37: S Avon 7J 115
Addison Pl. B46: Wat O 1B 24
Addison Rd. CV6: Cov 6A 50
CV22: Bil, Rugby 7D 74
Adelaide Ct. CV12: Bed 3G 41
Adelaide Rd. CV31: Lea S 7C 98
CV32: Lea S 7C 98
Adelaide St. CV1: Cov 1K 135 (3E 58)
(not continuous)
Adkins Cft. CV7: Fill 2C 38
Adkinson Av. CV22: Dunc 6C 86
ADLESTROP 3B 146
ADMINGTON 1A 146
Admington Dr. CV35: Hatt 5A 96
Admiral Gdns. CV8: Ken 3G 79
Admirals Way CV11: Bram 6G 33
Adrians' Cl. CV9: Man 5E 16
Adrians Ct. CV37: S Avon 3F 115
ADSTONE 3C 145
Agincourt Rd. CV3: Cov 1E 68
Aikman Grn. CV23: Gran 6G 105
AILSTONE 7E 124
Ainsbury Rd. CV5: Cov 7J 57
Ainsdale Cl. CV6: Ald G 2H 51
Aintree Cl. CV6: Cov 2E 58
CV12: Bed 1H 41
Aintree Dr. CV32: Lill 4G 99
Aintree Rd. CV37: S Avon 6C 114
Airport Way B26: Birm A 2C 44
Ajax Cl. CV21: Rugby 2H 75
Alandale Av. CV5: E Grn 3C 56
Alandale Ct. CV12: Bed 5C 40
Alan Higgs Way CV4: Tile H 7A 56
Alauna Av. B49: Alc 3C 112
Albany Ct. CV1: Cov 5A 58
Albany Rd. CV1: Cov 5A 58
CV5: Cov 6A 58
CV37: S Avon 5B 136 (5E 114)
Albany Ter. CV32: Lea S 6C 98
Albert Bean Cl. CV31: W'nsh 4E 102
Albert Cl. B80: Stud 3D 92
Albert Cres. CV6: Cov 3B 50
Albert Fearn Gdns. CV6: Cov 5F 51
Albert Rd. CV5: Mil W 6J 47
Albert Sq. CV21: Rugby 5H 75
Albert St. CV1: Cov 3E 58
CV10: Nun 1E 30
CV21: Rugby 5H 75
CV32: Lea S 6A 98
CV34: Warw 1F 101
Albert Ter. CV37: S Avon 2G 137
Albion Ct. CV11: Nun 1K 31
Albion Ind. Est. CV6: Cov 7D 50
Albion St. CV8: Ken 4E 78
Albion Ter. *B46: Wat O* *1B 24*
(off St Pauls Ct.)
B50: Broom 3F 123
Albrighton Wlk. CV11: Nun 2C 32
Albury Rd. B80: Stud 3D 92
ALCESTER 5B 112 (3B 142)
Alcester Heath B49: K Cou 2A 112
Alcester Rd. B80: Stud 3D 92
B95: Woot W 7G 93
CV37: Dray, S Avon 4A 114
Alcocks Rd. B49: Alc 4D 112
Alcott La. B37: Mars G 5A 34
Aldbourne Rd. CV1: Cov 2C 58
Aldbury Ri. CV5: Cov 3F 57
Alderbrooke Dr. CV11: Nun 3C 32
Alder Ct. CV9: Ath 2C 16
Alder Dr. B37: Chel W 4B 34
Alderman Gee Hall *CV12: Bed* *1G 41*
(off Dempster Rd.)
ALDERMAN'S GREEN 3H 51
Alderman's Grn. Ind. Est. CV2: Ald G 3K 51
Alderman's Grn. Rd. CV2: Ald G 4H 51
(not continuous)
Alder Mdw. Cl. CV6: Cov 2D 50
ALDERMINSTER 1B 146
Alderminster Gro. CV35: Hatt 5A 96
Alderminster Rd. CV5: E Grn 3E 56
Aldermoor La. CV3: Cov 6G 59
Alderney Cl. CV6: Cov 4B 50
CV11: Bram 6H 33
Alder Rd. CV6: Cov 4G 51
Alders, The CV12: Bed 3E 40
Aldersgate B78: K'bry 4E 12
CV11: Nun 1J 31
Alders La. CV10: Nun 4F 21
Alders Rd. CV34: Warw 4F 101
ALDERTON 3D 145
Alderton M. CV31: Lea S 2G 103
ALDINGTON 1A 146
Aldrich Av. CV4: Tile H 4C 56
ALDRIDGE 1B 138
Aldridge Cl. B78: B'moor 2C 10
Aldrin Way CV4: Canly 3H 67
Aldwick Cl. CV32: Lill 3E 98
Alec Wilson Sports Cen. 1H 41
Alexander Ct. CV34: Warw 1H 101

Alexander Rd. CV12: Bed . . . 2J 41
Alexandra Ct. CV3: Cov . . . 5G 59
CV8: Ken . . . 5E 78
CV9: Ath . . . 3D 16
CV21: Rugby . . . 5H 75
(off James St.)
Alexandra Rd. CV1: Cov . . . 3F 59
CV21: Rugby . . . 4H 75
CV31: Lea S . . . 2E 102
Alexandra St. CV11: Nun . . . 7C 22
Alexandra Ter. CV6: Cov . . . 4E 50
Alexandra Wlk. *CV21: Rugby . . . 5H 75*
(off James St.)
Alex Grierson Cl. CV3: Bin . . . 1A 70
Alfall Rd. CV2: Cov . . . 2H 59
Alfred Grn. Cl. CV22: Rugby . . . 6G 75
Alfred Rd. CV1: Cov . . . 3F 59
Alfred St. CV21: Rugby . . . 5F 75
Alfriston Rd. CV3: Finh . . . 4C 68
Algate Cl. CV6: Cov . . . 3C 50
Alice Arnold Ho. CV2: Cov . . . 5H 51
Alice Cl. CV12: Bed . . . 4F 41
Alicia Cl. CV22: Caw . . . 1A 86
Alison Sq. CV2: Ald G . . . 2H 51
ALKERTON . . . 1C 147
Allan Rd. CV6: Cov . . . 3K 57
Allans Cl. CV23: Clift D . . . 3C 76
Allans Dr. CV23: Clift D . . . 3C 76
Allans La. CV23: Clift D . . . 3C 76
Allard Ho. CV3: W'hall . . . 2H 69
Allard Way CV3: Bin, Cov . . . 1G 69
Allendale Av. B80: Stud . . . 4D 92
Allendale Ct. B80: Stud . . . 4D 92
Allendale Cres. B80: Stud . . . 4D 92
ALLEN END . . . 2C 139
Allens Cl. CV9: Bad E . . . 3F 15
Allerton Cl. CV2: Cov . . . 5A 60
ALLESLEY . . . 1F 57 (3D 139)
Allesley By-Pass CV5: Cov . . . 1F 57
Allesley Ct. CV5: Alle . . . 1E 56
Allesley Cft. CV5: Alle . . . 1E 56
Allesley Hall Dr. CV5: Alle, Cov . . . 2G 57
Allesley Old Rd. CV5: Cov . . . 2G 57
Allesley Rd. CV21: N'bld A . . . 2F 75
Alliance Cl. CV11: Nun . . . 1B 32
Alliance Trad. Est. CV4: Tile H . . . 6E 56
Alliance Way CV2: Cov . . . 2G 59
Allibone Cl. CV31: W'nsh . . . 4E 102
Allied Cl. CV6: Cov . . . 4D 50
Allimore La. B49: Alc . . . 4A 112
Allitt Gro. CV8: Ken . . . 4F 79
All Oaks La. CV23: Brin . . . 4D 62
All Saints Cl. CV7: Withy . . . 1D 54
All Saints La. *CV1: Cov . . . 4E 58*
(off Lwr. Ford St.)
CV1: Cov . . . 4E 58
(Oxford St.)
All Saints Rd. CV12: Bed . . . 4F 41
CV34: Warw . . . 6J 97
All Saints Sq. CV12: Bed . . . 2H 41
Allwoods Cl. B49: Alc . . . 4A 112
Alma Ct. CV11: Bram . . . 6H 33
Alma St. CV1: Cov . . . 3K 135 (4E 58)
Almond Av. CV10: Nun . . . 5H 21
CV32: Lea S . . . 4D 98
Almond Cl. CV23: Barby . . . 7E 88
Almond Gro. CV21: N'bld A . . . 1E 74
CV34: Warw . . . 6J 97
Almond Tree Av. CV2: Cov . . . 4H 51
Almshouses CV12: Bed . . . 2J 41
CV34: Warw . . . 2G 101
(off Castle Hill)
CV37: S Avon . . . 6F 137 (5F 115)
Alne Bank Rd. B49: Alc . . . 4D 112
Alne Cl. B95: Hen A . . . 2H 93
ALNE END . . . 3F 113
Alpha Bus. Pk. CV2: Cov . . . 5K 51
Alpha Ho. CV2: Cov . . . 3G 59
Alpine Ct. CV8: Ken . . . 3E 78
Alpine Ri. CV3: Cov . . . 3A 68
Alspath La. CV5: E Grn . . . 3D 56
Alspath Rd. CV7: Mer . . . 5E 46
Alstom Sports & Social Club . . . 7K 75
Althorpe Ind. Est. CV31: Lea S . . . 1E 102
Althorpe St. CV31: Lea S . . . 1E 102
Alton Cl. CV2: Cov . . . 4K 51
Alum Cl. CV6: Cov . . . 6D 50
ALVECHURCH . . . 1B 142
ALVECOTE . . . 3A 8 (1D 139)
Alvecote Cotts. B79: A'cte . . . 3A 8
Alvecote La. B79: A'cte . . . 3A 8
Alvecote Pools Nature Reserve . . . 5B 8
Alvecote Priory (remains of) . . . 4B 8
Alverley Rd. CV6: Cov . . . 1C 58
Alverstone Rd. CV2: Cov . . . 3G 59
ALVESTON . . . 2B 116 (3D 143)
ALVESTON HILL . . . 6K 115
Alveston La. CV37: A'ton . . . 2A 116
Alveston Leys CV37: A'ton . . . 1B 116
Alveston Pl. CV32: Lea S . . . 6E 98
Alvia Ho. CV1: Cov . . . 5H 135
Alvin Cl. CV3: Bin . . . 6B 60
Alvis Retail Pk. CV5: Cov . . . 4A 58
Alwyn Freeman Ct.
CV7: Ker E . . . 7A 40
(off Somers Rd.)
Alwyn Rd. CV22: Bil . . . 1C 86
Ambassador Ct. CV32: Lea S . . . 4D 98
Ambassador Rd. B26: Birm A . . . 2C 44
Amberley Av. CV12: Bulk . . . 2E 42
Ambien Rd. CV9: Ath . . . 4C 16
AMBLECOTE . . . 3A 138
Ambler Gro. CV2: Cov . . . 4J 59
Ambleside CV2: W'grve S . . . 4A 52
CV21: Brow . . . 1K 75
Ambleside Rd. CV12: Bed . . . 3G 41
Ambleside Way CV11: Nun . . . 5F 23
Ambrose Cl. CV21: Rugby . . . 2J 75
Amelia Cl. CV12: Bulk . . . 2E 42
Amersham Cl. CV5: Cov . . . 3F 57
AMF Bowling
Coventry . . . 4H 59
Amherst Bus. Cen. CV34: Warw . . . 1D 100
Amherst Rd. CV8: Ken . . . 2C 78
Amis Way CV37: S Avon . . . 6H 115
Amos Av. CV10: Nun . . . 2H 31
Amos-Jaques Rd. CV12: Bed . . . 1G 41
Amroth M. CV31: Lea S . . . 2G 103
Amy Cl. CV6: Longf . . . 2F 51
Anchorway Rd. CV3: Finh . . . 4A 68
Anderson Av. CV22: Rugby . . . 1G 87
Anderson Dr. CV31: W'nsh . . . 6E 102
Anderton Rd. CV6: Ald G . . . 1H 51
CV12: Bed . . . 4C 40
Andrew Cl. CV8: Bag . . . 6F 69
Anfield Ct. CV31: Lea S . . . 1F 103
Angela Av. CV2: W'grve S . . . 5A 52
Anglesey Av. B36: Cas B . . . 5B 24
Anglesey Cl. CV5: Alle . . . 7F 49
Angless Way CV8: Ken . . . 6D 78
Angus Cl. CV5: E Grn . . . 3E 56
CV8: Ken . . . 3G 79
Anker Ct. CV11: Nun . . . 1B 32
Anker Dr. CV23: Long L . . . 3B 74
Ankerside B78: Pole . . . 6D 8
Anker St. CV11: Nun . . . 1K 31
Anker Vw. B78: Pole . . . 2D 10
Anley Way CV6: Cov . . . 1C 58
Anne Cres. CV3: W'hall . . . 3J 69
Anne Hathaway's Cottage . . . 5B 114
Anns La. CV23: Stret U . . . 6G 55
Ansell Dr. CV6: Longf . . . 1G 51
Ansell Way CV34: Warw . . . 1F 101
ANSLEY . . . 7A 20 (2D 139)
ANSLEY COMMON . . . 3D 20
Ansley Comn. CV10: Ans C . . . 3D 20
Ansley La. CV7: Old A . . . 2C 28
CV10: Ansl . . . 6A 20
Ansley Rd. CV10: Nun . . . 1G 29
Anson Cl. CV22: Bil . . . 6C 74
CV35: Welle . . . 5G 117
Anson Way CV2: W'grve S . . . 6B 52
ANSTEY . . . 1C 141
Anstey Cft. B37: F'bri . . . 1A 34
ANSTY . . . 3F 53 (3A 140)
Ansty Rd. CV2: Cov . . . 3J 59
CV2: W'grve S . . . 1B 60
CV23: Brin, Stret U . . . 1A 62
Antelope Gdns. CV34: Warw . . . 7E 96
Anthony Way CV2: Cov . . . 5J 59
Antony Gardner Cres. CV31: W'nsh . . . 4E 102
Antrim Cl. CV5: Alle . . . 7E 48
Apollo Way CV34: Warw . . . 3B 102
Appleby Cl. B49: Gt Alne . . . 3F 113
Appleby Hill CV9: Aus . . . 6G 7
APPLEBY MAGNA . . . 1A 140
APPLEBY PARVA . . . 2K 7 (1A 140)
Applecross Cl. CV4: W'wd H . . . 2D 66
Appledore Dr. CV5: Alle . . . 2D 56
Apple Gro. CV22: Bil . . . 6B 74
Apple Pie La. CV10: Harts . . . 1G 21
APPLETREE . . . 1D 147
Appleyard Cl. CV12: Bed . . . 3H 41
Apollo Cinema . . . 7D 98
Approach, The CV31: Lea S . . . 2D 102
Aqua Pl. CV21: Rugby . . . 3J 75
Aragon Dr. CV34: Warw . . . 2A 102
Arboretum, The CV4: Canly . . . 5H 67
Arborfields Cl. CV8: Ken . . . 1F 79
Arbor Way B37: Chel W . . . 4C 34
Arbour Cl. CV8: Ken . . . 6F 79
CV22: Rugby . . . 2D 86
Arbours, The CV22: Rugby . . . 6J 75
Arbury Av. CV6: Cov . . . 4E 50
CV12: Bed . . . 2G 41
Arbury Cl. CV32: Lill . . . 4E 98
Arbury Gth. CV10: Nun . . . 1C 30
Arbury Hall . . . 5D 30
Arbury Rd. CV10: Nun . . . 2C 30
Arcade, The CV9: Ath . . . 3C 16
Archer Cl. B80: Stud . . . 3C 92
Archer Rd. CV8: Ken . . . 6C 78
Archers Spinney CV21: Hillm . . . 1D 88
Archery Flds. CV34: Warw . . . 2H 101
Archery Rd. CV7: Mer . . . 5D 46
CV31: Lea S . . . 7C 98
Arches Bus. Cen. CV21: Rugby . . . 3J 75
Arches Ind. Est. CV21: Rugby . . . 4K 75
Arches Ind. Est., The CV5: Cov . . . 4A 58
Arches La. CV21: Rugby . . . 3J 75
Arch Rd. CV2: Cov . . . 2A 60
Arden Av. CV9: Ath . . . 3D 16
Arden Bus. Cen. B49: Alc . . . 2B 112
Arden Cl. B95: Hen A . . . 2H 93
CV7: Mer . . . 5E 46
CV22: Bil . . . 4D 86
CV31: Lea S . . . 3F 103
CV34: Warw . . . 6J 97
CV37: Wilm . . . 5J 113
Arden Ct. B49: Alc . . . 2B 112
B92: H Ard . . . 7G 45
CV3: Bin W . . . 1F 71
CV37: S Avon . . . 1D 136
Arden Cft. B46: Col . . . 3F 25
Arden Forest Est. CV10: Ridge L . . . 1A 20
Arden Forest Ind. Est. B49: Kinw . . . 2C 112
Arden Leys B94: Tan A . . . 3A 90
Arden Rd. B49: Alc . . . 3A 112
B95: Hen A . . . 3H 93
CV8: Ken . . . 6F 79
CV11: Nun . . . 3C 32
CV12: Bulk . . . 3E 42
ARDENS GRAFTON . . . 1K 123 (3C 143)
Arden St. CV5: Cov . . . 6K 57
CV9: Ath . . . 4D 16
CV37: S Avon . . . 3C 136 (4E 114)
Arderne Dr. B37: F'bri . . . 4A 34
ARDLEY . . . 3D 147
Arena B40: Nat E C . . . 3E 44
Arena, The (Ice Rink) . . . 4F 135 (5B 58)
Argent Ct. CV4: Canly . . . 2G 67
Argyle St. CV21: Rugby . . . 5J 75
(not continuous)
Argyle Way CV33: Bis T . . . 5C 108
Argyll St. CV2: Cov . . . 4G 59
Ariel Way CV22: Bil . . . 3D 86
Arkle Dr. CV2: W'grve S . . . 7B 52
Arklet Cl. CV10: Nun . . . 6H 21
ARLESCOTE . . . 5E 128 (1C 147)
Arlescote Cl. CV35: Hatt . . . 5A 96
Arley La. CV7: Fill . . . 6D 28
CV10: Ansl . . . 2G 29
Arley M. CV32: Lea S . . . 6C 98
Arley Sports Cen. . . . 2C 28
Arlidge Cres. CV8: Ken . . . 5G 79
Arlington Av. CV32: Lea S . . . 5D 98
Arlington Ct. CV32: Lea S . . . 5D 98
Arlington M. CV32: Lea S . . . 5D 98
Arlington Way CV11: Nun . . . 2B 32
Arlon Av. CV10: Nun . . . 4J 21
Armarna Dr. CV5: Mil W . . . 6K 47
Armfield St. CV6: Cov . . . 5G 51
Armorial Rd. CV3: Cov . . . 2B 68
ARMSCOTE . . . 4G 127 (1B 146)
Armscote Gro. CV35: Hatt . . . 5A 96
Armscote Rd. CV36: Ilm . . . 6D 126
CV36: Tred . . . 6H 127
CV36: Wind . . . 6F 127
CV37: N'bld S . . . 3G 127
CV37: Wind, Arms . . . 6F 127
Armscott Rd. CV2: Cov . . . 1J 59
(not continuous)
Armson Rd. CV7: Exh . . . 5G 41
Armstrong Av. CV3: Cov . . . 6H 59
Armstrong Cl. CV22: Bil . . . 7E 74
CV31: W'nsh . . . 6E 102
Armstrong Dr. B36: Cas B . . . 3A 24
Arncliffe Cl. CV11: Nun . . . 2C 32
Arncliffe Way CV34: Warw . . . 6H 97
Arne Rd. CV2: W'grve S . . . 1C 60
ARNESBY . . . 2D 141
Arnhem Cnr. CV3: W'hall . . . 2K 69
Arnills Way CV23: Kils . . . 7J 89
Arno Ho. CV3: W'hall . . . 2H 69
Arnold Av. CV3: Cov . . . 3C 68
Arnold Cl. CV22: Rugby . . . 6G 75
Arnolds La. B46: Max . . . 1K 35
Arnold St. CV21: Rugby . . . 5H 75
Arnold Vs. CV21: Rugby . . . 5H 75
Arnside Cl. CV1: Cov . . . 3E 58
Arran Cl. CV10: Nun . . . 1F 31
Arran Way B36: Cas B . . . 5A 24
Arras Blvd. CV35: H Mag . . . 1C 100
ARROW . . . 6A 112 (3B 142)
Arrow Ct. B49: Alc . . . 3B 112
Arrow Cres. B49: Alc . . . 3B 112
Arrow Rdbt. B49: Arr . . . 6A 112
Artemis Dr. CV34: Warw . . . 3B 102
ARTHINGWORTH . . . 3D 141
Arthingworth Cl. CV3: Bin . . . 6A 60
Arthur Alford Ho. CV12: Bed . . . 4D 40
Arthur Rd. CV37: S Avon . . . 3E 114
Arthur Russell Ct. CV10: Nun . . . 1E 30
Arthur St. CV1: Cov . . . 1K 135 (3D 58)
CV8: Ken . . . 4E 78
Artillery Rd. CV11: Bram . . . 6H 33
Arundel Cl. CV34: Warw . . . 7H 97
Arundel Rd. CV3: Cov . . . 2D 68
CV12: Bulk . . . 2E 42
Arundel Way CV22: Caw . . . 1A 86
Ascot Cl. CV3: W'hall . . . 2J 69
CV12: Bed . . . 1H 41
CV37: S Avon . . . 6C 114
Ascote Way CV47: Sou . . . 6J 107
Ascot Ride CV32: Lill . . . 4G 99
ASCOTT-UNDER-WYCHWOOD . . . 3C 147
Ashbridge Rd. CV5: Cov . . . 3G 57
Ashbrook Ri. CV10: Harts . . . 1G 21
Ashburton Rd. CV2: Cov . . . 6A 52
Ashbury Ct. B95: Hen A . . . 1H 93
Ashby Cl. CV3: Bin . . . 7B 60
Ashby Ct. CV11: Nun . . . 1K 31
ASHBY FOLVILLE . . . 1D 141
ASHBY MAGNA . . . 2C 141
ASHBY PARVA . . . 3C 141
Ashby Rd. CV23: Kils . . . 7J 89
ASHBY ST LEDGARS . . . 2C 145
Ashcombe Dr. CV4: Tile H . . . 4D 56
Ash Ct. CV22: Rugby . . . 2E 86
Ash Cres. B37: K'hrst . . . 6A 24
Ashcroft Cl. CV2: W'grve S . . . 6C 52
Ashcroft Way CV2: W'grve S . . . 6D 52
Ashdale Cl. CV3: Bin W . . . 1G 71
Ashdene Gdns. CV8: Ken . . . 5F 79
Ashdown Cl. CV3: Bin . . . 7K 59
Ashdown Dr. CV10: Nun . . . 2F 31
Ash Dr. CV8: Ken . . . 5E 78
CV10: Harts . . . 3F 21
Ash End House Farm . . . 2C 139

Ashe Rd. CV10: Nun 1B 30
Ashfield Av. CV4: Tile H 6B 56
Ashfield Rd. CV8: Ken 6F 79
Ashford Dr. CV12: Bed 2G 41
Ashford Gdns. CV31: W'nsh 5D 102
Ashford Rd. CV31: W'nsh 6D 102
ASH GREEN 7C 40 (3A 140)
Ash Grn. La. CV7: Ash G 7C 40
Ash Gro. B78: K'bry 4E 12
CV7: Ash G 6C 40
CV7: Old A 2C 28
CV37: S Avon 2D 114
CV47: Sou 4H 107
Ashgrove CV36: Ship S 6H 131
Ashgrove Pl. CV31: Lea S 1E 102
Ashington Gro. CV3: Cov 2G 69
Ashington Rd. CV12: Bed 4C 40
Ash La. B79: No Hth 2F 7
CV37: Bear 7C 94
Ashlawn Railway Cutting Nature Reserve 1J 87
Ashlawn Rd. CV22: Hillm, Rugby 4F 87
Ashlea B78: Dord 5C 10
Ashleigh Cl. CV23: Barby 7E 88
Ashleigh Dr. CV11: Nun 3B 32
Ashley Cres. CV34: Warw 2K 101
Ashman Av. CV23: Long L 3B 74
Ashmore Rd. CV6: Cov 3B 58
ASHORNE 3A 144
Ashorne Cl. CV2: Cov 4J 51
(not continuous)
Ashorne Hall 3A 144
ASHOW 7J 79 (1A 144)
Ashow Cl. CV8: Ken 5F 79
Ash Priors Cl. CV4: Tile H 6F 57
Ash Ridge Cl. CV11: Nun 4B 32
Ashton Ct. CV32: Lill 4G 99
Ash Tree Av. CV4: Tile H 5E 56
Ash Tree Cl. CV35: Welle 3J 117
Ash Tree Gro. CV7: Shil 7G 43
Ashurst Cl. CV6: Longf 1H 51
ASHWOOD 3A 138
Ashwood Av. CV6: Cov 2K 57
Ashwood Ct. CV21: Rugby 4F 75
Ashwood Dr. B37: Chel W 2D 34
Ashwood Rd. CV10: Nun 5K 21
Aspects Pk. Ga. CV11: Nun 4G 23
Aspen Cl. B49: Alc 3B 112
CV4: Tile H 6B 56
Aspen Ct. *B95: Hen A 1H 93*
(off Chestnut Wlk.)
Aspen Dr. B37: Chel W 5C 34
CV6: Longf 7J 41
Aspens, The B78: K'bry 4E 12
Asplen Ct. CV8: Ken 5G 79
ASPLEY HEATH 3A 90
Aspley Heath La. B94: Tan A 3A 90
Assheton Cl. CV22: Bil 1C 86
ASTCOTE 3D 145
Aster Cl. CV11: Nun 3C 32
Aster Wlk. CV10: Nun 4G 31
Asthill Cft. CV3: Cov 7G 135 (7C 58)
Asthill Gro. CV3: Cov 7G 135 (7C 58)
ASTLEY 5J 29 (3A 140)
Astley Av. CV6: Cov 4E 50
Astley Castle 4J 29
Astley Cl. B98: Redd 1A 92
CV32: Lea S 5B 98
Astley La. CV7: Fill 2F 39
CV10: Asty, Nun 5J 29
(not continuous)
CV12: Bed 7A 30
Astley Pl. CV21: Hillm 2D 88
Astley Wlk. CV47: Temp H 2B 120
ASTON 2B 138
ASTON CANTLOW 2K 113 (3C 143)
Aston Cantlow Rd. B95: Aston C 4F 113
CV37: Wilm 4F 113
ASTON FIELDS 2A 142
ASTON FLAMVILLE 2B 140
Aston Hill CV37: Wilm 5G 113
ASTON LE WALLS 3B 144
ASTON MAGNA 2A 146
Aston Pk. Ind. Est. CV11: Nun 5C 22
Aston Rd. CV5: Cov 6K 57
CV11: Nun 6C 22
ASTON SOMERVILLE 2A 146
ASTON SUBEDGE 1A 146
ASTROP 2D 147
ASTWOOD BANK 2B 142
AT7 Sports Cen. 7G 51
Atcheson Cl. B80: Stud 3D 92
ATCH LENCH 3B 142
Athena Dr. CV34: Warw 3B 102
Athena Gdns. CV6: Cov 5G 51
ATHERSTONE 3C 16 (2A 140)
Atherstone Arts Cen. 3C 16
Atherstone By-Pass CV9: Ath 2A 16
Atherstone La. CV9: Bax, Hurl 7A 14
Atherstone Leisure Complex 2C 16
ATHERSTONE ON STOUR 7D 124 (3D 143)
Atherstone Rd. B46: Over W 1F 27
CV9: Hurl 7A 14
CV9: With 1E 16
CV10: Harts 1G 21 & 7G 17
DE12: App M 1K 7
Atherstone Station (Rail) 3B 16
Atherton Pl. CV4: Canly 2H 67
Atholl Ct. CV10: Nun 2E 30
Atholl Cres. CV10: Nun 2E 30
Athol Rd. CV2: W'grve S 1C 60
Atkins Wlk. B78: Pole 2D 10
Atterton La. CV9: With 3G 17
CV13: Att 3G 17
Attleboro La. B46: Wat O 2A 24
ATTLEBOROUGH 3K 31 (2A 140)
Attleborough By-Pass CV11: Nun 2K 31
Attleborough Flds. Ind. Est. CV11: Nun 1B 32
Attleborough Rd. CV11: Nun 1K 31
Attoxhall Rd. CV2: Cov 3A 60
Attwood Cres. CV2: Cov 7J 51
Atworth Cl. B98: Redd 2A 92
Auckland Dr. B36: Cas B 4A 24
Auden Cl. CV10: Gall C 7E 20
Augusta Pl. CV32: Lea S 7D 98
Augustine Av. B80: Stud 3B 92
Augustus Cl. B46: Col 3F 25
Augustus Dr. B49: Alc 5B 112
Augustus Rd. CV1: Cov 3F 59
Austen Cl. CV10: Gall C 6E 20
Austen Ct. CV32: Cubb 2J 99
Austen Rd. CV37: S Avon 7H 115
Austin Cl. CV9: Ath 4C 16
Austin Dr. CV6: Cov 7G 51
Austin Edwards Dr. CV34: Warw 7K 97
AUSTREY 7H 7 (1D 139)
Austrey La. B79: Newt R 5D 6
B79: No Hth 2F 7
Austrey Rd. B79: Wart 4H 9
CV9: App M 3J 7
DE12: App M 3J 7
Austwick Cl. CV34: Warw 6G 97
Autumn Ho. B37: K'hrst 7B 24
Avebury Cl. CV11: Nun 2B 32
Aventine Way CV21: Rugby 1F 75
Avenue, The CV3: Cov 2G 69
CV35: Row 5H 91
CV37: B'ton 2C 114
Avenue Farm CV37: S Avon 3D 114
Avenue Farm Ind. Est. CV37: S Avon 3D 114
Avenue Fld. Ind. Est. CV37: S Avon 3D 114
Avenue M. CV8: S'lgh P 6A 80
Avenue Rd. CV8: Ken 3B 78
CV11: Nun 2J 31
CV21: Rugby 4E 74
CV31: Lea S 1C 102
CV37: S Avon 1H 137 (4F 115)
Avery Ct. CV34: Warw 2H 101
Aviemore Cl. CV10: Nun 2G 31
Avocet Cl. CV2: Ald G 3H 51
CV23: Brow 6J 65
Avon Av. CV35: Mid T 7C 130
Avonbank CV37: S Avon 2J 137
Avonbank Dr. CV37: S Avon 7B 114
Avonbank Paddocks CV37: S Avon 7F 137
Avonbrook Cl. CV37: S Avon 3C 114
Avon Cvn. Pk. CV37: S Avon 2J 115
Avoncliffe CV37: Tidd 2A 116
Avon Cl. CV12: Bulk 6D 32
CV35: Barf 1C 108
CV37: Ett 2C 126
Avon Ct. CV21: Rugby 4G 75
CV32: Lea S 4D 98
Avon Cres. B49: Alc 3C 112
CV37: S Avon 6H 115
Avoncroft Ho. B37: Chel W 3A 34
Avondale Rd. CV5: Cov 7A 58
CV8: Bran 3H 71
CV32: Lill 3G 99
AVON DASSETT 3B 144
Avon Dassett Rd. CV47: Fen C 4F 121
Avon Dr. B36: Cas B 4A 24
Avon Flds. CV37: Ett 2C 126
Avonfields Cl. CV37: A'ton 2C 116
Avon Ho. CV37: S Avon 1F 137
Avonhurst CV37: Tidd 3J 115
Avon Ind. Est. CV21: Rugby 3J 75
CV37: S Avon 3E 114
Avonlea Ri. CV32: Lea S 5B 98
Avon Lodge CV11: Nun 6B 22
Avon Mdw. Cl. CV37: S Avon 6E 114
Avonmere CV21: N'bld A 1E 74
Avon Mill CV37: S Avon 1G 137
Avon Rd. CV4: Canly 2F 67
CV8: Ken 6C 78
CV31: W'nsh 5E 102
CV33: L Hth 2K 119
Avonside CV37: S Avon 6F 115
Avonside Cvn. Pk. CV37: Welf A 1A 124
Avon St. CV2: Cov 2H 59
CV21: Rugby 4G 75
CV23: Clift D 4A 76
CV34: Warw 1J 101
Avon Ter. CV8: Bubb 3J 81
Avon Vw. Pk. Homes
CV8: Rytn D 6A 70
Avon Way CV35: Mid T 7D 130
Awson St. CV6: Cov 1F 59
Axholme Rd. CV2: Cov 3A 60
Axminster Cl. CV11: Nun 6F 23
Aylesdene Ct. CV5: Cov 7K 57
Aylesford Dr. B37: Mars G 6A 34
Aylesford St. CV1: Cov 3E 58
CV31: Lea S 2E 102
AYLESTONE 1C 141
Aylstone Cl. CV37: Lwr Q 5H 125
AYLWORTH 3A 146
AYNHO 2D 147
Aynho Cl. CV5: E Grn 4E 56
Aysgarth Cl. CV11: Nun 2C 32

B

Babbacombe Rd. CV3: Cov 3D 68
Bablake Cl. CV6: Cov 6K 49
Bachelors Bench CV9: Ath 4C 16
Back La. B46: Shu 2B 26
B95: Hen A 1H 93
CV7: Mer 3A 56
CV23: Bird 5A 104
CV23: Harb M 4A 64
CV23: Long L 4A 74
CV34: Warw 2G 101
CV35: Mid T 6C 130
CV35: Oxh 1E 130
CV36: Long C 2D 134
CV37: Lwr Q 4J 125
OX17: Shotte 6G 129
Back St. CV11: Nun 6D 22
CV36: Ilm 7B 126
BACONS END 1B 34
Bacons End B37: K'hrst 7B 24
Bacon's Yd. CV6: Cov 4F 51
Badbury Cl. B80: Stud 3C 92
Badbury Gdns. B80: Stud 3C 92
BADBY 3C 145
Badby Leys CV22: Rugby 2F 87
BADDESLEY CLINTON 1D 143
Baddesley Clinton Hall 1D 143
Baddesley Cl. CV31: Lea S 3H 103
BADDESLEY ENSOR 2F 15 (2D 139)
Badger Rd. CV3: Bin 7K 59
Badgers Cres. CV36: Ship S 3H 131
Badgers La. CV35: Lwr T 4D 130
BADSEY 1A 146
Baffin Cl. CV22: Bil 7E 74
BAGGRAVE 1D 141
BAGINTON 6F 69 (1A 144)
Baginton Rd. CV3: Cov 2B 68
(not continuous)
Bagot Way CV34: H'cte 5C 102
Bagshaw Cl. CV8: Rytn D 7C 70
BAGWORTH 1B 140
Bailey's La. CV23: Long L 3A 74
Bakehouse La. CV21: Rugby 5F 75
OX17: Shotte 6H 129
Baker Av. CV31: Lea S 2D 102
CV37: S Avon 4C 114
Baker Dr. CV35: Welle 3G 117
Baker Ho. CV22: Bil 1C 86
Bakers Ct. CV9: Ath 3C 16
Bakers Cft. CV9: Bad E 2F 15
Bakers La. CV5: Cov 4J 57
Baker St. CV6: Longf 7H 41
Bakewell Cl. CV3: Bin 7B 60
Balcombe Ct. CV22: Hillm 1A 88
Balcombe Rd. CV22: Hillm 1K 87
Baldwin Cft. CV6: Cov 5H 51
Baldwins La. CV35: Up Tys 7C 130
Ballantine Rd. CV6: Cov 1B 58
BALLARDS GREEN 1B 28
Ballards La. CV36: Ilm 6C 126
Ballard Wlk. B37: K'hrst 6A 24
Ballingham Cl. CV4: Tile H 5E 56
Balliol Ho. B37: F'bri 3A 34
Balliol Rd. CV2: Cov 3H 59
Balmoral Cl. CV2: Cov 1B 60
Balmoral Ct. CV10: Nun 6K 21
Balmoral Rd. B36: Cas B 5A 24
Balmoral Way CV32: Cubb 1G 99
BALSALL 1D 143
BALSALL COMMON 1D 143
BALSCOTE 1C 147
Balthazar Cl. CV34: H'cte 4C 102
Bamburgh Gro. CV32: Lea S 4C 98
Banbrook Rd. WR11: Salf P 7B 122
BANBURY 1D 147
Banbury Rd. CV33: Bis T 4A 108
CV33: Gay, L Hth 4F 119
CV33: L Hth 1J 119
CV34: Warw 2H 101 & 4A 108
CV35: Gay 4F 119 & 1A 120
CV35: Kine 6D 120
CV35: Light 1J 119
CV35: Pill P 1B 126
CV37: Ett 1A 126
CV37: Ett, Pill P 1B 126
CV37: Gold, S Avon 5G 115
CV47: Gay, Lit D, Temp H 1A 120
CV47: Sou 6H 107 & 1C 110
OX17: Warm 3H 129
Banbury Rd. Hill CV34: Warw 3J 101
Banbury St. CV35: Kine 6D 120
Bancroft Pl. CV37: S Avon 4J 137 (4F 115)
Bangor Ho. B37: F'bri 1B 34
Banister Way CV36: Ship S 5H 131
Bank, The *B50: Bidf A 5G 123*
(off Friday Cl.)
B50: Bidf A 6G 123
(Tower Hill)
CV8: S'lgh 3C 80
CV35: Light 2G 119
Bank Cl. CV35: But M 7A 120
Bankcroft CV31: Lea S 3G 103
Bankfield Dr. CV32: Lea S 6A 98
Bank La. CV1: Cov 4A 58
Bank Rd. CV9: Ath 3D 16
Banks, The CV23: Kils 7J 89
Bankside Cl. CV3: Cov 2F 69
Banks Rd. CV6: Cov 2A 58
Bank St. CV21: Rugby 5G 75
Bank Vw. CV35: But M 7A 120
Banner La. CV4: Tile H 4B 56
Bannerlea Rd. B37: K'hrst 7A 24
BANNERS GATE 2B 138
Banquo App. CV34: H'cte 5D 102
Bantam Gro. CV6: Cov 3A 50
Bantock Rd. CV4: Tile H 5C 56
Barber Wlk. CV35: H Mag 1B 100

Barbican Ri. CV2: Cov . . . 5A 60
Barbridge Cl. CV12: Bulk . . . 3E 42
Barbridge Rd. CV12: Bulk . . . 2D 42
BARBY . . . 7E 88 (1C 145)
Barby La. CV22: Hillm . . . 1B 88
CV23: Barby . . . 4C 88
BARBY NORTOFT . . . 3H 89 (1C 145)
Barby Rd. CV22: Rugby . . . 6G 75
CV23: Barby, Kils . . . 6G 89
Barcherston Dr. CV35: Hatt . . . 4A 96
BARCHESTON . . . 6K 131 (1B 146)
Barcheston M. CV35: Hatt . . . 4A 96
Bardley Dr. CV6: Cov . . . 1C 58
BARDON . . . 1B 140
Bardon Vw. Rd. B78: Dord . . . 3D 10
Bard's Wlk. CV37: S Avon . . . 4F 137 (4F 115)
Bardswell Ct. CV37: S Avon . . . 3E 114
BARFORD . . . 2B 108 (2D 143)
Barford App. CV31: W'nsh . . . 6F 103
Barford Cl. CV3: Bin . . . 1K 69
Barford Hill CV35: Barf . . . 1D 108 & 7G 101
Barford M. CV8: Ken . . . 5F 79
Barford Rd. CV8: Ken . . . 6F 79
CV34: Warw . . . 7H 101
CV35: Sher . . . 1A 108
BARFORD ST JOHN . . . 2D 147
BARFORD ST MICHAEL . . . 2D 147
BARKBY . . . 1D 141
Barker's Butts La. CV6: Cov . . . 2K 57
Barkus Cl. CV47: Sou . . . 5J 107
Barle Gro. B36: Cas B . . . 5A 24
BARLESTONE . . . 1B 140
Barley Cl. B95: Hen A . . . 2G 93
CV21: Hillm . . . 1C 88
Barley Ct. CV32: Lea S . . . 5D 98
Barley Lea, The CV3: Cov . . . 7H 59
Barlichway B49: Alc . . . 4D 112
Barling Way CV10: Nun . . . 3H 31
Barlow Ct. B78: K'bry . . . 5E 12
Barlow Rd. CV2: Ald G . . . 3K 51
Barnack Av. CV3: Cov . . . 3B 68
Barnack Dr. CV34: Warw . . . 6G 97
BARNACLE . . . 7D 42 (3A 140)
Barnacle La. CV12: Bulk . . . 4E 42
Barnard Cl. B37: Chel W . . . 4D 34
CV32: Lill . . . 4G 99
Barn Cl. B78: Dord . . . 4C 10
CV5: Cov . . . 2G 57
CV31: W'nsh . . . 5F 103
CV37: Cliff C . . . 5C 124
Barncroft CV36: Long C . . . 3C 134
Barne Cl. CV11: Nun . . . 5D 32
Barn End Rd. B79: Wart . . . 6H 9
Barnes Ct. CV1: Cov . . . 1G 135 (3C 58)
Barnfield Av. CV5: Alle . . . 7E 48
BARNMOOR GREEN . . . 2A 94
Barnsley Cl. CV9: Ath . . . 4C 16
Barnstaple Cl. CV5: Alle . . . 3D 56
BARNT GREEN . . . 1B 142
Barnwell Cl. CV22: Dunc . . . 5C 86
Baron Leigh Dr. CV4: W'wd H . . . 2B 66
Barons Cft. CV3: Cov . . . 1E 68
CV10: Nun . . . 7H 21
Baron's Fld. Rd. CV3: Cov . . . 1D 68
Barpool Rd. CV10: Nun . . . 7A 22
Barracks Grn. CV35: Lox . . . 6C 116
Barrack St. CV34: Warw . . . 1G 101
Barracks Way CV1: Cov . . . 4H 135 (5C 58)
Barras Ct. CV2: Cov . . . 3G 59
Barras Grn. CV2: Cov . . . 3G 59
Barras Grn. Bungs. CV2: Cov . . . 3G 59
Barras La. CV1: Cov . . . 4B 58
Barrie Cl. CV37: S Avon . . . 6H 115
Barrington Rd. CV22: Bil . . . 6C 74
Barr La. CV13: High H . . . 1H 23
CV23: Brin . . . 3C 62
Bar Rd. CV3: Cov . . . 7E 58
Barrow Cl. CV2: W'grve S . . . 1D 60
Barrowfield Ct. CV8: Ken . . . 5D 78
Barrowfield La. CV8: Ken . . . 5D 78
Barrow Rd. CV8: Ken . . . 5D 78
Barry Ho. CV2: Cov . . . 5K 51
BARSBY . . . 1D 141
Barsby Cl. CV9: Ath . . . 4C 16
BARSTON . . . 1D 143
Barston Cl. CV6: Cov . . . 3G 51
Bartholomew Ct. CV3: Cov . . . 2F 69
Bartlett Cl. CV6: Cov . . . 4E 50
CV34: Warw . . . 1H 101
BARTLEY GREEN . . . 3B 138
BARTON
Alcester . . . 7J 123 (3C 143)
Cheltenham . . . 3A 146
Barton Cres. CV31: Lea S . . . 2G 103
Barton Flds. CV37: Welf A . . . 3A 124
BARTON IN THE BEANS . . . 1A 140
BARTON-ON-THE-HEATH . . . 2B 146
Barton Rd. CV6: Cov . . . 4F 51
CV10: Nun . . . 3J 31
CV12: Bed . . . 2G 41
CV22: Bil . . . 1D 86
CV36: Long C . . . 1A 134
CV37: Welf A . . . 4A 124
Bartons Ct. CV2: Cov . . . 3G 59
Barton's Mdw. CV2: Cov . . . 1H 59
BARWELL . . . 2B 140
Barwell Cl. CV32: Lea S . . . 4D 98
Basant Cl. CV34: Warw . . . 1J 101
BASCOTE . . . 1F 107 (2B 144)
Bascote Chase CV47: Bas . . . 1F 107
BASCOTE HEATH . . . 1J 109
Bascote Ri. CV47: Sou . . . 4G 107
Bascote Rd. CV47: Bas, Long I . . . 1F 107
Basely Way CV6: Longf . . . 2D 50
Basford Brook Dr. CV6: Longf . . . 1F 51
Basildon Wlk. CV2: W'grve S . . . 7C 52
Bassett Rd. CV6: Cov . . . 2A 58
BATCHLEY . . . 2B 142
Bateman Rd. B46: Col . . . 3F 25
Batemans Acre Sth. CV6: Cov . . . 3A 58
Bates La. B94: Tan A . . . 4C 90
Bates Rd. CV5: Cov . . . 1J 67
Bath Pl. CV31: Lea S . . . 1D 102
Bath Rd. CV9: Ath . . . 4D 16
CV11: Nun . . . 6D 22
Bath St. CV1: Cov . . . 1K 135 (3D 58)
CV21: Rugby . . . 5H 75
CV31: Lea S . . . 1D 102
Bath St. M. CV21: Rugby . . . 4H 75
Bathurst Cl. CV22: Bil . . . 1E 86
Bathurst Rd. CV6: Cov . . . 1A 58
Bathway Rd. CV3: Finh . . . 4A 68
BATSFORD . . . 2A 146
Batsford Cl. B98: Redd . . . 2A 92
Batsford Rd. CV6: Cov . . . 2K 57
Battalion Ct. CV6: Cov . . . 5A 50
Battle Ct. CV35: Kine . . . 5D 120
Battle of Edgehill Commemoration Stone . . . 3A 144
Bawnmore Ct. CV22: Bil . . . 1D 86
Bawnmore Pk. CV22: Bil . . . 2E 86
Bawnmore Rd. CV22: Bil . . . 1D 86
Baxter Cl. CV4: Tile H . . . 5E 56
CV9: Ath . . . 4D 16
Baxter Ct. CV31: Lea S . . . 1E 102
BAXTERLEY . . . 5G 15 (2D 139)
Bayley La. CV1: Cov . . . 4J 135 (5D 58)
Bayliss Av. CV6: Longf . . . 2G 51
BAYNARD'S GREEN . . . 3D 147
Bayton Ind. Est. CV7: Exh . . . 6G 41
Bayton Rd. CV7: Exh . . . 6G 41
Bayton Rd. Ind. Est. CV7: Exh . . . 5H 41
Bayton Way CV7: Exh . . . 6J 41
Baytree Cl. CV2: Cov . . . 5K 51
Bazzard La. CV11: Bram . . . 6H 33
CV12: Bulk . . . 6H 33
Beacon Cl. B49: Alc . . . 3C 112
Beacon Rd. CV6: Cov . . . 3C 50
Beaconsfield Av. CV22: Rugby . . . 7G 75
Beaconsfield Ct. CV11: Nun . . . 6E 22
Beaconsfield Rd. CV2: Cov . . . 5H 59
Beaconsfield St. CV31: Lea S . . . 1F 103
Beaconsfield St. W. CV31: Lea S . . . 7F 99
Beake Av. CV6: Cov . . . 5B 50
Beale Cl. CV33: Bis T . . . 5C 108
Beamish Cl. CV2: W'grve S . . . 1C 60
Beanfield Av. CV3: Finh . . . 4K 67
Bear Cl. B95: Hen A . . . 1G 93
Bear La. B95: Hen A . . . 1G 93
Bear La. Cl. B78: Pole . . . 7D 8
BEARLEY . . . 6D 94 (2C 143)
BEARLEY CROSS . . . 6B 94
Bearley Grange CV37: Bear . . . 6C 94
Bearley Grn. CV37: Bear . . . 6D 94
Bearley Rd. B95: Aston C . . . 2K 113
CV37: Snitt . . . 5F 95
Bearley Station (Rail) . . . 6B 94
BEARWOOD . . . 3B 138
Beatty Dr. CV22: Bil . . . 6D 74
Beaty's Gdns. CV32: Lill . . . 3E 98
Beauchamp Av. CV32: Lea S . . . 6D 98
Beauchamp Cl. B37: Chel W . . . 3B 34
Beauchamp Ct. B49: K Cou . . . 2A 112
CV32: Lea S . . . 6D 98
Beauchamp Gdns. CV34: Warw . . . 2K 101
Beauchamp Hill CV32: Lea S . . . 6C 98
Beauchamp Ho. CV1: Cov . . . 5G 135
Beauchamp Rd. B49: Alc . . . 3C 112
CV8: Ken . . . 7C 78
CV32: Lea S . . . 6D 98
CV34: Warw . . . 7K 97
Beaudesert Castle . . . 1J 93
Beaudesert La. B95: Hen A . . . 1H 93
Beaudesert Pl. B95: Hen A . . . 2H 93
Beaudesert Rd. CV5: Cov . . . 6A 58
Beaufell Cl. CV34: Warw . . . 6G 97
Beaufort Av. CV32: Cubb . . . 2G 99
Beaufort Cl. CV35: Welle . . . 4G 117
Beaufort Dr. CV3: Bin . . . 1B 70
Beaulieu Pk. CV31: Lea S . . . 2H 103
Beaumaris Cl. CV5: Alle . . . 2D 56
Beaumont Cl. CV47: Temp H . . . 2B 120
Beaumont Ct. *CV6: Cov . . . 3A 58*
(off Beaumont Cres.)
Beaumont Cres. CV6: Cov . . . 3A 58
BEAUMONT LEYS . . . 1C 141
Beaumont Pl. CV11: Nun . . . 7B 22
Beaumont Rd. CV7: Ker E . . . 7K 39
CV11: Nun . . . 6A 22
Beaurevoir Way CV34: Warw . . . 7J 97
BEAUSALE . . . 1D 143
Beausale Cft. CV5: E Grn . . . 4E 56
Beausale La. CV35: Beau, Hatt . . . 3A 96
Beche Way CV5: Cov . . . 2F 57
Beckbury Rd. CV2: W'grve S . . . 7B 52
Becket Cl. GL56: Tod . . . 5A 132
Beckfoot Cl. CV21: Brow . . . 7K 65
Beckfoot Dr. CV2: W'grve S . . . 5B 52
Beck's Cl. CV47: S'ton . . . 6C 106
Becks Cft. B95: Hen A . . . 2H 93
Becks La. CV7: Mer . . . 1J 47
CV47: S'ton . . . 6C 106
Bede Arc. CV12: Bed . . . 2H 41
Bede Rd. CV6: Cov . . . 1B 58
CV10: Nun . . . 1D 30
CV12: Bed . . . 1G 41
Bede Village CV12: Bed . . . 5C 40
Bedford Ho. B36: Cas B . . . 6B 24
Bedford Pl. CV32: Lea S . . . 7D 98
Bedford St. CV1: Cov . . . 5A 58
CV32: Lea S . . . 7D 98
Bedlam La. CV6: Longf . . . 4E 50
BEDWORTH . . . 2H 41 (3A 140)
Bedworth By-Pass CV7: Exh . . . 5F 41
CV10: Griff . . . 7G 31
CV12: Bed . . . 5F 41
Bedworth Cl. CV12: Bulk . . . 3D 42
BEDWORTH HEATH . . . 3E 40
Bedworth La. CV12: Bed . . . 1C 40
Bedworth Leisure Cen. . . . 4H 41
Bedworth Rd. CV6: Longf . . . 1G 51
CV12: Bulk . . . 3A 42
Bedworth Slough Local Nature Reserve . . . 2F 41
Bedworth Station (Rail) . . . 3J 41
BEDWORTH WOODLANDS . . . 2E 40
BEEBY . . . 1D 141
Beecham Rd. CV36: Ship S . . . 3H 131
Beecham Wlk. CV37: S Avon . . . 3B 114
Beech Av. B37: Chel W . . . 4B 34
Beech Cliffe CV34: Warw . . . 7H 97
Beech Cl. B49: Ove G . . . 6D 112
B78: K'bry . . . 4D 12
CV9: Hurl . . . 6K 13
CV10: Harts . . . 3F 21
CV35: Row . . . 6J 91
CV37: S Avon . . . 5H 115
CV47: Sou . . . 6G 107
Beech Ct. CV22: Hillm . . . 1B 88
CV34: H'cte . . . 6C 102
CV37: S Avon . . . 5G 115
Beech Cft. CV12: Bed . . . 4F 41
CV47: Long I . . . 2C 106
Beechcroft B95: Hen A . . . 1H 93
Beech Dr. CV8: Ken . . . 4F 79
CV22: Bil . . . 7C 74
CV23: Thurl . . . 6K 85
Beecher's Keep CV8: Bran . . . 3H 71
Beeches, The B78: Pole . . . 2D 10
CV12: Bed . . . 3E 40
CV23: Clift D . . . 3B 76
CV33: Har . . . 5G 109
Beeches Wlk. CV37: Tidd . . . 3K 115
Beech Gro. CV7: Old A . . . 2C 28
CV34: Warw . . . 6K 97
Beechnut Cl. CV4: Tile H . . . 5B 56
Beech Rd. CV6: Cov . . . 2B 58
CV35: Oxh . . . 1E 130
Beech Tree Av. CV4: Tile H . . . 5F 57
Beech Tree Pk. B50: Bidf A . . . 4H 123
Beechwood Av. CV5: Cov . . . 6J 57
Beechwood Ct. CV5: Cov . . . 7K 57
CV21: Rugby . . . 4F 75
Beechwood Cft. CV8: Ken . . . 7D 78
BEECHWOOD GARDENS . . . 7J 57
Beechwood Rd. CV10: Nun . . . 5J 21
CV12: Bed . . . 1J 41
Beehive Hill CV8: Ken . . . 2B 78
Beehive La. B76: Curd . . . 5C 18
Beeston Cl. CV3: Bin . . . 7B 60
BELBROUGHTON . . . 1A 142
Beldesert Cl. B95: Hen A . . . 2H 93
Belfry Golf Course, The . . . 1B 18
BELFRY JUNC. . . . 1C 18
Belgrade Theatre . . . 3G 135 (4C 58)
Belgrave Dr. CV21: Brow . . . 2K 75
Belgrave Rd. CV2: Cov . . . 3A 60
Belgrave Sq. CV2: Cov . . . 3A 60
Belgravia Ct. B37: K'hrst . . . 7A 24
Bellairs Av. CV12: Bed . . . 4E 40
Bellam Rd. CV35: H Mag . . . 1B 100
Bell Brook CV37: Snitt . . . 6G 95
Bellbrooke Cl. CV6: Cov . . . 5H 51
Bell Cl. B36: Cas B . . . 6B 24
Bell Ct. CV32: Lea S . . . 5D 98
Bell Ct. Shop. Cen. CV37: S Avon . . . 4F 137 (5F 115)
Bell Dr. CV7: Ash G . . . 6E 40
BELL END . . . 1A 142
Belle Vue CV10: Nun . . . 1E 30
Bellfield B94: Tan A . . . 3D 90
BELL GREEN . . . 6H 51
Bell Grn. Rd. CV6: Cov . . . 6G 51
Bellingham B77: Wiln . . . 1A 10
Bell La. B80: Stud . . . 3D 92
CV23: M Kirby . . . 3J 55
CV37: Shot . . . 5C 114
CV37: Snitt . . . 6H 95
Bell Mead B80: Stud . . . 3D 92
Bells La. OX15: Up Bra . . . 1F 133
Bell Tower M. CV32: Lea S . . . 4D 98
Bellview Way CV6: Cov . . . 5H 51
Bell Wlk. B37: F'bri . . . 4A 34
CV21: Hillm . . . 1D 88
Belmont Ct. CV32: Lill . . . 3E 98
Belmont Dr. CV32: Lill . . . 3E 98
Belmont M. CV8: Ken . . . 5D 78
CV32: Lill . . . 3E 98
Belmont Rd. CV6: Cov . . . 7F 51
(not continuous)
CV22: Rugby . . . 1G 87
Belvedere Rd. CV5: Cov . . . 7A 58
Benches Furlong CV23: Brow . . . 6K 65
Benedictine Ct. *CV1: Cov . . . 3J 135*
(off Priory Pl.)
Benedictine Rd. CV3: Cov . . . 1C 68
Benedict Sq. CV2: Cov . . . 6J 51
BENGEWORTH . . . 1A 146
Benjamins Yd. *CV36: Ship S . . . 5H 131*
(off Old Rd.)
Bennett Ct. CV8: Wols . . . 5H 71
Bennett Dr. CV34: Warw . . . 1K 101

Bennett Pl. CV36: Ilm 6C 126
Bennett's Rd. CV7: Ker E 7K 39
Bennett's Rd. Nth. CV7: Cor 5H 39
Bennett's Rd. Sth. CV6: Cov 3K 49
CV7: Ker E 3K 49
Bennett St. CV21: Rugby 5F 75
Bennet Way CV37: S Avon 7H 115
Bennfield Rd. CV21: Rugby 5G 75
Benn Rd. CV12: Bulk 3D 42
Benn St. CV22: Rugby 6J 75
Benson Rd. CV6: Cov 5A 50
CV37: S Avon 3F 115
Benthall Rd. CV6: Cov 4F 51
BENTLEY
Atherstone 7H 15 (2D 139)
Walsall 2A 138
Bentley Cl. CV32: Lill 4F 99
Bentley Ct. CV6: Cov 2C 50
BENTLEY HEATH 1C 143
Bentley La. B46: Max 3E 36
Bentley Rd. CV7: Exh 4G 41
CV11: Nun 7B 22
Bentree, The CV3: Cov 7H 59
BEOLEY 2B 142
Berenska Dr. CV32: Lea S 5E 98
Beresford Av. CV6: Cov 5D 50
Bericote Rd. CV32: B'dwn 1E 98
Berkeley Cl. CV11: Nun 1H 31
Berkeley Rd. CV8: Ken 3C 78
Berkeley Rd. Nth. CV5: Cov 6A 58
Berkeley Rd. Sth. CV5: Cov 7A 58
Berkett Rd. CV6: Cov 3B 50
Berkshire Cl. CV10: Nun 1E 30
BERKSWELL 1D 143
Berkswell Rd. CV6: Cov 4G 51
CV7: Mer 7E 46
BERMUDA 3G 31
Bermuda Bus. Pk. CV10: Griff 5F 31
Bermuda Ind. Est. CV10: Nun 4H 31
Bermuda Innovation Cen. CV10: Griff 6G 31
Bermuda Rd. CV10: Nun 2G 31
Bermuda Trade Cen., The CV10: Griff 5H 31
Berners Cl. CV4: Tile H 5C 56
Berrills La. CV36: Cher 7G 133
Berrington Rd. CV10: Nun 4H 21
Berrington Rd. CV31: Lea S 2F 103
Berry Av. CV36: Ship S 4G 131
Berrybanks CV22: Bil 7A 74
Berry Cl. CV36: Ship S 4G 131
Berry Flds. CV7: Fill 1C 38
Berry Mdw. CV47: Fen C 2G 121
Berry St. CV1: Cov 3E 58
Bertie Ct. CV8: Ken 5E 78
Bertie Rd. CV8: Ken 5D 78
Bertie Ter. CV32: Lea S 6C 98
Berwick Cl. CV5: E Grn 3F 57
CV34: Warw 5G 97
Berwicks La. B37: Chel W 4B 34
(not continuous)
Berwyn Av. CV6: Cov 5A 50
Berwyn Way CV10: Nun 7G 21
Best Av. CV8: Ken 3G 79
Beswick Gdns. CV22: Bil 2D 86
Betjeman Rd. CV37: S Avon 7H 115
Bettina Cl. CV10: Nun 6G 21
Bettman Cl. CV3: Cov 2E 68
Bettridge Pl. CV35: Welle 2H 117
Beverley Av. CV10: Nun 7G 21
Beverley Rd. CV32: Lea S 6B 98
Beverly Dr. CV4: Canly 6H 67
Bevington Cres. CV6: Cov 2J 57
Bewick Cft. CV2: Cov 2G 59
Bexfield Cl. CV5: Alle 1E 56
Biart Pl. CV21: Rugby 4K 75
BICKENHILL 5D 44 (3C 139)
Bickenhill Grn. Ct. B92: Bick 5D 44
Bickenhill La. B37: Mars G 7C 34
(not continuous)
B92: Cath B 7C 44
Bickenhill Parkway B40: Nat E C 7D 34
Bickenhill Rd. B37: Mars G 6A 34
Bickenhill Trad. Est. B40: Mars G 1D 44
BICKMARSH 3C 143
Bidavon Ind. Est. B50: Bidf A 4H 123
Bideford Rd. CV2: Cov 7J 51
BIDFORD-ON-AVON 6G 123 (3B 142)
Bidford Rd. B50: Broom 3F 123
Bigbury Cl. CV3: Cov 3E 68
Biggin Hall Cres. CV3: Cov 5H 59
Biggin Hall La. CV23: Thurl 7J 85
Bilberry Rd. CV2: Cov 4K 51
BILBROOK 1A 138
Billesden Cl. CV3: Bin 7A 60
BILLESDON 1D 141
BILLESLEY 7F 113 (3C 143)
Billesley Rd. CV37: Wilm 7H 113
Billing Rd. CV5: Cov 4H 57
Billington Cl. CV2: Cov 5A 60
BILSTON 2A 138
BILSTONE 1A 140
BILTON 1C 86 (1B 144)
Bilton Ind. Est. CV3: Cov 6F 59
Bilton La. CV22: Bil 6B 74
CV22: Dunc 5D 86
CV23: Long L 5B 74
Bilton Rd. CV22: Bil, Rugby 1D 86
BINLEY 7A 60 (1A 144)
Binley Av. CV3: Bin 1B 70
Binley Bus. Pk. CV3: Bin 6C 60
(not continuous)
Binley Gro. CV3: Bin 1B 70
Binley Rd. CV3: Bin, Cov 4F 59
(not continuous)
Binley Rd. CV3: Cov 5G 59
BINLEY WOODS 1E 70
Binns Cl. CV4: Tile H 7C 56
Binswood End CV33: Har 5G 109
Binswood Av. CV32: Lea S 5D 98
Binswood Cl. CV2: Cov 4K 51
Binswood Cres. CV32: Lea S 5D 98
Binswood Mans. CV32: Lea S 5D 98
Binswood St. CV32: Lea S 6C 98
BINTON 3C 143
Binton Bridges Cvn. Pk. CV37: Welf A 1A 124
Binton Rd. CV2: Cov 5K 51
CV37: Bint, Welf A 1A 124
Binton Vw. CV37: S Avon 3A 114
Birbeck Ho. B36: Cas B 6B 24
Birch Abbey B49: Alc 5B 112
Birch Cl. B78: K'bry 4E 12
CV5: Alle 1D 56
CV12: Bed 1K 41
Birch Ct. CV34: H'cte 6C 102
Birch Cft. B37: Chel W 4C 34
Birch Dr. CV22: Bil 6B 74
Birch End CV34: Warw 7K 97
Birches, The CV12: Bulk 1D 42
Birches La. CV8: Ken 6E 78
Birchfield Cl. CV9: Wood E 2K 13
Birchfield Rd. CV6: Cov 7K 49
CV37: S Avon 2F 115
Birchgrave Cl. CV6: Cov 7G 51
Birch Gro. B78: B'moor 3A 10
CV35: Welle 3J 117
BIRCHLEY HEATH 2D 139
Birch Mdw. Cl. CV34: Warw 1F 101
BIRCHMOOR 3B 10 (1D 139)
Birchmoor Rd. B78: B'moor 2B 10
Birch Tree Rd. CV10: Nun 5H 21
Birchway Cl. CV32: Lea S 6A 98
Birchwood Av. B78: Dord 3C 10
Birchwood Rd. CV3: Bin W 1E 70
BIRCHY CROSS 1E 90
Bird Gro. Ct. CV1: Cov 2D 58
Bird Haven Cl. CV33: L Hth 2K 119
Birdhope B77: Wiln 1A 10
Bird Ind. Pk. CV37: Long M 4G 125
BIRDINGBURY 5A 104 (2B 144)
Birdingbury Rd. CV23: Hill, Lea H 5B 104
CV23: Mart 2D 104
Bird Rd. CV33: L Hth 3K 119
CV34: H'cte 4A 102
Bird St. CV1: Cov 2J 135 (3D 58)
Birkdale Cl. CV6: Cov 2B 50
CV11: Nun 3C 32
BIRMINGHAM 3B 138
Birmingham Bus. Est. B37: Mars G 5E 34
BIRMINGHAM INTERNATIONAL AIRPORT 2C 44 (3C 139)
Birmingham International Station (Rail) 2D 44
Birmingham Rd. B37: K'hrst 7B 24
B46: Col 7C 24
B46: Neth W 4G 19
B46: Wat O 2A 24
B49: Alc 3A 112
B49: K Cou 1A 112
B76: Lea M 4G 19
B80: Map G, Stud 2D 92
B95: Hen A 1H 93
CV5: Mil W 3K 45
(Oak La.)
CV5: Alle 1E 56
(Rye Hill)
CV7: Mer 6G 47
(Church La.)
CV7: Mer 3K 45
(Kenilworth Rd.)
CV8: Ken 1A 78
CV8: S'lgh 2B 80
CV10: Ansl 5A 20
CV34: Warw 7D 96
CV35: Bud, Hatt, Wrox 5A 96
CV37: Bear 6B 94
CV37: B'ton, Path, S Avon 1D 136 (1C 114)
BIRSTALL 1C 141
Birstall Dr. CV21: Brow 2K 75
Birvell Ct. CV12: Bed 3J 41
BISHAMPTON 3A 142
Bishopgate Bus. Pk. CV1: Cov 2C 58
Bishops Bowl Lakes 7K 109
Bishops Cleeve CV9: Aus 7G 7
Bishops Cl. CV33: Bis T 5C 108
CV37: S Avon 3B 114
Bishop's Ct. B37: Mars G 5E 34
Bishops Ga. CV47: Bis I 5C 110
BISHOPSGATE GREEN 2D 58
Bishopsgate Ind. Est. CV1: Cov 2D 58
Bishops Hill CV35: Light 2G 119
BISHOP'S ITCHINGTON 6B 110 (3A 144)
BISHOP'S TACHBROOK 5C 108 (2A 144)
Bishop St. CV1: Cov 2H 135 (4C 58)
Bishop's Wlk. CV5: Cov 7F 135 (7B 58)
BISHOPTON 1C 114 (3C 143)
Bishopton Cl. CV5: E Grn 4F 57
Bishopton La. CV37: B'ton 3A 114
Bisset Cres. CV31: Lea S 2G 103
Bitham Rd. CV33: L Hth 1K 119
Bittern Wlk. CV2: Cov 4K 51
BITTESWELL 3C 141
Bixhill La. B46: Shu 2B 26
BLABY 2C 141
Black-a-Tree Ct. CV10: Nun 6A 22
Black-a-Tree Rd. CV10: Nun 7K 21
Blackbades Blvd. CV34: Warw 4D 100
BLACK BANK 4H 41
Black Bank CV7: Exh 4H 41
Blackberry Cl. CV23: Brow 7K 65
Blackberry La. CV2: Cov 1H 59
CV7: Ash G 1B 50
Blackbird Cft. B36: Cas B 5A 24
Blackburn Rd. CV6: Longf 3F 51
Blackcat Cl. B37: F'bri 2A 34
BLACKDOWN 2C 98
Blackfirs La. B37: Mars G 6C 34
Blackford Cl. B95: Hen A 2H 93
Blackford Way CV35: Oxh 1E 130
Blackgreaves La. B76: Lea M 2F 19
Black Hall La. CV7: Fill 1A 38
BLACKHEATH 3A 138
BLACK HILL 7K 95 (3D 143)
Blackhill Ind. Est. CV37: B Hill 7K 95
Black Horse Rd. CV6: Longf 1H 51
CV7: Exh 7G 41
Black La. CV32: Lea S 5F 99
Blacklow Rd. CV34: Warw 6J 97
Blackman Way CV21: Rugby 4F 75
Black Pad CV6: Cov 6C 50
Black Prince Av. CV3: Cov 1D 68
Blackshaw Dr. CV2: W'grve S 1B 60
Blacksmiths La. CV47: N'end 1D 120
Blackthorn Cl. CV4: Canly 3H 67
Blackthorn Ct. *B95: Hen A* *1H 93*
(off Chestnut Wlk.)
Blackthorn Gro. CV11: Nun 2B 32
Blackthorn Rd. CV8: Ken 6E 78
CV37: S Avon 2F 115
Blackthorn Way B49: Alc 3B 112
Blackwatch Rd. CV6: Cov 6C 50
BLACKWELL
Bromsgrove 1A 142
Shipston-on-Stour 6F 127 (1B 146)
Blackwell Business Pk. CV36: Wind 7F 127
Blackwell La. CV35: Hatt 5B 96
Blackwell Rd. CV6: Cov 6E 50
CV36: Tred 7H 127
Blackwood Av. CV22: Bil 7C 74
Blacon Way CV37: S Avon 4B 114
Bladon Cl. CV11: Nun 3G 23
Bladon Wlk. CV31: Lea S 2G 103
Blair Dr. CV12: Bed 4D 40
Blair Gro. B37: Chel W 4D 34
Blake Cl. CV10: Gall C 6F 21
CV22: Bil 7C 74
BLAKEDOWN 1A 142
Blakelands Av. CV31: Lea S 2F 103
BLAKENHALL 2A 138
BLAKESLEY 3D 145
Blandford Dr. CV2: W'grve S 2B 60
Blandford Rd. CV32: Lea S 6A 98
Blandford Way CV35: H Mag 1C 100
Bleaberry CV21: Brow 1J 75
Bleachfield St. B49: Alc 6B 112
BLEDINGTON 3B 146
Blenheim Av. CV6: Cov 4C 50
Blenheim Cl. B50: Bidf A 5G 123
CV11: Nun 2B 32
Blenheim Cres. CV31: Lea S 3G 103
Blenheim Wlk. CV6: Cov 2B 50
CV35: Welle 5G 117
BLETCHINGDON 3D 147
Bletchley Dr. CV5: Cov 3F 57
Blew Gates OX15: Lwr Bra 3G 133
Blick Rd. CV34: H'cte 4A 102
Blind La. B94: Tan A 3A 90
CV8: Ken 7D 66
Blindpit La. B76: Wis 3A 18
Bliss Cl. CV4: Tile H 4C 56
BLISWORTH 3D 145
BLOCKLEY 2A 146
Blockley Rd. CV12: Bed 1J 41
Blondvil St. CV3: Cov 1C 68
Bloxam Gdns. CV22: Rugby 6F 75
BLOXHAM 2D 147
Bloxham Pl. CV21: Rugby 5G 75
BLOXWICH 1B 138
Bluebell Cl. CV23: Brow 7K 65
Bluebell Dr. CV12: Bed 3E 40
Bluebell Wlk. CV4: Tile H 6D 56
Blue Cap Rd. CV37: S Avon 2F 115
Blue La. CV37: Lox 7C 116
Bluemel's Dr. CV8: Wols 4J 71
Blundells CV8: Ken 4E 78
Blundells, The CV8: Ken 4D 78
Blundells Cft. CV37: Welf A 2A 124
BLUNTINGTON 1A 142
BLUNT'S GREEN 4E 90
Blyth Cl. CV12: Bed 4C 40
CV22: Caw 1A 86
Blyth Ct. CV11: Nun 1J 31
Blythe Ct. B46: Col 5G 25
BLYTHE END 2J 25
Blythe Rd. B46: Col 5G 25
CV1: Cov 3E 58
Boar Cft. CV4: Tile H 5D 56
Boat La. CV37: Welf A 2A 124
Bockendon Rd. CV4: W'wd H 4B 66
Boddington Cl. CV32: Cubb 2J 99
BODICOTE 2D 147
Bodmin Rd. CV2: Cov 2B 60
Bodnant Way CV8: Ken 3G 79
BODYMOOR HEATH 7B 12 (2C 139)
Bodymoor Heath Rd. B76: Bod H, Mars 5A 12 & 1H 19
B78: Midd 5A 12
Bodymoor Heath Vis. Cen. 7B 12
Bohun St. CV4: Tile H 6D 56
BOLEHALL 1D 139
Boleyn Cl. CV34: Warw 2A 102
Bolingbroke Dr. CV34: H'cte 5C 102
Bolingbroke Rd. CV3: Cov 6G 59
Bolton Cl. CV3: Cov 3E 68

Bolus La. B46: Max 1D 36
Bolyfant Cres. CV31: W'nsh 6E 102
Bond End CV23: M Kirby 3J 55
Bond Ga. CV11: Nun 7D 22
Bonds Ct. CV1: Cov 3G 135 (4C 58)
Bond St. CV1: Cov 3G 135 (4C 58)
CV11: Nun 6D 22
CV21: Rugby 5F 75
BONEHILL 1C 139
BONEY HAY 1B 138
Bonneville Cl. CV5: Mil W 6K 47
Bonniksen Cl. CV31: Lea S 3D 102
Bonnington Cl. CV21: Hillm 7D 76
Bonnington Dr. CV12: Bed 1G 41
Boot Hill CV9: Gren 1F 15
Booths Flds. CV6: Cov 4E 50
Bordesley Ct. CV32: Lill 4E 98
Bordon Hill CV37: S Avon 6A 114
Bordon Pl. CV37: S Avon 6D 114
Borrowdale CV21: Brow 7J 65
Borrowdale Cl. CV6: Cov 6A 50
Borrowdale Dr. CV32: Lea S 5B 98
Borrowell La. CV8: Ken 5C 78
Borrowell Ter. CV8: Ken 5C 78
Boscastle Ho. CV12: Bed 4C 40
Bosley Cl. CV36: Ship S 6G 131
Boston Pl. CV6: Cov 6D 50
Boswell Dr. CV2: W'grve S 1C 60
Boswell Gro. CV34: Warw 6F 97
Boswell Rd. CV22: Rugby 2E 86
Bosworth Cl. CV8: Bag 5E 68
Bosworth Dr. B37: Chel W, F'bri 3A 34
BOTCHESTON 1B 140
Boteler Cl. B49: Alc 5B 112
Botoner Rd. CV1: Cov 5F 59
Bottom St. CV47: N'end 2D 120
Bottrill Ct. CV11: Nun 6C 22
Bottrill St. CV11: Nun 6C 22
Bott Rd. CV5: Cov 7H 57
Boucher Cl. CV37: Shot 6C 114
BOUGHTON 2D 145
Boughton La. Ind. Est. CV21: Rugby 2H 75
Boughton Rd. CV21: Rugby 1H 75
Boulters La. CV9: Wood E 2K 13
Boundary La. CV37: A'ton 5K 115
Boundary Rd. CV21: Rugby 6K 75
Boundary Rd. E. CV37: Long M 6F 125
Boundary Rd. Nth. CV37: Long M 4H 125
Boundary Rd. W. CV37: Long M 5F 125
BOURNBROOK 3B 138
Bourne Brook Cl. CV7: Fill 2B 38
Bournebrook Vw. CV7: Old A 3C 28
Bourne Cl. CV9: Ath 1D 16
Bourne End CV47: Sou 6G 107
Bourne Rd. CV3: Cov 6J 59
BOURNHEATH 1A 142
BOURNVILLE 3B 138
Bourton Dr. CV31: Lea S 3F 103
BOURTON ON DUNSMORE 7C 84 (1B 144)
BOURTON-ON-THE-HILL 2A 146
BOURTON-ON-THE-WATER 3A 146
Bourton Rd. CV23: F'ton 7B 84
Bowater Ct. CV3: Cov 2F 69
Bow Ct. CV5: Cov 7H 57
Bowden Way CV3: Bin 6B 60
Bowen Rd. CV22: Hillm 1K 87
Bowers Cft. CV32: Lill 3E 98
Bowet Cl. CV22: Caw 1K 85
Bow Fell CV21: Brow 1K 75
Bowfell Cl. CV5: E Grn 3E 56
Bow La. CV7: Withy 1D 54
CV23: M Kirby 1D 54
Bowleys La. DE12: App M 1K 7
Bowling Grn. La. CV12: Bed 6E 40
Bowling Grn. St. CV34: Warw 2F 101
Bowls Ct. CV5: Cov 4K 57
Bowness Cl. CV6: Cov 6A 50
Box Bush Cotts. CV37: Long M 2G 125
Box Cl. CV31: W'nsh 5F 103
Boxhill, The CV3: Cov 6H 59
Box Rd. B37: Chel W 5C 34
Boxwood Dr. CV23: Kils 6J 89
Boyce Way CV23: Long L 3B 74
Boyd Cl. CV2: W'grve S 6B 52
Bracadale Cl. CV3: Bin 4C 60
Bracebridge Rd. B78: K'bry 5D 12
CV9: Ath 4B 16
Bracebridge St. CV11: Nun 7C 22
Bracken Cl. CV22: Bil 7E 74
Bracken Cft. B37: Chel W 2C 34
Brackendale Dr. CV10: Nun 2F 31
Bracken Dr. CV22: Bil 7E 74
LE10: Wlvy 2H 33
Brackenhurst Rd. CV6: Cov 7K 49
Brackley Cl. CV6: Cov 7K 49
Bracknell Wlk. CV2: W'grve S 7C 52
BRADDEN 3D 145
Braddock Cl. CV3: Bin 6C 60
Brade Dr. CV2: W'grve S 7C 52
Bradestone Rd. CV11: Nun 3K 31
Bradfield Cl. CV5: Cov 2G 57
Bradford Cl. CV33: Bis T 5B 108
Brading Rd. CV10: Nun 5E 22
BRADLEY 2A 138
BRADLEY GREEN
Atherstone 5J 11 (1D 139)
Redditch 2A 142
BRADMORE 2A 138
Bradney Grn. CV4: Tile H 1C 66
Bradnick Pl. CV4: Tile H 6D 56
Braemar Cl. CV2: Cov 7A 52
Braemar Rd. CV32: Lill 3F 99
Braemar Way CV10: Nun 2G 31
Braeside Cft. B37: Chel W 3D 34
Brafield Leys CV22: Rugby 3G 87
Braids Cl. CV21: Rugby 4K 75
Brailes Ind. Est. OX15: Lwr Bra 3K 133
Brakesmead CV31: Lea S 3D 102
Bramble Cl. B46: Col 5F 25
CV11: Nun 2B 32
Bramble St. CV1: Cov 5E 58
Brambling Cl. CV23: Brow 7J 65
BRAMCOTE 6H 33 (3B 140)
Bramcote Cl. CV12: Bulk 3F 43
BRAMCOTE MAINS 2G 43
Bramdene Av. CV10: Nun 3D 22
Bramley Way B50: Bidf A 5G 123
Brampton Way CV12: Bulk 2D 42
Bramston Cres. CV4: Tile H 6D 56
Bramwell Gdns. CV6: Longf 1E 50
Brandfield Rd. CV6: Cov 6K 49
BRANDON 3H 71 (1B 144)
Brandon Ct. CV3: Bin 1C 70
Brandon La. CV3: W'hall 4K 69
CV8: Bran 3D 70
Brandon Marsh Nature Reserve 4C 70
Brandon Marsh Nature Reserve Vis. Cen. 4D 70
Brandon Pde. CV32: Lea S 7E 98
Brandon Rd. CV3: Bin 6B 60
CV23: Bret 2A 72
Branksome Rd. CV6: Cov 1J 57
Bransdale Av. CV6: Cov 3D 50
Bransford Av. CV4: Canly 3H 67
Branstree Dr. CV6: Cov 4D 50
BRATCH, THE 2A 138
Brathay Cl. CV3: Cov 2D 68
BRAUNSTON 2C 145
BRAUNSTONE 1C 141
Braunston Pl. CV22: Hillm 1K 87
Bray Bank B46: Over W 1F 27
Brayford Av. CV3: Cov 2C 68
Brays Cl. CV23: Brin 4C 62
Bray's La. CV2: Cov 4G 59
Braytoft Cl. CV6: Cov 4C 50
Brazil St. CV4: Tile H 5C 56
Breach La. CV35: Clav 2C 94
Breach Oak La. CV7: Cor 2G 39
Bread and Meat Cl. CV34: Warw 2F 101
Bream Cl. B37: Chel W 3C 34
Breaside Wlk. B37: Chel W 2C 34
BREDICOT 3A 142
Bredon Av. CV3: Bin 1B 70
Bree Cl. CV5: Alle 7E 48
Breeden Dr. B76: Curd 5B 18
Brendan Cl. B46: Col 7G 25
Brendon Way CV10: Nun 1A 30
Brentwood Av. CV3: Finh 5C 68
Brese Av. CV34: Warw 6H 97
BRETFORD 1B 72 (1B 144)
Bretford Rd. CV2: Cov 5J 51
CV8: Bran 2J 71
CV23: Brin 6C 62
BRETFORTON 1A 146
Bretts Cl. CV1: Cov 1K 135 (3E 58)
Bretts Hall Est. CV10: Ans C 4E 20
Brewer Rd. CV12: Bulk 4F 43
Brewers Cl. CV3: Bin 6C 60
Brewery Row GL56: Lit C 6B 134
Brewery St. CV37: S Avon 1E 136 (4E 114)
BREWOOD 1A 138
Brewster Cl. CV2: Cov 5A 60
Brians Way CV6: Cov 3E 50
Briar Cl. CV32: Lill 5F 99
Briar Cft. CV37: S Avon 4B 136 (5E 114)
Briardene Av. CV12: Bed 3H 41
Briar Gdns. CV32: Lill 5G 99
Briars Cl. CV2: Cov 5J 59
CV11: Nun 6F 23
CV23: Long L 4B 74
Brickall, The CV37: Long M 3G 125
Brickhill Cl. CV36: Ship S 4G 131
Brickhill Dr. B37: F'bri 3A 34
Brick Hill La. CV5: Alle 6B 48
Brickkiln La. CV9: Hurl 7J 13
Brick Kiln Way CV12: Bed 2J 41
Brickyard La. B80: Stud 2B 92
Brickyard Rd. CV47: Nap 2F 111
Bridgeacre Gdns. CV3: Bin 4B 60
Bridgecote CV3: W'hall 2A 70
Bridge Ct. CV47: Sou 6H 107
BRIDGE END 2H 101
Bridge End CV34: Warw 2H 101
CV47: Sou 5H 107
Bridge Foot CV37: S Avon 3H 137 (4F 115)
Bridgefoot Quay
CV37: S Avon 3J 137 (4F 115)
Bridge La. CV9: With 4G 17
CV47: Ladb 3C 110
Bridgeman Rd. CV6: Cov 2B 58
Bridge Rd. CV35: But M 7A 120
Bridge St. B78: Pole 1D 10
CV6: Cov 7F 51
CV8: Ken 4D 78
CV9: Hurl 7K 13
CV11: Nun 7D 22
(Church St.)
CV11: Nun 2J 31
(Henry St.)
CV21: Rugby 5J 75
CV34: Warw 7K 97
CV35: Barf 2B 108
CV35: H Lucy 2B 118
CV35: Kine 6C 120
CV35: Welle 3H 117
CV37: S Avon 4G 137 (4F 115)
CV47: Fen C 3G 121
BRIDGE TOWN 6G 115 (3D 143)
Bridgetown Rd. CV37: S Avon 6G 115
Bridget St. CV21: Rugby 5F 75
Bridgeway CV37: S Avon 2J 137 (4F 115)
Bridge Works Ind. Est. CV8: Ken 5E 78
BRIDGTOWN 1A 138
Bridle Brook La. CV5: Alle 2D 48
Bridle Path, The CV5: Alle 1F 57
Bridle Rd. CV21: Rugby 4E 74
CV33: L Hth 2K 119
Bridport Cl. CV2: W'grve S 2C 60
BRIERLEY HILL 3A 138
Brierley Rd. CV2: Cov 6J 51
Brightmere Rd. CV6: Cov 3B 58
Brighton St. CV2: Cov 4F 59
Bright St. CV6: Cov 1E 58
Bright Walton Rd. CV3: Cov 1D 68
Brill Cl. CV4: Canly 3G 67
Brindle Av. CV3: Cov 6J 59
Brindles All. CV36: Ship S 4H 131
Brindley Cl. CV9: Ath 2B 16
Brindley Paddocks CV1: Cov 1H 135 (3C 58)
Brindley Rd. CV7: Exh 6H 41
CV21: Hillm 7C 76
BRINKLOW 4C 62 (1B 144)
Brinklow Rd. CV3: Bin 5B 60
CV7: Ansty 2G 53
CV23: Brin 4E 62
Brisbane Cl. CV3: Cov 2E 68
Brisbane Ct. CV12: Bed 3G 41
Briscoe Rd. CV6: Cov 2C 50
Bristol Rd. CV5: Cov 5K 57
Bristol Way CV35: Welle 5G 117
Britannia St. CV2: Cov 4F 59
Briton Rd. CV2: Cov 3G 59
Britten Cl. CV11: Nun 5C 32
Brittons La. CV35: N Lin 1G 95
Brixham Cl. CV11: Nun 6G 23
Brixham Dr. CV2: Cov 1J 59
BRIXWORTH 1D 145
Brixworth Cl. CV3: Bin 7A 60
BROAD ALLEY 2A 142
BROAD CAMPDEN 2A 146
Broad Cl. CV33: Ufton 3F 109
Broadgate CV1: Cov 4H 135 (5C 58)
BROAD GREEN 1A 142
Broadhaven Cl. CV31: Lea S 1G 103
Broadlands Cl. CV5: Cov 5G 57
Broad La. B94: Tan A 3A 90
CV5: E Grn 3B 56
CV7: Berk 3A 56
CV7: Fill 1J 37
Broad La. Trad. Est. CV4: Tile H 3A 56
Broadlee B77: Wiln 1A 10
BROAD MARSTON 1A 146
Broadmead Ct. CV5: Cov 5G 57
Broadmeadow La. CV37: B'ton 3B 114
Broadmere Ri. CV5: E Grn 5E 56
Broadmoor La. CV36: Lit Wol 6D 132
Broad Oak Ct. CV32: Lea S 5E 98
Broad Pk. Rd. CV2: Cov 7K 51
Broad St. CV6: Cov 7E 50
CV23: Brin 4C 62
CV34: Warw 1H 101
CV36: Long C 2C 134
CV37: S Avon 7D 136 (5E 114)
Broad St. Jetty CV6: Cov 7E 50
Broad Wlk. CV37: S Avon 7C 136 (5E 114)
Broadwater CV5: Cov 7A 58
BROADWAY 2A 146
Broadway CV5: Cov 6A 58
CV32: Cubb 2J 99
Broadway Mans. CV5: Cov 6A 58
BROADWELL
Moreton-in-Marsh 3B 146
Rugby 2B 144
Broadwells Ct. CV4: W'wd H 2D 66
Broadwells Cres. CV4: W'wd H 3D 66
BROCKENCOTE 1A 142
Brockenhurst Way CV6: Longf 7H 41
BROCKHALL 2D 145
Brockhall Gro. B37: K'hrst 7A 24
BROCKHURST 3K 55
Brockhurst Dr. CV4: Tile H 5B 56
Brockhurst La. CV23: M Kirby 3K 55
BROCKMOOR 3A 138
Brodick Way CV10: Nun 1F 31
Bromage Av. B78: K'bry 5D 12
Brome Hall La. B94: Lapw 4J 91
BROMFORD 2C 139
Bromford Way CV37: S Avon 3C 114
Bromhurst Way CV34: Warw 4D 100
Bromleigh Dr. CV2: Cov 5J 59
Bromleigh Vs. CV8: Bag 6F 69
Bromley Cl. CV8: Ken 3C 78
BROMSGROVE 1A 142
Bromsgrove Rd. B80: Stud 4B 92
Bromwich Cl. CV3: Bin 7B 60
Bromwich Ct. B46: Col 2E 24
Bromwich Rd. CV21: Hillm 7B 76
Bronte Cl. CV10: Gall C 6E 20
CV21: Rugby 5J 75
Bronte Wlk. CV2: Cov 4K 59
Bronze Cl. CV11: Nun 4A 32
Brook Bus. Pk. CV35: Kine 5B 120
Brook Cl. B78: K'bry 6E 12
Brook Cl. CV1: Cov 4E 58
Brook Cott. Cl. B46: Over W 1F 27
Brook Cotts. CV36: W'ton 7K 131
Brook Cft. B37: Mars G 6B 34
Brookdale Rd. CV10: Nun 4E 22
Brooke Cl. CV34: Warw 3H 101
CV37: S Avon 6H 115

Brooke Ct. *CV21: Rugby* 5F 75
(off Lit. Pennington St.)
Brooke M. CV34: Warw 2H 101
BROOK END 3A 142
Brook End Cl. B95: Hen A 2G 93
Brook End Dr. B95: Hen A 2G 93
Brooke Rd. CV8: Ken 5F 79
Brook Farm Wlk. B37: Chel W 2D 34
Brookfield Ct. CV37: S Avon 4B 114
Brookfield Dr. LE10: Wlvy 2H 33
Brookfield Rd. CV32: Cubb 2J 99
Brookford Av. CV6: Cov 3A 50
Brookhampton CV35: Kine 6A 120
Brookhampton La. CV35: Kine 6B 120
Brookhurst Ct. CV32: Lea S 6B 98
Brooklands Way B37: Mars G 5B 34
Brook La. CV10: Nun 5D 22
CV35: More M 5C 118
CV37: N'bld S 1G 127
Brooklea CV12: Bed 3F 41
Brooklime Dr. CV23: Brow 7K 65
Brooklyn Rd. CV1: Cov 1D 58
Brook Rd. B95: Aston C 2K 113
Brooks Cl. CV23: W'hby 3H 105
Brookshaw Way CV2: W'grve S 6B 52
Brookside B95: Woot W 4J 93
CV23: Stret D 3H 83
CV37: Snitt 5G 95
Brookside Av. CV5: Cov 4G 57
CV8: Ken 5C 78
CV35: Welle 3J 117
Brookside Cl. CV22: Rugby 7G 75
CV37: S Avon 4C 114
Brookside Rd. CV37: S Avon 4C 114
Brookstray Flats CV5: E Grn 4F 57
Brook St. CV8: Wols 5J 71
CV12: Bed 7H 31
CV34: Warw 2G 101
CV47: Fen C 3G 121
Brookvale Av. CV3: Bin 6A 60
Brookvale Rd. CV37: S Avon 7A 136 (5D 114)
Brook Vw. CV22: Dunc 6C 86
Brook Wlk. CV9: Man 5E 16
BROOM 3F 123 (3B 142)
Broom Cl. CV22: Bil 7E 74
Broomcroft Rd. B37: K'hrst 7A 24
BROOME 1A 142
Broome Cft. CV6: Cov 3B 50
Broomey Croft Childrens Farm 4B 12
Broomfield Pl. CV5: Cov 5A 58
(not continuous)
Broomfield Ri. CV10: Nun 2F 31
Broomfield Rd. CV5: Cov 6K 57
BROOM HILL 1A 142
Broomybank CV8: Ken 3F 79
BROUGHTON 2D 147
BROUGHTON ASTLEY 2C 141
BROUGHTON GREEN 2A 142
BROUGHTON HACKETT 3A 142
Browett Rd. CV6: Cov 3K 57
BROWNHILLS 1B 138
Browning Av. CV34: Warw 3E 100
Browning Cl. CV10: Gall C 6F 21
CV37: S Avon 7H 115
Browning Rd. CV2: Cov 4J 59
CV21: Hillm 1D 88
Brownlow Dr. CV37: S Avon 6D 114
BROWNLOW GREEN 3A 96
Brownlow St. CV32: Lea S 5E 98
Brown's Bri. Rd. CV47: Sou 6H 107
BROWN'S GREEN 2B 138
Brownshill Ct. CV6: Cov 6K 49
BROWNSHILL GREEN 5H 49
Brownshill Grn. Rd. CV5: Alle 5H 49
CV6: Cov 5H 49
Brown's La. B78: Dord 5C 10
CV5: Alle 6E 48
BROWNSOVER 1K 75
Brownsover La. CV21: Brow 1H 75
Brownsover Rd. CV21: N'bld A, Rugby 1E 74
Broxell Cl. CV34: Warw 7E 96
Broxell Cl. Ind. Est. CV34: Warw 6E 96
Bruce Rd. CV6: Cov 6A 50
CV7: Exh 6F 41
Bruces Way CV37: S Avon 4A 114
Bruce Williams Way CV22: Rugby 6H 75
Brudenell Cl. CV22: Caw 1A 86
BRUERN ABBEY 3B 146
Brunel Cl. CV2: Cov 4F 59
CV31: W'nsh 5F 103
Brunel Wlk. B78: Pole 6D 8
Brunes Ct. CV21: Brow 1K 75
Brunswick Cl. CV21: Rugby 2J 75
Brunswick Ct. CV31: Lea S 3E 102
Brunswick Rd. CV1: Cov 5A 58
Brunswick St. CV31: Lea S 2E 102
BRUNTINGTHORPE 2D 141
Bruntingthorpe Way CV3: Bin 7A 60
Brunton Cl. CV3: Bin 6D 60
Brutus Dr. B46: Col 3E 24
Bryan M. B50: Bidf A 6H 123
Bryanston Cl. CV2: W'grve S 3C 60
Bryant Rd. CV7: Exh 6G 41
Brympton Rd. CV3: Cov 5J 59
Bryn Jones Cl. CV3: Bin 7B 60
Bryn Rd. CV6: Cov 7F 51
Bryony Cl. CV12: Bed 4E 40
BUBBENHALL 4J 81 (1A 144)
Bubbenhall Rd. CV8: Bag, Bubb 7F 69
BUBENHALL 4J 81
Buccleuch Cl. CV22: Dunc 5C 86
Buchanan Rd. CV22: Bil 7E 74
Buchan Cl. CV10: Gall C 7E 20
Buchan Cl. CV37: S Avon 7H 115
Buckden Cl. CV34: Warw 6H 97
Buckfast Cl. CV3: Cov 3E 68
Buckhold Dr. CV5: Cov 2F 57
Buckingham Cl. CV10: Nun 3H 31
Buckingham Ri. CV5: Cov 3F 57
Buckingham Rd. B36: Cas B 5A 24
BUCKLAND 2A 146
Buckland Rd. CV6: Cov 4B 50
BUCKLEY GREEN 2C 143
Buckley Rd. CV32: Lill 5F 99
Bucknill Cres. CV21: Hillm 1D 88
Bucks Hill CV10: Nun 4G 21
Buckwell La. CV23: Clift D 3C 76
BUDBROOKE 1B 100
Budbrooke Cl. CV2: Cov 4K 51
Budbrooke Ind. Est. CV34: Warw 1E 100
Budbrooke Rd. CV34: Warw 1D 100
BUGBROOKE 3D 145
BULKINGTON
Bedworth 3E 42 (3A 140)
Kenilworth 7D 78
Bulkington La. CV11: Nun 4C 32
Bulkington Rd. CV7: Shil 6G 43
CV12: Bed 3J 41
LE10: Wlvy 2G 33
Bullfield Av. CV4: Tile H 6C 56
Bullimore Gro. CV8: Ken 7E 78
Bull Ring CV10: Nun 2H 31
Bull Ring, The CV33: Har 6H 109
Bull Ring Farm Rd. CV33: Har 5H 109
Bull's Head La. CV3: Cov 5H 59
Bulls Head Yd. B49: Alc 5B 112
Bull St. CV11: Nun 2K 31
CV37: S Avon 7E 136 (6E 114)
CV47: Sou 5H 107
Bull Yd. CV1: Cov 4G 135 (5C 58)
Bull Yd., The CV47: Sou 5H 107
Bulwer Rd. CV6: Cov 7A 50
Bulwick Cl. CV3: Bin 6D 60
Bunkers Hill La. CV23: Bret, Chu L 3B 72
BURBAGE 2B 140
Burbage Av. CV37: S Avon 2E 114
Burbages La. CV6: Longf 1D 50
Burbury Cl. CV12: Bed 1J 41
CV32: Lill 5G 99
Burbury Ct. CV34: Warw 7K 97
BURDROP 2C 147
Burford M. CV31: Lea S 2G 103
Burford Rd. CV37: S Avon 5J 115
Burgage Pl. CV11: Nun 7D 22
Burgage Wlk. CV11: Nun 6C 22
(Friary St.)
CV11: Nun 7D 22
(Powell Way)
Burges, The CV1: Cov 2H 135 (4C 58)
Burges Gro. CV34: Warw 6H 97
Burghley Cl. CV11: Nun 2B 32
Burhill Way B37: F'bri 7B 24
Burlington Rd. CV2: Cov 3F 59
(not continuous)
CV10: Nun 5H 31
Burman Dr. B46: Col 7F 25
BURMINGTON 2B 146
Burnaby Cl. CV10: Nun 6G 21
Burnaby Rd. CV6: Cov 5B 50
Burnell Cl. B50: Bidf A 5F 123
Burnett Rd. CV33: L Hth 3K 119
Burnham Ri. CV11: Nun 5H 23
Burnham Rd. CV3: Cov 2G 69
Burnsall Cl. B37: F'bri 3A 34
Burnsall Gro. CV5: Cov 7H 57
Burnsall Rd. CV5: Cov 7G 57
Burns Av. CV34: Warw 3E 100
Burns Cl. CV37: S Avon 7H 115
Burnside CV3: Bin 5C 60
CV22: Rugby 6E 74
CV37: Shot 5B 114
Burns Rd. CV2: Cov 4J 59
CV32: Lill 3F 99
Burns Wlk. CV12: Bed 4J 41
Burnthurst La. CV23: Prin 7C 82
BURNTWOOD 1B 138
BURNTWOOD GREEN 1B 138
BURROUGH ON THE HILL 1D 141
Burrow Hill La. CV7: Cor 6G 39
Burrows, The CV37: N'bld S 1G 127
Burrows Cl. CV31: W'nsh 5F 103
Burton Cl. CV5: Alle 4G 49
BURTON DASSETT 4E 120
Burton Dassett Hills Country Pk. 2E 120 (3B 144)
BURTON GREEN 4B 66 (1D 143)
BURTON HASTINGS 4J 33 (3B 140)
Burton La. CV11: Burt H 5H 33
BURTON OVERY 2D 141
Bury, The *CV36: Ship S* 4H 131
(off Sheep St.)
Bury Ct. La. OX17: Shotte 6H 129
BURY END 2A 146
Bury Rd. CV31: Lea S 1C 102
Bury Way La. CV36: Long C 1C 134
Busby Cl. CV3: Bin 1B 70
Busbys Piece CV23: M Kirby 3K 55
Bushbery Av. CV4: Tile H 6D 56
BUSHBURY 1A 138
Bushbury Cft. B37: Chel W 2C 34
BUSHBY 1D 141
Bush Cl. CV4: Tile H 4D 56
Bushelton Cl. CV1: Cov 7K 135 (6D 58)
Bush Heath La. CV33: Har 6G 109
Bush Heath Rd. CV33: Har 7H 109
Bushley Cl. B98: Redd 1A 92
Bushy End CV34: H'cte 4C 102
Butchers Cl. CV23: Brin 4D 62
CV47: Bis I 6B 110
Butchers La. CV5: Alle 1G 57
OX15: Lwr Bra 3H 133
Butchers Rd. B92: H Ard 7G 45
Butler Cl. CV8: Ken 2G 79
BUTLER MARSTON 7A 120
Butlers Cl. CV36: Long C 2D 134
Butler's Cres. CV7: Exh 4G 41
Butlers La. CV9: Gren 1F 15
CV36: Long C 2C 134
Butlers Leap CV21: Rugby 3J 75
BUTLERS MARSTON 3A 144
Butlers Rd. CV36: Long C 3D 134
Butlin Rd. CV6: Cov 2C 50
CV21: Rugby 5K 75
Buttercup Way CV12: Bed 3D 40
Buttermere CV21: Brow 1K 75
Buttermere Av. CV11: Nun 5H 23
Buttermere Cl. CV3: Bin 1B 70
Butter St. B49: Alc 5C 112
Butterworth Dr. CV4: W'wd H 2E 66
Butt Hill CV47: Nap 1J 111
Butt La. CV5: Alle 7E 48
CV33: Har 6J 109
Butts CV1: Cov 5B 58
Butts, The CV34: Warw 1G 101
CV36: Long C 2C 134
CV47: Nap 2H 111
Butts Cl. CV9: Aus 6G 7
Butts La. B94: Tan A 3D 90
Butts Rd. CV1: Cov 5A 58
Butts Stadium 5A 58
BYFIELD 3C 145
Byfield Rd. CV6: Cov 2J 57
CV47: P Mars 6H 111
Byford Ct. CV10: Nun 7A 22
Byford St. CV10: Nun 7A 22
Byford Way B37: Mars G 5B 34
Byron Av. CV12: Bed 3K 41
CV34: Warw 4E 100
Byron Rd. CV37: S Avon 6G 115
Byron St. CV1: Cov 1J 135 (3D 58)
Byron Wlk. CV47: Temp H 2A 120
Bywater Cl. CV3: Cov 4B 68

C

Cadden Dr. CV4: Tile H 5F 57
CADEBY 1B 140
Cadman Cl. CV12: Bed 2J 41
Caen Cl. CV35: H Mag 1C 100
Caernarvon Dr. CV11: Nun 1K 31
Caesar Rd. CV8: Ken 6C 78
Caesar Way B46: Col 3F 25
Caithness Cl. CV5: E Grn 3E 56
CAKEBOLE 1A 142
Calcott Ho. CV3: W'hall 2H 69
Calcutt Mdw. CV47: Sou 5K 107
CALDECOTE 1B 22 (2A 140)
Caldecote Cl. CV10: Nun 4D 22
Caldecote Hall Dr. CV10: Cald 1A 22
Caldecote La. CV10: Cald 2A 22
Caldecote Rd. CV6: Cov 2C 58
Caldecott Ct. CV21: Rugby 4H 75
Caldecott Pl. CV21: Rugby 6J 75
Caldecott St. CV21: Rugby 6J 75
Calder Cl. CV3: Cov 1E 68
CV12: Bulk 3D 42
Calder Wlk. CV31: Lea S 2G 103
CALDESCOTE 3D 145
Caldwell Cvn. Pk. CV11: Nun 4K 31
Caldwell Ct. CV11: Nun 3K 31
Caldwell Rd. CV11: Nun 2J 31
Caliban M. CV34: H'cte 5C 102
Callaways Rd. CV36: Ship S 6H 131
Callendar Cl. CV11: Nun 4H 23
Callier Cl. CV22: Caw 1B 86
CALLOW HILL 2B 142
Calmere Cl. CV2: W'grve S 6B 52
Calpurnia Av. CV34: H'cte 6C 102
Caludon Castle 2A 60
Caludon Pk. Av. CV2: Cov 2A 60
Caludon Rd. CV2: Cov 3G 59
Calverstone Rd. CV22: Caw 2A 86
Calvert Cl. CV3: Cov 2D 68
CV21: Brow 1A 76
Camberwell Ter. CV31: Lea S 1E 102
Camborne Dr. CV11: Nun 6G 23
Cambridge Dr. B37: Mars G 5A 34
CV10: Nun 1E 30
Cambridge Gdns. CV32: Lea S 6E 98
Cambridge St. CV1: Cov 2E 58
CV21: Rugby 5J 75
Camden St. CV2: Cov 3G 59
Camelia Rd. CV2: Cov 4H 51
Camelot Gro. CV8: Ken 4G 79
Cameron Cl. CV5: Alle 7E 48
CV32: Lill 3E 98
Campbell Cl. CV10: Gall C 7F 21
Campbell St. CV21: Rugby 5E 74
Campden Gro. CV35: Hatt 5A 96
Campden Hill CV36: Ilm 7A 126
Campden Rd. CV36: Ship S 5F 131
CV37: Cliff C 7A 124
CV37: Lwr Q, Up Qui 7F 125
CAMP HILL 5J 21
Camp Hill Dr. CV10: Nun 4J 21
Camp Hill Rd. CV10: Nun 4G 21
Campion Cl. CV3: Cov 2D 68
CV12: Bed 3D 40
Campion Ct. CV32: Lea S 5E 98

Campion Grn. CV32: Lea S 5E 98
Campion Rd. CV32: Lea S 5E 98
Campion Ter. CV32: Lea S 6E 98
Campion Way CV23: Brow 7K 65
Camp La. OX17: Warm 5D 128 & 2F 129
Camplea Cft. B37: F'bri 3A 34
Campling Cl. CV12: Bulk 3D 42
Campriano Dr. CV34: Warw 7J 97
Campville Gro. B37: K'hrst 7A 24
Camville CV3: Bin 5C 60
Canada La. CV35: N Lin 3G 95
Canal Ho. CV1: Cov 1H 135 (3C 58)
Canal Rd. CV6: Cov 6F 51
Canalside CV6: Longf 7H 41
Canberra Cl. CV35: Welle 5G 117
Canberra Ct. CV12: Bed 3G 41
Canberra Rd. CV2: Ald G 2J 51
Canford Cl. CV3: Finh 5C 68
CANLEY 2G 67 (1A 144)
Canley Ford CV5: Cov 1J 67
(not continuous)
Canley Gdn. Cemetery & Crematorium CV4: Canly 2H 67
Canley Rd. CV5: Cov 6H 57
(Pilkington Rd.)
CV5: Cov 1H 67
(Riddings, The)
Canley Station (Rail) 6H 57
Cannas Ct. CV4: Canly 2H 67
CANNOCK 1A 138
Cannocks Cl. CV4: Canly 2H 67
CANNOCK WOOD 1B 138
Cannon Cl. CV4: Cov 2J 67
Cannon Hill Rd. CV4: Canly 3H 67
Cannon Pk. District Cen. CV4: Canly 2G 67
Cannon Pk. Rd. CV4: Canly 3J 67
Canon Dr. CV7: Ash G 7D 40
Canon Hudson Cl. CV3: W'hall 2J 69
CANONS ASHBY 3C 145
Canons Health Club 4B 102
Canon Young Rd. CV31: W'nsh 4F 103
Canterbury Cl. B80: Stud 3B 92
CV8: Ken 6G 79
Canterbury Dr. B37: Mars G 6A 34
Canterbury St. CV1: Cov 1K 135 (3E 58)
Canterbury Way CV11: Nun 3H 23
Cantlow Cl. CV5: E Grn 4E 56
Canton La. B46: Col 6G 19
CAPE, THE 7F 97
Cape Ind. Est. CV34: Warw 1G 101
Cape Rd. CV34: Warw 7F 97
Capmartin Rd. CV6: Cov 7B 50
Captain's Hill B49: Alc 3D 112
Capulet Cl. CV3: W'hall 2J 69
CV22: Bil 3E 86
Capulet Dr. CV34: H'cte 5C 102
Caradoc Cl. CV2: Cov 7K 51
Cardale Cft. CV3: Bin 6B 60
Cardiff Cl. CV3: W'hall 3K 69
Cardigan Rd. CV12: Bed 4B 40
Carding Cl. CV5: E Grn 3D 56
Carew Cl. CV37: S Avon 2D 114
Carew Wlk. CV22: Bil 7C 74
Carey St. CV6: Cov 5H 51
Cargill Cl. CV6: Longf 1F 51
Carisbrooke Av. B37: Chel W 3C 34
Carisbrook Rd. CV10: Nun 5E 22
CARLTON 1A 140
Carlton Cl. CV12: Bulk 2D 42
Carlton Ct. CV5: Cov 4K 57
CARLTON CURLIEU 2D 141
Carlton Gdns. CV5: Cov 7A 58
Carlton Ho. CV32: Lea S 7D 98
Carlton Rd. CV6: Cov 5F 51
CV22: Bil 7D 74
Carlyle Cl. CV10: Gall C 6E 20
Carlyon Rd. CV9: Ath 2D 16
Carlyon Rd. Ind. Est. CV9: Ath 2E 16
(not continuous)
Carmelite Rd. CV1: Cov 5E 58
Carnation Way CV10: Griff 4G 31
Carnbroe Av. CV3: Bin 1B 70
Carnegie Cl. CV3: W'hall 3H 69
Carnoustie Cl. CV11: Nun 4E 32
CAROL GREEN 1D 143
Caroline Cl. CV11: Nun 5B 32
Carolyn La. Ct. CV21: Rugby 4F 75
(off Blackman Way)
Carroll Cl. CV37: S Avon 7H 115
Carsal Cl. CV7: Ash G 1D 50
Carson Cl. GL56: Stret O 2C 132
Carter Dr. CV35: Barf 2B 108
Carter Rd. CV3: Cov 7G 59
Carters Cl. B37: Mars G 6A 34
Carters La. CV37: Tidd 2K 115
Carthusian Rd. CV3: Cov 7C 58
Cartmel Cl. CV5: E Grn 3E 56
Cart's La. CV9: Gren 1F 15
Carvell Cl. CV5: Alle 5F 49
Carver Cl. CV2: Cov 5A 60
Cascade Cl. CV3: Cov 2E 68
Cashmore Av. CV31: Lea S 3D 102
Cashmore Rd. CV8: Ken 5G 79
CV12: Bed 4E 40
Cash's Bus. Cen. CV1: Cov 2D 58
Cash's La. CV1: Cov 1D 58
Casita Gro. CV8: Ken 5G 79
Caspian Way CV2: W'grve S 6C 52
Cassandra Cl. CV4: Canly 5H 67
Cassandra Gro. CV34: H'cte 4B 102
CASTLE BROMWICH 3C 139
Castle Cl. B95: Hen A 2J 93
CV3: Cov 2D 68
CV7: Fill 3C 38
Castle Cl. CV34: Warw 2F 101
Castle Ct. CV8: Ken 3E 78
CV34: Warw 2G 101
Castle Cres. CV35: Kine 5C 120
Castle Dr. B46: Col 7F 25
CV10: Asty 5J 29
CASTLE END 6E 78
Castle Farm Recreation Cen. 5C 78
Castle Ga. M. CV34: Warw 1H 101
CASTLE GREEN 4B 78 (1D 143)
Castle Grn. CV8: Ken 4B 78
Castle Gro. CV8: Ken 5C 78
Castle Hill CV8: Ken 4C 78
CV34: Warw 2G 101
OX15: Up Bra 1G 133
Castle Hill La. OX15: Up Bra 3G 133
Castle La. B46: Max, Shu 2A 26
CV23: Wool 4H 105
CV34: Warw 2G 101
Castle M. CV21: Rugby 5H 75
Castle Mound CV23: Barby 7E 88
Castle Mound Way CV23: Brow 5K 65
Castle Pl. Ind. Est. CV1: Cov 1K 135 (3D 58)
Castle Rd. B49: Alc 3B 112
B80: Stud 3D 92
B95: Hen A 2J 93
CV8: Ken 4C 78
CV10: Harts 1G 21
CV10: Nun 4D 22
CV35: Kine 5C 120
Castle St. CV1: Cov 1K 135 (3E 58)
CV21: Rugby 5H 75
CV34: Warw 2G 101
Castle Vw. Pk. Mobile Homes CV10: Harts 2G 21
Castle Yd. CV1: Cov 4J 135
Caswell Rd. CV31: Lea S 2F 103
Catesby Ho. B37: K'hrst 7A 24
Catesby La. B94: Lapw 4G 91
Catesby Rd. CV6: Cov 6B 50
CV22: Rugby 7K 75
Cathedral Lanes Shop. Cen. CV1: Cov 3H 135 (4C 58)
CATHERINE-DE-BARNES 3C 139
Catherine de Barnes La. B92: Bick, Cath B 7C 44
Catherine St. CV2: Cov 4F 59
CATHIRON 6K 63
Cathiron La. CV23: Brin, Cath, Harb M, Lit L 4D 62
CATSHILL 1A 142
Cattell Rd. CV34: Warw 1G 101
CATTHORPE 1C 145
CAULCOTT 3D 147
CAUNSALL 3A 138
Cavalier Cl. CV11: Nun 2A 32
Cavans Cl. CV3: Bin 7C 60
Cavans Way CV3: Bin 7C 60
Cave Cl. CV22: Caw 1A 86
Cavell Ct. CV21: Rugby 5K 75
Cavendish Cl. CV22: Caw 7A 74
Cavendish Rd. CV4: Tile H 5C 56
Caversham Cl. CV11: Nun 4G 23
Cawnpore Rd. CV6: Cov 4B 50
CAWSTON 1A 86 (1B 144)
Cawston Grange Dr. CV22: Caw 1A 86
Cawston La. CV22: Caw, Dunc 2A 86
Cawston Way CV22: Bil 1C 86
Cawthorne Cl. CV1: Cov 3E 58
Cayzer Pl. CV35: Welle 3G 117
Cecil Ct. CV31: Lea S 7E 98
Cecil Leonard Knox Cres. CV11: Bram 6H 33
Cecily Rd. CV3: Cov 1D 68
Cedar Av. CV8: Rytn D 7D 70
Cedar Cl. CV32: Lill 3E 98
CV37: S Avon 3G 115
Cedar Ct. CV5: Alle 1E 56
Cedar Cres. B78: K'bry 5E 12
Cedar Dr. CV37: Snitt 5H 95
Cedar Gro. CV34: Warw 6J 97
Cedar Rd. CV10: Nun 5J 21
Cedars, The CV7: Exh 5G 41
CV32: Lea S 7B 98
Cedars Av. CV6: Cov 2J 57
Cedars M., The CV32: Lea S 7B 98
(off Cross Rd.)
Cedars Rd. CV7: Exh 4H 41
Cedar Wlk. B37: Chel W 3B 34
(off Chelmsley Wood Shop. Cen.)
Cedric Cl. CV3: W'hall 3J 69
Celandine CV23: Brow 7K 65
Celandine Rd. CV2: Cov 4K 51
Celandine Way CV12: Bed 3E 40
Celtic Way NN6: Crick 3K 89
Cemetery La. CV10: Harts 2G 21
Centaur Rd. CV5: Cov 5K 57
Centenary Bus. Cen. CV11: Nun 1A 32
Centenary Rd. CV4: Canly 1H 67
Central Av. CV2: Cov 5G 59
CV11: Nun 6C 22
CV31: Lea S 2D 102
Central Blvd. CV7: Ash G, Ker E 7K 39
Central Bldgs. CV3: Cov 6G 135 (6C 58)
Central Chambers CV37: S Avon 3F 137
Central City Ind. Est. CV6: Cov 2F 59
Central Dr. CV47: Bis I 6C 110
Central Pk. Dr. CV23: Brow 5J 65
Central Six Retail Pk. CV3: Cov 6F 135 (6B 58)
Centre Craft Yd. CV37: S Avon 3F 137
Centrovell Ind. Est. CV11: Nun 2J 31
Centurion Cl. B46: Col 3F 25
Century Pk. B37: Mars G 7C 34
Ceolmund Cres. B37: Chel W 3B 34
Chace Av. CV3: W'hall 3H 69
Chaceley Cl. CV2: W'grve S 6C 52
CHACOMBE 1D 147
CHADDESLEY CORBETT 1A 142
CHADLINGTON 3C 147
CHADSHUNT 3A 144
CHAD VALLEY 3B 138
Chadwick Cl. CV5: E Grn 4F 57
CHADWICK END 1D 143
Chadwick M. B98: Redd 1A 92
Chaffinch Dr. B36: Cas B 5B 24
Chalfont Cl. CV5: Cov 3F 57
CV12: Bed 1G 41
CHALK HILL 3A 146
Challenge Bus. Pk. CV1: Cov 2D 58
Challenge Cl. CV1: Cov 3D 58
Chamberlain Cl. CV32: Cubb 2H 99
Chamberlaine St. CV12: Bed 1H 41
Chamberlain Rd. CV21: Hillm 1D 88
Chamberlains Grn. CV6: Cov 7K 49
Chance Flds. CV31: Rad S 2K 103
Chancellors Cl. CV4: Canly 4H 67
Chancery Ct. CV10: Harts 4F 21
Chancery La. CV10: Harts 4G 21
Chanders Rd. CV34: Warw 6F 97
Chandler Ct. CV5: Cov 7B 58
Chandlers Rd. CV31: W'nsh 5E 102
Chandos St. CV2: Cov 4G 59
CV11: Nun 7B 22
CV32: Lea S 6D 98
Change Brook Cl. CV11: Nun 3G 23
Channel Way CV6: Longf 7H 41
Chantries, The CV1: Cov 2E 58
Chantry, The CV34: Warw 6J 97
Chantry Cres. B49: Alc 5B 112
Chantry Heath La. CV8: S'lgh 3E 80
CHAPEL BRAMPTON 2D 145
Chapel Cl. B50: Bidf A 6G 123
CV37: Welf A 3B 124
Chapel Ct. CV32: Lea S 7D 98
(off Windsor St.)
CV32: Lea S 7E 98
(Wood St.)
CHAPEL END 4G 21
Chapel Farm Cl. CV3: W'hall 2J 69
CHAPEL FIELDS 5K 57
Chapel Gdns. B50: Bidf A 6G 123
(off Salford Rd.)
GL56: Stret O 2C 132
CHAPEL GREEN
Coventry 6A 38 (3D 139)
Southam 3H 111 (2B 144)
Chapelhouse Rd. B37: F'bri 4A 34
Chapel La. B50: Bidf A 6G 123
(off High St.)
B95: Aston C 1K 113
B95: Ullen 5C 90
CV7: Barn 7D 42
CV8: Rytn D 6C 70
CV9: With 3G 17
CV23: Lilb 2J 77
CV35: Pill P 3B 128
CV37: N'bld S 1G 127
CV37: S Avon 6F 137 (5F 115)
CV47: Nap 2H 111
OX15: Ratl 7D 128
OX17: Shotte 7H 129
Chapel Row CV34: Warw 1G 101
Chapel St. CV1: Cov 2G 135 (4C 58)
CV11: Nun 7D 22
CV12: Bed 2H 41
(not continuous)
CV21: Rugby 5G 75
CV23: Kils 7J 89
CV23: Long L 4A 74
CV31: Lea S 1E 102
CV33: Har 6H 109
CV34: Warw 1G 101
CV35: Welle 3H 117
CV37: S Avon 5F 137 (5F 115)
CV37: Welf A 3A 124
CV47: Bis I 6B 110
OX17: Warm 2J 129
Chapel Wlk. B50: Bidf A 6G 123
(off Chapel Cl.)
Chapman Cl. CV31: Rad S 3J 103
Chapman Ct. CV34: Warw 7A 98
Chapman Way B49: Alc 3C 112
Chard Rd. CV3: Bin 7K 59
CHARINGWORTH 2B 146
Charingworth Dr. CV35: Hatt 5A 96
Chariot Way CV21: Rugby 1G 75
Charity Ho's., The CV23: C'over 1J 65
Charity Rd. CV7: Ker E 6A 40
CHARLBURY 3C 147
Charlbury M. CV31: Lea S 2G 103
CHARLECOTE 3C 118 (3D 143)
Charlecote Cl. CV37: Tidd 4K 115
Charlecote Flds. CV35: Welle 2H 117
Charlecote Gdns. CV31: Lea S 3H 103
Charlecote Mill 2B 118
Charlecote Pk. 4B 118
Charlecote Rd. CV6: Cov 4A 50
CV35: Char 2B 118
CV35: Welle 2H 117
Charlecote Wlk. CV11: Nun 4B 32
Charles Ct. CV34: Warw 7K 97
Charles Eaton Ct. CV12: Bed 2E 40
(off Charles Eaton Rd.)
Charles Eaton Rd. CV12: Bed 2F 41
Charlesfield Rd. CV22: Rugby 1G 87
Charles Gardner Rd. CV31: Lea S 2D 102
Charles Lakin Cl. CV7: Shil 1E 52
Charles Rd. CV9: Man 4E 16
Charles St. CV1: Cov 1K 135 (3E 58)
CV7: New A 4E 28
CV9: Hurl 6K 13

Charles St. CV11: Nun 6B 22
CV21: Rugby 5F 75
CV34: Warw 7J 97
Charles Warren Cl. CV21: Rugby 5H 75
Charles Watson Ct. CV32: Lill 5E 98
Charlewood Rd. CV6: Cov 4B 50
Charlotte St. CV21: Rugby 5H 75
CV31: Lea S 2D 102
CHARLTON 2D 147
Charminster Dr. CV3: Cov 4D 68
Charnwood Av. CV10: Nun 2D 30
Charnwood Dr. CV10: Harts 1F 21
Charnwood Way CV32: Lill 4G 99
Charter App. CV34: Warw 3F 101
Charter Av. CV4: Canly 1F 67
CV4: Tile H 1B 66
Charterhouse Rd. CV1: Cov 5E 58
Charter Rd. CV22: Hillm 1A 88
Chartwell Cl. CV11: Nun 3B 32
CHARWELTON 3C 145
Charwelton Dr. CV21: Brow 2A 76
Chase Cl. CV11: Nun 5E 22
Chase La. CV8: Ken 2A 78
CHASE TERRACE 1B 138
CHASETOWN 1B 138
Chassieur Wlk. B46: Col 4F 25
CHASTLETON 7A 134 (3B 146)
Chaters Orchard CV47: Long I 2C 106
Chatham Cl. CV3: Cov 6J 59
Chatillon Cl. CV34: H'cte 5C 102
CHATLEY 2A 142
Chatsworth Dr. CV11: Nun 2B 32
Chatsworth Gdns. CV31: Lea S 2H 103
Chatsworth Gro. CV8: Ken 4G 79
Chatsworth Ri. CV3: Cov 3E 68
CHATTLE HILL 2E 24
Chattle Hill B46: Col 2E 24
Chaucer Cl. CV37: S Avon 7J 115
Chaucer Dr. CV10: Gall C 6F 21
Chaucer Rd. CV22: Rugby 3F 87
Chauntry Pl. CV1: Cov 2J 135 (4D 58)
Chaytor Dr. CV10: Nun 4F 21
Chaytor Rd. B78: Pole 2D 10
Cheadle Cl. CV2: Ald G 2G 51
Cheam Cl. CV6: Cov 5G 51
Chelmar Cl. B36: Cas B 4A 24
Chelmarsh CV6: Cov 1C 58
Chelmsley Av. B46: Col 6F 25
Chelmsley Circ. B37: Chel W 3B 34
Chelmsley La. B37: Mars G 5A 34
(not continuous)
Chelmsley Rd. B37: Chel W, F'bri 2A 34
CHELMSLEY WOOD 3B 34
Chelmsley Wood Ind. Est. B37: F'bri 1B 34
Chelmsley Wood Shop. Cen. B37: Chel W 3B 34
Chelney Wlk. CV3: Bin 6C 60
Chelsea *B37: K'hrst* *7A 24*
(off Chilvers Gro.)
Chelsea Cl. CV11: Nun 4G 23
Chelsey Rd. CV2: Cov 6A 52
Cheltenham Cl. CV12: Bed 1H 41
Cheltenham Cft. CV2: W'grve S 7B 52
Chelveston Rd. CV6: Cov 2J 57
Chelwood Gro. CV2: W'grve S 5B 52
Chenies Cl. CV5: Cov 4F 57
Chepstow Cl. CV3: W'hall 3J 69
CV37: S Avon 6C 114
Chequer St. CV12: Bulk 3E 42
CHERINGTON 6G 133 (2B 146)
Cheriton Cl. CV5: Cov 3H 57
Cherry Blossom Gro. CV31: W'nsh 6F 103
Cherrybrook Way CV2: Cov 5J 51
Cherryburn Wlk. CV22: Bil 6E 74
Cherry Cl. CV6: Cov 4D 50
CV9: Hurl 7K 13
CV37: Ett 2B 126
Cherryfield Cl. CV10: Harts 1G 21
Cherry Gro. CV22: Bil 1E 86
Cherry La. CV35: H Mag 2B 100
CV37: Bear 7D 94
Cherry Orchard B95: Hen A 1G 93
CV8: Ken 4E 78
CV35: Welle 2H 117
CV36: Ship S 5H 131
CV37: S Avon 6D 114
Cherry St. CV34: Warw 1H 101
CV37: S Avon 6E 114
Cherry Tree Av. CV10: Nun 5K 21
Cherry Tree Cres. WR11: Salf P 7B 122
Cherry Tree La. CV23: Bour D 7C 84
Cherry Tree Wlk. CV47: Sou 4H 107
Cherry Way CV8: Ken 4E 78
Cherrywood Gro. CV5: Alle 2D 56
Cherwell Dr. B36: Cas B 4A 24
Cherwell Way CV23: Long L 4B 74
Chesford Cres. CV6: Cov 4H 51
CV34: Warw 6K 97
Chesford Gro. CV37: S Avon 3C 114
Chesham St. CV31: Lea S 1F 103
Cheshire Cl. CV22: Bil 1C 86
Chesholme Rd. CV6: Cov 3B 50
Chesils, The CV3: Cov 3C 68
CHESLYN HAY 1A 138
CHESSETTS WOOD 1C 143
Chessetts Wood Rd. B94: Lapw 1H 91
Chester Cl. B37: F'bri 3A 34
Chester Ct. *B37: Chel W* *3D 34*
(off Hedingham Gro.)
CHESTERFIELD 1C 139
Chester Rd. B36: Cas B 6A 24
B37: Chel W, F'bri 7B 24
B46: Col 6F 35
CV7: Lit P 6F 35
Chester St. CV1: Cov 4B 58
CV21: Rugby 4J 75
Chesterton Dr. CV10: Gall C 6E 20
CV31: Lea S 3G 103
CV37: S Avon 7H 115
CHESTERTON GREEN 3A 144
Chesterton Rd. CV6: Cov 7A 50
CV33: Har 6F 109
CV35: Light 2H 119
Chestnut Av. CV8: Ken 6D 78
Chestnut Cl. B78: K'bry 5E 12
Chestnut Ct. B49: Alc 5C 112
CV34: H'cte 6C 102
CV37: Ett 2C 126
Chestnut Cres. CV10: Nun 5K 21
Chestnut Dr. CV11: Nun 1A 32
Chestnut Fld. CV21: Rugby 5G 75
Chestnut Gro. B46: Col 5G 25
CV4: Tile H 5E 56
CV8: Wols 5J 71
Chestnut Ho. B37: Chel W 3B 34
Chestnut Pl. CV47: Sou 4H 107
Chestnut Rd. CV12: Bed 1K 41
Chestnuts, The CV3: Cov 7G 59
CV12: Bed 3E 40
Chestnut Sq. CV32: Lill 5F 99
CV35: Welle 3H 117
Chestnut Tree Av. CV4: Tile H 5E 56
Chestnut Wlk. *B37: Chel W* *3B 34*
(off Chelmsley Wood Shop. Cen.)
B95: Hen A 1G 93
CV37: S Avon 6D 136 (5E 114)
Cheswick Cl. CV6: Cov 7G 51
CHESWICK GREEN 1C 143
Chetton Av. CV6: Cov 2C 58
Chetwode Cl. CV5: Cov 3F 57
Chetwynd Av. B78: Pole 2D 10
Chetwynd Dr. CV11: Nun 5D 32
Cheveral Av. CV6: Cov 1B 58
Cheveral Rd. CV12: Bed 2G 41
Cheverel Pl. CV11: Nun 2H 31
Cheverel St. CV11: Nun 1H 31
Cheviot B77: Wiln 7A 8
Cheviot, The CV4: Canly 2H 67
Cheviot Cl. CV10: Nun 1B 30
Cheviot Ri. CV32: Lill 4G 99
CHEYLESMORE 1D 68
Cheylesmore CV1: Cov 5H 135 (5C 58)
Cheylesmore Shop. Pde. CV3: Cov 1D 68
Chichester Cl. CV11: Nun 4H 23
Chichester Gro. B37: Chel W 4A 34
(not continuous)
Chichester La. CV35: H Mag 2B 100
Chickabiddy La. *CV47: Sou* *5H 107*
(off Market Hill)
Chicory Dr. CV23: Brow 7K 65
Chideock Hill CV3: Cov 2A 68
Chiel Cl. CV5: E Grn 3D 56
CHILCOTE 1D 139
Childs Cl. CV37: S Avon 2D 114
CHILDSWICKHAM 2A 146
Chilham Dr. B37: Chel W 3C 34
Chillaton Rd. CV6: Cov 4B 50
CHILSON 3C 147
Chiltern Ct. CV6: Cov 2A 58
Chiltern Leys CV6: Cov 3A 58
Chiltern Rd. B77: Wiln 1A 10
Chilterns, The CV5: Cov 3F 57
CHILVERS COTON 1H 31
Chilvers Ct. CV11: Nun 7D 22
Chilvers Ri. CV10: Nun 2J 31
CV11: Nun 2J 31
Chilworth Cl. CV11: Nun 4A 32
Chines, The CV10: Nun 4E 22
CV11: Nun 2K 31
Chingford Rd. CV6: Longf 2G 51
Chingley Bank B95: Hen A 2J 93
CHIPPING CAMPDEN 2A 146
CHIPPING NORTON 3C 147
CHIPPING WARDEN 1D 147
Chiswick Wlk. B37: Chel W 3D 34
CHORLEY 1B 138
Chorley Way CV6: Cov 1C 58
Choyce Cl. CV9: Ath 1C 16
Christchurch Cl. CV10: Nun 3F 31
Christchurch Rd. CV6: Cov 1K 57
Christie Way CV37: S Avon 7H 115
Christine Ledger Sq. CV31: Lea S 2E 102
Christopher Hooke Ho. CV6: Cov 5E 50
Chudleigh Rd. CV2: Cov 7A 52
Church Av. B46: Wat O 1B 24
CHURCH BRAMPTON 2D 145
Church Cl. B37: K'hrst 6A 24
CV7: Old A 2C 28
CV8: Rytn D 6C 70
CV9: Wood E 2K 13
CV10: Harts 3G 21
CV23: Harb M 4B 64
CV31: W'nsh 4F 103
CV37: Ludd 1E 124
CV47: Bis I 6B 110
LE10: Wlvy 2J 33
Church Ct. CV6: Cov 5K 49
Churchdale Cl. CV10: Nun 7H 21
Church Dr. CV8: Ken 4D 78
CHURCH END
Birmingham 2E 26 (2D 139)
Coventry 4H 59
Nuneaton 2D 139
Church End CV31: Rad S 2J 103
CHURCH ENSTONE 3C 147
Church Farm Ct. CV35: Mid T 6D 130
Church Flds. B49: Wix 1E 122
CHURCH HILL 2B 142
Church Hill B46: Col 5G 25
B95: Ullen 6B 90
CV23: Stret D 4H 83
CV32: Cubb 2J 99
CV32: Lea S 7C 98
CV33: Bis T 5C 108
LE10: Wlvy 1J 33
OX17: Warm 2J 129
Church Hill Ct. CV35: Light 2G 119
CHURCHILL
Chipping Norton 3B 146
Kidderminster 1A 142
Worcester 3A 142
Churchill Av. CV6: Cov 5D 50
CV8: Ken 3E 78
Churchill Cl. CV37: Ett 1B 126
Churchill Rd. CV22: Rugby 7G 75
Churchlands Bus. Pk. CV33: Har 5J 109
Church La. B46: Max 3C 36
B76: Curd 5B 18
B76: Lea M 4G 19
B76: Wis 2A 18
B78: K'bry 6E 12
B79: No Hth 2G 7
B79: Shut 2B 8
B92: Bick 5D 44
B95: Aston C 2K 113
CV2: Cov 4H 59
CV5: E Grn 2A 56
CV7: Ash G 6E 40
CV7: Cor 6D 38
CV7: Fill 2C 38
CV7: Mer 6F 47
CV7: Old A 2C 28
CV8: S'lgh 3C 80
CV9: Aus 7H 7
CV10: Nun 4D 22
CV23: Thurl 7K 85
CV31: Rad S 2J 103
CV31: W'nsh 4F 103
CV32: Cubb 1J 99
CV32: Lill 4E 98
CV35: Barf 2C 108
CV35: Gay 7G 119
CV35: Leek W 1H 97
CV35: Light 2G 119
CV35: Oxh 1E 130
CV36: Whatc 3A 130
CV37: A'ton 2B 116
CV37: Bear 6D 94
CV37: Ett 2B 126
CV37: N'bld S 1G 127
CV37: Shot 4B 114
CV37: Snitt 5H 95
CV37: Welf A 2A 124
OX17: Shotte 7H 129
CHURCH LANGTON 2D 141
CHURCH LAWFORD 3G 73 (1B 144)
Church Lawford Bus. Cen. CV23: Chu L 3E 72
Church Lees CV33: Bis T 5C 108
CHURCH LENCH 3B 142
Church M. CV35: Kine 5D 120
CHURCHOVER 1J 65 (3C 141)
Church Pk. Cl. CV6: Cov 5K 49
Church Path CV35: H Mag 2B 100
Church Rd. B46: Shu 2B 26
B78: Dord 5D 10
B79: Wart 6G 9
B95: Ullen 7A 90
CV7: Shil 1G 53
CV8: Bag 6E 68
CV8: Bubb 3J 81
CV8: Rytn D 6D 70
CV9: With 3G 17
CV10: Harts 3G 21
CV10: Nun 1C 30
CV23: Chu L 3G 73
CV23: Gran 6H 105
CV35: Clav 2D 94
CV35: Gay 6G 119
CV35: N Lin 2G 95
CV35: Sher 1A 108
CV37: N'bld S 1G 127
CV37: Snitt 6H 95
CV37: Wilm 5J 113
CV47: Ladb 3B 110
CV47: Long I 2B 106
Church Row CV36: Cher 7G 133
GL56: Lit C 6C 134
Churchside Arc. *CV21: Rugby* *5G 75*
(off Lit. Church St.)
CHURCH STOWE 3D 145
Church St. B49: Alc 5C 112
B50: Bidf A 6H 123
B80: Stud 4D 92
CV1: Cov 3D 58
CV9: Ath 3C 16
CV11: Nun 7D 22
CV12: Bulk 3E 42
CV21: Rugby 5G 75
CV23: Clift D 3C 76
CV23: C'over 1H 65
(not continuous)
CV23: Mart 2D 104
CV31: Lea S 1E 102
CV33: Har 6H 109
CV34: Warw 2G 101
CV35: Barf 2B 108
CV35: H Lucy 2A 118
CV35: Welle 2H 117
CV36: Ship S 4H 131
CV37: S Avon 7E 136 (5E 114)

Church St. CV37: Welf A 2A 124
CV47: Fen C 3G 121
CV47: S'ton 6C 106
DE12: App M 1K 7
Church Ter. CV31: Lea S 1E 102
CV32: Cubb 2J 99
CV33: Har 5H 109
CV37: N'bld S 1G 127
Church Vw. B79: Wart 5H 9
CV8: Rytn D 6C 70
Church Wlk. B46: Col 5G 25
CV5: Alle 1G 57
CV9: Ath, Man 3D 16
CV11: Nun 2A 32
CV12: Bed 3H 41
CV21: Rugby 5G 75
CV22: Bil 1D 86
CV23: Barby 7E 88
CV23: Kils 6J 89
CV23: Thurl 6K 85
CV31: Lea S 1D 102
CV35: Welle 3H 117
Church Way CV12: Bed 2H 41
CHURCH WESTCOTE 3B 146
Chylds Ct. CV5: Cov 2E 56
Cicero App. CV34: H'cte 6C 102
Cicey La. CV11: Burt H 4J 33
Cinder La. CV9: Aus 1J 9
Cineworld Cinema
Rugby 2H 75
Circle, The CV10: Nun 7K 21
Circus Av. B37: Chel W 3C 34
City Arc. CV1: Cov 4G 135 (5C 58)
CLADSWELL 3B 142
Clapham Sq. CV31: Lea S 1F 103
Clapham St. CV31: Lea S 2F 103
Clapham Ter. CV31: Lea S 1F 103
CLAPTON-ON-THE-HILL 3A 146
Clara St. CV2: Cov 5G 59
Clare Cl. CV32: Lill 5G 99
Clare Ct. CV21: Rugby 5F 75
Clare Ho. B36: Cas B 5A 24
Claremont Cl. CV12: Bulk 1D 42
Claremont Rd. CV21: Rugby 5J 75
CV31: Lea S 2D 102
Claremont Wlk. CV5: Alle 1G 57
Clarence Mans. *CV32: Lea S* *6D 98*
(off Clarence Ter.)
Clarence Rd. CV21: Rugby 5E 74
CV37: S Avon 4C 114
Clarence St. CV1: Cov 3E 58
CV11: Nun 7B 22
CV31: Lea S 2E 102
Clarence Ter. *CV32: Lea S* *6D 98*
(off Warwick St.)
Clarendon Av. CV32: Lea S 6D 98
Clarendon Cres. CV32: Lea S 6C 98
Clarendon Pl. CV32: Lea S 6C 98
Clarendon Rd. CV8: Ken 6E 78
Clarendon Sq. CV32: Lea S 6C 98
(not continuous)
Clarendon St. CV5: Cov 6K 57
CV32: Lea S 6E 98
Clark Cl. CV36: Ship S 5H 131
Clarke's Av. CV8: Ken 6E 78
Clarks La. CV36: Long C 3D 134
Clarkson Dr. CV31: W'nsh 4E 102
Clark St. CV6: Cov 5G 51
Clark Wlk. CV37: Ett 2C 126
CLAVERDON 2D 94 (2C 143)
Claverdon Ho. CV34: Warw 7K 97
Claverdon Rd. CV5: E Grn 4F 57
Clay Av. CV11: Nun 4F 23
Claybrook Dr. B98: Redd 1D 92
CLAYBROOKE MAGNA 3B 140
CLAYBROOKE PARVA 3B 140
CLAY COTON 1C 145
CLAYDON 3B 144
Claydon Gro. CV35: Hatt 4A 96
CLAYHANGER 1B 138
Clayhill La. CV23: Lit L, Long L 2K 73
Claylands CV35: Gay 6B 119
Clay La. CV2: Cov 3G 59
CV5: Alle 2C 48
Clayton Rd. CV6: Cov 2J 57
Cleaver Gdns. CV10: Nun 5D 22
Clebe Rd. CV35: Clav 2D 94
CLEEVE PRIOR 3B 142
Cleeve Rd. B50: Marlc 7G 123
Cleeves Av. CV34: Warw 2A 102
Clematis Way CV10: Griff 4F 31
Clemens St. CV31: Lea S 1E 102
Clements Cl. CV8: Ken 4E 78
Clements St. CV2: Cov 4G 59
Clement St. CV11: Nun 1H 31
Clement Way CV22: Caw 1A 86
Clennon Ri. CV2: Cov 6K 51
CLENT 1A 142
Clent Dr. CV10: Nun 1B 30
Cleopatra Gro. CV34: H'cte 4C 102
Cleveland Ct. CV32: Lea S 5D 98
Cleveland Rd. CV2: Cov 3G 59
CV12: Bulk 2D 42
CLEVELEY 3C 147
Cleveley Dr. CV10: Nun 4J 21
Clifden Gro. CV8: Ken 3G 79
CLIFF 2D 12 (2D 139)
Cliffe Ct. CV32: Lea S 6B 98
Cliffe Rd. CV32: Lea S 6B 98
Cliffe Way CV34: Warw 7H 97
Cliff Hall La. B78: Cliff 2C 12
Clifford Bri. Rd. CV2: W'grve S 2B 60
CV3: Bin 5B 60
CLIFFORD CHAMBERS 5B 124 (3C 143)
Clifford Rd. CV37: Cliff C, S Avon 4C 124 & 7F 115
Cliff Pool Nature Reserve 3B 12
CLIFTON 2D 147
CLIFTON CAMPVILLE 1D 139
Clifton Rd. CV10: Nun 7A 22
CV21: Rugby 5H 75
Clifton St. CV1: Cov 3E 58
Clifton Ter. CV8: Ken 3E 78
CLIFTON UPON DUNSMORE 3C 76 (1C 145)
Clinic Dr. CV11: Nun 1J 31
Clinton Av. CV8: Ken 3B 78
CV35: H Mag 1C 100
Clinton La. CV8: Ken 2B 78
Clinton Rd. B46: Col 6F 25
CV6: Cov 4F 51
Clinton St. CV31: Lea S 1E 102
CLIPSTON 3D 141
Clipstone Rd. CV6: Cov 1J 57
Cliveden Wlk. CV11: Nun 4A 32
Clock La. B92: Bick 4D 44
Clock Towers Shop. Cen. CV21: Rugby 5G 75
Cloister Cft. CV2: W'grve S 1B 60
Cloister Crofts CV32: Lea S 4D 98
Cloisters, The B80: Stud 3C 92
CV32: Lea S 4D 98
CV47: Sou 5J 107
Cloister Way CV32: Lea S 4D 98
CLOPTON 2F 115
Clopton Ct. CV37: S Avon 1E 136 (4E 114)
Clopton Cres. B37: F'bri 1B 34
Clopton Rd. CV37: S Avon 1E 136 (4E 114)
Close, The CV8: Bran 3H 71
CV8: Ken 3E 78
CV31: Lea S 2E 102
CV35: H Lucy 2A 118
CV36: Half 3K 127
CV37: Cliff C 5C 124
CV37: Lwr Q 5H 125
CV37: Wilm 5K 113
Closers Bus. Cen. CV11: Nun 2K 31
Cloud Grn. CV4: Canly 3H 67
Cloudsley Bush La. LE10: Wlvy 1K 33
Clovelly Gdns. CV2: Cov 2J 59
Clovelly Rd. CV2: Cov 2H 59
Clovelly Way CV11: Nun 6F 23
Clover Av. B37: Chel W 3D 34
Clover Cl. CV23: Brow 7K 65
CV37: S Avon 2D 114
Cloverdale Cl. CV6: Cov 2B 50
Clover Way CV12: Bed 3D 40
Clunes Av. CV11: Nun 5F 23
Clyde Rd. CV12: Bulk 2C 42
Coach Ho. M. CV34: Warw 1H 101
Coach Ho's., The *B95: Hen A* *1H 93*
(off High St.)
Coach Ho. Way CV37: S Avon 1J 137 (4F 115)
COALPIT FIELD 3K 41
Coalpit Flds. Rd. CV12: Bed 3J 41
Coalpit La. CV8: Wols 4A 72
CV23: Law H 4A 72
COAL POOL 1B 138
Coat of Arms Bri. Rd. CV3: Cov 2K 67
Cobbs Rd. CV8: Ken 3B 78
Cobden Av. CV31: Lea S 3G 103
Cobden St. CV6: Cov 2E 58
Cobham Grn. CV31: W'nsh 4E 102
Cockerills Mdw. CV21: Hillm 1C 88
Cockermouth Cl. CV32: Lea S 5B 98
Cock Robin Wood Nature Reserve 3E 86
Cock's All. CV37: S Avon 4F 137
Cocksfoot Cl. CV37: S Avon 2D 114
Cocksparrow St. CV34: Warw 2F 101
Cockspur St. B78: B'moor 3B 10
CODSALL 1A 138
CODSALL WOOD 1A 138
Cofa Ct. CV1: Cov 5H 135
COFTON HACKETT 1B 142
Colbeck Cl. CV37: S Avon 6C 114
Colbek Ct. CV10: Gall C 7D 20
Colbourne Gro. CV32: Lea S 5B 98
Colchester St. CV1: Cov 4E 58
COLD ASHBY 1D 145
COLD ASTON 3A 146
Cold Comfort La. B49: Alc 4A 112
COLDHAM 1A 138
COLD HIGHAM 3D 145
Coldwells Ct. *CV22: Rugby* *6G 75*
(off Union St.)
Colebridge Cres. B46: Col 4F 25
Colebrook Cl. B49: Alc 5C 112
CV3: Bin 5B 60
Coleby Cl. CV4: W'wd H 1B 66
Cole Ct. B37: Chel W 3B 34
CV6: Cov 3A 58
COLE END 4F 25 (3D 139)
Coleford Dr. B37: F'bri 3A 34
Coleman St. CV4: Tile H 4D 56
Colemeadow Rd. B46: Col 5F 25
Coleridge Cl. CV37: S Avon 7H 115
Coleridge Rd. CV2: Cov 4J 59
Coleshaven B46: Col 6F 25
COLESHILL 5F 25 (3D 139)
COLESHILL HEATH 5C 34
Coleshill Heath Rd. B37: Mars G 6C 34
B46: Col 3E 34
Coleshill Ind. Est. B46: Col 2E 24
(not continuous)
Coleshill Leisure Cen. 6F 25
Coleshill Rd. B37: Mars G 6A 34
B46: Max 7K 25
B46: Over W, Shu 2E 26
B46: Shu 2K 25
Coleshill Rd. B46: Wat O 1B 24
B76: Curd 5B 18
(not continuous)
CV9: Ath, Bntly 7H 15
CV10: Ans C 4B 20
CV10: Harts 4F 21
Coleshill Station (Rail) 2F 25
Coleshill St. CV9: Ath 3C 16
Coleshill Trad. Est. B46: Col 3F 25
Colesleys, The B46: Col 6G 25
Colina Cl. CV3: W'hall 3J 69
Collector Rd. B36: Cas B 2A 24
B37: F'bri 7C 24
Colledge Cl. CV23: Brin 4C 62
Colledge Rd. CV6: Cov 5D 50
College Cl. CV37: Long M 3G 125
College Dr. CV32: Lea S 5D 98
College La. CV36: Long C 4D 134
CV37: S Avon 6E 114
College M. CV37: S Avon 6E 114
College Rd. CV23: W'hby 3J 105
College St. CV10: Nun 2H 31
CV37: S Avon 7F 137 (6E 114)
Collett Wlk. CV1: Cov 4B 58
CV8: Ken 5D 78
Colliers Way CV7: Gun H 4C 28
Colliery La. CV7: Exh 4H 41
Colliery La. Nth. CV7: Exh 4H 41
Collingham La. CV47: Long I 2D 106
COLLINGTREE 3D 145
Colling Wlk. B37: K'hrst 6A 24
Collingwood Av. CV22: Bil 7D 74
Collingwood Rd. CV5: Cov 5A 58
Collins Gro. CV4: Canly 3H 67
Collins Rd. CV34: H'cte 3B 102
Collins Way B49: Alc 4D 112
COLLYCROFT 1H 41
Columbia Gdns. CV12: Bed 3K 41
Columbine Way CV12: Bed 4E 40
Colyere Cl. CV7: Ker E 7A 40
COMBERFORD 1C 139
Combroke Gro. CV35: Hatt 5A 96
COMBROOK 3A 144
Comet Rd. B26: Birm A 2C 44
Commainge Cl. CV34: Warw 1F 101
Commander Cl. CV33: Bis T 5C 108
Commanders Cl. CV33: L Hth 1K 119
Commissary Rd. B26: Birm A 3A 44
COMMON, THE 2G 79
Common, The B94: Earls, Tan A 1D 90
CV9: Bad E, Gren, Bax 2F 15
Common La. B78: Dord, Pole 2D 10
CV7: Cor 7C 38
CV8: Ken 2F 79
CV35: Clav 1C 94
Common La. Ind. Est. CV8: Ken 2G 79
Common Way CV2: Cov 1G 59
Compass Ct. CV1: Cov 4B 58
COMPTON ABDALE 3A 146
Compton Cl. CV32: Lill 5G 99
Compton Ct. CV22: Dunc 3B 86
CV36: Long C 1C 134
Compton Cft. B37: Chel W 4D 34
Compton Rd. CV6: Cov 4D 50
CV33: L Hth 2K 119
Compton Verney 3A 144
Comrie Cl. CV2: Cov 1B 60
Comyn St. CV32: Lea S 6F 99
Concorde Rd. B26: Birm A 2C 44
CONDICOTE 3A 146
CONGERSTONE 1A 140
Congleton Cl. CV6: Cov 4E 50
CONGREVE 1A 138
Congreve Cl. CV34: Warw 5H 97
Congreve Wlk. CV12: Bed 3H 41
Congreve Way CV37: S Avon 7H 115
Conifer Cl. CV12: Bed 1J 41
Conifer Ct. CV12: Bed 1J 41
Conifer Gro. CV31: Lea S 3E 102
Conifer Paddock CV3: Bin 6A 60
Conifers, The CV8: Ken 6F 79
Coningsby Cl. CV31: Lea S 2G 103
Coniston Cl. CV12: Bulk 2E 42
CV21: Brow 2K 75
Coniston Ct. CV11: Nun 4G 23
Coniston Dr. CV5: E Grn 3B 56
Coniston Grange CV8: Ken 4E 78
Coniston Rd. CV5: Cov 6K 57
CV32: Lea S 6B 98
Coniston Way CV11: Nun 4G 23
Conrad Cl. CV22: Rugby 3F 87
Conrad Ho. CV37: S Avon 1D 136
Conrad Rd. CV6: Cov 7A 50
Constable Cl. CV12: Bed 7G 31
Constable Rd. CV21: Hillm 7D 76
Constance Cl. CV12: Bed 5F 41
Constance Dr. CV33: Har 6H 109
Constance Harris Cl. CV35: Welle 3H 117
Constantine La. B46: Col 3F 25
Consul Rd. CV21: Rugby 1F 75
Convent Cl. CV8: Ken 2E 78
CV9: Ath 4E 16
Convent La. CV9: Ath 4D 16
Conway Av. CV4: Tile H 7B 56
Conway Cft. B49: Dunn 3A 122
Conway Rd. B37: F'bri 2B 34
CV32: Lea S 7B 98
Conwy Cl. CV11: Nun 1K 31
Cook Cl. CV21: Brow 1J 75
Cooke Cl. CV6: Longf 2G 51
CV34: Warw 6H 97
COOKHILL 3B 142
COOKLEY 3A 138

Cooks Cl. CV9: Ath 3C 16
COOKSEY CORNER 2A 142
COOKSEY GREEN 2A 142
Cooks La. B37: K'hrst 2A 34
CV9: Bad E 1F 15
CV23: F'ton 7A 84
Cook St. CV1: Cov 2H 135 (4C 58)
Coombe Abbey 3G 61
Coombe Abbey Country Pk. 4E 60
Coombe Abbey Vis. Cen. 3G 61
Coombe Av. CV3: Bin 1B 70
Coombe Ct. CV3: Bin 5C 60
Coombe Dr. CV3: Bin W 1G 71
CV10: Nun 7G 21
Coombe Flds. Rd. CV2: W'grve S 4H 61
CV3: Bin 4H 61
CV7: Ansty 7H 53
Coombe Pk. Rd. CV3: Bin 5B 60
Coombe St. CV3: Cov 5H 59
Co-operative St. CV2: Ald G 3H 51
Coopers Cl. CV37: B'ton 2C 114
Cooper St. CV11: Nun 7E 22
Coopers Wlk. CV8: Bubb 3J 81
Cooper's Way CV47: Temp H 4A 120
Cope Arnolds Cl. CV6: Longf 2F 51
Copeland CV21: Brow 1J 75
Copeland Cl. B79: Wart 5H 9
Cope St. CV1: Cov 3K 135 (4D 58)
Copland Pl. CV4: Tile H 6C 56
Copperas St. CV2: Cov 4H 51
Copper Beech Cl. CV6: Cov 5E 50
Copperfield Rd. CV2: Cov 4H 59
Coppice, The CV3: Cov 7H 59
CV9: Man 5F 17
CV10: Nun 4D 22
Coppice Cl. CV8: Rytn D 1D 82
CV37: S Avon 2F 115
Coppice Dr. B78: Dord 3C 10
Coppice La. B79: Clift C 1A 6
Coppice Rd. CV31: W'nsh 5F 103
Coppice Way *B37: Chel W 3B 34*
(off Chelmsley Wood Shop. Cen.)
Copps Rd. CV32: Lea S 7B 98
Copse, The CV7: Exh 5G 41
Copse Dr. CV5: Alle 6K 47
Copsewood Av. CV11: Nun 5C 32
Copsewood Ter. CV3: Cov 5J 59
COPSTON MAGNA 3B 140
COPT GREEN 2C 143
Copthall Ter. CV1: Cov 6H 135 (6C 58)
COPT HEATH 1C 143
Copthorne Rd. CV6: Cov 6K 49
Copt Oak Cl. CV4: W'wd H 2A 66
Coral Cl. CV5: Cov 5G 57
Coralin Cl. B37: Chel W 3B 34
Corbet Rd. CV6: Cov 7C 50
Corbett Ho. CV37: Lwr Q 5H 125
Corbetts Cl. B92: H Ard 7H 45
Corbett St. CV21: Rugby 4J 75
Corbridge Pl. CV22: Caw 7K 73
Corbin Rd. B78: Dord 4C 10
Corbison Cl. CV34: Warw 6F 97
Corbizum Av. B80: Stud 3C 92
Cordelia Grn. CV34: H'cte 4C 102
Cordelia Way CV22: Bil 3E 86
Cord La. CV23: Eas 3K 63
Corelli Cl. CV37: S Avon 3C 114
Corfe Cl. CV2: W'grve S 2B 60
Corfe Way CV11: Nun 1H 31
Corinne Cft. B37: K'hrst 1A 34
Corinthian Ct. B49: Alc 5C 112
Corinthian Pl. CV2: Cov 1K 59
Coriolanus Sq. CV34: H'cte 5D 102
CORLEY 6G 39 (3A 140)
CORLEY ASH 5E 38 (3D 139)
CORLEY MOOR 7C 38 (3D 139)
Corley Vw. CV7: Ash G 6C 40
Corncrake Dr. B36: Cas B 4A 24
Cornel Cl. B37: Chel W 5C 34
Cornelius St. CV3: Cov 7D 58
Corner Ho., The *CV32: Lea S 6D 98*
(off Windsor St.)
Cornerstone Ho. CV1: Cov 1K 135
CORNETS END 7D 46
Cornets End La. CV7: Mer 6A 46
Cornfield, The CV3: Cov 6J 59
Cornfield Cft. B37: Chel W 2D 34
Corn Flower Dr. CV23: Brow 7K 65
Cornhill Gro. CV8: Ken 4G 79
Cornish Cl. CV10: Ans C 3E 20
Cornish Cres. CV10: Nun 2G 31
Corn Mdws. CV12: Bed 3J 41
Cornwall Cl. CV34: Warw 6H 97
Cornwall Ho. CV32: Lea S 6B 98
Cornwallis Rd. CV22: Bil 7B 74
Cornwall Pl. CV32: Lea S 6B 98
Cornwall Rd. CV1: Cov 6E 58
CORNWELL 3B 146
Cornwell Cl. B98: Redd 2A 92
Coronation Av. B78: Pole 7E 8
Coronation Ct. CV11: Nun 7B 22
Coronation Cres. B79: Shut 2C 8
Coronation La. OX17: Shotte 6G 129
Coronation Rd. CV1: Cov 3F 59
CV9: Hurl 7K 13
CV23: Chu L 7F 73
Coronation Wlk. CV10: Nun 5D 22
Coronel Av. CV6: Longf 2E 50
Corporation St. CV1: Cov 4G 135 (5C 58)
(not continuous)
CV11: Nun 6C 22
(not continuous)
CV21: Rugby 5G 75
Corrie Ho. *CV1: Cov 5B 58*
(off Meadow St.)
Corsham Rd. CV47: Temp H 3A 120
Corston M. CV31: Lea S 2G 103
Corunna Ct. *CV34: Warw 1E 100*
(off Corunna Rd.)
Corunna Rd. CV34: Warw 1E 100
COSBY 2C 141
COSELEY 2A 138
COSFORD 4F 65
Cosford Cl. CV32: Lill 4F 99
Cosford La. CV21: Cosf, Rugby 4F 65
(not continuous)
COSSINGTON 1D 141
Costard Av. CV34: H'cte 5C 102
CV36: Ship S 5G 131
Costock Cl. B37: Mars G 5B 34
Coten End CV34: Warw 1H 101
COTESBACH 3C 141
Cotman Cl. CV12: Bed 1G 41
COTON
Northampton 1D 145
Tamworth 1C 139
COTON LAWN 3D 30
Coton Pk. Dr. CV23: Brow 7J 65
Coton Rd. B46: Neth W 1H 19
B76: Lea M, Mars 1H 19
CV11: Nun 7D 22
CV21: Hillm 1C 88
CV23: C'over 3K 65
Cotswold Cl. CV36: Tred 6H 127
Cotswold Cres. CV10: Nun 1B 30
Cotswold Dr. CV3: Finh 5C 68
Cotswolds, The CV32: Lea S 4D 98
Cottage Cl. CV11: Nun 7E 22
CV31: Lea S 2G 103
Cottage Farm Ct. GL56: Stret O 1C 132
Cottage Farm Lodge CV6: Cov 5A 50
Cottage Farm Rd. CV6: Cov 5A 50
Cottage La. B46: Neth W 5K 19
CV37: Shot 5B 114
Cottage Leap CV21: Rugby 4K 75
Cottage Sq. CV31: Lea S 2G 103
Cotterell Rd. CV21: N'bld A 2F 75
Cotterills Cl. CV31: W'nsh 5F 103
Cotters Cft. CV47: Fen C 3G 121
Cottesbrook Cl. CV3: Bin 6A 60
COTTESBROOKE 1D 145
Cotton Dr. CV8: Ken 3G 79
Cotton Mill Spinney CV32: Cubb 1J 99
Cottrells M. B46: Wat O 2B 24
COUGHTON 2B 142
Coughton Cl. CV11: Nun 5B 32
Coughton Court 2B 142
Coughton Dr. CV31: Lea S 3H 103
Coughton Flds. La. B49: Cou, Kinw 1D 112
Council Ho's. CV23: Mart 2E 104
COUNDON 1K 57
Coundon Grn. CV6: Cov 7J 49
Coundon Rd. CV1: Cov 3B 58
Coundon St. CV1: Cov 3B 58
Coundon Wedge Dr. CV5: Alle 1G 57
Countess Cft., The CV3: Cov 1D 68
Countess Rd. CV11: Nun 7B 22
COUNTESTHORPE 2C 141
Courtaulds Ind. Est. CV6: Cov 1D 58
Courtaulds Way CV6: Cov 1D 58
Court Cl. CV33: Bis T 5B 108
OX17: Warm 2J 129
Courthouse Cft. CV8: Ken 5G 79
COURT HOUSE GREEN 6G 51
Courtland Av. CV6: Cov 2K 57
Court Leet CV3: Bin W 1F 71
Court Leet Rd. CV3: Cov 1E 68
Courtney Cl. CV11: Nun 4G 23
Court St. CV31: Lea S 1E 102
Court Way B50: Bidf A 6G 123
Courtyard, The B46: Col 2F 25
CV8: Ken 5G 79
CV34: Warw 2H 101
CV37: S Avon 3C 114
Court Yd, The CV35: Lit K 6C 120
COVEN 1A 138
COVEN HEATH 1A 138
COVENTRY 4H 135 (1A 144)
Coventry Airpark CV3: W'hall 7H 69
COVENTRY AIRPORT 6G 69 (1A 144)
Coventry Bus. Pk. CV5: Cov 6H 57
(Elliott Ct.)
CV5: Cov 6G 57
(Renown Av.)
Coventry Canal Basin CV1: Cov 1H 135
Coventry Cathedral 3J 135 (4D 58)
Coventry City Farm 3E 58
Coventry City FC 2E 50
Coventry Eastern By-Pass CV2: W'grve S 2D 60
CV3: Bin, Bin W, W'hall 4C 60
Coventry Golf Course 6D 68
Coventry Point CV1: Cov 4G 135 (5C 58)
Coventry Rd. B46: Col 2G 35
B46: Neth W 2K 19
B78: K'bry 7E 12
B92: Bick 3A 44
CV7: Ald G 6B 42
CV7: Exh 6G 41
CV7: Fill 2C 38
CV8: Bag 5E 68
CV8: Ken 3D 78
CV8: S'lgh 3C 80
CV8: Stare 5E 80
CV10: Griff, Nun 7H 31
CV11: Nun 5J 31
CV12: Bed 4H 41
Coventry Rd. CV12: Bulk 6B 42
CV22: Caw 4G 85
CV22: Dunc 5K 85
CV23: Brin 4K 61
CV23: Chu L 2C 72
CV23: Dunc, Thurl 4G 85
CV23: Long L 4G 73
CV23: Mart 1D 104
CV23: S Ash 5H 55
CV32: Cubb 1J 99
CV34: Guys C, Warw 1H 101
CV47: Sou 3H 107
LE10: Wlvy 2H 33
Coventry RUFC 5A 58
Coventry Skydome 4F 135 (5B 58)
Coventry Sports Cen. 3K 135 (4D 58)
Coventry Stadium 1H 71
Coventry Station (Rail) 7G 135 (6C 58)
Coventry St. CV2: Cov 3G 59
CV11: Nun 7D 22
Coventry Toy Mus., The 5K 135 (5D 58)
Coventry Trad. Est. CV3: W'hall 5J 69
Coventry Transport Mus. 2H 135 (4C 58)
Coventry University
Caradoc Hall 7K 51
Priory St. 3J 135 (4D 58)
Coventry University for the Performing Arts 4J 67
Coventry University (Lanchester Gallery)
Gosford St. 4K 135 (5D 58)
Coventry University Library 4K 135 (5E 58)
Coventry University Sports Cen. 4E 58
Coventry University Technology Pk.
CV1: Cov 6J 135 (6D 58)
(Puma Way)
CV1: Cov 7J 135 (6D 58)
(Quinton Rd.)
Cove Pl. CV2: Cov 7J 51
Coverley Pl. CV22: Rugby 5E 74
Covers, The B80: Stud 1D 92
Cowan Cl. CV22: Bil 7C 74
Cowdray Cl. CV31: Lea S 1G 103
Cow La. B78: What 1G 13
OX15: Lwr Bra 3H 133
Cowley Cl. B36: Cas B 3A 24
Cowley Rd. CV2: Cov 3K 59
Cowley Way CV23: Kils 7H 89
Cowper Cl. CV34: Warw 6H 97
Cox Cl. B50: Bidf A 5H 123
Cox Cres. CV22: Dunc 5C 86
Coxs Cl. CV10: Nun 1H 31
Cox's La. CV47: Nap 3H 111
Cox's Orchard CV31: W'nsh 4E 102
Cox St. CV1: Cov 4K 135 (5D 58)
(Gosford St.)
CV1: Cov 2K 135 (4D 58)
(White St.)
Cox's Yard 4J 137 (5G 115)
Cozens Cl. CV12: Bed 1G 41
CRABBS CROSS 2B 142
Crabmill La. CV6: Cov 7F 51
Crabtree Dr. B37: F'bri 3A 34
Crabtree Gro. CV31: Lea S 2G 103
CRACKLEY 2F 79 (1D 143)
Crackley Cotts. CV8: Ken 1F 79
Crackley Cres. CV8: Ken 1F 79
Crackley Hill CV8: Ken 2F 79
Crackley La. CV8: Ken 4C 66
Crackthorne Dr. CV23: Brow 6K 65
Craddock Ct. CV10: Nun 4H 21
Craddock Dr. CV10: Nun 4H 21
CRADLEY 3A 138
Craig Cl. CV31: Lea S 2F 103
Craig Cft. B37: Chel W 3D 34
Craigends Av. CV3: Bin 2B 70
Crakston Cl. CV2: Cov 5A 60
Crampers Fld. CV6: Cov 2A 58
Cranborne Chase CV2: W'grve S 2B 60
Crane Cl. CV34: Warw 6F 97
CV37: B'ton 2B 114
Craner's Rd. CV1: Cov 3F 59
Cranford Rd. CV5: Cov 3H 57
Cranmer Gro. CV34: H'cte 5B 102
Crantock Way CV11: Nun 7G 23
Cranwell Dr. CV35: Welle 5G 117
Crathie Cl. CV2: Cov 1B 60
Craven Av. CV3: Bin W 1E 70
Craven Ct. *CV47: Sou 5H 107*
(off Craven La.)
Craven Hgts. B92: H Ard 7G 45
Craven La. CV47: Sou 5H 107
Craven Rd. CV21: Rugby 4H 75
Craven St. CV5: Cov 5K 57
Crawford Cl. B50: Bidf A 6F 123
CV32: Lill 2F 99
CREATON 1D 145
Crecy Rd. CV3: Cov 1E 68
Crediton Cl. CV11: Nun 6G 23
Crendon Cl. B80: Stud 2D 92
Crescent, The B37: Mars G 5E 34
B46: Wat O 1B 24
B50: Bidf A 5G 123
B92: H Ard 7H 45
B95: Woot W 6A 94
CV7: Ker E 7K 39
CV9: Bad E 7F 11
CV23: Brin 3D 62
CV23: Law H 3G 85
CV35: Char 2E 118
CV47: Nap 3J 111
Crescent Av. CV3: Cov 5J 59
Cressage Rd. CV2: W'grve S 1C 60
Cressida Cl. CV34: H'cte 5D 102
Cresswell Cl. CV10: Nun 3D 22

Cresswell Pl. CV22: Caw .7A **74**
Crest, The CV32: Lill .4G **99**
CRESWELL GREEN .1B **138**
Crew La. CV8: Ken .3G **79**
CRICK .1C **145**
Cricket Cl. CV5: Cov .4K **57**
Crick Rd. CV21: Hillm .1D **88**
CV23: Hillm .2F **89**
Crigdon B77: Wiln .7A **8**
CRIMSCOTE .1B **146**
Crimscote Sq. CV35: Hatt .4A **96**
Critchley Dr. CV22: Dunc .6D **86**
Crockwell St. CV36: Long C .1C **134**
CROFT .2C **141**
Croft, The B79: Wart .5H **9**
B95: Hen A .2H **93**
CV6: Longf .2F **51**
CV7: Mer .5E **46**
CV12: Bulk .3D **42**
Croft Cl. CV23: Stret D .3H **83**
CV33: Bis T .5C **108**
CV34: Warw .1A **102**
LE10: Wlvy .2J **33**
Croft Fld. CV47: Nap .3H **111**
Croft Flds. CV12: Bed .3H **41**
Croft Ind. Est. B37: Chel W .3D **34**
Croft Mead CV10: Ansl .1G **29**
Croft M. CV10: Nun .7B **22**
Croft Pool CV12: Bed .3F **41**
Croft Rd. CV1: Cov .4F **135** (5B **58**)
CV9: Ath .2C **16**
CV10: Nun .2E **30**
CV12: Bed .3F **41**
CV35: Leek W .1J **97**
Cromarty Cl. CV5: E Grn .3E **56**
Cromdale B77: Wiln .1A **10**
Cromdale Cl. CV10: Nun .1A **30**
Cromer Rd. CV32: Lill .5F **99**
Cromes Wood CV4: Tile H .6B **56**
Crompton Av. B50: Bidf A .5H **123**
Crompton St. CV34: Warw .2F **101**
Cromwell Ct. OX15: E'hill .7B **128**
Cromwell La. CV4: Tile H, W'wd H .2A **66**
CV8: Burt G .4A **66**
Cromwell Pl. CV33: L Hth .2K **119**
Cromwell Rd. CV22: Rugby .7J **75**
Cromwell St. CV6: Cov .1F **59**
Crondal Rd. CV7: Exh .5H **41**
Crook Ho. Yd. CV23: Brin .3D **62**
Crooks La. B49: Alc .3C **112**
B80: Stud .3C **92**
Crooks La. Bus. Pk. B80: Stud .3C **92**
Croome Cl. CV6: Cov .3K **57**
CROPREDY .1D **147**
CROPSTON .1C **141**
Crosbie Rd. CV5: Cov .4J **57**
Cross Cheaping CV1: Cov .3H **135** (4C **58**)
(not continuous)
Crossfields Rd. CV34: Warw .7H **97**
CROSS GREEN .1A **138**
Cross Grn. Flats CV47: Bis I .7B **110**
Crosslands CV35: Welle .5G **117**
Cross La. CV32: Cubb .3J **99**
Crossley Ct. CV6: Cov .7F **51**
Cross Leys CV36: Ilm .6D **126**
Cross Point Bus. Pk. CV2: W'grve S .6D **52**
(not continuous)
Cross Rd. B49: Alc .5B **112**
CV6: Cov .6E **50**
CV7: Ker E .7K **39**
CV32: Lea S .7B **98**
Cross Rd. Ind. Est. CV6: Cov .7F **51**
Cross St. CV1: Cov .1K **135** (3D **58**)
CV10: Nun .1D **30**
CV21: Rugby .4J **75**
CV23: Long L .3A **74**
CV32: Lea S .6E **98**
CV34: Warw .1H **101**
Cross Wlk. B78: Dord .4D **10**
Crossway Rd. CV3: Finh .4B **68**
Crossways Cotts. CV7: Fill .1E **38**
CROUGHTON .2D **147**
Crowhill Rd. CV11: Nun .2B **32**
CROWLE .3A **142**
CROWLE GREEN .3A **142**
Crowley's Cl. B95: Ullen .6B **90**
Crowmere Rd. CV2: W'grve S .7B **52**
Crown Cl. *CV33: Har* .5J **109**
(off Crown St.)
Crown Grn. CV6: Cov .4E **50**
Crown St. CV33: Har .5J **109**
Crown Ter. CV31: Lea S .1D **102**
Crown Way CV32: Lill .4F **99**
Crows Furlong CV23: Brow .6K **65**
Crowthorns CV21: Brow .1J **75**
CROXALL .1C **139**
Croxall Dr. B46: Shu .2C **26**
Croxhall St. CV12: Bed .3J **41**
Croydon Cl. CV3: Cov .2E **68**
Crucible Ho. CV37: S Avon .1E **136**
Crummock Cl. CV6: Cov .3D **50**
Crutchley Way CV31: W'nsh .6E **102**
Cryfield Grange Rd. CV4: Canly .6G **67**
Cryfield Halls CV4: Canly .4F **67**
Cryfield Hgts. CV4: Canly .6G **67**
Cryfield Hurst Flats CV4: Canly .4F **67**
Cryfield Redfern Flats CV4: Canly .5F **67**
CUBBINGTON .2J **99** (2A **144**)
Cubbington Rd. CV6: Cov .4G **51**
CV32: Lill .4E **98**
Cuckoo La. CV1: Cov .3J **135** (4D **58**)
Culey Wlk. B37: Chel W .3D **34**
Culpepper Cl. CV10: Nun .7K **21**
CULWORTH .3C **145**
Culworth Cl. CV21: Brow .1A **76**
CV31: Lea S .3D **102**
(not continuous)
Culworth Ct. CV6: Cov .7E **50**
CV31: Lea S .3E **102**
Culworth Row CV6: Cov .6E **50**
Cumberland Cres. CV32: Lill .4H **99**
Cumberland Dr. CV10: Nun .1E **30**
Cumbernauld Wlk. CV2: W'grve S .1C **60**
Cumbria Cl. CV1: Cov .4A **58**
Cumming St. CV31: Lea S .1E **102**
Cundall Cl. CV31: Lea S .2F **103**
Cunnery, The CV8: S'lgh P .6A **80**
Cunningham Way CV22: Bil .6C **74**
CURBOROUGH .1C **139**
CURDWORTH .5B **18** (2C **139**)
Curdworth La. B76: Wis .2A **18**
Curie Cl. CV21: Rugby .5K **75**
Curlew Cl. B79: Wart .5H **9**
CV37: B'ton .3B **114**
Curlieu Cl. CV35: H Mag .1C **100**
Curlieu La. CV35: N Lin .2F **95**
Curran Cl. CV31: W'nsh .5F **103**
Curriers Cl. CV4: Tile H .1B **66**
Curriers Cl. Ind. Est. CV4: Tile H .1B **66**
Curtis Rd. CV2: Cov .1K **59**
Curzon Av. CV6: Cov .6E **50**
Curzon Gro. CV31: Lea S .2G **103**
CUTNALL GREEN .2A **142**
CUTSDEAN .2A **146**
Cuttle Mill La. B76: Wis .1D **18**
Cygnet Ho. CV1: Cov .1K **135**
Cymbeline Way CV22: Bil .3D **86**
CV34: H'cte .4C **102**
Cypress Cft. CV3: Bin .7B **60**
Cypress La. CV31: W'nsh .5F **103**
Cypress Way CV10: Nun .5J **21**

D

Dadglow Rd. CV47: Bis I .6C **110**
DADLINGTON .2B **140**
Daffern Av. CV7: New A .4E **28**
Daffern Rd. CV7: Exh .4G **41**
Daffodil Dr. CV12: Bed .3D **40**
DAGTAIL END .2B **142**
Dahlia Wlk. CV10: Nun .4G **31**
Daimler Rd. CV6: Cov .2C **58**
Daintree Cft. CV3: Cov .1C **68**
DAISY BANK .2B **138**
Daisy Cft. CV12: Bed .3D **40**
Dalby Cl. CV3: Bin .7A **60**
Dale, The B95: Woot W .5H **93**
Dale Av. CV37: S Avon .6H **115**
Dale Cl. CV34: Warw .7J **97**
CV47: Long I .2B **106**
Dale End CV10: Nun .6K **21**
Dalehouse La. CV8: Ken .3F **79**
Dalehouse La. Ind. St. CV8: Ken .3G **79**
Dale St. CV21: Rugby .4G **75**
CV32: Lea S .7C **98**
Daleway Rd. CV3: Finh .5B **68**
Dalewood Rd. B37: K'hrst .7A **24**
Dalkeith Av. CV22: Bil .2D **86**
Dallas Burstone Polo Grounds .2K **109**
Dallington Rd. CV6: Cov .1J **57**
Dalmahoy Cl. CV11: Nun .4E **32**
Dalmeny Rd. CV4: Tile H .1B **66**
DALSCOTE .3D **145**
Dalton Cl. CV23: Chu L .2F **73**
Dalton Gdns. CV2: Cov .3B **60**
Dalton Rd. CV5: Cov .7B **58**
CV12: Bed .3F **41**
Dalwood Way CV6: Ald G .2H **51**
Daly Av. CV35: H Mag .2B **100**
Dame Agnes Gro. CV6: Cov .6H **51**
Damson Parkway B91: Sol .7A **44**
B92: Sol .5A **44**
Damson Rd. CV35: H Mag .2B **100**
Dancers Dr. CV35: Lox .7D **116**
Dane Rd. CV2: Cov .3G **59**
Danesbury Cres. CV31: Lea S .2H **103**
Danes Way NN6: Crick .1K **89**
Daneswood Rd. CV3: Bin W .1G **71**
Daniel Av. CV10: Nun .1C **30**
Daniell Rd. CV35: Welle .2H **117**
Daniel Rd. CV9: Man .4E **16**
Danzey Cl. B98: Redd .2A **92**
DANZEY GREEN .2C **143**
Danzey Grn. La. B94: Tan A .4E **90**
Daphne Cl. CV2: Cov .3J **51**
Darfield Ct. CV8: Bubb .4J **81**
Dark La. B78: B'moor .2B **10**
CV1: Cov .3C **58**
CV12: Bed .4D **40**
CV37: Tidd .3K **115**
Dark La. Cotts. B78: B'moor .2B **10**
DARLASTON .2A **138**
Darlaston Ct. CV7: Mer .5F **47**
Darlaston Row CV7: Mer .5D **46**
Darlingscote Rd. CV36: Ship S .2F **131**
DARLINGSCOTT .1B **146**
Darlow Dr. CV37: S Avon .4C **114**
Darnbrook B77: Wiln .1A **10**
Darnford Cl. CV2: W'grve S .7B **52**
Darnley Cl. CV36: Ship S .3G **131**
Darrach Cl. CV2: W'grve S .5A **52**
Dartington Way CV11: Nun .4B **32**
Dartmouth Rd. CV2: Cov .2J **59**
Darwin Cl. CV2: W'grve S .1C **60**
Darwin Ct. CV12: Bed .3G **41**
Darwin Ho. B37: Chel W .4C **34**
Dassett Cl. CV35: Hatt .4A **96**
Dassett Rd. OX17: Farn .6G **121**
Datchet Cl. CV5: Cov .3G **57**
D'Aubeny Rd. CV4: Canly .1G **67**
Davenport Rd. CV5: Cov .7F **135** (7B **58**)
DAVENTRY .2C **145**
Daventry Intl. Rail Freight Terminal NN6: Crick .2K **89**
(Danes Way)
NN6: Crick .3K **89**
(Railport App.)
Daventry Rd. CV3: Cov .1C **68**
CV22: Dunc .6D **86**
CV23: Barby .7E **88**
CV23: Kils .7J **89**
CV23: Wool .7E **86** & 1G **105**
CV47: Sou, S'ton .5J **107** & 1F **111**
Daventry St. CV47: Sou .5H **107**
David Rd. CV1: Cov .5E **58**
CV7: Exh .5F **41**
CV22: Bil .1D **86**
Davidson Av. CV31: Lea S .1E **102**
Davies Rd. CV7: Exh .5F **41**
Davis Cl. CV32: Lea S .5B **98**
Davy Ct. CV23: Brow .5J **65**
Dawes Cl. CV2: Cov .3G **59**
Dawley Cres. B37: Mars G .4B **34**
Dawley Wlk. CV2: W'grve S .7C **52**
Dawlish Cl. CV11: Nun .6F **23**
Dawlish Dr. CV3: Cov .3D **68**
Daw Mill La. B46: Shu .3E **26**
CV7: Old A .4G **27**
Dawson Cl. CV31: W'nsh .6E **102**
Dawson Rd. CV3: Cov .6H **59**
DAYHOUSE BANK .1A **142**
DAYLESFORD .3B **146**
Days Cl. CV1: Cov .4E **58**
Day's La. CV1: Cov .4E **58**
Daytona Dr. CV5: Mil W .6K **47**
Deacon Cl. CV22: Rugby .7J **75**
Deacon St. CV11: Nun .1J **31**
Deane Pde. CV21: Hillm .1C **88**
Deane Rd. CV21: Hillm .1C **88**
Deanston Cft. CV2: W'grve S .5B **52**
Dean St. CV2: Cov .4G **59**
Deans Way CV7: Ash G .7D **40**
Deansway CV34: Warw .6F **97**
Deasy Ho. CV3: W'hall .3H **69**
Deasy Rd. CV1: Cov .6K **135** (6D **58**)
Debden Cl. CV35: Welle .5G **117**
De Compton Cl. CV7: Ker E .6A **40**
DEDDINGTON .2D **147**
Deedmore Rd. CV2: Cov, W'grve S .6J **51**
Deegan Cl. CV2: Cov .2G **59**
Deepdale B77: Wiln .7A **8**
Deepmore Rd. CV22: Bil .1D **86**
Deerdale Ter. CV3: Bin .7B **60**
Deerdale Way CV3: Bin .7B **60**
Deerhill B77: Wiln .1A **10**
Deerhurst Cl. GL56: Lit C .6B **134**
Deerhurst M. CV22: Dunc .6C **86**
Deerhurst Rd. CV6: Cov .4B **50**
Deerings Rd. CV21: Hillm .1B **88**
Deer Leap, The CV8: Ken .3F **79**
Deerpark Dr. CV34: Warw .7F **97**
Dee Wlk. B36: Cas B .4A **24**
(not continuous)
DeHavilland Cl. CV11: Nun .6C **22**
Deighton Gro. CV3: W'hall .2J **69**
Delage Cl. CV6: Ald G .2H **51**
Delamere Rd. CV12: Bed .3F **41**
Delamere Way CV32: Lill .3G **99**
Delaware Rd. CV3: Cov .3C **68**
Delf Ho. CV2: Cov .5K **51**
Delhi Av. CV6: Cov .5D **50**
Delius St. CV4: Tile H .4C **56**
Dell, The B36: Cas B .3A **24**
B95: Woot W .4J **93**
Dell Cl. CV3: W'hall .3J **69**
Dell Ct. B95: Hen A .1H **93**
Delphi Cl. CV34: Warw .4C **102**
Delves Cres. CV9: Wood E .2K **13**
DELVES, THE .2B **138**
De Montfort Ct. B95: Hen A .2H **93**
De Montfort M. B46: Col .6F **25**
De Montfort Rd. CV8: Ken .3C **78**
De Montfort Way CV4: Canly .2G **67**
Dempster Ct. CV11: Nun .7E **22**
Dempster Rd. CV12: Bed .1G **41**
Denbigh Rd. CV6: Cov .1J **57**
Denby Bldgs. CV32: Lea S .7D **98**
Denby Cl. CV32: Lill .5G **99**
Dencer Dr. CV8: Ken .4G **79**
Dene Cl. CV35: Kine .6C **120**
Denehurst Way CV10: Nun .1F **31**
Denemoor Ct. CV8: Ken .4F **79**
Dene Valley Bus. Cen. CV35: Kine .6B **120**
Denewood Way CV8: Ken .3G **79**
(not continuous)
Denham Av. CV5: Cov .3F **57**
Denham Ct. CV9: Ath .3D **16**
Denise Dr. B37: K'hrst .1A **34**
Denne Cl. CV37: S Avon .2F **115**
Dennett Cl. CV34: Warw .5H **97**
Dennis Rd. CV2: Cov .2H **59**
Denshaw Cft. CV2: W'grve S .6C **52**
Denton Cl. CV8: Ken .3B **78**
Denville Rd. CV32: Lea S .4E **98**
Derby Dr. B37: Chel W .3B **34**
Derby La. CV9: Ath .3C **16**
Dereham Ct. CV32: Lea S .5E **98**
Derek Av. B78: Dord .5D **10**
Dering Cl. CV2: Cov .6J **51**

Deronda Cl. CV12: Bed 2G 41
Derry Cl. CV8: Wols 4J 71
Dersingham Dr. CV6: Cov 4H 51
Derwent Cl. CV5: E Grn 3C 56
CV21: Brow 2J 75
CV32: Lea S 6B 98
Derwent Rd. CV6: Cov 4A 50
CV12: Bed 3G 41
Derwent Way CV11: Nun 5G 23
Desdemona Av. CV34: H'cte 4C 102
DESFORD 1B 140
Despard Rd. CV5: E Grn 2B 56
Devere Ct. *CV37: S Avon 4E 114*
(off Clopton Rd.)
Devereux Cl. CV4: Tile H 6A 56
DEVITTS GREEN 3A 28 (2D 139)
Devitts Grn. La. CV7: Old A 3J 27
Devon Cl. CV10: Nun 1F 31
Devon Gro. CV2: Cov 1H 59
Devonish Cl. B49: Alc 3C 112
Devon Ox Rd. CV23: Kils 7H 89
Devonshire Cl. CV22: Caw 7B 74
Devoran Cl. CV7: Exh 5H 41
Dewar Gro. CV21: Hillm 6A 76
Dew Cl. CV22: Dunc 6C 86
Dewis Ho. CV2: Cov 5H 51
Dewsbury Av. CV3: Cov 3B 68
Dexter Ct. CV9: Hurl 7K 13
Dexter La. CV9: Hurl 7K 13
Dexter Way B78: B'moor 2C 10
Dey Cft. CV34: Warw 4D 100
Dialhouse La. CV5: E Grn 3D 56
Diana Dr. CV2: W'grve S 5A 52
Dickens Cl. CV10: Gall C 7F 21
CV37: S Avon 7H 115
Dickens Rd. CV6: Cov 5A 50
CV22: Rugby 3F 87
CV33: Har 6G 109
Dickinson Ct. CV22: Rugby 7G 75
Dickins Rd. CV34: Warw 7K 97
Dick's La. CV35: Row 6F 91
DIDBROOK 2A 146
Diddington La. B92: Bick, H Ard 6J 45
Didgley Gro. B37: K'hrst 7A 24
Didgley La. CV7: Fill 1A 38
Didsbury Rd. CV7: Exh 4G 41
Digby Cl. CV5: Alle 1F 57
Digby Cres. B46: Wat O 1B 24
Digby Dr. B37: Mars G 7B 34
Digby Pl. CV7: Mer 5E 46
Digby Rd. B46: Col 6F 25
Dighton Cl. CV37: Cliff C 5C 124
Dilcock Way CV4: Tile H 1D 66
Dillam Cl. CV6: Longf 2G 51
Dillington Ho. B37: Chel W 3B 34
Dillon Ct. CV11: Nun 6C 22
Dillotford Av. CV3: Cov 1C 68
Dingle, The CV10: Nun 5K 21
Dingle Cl. CV6: Cov 1A 58
Dingle La. B79: No Hth 2H 7
DE12: App M 2H 7
Dingles Way CV37: S Avon 2F 115
Dingley Rd. CV12: Bulk 3D 42
Discovery Way CV3: Bin 1C 70
Ditton Cl. CV22: Bil 7C 74
Dobbie Rd. CV37: Up Qui 7H 125
Dobson La. CV31: W'nsh 4E 102
Doctors Cl. B94: Tan A 3D 90
Doctor's Hill B94: Tan A 3D 90
Doctors La. B95: Hen A 1H 93
Dodd Av. CV34: Warw 1A 102
DODFORD
Bromsgrove 1A 142
Northampton 2D 145
Dodgson Cl. CV6: Longf 2G 51
Dodwells Bri. Ind. Est. LE10: Hinc 3K 23
Doe Bank La. CV1: Cov 4A 58
Dogberry Cl. CV3: W'hall 2J 69
Dogberry Way CV34: H'cte 6D 102
Doglands, The CV31: W'nsh 4F 103
Dog La. B76: Bod H 6A 12
CV47: Fen C 3G 121
CV47: Nap 3J 111
Dolomite Av. CV5: Cov 6H 57
Donalbain Cl. CV34: H'cte 5D 102
Doncaster Cl. CV2: Cov 7K 51
Done-Cerce Cl. CV22: Dunc 6C 86
Donegal Cl. CV4: Tile H 1E 66
Dongan Rd. CV34: Warw 1G 101
DONINGTON LE HEATH 1B 140
DONNINGTON 3A 146
Donnington Av. CV6: Cov 2J 57
Donnington Rd. CV36: Ship S 3H 131
Donnithorne Av. CV10: Nun 3J 31
CV11: Nun 3J 31
Donnybrook Dr. CV3: Bin 6D 60
Doone Cl. CV2: Cov 1A 60
Dorcas Cl. CV11: Nun 4E 32
Dorchester Av. CV35: H Mag 2B 100
Dorchester Way CV2: W'grve S 2B 60
CV11: Nun 4H 23
DORDON 5D 10 (1D 139)
Dordon Rd. B78: Dord 2C 10
Doris Rd. B46: Col 4F 25
Dorlecote Ct. CV10: Nun 3J 31
Dorlecote Pl. CV10: Nun 4J 31
Dorlecote Rd. CV10: Nun 3J 31
Dormer Harris Av. CV4: Tile H 6D 56
Dormer Pl. CV32: Lea S 7D 98
DORMSTON 3A 142
DORN 2B 146
Dorney Cl. CV5: Cov 7J 57
Dorothy Powell Way CV2: W'grve S 5B 52
DORRIDGE 1C 143
Dorset Cl. CV10: Nun 1F 31
CV22: Caw 7B 74
Dorset Rd. CV1: Cov 2C 58
DORSINGTON 1A 146
Dorsington Cl. CV35: Hatt 4A 96
Dorsington Rd. CV37: Long M, Peb 3F 125
Douglas Ho. CV1: Cov 1K 135
Douglas Rd. CV21: Rugby 2J 75
Doulton Cl. CV2: W'grve S 5A 52
Dove Cl. CV12: Bed 1E 40
Dovecote Cl. CV6: Cov 2H 57
Dovecotes, The CV5: Cov 2F 57
Dovedale Av. CV6: Cov 4F 51
Dovedale Cl. CV21: Brow 1J 75
Dovedale Ct. B46: Wat O 1A 24
Dovehouse Dr. CV35: Welle 4G 117
Dovehouse La. CV33: Har 6J 109
DOVERDALE 2A 142
Dover St. CV1: Cov 3F 135 (4B 58)
Dovestone B77: Wiln 1A 10
Dowley Cft. CV3: Bin 6D 60
Downderry Way CV6: Cov 1G 59
Downing Cres. CV12: Bed 1J 41
Downing Ho. B37: Chel W 4B 34
Downton Cl. CV2: W'grve S 6C 52
Dowty Av. CV12: Bed 4D 40
Doyle Dr. CV6: Longf 3F 51
Dragons Health Club 6E 74
Drake Cft. B37: Chel W 2D 34
DRAKES BROUGHTON 3A 142
DRAKES CROSS 1B 142
Drake St. CV6: Cov 7D 50
Draper Cl. CV8: Ken 5G 79
Drapers Ct. CV1: Cov 1H 135 (3C 58)
DRAPER'S FIELD 1H 135 (3C 58)
Drapers Flds. CV1: Cov 1H 135 (3C 58)
DRAYCOTE 2B 144
Draycote Water Country Pk. 2B 144
DRAYCOTT
Moreton-in-Marsh 2A 146
Worcester 3A 142
Draycott Rd. CV2: Cov 7H 51
DRAYTON
Banbury 1D 147
Daventry 2C 145
Stratford-upon-Avon 3C 143
Stourbridge 1A 142
Drayton Av. CV37: S Avon 3B 114
DRAYTON BASSETT 1C 139
Drayton Cl. B50: Bidf A 5F 123
CV10: Harts 3F 21
CV37: S Avon 3C 114
Drayton Ct. CV10: Nun 5H 21
CV34: Warw 5H 97
Drayton Cres. CV5: E Grn 2B 56
Drayton La. CV13: Fen D 5J 17
Drayton Leys CV22: Rugby 2G 87
Drayton Rd. CV12: Bed 3K 41
Drayton Way CV10: Nun 4H 21
Drew Cres. CV8: Ken 5E 78
Dreyer Cl. CV22: Bil 6C 74
Driftway, The CV36: Ship S 4H 131
Drinkwater Cl. CV33: Har 6J 109
Drinkwater Ho. *CV1: Cov 5B 58*
(off Meadow St.)
Drive, The B46: Col 6G 25
CV2: Cov 4K 59
CV22: Dunc 5D 86
Drivers La. GL56: Lit C 6C 134
DROITWICH SPA 2A 142
Dronfield Rd. CV2: Cov 4H 59
Drovers Way CV47: Sou 5J 107
Droylesdon Pk. Rd. CV3: Finh 5B 68
Druid Rd. CV2: Cov 4H 59
DRUID'S HEATH 1B 138
Drummond Cl. CV6: Cov 7K 49
Drummond Rd. CV22: Caw 1K 85
Drummond Way B37: Chel W 3C 34
Drury La. CV21: Rugby 5G 75
Dryden Cl. CV8: Ken 6D 78
CV10: Gall C 6E 20
Dryden Pl. CV22: Rugby 5E 74
Dryden Wlk. CV22: Rugby 5E 74
Dryden Way CV37: S Avon 7H 115
Dtratford Rd. CV33: L Hth 2J 119
Duckham Ct. CV6: Cov 3A 58
Duck La. CV37: Welf A 2B 124
DUDLEY 3A 138
Dudley Grn. CV32: Lill 5F 99
Dudley Rd. CV8: Ken 7C 78
Dudley St. CV6: Cov 5G 51
CV9: Ath 4C 16
Dudley Ter. CV8: S'lgh 3B 80
Duffins Pl. CV37: Snitt 6G 95
Duffus Hill CV35: More M 4C 118
Duffy Pl. CV21: Hillm 1C 88
Dugard Pl. CV35: Barf 3C 108
Dugdale Av. B50: Bidf A 5F 123
CV37: S Avon 2F 115
Dugdale Ct. CV31: Lea S 2E 102
Dugdale Rd. CV6: Cov 1B 58
Dugdale St. CV11: Nun 7D 22
(not continuous)
Duggins La. CV4: Tile H 7A 56
Duke Barn Fld. CV2: Cov 2G 59
DUKE END 1K 35
Dukes Jetty CV21: Rugby 5G 75
Dukes Rd. B78: Dord 4C 10
Duke St. CV5: Cov 5K 57
CV11: Nun 7B 22
CV21: Rugby 4G 75
CV32: Lea S 6E 98
Dulverton Av. CV5: Cov 2H 57
Dulverton Ct. CV5: Cov 3H 57
Dunblane Dr. CV32: Cubb 2G 99
Duncan Dr. CV22: Bil 3D 86
DUNCHURCH 6C 86 (1B 144)
Dunchurch Hall CV22: Dunc 6C 86
Dunchurch Highway CV5: Alle, Cov 1E 56
Dunchurch Rd. CV22: Rugby 3E 86
Dunchurch Trad. Est. CV23: Dunc 4H 85
Duncombe Grn. B46: Col 5F 25
DUNCOTE 3D 145
Dun Cow Cl. CV23: Brin 4C 62
Duncroft Av. CV6: Cov 7K 49
DUNHAMPTON 2A 142
Dunhill Av. CV4: Tile H 4C 56
Dunkirk Pl. CV3: Bin 1B 70
Dunnerdale CV21: Brow 1K 75
DUNNINGTON 2A 122 (3B 142)
Dunnose Cl. CV6: Cov 6E 50
Dunn's La. B78: Dord 4E 10
Dunrose Cl. CV2: Cov 5A 60
DUNSLEY 3A 138
Dunsmore Av. CV3: W'hall 2J 69
CV22: Hillm 1A 88
Dunsmore Heath CV22: Dunc 6C 86
Dunstall Cres. CV33: Bis T 5B 108
DUNSTALL HILL 2A 138
Dunster Cl. CV22: Rugby 6E 74
Dunster Pl. CV6: Cov 3D 50
Dunster Rd. B37: Chel W 2C 34
DUNS TEW 3D 147
Dunsville Dr. CV2: W'grve S 6B 52
DUNTON BASSETT 2C 141
DUNTON INTERCHANGE 3D 18
Dunton La. B76: Wis 2B 18
Dunvegan Cl. CV3: Bin 5C 60
CV8: Ken 5G 79
Durbar Av. CV6: Cov 6D 50
Durbar Av. Ind. Est. CV6: Cov 6D 50
Durham Cl. CV7: Ker E 2K 49
Durham Cres. CV5: Alle 7E 48
Durham Cft. B37: Chel W 3B 34
Durrell Dr. CV22: Caw 1A 86
DUSTON 2D 145
Dutton Rd. CV2: Ald G 3K 51
Duttons Cl. CV37: Snitt 5G 95
Duxford Cl. CV35: Welle 4G 117
Dwarris Wlk. CV34: Warw 5G 97
Dyer's La. CV8: Wols 5J 71
Dyers Rd. CV11: Bram 6H 33
Dymond Rd. CV6: Cov 3C 50
Dysart Cl. CV1: Cov 3E 58
Dyson Cl. CV21: Hillm 7B 76
Dyson St. CV4: Tile H 4C 56

E

Eacott Cl. CV6: Cov 3A 50
Eadie St. CV10: Nun 7J 21
Eagle Cl. CV11: Nun 4D 32
Eagle Ct. *CV34: Warw 1F 101*
(off Saltisford)
Eagle Gro. B36: Cas B 4A 24
Eagle La. CV8: Ken 6D 78
Eagle St. CV1: Cov 2D 58
CV31: Lea S 2E 102
Eagle St. E. CV1: Cov 2D 58
Earles Cl. CV47: S'ton 6C 106
Earl Pl. Bus. Pk. CV4: Tile H 6F 57
Earl Rivers Av. CV34: H'cte 5B 102
EARLS COMMON 3A 142
Earl's Cft., The CV3: Cov 1C 68
EARLSDON 7K 57 (1A 144)
Earlsdon Av. Nth. CV5: Cov 5K 57
Earlsdon Av. Sth. CV5: Cov 6A 58
Earlsdon Bus. Cen. CV5: Cov 7K 57
Earlsdon St. CV5: Cov 7K 57
EARL SHILTON 2B 140
Earls Rd. CV11: Nun 6B 22
Earl St. CV1: Cov 4J 135 (5D 58)
CV12: Bed 3J 41
CV21: Rugby 5H 75
CV32: Lea S 6E 98
Earls Wlk. CV3: Bin W 1F 71
EARLSWOOD 1C 143
Easedale Cl. CV3: Cov 2B 68
CV11: Nun 5H 23
EASENHALL 3J 63 (1B 144)
Easenhall Rd. CV23: Harb M 4A 64
EASINGTON 2D 147
East Av. CV2: Cov 4G 59
CV12: Bed 3K 41
Eastboro Flds. CV11: Nun 7G 23
Eastborough Ct. CV11: Nun 2A 32
Eastboro' Way CV11: Nun 2A 32
Eastbourne Cl. CV6: Cov 1J 57
E. Car Pk. Rd. B40: Nat E C 2F 45
EASTCOTE
Solihull 1C 143
Towcester 3D 145
Eastcotes CV4: Tile H 6F 57
East Dene CV32: Lill 5F 99
Eastern Grn. Rd. CV5: E Grn 4D 56
EAST FARNDON 3D 141
Eastfield Cl. CV37: S Avon 2E 114
Eastfield Pl. CV21: Rugby 5G 75
Eastfield Rd. CV10: Nun 5E 22
CV32: Lea S 7E 98
Eastgate M. CV34: Warw 2G 101
EAST GOSCOTE 1D 141
East Grn. Dr. CV37: S Avon 4B 114
East Gro. CV31: Lea S 2E 102

EAST HADDON ... 2D 145
East Ho. Dr. CV9: Hurl ... 7A 14
Eastlands Ct. CV21: Rugby ... 5J 75
Eastlands Gro. CV5: Cov ... 3J 57
Eastlands Pl. CV21: Rugby ... 5K 75
Eastlands Rd. CV21: Rugby ... 5K 75
Eastlang Rd. CV7: Fill ... 2C 38
EAST LANGTON ... 2D 141
Eastleigh Av. CV5: Cov ... 1K 67
Eastley Cres. CV34: Warw ... 7D 96
Eastnor Gro. CV31: Lea S ... 1F 103
East St. CV1: Cov ... 4E 58
CV21: Rugby ... 4K 75
CV36: Long C ... 2C 134
E. Union St. CV22: Rugby ... 6G 75
Eastway B40: Nat E C ... 3F 45
B92: Bick ... 3F 45
Eastwood Bus. Village CV3: Bin ... 6B 60
Eastwood Cl. CV31: Lea S ... 2H 103
Eastwood Gro. CV21: Hillm ... 1E 88
Easy La. CV21: Rugby ... 5F 75
EATHORPE ... 1A 104 (2A 144)
Eathorpe Cl. CV2: Cov ... 5J 51
Eathorpe Pk. CV33: Eat ... 1B 104
Eaton Cl. CV32: Lea S ... 5B 98
Eaton Rd. CV1: Cov ... 6G 135 (6C 58)
EAVES GREEN ... 4H 47 (3D 139)
Eaves Grn. La. CV7: Mer ... 5G 47
Eaves Grn. Pk. CV7: Mer ... 4H 47
Ebbw Va. Ter. CV3: Cov ... 1D 68
Eborall Cl. CV34: Warw ... 5G 97
Ebourne Cl. CV8: Ken ... 5E 78
EBRINGTON ... 1A 146
Ebrington Dr. CV35: Hatt ... 5A 96
Ebro Cres. CV3: Bin ... 6B 60
Ebsdorf Cl. B50: Bidf A ... 5G 123
Eburne Rd. CV2: Ald G ... 3H 51
Eccles Cl. CV2: Cov ... 6J 51
Echills Wood Railway ... 5A 80
(off Avenue M.)
Eclipse Rd. B49: Alc ... 4A 112
Ecton Leys CV22: Rugby ... 2G 87
Edale Way CV6: Cov ... 7G 51
Eddie Miller Ct. CV12: Bed ... 3G 41
Eddison Rd. B46: Col ... 7E 18
Eden Cl. B80: Stud ... 4C 92
Eden Ct. CV10: Nun ... 4H 21
CV32: Lill ... 4H 99
Eden Cft. CV8: Ken ... 5F 79
Eden Gro. B37: Chel W ... 4D 34
Eden Rd. CV2: W'grve S ... 5C 52
CV21: Hillm ... 7B 76
Eden St. CV6: Cov ... 7F 51
EDGBASTON ... 3B 138
Edgecote Cl. CV21: Hillm ... 7B 76
Edgefield Rd. CV2: W'grve S ... 6C 52
EDGE HILL ... 1K 13
EDGEHILL ... 7B 128
Edge Hill CV9: Wood E ... 1H 13
Edgehill Country Pk. ... 2F 129
Edgehill Pl. CV4: Tile H ... 6A 56
Edge Hill Rd. CV33: L Hth ... 2J 119
Edge La. B95: Hen A ... 2J 93
EDGIOCK ... 2B 142
EDGWICK ... 6E 50
Edgwick Pk. Ind. Est. CV6: Cov ... 6E 50
Edgwick Rd. CV6: Cov ... 7F 51
Edinburgh Cres. CV31: Lea S ... 2D 102
Edinburgh Rd. CV9: Hurl ... 6K 13
CV10: Nun ... 5H 21
Edinburgh Vs. CV8: Bag ... 5F 69
Edinburgh Way CV23: Long L ... 3B 74
EDINGALE ... 1D 139
Edingale Rd. CV2: W'grve S ... 5B 52
Edkins Cvn. Site CV37: Wilm ... 5H 113
Edmondes Cl. CV34: Warw ... 6H 97
Edmonds Cl. CV37: Up Qui ... 6H 125
Edmondscote Rd. CV32: Lea S ... 7A 98
Edmondson Cl. CV22: Dunc ... 5D 86
Edmund Rd. CV1: Cov ... 2D 58
EDSTONE ... 4D 94 (2C 143)
Edstone Aqueduct ... 2C 143
Edward Bailey Cl. CV3: Bin ... 1A 70
Edward Ct. CV21: Rugby ... 5H 75
(off Pinders La.)
Edward Rd. B46: Wat O ... 1C 24
CV6: Cov ... 3A 50
CV12: Bed ... 2J 41
Edwards Gro. CV8: Ken ... 4G 79
Edward St. CV6: Cov ... 2E 58
CV11: Nun ... 7C 22
CV21: Rugby ... 4F 75
CV32: Lea S ... 6A 98
CV34: Warw ... 1F 101
Edward Tyler Rd. CV7: Exh ... 4G 41
Edwin Cl. CV22: Caw ... 2A 86
Edyth Rd. CV2: Cov ... 3A 60
Edyvean Cl. CV22: Bil ... 3E 86
Edyvean Walker Ct. CV11: Nun ... 6C 22
EGDON ... 3A 142
Egerton Cl. CV21: N'bld A ... 2F 75
Eglamour Way CV34: H'cte ... 5D 102
Egret Wlk. CV2: Ald G ... 3H 51
Eileen Gdns. B37: K'hrst ... 1A 34
Elan Cl. CV32: Lill ... 4G 99
Elborow St. CV21: Rugby ... 5G 75
Elderberry Way CV2: Cov ... 1H 59
Elder Cl. B78: K'bry ... 4E 12
CV22: Bil ... 7B 74
Eldorado Cl. B80: Stud ... 3C 92
Eld Rd. CV6: Cov ... 7E 50
ELFORD ... 1C 139
Elford Gro. B37: Mars G ... 4B 34
Elgar Cl. CV11: Nun ... 5C 32
Elgar Rd. CV6: Cov ... 6H 51
Eliot Cl. CV34: Warw ... 5G 97
CV37: S Avon ... 7H 115
Eliot Ct. CV22: Rugby ... 5E 74
Eliot Way CV10: Nun ... 2H 31
Elizabeth Av. B78: Pole ... 7D 8
Elizabeth Ct. CV34: Warw ... 2K 101
Elizabeth Ho. CV37: S Avon ... 1D 136
Elizabeth Rd. CV31: Lea S ... 2C 102
Elizabeth Sports Cen. ... 2J 41
Elizabeth Way CV2: W'grve S ... 7B 52
CV8: Ken ... 4C 78
CV23: Long L ... 3B 74
ELKINGTON ... 1D 145
Elkington La. CV23: Barby ... 7D 88
Elkington St. CV6: Cov ... 6F 51
Ellacombe Rd. CV2: Cov ... 6K 51
Ellerman Gdns. CV6: Longf ... 3F 51
Ellesmere Rd. CV12: Bed ... 3G 41
Ellice Dr. B36: Cas B ... 5B 24
Ellidon Rd. CV47: P Mars ... 6H 111
Elliots Fld. Retail Pk.
CV21: Rugby ... 1H 75
Elliott Cl. B50: Bidf A ... 5F 123
Elliott Ct. CV5: Cov ... 6H 57
Elliott Dr. CV35: Welle ... 3G 117
(not continuous)
Elliotts Orchard CV35: Barf ... 2B 108
Ellis Pk. Dr. CV3: Bin ... 6D 60
Elliston Gro. CV31: Lea S ... 2G 103
ELLISTOWN ... 1B 140
Ell La. CV23: Brin ... 3D 62
Ellys Rd. CV1: Cov ... 2C 58
Elmbank CV47: Sou ... 6H 107
Elm Bank Cl. CV32: Lill ... 3E 98
Elmbank Rd. CV8: Ken ... 3C 78
ELMBRIDGE ... 2A 142
Elm Cl. CV3: Bin W ... 1E 70
CV36: Ilm ... 6C 126
CV47: Sou ... 6H 107
Elm Ct. CV5: Alle ... 6A 48
CV37: S Avon ... 2D 136
Elmdene Cl. CV8: Wols ... 4J 71
Elmdene Rd. CV8: Ken ... 5F 79
ELMDON ... 3A 44 (3C 139)
Elmdon Ct. B37: Mars G ... 6A 34
ELMDON HEATH ... 3C 139
Elmdon La. B26: Birm A ... 3A 44
B37: Mars G ... 6A 34
Elmdon Rd. B37: Mars G ... 6A 34
Elmdon Trad. Est. B37: Mars G ... 1C 44
Elm Dr. B49: Ove G ... 5D 112
ELMESTHORPE ... 2B 140
Elm Farm Av. B37: Mars G ... 6A 34
Elmfield Rd. B36: Cas B ... 5A 24
CV10: Nun ... 4D 22
Elm Gro. B37: K'hrst ... 6A 24
CV7: Old A ... 2C 28
CV9: Hurl ... 7K 13
ELMHURST ... 1C 139
Elmhurst Rd. CV6: Longf ... 2G 51
ELMLEY LOVETT ... 2A 142
Elm Lodge B92: H Ard ... 7G 45
Elmore Cl. B37: F'bri ... 1A 34
CV3: Bin ... 7K 59
Elmore Rd. CV22: Bil ... 7F 75
Elm Rd. CV32: Lill ... 4F 99
CV36: Ship S ... 6H 131
CV37: S Avon ... 2E 114
Elm Row CV47: S'ton ... 6C 106
Elms, The CV12: Bed ... 3E 40
CV35: Leek W ... 1H 97
CV37: S Avon ... 3F 115
Elms Cvn. Pk., The CV37: Tidd ... 2J 115
Elms Ct. CV9: Aus ... 6G 7
Elmsdale Av. CV6: Cov ... 4E 50
Elms Dr. CV9: Aus ... 6G 7
CV22: Hillm ... 1B 88
Elms Paddock, The CV23: Clift D ... 3B 76
Elm Tree Av. CV4: Tile H ... 5E 56
Elm Tree Cl. B78: K'bry ... 5E 12
Elm Tree Ri. B92: H Ard ... 7G 45
Elm Tree Rd. CV12: Bulk ... 3F 43
Elm Way CV10: Harts ... 3F 21
Elmwood Av. CV6: Cov ... 2K 57
Elmwood Ct. CV1: Cov ... 1G 135 (3C 58)
Elphin Cl. CV6: Cov ... 3A 50
Elsee Rd. CV21: Rugby ... 5H 75
Elsinore CV37: S Avon ... 1G 137
Elstop Av. CV23: Brow ... 6K 65
Elter Cl. CV21: Brow ... 1K 75
Eltham Rd. CV3: Cov ... 1E 68
Elton Cl. CV32: Lill ... 5G 99
Elva Cft. B36: Cas B ... 3A 24
Elwy Circ. CV7: Ash G ... 6B 40
Ely Cl. B37: Chel W ... 3B 34
CV2: W'grve S ... 1C 60
Ely Cotts. CV37: S Avon ... 5F 137
Ely Gdns. CV37: S Avon ... 5E 136
Ely St. CV37: S Avon ... 4E 136 (5E 114)
Embassy Wlk. CV2: Cov ... 6K 51
Emerald Way CV31: Lea S ... 3D 102
Emerson Av. CV37: S Avon ... 4C 114
Emerson Rd. CV2: Cov ... 4J 59
Emery Cl. CV2: Cov ... 7A 52
Emily Smith Ho. CV2: Cov ... 5H 51
(off Roseberry Av.)
Emmott Dr. CV31: Lea S ... 2F 103
Emperor Way CV21: Rugby ... 1F 75
Empire Rd. CV4: Tile H ... 5C 56
Empress Arc. CV3: Cov ... 5H 59
EMSCOTE ... 7H 97
Emscote Rd. CV3: Cov ... 5J 59
CV34: Warw ... 1J 101
Ena Rd. CV1: Cov ... 2D 58
Endemere Rd. CV6: Cov ... 6D 50
ENDERBY ... 2C 141
Endsleigh Gdns. CV31: Lea S ... 2F 103
Enfield Rd. CV2: Cov ... 4H 59
England Cres. CV31: Lea S ... 1C 102
Engleton Rd. CV6: Cov ... 1A 58
Ennerdale CV21: Brow ... 1J 75
Ennerdale Cl. CV32: Lea S ... 5B 98
Ennerdale Cres. CV11: Nun ... 5G 23
Ennerdale La. CV2: Cov ... 3B 60
Ennersdale Bungs. B46: Col ... 3F 25
Ennersdale Cl. B46: Col ... 3F 25
Ennersdale Rd. B46: Col ... 3F 25
Enright Cl. CV32: Lea S ... 5C 98
Ensign Bus. Cen. CV4: W'wd H ... 2D 66
Ensign Cl. CV4: Tile H ... 6B 56
Ensor Cl. CV11: Nun ... 6H 23
Ensor Dr. B78: Pole ... 1C 10
ENSTONE ... 3C 147
Enville Cl. B37: Mars G ... 4B 34
Epperston Ct. CV31: Lea S ... 1D 102
Epping Way CV32: Lill ... 3G 99
Epsom Cl. CV12: Bed ... 1H 41
Epsom Dr. CV3: W'hall ... 2J 69
Epsom Rd. CV22: Bil ... 7D 74
CV32: Lill ... 3G 99
EPWELL ... 1C 147
Epwell Rd. CV35: Up Tys ... 7C 130
ERDINGTON ... 2C 139
Erdington Rd. CV9: Ath ... 4C 16
Erica Av. CV12: Bed ... 3F 41
Erica Dr. CV31: W'nsh ... 6F 103
Eric Grey Cl. CV2: Cov ... 2G 59
Eric Inott Ho. CV3: Cov ... 2E 68
Erithway Rd. CV3: Finh ... 4B 68
Ernest Richards Rd. CV12: Bed ... 1H 41
Ernsford Av. CV3: Cov ... 6H 59
Esher Dr. CV3: Cov ... 1E 68
Eskdale CV21: Brow ... 7J 65
Eskdale Wlk. CV3: W'hall ... 1K 69
Esporta Health Club
Rugby ... 2H 75
Whitley ... 1F 69
Essen La. CV23: Kils ... 6H 89
Essex Cl. CV5: E Grn ... 4F 57
CV8: Ken ... 7C 78
Essex Ct. CV34: Warw ... 7G 97
Essex Grn. CV47: Temp H ... 2A 120
Essex St. CV21: Rugby ... 4G 75
ESSINGTON ... 1A 138
Esterton Cl. CV6: Cov ... 4C 50
Ethelfield Rd. CV2: Cov ... 4H 59
Etone Ct. CV11: Nun ... 6C 22
Etone Sports Cen. ... 6E 22
Eton Rd. CV37: S Avon ... 6H 115
Ettingley Cl. B98: Redd ... 2A 92
ETTINGTON ... 2B 126 (1B 146)
Ettington Cl. CV35: Welle ... 4H 117
Ettington Rd. CV5: E Grn ... 4E 56
CV35: Welle ... 4H 117
(not continuous)
Europa Way CV34: Warw ... 7K 101
Eustace Rd. CV12: Bulk ... 4F 43
Euston Cres. CV3: W'hall ... 1J 69
Euston Pl. CV32: Lea S ... 7D 98
Euston Sq. CV32: Lea S ... 7D 98
Evans Cl. CV12: Bed ... 2J 41
CV37: Shot ... 6C 114
Evans Gro. CV31: W'nsh ... 6E 102
Evans Rd. CV22: Bil ... 6C 74
Evelyn Av. CV6: Cov ... 4E 50
EVENLODE ... 3B 146
Evenlode Cl. CV37: S Avon ... 6H 115
Evenlode Cres. CV6: Cov ... 2K 57
Everard Cl. CV23: Clift D ... 3C 76
Everard Ct. CV11: Nun ... 2A 32
EVERDON ... 3C 145
Everdon Cl. CV22: Hillm ... 1K 87
Everdon Rd. CV6: Cov ... 4B 50
(not continuous)
Everest Rd. CV22: Rugby ... 1E 86
Everglade Rd. CV9: Wood E ... 1J 13
Evergreens, The CV10: Nun ... 5A 22
Eversleigh Rd. CV6: Cov ... 7J 49
Evesham Pl. CV37: S Avon ... 7C 136 (5E 114)
Evesham Rd.
CV37: Bint, D'wll, S Avon ... 7A 136 & 6A 114 (1A 124)
WR11: Salf P ... 7B 122
Evesham St. B49: Alc, Arr ... 6A 112
Evesham Wlk. CV4: Canly ... 3H 67
EVINGTON ... 1D 141
Evreux Way CV21: Rugby ... 5G 75
Exbury Way CV11: Nun ... 4A 32
Exeter Cl. CV3: Bin ... 7K 59
Exeter Dr. B37: Mars G ... 5A 34
EXHALL
Alcester ... 1G 123 (3C 143)
Coventry ... 6G 41
Exhall CV7: Exh ... 4G 41
Exhall Basin CV6: Longf ... 1H 51
Exhall Cl. CV37: S Avon ... 6J 115
Exhall Grn. CV7: Exh ... 6F 41
EXHALL HALL GREEN ... 6F 41
Exhall Mobile Homes CV7: Ash G ... 6B 40
Exhall Rd. CV7: Ker E ... 7K 39
Exham Cl. CV34: Warw ... 6G 97
Exhibition Way B40: Nat E C ... 2D 44
Exis Ct. CV11: Nun ... 2A 32
Exminster Rd. CV3: Cov ... 3E 68
Exmoor Dr. CV32: Lill ... 3G 99

Exmouth Cl. CV2: Cov 7J 51
Exton Cl. CV7: Ash G 6C 40
EYDON 3C 145
Eydon Cl. CV21: Brow 2A 76
Eyffler Cl. CV34: Warw 1F 101

F

Fabian Cl. CV3: W'hall 1K 69
Fairbanks Cl. CV2: W'grve S 7C 52
Fairbourne Way CV6: Cov 6J 49
Fair Cl. CV23: F'ton 7A 84
Faircroft CV8: Ken 6D 78
Fairfax Cl. CV35: Barf 2B 108
Fairfax Ct. CV34: Warw 1H 101
Fairfax St. CV1: Cov 3J 135 (4D 58)
FAIRFIELD 1A 142
Fairfield CV7: Exh 4G 41
Fairfield Ct. CV3: Cov 1G 69
Fairfield Ri. CV7: Mer 5E 46
Fairfields Hill B78: Pole 2C 10
Fairfields Wlk. CV37: S Avon 4C 114
Fairhurst Dr. CV32: Lea S 4C 98
Fair Isle Dr. CV10: Nun 1F 31
Fairlands Pk. CV4: Canly 3J 67
Fairlawn Cl. CV32: Lea S 6B 98
Fairmile Cl. CV3: Bin 7J 59
Fairview Ind. Est. B76: Curd 4B 18
Fairview Wlk. CV6: Longf 4E 50
Fairwater Cres. B49: Alc 4D 112
Fairway CV11: Nun 3D 32
Fairway Ct. CV21: Rugby 4K 75
Fairway Ri. CV8: Ken 3G 79
Fairways, The CV32: Lea S 5B 98
Fairways Cl. CV5: Alle 1E 56
Falcon Av. CV3: Bin 7B 60
Falcon Cl. CV11: Nun 4D 32
Falcon Ct. *CV47: Sou* *5H 107*
(off Bull St.)
Falcon Cres. B50: Bidf A 5H 123
Falkener Ho. CV6: Cov 7E 50
Falkland Cl. CV4: Tile H 1B 66
Falkland Pl. CV47: Temp H 2B 120
Falkland Way B36: Cas B 7B 24
Fallowfields Cres. CV6: Cov 2B 50
Fallow Hill CV31: Lea S 2G 103
Falmouth Cl. CV11: Nun 6H 23
Falstaff Cl. CV11: Nun 3C 32
(not continuous)
Falstaff Ct. CV37: S Avon 1F 137 (4F 115)
Falstaff Dr. CV22: Bil 4D 86
Falstaff Gro. CV34: H'cte 5C 102
Falstaff Rd. CV4: Tile H 5C 56
Falstaff's Experience 4G 137
Fancott Dr. CV8: Ken 3D 78
Fant Hill OX15: Up Bra 1F 133
Faraday Av. B46: Col 6E 18
B76: Curd 6E 18
Faraday Rd. CV22: Rugby 7J 75
Farber Rd. CV2: W'grve S 1C 60
FAR COTTON 3D 145
Farcroft Av. CV5: E Grn 3B 56
Fareham Av. CV22: Hillm 1A 88
FAREWELL 1B 138
Far Gosford St. CV1: Cov 5E 58
Farley Av. CV33: Har 6G 109
Farley St. CV31: Lea S 1F 103
Farlow Cl. CV6: Cov 1G 59
Farman Rd. CV5: Cov 5K 57
Farm Cl. CV6: Cov 3B 50
CV33: Har 6G 109
CV36: Ship S 4G 131
FARMCOTE 3A 146
Farmcote Lodge *CV2: Ald G* *2H 51*
(off Farmcote Rd.)
Farmcote Rd. CV2: Ald G 2H 51
Farmer Ward Rd. CV8: Ken 6E 78
Farm Gro. CV22: Rugby 7J 75
Farm La. CV9: Gren 3J 11
CV23: Eas 3J 63
Farm Pl. CV3: Cov 7J 59
Farm Rd. CV8: Ken 7C 78
CV32: Lill 4F 99
Farmside CV3: W'hall 3K 69
Farmstead, The CV3: Cov 7J 59
Farm St. CV33: Har 5G 109
Farm Wlk. CV33: Bis T 4C 108
FARNBOROUGH 6H 121 (1D 147)
Farnborough Av. CV22: Rugby 6E 74
Farnborough Hall 7G 121
Farnborough Rd. CV35: Rad 5B 128
Farndale Av. CV6: Cov 3D 50
Farndon Av. B37: Mars G 6B 34
Farndon Cl. CV12: Bulk 2D 42
Farnell Dr. CV37: S Avon 4C 114
Far Pool Mdw. CV35: Clav 2C 94
Farr Dr. CV4: Tile H 5F 57
Farren Rd. CV2: Cov 3K 59
Farriers Ct. CV23: Stret U 7F 55
Farriers Way CV11: Nun 2B 32
Farrington Cl. CV35: Welle 4G 117
Farrington Ct. *CV35: Welle* *4H 117*
(off Farrington Cl.)
Farther Sand Cl. CV35: H Lucy 2A 118
FARTHINGHOE 2D 147
Farthing La. B76: Curd 5C 18
FARTHINGSTONE 3D 145
Farthing Wlk. CV4: W'wd H 2B 66
Farzens Av. CV34: Warw 5D 100
Faseman Av. CV4: Tile H 4D 56
Faulconbridge Av. CV5: E Grn 3C 56
Faulconbridge Way CV34: H'cte 5C 102
Faultlands Cl. CV11: Nun 4B 32
(not continuous)
FAWLER 3C 147
Fawley Cl. CV3: W'hall 2K 69
Fawsley Leys CV22: Rugby 2G 87
Faygate Cl. CV3: Bin 4C 60
FAZELEY 1C 139
Featherbed La. CV4: W'wd H 3E 66
CV7: Withy 1D 54
CV21: Hillm 1C 88
CV36: Cher 6G 133
CV36: Ilm 7C 126
CV37: Path, Wilm 5K 113
CV47: Bas H 1J 109
FEATHERSTONE 1A 138
Featherstone Cl. CV10: Nun 2J 31
FECKENHAM 2B 142
Fein Bank CV4: Tile H 5A 56
Feldon Edge CV36: Half 3K 127
Feldon Vw. CV37: N'bld S 1G 127
Fell Gro. CV32: Lill 4G 99
Fell Mill La. CV36: H'ton, Ship S 1K 131
Fellmore Gro. CV31: Lea S 1G 103
Fellows Way CV21: Hillm 2B 88
Fell's La. CV47: Nap 2J 111
Felton Cl. CV2: W'grve S 5A 52
Fencote Av. B37: F'bri 1A 34
FEN END 1D 143
Fennell Ho. *CV1: Cov* *5B 58*
(off Meadow St.)
FENNY COMPTON 3G 121 (3B 144)
FENNY DRAYTON 2A 140
Fenside Av. CV3: Cov 4D 68
Fentham Cl. B92: H Ard 7H 45
Fentham Grn. B92: H Ard 7G 45
Fentham Rd. B92: H Ard 7G 45
Fenwick Cl. B49: Alc 3D 112
Fenwick Dr. CV21: Hillm 1C 88
Ferguson Cl. CV37: Ett 2C 126
Fern Cl. CV2: Cov 4J 51
CV23: Brow 7K 65
Ferndale Cl. CV11: Nun 6F 23
Ferndale Ct. B46: Col 7G 25
Ferndale Dr. CV8: Ken 7E 78
Ferndale M. B46: Col 7G 25
Ferndale Rd. B46: Col 7G 25
CV3: Bin W 1F 71
Ferndown Cl. CV4: Tile H 4D 56
Ferndown Ct. CV22: Bil 7E 74
Ferndown Rd. CV22: Bil 7E 74
Ferndown Ter. CV22: Bil 7E 74
Fern Gro. CV12: Bed 3E 40
Fernhill Cl. CV8: Ken 3C 78
Fernhill Dr. CV32: Lea S 6F 99
FERNHILL HEATH 3A 142
Fern Hill Way LE10: Wlvy 2H 33
Fernwood Cl. B98: Redd 2A 92
Ferrers Cl. CV4: Tile H 5D 56
Ferrieres Cl. CV22: Dunc 6C 86
Ferry La. CV37: A'ton 2C 116
Fetherston Ct. CV31: Lea S 2D 102
Fetherston Cres. CV8: Rytn D 7D 70
FEWCOTT 3D 147
Fiddlers Grn. B92: H Ard 7G 45
Fld. Barn Rd. CV35: H Mag 1B 100
Field Cl. CV8: Ken 4F 79
CV33: Ufton 3F 109
CV34: Warw 1K 101
Field Ct. CV2: Cov 7J 51
Fieldfare Cl. CV23: Brow 7J 65
Fieldfare Cft. B36: Cas B 4A 24
Field Ga. La. CV47: Fen C 2H 121
Fieldgate La. CV8: Ken 3C 78
CV31: W'nsh 6F 103
Fieldgate Lawn CV8: Ken 3D 78
FIELD HEAD 1B 140
Fieldhead La. CV34: Warw 2K 101
Fieldhouse Cl. B95: Hen A 2H 93
Fielding Cl. CV2: W'grve S 1C 60
CV9: Ath 1C 16
Fielding Way CV10: Gall C 6F 21
Field March CV3: W'hall 3A 70
Fields Ct. CV34: Warw 7H 97
Fieldside La. CV3: Bin 4B 60
Fields Pk. Dr. B49: Alc 4D 112
Field Vw. CV22: Caw 1B 86
Field Vw. Cl. CV7: Exh 5G 41
Fife Rd. CV5: Cov 5K 57
Fife St. CV11: Nun 7B 22
FIFIELD 3B 146
Fifield Cl. CV11: Nun 2K 31
Fighting Cl. CV35: Kine 5D 120
Fillingham Cl. B37: Chel W 4D 34
FILLONGLEY 2C 38 (3D 139)
Fillongley Rd. B46: Max 7C 26
CV7: Fill 7C 26
CV7: Mer 5E 46
Finch Cl. CV6: Cov 4C 50
Findley Cl. CV9: Man 5E 16
Findon Cl. CV12: Bulk 2E 42
Fineacre La. CV8: Rytn D 4E 82
CV23: Stret D 4E 82
Fingal Cl. CV3: W'hall 2J 69
Fingest Cl. CV5: Cov 3F 57
FINHAM 5C 68
Finham Cres. CV8: Ken 3F 79
Finham Flats CV8: Ken 3F 79
Finham Grn. Rd. CV3: Finh 5B 68
Finham Gro. CV3: Finh 5C 68
Finham Pk. CV3: Finh 6C 68
Finham Rd. CV8: Ken 3F 79
Finings Ct. CV32: Lea S 5D 98
Finlay Ct. CV1: Cov 6H 135 (6D 58)
Finmere CV21: Brow 2K 75
Finnemore Cl. CV3: Cov 3B 68
FINSTALL 1A 142
FINSTOCK 3C 147
FINWOOD 2C 143
Finwood Rd. CV35: Row 7G 91
Fircroft B78: K'bry 4D 12
Fircroft Ho. B37: Chel W 3A 34
Firedrake Cft. CV1: Cov 5F 59
Fire Sta. Rd. B26: Birm A 1A 44
Firethorn Cres. CV31: W'nsh 6E 102
Fir Gro. CV4: Tile H 5E 56
Firleigh Dr. CV12: Bulk 2F 43
(not continuous)
Firs, The B78: K'bry 4E 12
CV5: Cov 7A 58
CV7: Mer 5D 46
CV12: Bed 3E 40
CV37: Lwr Q 5J 125
Firs Dr. CV22: Rugby 6F 75
Firs Est. CV5: Cov 7B 58
First Av. CV3: Cov 6J 59
First Exhibition Av. B40: Nat E C 2D 44
Fir Tree Av. CV4: Tile H 5E 56
Fir Tree Gro. CV11: Nun 3K 31
Firtree La. CV7: New A 4E 28
Fisher Av. CV22: Hillm 1A 88
Fisher Rd. CV6: Cov 6E 50
CV47: Bis I 6B 110
Fishers Cl. CV23: Kils 7H 89
Fishers Ct. CV34: Warw 4F 101
Fishers Wlk. CV9: Ath 4C 16
Fishpond La. CV7: Lit P 7H 35
Fishponds Rd. CV8: Ken 6C 78
Fitness First Health Club
Canley *2G 67*
(in Cannon Pk. District Cen.)
Fitton St. CV11: Nun 1H 31
Fitzalan Cl. CV23: Chu L 2F 73
Fitzroy Cl. CV2: W'grve S 1D 60
Fivefield Rd. CV7: Ker E 1H 49
FIVE WAYS 1D 143
FLADBURY 3A 142
Flamborough Cl. CV3: Bin 7B 60
Flaunden Cl. CV5: Cov 3F 57
Flavel Ct. CV9: Aus 7G 7
Flavel Cres. CV31: Lea S 1D 102
Flaxdown Gdns. *CV23: Brow* *6K 65*
(off Tower Furlong)
FLECKNEY 2D 141
FLECKNOE 2C 145
Flecknose St. CV3: W'hall 2J 69
Fleet Cres. CV21: Hillm 6A 76
Fleet Ho. CV1: Cov 4G 135 (5C 58)
Fleet St. CV1: Cov 3G 135 (4C 58)
Fletchamstead Highway CV4: Cov 5G 57
Fletchamstead Highway Ind. Est. CV4: Cov 1H 67
Fletchers Way CV35: Welle 3G 117
Fletchworth Ga. CV5: Cov 7H 57
Fleur-de-Lys Ct. CV34: Warw 7K 97
Flint Cl. CV9: Ath 1D 16
FLINT'S GREEN 3A 56
FLORE 2D 145
Florence Cl. CV9: Ath 2C 16
CV12: Bed 5F 41
Florence Rd. CV3: Bin 5C 60
Florin Pl. CV21: Hillm 1C 88
Flower Ct. CV37: S Avon 6E 114
Flowerdale Dr. CV2: Cov 1H 59
Flower Rd. CV37: S Avon 1E 114
Flude Rd. CV7: Ash G 7C 40
FLYFORD FLAVELL 3A 142
Flying Flds. Rd. CV47: Sou 5J 107
Flynt Av. CV5: Alle 1E 56
Fold, The CV37: S Avon 2G 137 (4F 115)
FOLESHILL 5H 51 (3A 140)
Foleshill Ent. Pk. CV6: Cov 1D 58
Foleshill Leisure Cen. 7D 50
Foleshill Rd. CV1: Cov 1H 135 (2D 58)
CV6: Cov 3C 58
Folkland Grn. CV6: Cov 7K 49
Follager Rd. CV21: Rugby 4E 74
Folly La. CV9: Ath 3G 15
CV47: Nap 3G 111
Fontmell Cl. CV2: W'grve S 3C 60
FOOTHERLEY 1C 139
FORD 3A 146
FORDBRIDGE 2A 34
Fordbridge Rd. B37: K'hrst 1A 34
Forde Hall La. B95: Ullen 4A 90
Forders La. CV12: Bulk 7B 32
Fordham Av. CV37: S Avon 3F 115
FORDHOUSES 1A 138
Fordington Pl. CV35: Kine 5D 120
Fordrift, The B37: Mars G 1A 44
Ford St. CV1: Cov 2K 135 (4D 58)
CV10: Nun 7K 21
Fordway, The CV37: Lwr Q 5G 125
Fordwell Cl. CV5: Cov 4K 57
Foredraught B80: Stud 3D 92
Foreland Way CV6: Cov 3A 50
Foresters Pl. CV21: Hillm 2D 88
Foresters Rd. CV3: Cov 2E 68
Forest of Arden Golf Course 6A 36
Forest Way CV10: Nun 2E 30
Forfield Pl. CV31: Lea S 1E 102
Forfield Rd. CV6: Cov 1J 57
Forge La. OX17: Farn 6H 121
Forge Rd. B46: Shu 2C 26
CV8: Ken 3E 78
Forge Way CV6: Cov 3C 50
Forknell Av. CV2: Cov 2J 59
Fornside Cl. CV21: Brow 1K 75

Forrest Rd. CV8: Ken 5C 78
Forth Dr. B37: F'bri 1B 34
Forum B40: Nat E C 3E 44
Forum Dr. CV21: Rugby 2G 75
Forward Rd. B26: Birm A 3A 44
Fosberry Cl. CV34: Warw 7K 97
FOSCOT 3B 146
Fosse, The CV8: Wols 4A 72
Fosse Cres. CV23: Prin 6G 83
Fosse Way CV23: Bret 3B 72
(Bunkers Hill La.)
CV23: Bret 1C 72
(Kings Newnham La.)
CV23: Prin, Stret D 7F 83
(not continuous)
CV33: Eat, Off, Rad S 3A 104
CV35: More M 7C 118
CV36: Half, Tred, Wind 1F 131 & 7G 127
CV37: C'brk, Ett 3D 126
CV37: Ett 1K 127
Fosseway Cres. CV36: Tred 6J 127
Fosseway Rd. CV3: Finh 4B 68
Foster Av. B80: Stud 4C 92
Fosterd Rd. CV21: N'bld A 3F 75
Foster Rd. CV6: Cov 7A 50
Fosters Wharf B78: Pole 1C 10
FOSTON 2D 141
Founder Cl. CV4: Tile H 7D 56
Foundry Ct. CV37: S Avon 2D 136
Fountain Gdns. CV35: Welle 2H 117
Fountain Way CV37: S Avon 4E 136 (5E 114)
FOUR ASHES 1A 138
FOUR CROSSES 1A 138
Fourfields Way CV7: Gun H 5D 28
FOUR LANES END 4D 40
FOUR OAKS 3D 139
Four Pounds Av. CV5: Cov 4K 57
Four Shire Stone, The 2B 146
Fourways Rd. CV9: Ath 3E 16
Fowler Rd. CV6: Cov 2B 58
Fow Oak CV4: Tile H 5A 56
Fox Av. CV10: Nun 3D 22
Fox Cl. CV21: Hillm 7D 76
CV33: Har 6H 109
Foxcote Hill CV36: Ilm 7B 126
Foxdale Wlk. CV31: Lea S 2G 103
Foxes La. CV37: Wilm 5J 113
Foxes Way CV34: Warw 4F 101
Foxford Cres. CV2: Ald G 2H 51
Foxglove Cl. CV6: Cov 4C 50
CV12: Bed 4E 40
CV23: Brow 7K 65
Foxhills Cl. CV11: Nun 3E 32
Foxland Cl. B37: Chel W 3D 34
FOXLEDIATE 2B 142
FOXLEY 3D 145
Foxon's Barn Rd. CV21: Brow 2J 75
Foxtail Cl. CV37: S Avon 2C 114
FOXTON 3D 141
Foxton Rd. CV3: Bin 6A 60
Foxwood Dr. CV3: Bin W 1F 71
Foxwood Gro. B37: K'hrst 7A 24
Foxwood Rd. B78: B'moor 2C 10
FRADLEY 1C 139
FRADLEY SOUTH 1C 139
Framlingham Gro. CV8: Ken 3G 79
Frampton Cl. B37: Chel W 2D 34
Frampton Wlk. CV2: W'grve S 3B 60
Frances Av. CV34: Warw 1J 101
Frances Cres. CV12: Bed 2G 41
Frances Gibbs Gdns. CV31: W'nsh 4E 102
Frances Havergal Cl. CV31: Lea S 2D 102
Frances Rd. CV33: Har 6J 109
Franciscan Rd. CV3: Cov 7C 58
Francis Cl. B78: Pole 7D 8
Francis Dr. CV22: Caw 1A 86
Francis Rd. CV8: Bag 5E 68
Francis St. CV6: Cov 7E 50
Frankel Gdns. CV34: Warw 6H 97
Frankland Rd. CV6: Cov 5G 51
FRANKLEY 3A 138
Franklin Ct. CV11: Nun 3K 31
Franklin Gro. CV4: Tile H 6C 56
Franklin Rd. CV11: Nun 3K 31
CV31: W'nsh 5E 102
Franklins Gdns. CV3: Bin 6D 60
Frankpledge Rd. CV3: Cov 1E 68
Frank St. CV11: Nun 1H 31
FRANKTON 7B 84 (1B 144)
Frankton Av. CV3: Cov 3C 68
Frankton La. CV23: Stret D 4J 83
Frankton Rd. CV23: Bour D 6C 84
Frank Walsh Ho. CV1: Cov 3D 58
Frankwell Dr. CV2: W'grve S 5A 52
Fraser Cl. CV10: Nun 5G 21
Fraser Rd. CV6: Cov 5A 50
Fraser Way CV37: Welf A 3B 124
Frederick Neal Av. CV5: E Grn 3B 56
Frederick Press Way CV21: Rugby 5F 75
Frederick Rd. CV7: New A 4D 28
Frederick St. CV21: Rugby 5F 75
Fred Lee Gro. CV3: Cov 4D 68
Freeboard La. CV8: Rytn D 2G 83
Freeburn C'way. CV4: Canly 1G 67
Freehold St. CV1: Cov 2F 59
Freeman Cl. CV10: Nun 7J 21
Freeman Ct. CV37: S Avon 3E 114
Freemans Cl. CV32: Lea S 6C 98
Freeman St. CV6: Cov 1F 59
Freeman's Way CV1: Cov 5G 135 (5C 58)
Freemantle Rd. CV22: Bil 6C 74
Free Port B26: Birm A 3A 44
Freers M. CV34: Warw 4D 100
Freer St. CV11: Nun 2A 32
Freesland Ri. CV10: Nun 5G 21
Frensham Cl. B37: Chel W 3C 34
Frensham Dr. CV10: Nun 6G 21
Freshfield Cl. CV5: Alle 5G 49
Freshwater Gro. CV31: Lea S 2G 103
Fretton Cl. CV6: Cov 7F 51
Frevill Rd. CV6: Cov 6H 51
Frewen Rd. CV22: Caw 1K 85
Friars Cl. CV3: Bin W 1G 71
Friar's Ga. CV9: Ath 3C 16
Friars La. OX15: Lwr Bra 3J 133
Friars Rd. CV1: Cov 6H 135 (5C 58)
Friars St. CV34: Warw 2F 101
Friars Wlk. B37: Chel W 3D 34
Friary Cl. CV35: H Mag 2A 100
Friary Rd. CV9: Ath 2C 16
Friary St. CV11: Nun 6C 22
Friday Cl. B50: Bidf A 5G 123
CV37: Lwr Q 5J 125
Friday Furlong B50: Bidf A 5G 123
Friends Cl. CV8: Bag 5D 68
Frilsham Way CV5: Cov 3F 57
Frisby Ct. CV11: Nun 2A 32
Frisby Rd. CV4: Tile H 5C 56
Friswell Dr. CV6: Cov 6F 51
Friswell Ho. CV2: Cov 6K 51
FRITWELL 3D 147
Frobisher Rd. CV3: Cov 3C 68
CV22: Bil 7C 74
Frog La. CV36: Ilm 7B 126
CV37: Welf A 3B 124
Frogmere Cl. CV5: Alle 1F 57
Frogmore Rd. CV37: Snitt 6G 95
FROLESWORTH 2C 141
Front St. CV36: Ilm 7B 126
Frost Rd. CV35: Welle 2H 117
Fryer Av. CV32: Lea S 5C 98
Frythe Cl. CV8: Ken 3G 79
Fuchsia Cl. CV2: Cov 4H 51
Fulbrook La. CV35: Lwr F, Sher 1A 108 & 7C 100
Fulbrook Rd. CV2: Cov 5J 51
Fullers Cl. CV6: Cov 7K 49
Fullwood Cl. CV2: Ald G 4A 52
Fulwell M. B37: Mars G 5B 34
Furlong Mdw. CV36: Ship S 6H 131
Furlong Rd. CV1: Cov 7K 135 (6D 58)
Furnace Cl. CV12: Bed 1K 41
FURNACE END 1F 27
Furnace Rd. CV12: Bed 1K 41
Furness Cl. CV21: Brow 1K 75
Furr Marsh, The CV34: Warw 4D 100
Furrow Cl. CV21: Rugby 4K 75
Furrows, The CV47: Sou 4J 107
Furze Hill CV36: Ship S 6H 131
Furze Hill Rd. CV36: Ship S 6H 131
Fuschia Cl. CV10: Nun 4G 31
Futures Wlk. CV3: W'hall 2K 69
Fylde Ho. CV2: Cov 3K 59
Fynford Rd. CV6: Cov 2B 58

G

Gable Cl. CV22: Bil 1D 86
Gable M. B50: Bidf A 6F 123
Gables, The B78: Pole 7D 8
Gabor Cl. CV21: Rugby 2J 75
GADDESBY 1D 141
Gadsby Ct. CV11: Nun 1A 32
Gadsby St. CV11: Nun 1K 31
Gadshill CV34: H'cte 4C 102
GAGINGWELL 3D 147
GAILEY 1A 138
Gainford Ri. CV3: Bin 4B 60
Gainsborough Cres. CV21: Hillm 7D 76
Gainsborough Dr. CV12: Bed 1G 41
CV31: Lea S 2G 103
Gainsborough Rd. CV37: Shot 6C 114
Gainsborough Trad. Est. CV47: Sou 6G 107
Gala Bingo
Coventry 3K 135 (4D 58)
Radford 1B 58
Rugby 5G 75
Walsgrave on Sowe 7D 52
Galey's Rd. CV3: Cov 7D 58
Gallagher Bus. Pk. CV6: Longf 1E 50
CV34: H'cte 5B 102
Gallagher Retail Pk. CV6: Cov 6F 51
Gallagher Rd. CV12: Bed 3G 41
Gallagher Way CV6: Cov 7F 51
CV34: H'cte 5B 102
GALLEY COMMON 6E 20 (2A 140)
Galliards, The CV4: Canly 4H 67
GALLOWS GREEN 2A 142
Gallows Hill CV34: Warw 3J 101
Galmington Dr. CV3: Cov 2B 68
Gamecock Barracks CV11: Bram 7H 33
GANBOROUGH 3A 146
Gannaway Ct. CV35: N Lin 1F 95
Gannaway Rd. CV35: N Lin 1F 95
Garden Ct. CV34: Warw 7A 98
(Bridge St.)
CV34: Warw 1G 101
(Priory Rd.)
Garden Flats CV5: E Grn 2B 56
Garden Gro. CV12: Bed 5F 41
Gardenia Dr. CV5: Alle 1E 56
Garden Row CV35: Welle 3H 117
CV37: S Avon 5E 136
Gardens, The CV8: Ken 6E 78
CV23: Thurl 6K 85
CV31: Rad S 3J 103
Gardens, The CV37: S Avon 5E 136 (5E 114)
Garden Ter. CV35: Welle 3H 117
Gardner Ho. *CV1: Cov 5B 58*
(off Vincent St.)
Gardner Way CV8: Ken 7E 78
Garlands Cft. CV7: Ker E 7A 40
Garlick Dr. CV8: Ken 3G 79
Garnette Cl. CV10: Nun 6G 21
Garrard Cl. WR11: Salf P 7C 122
Garratt Cl. CV23: Long L 3B 74
Garrett St. CV11: Nun 2A 32
Garrick Cl. CV5: E Grn 3A 56
Garrick Way CV37: S Avon 6D 114
Garth Cres. CV3: Bin 7K 59
Garth Ho. CV3: Bin 1K 69
Garway Cl. CV32: Lill 3D 98
Garyth Williams Cl. CV22: Bil 1E 86
Gas Ho. La. B49: Alc 5C 112
Gas St. CV21: Rugby 5H 75
CV31: Lea S 1D 102
Gate Farm Dr. CV23: M Kirby 3K 55
Gatehouse, The CV31: Lea S 1B 102
Gatehouse Cl. CV21: Hillm 1C 88
Gatehouse La. CV12: Bed 3G 41
Gateside Rd. CV6: Cov 4E 50
GAULBY 1D 141
Gaulby Wlk. CV3: Bin 6C 60
Gaveston Cl. CV34: Warw 7H 97
Gaveston Rd. CV6: Cov 1J 57
CV32: Lea S 6C 98
GAYDON 7G 119 (3A 144)
Gaydon Cl. CV6: Cov 6G 51
Gaydon Rd. CV47: Bis I 7A 110
Gaydon Vehicle Proving Ground CV33: L Hth 3K 119
Gayer St. CV6: Cov 5G 51
Gayhurst Cl. CV3: Bin 7A 60
GAYTON 3D 145
Gaza Cl. CV4: Tile H 6E 56
Gazelle Cl. CV1: Cov 2K 135 (4E 58)
Gentian Way CV23: Brow 7K 65
Gentlemans La. B95: Ullen 4A 90
GENTLESHAW 1B 138
Geoffrey Cl. CV2: Cov 2H 59
George Birch Cl. CV23: Brin 4C 62
George Eliot Av. CV12: Bed 3K 41
George Eliot Bldgs. *CV11: Nun 7D 22*
(off Mill St.)
George Eliot Rd. CV1: Cov 2D 58
George Eliot St. CV11: Nun 2J 31
George Hodgkinson Cl. CV4: Tile H 4D 56
George Marston Rd. CV3: Bin 6A 60
George Pk. Cl. CV2: Cov 5J 51
George Poole Ho. *CV1: Cov 5B 58*
(off Windsor St.)
George Rd. B46: Wat O 1C 24
CV34: Warw 7J 97
George Robertson Cl. CV3: Bin 1A 70
George Row CV23: Kils 6J 89
George's Elm La. B50: Bidf A 3G 123
George St. CV1: Cov 2D 58
CV7: New A 4E 28
CV11: Nun 2A 32
CV12: Bed 2H 41
CV21: Rugby 5F 75
CV31: Lea S 1E 102
CV47: S'ton 6C 106
George St. Ringway CV12: Bed 2H 41
Georgian Cl. B49: Alc 4B 112
Gerard Av. CV4: Canly 7F 57
Gerard Ct. CV22: Caw 1A 86
Gerard Pl. CV22: Caw 1A 86
Gerard Rd. B49: Alc 3D 112
CV22: Caw 1A 86
Gerrards Rd. CV36: Ship S 5H 131
Gerrard St. CV34: Warw 2G 101
GIBBET HILL 6H 67
Gibbet Hill Rd. CV4: Canly 3F 67
Gibbons Cl. CV4: Tile H 5D 56
Gibbs Cl. CV2: W'grve S 1D 60
Gibson Cres. CV12: Bed 4G 41
Gibson Dr. CV21: Hillm 7C 76
Gielgud Way CV2: W'grve S 6D 52
Giffard Wlk. *CV22: Caw 1A 86*
(off Frewen Rd.)
Giffard Way CV34: Warw 6G 97
Gifford Rd. CV33: L Hth 1K 119
Gifford Wlk. CV37: S Avon 3B 114
GIGGETTY 2A 138
Gigg La. B76: Wis 1B 18
Gilbert Av. CV22: Bil 6D 74
Gilbert Cl. CV1: Cov 4E 58
CV12: Bed 4H 41
CV37: S Avon 1E 114
GILBERT'S GREEN 2B 90 (1C 143)
Giles Cl. CV6: Cov 4C 50
Gilfil Rd. CV10: Nun 3H 31
Gilkes La. CV35: Oxh 1E 130
Gillett Cl. CV11: Nun 1H 31
Gillett's La. OX15: Up Bra 2F 133
Gillian's Wlk. CV2: W'grve S 6C 52
Gillquart Way CV1: Cov 7K 135 (6D 58)
GILMORTON 3C 141
GILSON 3D 24
Gilson Dr. B46: Col 5D 24
Gilson Rd. B46: Col 3D 24
Gilson Way B37: K'hrst 7A 24
Gingles Ct. CV21: Hillm 1C 88
Ginkgo Wlk. CV31: Lea S 3D 102
Gipsy La. CV10: Nun 6J 31
CV11: Nun 6J 31
Girdlers Cl. CV3: Cov 3B 68
Girtin Cl. CV12: Bed 1G 41
Girton Ho. B36: Cas B 4A 24

Girvan Gro. CV32: Cubb 2G 99
Gisburn Cl. CV34: Warw 6H 97
Givens Ho. *CV1: Cov 5B 58*
(off Meadow St.)
Glade, The CV5: E Grn 4D 56
Gladiator Way CV21: Rugby 1F 75
Gladstone Ct. CV32: Lea S 6D 98
Gladstone St. CV21: Rugby 4F 75
Glaisdale Av. CV6: Cov 3E 50
Glamorgan Cl. CV3: W'hall 3K 69
Glaramara Cl. CV21: Brow 1K 75
GLASCOTE 1D 139
Glasshouse La. CV8: Ken 4G 79
Gleave Rd. CV31: W'nsh 5E 102
Glebe, The B95: Woot W 5H 93
CV7: Cor 6F 39
Glebe Av. CV12: Bed 4E 40
Glebe Cl. B50: Bidf A 6G 123
CV4: Tile H 1E 66
CV47: S'ton 6C 106
Glebe Cres. CV8: Ken 6E 78
CV21: Rugby 5E 74
Glebe Est. CV37: Wilm 5H 113
Glebe Farm Gro. CV3: Bin 4B 60
Glebe Farm Ind. Est. CV21: Rugby 1F 75
Glebe Farm Mus. 5J 113
Glebe Farm Rd. CV21: Rugby 1F 75
Glebe Flds. B76: Curd 5B 18
Glebe La. CV11: Nun 5G 23
(not continuous)
Glebe Pl. CV31: Lea S 1F 103
Glebe Ri. CV9: Aus 7H 7
Glebe Rd. CV11: Nun 7E 22
CV37: S Avon 3B 114
CV47: Sou 4G 107
Gleeson Dr. CV34: Warw 6G 97
Glen Cl. CV36: Ship S 4H 131
Glencoe Rd. CV3: Cov 5H 59
Glendale Av. CV8: Ken 3E 78
Glendale Way CV4: Tile H 5A 56
Glendon Gdns. CV12: Bulk 2E 42
Glendower CV37: S Avon 1H 137
Glendower App. CV34: H'cte 5C 102
Glendower Av. CV5: Cov 5H 57
Gleneagles Cl. CV11: Nun 3E 32
Gleneagles Rd. CV2: Cov 1A 60
Glenfern Gdns. CV8: Rytn D 6A 70
GLENFIELD 1C 141
Glenfield Av. CV10: Nun 4D 22
Glenhurst Rd. B95: Hen A 3G 93
Glenmore Dr. CV6: Longf 1F 51
Glenmount Av. CV6: Longf 1F 51
Glenn St. CV6: Cov 3D 50
GLEN PARVA 2C 141
Glenridding Cl. CV6: Longf 1F 51
Glenrosa Wlk. CV4: Tile H 1E 66
Glenroy Cl. CV2: Cov 1A 60
Glentworth Av. CV6: Cov 4A 50
Glenville Av. CV9: Wood E 2K 13
Glenwood Gdns. CV12: Bed 1G 41
Globe Ct. B49: Alc 5B 112
GLOOSTON 2D 141
Gloster Dr. CV8: Ken 3D 78
Gloster Gdns. CV35: Welle 5G 117
Glosters Grn. CV35: Kine 5D 120
Gloucester Cl. CV11: Nun 4H 23
Gloucester Ct. CV37: S Avon 3G 137 (4F 115)
Gloucester St. CV1: Cov 4B 58
Gloucester St. CV31: Lea S 1E 102
Gloucester Way B37: Mars G 4A 34
Glover Cl. CV34: Warw 4D 100
Glovers Cl. CV7: Mer 5E 46
CV9: Man 4E 16
Glovers Cft. B37: F'bri 2A 34
Glover St. CV3: Cov 7D 58
GLYMPTON 3D 147
GOADBY 2D 141
Godfrey Cl. CV31: Rad S 3J 103
Godiva Pl. CV1: Cov 4E 58
Godiva Trading Est. CV6: Cov 6F 51
Godsons La. CV47: Nap 2J 111
Goldacre Cl. CV31: W'nsh 4D 102
Gold Av. CV22: Caw 1B 86
Gold Cl. CV11: Nun 4A 32
Goldcrest Cft. B36: Cas B 4A 24
Golden Acres La. CV3: Bin 1B 70
Goldicote Rd. CV35: Lox 7C 116
Goldsmith Av. CV22: Rugby 2F 87
CV34: Warw 3E 100
Goldthorn Cl. CV5: E Grn 3B 56
Golf Dr. CV11: Nun 4C 32
Golf La. CV31: W'nsh 5F 103
Gooch's Way CV31: W'nsh 4E 102
Goodacre Cl. CV23: Clift D 3C 76
Goode Cl. CV34: Warw 1E 100
Goode Cft. CV4: Tile H 5D 56
Goodere Av. B78: Pole 2D 10
Goodere Dr. B78: Pole 7D 8
Goodfellow St. CV32: Lea S 6A 98
Goodman Way CV4: Tile H 6A 56
Goodway Ho. CV32: Lea S 7B 98
Goodwood Cl. CV3: W'hall 2J 69
CV37: S Avon 6C 114
GOODYERS END 5C 40
Goodyers End La. CV12: Bed 5C 40
GOOM'S HILL 3B 142
GORCOTT HILL 2B 142
Gordon Cl. CV12: Bed 1H 41
Gordon Pas. CV31: Lea S 1E 102
Gordon St. CV1: Cov 6A 58
CV31: Lea S 1E 102
Goring Rd. CV2: Cov 3G 59
GORNALWOOD 2A 138
Gorse Cl. B37: F'bri 3A 34
CV22: Bil 7E 74
Gorse Farm Rd. CV11: Nun 4D 32
Gorse La. B95: Woot W 4G 93
CV37: Lwr Q, Up Qui 6H 125
Gorse Lea CV47: Sou 4G 107
Gorseway CV5: Cov 4G 57
Gorsey La. B46: Col 2E 24
Gorsey Way B46: Col 2E 24
Gorsy Way CV10: Nun 6J 21
GOSFORD GREEN 5F 59
Gosford Ind. Est. CV1: Cov 5F 59
Gosford St. CV1: Cov 4K 135 (5D 58)
GOSPEL END VILLAGE 2A 138
Gospel Oak La. CV37: Snitt 7F 95
Gospel Oak Rd. CV6: Cov 2B 50
Gosport Rd. CV6: Cov 6E 50
Gossett La. CV3: Bin W 1G 71
Gould Rd. CV35: H Mag 1C 100
Governor's Ct. CV34: Warw 7F 97
Gower Memorial, The 4J 137
Grace Rd. CV5: Mil W 6J 47
Grafton Cl. B98: Redd 1A 92
CV8: Ken 6E 78
GRAFTON FLYFORD 3A 142
Grafton La. B50: Bidf A 5J 123
GRAFTON REGIS 3D 145
Grafton Rd. B49: Ard G, Wix 1F 123
B50: Ard G 1F 123
Grafton St. CV1: Cov 5E 58
Graham Cl. CV6: Cov 5H 51
Graham Rd. CV21: Rugby 4J 75
Graham St. CV11: Nun 6D 22
Gramer Ct. CV9: Man 5E 16
Granborough Cl. CV3: Bin 7B 60
Granborough Ct. CV32: Lill 4E 98
Granby Rd. CV10: Nun 1F 31
CV36: H'ton 1K 131
GRANDBOROUGH 6H 105 (2B 144)
Grandborough Flds. Rd. CV23: Gran, Gran F 7F 105
Grand Dpt. Rd. CV11: Bram 6H 33
Grandys Cft. B37: F'bri 2A 34
Grange, The CV32: Cubb 2K 99
CV32: Lea S 6F 99
CV34: Warw 1K 101
Grange Av. CV3: Bin 1B 70
CV3: Finh 5C 68
CV8: Ken 2C 78
Grange Cl. CV10: Nun 4H 21
CV34: Warw 7A 98
CV47: Sou 4H 107
OX15: Ratl 6C 128
Grange Farm Dr. CV47: S'ton 6C 106
Grange Gdns. CV35: Welle 3H 117
Grange M., The CV32: Lea S 6B 98
Grangemouth Rd. CV6: Cov 1B 58
Grange Pk. CV37: S Avon 3F 115
Grange Rd. B50: Bidf A 6H 123
CV6: Longf 2G 51
CV10: Harts 1G 21
CV21: N'bld A 2E 74
CV32: Lill 4E 98
CV37: Bear 6C 94
Grange Wlk. CV6: Longf 1H 51
Granleigh Ct. CV32: Cubb 2J 99
Granoe Cl. CV3: Bin 7A 60
Grantham St. CV2: Cov 4F 59
Grantley Dr. B37: F'bri 2B 34
Grant Rd. CV3: Cov 5H 59
CV7: Exh 5G 41
Grants Cl. CV47: Fen C 3G 121
Granville Ct. CV36: Ship S 4H 131
Granville Rd. CV35: Welle 3G 117
Granville St. CV32: Lea S 5E 98
Grapes Cl. CV6: Cov 2B 58
Grasmere Av. CV3: Cov 2K 67
Grasmere Cl. CV21: Brow 2K 75
Grasmere Ct. CV37: S Avon 1H 137
Grasmere Cres. CV11: Nun 4G 23
Grasmere Rd. CV12: Bed 3H 41
Grasscroft Dr. CV3: Cov 2E 68
Grassington Av. CV34: Warw 6H 97
Grassington Dr. B37: F'bri 4A 34
CV11: Nun 2C 32
Gratton Ct. CV3: Cov 2K 67
Gravel, The B76: Wis 1B 18
Gravel Hill CV4: Tile H 6C 56
GRAVELLY HILL 2C 139
Graylands, The CV3: Finh 4C 68
Grayling Wlk. B37: Chel W 2C 34
Grays Orchard CV23: Thurl 7K 85
Grayswood Av. CV5: Cov 3H 57
GREAT ALNE 3F 113 (3C 143)
Gt. Balance CV23: Brin 4B 62
GREAT BARR 2B 138
Great Borne CV21: Brow 7J 65
GREAT BOURTON 1D 147
GREAT BOWDEN 3D 141
GREAT BRINGTON 2D 145
Gt. Central Way CV21: Rugby 4K 75
Gt. Central Way Ind. Est. CV21: Rugby 3K 75
Great Garden of New Place, The 5G 137
GREAT GLEN 2D 141
GREAT HEATH 1E 58 (3A 140)
Greatheed Rd. CV32: Lea S 6C 98
GREAT OXENDON 3D 141
GREAT RISSINGTON 3A 146
GREAT ROLLRIGHT 2C 147
GREAT SAREDON 1A 138
GREAT TEW 3C 147
Gt. William St. CV37: S Avon 2F 137 (4F 115)
GREAT WOLFORD 7A 132 (2B 146)
GREATWORTH 1D 147
GREAT WYRLEY 1A 138
Greaves Cl. CV34: Warw 1A 102
Greaves Way, The CV47: Bis I 6C 110
GREEN, THE 6G 95
Green, The B46: Shu 2B 26
B76: Lea M 4G 19
B78: K'bry 5D 12
B79: Seck 5A 6
B94: Tan A 3D 90
B96: Sam 7B 92
CV7: Mer 5D 46
CV8: S'lgh 3C 80
CV9: Aus 7H 7
CV9: Man 5F 17
CV10: Harts 1G 21
CV11: Nun 2A 32
CV22: Bil 1C 86
CV22: Dunc 6C 86
CV23: Barby 7E 88
CV23: C'over 1H 65
CV23: Harb M 4B 64
CV23: Lilb 2J 77
CV23: Long L 4A 74
CV35: Clav 1D 94
CV35: Light 2G 119
CV35: Lit K 7C 120
CV35: Mid T 6C 130
CV35: Rad 5A 128
CV36: Lit Wol 7D 132
CV37: A'ton 1C 116
CV37: Snitt 7F 95
CV37: Wilm 5J 113
CV47: Long I 2C 106
CV47: P Mars 6G 111
GL56: Stret O 2C 132
OX17: Warm 2J 129
Green Cl. B80: Stud 4D 92
CV23: Long L 4K 73
CV31: W'nsh 4F 103
Green Ct. CV21: Rugby 4K 75
Greendale Cl. CV9: Ath 4D 16
Greendale Rd. CV5: Cov 4H 57
CV9: Ath 4D 16
GREEN END 4H 37 (3D 139)
Green End CV47: Long I 2C 106
Grn. End Rd. CV7: Fill 3E 36
Grn. Farm Cl. CV23: Lilb 2J 77
Grn. Farm End CV35: Kine 5D 120
Green Fld., The CV3: Cov 7H 59
Greenfields Cl. CV36: Ship S 5H 131
Greenfinch Rd. B36: Cas B 4A 24
Green Gates B95: Hen A 1H 93
GREEN HEATH 1A 138
GREENHILL 1A 142
Greenhill Rd. CV22: Bil 7F 75
CV31: W'nsh 4F 103
Greenhill St. CV37: S Avon 3D 136 (4E 114)
Greenland Av. CV5: Alle 2D 56
Greenland Ct. CV5: Alle 2D 56
GREENLANDS 2B 142
Greenlands Rd. B37: Chel W 3B 34
GREEN LANE
Coventry 4B 68
Redditch 1B 92 (2B 142)
Green La. B46: Col 7F 25
(Castle Dr., not continuous)
B46: Col 4B 24
(Collector Rd., not continuous)
B46: Col 1D 34
(Ryeclose Cft.)
B77: Wiln 3A 10
(not continuous)
B78: B'moor 3A 10
B80: Stud 2A 92
CV3: Cov, Finh 2A 68
CV3: Finh 4B 68
CV7: Cor 7B 38
CV7: Fill 2D 38
CV8: Bran 1H 71
CV9: Gren 5J 11
CV10: Nun 5H 21
CV23: Brin 3B 62
CV23: Chu L 3G 73
CV34: Warw 7H 97
CV35: Oxh 1D 130
CV36: Ship S 5H 131
Green La. Cl. CV36: Ship S 5H 131
Greenleaf Cl. CV5: E Grn 4E 56
Greenmoor Rd. CV10: Nun 7B 22
Greenodd Dr. CV6: Longf 1F 51
Greens Cl. CV23: C'over 1J 65
Greenside Cl. CV11: Nun 3D 32
Greensleeves Cl. CV6: Cov 4B 50
GREENS NORTON 3D 145
Green's Rd. CV6: Cov 5A 50
Greensward, The CV3: Bin 5C 60
Greensward Cl. CV8: Ken 3F 79
Greenswood CV37: Bear 6D 94
Greens Yd. CV12: Bed 2H 41
Greenway B78: Pole 6D 8
CV11: Nun 4D 32
CV34: Warw 6G 97
Greenway, The B37: Mars G 7A 34
Greenway Cl. CV36: Ship S 4G 131
Greenway Rd. CV36: Ship S 4G 131
Greenways CV4: Tile H 5A 56
Greenways, The CV32: Lill 4F 99
Greenways Ct. CV36: Ship S 4G 131
Greenwood Cl. CV23: Long L 3A 74
Greenwood Ct. CV11: Nun 1B 32
CV32: Lea S 6F 99
Greenwood Sq. *B37: Chel W 3B 34*
(off Chelmsley Wood Shop. Cen.)

Greenwood Way *B37: Chel W* 3B 34
(off Chelmsley Wood Shop. Cen.)
Gregory Av. CV3: Cov 2A 68
Gregory Hood Rd. CV3: Cov 3D 68
Greig Cen., The 4C 112
GRENDON
Baddesley Ensor 7G 11
Bradley Green 4J 11 (2D 139)
Grendon Cl. CV4: Tile H 6A 56
GRENDON COMMON 1F 15 (2D 139)
Grendon Dr. CV21: Brow 1A 76
Grendon Rd. B78: Pole 1D 10
Grenfell Cl. CV31: Lea S 2H 103
Grenville Av. CV2: Cov 4H 59
Grenville Cl. CV22: Bil 7C 74
Gresham Av. CV32: Lill 5F 99
Gresham Pl. CV32: Lill 5F 99
Gresham Rd. CV10: Nun 4H 31
Gresham St. CV2: Cov 5G 59
Gresley Rd. CV2: Cov 7K 51
Greswold Cl. CV4: Tile H 6D 56
Greswoldes, The CV31: Rad S 2K 103
Gretna Rd. CV3: Finh 4K 67
Greville Ho. *CV34: Warw* 1H 101
(off Yeomanry Cl.)
Greville Rd. B49: Alc 3A 112
CV8: Ken 5D 78
CV34: Warw 6K 97
Greville Smith Av. CV31: W'nsh 4F 103
Greycoat Rd. CV6: Cov 4A 50
Greyfriars Ct. CV6: Cov 7A 50
Greyfriars La. CV1: Cov 5H 135 (5C 58)
Greyfriars Rd. CV1: Cov 5G 135 (5C 58)
Grey Mill La. B95: Woot W 7G 93
Greys Rd. B80: Stud 4D 92
GRIFF 6G 31 (3A 140)
Griff Cvn. Site CV10: Nun 5J 31
GRIFF HOLLOW 4K 31
Griffin, Cen., The 5H 75
Griffin Rd. CV34: Warw 1A 102
Griffiths Ho. *CV21: Brow* 1J 75
(off Dovedale Cl.)
Griff La. CV10: Griff 5F 31
(not continuous)
Griff Way CV10: Nun 5H 31
GRIMSCOTE 3D 145
Grimshaw Hill B95: Ullen 7C 90
Grimston Cl. CV3: Bin 5C 60
Grindal Pl. CV22: Caw 1K 85
Grindle Rd. CV6: Longf 2F 51
Grindley Ho. *CV1: Cov* 5B 58
(off Windsor St.)
Grizebeck Dr. CV5: Alle 2E 56
Grizedale CV21: Brow 1J 75
GROBY 1C 141
Grosvenor Ct. CV32: Lea S 6D 98
Grosvenor Ho. CV1: Cov 6F 135 (5B 58)
Grosvenor Lwr. Rd. CV1: Cov 6F 135 (6B 58)
Grosvenor Rd. CV1: Cov 6F 135 (6B 58)
CV21: Rugby 5H 75
CV31: Lea S 3E 102
Grounds Farm La. CV8: Ken 5B 78
Grouse Cl. CV37: B'ton 2B 114
Grove, The B46: Col 1F 35
B80: Stud 4C 92
(not continuous)
B92: H Ard 5G 45
CV12: Bed 2H 41
Grove Ct. CV5: Cov 7B 58
Grove Cft. CV35: H Hill 3A 100
GROVE END 3G 133
Grove Flds. CV10: Nun 3D 22
Grove Ho. CV37: S Avon 4D 136 (5E 114)
Grovehurst Pk. CV8: S'lgh P 7B 80
Grovelands Ind. Est. CV7: Exh 7G 41
Grove La. B76: Wis 1A 18 & 2A 18
B94: Lapw 1F 91
CV7: Ker E 6K 39
Grove Pk. CV35: H Hill 3A 100
Grove Pl. CV10: Nun 1D 30
CV31: Lea S 2E 102
(not continuous)
Grove Rd. CV7: Ansty 3E 52
CV9: Ath 4C 16
CV10: Nun 1D 30
CV37: S Avon 6C 136 (5E 114)
Grove St. CV1: Cov 3K 135 (4D 58)
CV32: Lea S 7C 98
Grump St. CV36: Ilm 7B 126
Guardhouse Rd. CV6: Cov 6B 50
Guernsey Dr. B36: Cas B 6B 24
Guild Chapel, The 6F 137
Guild Cotts., The *CV34: Warw* 2G 101
(off Bowling Grn. St.)
Guildford Ct. CV6: Cov 7D 50
Guildford Cft. B37: Mars G 5A 34
Guild Rd. B95: Aston C 2K 113
CV6: Cov 7D 50
Guild St. CV37: S Avon 2F 137 (4F 115)
Guillemard Ct. B37: Chel W 4B 34
GUILSBOROUGH 1D 145
Guilsborough Rd. CV3: Bin 7A 60
Guinea Cres. CV4: W'wd H, 2B 66
GUITING POWER 3A 146
Gulistan Ct. CV32: Lea S 6C 98
Gulistan Rd. CV32: Lea S 6C 98
Gullet, The B78: Pole 1C 10
Gulliman's Way CV31: Lea S 2H 103
Gulson Rd. CV1: Cov 5K 135 (5E 58)
GUMLEY 2D 141
Gundry Cl. CV31: Lea S 1E 102
GUN HILL 5D 28
Gun Hill CV7: New A 4E 28
Gun La. CV2: Cov 2G 59
Gunn Ct. B49: Gt Alne 2F 113
Gunn End CV36: Ship S 3H 131
Gunners La. B80: Stud 3D 92
Gunnery Ter. CV32: Lea S 6B 98
Gunnings Rd. B49: Alc 4C 112
GUNSTONE 1A 138
Gunton Av. CV3: W'hall 2J 69
Guphill Av. CV5: Cov 4H 57
Gurney Cl. CV4: Tile H 4C 56
Gutteridge Av. CV6: Cov 4A 50
Guy Pl. E. CV32: Lea S 6D 98
Guy Pl. W. CV32: Lea S 6D 98
Guy Rd. CV8: Ken 7D 78
GUY'S CLIFFE 4J 97
Guy's Cliffe Av. CV32: Lea S 5A 98
Guy's Cliffe House 5J 97
Guy's Cliffe Rd. CV32: Lea S 6B 98
Guy's Cliffe Ter. CV34: Warw 1H 101
Guys Cl. CV34: Warw 7H 97
Guys Cross Pk. Rd. CV34: Warw 7H 97
Guy St. CV32: Lea S 6D 98
CV34: Warw 1H 101
Gypsy La. B46: Wat O 2D 24
B78: Dord 6D 10
CV8: Ken 7D 78
CV9: Ath 1C 16
CV9: Bad E 6D 10

H

Hackwell St. CV47: Nap 2H 111
Haddon End CV3: Cov 2E 68
Haddon Rd. CV32: Lill 5F 99
Haddon St. CV6: Cov 6G 51
HADEMORE 1C 139
Hadfield Cl. CV23: Clift D 3C 76
Hadfield Way B37: F'bri 1A 34
Hadleigh Rd. CV3: Finh 5C 68
HADLEY 2A 142
Hadleys Cft. B78: K'bry 6E 12
Hadrian Cl. CV32: Lill 3F 99
Hadrian Dr. B46: Col 3F 25
Hadrians Wlk. B49: Alc 5A 112
Hadrians Way CV21: Rugby 1F 75
HADZOR 2A 142
HAGLEY 3A 138
Haig Ct. CV22: Bil 7E 74
HAILES 2A 146
Hales Cl. CV37: Snitt 5G 95
Hales Ind. Pk. CV6: Longf 2E 50
HALESOWEN 3A 138
Hales St. CV1: Cov 2H 135 (4C 58)
(not continuous)
HALFORD 2J 127 (1B 146)
Halford Gro. CV35: Hatt 5A 96
Halford La. CV6: Cov 5A 50
Halford Lodge CV6: Cov 4A 50
Halford Rd. CV37: Arms 4G 127
CV37: Ett 2B 126
CV37: S Avon 6D 114
Halfway La. CV22: Dunc 6B 86
Halifax Cl. CV5: Alle 7E 48
CV35: Welle 5F 117
Hallam Rd. CV6: Cov 3B 50
Hallam's Cl. CV8: Bran 3H 71
Hallbrook Rd. CV6: Cov 3A 50
Hall Cl. CV8: S'lgh 3B 80
CV23: Kils 6J 89
Hall Cl., The CV22: Dunc 7C 86
Hall Ct. B78: Pole 1D 10
Hall Dr. B37: Mars G 6A 34
CV8: Bag 5E 68
HALL END 5C 10
HALLEND 6E 90
Hall End CV11: Nun 2K 31
Hall End Pl. CV11: Nun 2K 31
Hallfields CV31: Rad S 3J 103
HALL GREEN
Birmingham 3C 139
Coventry 4H 51
Hall Grn. Rd. CV6: Cov 4H 51
Hall Gro. CV23: Brin 3C 62
Hall La. CV2: W'grve S 1B 60
CV9: With 3G 17
CV33: Har 5H 109
LE10: Wlvy 2H 33
Hall Rd. CV32: Lea S 6D 98
LE10: Wlvy 2H 33
Hall's Cl. CV31: W'nsh 5F 103
Halls Croft 7F 137 (5F 115)
Hall Wlk. B46: Col 7E 24
(not continuous)
Hallway Dr. CV7: Shil 7G 43
HALSTEAD 1D 141
Hamar Way B37: Mars G 4B 34
Hambridge Rd. CV47: Bis I 6C 110
Hames La. B79: Newt R 4D 6
HAM GREEN 2B 142
HAMILTON 1D 141
Hamilton Cl. CV10: Nun 7J 21
CV12: Bed 4C 40
Hamilton Ct. CV10: Nun 7J 21
Hamilton Dr. B80: Stud 4C 92
Hamilton Rd. CV2: Cov 4G 59
CV31: Rad S 3J 103
CV37: Tidd 4K 115
Hamilton Ter. CV32: Lea S 7D 98
Hamlet, The CV35: Leek W 1J 97
Hamlet Cl. CV11: Nun 3C 32
CV22: Bil 3D 86
Hammersley St. CV12: Bed 4E 40
Hammerton Way CV35: Welle 5G 117
HAMMERWICH 1B 138
Hammond Bus. Cen. CV11: Nun 1A 32
Hammond Cl. CV11: Nun 1A 32
Hammond Grn. CV35: Welle 2H 117
Hammond Rd. CV2: Cov 3F 59
Hammonds Ter. CV8: Ken 4B 78
Hampden Ct. CV47: Temp H 2B 120
Hampden Way CV22: Bil 2C 86
Hampdon Way CV35: Welle 4G 117
HAMPEN 3A 146
Hampshire Cl. CV3: Bin 7B 60
Hampton Av. CV10: Nun 7G 21
Hampton Cl. B98: Redd 1A 92
CV6: Cov 1F 59
Hampton Ct. B92: H Ard 7H 45
Hampton Cft. CV35: H Hill 3A 100
Hampton Grange CV7: Mer 5D 46
Hampton Gro. CV32: Lea S 6F 99
HAMPTON IN ARDEN 7G 45 (3D 139)
Hampton in Arden Station (Rail) 7H 45
Hampton La. CV7: Mer 6A 46
HAMPTON LOVETT 2A 142
HAMPTON LUCY 2B 118 (3D 143)
HAMPTON MAGNA 2B 100 (2D 143)
HAMPTON ON THE HILL 4J 81 (2D 143)
HAMPTON-ON-THE-HILL 2A 100
Hampton Rd. CV6: Cov 1F 59
CV34: Warw 3B 100
CV35: H Hill 3B 100
Hampton St. CV34: Warw 2F 101
HAMS HALL 7H 19
Hams Hall Distribution Pk. B46: Col 7H 19
(Faraday Av.)
B46: Col 6F 19
(Hams La.)
Hams La. B76: Lea M 6E 18
HAMSTEAD 2B 138
HANBURY 2A 142
Hanbury Cl. CV35: Kine 5D 120
Hanbury Pl. CV6: Cov 4G 51
Hanbury Rd. CV12: Bed 1J 41
Hancock Grn. CV4: Tile H 7D 56
Handcross Gro. CV3: Finh 3A 68
Handley Gro. CV34: Warw 6F 97
Handleys Cl. CV8: Rytn D 7C 70
Hands Paddock CV37: N'bld S 1G 127
HANDSWORTH 2B 138
Handsworth Cres. CV5: E Grn 3C 56
Hanford Cl. CV6: Cov 1E 58
Hanford Cl. Ind. Est. CV6: Cov 1E 58
Hangar Rd. B26: Birm A 3A 44
HANGING HAUGHTON 1D 145
Hangman's La. B79: Seck 4A 6
Hanover Gdns. CV21: Rugby 4H 75
CV32: Lea S 6E 98
Hanover Glebe CV11: Nun 2J 31
Hans Cl. CV2: Cov 3F 59
Hanson Av. CV36: Ship S 5G 131
Hanson Way CV6: Longf 2G 51
HANWELL 1D 147
Hanwood Cl. CV5: E Grn 3A 56
Hanworth Cl. CV32: Lill 4G 99
Hanworth Rd. CV34: Warw 7F 97
Harbet Dr. B40: Nat E C 2E 44
HARBORNE 3B 138
Harborough Cotts. B94: Lapw 3H 91
HARBOROUGH MAGNA 4B 64 (1B 144)
HARBOROUGH PARVA 4B 64
Harborough Rd. CV6: Cov 4B 50
CV23: Harb M 7C 64
Harbour Cl. B50: Bidf A 6F 123
Harbourne Cl. CV8: Ken 4E 78
HARBOURS HILL 2A 142
HARBURY 6H 109 (2A 144)
Harbury La. CV33: Bis T, Ches 6D 102
CV34: H'cte 4A 102
Harbury Rd. CV47: Ladb 2A 110
Harbury Spoilbank Nature Reserve 5K 109
Harby Cl. B37: Mars G 5B 34
Harcourt CV3: W'hall 3A 70
Harcourt Gdns. CV11: Nun 1J 31
Hardingwood La. CV7: Fill 3G 37
HARDWICK 2B 138
Hardwick Cl. CV5: E Grn 3E 56
Hardwick Rd. CV47: P Mars 7F 111
Hardwyn Cl. CV3: Bin 6D 60
Hardy Cl. CV10: Gall C 7F 21
CV22: Bil 6C 74
Hardy Rd. CV6: Cov 7A 50
Hare & Hounds La. CV10: Nun 2G 31
Harebell Wlk. B37: Chel W 3D 34
Harebell Way CV23: Brow 7K 65
Harefield Ho. CV2: Cov 4H 59
Harefield La. CV10: Arb, Nun 4E 30
Harefield Rd. CV2: Cov 4H 59
CV11: Nun 7D 22
Hareway La. CV35: Barf 7A 108
Harewood Rd. CV5: Cov 4G 57
Harger Ct. CV8: Ken 5D 78
Harger M. CV8: Ken 5D 78
Hargrave Cl. B46: Wat O 1B 24
CV3: Bin 6C 60
CV23: Gran 6H 105
HARLASTON 1D 139
Harlech Cl. CV8: Ken 4G 79
HARLESTONE 2D 145
Harley St. CV2: Cov 4G 59
Harlow Wlk. CV2: W'grve S 7C 52
Harmar Cl. CV34: Warw 6F 97
Harmer Cl. CV2: W'grve S 7C 52
Harmony Ct. CV10: Nun 2H 31
Harnall La. CV1: Cov 1K 135 (3D 58)

Harnall La. E. CV1: Cov 1K **135** (3D **58**)
Harnall La. Ind. Est. CV1: Cov 1K **135** (3D **58**)
Harnall La. W. CV1: Cov 1H **135** (3D **58**)
Harnall Row *CV1: Cov* *5E 58*
(off Far Gosford St.)
CV1: Cov 4E **58**
(West St.)
Harold Cox Pl. CV22: Bil 3E **86**
Harold Rd. CV2: Cov 5K **59**
Harold's Orchard GL56: Stret O 2B **132**
Harold St. CV11: Nun 1J **31**
Harpenden Dr. CV5: Alle 2E **56**
Harper Rd. CV1: Cov 5E **58**
Harper's La. CV9: Man 5F **17**
HARPOLE 2D 145
Harrington Rd. CV6: Cov 2A **58**
Harrington Way CV10: Griff 5G **31**
Harriott Dr. CV34: H'cte 4B **102**
Harris Cl. B95: Hen A 2H **93**
Harris Dr. CV22: Rugby 1F **87**
Harris M. B95: Hen A 2H **93**
Harrison Cl. CV21: Hillm 1D **88**
Harrison Cres. CV12: Bed 3G **41**
Harrison Way CV31: Lea S 3D **102**
Harris Rd. CV3: Cov 5H **59**
CV34: Warw 7E **96**
Harrow Cl. CV6: Longf 2G **51**
Harrow Hill CV36: Long C 1C **134**
Harrow Rd. CV31: W'nsh 5F **103**
Harry Caplan Ho. CV5: Alle 1F **57**
Harry Edwards Ho. CV2: Cov 6K **51**
Harry Rose Rd. CV2: Cov 4A **60**
Harry Salt Ho. *CV1: Cov* *4E 58*
(off Canterbury St.)
Harry Stanley Ho. CV6: Cov 6G **51**
Harry Truslove Cl. CV6: Cov 7A **50**
Harry Weston Rd. CV3: Bin 6B **60**
Hart Cl. CV21: Hillm 6K **75**
Hartington Cres. CV5: Cov 6J **57**
Hartland Av. CV2: Cov 1H **59**
HARTLE 1A 142
HARTLEBURY 1A 142
Hartlepool Rd. CV1: Cov 1K **135** (3E **58**)
Hartley Gdns. CV47: Sou 6G **107**
Hartridge Wlk. CV5: Cov 3F **57**
HARTSHILL 3F 21 (2A 140)
Hartshill Hayes Country Pk. 2F 21
Hartshill Hayes Country Pk. Vis. Cen. 2E 20
Harvard Cl. CV35: Welle 5G **117**
Harvard House 4F 137
Harvesters Cl. CV3: Bin 5C **60**
Harvest Hill Cl. CV31: Lea S 2G **103**
Harvest Hill La. CV5: Alle 2J **47**
CV7: Mer 2J **47**
Harvey Cl. CV5: Alle 7E **48**
HARVINGTON
Evesham 3B 142
Kidderminster 1A 142
HASELBECH 1D 145
Haselbech Rd. CV3: Bin 6B **60**
Haselbury Cnr. CV10: Nun 3F **31**
HASELEY 2D 143
Haseley Cl. CV31: Lea S 3F **103**
Haseley Rd. CV2: Cov 5J **51**
HASELOR 3C 143
Haselor Cl. B49: Alc 4D **112**
Haselour Rd. B37: K'hrst 7A **24**
Hasilwood Sq. CV3: Cov 5H **59**
Hassall Cl. CV33: Bis T 5C **108**
Hastang Flds. CV31: Lea S 3G **103**
Hastings Rd. CV2: Cov 3G **59**
CV35: Welle 2H **117**
Haswell Cl. CV22: Rugby 6J **75**
Hatchford Wlk. B37: Chel W 4B **34**
HATFIELD 3A 142
Hathaway Dr. CV11: Nun 3C **32**
CV34: Warw 5F **97**
Hathaway Grn. La. CV37: S Avon 4A **114**
Hathaway Hamlet CV37: Shot 4B **114**
Hathaway La. CV37: Shot 5C **114**
Hathaway Rd. CV4: Tile H 6B **56**
Hatherell Rd. CV31: Rad S 3J **103**
HATHERTON 1A 138
Hatters Ct. CV12: Bed 3J **41**
Hatters Dr. CV9: Ath 1C **16**
HATTON 2D 143
Hatton Cl. CV35: Hatt 5A **96**
Hatton Country World 2D 143
Hatton Lock Flight 2D 143
HATTON PARK 4A 96
Hatton Ter. CV35: Hatt 5A **96**
Hauley Gro. CV31: W'nsh 4E **102**
Haunch La. B76: Lea M 3G **19**
Haunchwood Pk. Dr. CV10: Gall C 7D **20**
Haunchwood Pk. Ind. Est. CV10: Gall C 7D **20**
Haunchwood Rd. CV10: Nun 7J **21**
HAUNTON 1D 139
Haven Cvn. Pk. B92: Bick 4C **44**
Havendale Cl. CV6: Cov 2B **58**
Hawk Cl. CV11: Nun 4D **32**
HAWKESBURY 7H 41
Hawkes Dr. CV34: H'cte 4B **102**
HAWKES END 4F 49 (3D 139)
Hawkeshead CV21: Brow 1K **75**
Hawkes Mill La. CV5: Alle 4E **48**
Hawkeswell La. B46: Col 2G **35**
Hawkesworth Dr. CV8: Ken 3E **78**
Hawkins Cl. CV22: Bil 7E **74**
Hawkins Rd. CV5: Cov 5A **58**
Hawksworth Cres. B37: Chel W 2D **34**
Hawksworth Dr. CV1: Cov 4A **58**
Hawlands CV21: Brow 2J **75**
HAWLING 3A 146
Hawthorn Av. CV9: Hurl 6K **13**
Hawthorn Cl. B49: Alc 3B **112**
Hawthorn Ct. CV4: Tile H 5C **56**
Hawthorne Av. CV7: New A 4F **29**
Hawthorne Cl. CV8: Wols 4J **71**
Hawthorne Ter. CV10: Nun 6K **21**
Hawthorn La. CV4: Tile H 4C **56**
(Delius St.)
CV4: Tile H 5C **56**
(Roosevelt Dr.)
Hawthorn Rd. CV31: Lea S 2D **102**
Hawthorns, The B78: K'bry 4D **12**
Hawthorn Ter. CV23: Harb M 4B **64**
Hawthorn Way CV10: Harts 3F **21**
CV22: Bil 7B **74**
CV36: Ship S 6H **131**
Haydock Cl. CV6: Ald G 2H **51**
CV37: S Avon 6C **114**
Haydon Cl. B80: Stud 3D **92**
Haydon Way B49: Cou 6E **92**
Hayes Cl. CV21: Brow 1K **75**
Hayes Grn. Rd. CV12: Bed 4F **41**
Hayes La. CV7: Exh 5F **41**
Hayes Rd. CV10: Harts 3F **21**
Hay La. CV1: Cov 4J **135** (5D **58**)
Hayle Av. CV34: Warw 6H **97**
Hayle Cl. CV11: Nun 6H **23**
HAYLEY GREEN 3A 138
Hay Mdw. CV36: Ship S 4G **131**
Haynestone Rd. CV6: Cov 1J **57**
Haynes Way CV21: Rugby 7F **65**
Hay Pool OX17: Farn 5J **121**
Hayton Grn. CV4: Tile H 7D **56**
(not continuous)
Haytor Ri. CV2: Cov 7J **51**
Hayward Cl. CV35: H Mag 2B **100**
Haywards Grn. CV6: Cov 7A **50**
Haywood La. CV35: Row 4K **91**
Hazel Cl. CV10: Harts 4F **21**
CV32: Lea S 5E **98**
Hazel Cft. B37: Chel W 4B **34**
Hazelcroft B78: K'bry 4D **12**
Hazel Gro. CV12: Bed 2K **41**
Hazell Way CV10: Nun 3G **31**
Hazell Way Ind. Est. CV10: Nun 3G **31**
Hazelmere Cl. CV5: Cov 3F **57**
Hazel Rd. CV6: Cov 5H **51**
CV10: Nun 6J **21**
HAZELSLADE 1B 138
Hazelwood Cl. CV22: Dunc 6B **86**
HAZLETON 3A 146
Hazlewood Cl. B49: Alc 5A **112**
Headborough Rd. CV2: Cov 2G **59**
Headington Av. CV6: Cov 4A **50**
Headland Cl. CV37: Welf A 3A **124**
Headland Ri. CV37: Welf A 3A **124**
Headland Rd. CV37: Welf A 2A **124**
Headlands, The CV5: Cov 3H **57**
HEADLESS CROSS 2B 142
HEADLEY HEATH 1B 142
Healey Cl. CV21: Brow 1J **75**
Healey Ct. CV34: Warw 1H **101**
Health Cen. Rd. CV4: Canly 4G **67**
Heanley La. CV9: Hurl 4A **14**
Hearsall Comn. CV5: Cov 5J **57**
Hearsall Ct. CV4: Cov 5H **57**
Hearsall La. CV5: Cov 5K **57**
Heart of England Crematorium CV11: Nun 1C **32**
Heart of England Way CV11: Nun 1B **32**
HEATH 5C 86
Heath, The CV22: Dunc 6C **86**
Heath Av. CV12: Bed 4E **40**
Heath Bus. Pk. CV8: Wols 7B **72**
HEATHCOTE 5C 102
Heathcote Ind. Est. CV34: H'cte 3A **102**
Heathcote La. CV34: H'cte 4A **102**
Heathcote Pk. CV34: H'cte 6C **102**
Heathcote Rd. CV31: W'nsh 5D **102**
Heathcote St. CV6: Cov 1A **58**
Heathcote Way CV34: H'cte 4B **102**
Heath Cres. CV2: Cov 1G **59**
HEATHENCOTE 3D 145
HEATH END
Nuneaton 2E 31
Walsall 1B 138
Heath End Rd. CV10: Nun 2E **30**
HEATHER 1A 140
Heather Cl. B36: Cas B 4A **24**
CV10: Nun 1F **31**
CV22: Bil 7E **74**
CV37: S Avon 4C **114**
CV47: Sou 4H **107**
Heather Ct. CV9: Ath 2C **16**
Heather Dr. CV12: Bed 3E **40**
Heather Rd. CV2: Cov 4J **51**
CV3: Bin W 1E **70**
Heath Farm La CV33: Light 2H **119**
Heath Farm La. CV35: Light 2H **119**
Heathfield Rd. CV5: Cov 5G **57**
HEATH GREEN 1B 142
Heathgreen Cl. B37: Chel W 2D **34**
Heath Grn. Way CV4: W'wd H 2D **66**
HEATH HAYES 1B 138
Heath La. CV23: Brin 7A **62**
Heathmere Dr. B37: F'bri 3A **34**
Heath Rd. CV2: Cov 3F **59**
CV12: Bed 4F **41**
Heath Ter. CV32: Lea S 6C **98**
HEATH TOWN 1A 138
Heath Way CV22: Hillm 1K **87**
Hebden Av. CV34: Warw 6G **97**
Hebden Way CV11: Nun 2C **32**
Heber Dr. CV33: Har 6G **109**
Heckley Rd. CV7: Exh 6G **41**
Heddle Gro. CV6: Cov 6H **51**
Hedge Cl. CV47: Ladb 3C **110**
Hedgefield Way CV4: Tile H 7D **56**
Hedgerows, The CV10: Nun 5A **22**
Hedgerow Wlk. CV6: Cov 2B **50**
Hedgetree Cft. B37: Chel W 3C **34**
Hedge Way CV10: Nun 4H **21**
Hedingham Gro. B37: Chel W 3D **34**
HEDNESFORD 1B 138
Heemstede La. CV32: Lea S 5E **98**
Heera Cl. CV6: Cov 7D **50**
Helena Cl. CV10: Nun 1F **31**
Helen St. CV6: Cov 1F **59**
Hele Rd. CV3: Cov 2D **68**
HELLIDON 3C 145
Hellidon Cl. CV32: Lill 5E **98**
Helmdon Cl. CV21: Brow 2K **75**
Helmsdale Rd. CV32: Lill 3F **99**
Helmswood Dr. B37: Chel W 5C **34**
Helston Cl. CV11: Nun 6H **23**
Helvellyn Way CV21: Brow 1K **75**
Hemdale CV11: Nun 7H **23**
Hemingford Rd. CV2: W'grve S 6B **52**
Heming Rd. B98: Redd 1D **92**
Hemlingford Cft. B37: Mars G 6A **34**
Hemlingford Rd. B78: K'bry 7E **12**
Hemmin Gdns. Mill CV35: Barf 2B **108**
Hemmings Cl. CV31: Rad S 3J **103**
Hempit La. B76: Wis 4A **18**
HEMPTON 2D 147
Hemsby Cl. CV4: Canly 1E **66**
Hemsworth Dr. CV12: Bulk 3D **42**
Henbrook La. OX15: Up Bra 3G **133**
Henbury Dr. B37: Chel W 1D **34**
Henderson Cl CV5: Alle 7G **49**
Hendre Cl. CV5: Cov 5G **57**
Hen La. CV6: Cov 3C **50**
Henley Cl. CV11: Nun 3G **23**
Henley Ct. B49: Alc 4C **112**
CV2: Cov 7K **51**
HENLEY GREEN 6K 51
HENLEY-IN-ARDEN 2H 93 (2C 143)
Henley-in-Arden Station (Rail) 2G 93
Henley Ind. Pk. CV2: Cov 7A **52**
Henley Mill La. CV2: Cov 7H **51**
Henley Rd. B49: Gt Alne 3F **113**
B95: Hen A, Ullen 7D **90**
B95: Ullen 6B **90**
CV2: Cov, W'grve S 5H **51**
CV31: Lea S 3F **103**
CV35: Clav 1B **94**
CV35: H Hill, N Lin . . . . 1F **95** & 4A **100**
Henley St. B49: Alc 4C **112**
CV37: S Avon 2E **136** (4E **114**)
Henley Wlk. CV2: Cov 6K **51**
Henrietta St. CV6: Cov 2E **58**
Henry Boteler Rd. CV4: Canly 1F **67**
Henry St. CV1: Cov 2H **135** (4C **58**)
CV8: Ken 4E **78**
CV11: Nun 2J **31**
CV21: Rugby 5G **75**
Henry's Way *CV31: W'nsh* *4E 102*
(off Dobson La.)
Henry Tanday Ct. CV32: Lea S 6C **98**
Henson Rd. CV12: Bed 4E **40**
Henwoods Ct. *CV36: Ship S* *3H 131*
(off Mayo Rd.)
Hepworth Rd. CV3: Bin 5D **60**
Herald Av. CV5: Cov 6G **57**
Herald Bus. Pk. CV3: Bin 1B **70**
Herald Rd. B26: Birm A 2C **44**
Heralds Ct. CV34: Warw 7K **97**
Herald Way CV3: Bin 1C **70**
Herbert Art Gallery, The & Mus. 4J 135 (5D 58)
Herberts La. CV8: Ken 4E **78**
Herbert St. CV10: Nun 1E **30**
Hercules La. CV35: Clav, Yarn C 1B **94**
Herdwycke Cl. CV47: Sou 5K **107**
Hereford Cl. CV10: Nun 7K **21**
Hereford Rd. CV11: Bram 6H **33**
Hereford Wlk. B37: Mars G 4A **34**
Heritage Ct. CV4: Canly 5H **67**
Heritage Dr. CV6: Longf 7J **41**
Heritage Motor Cen. 5F 119
Hermes Cl. CV34: Warw 3C **102**
Hermes Ct. CV34: Warw 3C **102**
Hermes Cres. CV2: Cov 7K **51**
Hermes Rd. B26: Birm A 2C **44**
Hermione Cl. CV34: H'cte 5D **102**
Hermitage Cl. B78: Pole 1C **10**
Hermitage La. B78: B'moor 1B **10**
Hermitage Rd. CV2: Cov 3J **59**
Hermitage Way CV8: Ken 6E **78**
Hermit's Cft. CV3: Cov 7K **135** (7D **58**)
Heronbank CV4: Tile H 5A **56**
Heron Cl. B49: Alc 3B **112**
Heron Ho. CV2: Cov 4H **59**
Heron La. CV37: B'ton 2B **114**
Heron Way CV37: N'bld S 1G **127**
Herrick Rd. CV2: Cov 4K **59**
Herring Rd. CV9: Ath 4D **16**
Hertford Pl. CV1: Cov 5F **135** (5B **58**)
Hertford Rd. B49: Alc 3C **112**
CV37: S Avon 6E **114**
Hertford St. CV1: Cov 4H **135** (5C **58**)
Heslop Cl. CV3: Bin 7B **60**
Hetton Cl. CV34: Warw 6H **97**
Hewitt Av. CV6: Cov 2B **58**
Hexby Cl. CV2: W'grve S 1C **60**
Hexworthy Av. CV3: Cov 3B **68**
Heybrook Cl. CV2: Cov 7J **51**
Heycroft CV4: Canly 4H **67**

Heyford Cl. CV2: Ald G . . . 3K 51
Heyford Leys
CV22: Rugby . . . 3F 87
HEYTHROP . . . 3C 147
Heyville Cft. CV8: Ken . . . 6G 79
Heywood Cl. CV6: Cov . . . 7G 51
Hibberd Ct. CV8: Ken . . . 5D 78
Hibbert Cl. CV22: Rugby . . . 7F 75
Hickey La. B79: Newt R . . . 5C 6
Hickman Rd. CV10: Gall C . . . 7D 20
Hicks Cl. CV34: Warw . . . 5H 97
HIDCOTE BARTRIM . . . 1A 146
HIDCOTE BOYCE . . . 1A 146
Hidcote Cl. CV11: Nun . . . 4B 32
CV22: Rugby . . . 6E 74
CV31: Lea S . . . 3G 103
Hidcote Gro. B37: Mars G . . . 6A 34
Hidcote Rd. CV8: Ken . . . 3G 79
Higham La. CV11: Nun . . . 6F 23
HIGHAM ON THE HILL . . . 2A 140
High Ash Cl. CV7: Exh . . . 6F 41
High Beech CV5: Alle . . . 1E 56
High Brink Rd. B46: Col . . . 5F 25
Highbury Grn. CV10: Nun . . . 4H 21
High Cft. CV35: Clav . . . 2C 94
Highcroft Cres. CV32: Lea S . . . 6A 98
Highdown Rd. CV31: Lea S . . . 2F 103
Highfield CV7: Mer . . . 5E 46
CV35: Hatt . . . 4A 96
Highfield Cl. CV8: Ken . . . 5C 78
CV37: Snitt . . . 5G 95
Highfield La. CV7: Cor . . . 4F 39
Highfield Rd. B80: Stud . . . 3C 92
CV2: Cov . . . 3F 59
CV11: Nun . . . 2K 31
CV37: S Avon . . . 2D 114
Highfield Ter. CV32: Lea S . . . 6B 98
Highgrove CV4: W'wd H . . . 3D 66
CV22: Bil . . . 2D 86
Highland Rd. CV5: Cov . . . 6K 57
CV8: Ken . . . 2F 79
CV32: Lill . . . 3F 99
Highlands Cl. CV34: Warw . . . 7H 97
High La. OX15: Up Bra . . . 4G 133
Highley Dr. CV6: Cov . . . 7C 50
High Pk. Cl. CV5: E Grn . . . 4D 56
High St. B46: Col . . . 4F 25
B49: Alc . . . 5B 112
B50: Bidf A . . . 6G 123
B50: Broom . . . 3E 122
B78: Pole . . . 7D 8
B80: Stud . . . 3D 92
B92: H Ard . . . 7G 45
B95: Hen A . . . 2H 93
CV1: Cov . . . 4H 135 (5C 58)
CV6: Cov . . . 5K 49
CV8: Ken . . . 4C 78
CV8: Rytn D . . . 7D 70
CV9: Hurl . . . 6K 13
CV11: Nun . . . 7C 22
CV12: Bed . . . 3H 41
CV21: Hillm . . . 1B 88
CV21: Rugby . . . 5G 75
CV23: Mart . . . 2D 104
CV31: Lea S . . . 1D 102
CV32: Cubb . . . 2J 99
CV33: Har . . . 6H 109
CV34: Warw . . . 2G 101
CV35: Barf . . . 1C 108
CV36: Ship S . . . 4H 131
CV37: S Avon . . . 5G 137 (5F 115)
CV37: Welf A . . . 2A 124
CV47: Bis I . . . 6B 110
CV47: Fen C . . . 3G 121
CV47: Nap . . . 3H 111
CV47: Sou . . . 5H 107
CV47: S'ton . . . 6C 106
OX15: Lwr Bra . . . 3H 133
OX15: Ratl . . . 7D 128
HIGH TOWN . . . 1A 138
High Town CV23: Prin . . . 7G 83
Highview CV9: Hurl . . . 7K 13
High Vw. Dr. CV7: Ash G . . . 6C 40
High Vw. Rd. CV32: Cubb . . . 2G 99
Highwayman's Cft. CV4: Canly . . . 3H 67
Hiker Gro. B37: Chel W . . . 3D 34
Hilary Rd. CV4: Canly . . . 2H 67
CV10: Nun . . . 6A 22
Hilditch Way CV11: Nun . . . 3A 32
HILL
Pershore . . . 3A 142
Rugby . . . 7E 104 (2B 144)
Hill, The CV47: S'ton . . . 5C 106
Hillary Rd. CV22: Rugby . . . 1E 86
Hill Cl. CV32: Lill . . . 4E 98
Hill Cl. CV47: N'end . . . 1D 120
Hill Cres. CV23: Stret D . . . 3H 83
Hillcrest CV32: Cubb . . . 2J 99
Hill Crest Farm Cl. B79: Wart . . . 5H 9
Hillcrest Rd. B78: Dord . . . 3D 10
CV10: Nun . . . 5J 21
Hill Farm Av. CV11: Nun . . . 3D 32
Hillfield Rd. CV22: Bil . . . 7C 74
HILLFIELDS . . . 1K 135 (3E 58)
Hillfields Ho. CV1: Cov . . . 4E 58
Hillfray Dr. CV3: Cov . . . 3G 69
HILL FURZE . . . 3A 142
Hilliard Cl. CV12: Bed . . . 1G 41
HILLIARD'S CROSS . . . 1C 139
Hill La. CV37: Up Qui . . . 7H 125
OX15: Up Bra . . . 1F 133
Hillman Way CV37: Ett . . . 2C 126
HILLMORTON . . . 1C 88 (1C 145)
Hillmorton La. CV23: Clift D . . . 6C 76
CV23: Lilb . . . 3H 77
Hillmorton Rd. CV2: Cov . . . 4J 51
CV22: Rugby . . . 6G 75
Hill Rd. CV7: Ker E . . . 7K 39
CV23: Gran . . . 6F 105
Hill Side B78: K'bry . . . 7E 12
Hillside CV2: Cov . . . 1G 59
CV10: Harts . . . 3F 21
CV33: Har . . . 5G 109
CV47: Nap . . . 1H 111
Hillside Cl. CV37: S Avon . . . 3A 114
Hillside Cft. CV47: Nap . . . 1H 111
Hillside Dr. B37: K'hrst . . . 1A 34
CV10: Nun . . . 4H 21
Hillside Gdns. B37: K'hrst . . . 1A 34
Hillside Nth. CV2: Cov . . . 1G 59
Hillside Rd. CV37: S Avon . . . 3B 114
Hill St. CV1: Cov . . . 3F 135 (4B 58)
CV10: Nun . . . 7J 21
CV12: Bed . . . 7H 31
CV21: Rugby . . . 4F 75
CV32: Lea S . . . 6E 98
CV34: Warw . . . 7K 97
HILL TOP . . . 3F 29
Hill Top CV1: Cov . . . 3J 135 (4D 58)
CV9: Bad E . . . 1E 14
CV35: Lox . . . 6D 116
Hilltop Cl. CV47: Sou . . . 4G 107
Hilltop Pk. CV23: Prin . . . 7H 83
Hill Vw. CV37: S Avon . . . 3A 114
CV47: Bis I . . . 7B 110
Hill Vw. Rd. B50: Bidf A . . . 5H 123
Hill Wooton Rd. CV32: B'dwn . . . 1J 97
HILL WOOTTON . . . 1A 98 (2A 144)
Hill Wootton Rd. CV35: Hill W, Leek W . . . 1J 97
Hillyard Rd. CV47: Sou . . . 4G 107
HILTON . . . 1B 138
Hilton Av. CV10: Nun . . . 5G 21
Hilton Ct. CV5: Cov . . . 5K 57
HIMBLETON . . . 3A 142
HIMLEY . . . 2A 138
Himley Rd. CV12: Bed . . . 3D 40
HINCHWICK . . . 2A 146
HINCKLEY . . . 2B 140
Hinckley Rd. CV2: W'grve S . . . 7C 52
CV7: Ansty . . . 4E 52
CV11: Burt H . . . 4J 33
CV11: Nun . . . 6E 22
Hind Cl. CV34: Warw . . . 5H 97
Hinde Cl. CV21: Brow . . . 1J 75
HINDLIP . . . 3A 142
HINKSFORD . . . 3A 138
HINTON . . . 3C 145
HINTS . . . 1C 139
Hipsley La. CV9: Bax, Hurl . . . 6B 14
Hipswell Highway CV2: Cov . . . 3K 59
Hiron, The CV3: Cov . . . 7C 58
Hiron Cft. CV3: Cov . . . 7C 58
Hiron Way CV34: Warw . . . 1D 100
Hirsel Gdns. CV32: Lea S . . . 5D 98
Hirst Cl. CV23: Long L . . . 3A 74
Hitchman Ct. CV31: Lea S . . . 3E 102
Hitchman M. CV31: Lea S . . . 3E 102
Hitchman Rd. CV31: Lea S . . . 2E 102
Hithersand Cl. CV35: H Lucy . . . 2B 118
HMP Rye Hill CV23: W'hby . . . 7K 87
HM Young Offenders Institution Onley CV23: W'hby . . . 7J 87
Hoarestone Av. CV11: Nun . . . 5C 32
Hobbins, The CV36: Ship S . . . 5G 131
Hobgoblin La. CV7: Fill . . . 3D 38
Hob La. CV8: Burt G . . . 5A 66
Hobley Cl. CV22: Bil . . . 2D 86
Hockett St. CV3: Cov . . . 7K 135 (7D 58)
Hocking Rd. CV2: Cov . . . 2K 59
HOCKLEY
Coventry . . . 3A 56 (1D 143)
Tamwork . . . 1D 139
Hockley Cl. CV23: Gran . . . 6H 105
HOCKLEY HEATH . . . 1C 143
Hockley La. CV5: E Grn . . . 3A 56
CV37: Ett . . . 2C 126
Hodgett's La. CV8: Burt G . . . 3A 66
Hodgson Rd. CV37: S Avon . . . 2E 114
Hodnell Dr. CV47: Sou . . . 6J 107
Hodnet Cl. CV8: Ken . . . 4F 79
Hogan Ho. CV22: Bil . . . 1C 86
Hogarth Cl. CV12: Bed . . . 1G 41
Hogarth Rd. CV37: Shot . . . 6C 114
HOGGRILL'S END . . . 7K 19 (2D 139)
Hoggrills End La. B46: Neth W . . . 1B 26
Holbeche Cres. CV7: Fill . . . 2C 38
Holbein Cl. CV12: Bed . . . 1G 41
HOLBERROW GREEN . . . 3B 142
Holborn Av. CV6: Cov . . . 4C 50
Holbrook Av. CV21: Rugby . . . 4G 75
Holbrook Gro. B37: Mars G . . . 4B 34
Holbrook La. CV6: Cov . . . 3C 50
(Beacon Rd.)
CV6: Cov . . . 6D 50
(Holbrook Pk. Est., not continuous)
Holbrook Pk. Est. CV6: Cov . . . 6D 50
Holbrook Rd. CV23: Long L . . . 3B 74
CV37: S Avon . . . 4B 114
HOLBROOKS . . . 3C 50
Holbrook Way CV6: Cov . . . 5D 50
Holcot Leys CV22: Rugby . . . 2G 87
HOLDENBY . . . 2D 145
Holder Cl. B50: Bidf A . . . 5G 123
Holioake Dr. CV34: Warw . . . 2J 101
Holland Cl. B50: Bidf A . . . 6G 123
Holland Cft. B76: Mars . . . 1H 19
Holland Mdw. CV37: Welf A . . . 4A 124
HOLLAND PARK . . . 1B 138
Holland Rd. CV6: Cov . . . 1A 58
Hollands Bldgs. CV9: Ath . . . 3D 16
Holliars Gro. B37: K'hrst . . . 7A 24
Hollick Cres. CV7: New A . . . 4E 28
Hollick Way LE10: Wlvy . . . 2H 33
Hollicombe Ter. CV2: Cov . . . 6K 51
Hollies Rd. B78: Pole . . . 2E 10
Hollinwell Cl. CV11: Nun . . . 4E 32
Hollis La. CV8: Ken . . . 7C 66
Hollis Rd. CV3: Cov . . . 5G 59
Holloway CV47: Nap . . . 2H 111
Holloway, The CV34: Warw . . . 2F 101
CV47: P Mars . . . 6G 111
Holloway Fld. CV6: Cov . . . 1K 57
Holloway Hill OX15: Lwr Bra . . . 4J 133
Holloway La. OX15: Lwr Bra . . . 4K 133
HOLLOW COURT . . . 3A 142
Hollow Cres. CV6: Cov . . . 2B 58
HOLLOWELL . . . 1D 145
Hollowell Way CV21: Brow . . . 1J 75
Hollows, The CV11: Nun . . . 3B 32
Hollybank CV5: Cov . . . 7A 58
Holly Bank Est. CV9: Aus . . . 6H 7
HOLLYBERRY END . . . 2A 48
Hollybush Ho. *CV11: Nun . . . 7D 22*
(off Bond Ga.)
Holly Bush La. CV47: P Mars . . . 6G 111
Hollybush La. CV6: Longf . . . 2G 51
Holly Dr. CV8: Rytn D . . . 7D 70
CV9: Hurl . . . 7A 14
Hollyfast La. CV7: Cor . . . 2F 49
Hollyfast Rd. CV6: Cov . . . 7J 49
Holly Gro. CV4: Tile H . . . 5F 57
CV23: Chu L . . . 3F 73
Hollyhurst B46: Wat O . . . 1C 24
CV12: Bed . . . 4F 41
Hollyland B46: Shu . . . 3B 26
Holly La. CV9: Ath . . . 2A 16
(not continuous)
Holly La. Ind. Est. CV9: Ath . . . 2B 16
Holly Lodge CV35: Welle . . . 3H 117
Holly Lodge Wlk. B37: F'bri . . . 3A 34
Holly Orchard Cl. CV37: S Avon . . . 3F 115
Holly Rd. CV36: Ship S . . . 6H 131
Holly Stitches Rd. CV10: Nun . . . 5K 21
Holly St. CV32: Lea S . . . 6E 98
Holly Wlk. CV8: Bag . . . 6E 68
CV11: Nun . . . 2B 32
CV32: Lea S . . . 7D 98
(not continuous)
CV37: S Avon . . . 3B 114
HOLLYWOOD . . . 1B 142
Holman Way CV11: Nun . . . 1K 31
Holman Way Ind. Est. CV11: Nun . . . 1K 31
Holmcroft CV2: W'grve S . . . 6B 52
Holme Cl. CV21: Brow . . . 2J 75
Holmes Ct. CV8: Ken . . . 4D 78
Holmes Dr. CV5: E Grn . . . 2B 56
Holmes Rd. CV31: W'nsh . . . 5F 103
Holme Way CV23: Barby . . . 7F 89
Holmewood Cl. CV8: Ken . . . 4F 79
Holmfield Rd. CV2: Cov . . . 4H 59
Holmsdale Rd. CV6: Cov . . . 7E 50
Holroyd Ho. CV4: Tile H . . . 5D 56
Holsworthy Cl. CV11: Nun . . . 6F 23
Holt, The CV32: Lill . . . 4F 99
Holt Av. CV33: Bis T . . . 5B 108
HOLT END . . . 2B 142
Holte Rd. CV9: Ath . . . 2C 16
Holt Gdns. B80: Stud . . . 5D 92
Holt Leys CV47: Sou . . . 5J 107
Holtom St. CV37: S Avon . . . 6E 114
Holt Rd. B80: Stud . . . 5D 92
HOLY CROSS . . . 1A 142
Holy Cross Ct. CV2: Cov . . . 3A 60
Holyhead Rd. CV1: Cov . . . 3F 135 (4A 58)
CV5: Cov . . . 2H 57
Holyoak Cl. CV12: Bed . . . 4F 41
Holyoak Cl. CV22: Bil . . . 1C 86
Holyoke Gro. CV31: W'nsh . . . 6F 103
Holyrood Ct. CV10: Nun . . . 6K 21
Holy Trinity Church (Shakespeare's Tomb) . . . 6F 115
HOLYWELL . . . 2C 143
Holywell Cl. CV4: Tile H . . . 6B 56
Holywell Rd. CV47: Sou . . . 5G 107
Home Cl. CV8: Bubb . . . 3J 81
Home Farm CV35: Leek W . . . 1H 97
Home Farm Cl. CV9: With . . . 3G 17
Home Farm Cres. CV31: W'nsh . . . 4F 103
Homefield La. CV22: Dunc . . . 5D 86
Home Furlong CV35: Welle . . . 5G 117
Home Mdw. CV35: Clav . . . 3D 94
Home Pk. Rd. CV11: Nun . . . 1J 31
Homer Cl. CV34: Warw . . . 3C 102
Homestalls Mdw. CV35: Pill P . . . 3B 128
Homeward Way CV3: Bin . . . 6C 60
HONEYBOURNE . . . 1A 146
Honeybourne Cl. CV5: E Grn . . . 4F 57
Honeybourne Rd. B50: Bickm . . . 7H 123
B50: Bidf A . . . 6G 123
Honeyfield Rd. CV1: Cov . . . 2D 58
Honeysuckle Cl. CV23: Brow . . . 7K 65
Honeysuckle Dr. CV2: Cov . . . 4H 51
HONILEY . . . 1D 143
Honiley Way CV2: Cov . . . 5K 51
HONINGTON . . . 1J 131 (1B 146)
Honington Cl. CV35: Hatt . . . 5B 96
Honington Hall . . . 1J 131
Honiton Rd. CV2: Cov . . . 2H 59
Honiwell Cl. CV33: Har . . . 6G 109
Hood La. CV10: Ansl . . . 1D 28
Hood St. CV1: Cov . . . 4E 58

Hood's Way CV22: Bil . . . 6D 74
HOOK NORTON . . . 2C 147
Hope Aldridge Bus. Cen. CV10: Nun . . . 5D 22
Hope Cl. CV7: Ker E . . . 6A 40
Hopedale Cl. CV2: Cov . . . 4A 60
Hope St. CV1: Cov . . . 5B 58
Hopkins Fld. CV37: Long M . . . 2G 125
Hopkins Pct., The B49: Alc . . . 4C 112
Hopkins Rd. CV6: Cov . . . 3A 58
Hopkins Way CV35: Welle . . . 1H 117
Hopper's La. CV35: Welle . . . 2H 117
HOPSFORD . . . 1A 54
Hopton Cl. CV5: E Grn . . . 3E 56
Hopton Crofts CV32: Lea S . . . 5A 98
HOPWAS . . . 1C 139
Hopwas Gro. B37: K'hrst . . . 7A 24
HOPWOOD . . . 1B 142
HORESTON GRANGE . . . 6F 23
Horeston Grange Shop. Cen. CV11: Nun . . . 6H 23
HORLEY . . . 1D 147
Hornbeam Dr. CV4: Tile H . . . 6B 56
Hornbeam Gro. CV31: Lea S . . . 2G 103
Hornchurch Cl. CV1: Cov . . . 7H 135 (6C 58)
Hornchurch Cl. Ind. Est. CV1: Cov . . . 7H 135 (6C 58)
Horndean Cl. CV6: Cov . . . 6E 50
Horne Cl. CV21: Hillm . . . 1D 88
Horninghold Cl. CV3: Bin . . . 7A 60
Hornsey Cl. CV2: Cov . . . 7A 52
HORNTON . . . 1C 147
Hornton Gro. CV35: Hatt . . . 5A 96
Horobins Yd. CV12: Bed . . . 7H 31
HORSEBROOK . . . 1A 138
Horse Fair CV36: Ship S . . . 4H 131
Horsefair, The *B95: Hen A* . . . *2H 93*
(off High St.)
Horsepool, The CV23: Lilb . . . 1J 77
Horsepool Hollow CV31: Lea S . . . 3G 103
Horseshoe Cl. CV36: Ship S . . . 4H 131
Horse Shoe Rd. CV6: Longf . . . 2G 51
Horsewell CV47: Sou . . . 5H 107
Horsford Rd. CV3: Cov . . . 2D 68
Horton Cl. B49: Alc . . . 3C 112
CV7: Exh . . . 6F 41
Horton Cres. CV22: Rugby . . . 6G 75
Hosiery St. CV12: Bed . . . 3J 41
Hoskyn Cl. CV21: Hillm . . . 1B 88
Hospital La. CV12: Bed . . . 3B 40
Hotchkiss Cl. CV35: Welle . . . 4G 117
Hotchkiss Way CV3: Bin . . . 1C 70
Hothorpe Cl. CV3: Bin . . . 6B 60
HOUGHTON ON THE HILL . . . 1D 141
Houldsworth Cres. CV6: Cov . . . 2C 50
Houston Rd. CV21: Rugby . . . 2J 75
Hove Av. CV5: E Grn . . . 3C 56
Hovelands Cl. CV2: Cov . . . 6J 51
Howard Cl. B50: Bidf A . . . 6F 123
CV5: E Grn . . . 3C 56
CV22: Dunc . . . 5D 86
Howard Ho. B92: H Ard . . . 7H 45
Howard Rd. CV10: Nun . . . 1G 31
Howard St. CV1: Cov . . . 1J 135 (3D 58)
Howard Wlk. CV34: Warw . . . 2B 102
Howat Rd. CV7: Ker E . . . 6K 39
Howcombe La. CV47: Nap . . . 2H 111
Howcotte Grn. CV4: Tile H . . . 1C 66
HOWE GREEN . . . 7H 29 (3A 140)
Howe Grn. La. CV7: Cor . . . 1H 39
CV10: Asty . . . 1H 39
Howells Cl. CV12: Bed . . . 4D 40
Howes La. CV3: Finh . . . 6C 68
Howkins Rd. CV21: Rugby . . . 2J 75
Howlette Rd. CV4: Tile H . . . 5C 56
Hoylake Cl. CV11: Nun . . . 3D 32
Huckson Rd. CV47: Bis I . . . 6C 110
HUDDINGTON . . . 3A 142
HUDDLESFORD . . . 1C 139
Hudisdon Cl. CV34: Warw . . . 6H 97
Hudson Av. B46: Col . . . 6F 25
Hudson Rd. CV22: Bil . . . 7E 74
HUGGLESCOTE . . . 1B 140
Hughes, The CV34: Warw . . . 2G 101
Hughes Cl. CV31: W'nsh . . . 6E 102
CV34: Warw . . . 5F 97
Hugh Rd. CV3: Cov . . . 5G 59
HULCOTE . . . 3D 145
Hulme Cl. CV3: Bin . . . 6D 60
Humber Av. CV1: Cov . . . 6E 58
CV3: Cov . . . 6F 59
Humber Gro. B36: Cas B . . . 3A 24
Humber Rd. CV3: Cov . . . 6F 59
HUMBERSTONE . . . 1D 141
Humberstone Rd. CV6: Cov . . . 2A 58
Humphrey Burton's Rd. CV3: Cov . . . 7C 58
Humphrey-Davy Rd. CV12: Bed . . . 5D 40
Humphris St. CV34: Warw . . . 7K 97
HUNCOTE . . . 2C 141
HUNGARTON . . . 1D 141
Hunger Hill B95: Hen A . . . 2F 93
HUNNINGHAM . . . 2A 144
HUNNINGTON . . . 3A 138
Hunt Cl. CV35: H Mag . . . 2B 100
HUNT END . . . 2B 142
Hunters Cl. CV3: Bin . . . 5C 60
Hunters La. CV21: Rugby . . . 3G 75
Hunters La. Ind. Est. CV21: Rugby . . . 3G 75
Hunters Pk. CV9: Bad E . . . 2F 15
Hunter St. CV21: Rugby . . . 4J 75
Hunters Wlk. CV9: With . . . 4G 17
Hunter Ter. CV5: Cov . . . 7H 57
Hunt Hall La. CV37: Welf A . . . 4A 124
Huntingdon Rd. CV5: Cov . . . 6A 58
Huntingdon Way CV10: Nun . . . 1E 30
HUNTINGTON . . . 1A 138
Huntington Ct. CV35: Welle . . . 4H 117
Hunt La. CV9: With . . . 4G 17
Hunt Paddocks CV8: Ken . . . 7C 78
HUNTS GREEN . . . 2C 139
Hunts Rd. CV37: S Avon . . . 6G 115
Hunt Ter. CV4: Canly . . . 1F 67
Hurdlers La. CV37: Snitt . . . 6G 95
Hurlbutt Rd. CV34: H'cte . . . 4A 102
HURLEY . . . 7K 13 (2D 139)
Hurley Cl. CV32: Lea S . . . 5E 98
HURLEY COMMON . . . 4K 13
Hurley Comn. CV9: Hurl . . . 6J 13
Hurley La. CV9: Hurl . . . 7H 13
Hurn Way CV6: Ald G . . . 2H 51
Hurst Rd. CV6: Longf . . . 2G 51
(not continuous)
CV12: Bed . . . 2H 41
CV47: Sou . . . 6G 107
Hurst Wlk. CV6: Longf . . . 2G 51
Husbandmans Cl.
CV36: Ship S . . . 4H 131
HUSBANDS BOSWORTH . . . 3D 141
HYDE . . . 3A 146
Hyde Pl. CV32: Lea S . . . 7C 98
Hyde Rd. CV2: Cov . . . 3A 60
CV8: Ken . . . 4D 78
Hypericum Gdns. CV2: Cov . . . 3J 59

I

Iago Way CV34: H'cte . . . 5B 102
Ibex Cl. CV3: Bin . . . 6B 60
IBSTOCK . . . 1B 140
Ibstock Rd. CV6: Longf . . . 1G 51
Icknield Cl. B50: Bidf A . . . 6H 123
Icknield Ct. B50: Bidf A . . . 6H 123
Icknield Row B49: Alc . . . 4A 112
Icknield St. B50: Bidf A . . . 6H 123
Icknield St. Dr. B98: Redd . . . 1D 92
ICOMB . . . 3B 146
IDBURY . . . 3B 146
Iden Rd. CV1: Cov . . . 3E 58
IDLICOTE . . . 1B 146
Idlicote Rd. CV36: Half . . . 2K 127
CV36: Whatc . . . 3A 130
Ilam Ct. CV22: Bil . . . 6E 74
Ilam Pk. CV8: Ken . . . 4G 79
Ilex Ct. CV34: Warw . . . 1J 101
Ilford Cl. CV12: Bed . . . 2G 41
Ilford Ct. CV3: Bin W . . . 1F 71
Ilford Dr. CV3: Cov . . . 2B 68
Ilfracombe Gro. CV3: Finh . . . 3A 68
ILLEY . . . 3A 138
ILLSTON ON THE HILL . . . 2D 141
Ilmer Cl. CV21: Brow . . . 1A 76
ILMINGTON . . . 6C 126 (1B 146)
Ilmington Cl. CV3: Cov . . . 3B 68
CV35: Hatt . . . 5A 96
Ilmington Rd. CV36: Wind . . . 7F 127
CV37: Arms . . . 4F 127
Imogen Gdns. CV34: H'cte . . . 5C 102
Imperial Ri. B46: Col . . . 2E 24
Inca Cl. CV3: Bin . . . 7B 60
Inchbrook Rd. CV8: Ken . . . 2G 79
Inchcape Cl. CV22: Caw . . . 1B 86
Inchford Av. CV34: Warw . . . 5G 97
Inchford Cl. CV11: Nun . . . 3B 32
Independent St. CV23: Kils . . . 6J 89
Ingle Ct. CV31: Lea S . . . 1C 102
Ingleton Cl. CV11: Nun . . . 2C 32
Inglewood Cl. CV32: Lill . . . 4E 98
INGON . . . 1J 115 (3D 143)
Ingon La. CV37: Ing . . . 7G 95 & 1J 115
Ingram Rd. CV5: Cov . . . 7H 57
INKBERROW . . . 3B 142
INKFORD . . . 1B 142
Innage Cl. CV31: Lea S . . . 7E 98
Innage Pk. CV9: Ath . . . 2B 16
Innage Ter. CV9: Ath . . . 3C 16
Innis Rd. CV5: Cov . . . 7J 57
Instone Rd. CV6: Cov . . . 5A 50
International Ho. B37: Mars G . . . 1D 44
CV4: Canly . . . 4F 67
International Sq.
B37: Mars G . . . 7C 34
Inverary Cl. CV8: Ken . . . 5G 79
Inverness Cl. CV5: E Grn . . . 3E 56
Invicta Rd. CV3: Bin . . . 7B 60
Ipswich Wlk. B37: Chel W . . . 3B 34
Ireton Cl. CV4: Tile H . . . 6A 56
Ironbridge Way CV6: Longf . . . 7H 41
IRON CROSS . . . 3B 142
Iron Ga. Cotts. *CV37: Up Bil* . . . *7H 113*
(off Billesley Rd.)
Ironmonger Row CV1: Cov . . . 3H 135 (4C 58)
Irving Rd. CV1: Cov . . . 5E 58
Isambard Dr. CV6: Longf . . . 1F 51
Isis Gro. B36: Cas B . . . 4A 24
Island Mdw. Cvn. Pk.
B95: Lit Al . . . 2J 113
Ivanhoe Av. CV11: Nun . . . 3A 32
Ivor Rd. CV6: Cov . . . 4F 51
CV9: Ath . . . 4E 16
Ivybridge Rd. CV3: Cov . . . 2D 68
Ivycroft Rd. B79: Wart . . . 6H 9
Ivy Farm La. CV4: Canly . . . 2H 67
Ivy Grange CV22: Bil . . . 1C 86
Ivy Gro. CV10: Nun . . . 5J 21
Ivy La. CV33: Har . . . 6H 109
CV37: Ett . . . 2B 126
Ivy Lodge Cl. B37: Mars G . . . 6A 34
Izod Rd. CV21: Rugby . . . 4F 75

J

Jack Ball Ho. CV2: W'grve S . . . 5B 52
Jackdaw Dr. B36: Cas B . . . 4A 24
Jacker's Rd. CV2: Ald G . . . 2H 51
Jacklin Dr. CV3: Finh . . . 4C 68
Jack O'Watton Ind. Est. B46: Wat O . . . 1D 24
Jackson Cl. CV7: Ker E . . . 6A 40
CV35: H Mag . . . 2A 100
Jackson Gro. CV8: Ken . . . 5G 79
Jackson La. CV47: Nap . . . 3J 111
Jackson Rd. CV6: Cov . . . 5D 50
CV21: Hillm . . . 7C 76
Jacksons Mdw. B50: Bidf A . . . 4F 123
Jacksons Orchard CV37: Long M . . . 2G 125
Jack Thomson Cft. WR11: Salf P . . . 7B 122
Jackwood Grn. CV12: Bed . . . 5C 40
Jacob Dr. CV4: Canly . . . 2H 67
Jacox Cres. CV8: Ken . . . 4G 79
Jacquard Cl. CV3: Cov . . . 4D 68
Jacquard Ho. CV1: Cov . . . 3E 58
Jade Cl. CV1: Cov . . . 3D 58
Jago La. CV37: Snitt . . . 5J 95
Jake Cade Way CV34: H'cte . . . 4C 102
James Ct. *CV21: Rugby* . . . *5H 75*
(off James Wlk.)
CV34: Warw . . . 1H 101
Jamescroft CV3: W'hall . . . 2A 70
James Dawson Dr. CV5: Mil W . . . 6K 47
James Diskin Ct. CV11: Nun . . . 2A 32
James Galloway Cl. CV3: Bin . . . 1A 70
James Gilbert Rugby Football Mus., The . . . 5G 75
James Grn. Rd. CV4: Tile H . . . 5D 56
James Ho. CV2: Cov . . . 6J 51
James Rd. B46: Col . . . 4F 25
James St. CV7: New A . . . 4E 28
CV11: Nun . . . 6B 22
CV21: Rugby . . . 5H 75
James Wlk. CV21: Rugby . . . 5H 75
Jaques Cl. B46: Wat O . . . 2B 24
Jardine Cres. CV4: Tile H . . . 5D 56
Jardine Shop. Cen. CV4: Tile H . . . 5D 56
Jasmine Gro. CV3: Cov . . . 7J 59
CV32: Lea S . . . 5E 98
Jasmine Way CV12: Bed . . . 3D 40
Jean St. CV9: Bad E . . . 2F 15
Jedburgh Gro. CV3: Finh . . . 4A 68
Jeffrey Cl. CV12: Bed . . . 5D 40
Jeffs Cl. CV35: Up Tys . . . 7C 130
OX15: Lwr Bra . . . 3H 133
Jeliff St. CV4: Tile H . . . 5D 56
Jenkins Av. CV5: E Grn . . . 3D 56
Jenkins Rd. CV21: Hillm . . . 7C 76
Jenner St. CV1: Cov . . . 1K 135 (3D 58)
Jenton Rd. CV31: Lea S . . . 2F 103
Jephcott Cl. B49: Alc . . . 4A 112
Jephcott Ho. *CV1: Cov* . . . *4E 58*
(off Kildale Clo.)
Jephson Ct. CV2: Ald G . . . 2J 51
Jephson Pl. CV31: Lea S . . . 1F 103
Jersey Cft. B36: Cas B . . . 6B 24
Jesmond Rd. CV1: Cov . . . 3F 59
Jill La. B80: Stud . . . 5A 92
B96: Sam . . . 5A 92
Jim Forrest Cl. CV3: Bin . . . 7B 60
Jitty, The CV34: Warw . . . 2F 101
JM Halls CV4: Canly . . . 4G 67
Joanna Dr. CV3: Finh . . . 5C 68
Joan of Arc Ho. CV3: Cov . . . 2E 68
Joans Cl. CV31: Lea S . . . 2G 103
Joan Ward St. CV3: Cov . . . 7J 135 (7D 58)
Job's La. CV4: Tile H . . . 4E 56
Jodrell St. CV11: Nun . . . 6C 22
Joe O'Brien Cl. CV3: W'hall . . . 2J 69
Joe Williams Cl. CV3: Bin . . . 7B 60
John Grace St. CV3: Cov . . . 7D 58
John Knight Rd. CV12: Bed . . . 1H 41
John McGuire Cres. CV3: Bin . . . 1A 70
John Nash Sq. CV8: Ken . . . 6D 78
John of Gaunt Ho. CV3: Cov . . . 1E 68
John O'Gaunt Rd. CV8: Ken . . . 6C 78
John Rous Av. CV4: Canly . . . 1F 67
John's Cl. B80: Stud . . . 3B 92
John Shelton Dr. CV6: Cov . . . 2C 50
John Simpson Cl. CV8: Wols . . . 5J 71
John Sinclair Ho. CV1: Cov . . . 1H 135
Johnson Av. CV22: Rugby . . . 6D 74
Johnson Pl. B95: Hen A . . . 1H 93
Johnson Rd. CV6: Cov . . . 6G 51
CV12: Bed . . . 2J 41
Johnson St. CV9: Wood E . . . 2K 13
John St. CV10: Nun . . . 1E 30
CV11: Nun . . . 2J 31
CV12: Bed . . . 3G 41
CV32: Lea S . . . 7D 98
CV37: S Avon . . . 3G 137 (4F 115)
John Thwaites Cl. CV22: Rugby . . . 6G 75
John Tofts Ho. CV1: Cov . . . 1H 135 (3C 58)
Jolyffe Ct. CV37: S Avon . . . 3E 114
Jolyffe Pk. Rd. CV37: S Avon . . . 3E 114
Jonathan Rd. CV2: W'grve S . . . 6B 52
Jones Rd. CV7: Exh . . . 4G 41
Jordan Cl. CV8: Ken . . . 7F 79
Jordans, The CV5: Cov . . . 3G 57
Jordan Well CV1: Cov . . . 4J 135 (5D 58)
Joseph Creighton Cl. CV3: Bin . . . 1A 70
Joseph Halpin Ho. CV1: Cov . . . 1K 135
Joseph Latham Ho. CV2: Cov . . . 5H 51
Joseph Luckman Rd. CV12: Bed . . . 1G 41
Joseph Way CV37: S Avon . . . 2D 114
Jourdain Pk. CV34: H'cte . . . 5C 102
Joyce Pool CV34: Warw . . . 1G 101

Joyce Way CV22: Caw 1A 86
Jubilee Cl. B50: Bidf A 5H 123
Jubilee Ct. B49: Alc 3C 112
B78: K'bry 6E 12
(not continuous)
Jubilee Cres. CV6: Cov 6B 50
Jubilee Gardens 5G 75
(off Regent St.)
Jubilee Sports Cen. 1G 31
Jubilee St. CV21: Rugby 5E 74
Jubilee Ter. CV12: Bed 1H 41
Jubilee Wlk. CV37: Shot 5C 114
Judd Cl. CV12: Bed 2F 41
Judd's La. CV6: Longf 2E 50
Judge Cl. CV23: Long L 3A 74
Judith Quiney's House (site of) 4G 137
Judith Way CV22: Caw 1A 86
Julian Cl. CV2: W'grve S 6B 52
Juliet Cl. CV11: Nun 3C 32
Juliet Dr. CV22: Bil 3D 86
CV34: H'cte 5D 102
Julius Dr. B46: Col 3F 25
Junction One CV21: Rugby 2H 75
Junction St. CV1: Cov 5F 135 (5B 58)
Junewood Cl. CV21: Brow 1K 75
Juniper Cl. CV12: Bed 3E 40
Juniper Dr. CV5: Alle 2D 56
Juno Dr. CV31: Lea S 3D 102
Jury St. CV34: Warw 2G 101
Justice Cl. CV31: W'nsh 4E 102
Justice Wlk. CV11: Nun 7D 22
Justins Av. CV37: S Avon 2D 114

K

Kalfs Dr. CV22: Caw 1B 86
Kanzan Rd. CV2: Ald G 2H 51
Kareen Gro. CV3: Bin W 1E 70
Karen Cl. CV10: Nun 4K 21
Karlingford Cl. CV5: Cov 7H 57
Kathleen Av. CV12: Bed 4E 40
Katrine Cl. CV10: Nun 6H 21
Kay Cl. CV21: Brow 1J 75
Kaysbrook Dr. CV23: Stret D 3J 83
Keats Cl. CV10: Gall C 6F 21
Keats Rd. CV2: Cov 5K 59
CV37: S Avon 6G 115
Keble Ho. B37: F'bri 3A 34
Kebull Grn. CV4: Tile H 7C 56
Kedleston Ct. CV22: Rugby 6E 74
Keele Ho. B37: F'bri 1B 34
Keeling Rd. CV8: Ken 4F 79
Keenan Dr. CV12: Bed 4D 40
Keepers Cl. B46: Col 1F 35
Keepers Wlk. CV12: Bed 4D 40
Keetley Cl. CV36: Ship S 6H 131
Kegworth Cl. CV6: Longf 2G 51
Keir Cl. CV32: Lea S 5E 98
Keith Rd. CV32: Lill 3F 99
Kele Rd. CV4: Tile H 1D 66
KELMARSH 1D 145
Kelmscote Rd. CV6: Cov 6K 49
Kelsey Cl. CV11: Nun 1A 32
Kelsey's Cl. CV8: Wols 5H 71
Kelsull Cft. B37: F'bri 3A 34
Kelvin Av. CV2: Cov 2K 59
Kelvin Rd. CV32: Lill 2F 99
Kelway CV3: Bin 5C 60
Kemp Cl. CV34: Warw 1J 101
Kempley Av. CV2: Cov 4J 59
KEMPSEY 3A 142
Kempsey Cl. B98: Redd 1A 92
KEMPS GREEN 1C 143
Kempton Cl. CV37: S Avon 7D 114
Kempton Cres. CV32: Lill 3G 99
Kem St. CV11: Nun 2K 31
Kendal Av. B46: Col 5F 25
CV32: Lea S 5A 98
Kendal Cl. CV11: Nun 5H 23
Kendall Av. CV37: S Avon 1F 137 (4E 114)
Kendal Ri. CV5: Cov 3G 57
Kendon Av. CV6: Cov 1J 57
Kendrick Cl. CV6: Longf 2G 51
Kenelm Ct. CV3: W'hall 3J 69
Kenilcourt CV8: Ken 3B 78
KENILWORTH 5D 78 (1D 143)
Kenilworth By-Pass CV3: Finh 7G 79
CV8: Ken 7G 79
CV35: Ken, Leek W 2J 97
Kenilworth Castle 4B 78
Kenilworth Ct. CV3: Cov 7C 58
Kenilworth Dr. CV11: Nun 1H 31
Kenilworth M. CV8: Ken 4D 78
Kenilworth Rd. B46: Col 4G 35
B92: H Ard 7K 45
CV3: Cov 2K 67
CV4: Canly 1F 79
CV7: Mer 4J 45
CV8: Ken 1F 79
CV32: B'dwn, Lea S 1C 98
CV32: Cubb 1G 99
CV33: L Hth 2K 119
Kenilworth St. CV32: Lea S 6D 98
Ken Marriot Leisure Cen. 7H 75
Kennan Av. CV31: Lea S 1D 102
Kennedy Dr. CV22: Bil 6C 74
Kennedy Sq. CV32: Lea S 6E 98
Kennel La. CV9: With 4G 17
Kennet Cl. CV2: Cov 6J 51
Kennet Gro. B36: Cas B 4A 24
Kenpas Highway CV3: Cov 2K 67
Kensington Ct. CV5: Cov 6A 58
Kensington Ct. CV10: Nun 5H 21
Kensington Rd. CV5: Cov 6K 57
Kent, The CV21: Hillm 6C 76
Kent Cl. CV3: Cov 2E 68
Kenthurst Cl. CV5: E Grn 3A 56
Kentmere Cl. CV2: W'grve S 4A 52
Kents La. CV37: Ett 1B 126
Kenwyn Grn. CV7: Exh 5H 41
Keppel Cl. CV22: Bil 7C 74
Keppel St. CV1: Cov 2E 58
KERESLEY 5K 49 (3A 140)
Keresley Brook Rd. CV6: Cov 4K 49
Keresley Cl. CV6: Cov 4K 49
Keresley Grn. Rd. CV6: Cov 5K 49
KERESLEY NEWLAND 7K 39 (3A 140)
Keresley Rd. CV6: Cov 6K 49
Kerns Ter. CV37: S Avon 1G 137 (4F 115)
Kerris Way CV3: Bin 6C 60
Kerrys Ho. CV1: Cov 5B 58
(off Windsor St.)
KERSWELL GREEN 3A 142
Kestrel Cl. CV37: S Avon 2F 115
Kestrel Cft. CV3: Bin 7B 60
Keswick Cl. CV11: Nun 5H 23
Keswick Dr. CV21: Brow 7J 65
Keswick Grn. CV32: Lea S 6B 98
Keswick Wlk. CV2: Cov 3B 60
KETTLEBROOK 1D 139
Kettlewell Cl. CV34: Warw 6G 97
Kettlewell Way B37: F'bri 4A 34
Keviliok St. CV3: Cov 2D 68
Kew Cl. B37: K'hrst 2A 34
CV8: Ken 4G 79
Kew Rd. CV21: Rugby 4G 75
Keyes Dr. CV22: Bil 6C 74
KEYHAM 1D 141
Keys Hill CV9: Bad E 2F 15
Keys La. CV47: P Mars 5H 111
Keyte Rd. CV36: Ilm 6D 126
Keyte's La. CV35: Barf 2C 108
Kiblers La. CV35: Pill P 3B 128
KIBWORTH BEAUCHAMP 2D 141
KIBWORTH HARCOURT 2D 141
KIDDEMORE GREEN 1A 138
KIDDINGTON 3D 147
Kielder Dr. CV10: Nun 2E 30
Kilburn Dr. CV5: Cov 4K 57
KILBY 2D 141
Kilby Gro. CV31: Lea S 3G 103
Kildale Cl. CV1: Cov 4E 58
Kilderkin Ct. CV1: Cov 7K 135 (6D 58)
Kildwick Way CV34: Warw 6G 97
Kiln Cl. B80: Stud 3B 92
CV10: Nun 1E 30
CV32: Lea S 5E 98
Kiln La. CV23: Stret D 3K 83
Kilnsey Gro. CV34: Warw 6G 97
Kiln Way B78: Pole 1C 10
KILSBY 6J 89 (1C 145)
Kilsby La. CV21: Hillm 2E 88
Kilsby Rd. CV23: Barby 7E 88
Kilworth Ho. CV32: Lea S 6D 98
(off Windsor St.)
Kilworth Rd. CV21: Hillm 2D 88
Kimberley Cl. CV5: E Grn 3D 56
Kimberley Rd. CV8: Bag 6E 68
CV12: Bed 1J 41
CV21: Rugby 4H 75
Kimble Cl. CV5: Cov 3F 57
KIMCOTE 3C 141
KINETON
Cheltenham 3A 146
Warwick 5D 120 (3A 144)
Kineton Community Sports Cen. 5E 120
Kineton Rd. CV2: Cov 1J 59
CV8: Ken 5G 79
CV35: Gay 7F 119
CV35: Lit K 7C 120
CV35: Oxh 1E 130
CV35: Pill P 3B 128
CV35: Welle 3J 117
CV47: Sou 6G 107
(Hurst Rd.)
CV47: Sou 7F 107
(Station Rd.)
Kineton Rd. Ind. Est. CV47: Sou 6G 107
King Edward Rd. CV1: Cov 3E 58
CV11: Nun 7E 22
CV21: Rugby 4H 75
Kingfield Ind. Est. CV1: Cov 1C 58
Kingfield Rd. CV1: Cov 1C 58
CV6: Cov 1C 58
Kingfisher Av. CV10: Nun 6H 21
Kingfisher Ct. CV37: S Avon 2G 137
Kingfisher Dr. B36: Cas B 4A 24
Kingfisher Way B49: Alc 3B 112
King George's Av. CV6: Cov 4E 50
CV12: Bed 7H 31
King George's Ct. CV23: Long L 3A 74
KINGHAM 3B 146
King John's La. CV35: Rad 6A 128
OX15: Rad 6A 128
King John's Rd. CV35: Kine 5C 120
Kingland Dr. CV32: Lea S 6A 98
Kingley Av. B49: Alc 3C 112
King Richard St. CV2: Cov 4F 59
Kings Av. CV9: Ath 3D 16
Kingsbridge Rd. CV10: Nun 5E 22
KINGSBURY 6E 12 (2D 139)
Kingsbury Link B78: Picc 2H 13
Kingsbury Rd. B76: Curd, Mars 3D 18
B76: K'bry, Mars 1H 19
B76: Min, Curd 5A 18
Kingsbury Rd. B78: K'bry 1H 19
CV6: Cov 1H 57
Kingsbury Water Camping & Caravaning Site
B76: Bod H 5B 12
Kingsbury Water Pk. 4B 12
Kingscote Gro. CV3: Finh 4K 67
KING'S COUGHTON 2A 112 (3B 142)
Kings Coughton La. B49: K Cou 2A 112
King's Ct. B37: Mars G 4E 34
Kingsford Rd. CV6: Cov 1C 58
Kings Gdns. CV12: Bed 3J 41
Kingsgate Ho. B37: Chel W 3A 34
Kings Gro. CV2: Cov 4H 59
KING'S HEATH 3B 138
King's Hill La. CV3: Finh 7K 67
Kingsholm Cl. CV3: Bin 6D 60
KINGSHURST 7A 24 (3C 139)
Kingshurst CV31: Rad S 2J 103
Kingshurst Way B37: K'hrst 7A 24
Kingsland Av. CV5: Cov 5K 57
King's La. B50: Broom 3E 122
B79: Newt R 3D 6
CV37: Lwr Clop, Snitt 1D 114
CV37: Snitt 7F 95
Kingsley Av. CV21: Hillm 7A 76
Kingsley Ct. CV3: Bin W 2F 71
Kingsley Cres. CV12: Bulk 2D 42
Kingsley Orchard CV21: Hillm 7A 76
Kingsley Rd. CV33: Bis T 5B 108
Kingsley Sports Cen. 1B 92
Kingsley Ter. CV2: Cov 6A 52
Kingsley Wlk. CV2: W'grve S 6B 52
Kingsmead M. CV3: W'hall 2K 69
Kings Mdw. CV10: Nun 1A 30
KING'S NEWNHAM 1G 73 (1B 144)
Kings Newnham La. CV23: Bret, K New 1C 72
Kings Newnham Rd. CV23: Chu L, K New 1F 73
KING'S NORTON
Birmingham 1B 142
Leicester 1D 141
Kings Pk. Dr. CV3: Bin 6D 60
KING'S SUTTON 2D 147
KINGSTANDING 2B 138
Kingston M. CV31: Lea S 2G 103
Kingston Rd. CV5: Cov 5K 57
King St. CV12: Bed 3H 41
(not continuous)
CV21: Rugby 4G 75
CV32: Lea S 6E 98
Kingsway B78: K'bry 5D 12
CV2: Cov 4G 59
CV11: Nun 7C 22
CV22: Rugby 7G 75
CV31: Lea S 2C 102
CV33: L Hth 3K 119
KINGSWINFORD 3A 138
KINGSWOOD 3J 91 (1C 143)
Kingswood Av. CV7: Cor 6F 39
KINGSWOOD BROOK 4K 91
Kingswood Cl. B94: Lapw 1K 91
CV6: Cov 5D 50
Kingswood Ct. CV10: Nun 7G 21
Kingswood Gdns. CV10: Nun 7G 21
Kingswood Rd. CV10: Nun 7F 21
KINGTON
Warwick 3A 94
Worcester 3A 142
Kington Gdns. B37: F'bri 4A 34
Kington La. CV35: Clav 3A 94
Kington Ri. CV35: Clav 4A 94
King William St. CV1: Cov 3E 58
Kinman Way CV21: Rugby 2J 75
Kinmond Ct. CV32: Lea S 6D 98
Kinross Cl. CV10: Nun 2F 31
Kinross Rd. CV32: Lill 3F 99
Kintyre, The CV2: W'grve S 7D 52
Kinver Cl. CV2: W'grve S 5A 52
Kinver M. B37: Mars G 5A 34
KINWALSEY 6H 37
Kinwalsey La. CV7: Mer 1D 46
KINWARTON 4D 112 (3C 143)
Kinwarton Farm Rd. B49: Kinw 2C 112
Kinwarton Rd. B49: Alc 4C 112
Kinwarton Workshops B49: Kinw 2C 112
Kipling Av. CV34: Warw 4E 100
Kipling Cl. CV10: Gall C 6F 21
Kipling Rd. CV6: Cov 6A 50
CV37: S Avon 7G 115
Kirby Av. CV34: Warw 6H 97
Kirby Cl. CV1: Cov 1D 58
CV8: Bran 3H 71
KIRBY CORNER 3F 67
Kirby Cnr. CV4: Canly 2G 67
Kirby Cnr. Rd. CV4: Canly 3F 67
KIRBY FIELDS 1C 141
Kirby La. CV7: Withy 1D 54
KIRBY MUXLOE 1C 141
Kirby Rd. CV5: Cov 5K 57
Kirkby Cl. CV21: Brow 2A 76
KIRKBY MALLORY 1B 140
Kirkby Rd. CV21: Hillm 7B 76
Kirkdale Av. CV6: Cov 3D 50
Kirkstone CV21: Brow 1K 75
Kirkstone Rd. CV12: Bed 3G 41
Kirkstone Wlk. CV11: Nun 5H 23
Kirkwall CV47: Sou 5H 107
Kirtland Cl. CV9: Aus 7H 7
KIRTLINGTON 3D 147
Kirton Cl. CV6: Cov 5K 49
CV31: W'nsh 5F 103
KISLINGBURY 3D 145
Kissing Tree La. CV37: A'ton 2B 116
Kissing Tree Way CV37: A'ton 2B 116

Kitchener Rd. CV6: Cov 6E 50
KITE GREEN 1K 93
Kitegreen Cl. B37: Chel W 1D 34
Kites Cl. CV34: Warw 5G 97
KITES HARDWICK 2B 144
Kites Nest La. CV35: Beau 2A 96
Kittermaster Rd. CV7: Mer 5E 46
Kitwood Av. B78: Dord 4C 10
Klevedon Cl. CV11: Nun 3C 32
Knebley Cres. CV10: Nun 3J 31
Knibbs Shop. Cen., The *CV34: Warw* *1G 101*
(off Smith St.)
Knight Av. CV1: Cov 6E 58
KNIGHTCOTE 3B 144
Knightcote Dr. CV32: Lea S 7C 98
Knightcote Rd. CV47: Bis I 7B 110
Knight Ct. CV37: S Avon 4E 136
Knightley Cl. CV32: Cubb 2J 99
Knightlow Av. CV3: W'hall 2J 69
Knightlow Cl. CV8: Ken 5G 79
KNIGHTLOW HILL 1H 83 (1B 144)
Knightlow Lodge CV3: W'hall 2J 69
Knightlow Way CV33: Har 6H 109
KNIGHTON
Alcester 3B 142
Leicester 1D 141
Knightsbridge Av. CV12: Bed 7J 31
Knightsbridge Ho. B37: K'hrst 7A 24
Knights Ct. CV34: Warw 2F 101
Knights La. CV37: Tidd 3K 115
Knights Templar Way CV4: Tile H 6E 56
Knob Hill CV23: Stret D 3H 83
Knole Cl. CV22: Rugby 6E 74
Knoll Cft. CV3: Cov 2C 68
Knoll Dr. CV3: Cov 2C 68
CV34: Warw 6G 97
Knottesford Cl. B80: Stud 4B 92
Knotting Way CV3: Cov 6J 59
KNOWLE 1C 143
Knowlebury Cross B94: Tan A 3D 90
Knowle Hill CV8: Ken 3G 79
CV9: Hurl 7J 13
Knowles Av. CV10: Nun 7H 21
Knox Cres. CV11: Nun 3G 23
Kynner Way CV3: Bin 7C 60

L

Laburnum Av. B37: K'hrst 6A 24
CV6: Cov 2K 57
CV8: Ken 5E 78
Laburnum Cl. B37: K'hrst 6A 24
B78: K'bry 5E 12
CV12: Bed 3E 40
Laburnum Cotts. CV37: S Avon 4D 136 (5E 114)
Laburnum Dr. CV31: W'nsh 5F 103
Laburnum Gro. CV10: Nun 5J 21
CV22: Bil 1D 86
CV34: Warw 6K 97
Lacell Cl. CV34: Warw 6F 97
LADBROKE 3C 110 (3B 144)
Ladbroke By-Pass CV47: Ladb 2C 110
Ladbroke Hall CV47: Ladb 3D 110
Ladbroke Pk. CV34: Warw 6G 97
Ladbroke Rd. CV47: Bis I, Dep B 2A 110
Ladbrook Rd. CV5: E Grn 3E 56
Ladycroft CV32: Cubb 3J 99
Ladyfields Way CV6: Cov 2B 50
Lady Godiva's Statue 4H 135
Lady Grey Av. CV34: H'cte 5C 102
Lady Herbert's Homes CV1: Cov 2J 135 (4D 58)
Lady La. CV6: Longf 2F 51
CV8: Ken 5D 78
Lady Lane Mobile Home Pk. CV6: Longf 2F 51
Ladymead Dr. CV6: Cov 4B 50
Ladysmock CV23: Brow 7K 65
Ladywalk Bird Sanctuary 7J 19
Lady Warwick Av. CV12: Bed 3J 41
LADYWOOD
Birmingham 3B 138
Droitwich 2A 142
Laertes Gro. CV34: H'cte 6D 102
Laggan Cl. CV10: Nun 6H 21
Lair, The B78: B'moor 2C 10
Lairhillock Pk. CV23: Mart 3E 104
Lakeland Ho. CV34: Warw 1J 101
Lakeside B95: Woot W 4J 93
CV12: Bed 3G 41
Lakeside Residences CV4: Canly 4E 66
Lakeside Superbowl 6H 31
Lake Vw. Rd. CV5: Cov 3J 57
Lakin Ct. CV34: Warw 7H 97
Lakin Dr. CV47: Bis I 6B 110
Lakin Rd. CV34: Warw 7H 97
Lambert Ct. B50: Bidf A 5F 123
Lambeth Cl. B37: F'bri 1B 34
CV2: Cov 7A 52
Lambourn Cres. CV31: Lea S 2G 103
Lambourne Cl. B50: Bidf A 5G 123
CV5: E Grn 3E 56
Lamb St. CV1: Cov 2G 135 (4C 58)
Lamintone Dr. CV32: Lea S 4B 98
Lammas Ct. CV8: Wols 5J 71
CV34: Warw 2F 101
Lammas Cft. CV31: W'nsh 5E 102
Lammas Ho. CV6: Cov 3A 58
Lammas Rd. CV6: Cov 3K 57
Lammas Wlk. CV34: Warw 1F 101
Lammerton Cl. CV2: Cov 1J 59
Lamorna Cl. CV11: Nun 7G 23
Lamp La. CV7: Gun H 5D 28
Lancaster Cl. CV9: Ath 2D 16
Lancaster Cl. CV35: Welle 4G 117
Lancaster Pl. CV8: Ken 7C 78
Lancaster Rd. CV21: Rugby 4G 75
Lanchester Rd. CV6: Cov 1B 58
Lanchester Way B36: Cas B 3A 24
Lancia Cl. CV6: Ald G 2H 51
Lancing Rd. CV12: Bulk 2E 42
Lancut Hill CV23: Brow, Newt 6K 65
Land La. B37: Mars G 6A 34
Landor Ho. CV31: W'nsh 6E 102
Landor Rd. CV31: W'nsh 5E 102
CV34: Warw 7F 97
Landrail Wlk. B36: Cas B 4A 24
(not continuous)
Landseer Cl. CV21: Hillm 7D 76
LANDYWOOD 1A 138
Lane, The CV36: Lit Wol 7D 132
Laneside CV3: W'hall 2A 70
LANEY GREEN 1A 138
Langbank Av. CV3: Bin 7J 59
Langbay Ct. CV2: W'grve S 1B 60
Langcliffe Av. CV34: Warw 6H 97
Langdale Av. CV6: Cov 3D 50
Langdale Cl. CV21: Brow 1J 75
CV32: Lill 4H 99
Langdale Dr. CV11: Nun 5H 23
Langdon La. CV35: Rad 4A 128
Langlands, The CV35: H Lucy 2A 118
Langlands Pl. CV23: Brow 6K 65
LANGLEY 2C 143
Langley Cft. CV4: Tile H 5E 56
LANGLEY GREEN 2C 143
Langley Rd. CV31: W'nsh 4E 102
CV35: Clav 3B 94
Langlodge Rd. CV6: Cov 4B 50
Langnor Rd. CV2: Cov 1J 59
Langton Cl. B36: Cas B 6B 24
CV3: Bin 7A 60
Langton Rd. CV21: Hillm 7A 76
Langwood Cl. CV4: Canly 1F 67
Lankett, The CV47: Fen C 3G 121
Lansbury Cl. CV2: Cov 7A 52
Lansdale Av. B92: Sol 6A 44
Lansdowne Cir. CV32: Lea S 6E 98
Lansdowne Cl. CV12: Bed 2G 41
Lansdowne Cres. B80: Stud 4C 92
CV32: Lea S 6E 98
Lansdowne Pl. CV21: Rugby 6K 75
Lansdowne Rd. B80: Stud 4C 92
CV32: Lea S 6E 98
Lansdowne St. CV2: Cov 4F 59
CV32: Lea S 6E 98
LAPLEY 1A 138
Lapwing Dr. B92: H Ard 7H 45
LAPWORTH 1C 143
Lapworth Oaks B94: Lapw 3J 91
Lapworth Rd. CV2: Cov 4J 51
Lapworth Station (Rail) 2J 91
Lapworth St. B94: Lapw 3G 91
Larch Cl. B49: Alc 3B 112
CV22: Bil 6B 74
CV37: S Avon 3F 115
Larch Cft. B37: Chel W 3B 34
Larches, The B78: K'bry 4E 12
CV7: Exh 5G 41
Larchfields CV8: Wols 4J 71
Larch Gro. CV34: Warw 6J 97
Larch Tree Av. CV4: Tile H 4E 56
Larchwood Rd. CV7: Exh 5H 41
Larkfield Way CV5: Alle 1E 56
Larkin Cl. CV12: Bulk 2D 42
Larkin Gro. CV2: W'grve S 1B 60
Larkspur CV23: Brow 7K 65
Larkspur Ct. CV12: Bed 5C 40
Larkspur Gro. CV12: Bed 3D 40
Latham Rd. CV5: Cov 5A 58
Latimer Cl. CV8: Ken 7D 78
Lauderdale Av. CV6: Cov 3D 50
Lauderdale Cl. CV23: Long L 4B 74
LAUGHTON 3D 141
Launce Gro. CV34: H'cte 6D 102
Launceston Dr. CV11: Nun 7G 23
Laurel Av. B78: Pole 2D 10
Laurel Cl. CV2: W'grve S 4A 52
Laurel Dr. CV10: Harts 3F 21
CV22: Bil 7B 74
CV47: S'ton 6B 106
Laurel Gdns. CV22: Rugby 1F 87
Laurels, The B78: K'bry 4E 12
CV12: Bed 3E 40
Lavender Av. CV6: Cov 2J 57
Lavender Cl. CV12: Bed 4E 40
CV23: Brow 7K 65
Lavenham Cl. CV11: Nun 4E 32
LAVERTON 2A 146
Lawford Cl. CV3: Bin 6A 60
LAWFORD HEATH 2H 85
Lawford Heath Ind. Est. CV23: Law H 2G 85
Lawford Heath La. CV23: Law H, Long L 3F 85
Lawford La. CV22: Bil 7B 74
Lawford Rd. CV21: Rugby 4C 74
CV31: Lea S 3F 103
Lawley Cl. CV4: Tile H 5E 56
Lawns, The B95: Woot W 5J 93
CV12: Bed 3D 40
CV23: Kils 7H 89
Lawnsdale Cl. B46: Col 5F 25
Lawrence Cl. CV47: Nap 3J 111
Lawrence Gdns. CV8: Ken 3D 78
Lawrence Mackie Gdns. CV35: Welle 2J 117
Lawrence Mackie Ho. CV35: Welle 1J 117
Lawrence Rd. CV7: Exh 5G 41
CV21: Rugby 5K 75
Lawrence Saunders Rd. CV6: Cov 2A 58
Lawrence Sheriff St. CV22: Rugby 5G 75
Lawson Av. CV37: Tidd 3K 115
Lay Gdns. CV31: Rad S 3J 103
Lea Cl. B49: Alc 3C 112
CV37: S Avon 3A 114
Lea Ct. CV37: S Avon 6E 114
Lea Cres. CV21: N'bld A 2D 74
Leacrest Rd. CV6: Cov 4A 50
LEA END 1B 142
Leaf Ct. CV3: Cov 4D 68
Leafield Cl. CV2: W'grve S 5B 52
Leaf La. CV3: Cov 4E 68
Leagh Cl. CV8: Ken 2F 79
LEA HALL 3C 139
Leaholme Ct. CV5: Cov 7K 57
LEA MARSTON 4G 19 (2D 139)
Lea Marston Leisure Cen. 2G 19
Leam Cl. CV11: Nun 3B 32
Leam Grn. CV4: Canly 3H 67
LEAMINGTON HASTINGS 6D 104 (2B 144)
Leamington Hastings Rd. CV23: Bird 5A 104
Leamington Rd. CV3: Cov 1C 68
CV8: Ken 7E 78
CV8: Rytn D 1C 82
CV23: Prin 7C 82
CV47: Long I 1A 106
CV47: Sou 6F 107
LEAMINGTON SPA, ROYAL 2A 144
Leamington Spa Station (Rail) 1D 102
LEAMONSLEY 1C 139
Leam Rd. CV31: Lea S 1B 102
CV33: L Hth 2K 119
Leam St. CV31: Lea S 1F 103
Leam Ter. CV31: Lea S 1E 102
Lear Gro. CV34: H'cte 4C 102
Leas Cl. CV12: Bed 2G 41
Leasowes Av. CV3: Finh 4K 67
Leathermill La. CV10: Harts 1H 21 & 7J 17
Leather St. CV47: Long I 2D 106
Lea Wlk. CV8: Rytn D 7D 70
Leaward Cl. CV10: Nun 2E 30
Ledbrook Rd. CV32: Cubb 2H 99
Ledbury Rd. CV31: Lea S 2G 103
LEDWELL 3D 147
Lee, The CV5: Cov 3G 57
Lee Cl. CV34: Warw 5G 97
Leeder Cl. CV6: Cov 4C 50
LEEK WOOTTON 1H 97 (2D 143)
Lee Meadowe CV34: Warw 4D 100
Leeming Cl. CV4: Canly 2G 67
Lee Rd. CV31: Lea S 1C 102
Lees, The CV33: Bis T 5B 108
Le Haunche Cl. CV7: Ker E 6A 40
LEICESTER 1C 141
Leicester C'way. CV1: Cov 3D 58
Leicester Ct. CV12: Bulk 3E 42
CV32: Lea S 6F 99
Leicester Cres. CV9: Ath 2D 16
LEICESTER FOREST EAST 1C 141
Leicester La. CV32: Cubb, Lill 2E 98 & 7E 80
Leicester Rd. CV2: W'grve S 6C 52
CV7: Shil, Wlvy 1G 53
CV11: Nun 6E 22
CV12: Bed 1H 41
CV21: Brow, Rugby 3G 75
LE10: Wlvy 1J 33
Leicester Row CV1: Cov 1H 135 (3C 58)
Leicester St. CV12: Bed 2H 41
CV12: Bulk 3E 42
CV32: Lea S 6E 98
Leigh Av. CV3: Finh 5C 68
Leigh Cres. CV47: Long I 3D 106
Leigh Rd. CV21: Rugby 7F 65
Leigh St. CV1: Cov 3E 58
Leighton Cl. CV4: Canly 6H 67
CV32: Lill 3G 99
LEIRE 2C 141
LENCHWICK 3B 142
Lennon Cl. CV21: Hillm 1E 88
Lennox Cl. CV3: W'hall 2A 70
Lenton's La. CV2: Ald G 2K 51
Leofric St. CV6: Cov 2A 58
Leonard Perkins Ho. *CV12: Bulk* *3F 43*
(off Elm Tree Rd.)
Leontes Mdws. CV34: H'cte 5C 102
Leopold Rd. CV1: Cov 3F 59
Lesingham Dr. CV4: Tile H 6C 56
Lestock Cl. CV22: Bil 6C 74
Letchlade Cl. CV2: Cov 7J 51
Leven Way CV2: W'grve S 6C 52
Lever Rd. CV21: Hillm 7C 76
Levy Cl. CV21: Rugby 5F 75
Lewis Cl. CV9: Man 5E 16
Lewis Rd. CV1: Cov 2D 58
CV31: Rad S 4J 103
Lexington Ct. CV11: Nun 6C 22
Leyburn Cl. CV6: Cov 4D 50
CV11: Nun 2C 32
CV34: Warw 6G 97
Leycester Cl. CV33: Har 5G 109
Leycester Pl. CV34: Warw 2G 101
Leycester Rd. CV8: Ken 7D 78
Leyes La. CV8: Ken 4F 79
(not continuous)
LEYFIELDS 1D 139
Leyfields Cres. CV34: Warw 4F 101
Leyland Rd. CV5: Cov 3H 57
CV11: Nun 3A 32
CV12: Bulk 3D 42
Leylands Way CV34: Warw 4D 100
Leymere Cl. CV7: Mer 5E 46
Leys, The B50: Bidf A 5H 123

Leys, The CV36: Half . . . 2K 127
CV36: Lit Wol . . . 6D 132
CV36: Whatc . . . 3B 130
Leys Cl. CV47: N'end . . . 2D 120
Leyside CV3: W'hall . . . 3A 70
Leys La. CV7: Mer . . . 5E 46
Leys Rd. CV21: Hillm . . . 2E 88
LIBBERY . . . 3A 142
Liberty Way CV11: Nun . . . 1B 32
Library Rd. CV4: Canly . . . 4F 67
Lichen Grn. CV4: Canly . . . 3H 67
LICHFIELD . . . 1C 139
Lichfield Cl. CV7: Gun H . . . 4E 28
CV11: Nun . . . 4H 23
Lichfield Rd. B46: Col, Wat O . . . 7D 18
B76: Curd, Wis . . . 1C 18
CV3: Cov . . . 7D 58
LICKEY . . . 1A 142
LICKEY END . . . 1A 142
LIDSTONE . . . 3C 147
LIFFORD . . . 3B 138
Lifford Way CV3: Bin . . . 1C 70
LIGHTHORNE . . . 2G 119 (3A 144)
LIGHTHORNE HEATH . . . 2K 119
Lighthorne Rd. CV35: Kine . . . 4C 120
Light La. CV1: Cov . . . 1G 135 (3C 58)
Lilac Av. CV6: Cov . . . 2K 57
Lilac Dr. CV22: Bil . . . 6B 74
Lilac Gro. CV34: Warw . . . 6J 97
Lilac Rd. CV12: Bed . . . 7K 31
Lilacvale Way CV4: Canly . . . 3H 67
LILBOURNE . . . 2J 77 (1C 145)
Lilbourne Rd. CV23: Clift D . . . 3D 76
Lilleburn Dr. CV10: Nun . . . 4F 21
Lilley Cl. CV6: Cov . . . 4C 50
LILLINGTON . . . 4F 99
Lillington Av. CV32: Lea S . . . 5D 98
Lillington Cl. CV32: Lill . . . 4E 98
Lillington Rd. CV2: Cov . . . 5K 51
CV32: Lea S, Lill . . . 5E 98
Limbrick Av. CV4: Tile H . . . 6D 56
Lime Av. CV32: Lill . . . 3E 98
Lime Gro. B37: Chel W . . . 4B 34
B79: Newt R . . . 5D 6
CV4: Tile H . . . 5F 57
CV8: Ken . . . 5E 78
CV9: Hurl . . . 7J 13
CV10: Nun . . . 6K 21
Lime Kilns B78: Pole . . . 2D 10
Lime Rd. CV47: Sou . . . 4H 107
Limes, The CV6: Cov . . . 2J 57
CV12: Bed . . . 3E 40
CV37: S Avon . . . 4B 136
Limes Av. CV37: S Avon . . . 6C 114
Limes Coppice CV10: Ans C . . . 4D 20
Limestone Hall La. CV23: Chu L . . . 7D 72
Lime Tree Av. CV4: Tile H . . . 5E 56
CV22: Bil . . . 2B 86
Limetree Dr. CV35: More M . . . 6B 118
LIME TREE PARK . . . 5F 57
Linacre Ho. B37: F'bri . . . 3A 34
Linaker Rd. CV3: W'hall . . . 3J 69
Lincoln Av. CV10: Nun . . . 4G 21
Lincoln Cl. CV34: Warw . . . 6G 97
CV35: Welle . . . 4G 117
Lincoln Gro. B37: Mars G . . . 4A 34
Lincoln St. CV1: Cov . . . 1H 135 (3D 58)
Lincroft Cres. CV5: Cov . . . 3H 57
Lindale CV21: Brow . . . 7K 65
Linden Av. CV35: Welle . . . 3J 117
Linden Cl. CV34: Warw . . . 5G 97
Linden Lea CV12: Bed . . . 2H 41
Lindfield, The CV3: Cov . . . 7J 59
Lindisfarne Dr. CV8: Ken . . . 5F 79
Lindley Rd. CV3: Cov . . . 5H 59
CV12: Bed . . . 3D 40
Lindop Cl. CV32: Cubb . . . 2G 99
Lindsay Wlk. CV47: Temp H . . . 2A 120
Lindsey Cres. CV8: Ken . . . 7D 78
Linehoit Cl. B98: Redd . . . 1A 92
Linen St. CV34: Warw . . . 2F 101
Linford Wlk. CV2: W'grve S . . . 5B 52
Lingfield Ct. CV6: Ald G . . . 2H 51
Lingfield Cres. CV37: S Avon . . . 7D 114
Lingwood Dr. CV10: Nun . . . 1F 31
Links Rd. CV6: Cov . . . 6A 50
Linkway CV31: Lea S . . . 2C 102
Linley Rd. CV47: Sou . . . 3H 107
Linnell Rd. CV21: Hillm . . . 6A 76
Linnet Cl. CV3: W'hall . . . 3K 69
CV23: Brow . . . 6J 65
Linstock Way CV6: Ald G . . . 2H 51
Linwood Dr. CV2: W'grve S . . . 5B 52
Lion Flds. Av. CV5: Alle . . . 1F 57
Lion Tuery B49: Alc . . . 5B 112
Liskeard Cl. CV11: Nun . . . 6H 23
Lisle Ct. CV31: Lea S . . . 2E 102
Lisle Gdns. CV33: Bis T . . . 5C 108
Lismore Cft. CV2: W'grve S . . . 7D 52
Lister Rd. CV9: Ath . . . 2C 16
Lister St. CV11: Nun . . . 1K 31
LITCHBOROUGH . . . 3D 145
Littimore Rd. CV37: S Avon . . . 2D 114
LITTLE ALNE . . . 2C 143
LITTLE ASTON . . . 1B 138
LITTLE BEDWORTH HEATH . . . 4E 40
LITTLE BOURTON . . . 1D 147
LITTLE BOWDEN . . . 3D 141
LITTLE BRINGTON . . . 2D 145
LITTLE BRITAIN . . . 1K 123
Little Brum CV9: Gren . . . 1F 15
Lit. Church St. CV1: Cov . . . 3D 58
CV21: Rugby . . . 5G 75
LITTLE COMPTON . . . 6C 134 (2B 146)
Little Cryfield CV4: Canly . . . 6G 67
LITTLE DASSETT . . . 2D 120
Lit. Duke St. CV11: Nun . . . 7C 22
Lit. Elborow St. CV21: Rugby . . . 5G 75
(not continuous)
LITTLE EVERDON . . . 3C 145
Little Farm CV3: W'hall . . . 3K 69
Little Fields CV2: Cov . . . 2G 59
Little Gro. CV22: Rugby . . . 7J 75
LITTLE HAY . . . 1C 139
LITTLE HEATH . . . 4F 51 (3A 140)
Lit. Heath Ind. Est. CV6: Cov . . . 4F 51
LITTLE HONINGTON . . . 1K 131
LITTLE KINETON . . . 7C 120 (3A 144)
LITTLE LAWFORD . . . 1K 73 (1B 144)
Lit. Lawford La. CV21: N'bld A . . . 1J 73
CV23: Lit L . . . 1J 73
LITTLE LONDON . . . 2C 38
Lit. Orchard CV22: Bil . . . 7B 74
LITTLE ORTON . . . 1A 140
LITTLE PACKINGTON . . . 7K 35 (3D 139)
Little Pk. CV47: Sou . . . 5H 107
Lit. Park St. CV1: Cov . . . 5J 135 (5D 58)
Lit. Pennington St. CV21: Rugby . . . 5F 75
Lit. Pittern CV35: Kine . . . 5C 120
LITTLE PRESTON . . . 3C 145
LITTLE RISSINGTON . . . 3A 146
LITTLE ROLLRIGHT . . . 2B 146
LITTLE SAREDON . . . 1A 138
Lit. South St. CV1: Cov . . . 4E 58
LITTLE STRETTON . . . 1D 141
LITTLE TEW . . . 3C 147
LITTLETHORPE . . . 2C 141
Littlethorpe CV3: W'hall . . . 2K 69
Littleton Cl. CV8: Ken . . . 3E 78
LITTLE TWYCROSS . . . 1A 140
LITTLE WARTON . . . 6H 9
Lit. Warton Rd. B79: Wart . . . 5J 9
LITTLE WOLFORD . . . 7D 132 (2B 146)
LITTLEWOOD GEEN . . . 5D 92
Littlewood Grn. B80: Stud . . . 5C 92
LITTLEWORTH
Broadway . . . 2A 146
Cannock . . . 1B 138
Warwick . . . 2J 95
Worcester . . . 3A 142
Redditch . . . 2A 142
Littleworth B95: Hen A . . . 3H 93
Littleworth Cft. CV31: Lea S . . . 4G 103
LITTLE WYRLEY . . . 1B 138
Liverpool Cft. B37: Mars G . . . 5A 34
Livery St. CV32: Lea S . . . 7D 98
Livingstone Av. CV23: Long L . . . 4K 73
Livingstone Rd. CV6: Cov . . . 7D 50
Liza Ct. CV21: Brow . . . 7J 65
Llewellyn Rd. CV31: Lea S . . . 2E 102
Lloyd Cl. CV11: Nun . . . 2K 31
CV35: H Mag . . . 2B 100
Lloyd Cres. CV2: Cov . . . 4A 60
Lloyd Rd. CV21: Brow . . . 2J 75
Lloyds Way CV37: B'ton, S Avon . . . 2C 114
Loach Dr. CV2: Ald G . . . 2H 51
Loch St. CV3: Cov . . . 6J 59
Lock Cl. CV37: S Avon . . . 2G 137 (4F 115)
Locke Cl. CV6: Cov . . . 5A 50
Lockhart Cl. CV8: Ken . . . 5E 78
Lockheed Cl. CV31: Lea S . . . 3D 102
Lock Ho. La. B76: Curd . . . 2D 18
Lockhurst La. CV6: Cov . . . 6D 50
Lock La. CV34: Warw . . . 6F 97
Locks, The CV21: Hillm . . . 7D 76
Loder Cl. CV4: Tile H . . . 4D 56
Lodge Cl. CV9: Man . . . 5F 17
Lodge Ct. CV37: S Avon . . . 4D 114
Lodge Cres. CV34: Warw . . . 4F 101
LODGE GREEN . . . 3G 47
Lodge Grn. La. CV7: Mer . . . 3G 47
Lodge Grn. La. Nth. CV7: Mer . . . 3G 47
Lodge Rd. CV3: Cov . . . 6H 59
CV21: Rugby . . . 4H 75
CV37: S Avon . . . 4C 114
Loft Theatre, The . . . 1D 102
Logan Rd. CV2: Cov . . . 7A 52
Lole Cl. CV6: Longf . . . 2G 51
Lollard Cft. CV3: Cov . . . 7D 58
Lomond Way CV10: Nun . . . 6H 21
Lomsey Cl. CV4: Tile H . . . 6E 56
London Rd. CV1: Cov . . . 6K 135 (6E 58)
CV3: Cov, W'hall . . . 2G 69
CV3: W'hall . . . 4K 69
CV23: Bour D, Dunc, Stret D, Thurl . . . 7E 70
CV23: W'hby . . . 2J 105
CV36: Ship S . . . 5H 131
LONGBOROUGH . . . 3A 146
LONGBRIDGE
Birmingham . . . 1B 142
Warwick . . . 6D 100 (2D 143)
LONG BUCKBY . . . 2D 145
LONG BUCKBY WHARF . . . 2D 145
Long Cast Pk. Homes CV37: Welf A . . . 4A 124
Long Cl. Av. CV5: Alle . . . 1F 57
LONG COMPTON . . . 2C 134 (2B 146)
Longdon Cl. B98: Redd . . . 1A 92
LONGDON GREEN . . . 1B 138
Longdown La. CV23: Barby, W'hby . . . 2J 105
Longfellow Av. CV34: Warw . . . 4E 100
Longfellow Ct. CV2: Cov . . . 4J 59
Longfellow Rd. CV2: Cov . . . 4J 59
CV37: S Avon . . . 7H 115
Longfield Ho. CV6: Cov . . . 6G 51
Longfield Rd. CV31: Lea S . . . 2F 103
LONGFORD . . . 2G 51 (3A 140)
Longford Cl. B50: Bidf A . . . 5J 123
Longford Rd. CV6: Longf . . . 3F 51
CV7: Exh . . . 7G 41
Longford Sq. CV6: Longf . . . 2F 51
Long Furlong CV22: Rugby . . . 2F 87
Long Hassocks CV23: Brow, Newt . . . 6K 65
LONG ITCHINGTON . . . 2C 106 (2B 144)
Long La. CV5: Alle . . . 4H 49
CV7: Ker E . . . 4H 49
LONG LAWFORD . . . 3A 74 (1B 144)
Longleat Gro. CV31: Lea S . . . 2G 103
Long Leys Ct. B46: Wat O . . . 2B 24
Longleys Cft. B46: Wat O . . . 2B 24
Longley Wlk. B37: Chel W . . . 3C 34
LONG MARSTON . . . 2G 125 (1A 146)
Long Marston Rd. CV37: Long M . . . 1G 125
CV37: Welf A . . . 3A 124
Longmoor Dr. CV3: Cov . . . 6J 59
Longrood Rd. CV22: Bil . . . 3D 86
Long Shoot, The CV11: Nun . . . 6H 23
Longstork Rd. CV23: Brow . . . 6K 65
Long St. B78: Dord . . . 5D 10
CV9: Ath . . . 3C 16
CV12: Bulk . . . 3F 43
Longwood Cl. CV4: W'wd H . . . 2D 66
Lonscale Dr. CV3: Cov . . . 3B 68
Lonsdale Rd. CV32: Lill . . . 3F 99
Lord Leycester Hospital . . . 2G 101
Lord Lytton Av. CV2: Cov . . . 5K 59
Lords La. B80: Stud . . . 4D 92
Lord St. CV5: Cov . . . 5K 57
Lorenzo Cl. CV3: W'hall . . . 2K 69
Lotus Wlk. B36: Cas B . . . 3A 24
Loudon Av. CV6: Cov . . . 2A 58
Loudon Ga. CV11: Nun . . . 3B 32
Louisa Ward Cl. CV23: Mart . . . 2D 104
Loveday Cl. CV9: Ath . . . 1C 16
Loveday Dr. CV32: Lea S . . . 5C 98
Love La. CV8: Ken . . . 3D 78
Lovell Cl. CV7: Exh . . . 5G 41
Lovell Rd. CV12: Bed . . . 2G 41
Loverock Cres. CV21: Hillm . . . 6A 76
Lower Av. CV31: Lea S . . . 1D 102
LOWER BENTLEY . . . 2A 142
LOWER BODDINGTON . . . 3B 144
LOWER BRAILES . . . 3H 133 (2C 147)
Lower Cape CV34: Warw . . . 6F 97
LOWER CATESBY . . . 3C 145
LOWER CLOPTON . . . 3C 143
LOWER EASTERN GREEN . . . 3D 56
Lwr. Eastern Grn. La. CV5: E Grn . . . 3D 56
Lower End CV8: Bubb . . . 3J 81
CV37: A'ton . . . 1B 116
Lwr. Ford St. CV1: Cov . . . 5E 58
(Far Gosford St.)
CV1: Cov . . . 2K 135 (4D 58)
(Ford St.)
Lower Friars CV34: Warw . . . 3F 101
LOWER GREEN . . . 1A 138
LOWER HEYFORD . . . 3D 147
Lwr. Hillmorton Rd. CV21: Hillm, Rugby . . . 5H 75
Lwr. Holyhead Rd. CV1: Cov . . . 3F 135 (4B 58)
Lwr. House La. CV9: Bad E . . . 2B 14
LOWER LADYES HILLS . . . 4E 78
Lwr. Ladyes Hills CV8: Ken . . . 3E 78
Lwr. Leam St. CV31: Lea S . . . 7F 99
Lwr. Lea Pl. CV21: Hillm . . . 1D 88
LOWER LEMINGTON . . . 2B 146
Lower Mall *CV32: Lea S* . . . *7D 98*
(in Royal Priors Shop. Cen.)
LOWER MOOR . . . 3A 142
LOWER NORTON . . . 1H 95
Lowe Rd. CV6: Cov . . . 4K 49
LOWER ODDINGTON . . . 3B 146
LOWER PENN . . . 2A 138
Lower Pct. CV1: Cov . . . 3G 135 (4C 58)
LOWER QUINTON . . . 5H 125 (1A 146)
Lower Rd. CV7: Barn . . . 7D 42
LOWER SHUCKBURGH . . . 2B 144
LOWER SLAUGHTER . . . 3A 146
LOWER STOKE . . . 5G 59
LOWER STONNALL . . . 1B 138
Lower St. CV21: Hillm . . . 7D 76
CV23: W'hby . . . 2H 105
LOWER SWELL . . . 3A 146
LOWER TYSOE . . . 4D 130 (1C 147)
Lwr. Villiers St. CV32: Lea S . . . 6E 98
Lowes Av. CV34: Warw . . . 6G 97
LOWESBY . . . 1D 141
Lowes La. CV35: Welle . . . 4H 117
Loweswater Cl. CV11: Nun . . . 5H 23
Loweswater Rd. CV3: Bin . . . 6A 60
Lowfield Rd. CV3: Cov . . . 6J 59
Lowry Cl. CV12: Bed . . . 1G 41
LOWSONFORD . . . 2C 143
Lowther St. CV2: Cov . . . 3F 59
LOXLEY . . . 6D 116 (3D 143)
Loxley Cl. CV2: Cov . . . 4K 51
CV35: Welle . . . 4G 117
Loxley Ct. CV2: Cov . . . 4K 51
Loxley Flds. CV35: Lox . . . 6D 116
Loxley Paddocks CV35: Lox . . . 7F 117
Loxley Rd. CV35: Welle . . . 4E 116
CV37: S Avon, A'ton . . . 5G 115
Loxley Way CV32: Lill . . . 5E 98
LUBENHAM . . . 3D 141
Lucas Ct. CV21: Rugby . . . 4H 75
CV32: Lea S . . . 7B 98
Lucerne Cl. CV2: Ald G . . . 3J 51
Lucian Cl. CV2: W'grve S . . . 7D 52
Lucy's Mill Ho's. CV37: S Avon . . . 6F 115
LUDDINGTON . . . 1E 124 (3C 143)
Luddington Rd. CV37: S Avon . . . 7A 114

Ludford Cl. CV10: Ansl 7A 20
CV37: S Avon 3A 114
Ludford Rd. CV10: Nun 5H 21
Ludgate Cl. B46: Wat O 1A 24
Ludham Pl. CV22: Caw 1A 86
Ludlow Cl. B37: Chel W 3C 34
Ludlow Rd. CV5: Cov 5A 58
Ludworth Av. B37: Mars G 4B 34
Luff Cl. CV3: Cov 7H 59
LULLINGTON 1D 139
Lulworth Pk. CV8: Ken 3G 79
Lumley Gro. B37: Chel W 3D 34
Lumsden Cl. CV2: W'grve S 6B 52
Lunar Cl. CV4: Canly 3H 67
Lundy Vw. B36: Cas B 7B 24
Lunn Av. CV8: Ken 6C 78
Lunt Roman Fort Mus. 5E 68
Lupin Wlk. CV10: Nun 4G 31
Lupton Av. CV3: Cov 1C 68
Luscombe Rd. CV2: Cov 6A 52
Luther Way CV5: E Grn 3D 56
LUTTERWORTH 3C 141
Lutterworth Rd. CV2: Cov 2J 59
CV11: Bram, Nun, Burt H 2A 32 & 1G 33
CV23: Brin 3D 62
CV23: C'over 1J 65
LE10: Wlvy 2A 32
Luxor La. CV5: Mil W 6K 47
Lydford Cl. CV2: Cov 7J 51
Lydgate Ct. CV11: Nun 1J 31
CV12: Bed 1G 41
Lydgate Rd. CV6: Cov 2B 58
LYDIATE ASH 1A 142
Lydstep Gro. CV31: Lea S 1G 103
LYE 3A 138
Lyecroft Av. B37: Chel W 3D 34
LYE GREEN 1D 94
Lye Grn. Rd. CV35: Clav 1D 94
Lymesy St. CV3: Cov 2D 68
Lymington Cl. CV6: Cov 6D 50
Lymington Dr. CV6: Longf 7H 41
Lymore Cft. CV2: W'grve S 6C 52
Lynbrook Rd. CV5: Cov 7H 57
Lynch, The B78: Pole 1C 10
CV11: Nun 2K 31
Lynchgate Ct. CV4: Canly 2G 67
Lynchgate Rd. CV4: Canly 2G 67
Lyndale Cl. CV5: Cov 4G 57
(Harewood Rd.)
CV5: Cov 4G 57
(Overdale Rd.)
Lyndale Rd. CV5: Cov 4G 57
Lyndhurst Cl. CV6: Longf 1H 51
Lyndhurst Cft. CV5: E Grn 3A 56
Lyndhurst Rd. CV21: Hillm 1B 88
Lyndon Ct. CV32: Lea S 7C 98
Lyndon Cft. B37: Mars G 6B 34
LYNEHAM 3B 146
Lyne Ho. CV2: Cov 5K 51
Lyng Cl. CV5: E Grn 4E 56
Lynmouth Cl. CV11: Nun 6F 23
Lynmouth Rd. CV2: Cov 6A 52
LYNN 1B 138
Lynnon Fld. CV34: Warw 4D 100
Lynton Cl. CV34: Warw 6F 97
Lynton Rd. CV6: Cov 5F 51
Lynwood Wlk. CV31: Lea S 2G 103
Lysander Cl. CV35: Welle 4G 117
Lysander Ct. CV37: S Avon 5F 137 (5E 114)
Lyster Cl. CV34: Warw 7D 96
Lythall Cl. CV31: Rad S 3K 103
Lythalls La. CV6: Cov 4D 50
Lythalls La. Ind. Est. CV6: Cov 5E 50
Lytham Rd. CV22: Bil 7D 74
Lyttelton Rd. CV34: Warw 7G 97
Lyttleton Cl. CV3: Bin 6C 60

M

Macaulay Rd. CV2: Cov 3K 59
CV22: Rugby 2E 86
Macbeth App. CV34: H'cte 5B 102
Macbeth Cl. CV22: Bil 3E 86
Macdonald Rd. CV2: Cov 4K 59
McDonnell Dr. CV7: Exh 7F 41
Macefield Cl. CV2: Ald G 3K 51
Mackenzie Cl. CV5: Alle 7E 48
McKinnell Cres. CV21: Hillm 6A 76
Mackley Way CV33: Har 6G 109
McMahon Rd. CV12: Bed 5E 40
Madden Pl. CV22: Bil 6C 74
Madeira Cft. CV5: Cov 5J 57
MADELEY HEATH 1A 142
Maffey Ct. CV22: Rugby 6G 75
Magdalen Cl. CV37: Lwr Q 5H 125
Magdalen Rd. CV23: W'hby 3J 105
MAGNA PARK 3C 141
Magnet La. CV22: Bil 1C 86
Magneto Rd. CV3: Cov 6J 59
Magnolia Cl. CV3: Cov 3B 68
Magpie Ho. CV5: E Grn 2B 56
Maguire Ind. Est. CV4: Tile H 7D 56
Magyar Cres. CV11: Nun 5B 32
Maidavale Cres. CV3: Cov 3C 68
Maidenhair Dr. CV23: Brow 7K 65
Maidenhead Cl. CV37: S Avon 3F 115
Maidenhead Rd. CV37: S Avon 1G 137 (4F 115)
MAIDFORD 3D 145
MAIDWELL 1D 145
Main Rd. B26: Birm A 3A 44
B79: Newt R, Shut 2B 8
CV7: Ansty 3F 53
Main Rd. CV7: Mer 5E 46
CV9: Aus 7H 7
CV9: Bax 4C 14
CV23: Kils 6H 89
CV37: Lwr Q 5H 125
Main St. CV7: Withy 1C 54
CV8: Wols 4H 71
CV21: N'bld A 1D 74
CV22: Bil 1C 86
CV23: Bird 5A 104
CV23: Bour D 7C 84
CV23: Clift D 3B 76
CV23: Eas 3J 63
CV23: F'ton 7B 84
CV23: Gran 6H 105
CV23: Harb M 4A 64
CV23: Long L 4A 74
CV23: M Kirby 3J 55
CV23: Stret U 7F 55
CV23: Thurl 7K 85
CV23: W'hby 3H 105
CV35: N Lin 2G 95
CV35: Oxh 1E 130
CV35: Up Tys, Mis T 7C 130
CV36: Long C 1C 134
CV37: A'ton, Tidd 3K 115
MAJOR'S GREEN 1C 143
Makepeace Av. CV34: Warw 6H 97
Malam Cl. CV4: Tile H 6E 56
Maldale B77: Wiln 1A 10
Maldens, The CV36: Ship S 5H 131
Maletts Cl. CV35: Mid T 7C 130
Malham Cl. CV11: Nun 2C 32
Malham Rd. B77: Wiln 2A 10
CV34: Warw 6H 97
Malin Ct. B49: Alc 4B 112
Malins, The CV34: Warw 2K 101
Mallard Av. CV10: Nun 6H 21
Mallard Cl. CV37: B'ton 2B 114
Mallard Rd. B80: Stud 3E 92
Mallerin Cft. CV10: Nun 6G 21
Mallory Dr. CV34: Warw 1F 101
Mallory Rd. CV33: Bis T 5A 108
CV33: L Hth 2K 119
Mallory Way CV6: Longf 2E 50
Mallow Cft. CV12: Bed 3E 40
Mallow Way CV23: Brow 7J 65
Malmesbury Rd. CV6: Cov 4A 50
Malt Ho. Cl. B50: Broom 3F 123
Malthouse Cl. CV10: Ansl 7A 20
CV47: N'end 2D 120
Malthouse Ct. CV34: Warw 1F 101
Malthouse La. CV8: Ken 2C 78
CV36: Long C 2C 134
CV47: N'end 2D 120
Malt Ho. Row B37: Mars G 5A 34
Maltings, The B80: Stud 3C 92
CV11: Nun 6F 23
CV32: Lea S 5D 98
(not continuous)
CV37: S Avon 5F 137 (5F 115)
Maltings Ct. CV37: S Avon 1E 136
Malt Mill Cl. CV23: Kils 7J 89
Malt Mill Grn. *CV23: Kils 7J 89*
(off Main Rd.)
Maltmill La. B49: Alc 5C 112
Malt Shovel Ct. *CV47: Bis I 6B 110*
(off Fisher Rd.)
Malvern Av. CV10: Nun 1B 30
CV22: Rugby 7K 75
Malvern Rd. CV5: Cov 3K 57
MANCETTER 5F 17 (2A 140)
Mancetter Rd. CV9: Man 4E 16
(not continuous)
CV10: Nun 4J 21
Mandale Cl. CV47: Bis I 7B 110
Mander Gro. CV34: Warw 4D 100
Manderley Cl. CV5: E Grn 2A 56
Mandrake Cl. CV6: Cov 2D 50
MANEY 2C 139
Manfield Av. CV2: W'grve S 7C 52
Manning Wlk. *CV21: Rugby 5G 75*
(in Clock Towers Shop. Cen.)
Mann's Cl. CV8: Rytn D 1D 82
Manor Barns CV36: Ilm 6C 126
Manor Cl. CV9: Bad E 1E 14
Manor Ct. B49: Gt Alne 3F 113
CV8: Ken 3E 78
CV31: Lea S 1D 102
CV37: Ett 2B 126
CV47: Fen C 3G 121
Manor Ct. Av. CV11: Nun 6C 22
Manor Ct. Rd. CV11: Nun 7B 22
Manor Dr. CV23: Stret D 3H 83
CV37: Wilm 6K 113
Manor Est. CV8: Wols 5H 71
Mnr. Farm Cl. CV23: Barby 7E 88
Mnr. Farm Cotts. CV37: Ludd 1E 124
Mnr. Farm Rd. CV36: Tred 6J 127
Manor Grn. CV37: S Avon 5H 115
Mnr. Hall M. CV3: W'hall 2K 69
Manor Ho. CV2: W'grve S 7B 52
CV31: Lea S 1D 102
Manor Ho. Cl. CV21: N'bld A 1D 74
Manor Ho. Dr. CV1: Cov 6G 135 (5C 58)
Manor Ho. La. B46: Wat O 1B 24
Manor La. CV23: Clift D 2C 76
CV35: Kine 6D 120
CV35: Lox 6D 116
CV36: Ship S 4H 131
CV37: Ett 2B 126
Manor M. B80: Stud 3D 92
Manor Orchard CV33: Har 6G 109
Manor Pk. Rd. CV11: Nun 6B 22
Manor Rd. B80: Stud 3D 92
CV1: Cov 6G 135 (6C 58)
CV8: Ken 3D 78
CV9: Man 4D 16
CV21: Rugby 4H 75
CV23: Kils 6J 89
CV32: Lill 4F 99
CV33: Har 6H 109
CV35: Clav 1E 94
CV37: S Avon 5H 115
CV47: Bis I 6B 110
CV47: S'ton 6C 106
Manor Rd. Ind. Est. CV9: Man 4D 16
Manor Ter. CV1: Cov 5H 135 (5C 58)
Manor Yd. CV1: Cov 5H 135 (5C 58)
Mansard Ct. B46: Col 5G 25
Manse Cl. CV7: Exh 4G 41
Manse Gdns. B80: Stud 3D 92
Mansell St. CV37: S Avon 2D 136 (4E 114)
Mansel St. CV6: Cov 6E 50
Mansfield Ho. B37: Chel W 2C 34
Mansion Ho., The CV35: Lit K 6C 120
Mansions Cl. CV47: Bis I 6B 110
Mansley Bus. Cen., The CV37: S Avon 3C 114
Manston Dr. CV35: Welle 4G 117
Mantilla Dr. CV3: Cov 3A 68
Mantua CV37: S Avon 1H 137
Maple Av. CV7: Exh 4H 41
Maplebeck Cl. CV5: Cov 4A 58
Maple Dr. B78: K'bry 4E 12
Maple Gro. B37: K'hrst 6A 24
CV21: Rugby 4G 75
CV34: Warw 6J 97
CV37: S Avon 2E 114
Maple Leaf Dr. B37: Mars G 5B 34
Maple Rd. CV10: Nun 6K 21
CV31: Lea S 2D 102
Maples, The CV12: Bed 3E 40
Mapleton Rd. CV6: Cov 6K 49
Maple Wlk. *B37: Chel W 3B 34*
(off Chelmsley Wood Shop. Cen.)
CV6: Longf 1F 51
Mapperley Cl. CV2: W'grve S 6C 52
MAPPLEBOROUGH GREEN 2B 142
Marble All. B80: Stud 3D 92
March Ct. CV22: Rugby 7G 75
Marchfont Cl. CV11: Nun 2C 32
March Way CV3: Bin 1K 69
MARCLIFF 7G 123
Marcroft Pl. CV31: Lea S 2H 103
Mardol Cl. CV2: Cov 7K 51
MAREFIELD 1D 141
Margaret Av. CV12: Bed 2G 41
Margaret Cl. CV33: Har 6H 109
Margaret Rd. CV9: Ath 4D 16
Margeson Cl. CV2: Cov 5A 60
Margetts Cl. CV8: Ken 5D 78
Marie Brock Cl. CV4: Tile H 6F 57
Marie Cl. CV9: Man 4F 17
Marigold Wlk. CV10: Griff 4G 31
Marina Cl. CV4: Tile H 1C 66
Marion Rd. CV6: Cov 7D 50
Mark Antony Dr. CV34: H'cte 4B 102
MARKET BOSWORTH 1B 140
Market Cnr. CV8: Bag 6F 69
CV31: Lea S 2D 102
Market Cross *CV37: S Avon 4G 137*
(off Bridge St.)
MARKET END 3D 40 (3A 140)
Mkt. End Cl. CV12: Bed 4D 40
MARKET HARBOROUGH 3D 141
Market Hill CV47: Sou 5H 107
Market Mall *CV21: Rugby 5G 75*
(in Clock Towers Shop. Cen.)
Market Pl. B49: Alc 5B 112
CV9: Ath 3C 16
(off Market St.)
CV11: Nun 7D 22
CV21: Rugby 5G 75
CV34: Warw 2G 101
CV36: Ship S 4H 131
CV47: Sou 5H 107
Market Sq. CV35: Kine 5D 120
Market St. B78: Pole 1D 10
CV9: Ath 3C 16
CV21: Rugby 4H 75
CV34: Warw 2F 101
Market Way CV1: Cov 4G 135 (5C 58)
MARKFIELD 1B 140
Markham Dr. CV31: W'nsh 5F 103
Marks M. CV34: Warw 2G 101
Marlborough Dr. CV31: Lea S 2H 103
Marlborough M. B80: Stud 3D 92
Marlborough Rd. CV2: Cov 5G 59
CV11: Nun 7C 22
CV22: Bil 7E 74
MARLCLIFF 3B 142
Marlcroft CV3: W'hall 2A 70
Marleigh Rd. B50: Bidf A 5G 123
Marlene Cft. B37: Chel W 4C 34
Marler Rd. CV4: Tile H 1D 66
Marlissa Dr. CV6: Cov 4E 50
Marloes Wlk. CV31: Lea S 2G 103
Marlow Cl. CV5: Cov 3F 57
Marlowe Cl. CV10: Gall C 6E 20
Marlowe Rd. CV37: S Avon 7H 115
Marlow Rd. CV9: Hurl 6K 13
Marlston Wlk. CV5: Cov 3F 57
Marlwood Cl. CV6: Longf 2F 51
Marne Cl. CV34: Warw 7J 97
Marner Cres. CV6: Cov 1B 58
Marner Rd. CV10: Nun 3H 31

Marner Rd. CV12: Bed 2G 41
Marnhull Cl. CV2: W'grve S 3B 60
Marram Ct. CV37: S Avon 3D 114
Marrick B77: Wiln 2A 10
Marriner's La. CV5: Cov 2F 57
Marriott Forest of Arden Golf Course 6B 36
Marriott Rd. CV6: Cov 3A 58
CV12: Bed 3D 40
Marsdale Dr. CV10: Nun 1E 30
Marsett B77: Wiln 3A 10
Marshall Av. CV36: Ship S 5H 131
Marshall Rd. CV7: Exh 5F 41
Marsham Cl. CV34: Warw 7K 97
Marshbrook Cl. CV2: Ald G 4K 51
Marshdale Av. CV6: Cov 3E 50
Marshfield Dr. CV4: Canly 6H 67
Marsh Ho. CV2: W'grve S 7C 52
Marsh La. B46: Wat O 1B 24
B76: Curd 6C 18
B92: H Ard 7G 45
(not continuous)
CV37: S Avon 2D 114
Marsh Rd. CV37: Wilm 5G 113
MARSTON
Birmingham 1H 19 (2D 139)
Coventry 3A 72
Marston Av. CV33: L Hth 2K 119
Marston Cl. CV32: Lill 5F 99
Marston Cft. B37: Mars G 6A 34
MARSTON DOLES 3B 144
Marston Dr. B37: K'hrst 7A 24
MARSTON GREEN 5A 34 (3C 139)
Marston Hill CV47: P Mars 5H 111
MARSTON JABBETT 7B 32 (3A 140)
Marston La. B76: Curd 2E 18
CV11: Nun 2A 32
CV12: Bed, Bulk 1H 41
MARSTON ST LAWRENCE 1D 147
MARSTON TRUSSELL 3D 141
Marten Cl. CV35: H Mag 1C 100
Martin Cl. CV5: E Grn 3C 56
CV37: S Avon 2F 115
Martindale Rd. CV7: Exh 5J 41
MARTIN HUSSINGTREE 2A 142
Martinique Sq. CV34: Warw 2F 101
Martin La. CV22: Bil 2D 86
Martins Dr. CV9: Ath 1C 16
Martins Rd. CV12: Bed 4E 40
MARTON 2D 104 (2B 144)
Marton Ct. CV22: Dunc 2B 86
Marton Rd. CV23: Bird 5A 104
CV47: Long I 1C 106
Martyrs Cl., The CV3: Cov 7D 58
Marwood Cl. CV11: Nun 5A 32
Mary Arden's House 5J 113
Mary Herbert St. CV3: Cov 1D 68
Mary Slessor St. CV3: W'hall 2J 69
Marystow Cl. CV5: Alle 6F 49
Masefield Av. CV34: Warw 4E 100
Masefield Rd. CV37: S Avon 6G 115
Mason Av. CV32: Lill 4G 99
Mason Cl. B50: Bidf A 5H 123
Mason Rd. CV6: Cov 5F 51
Masons Cl. CV37: Wilm 5J 113
Masons Ct. CV37: S Avon 5D 136
Masons Rd. CV37: S Avon 3C 114
Masons Rd. Ind. Est. CV37: S Avon 3C 114
Masons Way CV37: S Avon 3C 114
Masser Rd. CV6: Cov 2C 50
Masters Rd. CV31: W'nsh 3E 102
Master's Yd. CV23: Bird 5A 104
Mathecroft CV31: Lea S 3G 103
Matlock Cl. CV21: Brow 1J 75
Matlock Rd. CV1: Cov 1D 58
Matterson Rd. CV6: Cov 2A 58
Matthews Cl. CV37: S Avon 3F 115
Maud Rd. B46: Wat O 1D 24
Maudslay Rd. CV5: Cov 5J 57
MAUGERSBURY 3A 146
Maureen Cl. CV4: Tile H 6A 56
Maurice Mead Ct. CV31: Lea S 2E 102
Mavor Dr. CV12: Bed 4D 40
Mawnan Cl. CV7: Exh 5H 41
Max Rd. CV6: Cov 2K 57
MAXSTOKE 3D 36 (3D 139)
Maxstoke Castle 5A 26
Maxstoke Cl. CV7: Mer 5D 46
Maxstoke Ct. B46: Col 1G 35
Maxstoke Gdns. CV31: Lea S 2D 102
Maxstoke La. B46: Col 6G 25
CV7: Mer 5D 36
(not continuous)
Maybird Cen., The CV37: S Avon 3E 114
Maybrook Ind. Est. CV37: S Avon 3E 114
Maybrook Rd. CV37: S Avon 3E 114
Maycock Rd. CV6: Cov 7D 50
Mayfair *B37: K'hrst 7A 24*
(off Haselour Rd.)
Mayfair Dr. CV10: Gall C 7E 20
Mayfield B77: Wiln 2A 10
CV12: Bed 2H 41
Mayfield Av. CV37: S Avon 3F 115
Mayfield Cl. CV12: Bed 2H 41
CV31: Lea S 2G 103
Mayfield Ct. CV37: S Avon 4F 115
Mayfield Dr. B95: Hen A 1G 93
CV8: Ken 5G 79
Mayfield Rd. CV5: Cov 7A 58
CV11: Nun 2A 32
CV47: Sou 4H 107
Mayflower Dr. CV2: Cov 5K 59
May La. CV22: Bil 7D 74
Maynard Av. CV12: Bed 5D 40
Maynard Av. CV34: Warw 1J 101
Mayne Cl. CV35: H Mag 2B 100
Mayo Dr. CV8: Ken 5E 78
Mayo Rd. CV36: Ship S 3H 131
Mayor's Cft. CV4: Canly 1F 67
Maypole La. CV9: Gren 2F 15
Maypole Rd. B79: Wart 5H 9
May St. CV6: Cov 6E 50
Mayswood Rd. B95: Hen A, Woot W 3F 93
Maytree Cl. B37: F'bri 3A 34
Maywell Dr. B92: Sol 6A 44
Meadfoot Rd. CV3: W'hall 2K 69
Meadow Cl. B78: K'bry 6E 12
CV7: Ansty 3F 53
CV23: Stret D 3J 83
CV32: Lill 3G 99
CV37: S Avon 4C 114
LE10: Wlvy 2H 33
Meadow Ct. CV11: Nun 6C 22
Meadow Cft. CV7: Old A 3C 28
Meadowcroft Cl. CV4: Tile H 7D 56
Meadow Crofts CV47: Bis I 5C 110
Meadow Dr. B92: H Ard 7H 45
Mdw. Furlong CV23: Brow 6K 65
Meadow Gdns. CV9: Bad E 3F 15
Meadow Ho. CV1: Cov 4B 58
Meadow La. B94: Lapw 3J 91
Meadow Lea CV37: S Avon 4C 114
Meadow Ri. B95: Ullen 6B 90
Meadow Rd. B49: Alc 3B 112
B95: Hen A 2H 93
CV6: Cov 2B 50
CV8: Wols 4J 71
CV9: Hurl 6K 13
CV10: Harts 3F 21
CV21: N'bld A 2D 74
CV34: Warw 1J 101
CV47: Sou 4H 107
Meadows, The B50: Bidf A 5F 123
CV35: Leek W 1J 97
Meadowside CV11: Nun 3D 32
Meadow St. CV1: Cov 5B 58
CV9: Ath 4C 16
CV11: Nun 6C 22
Meadowsweet CV23: Brow 7J 65
Meadow Sweet Rd. CV37: S Avon 2D 114
Meadow Vw. Cl. B49: Alc 4C 112
Meadow Way CV23: Harb M 4B 64
CV47: Fen C 2H 121
Meadway CV2: Cov 1H 59
Meadway Nth. CV2: Cov 1H 59
Meakins Cl. CV34: Warw 4D 100
MEASHAM 1A 140
Medhurst Cl. CV22: Dunc 6B 86
Medina Rd. CV6: Cov 5E 50
Medland Av. CV3: Finh 3K 67
Medley Gro. CV31: W'nsh 5D 102
Medway Cft. B36: Cas B 5A 24
MEER END 1D 143
Meer St. CV37: S Avon 3E 136 (4F 115)
Meeting La. B49: Alc 4C 112
Megabowl
Royal Leamington Spa 2C 102
Walsgrave on Sowe 6D 52
Melbourne Cl. CV11: Nun 4A 32
Melbourne Ct. CV12: Bed 3G 41
Melbourne Rd. CV5: Cov 5A 58
Meldrum Ct. CV47: Temp H 2A 120
Meldrum Rd. CV10: Nun 1D 30
Melford Ct. CV22: Bil 6E 74
Melfort Cl. CV3: Bin 5B 60
CV10: Nun 6H 21
Mellish Ct. CV22: Bil 7E 74
Mellish Rd. CV22: Bil 7E 74
Mellor Rd. CV21: Hillm 1D 88
Mellowdew Rd. CV2: Cov 3J 59
Mellowship Rd. CV5: E Grn 2A 56
Mellwaters B77: Wiln 2A 10
Melmerby B77: Wiln 2A 10
Melrose Av. CV12: Bed 5D 40
Melton Ct. CV22: Caw 1K 85
Melton Rd. CV32: Lill 3E 98
Melville Cl. CV7: Exh 5G 41
CV22: Bil 7E 74
Melville Rd. CV1: Cov 4A 58
Memorial Rd. CV47: Fen C 3G 121
Menai Wlk. B37: F'bri 1B 34
Mendip Dr. CV10: Nun 1B 30
Mendip Way B77: Wiln 1A 10
Meon Cl. CV37: Up Qui 7H 125
Mercer Av. B46: Wat O 1A 24
CV2: Cov 2G 59
Mercer Ct. CV22: Hillm 1B 88
Mercers Mdw. CV7: Ker E 7A 40
Mercia Av. CV8: Ken 5C 78
Mercia Bus. Village CV4: W'wd H 2D 66
Mercia Ho. CV1: Cov 3G 135 (4C 58)
Mercia Way CV34: Warw 1K 101
Mercot Cl. B98: Redd 1A 92
Meredith Rd. CV2: Cov 4K 59
MERE GREEN
Droitwich 2A 142
Sutton Coldfield 2C 139
Merestone Cl. CV47: Sou 3H 107
Merevale Av. CV11: Nun 7B 22
Merevale Ct. CV11: Nun 7B 22
Merevale La. CV9: Ath 4H 15
Merevale Rd. CV9: Ath 2B 16
Merevale Vw. CV9: Ath 4B 16
MERIDEN 5E 46 (3D 139)
Meriden Dr. B37: K'hrst 6A 24
Meriden Pk. Homes CV7: Mer 6E 46
Meriden Rd. B92: H Ard 7H 45
Meriden Rd. CV7: Fill 6J 37
CV7: Mer 7H 45
Meriden St. CV1: Cov 4B 58
Meridian Point CV1: Cov 5H 135
Merlin Av. CV10: Nun 5G 21
Merlin Cl. CV23: Brow 7J 65
Merrivale Rd. CV5: Cov 4J 57
Merryfields Way CV2: W'grve S 5B 52
MERRY LEES 1B 140
Mersey Rd. CV12: Bulk 3C 42
Merton Ho. B37: F'bri 3A 34
Merttens Dr. CV22: Rugby 6F 75
Merynton Av. CV4: Canly 2J 67
Meschede Way CV1: Cov 4J 135 (5D 58)
Meschines St. CV3: Cov 2D 68
Mews, The CV8: Ken 6C 78
CV9: Ath 3D 16
CV12: Bed 3H 41
CV21: Hillm 7C 76
Mews Rd. CV32: Lea S 7B 98
Michaelmas Rd. CV3: Cov 7G 135 (6C 58)
Michel Ho. CV1: Cov 1K 135 (3D 58)
Michell Cl. CV3: Cov 7H 59
Mickle Mdw. B46: Wat O 1B 24
MICKLETON 1A 146
Mickleton Dr. CV35: Hatt 5A 96
Mickleton Rd. CV5: Cov 6A 58
CV36: A'ton, Ilm 5A 126
Middelburg Cl. CV11: Nun 3C 32
MIDDLE ASTON 3D 147
MIDDLE BARTON 3D 147
Middle Bickenhill La. B92: Bick 1G 45
Middleborough Rd. CV1: Cov 2F 135 (4B 58)
Middlecotes CV4: Tile H 6F 57
Middlefield Dr. CV3: Bin 6C 60
Middlefield La. CV37: N'bld S 1F 127
Middle La. B46: Neth W 5K 19
OX17: Shotte 6H 129
MIDDLE LITTLETON 3B 142
Middle Lock La. CV35: Hatt 5A 96
Middlemarch Bus. Pk. CV3: W'hall 4J 69
(London Rd.)
CV3: W'hall 7J 69
(Siskin Parkway E.)
Middlemarch Rd. CV6: Cov 1B 58
CV10: Nun 3H 31
Middlemore Cl. B80: Stud 4C 92
Middle Ride CV3: W'hall 2K 69
Middle Rd. CV33: Har 5F 109
Middlesmoor B77: Wiln 2A 10
MIDDLE STOKE 4G 59
Middle St. CV23: Kils 6J 89
CV36: Ilm 7C 126
CV37: Arms 4F 127
MIDDLETON 2C 139
MIDDLETON CHENEY 1D 147
Middleton Cl. CV35: Mid T 7C 130
Middleton Hall 2A 12
MIDDLETON STONEY 3D 147
MIDDLETOWN 6C 92
Middletown B80: Stud 6C 92
CV35: More M 4C 118
Middletown La. B80: Stud 7B 92
B96: Sam 7B 92
MIDDLE TYSOE 6C 130 (1C 147)
Midland Air Mus. 5H 69
Midland Oak Trad. Est. CV6: Cov 4E 50
Midland Rd. CV6: Cov 2E 58
CV11: Nun 6B 22
Midlands Hydroplane Club, The 7C 12
Midland Sports Cen. 1A 66
Midland Trad. Est. CV21: Rugby 2G 75
Milby Ct. CV11: Nun 2J 31
Milby Dr. CV11: Nun 3G 23
MILCOMBE 2D 147
Milcote Rd. CV37: Cliff C, Milc 5A 124
CV37: Welf A, W Avon 4B 124
Mildmay Cl. CV37: S Avon 7D 114
Mile End B94: Tan A 3C 90
Mile La. CV1: Cov 6J 135 (6D 58)
CV3: Cov 6J 135 (6D 58)
Miles Mdw. CV6: Cov 5H 51
CV37: N'bld S 1G 127
Milestone Dr. CV22: Rugby 1F 87
Milestone Ho. *CV1: Cov 5B 58*
(off Windsor St.)
Milestone Rd. CV37: S Avon 7J 115
Milford Cl. CV5: Alle 1F 57
Milford St. CV10: Nun 2H 31
Milking La. B95: Hen A 2G 93
Millais Cl. CV12: Bed 1G 41
Mill Bank B46: Over W 1F 27
Millbank CV34: Warw 6J 97
Millbank M. CV8: Ken 3F 79
Millbeck CV21: Brow 1K 75
Millburn Hill Rd. CV4: Canly 2F 67
Mill Cl. B50: Broom 3E 122
CV2: Ald G 3H 51
CV8: Wols 5H 71
CV11: Nun 3B 32
CV35: N Lin 2F 95
CV47: Sou 4G 107
Mill Cotts. CV21: Rugby 2K 75
Mill Ct. CV36: Ship S 5H 131
Mill Cres. B78: K'bry 6E 12
CV35: Kine 5D 120
CV47: Sou 4G 107
MILL END 3F 79
Mill End CV8: Ken 3E 78
Millennium Way CV8: Wols 5H 71
Millers Bank B50: Broom 3E 122
Millers Cl. CV22: Dunc 5A 86
CV37: Welf A 3A 124

Millers Dale Cl. CV21: Brow 1J 75
Miller's La. CV23: M Kirby 3G 55
Millers Rd. CV34: Warw 7F 97
Millers Wharf B78: Pole 1C 10
Mill Farm Cvn. Pk. CV12: Bulk 6D 32
Mill Farm Cl. CV22: Dunc 6C 86
Millfield CV31: Lea S 7E 98
Mill Fld. Cvn. Site CV37: Welf A 3A 124
Millfield Cl. CV37: Lwr Q 5H 125
Millfields Av. CV21: Hillm 1B 88
Mill Furlong CV23: Brow 6K 65
Mill Gdns. CV10: Nun 2H 31
Mill Hill CV8: Bag 4D 68
Millholme Cl. CV47: Sou 5J 107
Mill Ho. Cl. CV32: Lea S 7A 98
Mill Ho. Ct. CV6: Cov 7F 51
Mill Ho. Dr. CV32: Lea S 7A 98
Mill Ho. Ter. CV32: Lea S 7A 98
Mill Ind. Pk., The B49: K Cou 1A 112
Milliners Ct. CV9: Ath 3C 16
MILLISON'S WOOD 6K 47
Mill La. B49: Aston C 4J 113
B49: Gt Alne 3G 113
B49: Ove G 6B 112
B50: Broom 3E 122
B94: Lapw 3H 91
B95: Aston C 4J 113
CV3: Bin 5B 60
CV7: Fill 7A 28
CV9: Man 5F 17
CV9: With 3F 17
CV11: Burt H 4H 33
CV12: Bulk 2C 42
CV23: Clift D 2A 76
CV32: Cubb 2K 99
CV33: Har 5H 109
CV35: Barf 2B 108
CV35: Kine 5D 120
CV35: Row 6H 91
CV36: Half 2J 127
CV36: Tred 6J 127
CV37: A'ton 1B 116
CV37: N'bld S 2H 127
CV37: S Avon 6F 115
CV37: Welf A 2A 124
CV47: Fen C 3G 121
LE10: Wlvy 1K 33
Mill Pleck B80: Stud 4D 92
Mill Race La. CV6: Cov 3G 51
Mill Race Vw. CV9: Ath 1C 16
Mill Rd. CV21: Rugby 3J 75
CV31: Lea S 7E 98
CV47: Nap 2H 111
CV47: Sou 4G 107
Mill Row LE10: Wlvy 1K 33
Mill St. CV1: Cov 1F 135 (4B 58)
CV11: Nun 7D 22
CV12: Bed 2H 41
CV31: Lea S 1E 102
CV33: Har 5G 109
CV34: Warw 2H 101
CV35: Kine 5D 120
CV36: Ship S 4H 131
Mill Ter. CV12: Bed 7H 31
Mill Wlk. CV11: Nun 7D 22
Millway Dr. CV33: Bis T 4C 108
Milner Cl. CV12: Bulk 3F 43
Milner Cres. CV2: W'grve S 5A 52
Milner Dr. B79: Shut 2B 8
Milrose Way CV4: Tile H 7D 56
MILTHORPE 3C 145
MILTON 2D 147
Milton Av. CV34: Warw 3E 100
Milton Cl. CV12: Bed 4K 41
MILTON MALSOR 3D 145
Milton Rd. CV37: S Avon 7H 115
Milton St. CV2: Cov 2G 59
MILTON-UNDER-WYCHWOOD 3B 146
MILVERTON 6A 98 (2A 144)
Milverton Ct. CV32: Lea S 7C 98
Milverton Cres. CV32: Lea S 6C 98
Milverton Cres. W. CV32: Lea S 6C 98
Milverton Hill CV32: Lea S 7C 98
Milverton Lodge *CV32: Lea S* *6C 98*
(off Milverton Cres. W.)
Milverton Rd. CV2: Cov 4J 51
Milverton Ter. CV32: Lea S 7C 98
Mimosa Cl. CV10: Nun 4G 31
Miners Wlk. B78: Pole 1C 10
Minerva M. B49: Alc 4B 112
Minerva Mill Technology Cen. *B49: Alc* *4B 112*
(off Station Rd.)
Minions Cl. CV9: Ath 3C 16
Minories, The CV37: S Avon 3E 136 (4E 114)
Minshills Ct. CV37: S Avon 1F 137
Minster Cl. CV35: H Mag 2B 100
Minster Rd. CV1: Cov 4B 58
Minton Rd. CV2: W'grve S 6A 52
MINWORTH 2C 139
Minworth Rd. B46: Wat O 1A 24
Mira Dr. CV10: Fen D 1D 22
Miranda Cl. CV3: W'hall 1K 69
Miranda Dr. CV34: H'cte 6C 102
MISTERTON 3C 141
Mitchell Av. CV4: Canly 1E 66
Mitchell Ct. CV23: Brow 5J 65
Mitchell Rd. CV12: Bed 3J 41
Moat Av. CV3: Finh 4K 67
Moat Cl. CV8: Bubb 3J 81
CV23: Thurl 7K 85
Moat Cft. B37: F'bri 3A 34
Moat Farm Dr. CV12: Bed 5C 40
CV21: Hillm 2C 88
Moat Farm La. B95: Ullen 4C 90
Moat Grn. CV35: Sher 7C 100
Moat Ho. La. B46: Shu 3B 26
CV4: Canly 1G 67
Moat La. LE10: Wlvy 1J 33
Modbury Cl. CV3: Cov 3D 68
MODEL VILLAGE 1G 107
Model Village, The CV47: Long I 1G 107
Molesworth Av. CV3: Cov 6G 59
MOLLINGTON 1D 147
Mollington Gro. CV35: Hatt 5A 96
Mollington La. OX17: Shotte 6H 129
OX17: Warm, Farn 2J 129
Mollington Rd. CV31: W'nsh 5E 102
OX17: Shotte 6G 129
Momus Blvd. CV2: Cov 5J 59
Moncrieff Dr. CV31: Lea S 3G 103
Monks Cl. CV22: Caw 1A 86
Monks Cft., The CV3: Cov 1C 68
Monks Dr. B80: Stud 3C 92
Monk's Fld. Cl. CV4: Tile H 6E 56
MONKS KIRBY 3J 55 (3B 140)
Monks Kirby La. CV23: M Kirby 2J 55
MONKSPATH 1C 143
Monks Rd. CV1: Cov 5F 59
CV3: Bin W 1E 70
Monks Way CV34: Warw 2F 101
Monkswood Cres. CV2: Cov 6K 51
Monmouth Cl. CV5: E Grn 4F 57
CV8: Ken 3D 78
Monmouth Gdns. CV10: Nun 1E 30
Montague Dr. CV23: Kils 6J 89
Montague Rd. CV22: Bil 4D 86
CV34: Warw 6J 97
Montalt Rd. CV3: Cov 1D 68
Montana Wlk. CV10: Nun 1E 30
Montfort Rd. B46: Col 7F 25
Montgomery Av. CV35: H Mag 2A 100
Montgomery Cl. CV3: W'hall 4J 69
CV37: Shot 6D 114
Montgomery Ct. CV34: Warw 1H 101
Montgomery Dr. CV22: Bil 7C 74
Montgomery Rd. CV31: W'nsh 4D 102
Montilo La. CV23: Harb M 3B 64
Montjoy Cl. CV3: W'hall 1K 69
Montpelier Ho. *CV8: Ken* *4D 78*
(off Southbank Rd.)
Montpellier Cl. CV3: Cov 2C 68
Montrose Av. CV32: Lill 3E 98
Montrose Dr. CV10: Nun 1F 31
Montrose Rd. CV22: Rugby 7G 75
Monument Vw. B78: Pole 2D 10
Monument Way CV37: S Avon 2F 115
MONWODE LEA 1K 27
Monwode Lea La. B46: Over W 1K 27
Moorbrooke CV10: Harts 4F 21
Moorcroft Cl. CV11: Nun 3D 32
Moore Cl. CV6: Longf 2G 51
CV34: Warw 5G 97
Moorend Av. B37: Chel W, Mars G 5A 34
Moore Wlk. CV34: Warw 1A 102
Moor Farm Cl. CV23: Stret D 3H 83
Moorfield, The CV3: Cov 7G 59
Moorfield Rd. B49: Alc 5B 112
Moorfields B49: Alc 4B 112
Moorhill Rd. CV31: W'nsh 5E 102
Moorings, The CV31: Lea S 1B 102
Moorlands Av. CV8: Ken 6D 78
Moorlands Lodge CV8: Ken 6D 78
Moor La. CV23: W'hby 4G 105
Moorpark Cl. CV11: Nun 4E 32
Moor Rd. CV10: Harts 3F 21
MOORS, THE 4B 112
Moor's La. CV23: Hillm 1E 88
Moor St. CV5: Cov 6K 57
Moorwood Cres. CV10: Harts 3F 21
Moorwood La. CV10: Harts 3E 20
(not continuous)
Mordaunt Rd. CV35: Welle 2J 117
Moreall Mdws. CV4: Canly 5H 67
Morecroft Dr. CV34: Warw 4D 100
Moreton Cl. CV37: S Avon 5J 115
Moreton Hall Bungalows CV35: More M 5B 118
MORETON-IN-MARSH 2B 146
MORETON MORRELL 5C 118 (3A 144)
Moreton Morrell La. CV35: Light, More M 5E 118
Moreton Morrell Tennis Court Club 6C 118
MORETON PADDOX 7B 118
MORETON PINKNEY 3C 145
Morey St. CV6: Cov 7E 50
Morfa Gdns. CV6: Cov 2H 57
Morgan Cl. B80: Stud 5D 92
CV7: Gun H 4D 28
CV35: N Lin 2F 95
Morgan Gro. B36: Cas B 3A 24
Morgans Rd. CV5: E Grn 3A 56
Morland Cl. CV12: Bulk 3F 43
Morland Rd. CV6: Cov 4C 50
Morningside CV5: Cov 7B 58
Mornington Ct. B46: Col 5G 25
Morrell St. CV32: Lea S 6D 98
Morris Av. CV2: Cov 3K 59
Morris Cl. CV21: N'bld A 2F 75
Morris Dr. CV11: Nun 3K 31
CV31: W'nsh 6F 103
Morris Hill B78: Pole 3C 10
Morse Rd. CV31: W'nsh 5E 102
Morson Cres. CV21: Hillm 6A 76
Mortimer Rd. CV8: Ken 7D 78
MORTON BAGOT 2C 143
Morton Cl. CV6: Cov 5A 50
Morton Ct. CV21: Hillm 1B 88
CV37: S Avon 1H 137
Morton Gdns. CV21: Rugby 6H 75
Morton St. CV32: Lea S 6D 98
Mosedale CV21: Brow 1K 75
MOSELEY
Birmingham 3B 138
Wolverhampton 1A 138
Moseley Av. CV6: Cov 3A 58
Moseley Rd. CV8: Ken 6F 79
Moss Cl. CV22: Bil 7E 74
Mossdale Cl. CV6: Cov 1A 58
Mossdale Cres. CV10: Nun 2F 31
Moss Gro. CV8: Ken 2F 79
Moss La. CV37: N'bld S 1G 127
Mossop Ct. CV37: S Avon 4D 114
Mosspaul Cl. CV32: Lea S 5B 98
Moss St. CV31: Lea S 1E 102
Mottistone Cl. CV3: Cov 2D 68
Motts Way B46: Col 7G 25
Moultrie Rd. CV21: Rugby 6H 75
Mount, The B76: Curd 5C 18
CV3: Cov 7D 58
Mountbatten Av. CV8: Ken 5G 79
Mountbatten Cl. CV37: Shot 6C 114
Mount Cres. CV37: S Avon 4B 114
Mount Dr. CV12: Bed 2G 41
Mount Fld, Ct. *CV1: Cov* *1K 135*
(off Charles St.)
Mountfield Gdns. *CV47: Sou* *5H 107*
(off The Bull Yd.)
Mountford Cl. CV35: Welle 2J 117
Mountford Ri. CV35: Light 2G 119
(not continuous)
Mount Gdns. CV5: Cov 7B 58
Mt. Nod Way CV5: E Grn 4E 56
MOUNT PLEASANT 2G 41
Mt. Pleasant CV37: S Avon 4B 114
CV47: Bis I 6B 110
CV47: S'ton 6C 106
Mt. Pleasant Cl. CV47: S'ton 6C 106
Mt. Pleasant La. B95: Ullen 6C 90
Mt. Pleasant Rd. CV12: Bed 1G 41
Mt. Pleasant Ter. CV10: Nun 5A 22
Mount Rd. B95: Hen A 2H 93
Mount St. CV5: Cov 5K 57
CV11: Nun 7C 22
Mount St. Pas. CV11: Nun 7C 22
Mowbray St. CV2: Cov 4F 59
Mowe Cft. B37: Mars G 6A 34
MOWMACRE HILL 1C 141
MOWSLEY 3D 141
Moxhull Rd. B37: K'hrst 7A 24
Moyeady Av. CV22: Hillm 1A 88
Moyle Cres. CV5: E Grn 3C 56
Much Pk. St. CV1: Cov 4J 135 (5D 58)
MUCKLEY CORNER 1B 138
Muirfield Cl. CV11: Nun 4E 32
Mulberry Cl. CV32: Lill 5E 98
Mulberry Ct. CV8: Ken 5D 78
CV37: S Avon 1F 137 (4F 115)
Mulberry Dr. CV34: Warw 7H 97
Mulberry Rd. CV6: Cov 7G 51
CV22: Bil 6B 74
Mulberry St. CV37: S Avon 1F 137 (4F 115)
Mulberry Tree Shop. Cen., The CV37: S Avon 3H 137
Mulberry Way CV10: Harts 3F 21
Mullard Dr. CV31: W'nsh 5F 103
Mull Cft. B36: Cas B 5A 24
Mullens Gro. Rd. B37: K'hrst 7A 24
Mulliners Cl. B37: Chel W 3C 34
Mulliner St. CV6: Cov 2F 59
MURCOT 1A 146
Murcott Ct. CV31: W'nsh 5E 102
Murcott Rd. E. CV31: W'nsh 5E 102
Murcott Rd. W. CV31: W'nsh 5E 102
Murrayfield Way CV3: Bin 6D 60
Murrayian Cl. CV21: Rugby 5H 75
Murray Rd. CV6: Cov 7A 50
CV21: Rugby 5H 75
MUSCOTT 2D 145
Musson Grn. B37: Mars G 5B 34
MUSTOW GREEN 1A 142
Myers Rd. CV21: Hillm 1E 88
Mylgrove CV3: Finh 5D 68
Myrtle Gro. CV5: Cov 6K 57
Mythe La. CV9: With 1F 17
Mythe Vw. CV9: Ath 2D 16
MYTON 2K 101
Myton Cres. CV34: Warw 2K 101
Myton Crofts CV31: Lea S 1B 102
Myton Gdns. CV34: Warw 2J 101
Myton La. CV34: Warw 2K 101
Myton Rd. CV31: Lea S 2J 101
CV34: Lea S, Warw 2J 101
Mytton Rd. B46: Wat O 1A 24

N

Nailcote Av. CV4: Tile H 6A 56
NAILSTONE 1B 140
Nairn Cl. CV10: Nun 2G 31
Napier St. CV1: Cov 4E 58
Napier St. Ind. Est. *CV1: Cov* *4E 58*
(off Napier St.)
Napton Ct. CV22: Dunc 3B 86
Napton Dr. CV32: Lill 5E 98
Napton Grn. CV5: E Grn 4E 56
Napton Ind. Est. CV47: Nap 2F 111
NAPTON ON THE HILL 1H 111 (2B 144)
Napton Ri. CV47: Sou 5K 107
Napton Rd. CV47: S'ton 5B 106
Narberth Way CV2: W'grve S 7B 52
NARBOROUGH 2C 141

Narborough Ct. CV32: Lea S 7B 98
Nares Cl. CV22: Bil 7E 74
Narrowboat Cl. CV6: Longf 7H 41
Narrow Hall Mdw. CV34: Warw 4D 100
Narrow La. CV37: S Avon 7D 136 (6E 114)
NASEBY 1D 145
Naseby Cl. CV3: Bin 7B 60
Naseby Rd. CV22: Rugby 7J 75
Nash Cft. B37: Mars G 5B 34
Nashes, The CV37: Cliff C 5B 124
Nash's House 5F 137 (5F 115)
Nason Gro. CV8: Ken 4F 79
National Agricultural Cen. CV8: S'lgh P 5K 79
National Exhibition Cen. 1D 44
National Herb Cen., The 3J 129
National Motorcycle Mus. 4G 45
Naul's Mill Ho. CV1: Cov 1F 135 (3B 58)
NAUNTON 3A 146
NAUNTON BEAUCHAMP 3A 142
Navigation Way CV6: Cov 6G 51
Nayler Cl. CV21: Rugby 2J 75
Neal Ct. CV2: W'grve S 6C 52
Neale Av. CV5: Alle 1E 56
Neale Cl. CV12: Bulk 4E 42
Neale's Cl. CV33: Har 5J 109
NEAL'S GREEN 7D 40 (3A 140)
NEC House B40: Nat E C 1D 44
Needle Cl. B80: Stud 3D 92
Needles Ho. B80: Stud 2D 92
Neilston St. CV31: Lea S 1E 102
NEITHROP 1D 147
Nellands Cl. CV36: Ilm 7C 126
Nelson Av. CV34: Warw 7J 97
Nelson Cl. CV37: Ett 1B 126
Nelson La. CV34: Warw 7H 97
Nelson St. CV1: Cov 3E 58
Nelson Tuery B49: Alc 5B 112
Nelson Way CV22: Bil 7C 74
Nene Cl. CV3: Bin 1K 69
Nene Ct. CV23: Long L 4C 74
Nene Way B36: Cas B 4A 24
Nesfield Gro. B92: H Ard 7H 45
NETHERCOTE
Cheltenham 3A 146
Rugby 2C 145
Nethercote Mdw. CV36: Long C 1C 134
NETHERCOTT 3D 147
NETHER HEYFORD 3D 145
Nethermill Rd. CV6: Cov 2A 58
NETHERSEAL 1D 139
Nethersole St. B78: Pole 7D 8
NETHERTON 3A 138
NETHER WESTCOTE 3B 146
NETHER WHITACRE 2D 139
Netherwood Ind. Est. CV9: Ath 2E 16
NETHER WORTON 2D 147
Nevada Way B37: Chel W 4C 34
Nevill Cl. CV31: Lea S 2D 102
Neville Ct. CV34: Warw 2G 101
Neville Gro. CV34: Warw 6H 97
Newall Cl. CV23: Clift D 3A 76
NEW ARLEY 4E 28 (3D 139)
New Ash Dr. CV5: Alle 2D 56
NEW BILTON 5E 74
Newbold Cl. CV3: Bin 6B 60
Newbold Comyn Leisure Cen. 7G 99
Newbold Footpath CV21: Rugby 4E 74
(Edward St.)
CV21: Rugby 5F 75
(Oliver St.)
NEWBOLD ON AVON 2E 74 (1B 144)
NEWBOLD ON STOUR 1G 127 (1B 146)
NEWBOLD PACEY 3D 143
Newbold Pl. CV32: Lea S 7D 98
CV35: Welle 2J 117
Newbold Rd. CV21: N'bld A, Rugby 1E 74
CV35: Welle 2J 117
CV37: Arms 3G 127
Newbold St. CV32: Lea S 7E 98
Newbold Ter. CV32: Lea S 7D 98
Newbold Ter. E. CV32: Lea S 7E 98
NEWBOLD VERDON 1B 140
Newborough Cl. CV9: Aus 6G 7
NEWBOTTLE 2D 147
New Broad St. CV37: S Avon 7C 136 (6E 114)
New Brook St. CV32: Lea S 7C 98
New Bldgs. CV1: Cov 3H 135 (4D 58)
Newburgh Cres. CV34: Warw 7G 97
Newbury Cl. CV31: Lea S 2H 103
Newbury Dr. CV37: S Avon 6D 114
Newby Cl. CV3: Cov 2E 68
Newby Gro. B37: F'bri 7B 24
New Century Pk. CV3: Cov 6K 59
New Century Way CV11: Nun 7C 22
New Cl. CV35: H Mag 2B 100
Newcombe Cl. CV22: Dunc 6C 86
Newcombe Rd. CV5: Cov 6K 57
Newcomen Cl. CV12: Bed 5D 40
Newcomen Rd. CV12: Bed 4D 40
New Cotts. CV10: Nun 1F 31
CV37: S Avon 5D 114
Newdegate Pl. CV11: Nun 7D 22
Newdegate Rd. CV12: Bed 1G 41
Newdegate St. CV11: Nun 7D 22
Newdigate CV31: Lea S 3G 103
Newdigate Cl. CV12: Bed 2G 41
Newdigate Rd. CV6: Cov 2F 59
NEW DUSTON 2D 145
NEW END
Alcester 3B 142
Henley-in Arden 2C 143
New End Rd. B46: Max 1C 36
Newey Av. CV12: Bed 5D 40
Newey Dr. CV8: Ken 7E 78
Newey Rd. CV2: Cov 3K 59
Newfield Av. CV8: Ken 6F 79
Newfield Rd. CV1: Cov 2C 58
Newgale Wlk. CV31: Lea S 1G 103
Newgate Ct. CV1: Cov 5K 135 (5D 58)
New Grn. Pk. Cvn. Site CV2: Cov 7K 51
NEWHALL GREEN 4J 37
Newhall Rd. CV2: Cov 7K 51
Newham Grn. CV10: Nun 4H 21
Newhaven Cl. CV6: Cov 2J 57
Newington Cl. CV6: Cov 1H 57
Newington Rd. B37: Mars G 5B 34
Newland Cl. B98: Redd 1A 92
Newland La. CV7: Ash G 6B 40
Newland Rd. CV1: Cov 2D 58
CV32: Lill 4G 99
Newlands, The B80: Stud 4C 92
Newlands Ct. *CV3: Cov 5F 59*
(off School Cl.)
Newlands La. B37: Mars G 7A 34
Newlands Rd. CV9: Bad E 3F 15
Newland St. CV22: Rugby 5E 74
Newlyn Cl. CV11: Nun 7G 23
Newman Cl. CV12: Bed 1H 41
Newmarket Cl. CV6: Ald G 2H 51
CV37: S Avon 7D 114
NEWNHAM
Daventry 3C 145
Henley-in-Arden 2C 143
Newnham Ho. B36: Cas B 7B 24
Newnham La. CV23: Brin, K New 5D 62
Newnham Rd. CV1: Cov 2F 59
CV32: Lill 4F 99
NEW OSCOTT 2C 139
New Pk. Cotts. OX15: Lwr Bra 3J 133
New Place 5F 137
Newport Dr. B49: Alc 5B 112
Newport Rd. CV6: Cov 5D 50
Newquay Cl. CV11: Nun 6G 23
New River Wlk. CV31: Lea S 7B 98
CV32: Lea S 7B 98
New Rd. B46: Wat O 1B 24
B79: Shut 1B 8
B80: Stud 3D 92
B95: Hen A 3G 93
CV6: Cov 5K 49
CV7: Ash G 7C 40
CV9: Ath 4C 16
CV12: Bed 1K 39
(not continuous)
CV35: N Lin 2G 95
DE12: App M 2K 7
OX15: Ratl 6D 128
OX17: Shotte 6G 129
New Row CV37: Lwr Q 5H 125
Newsholme Cl. CV34: Warw 6H 97
(not continuous)
Newstead Cl. CV11: Nun 2B 32
Newstead Dr. CV47: Sou 6G 107
Newstead Way CV3: Bin 6D 60
New St. B78: B'moor 3B 10
B78: Dord 5D 10
CV8: Ken 3D 78
CV9: Bad E 2F 15
CV12: Bed 3J 41
CV12: Bulk 3E 42
CV22: Rugby 5E 74
CV31: Lea S 1E 102
CV32: Cubb 2J 99
CV34: Warw 2G 101
CV36: Ship S 5H 131
CV37: S Avon 6E 114
CV37: Tidd 3K 115
CV47: Nap 3H 111
NEWTON 1C 145
Newton Bldgs. CV12: Bed 3H 41
NEWTON BURGOLAND 1A 140
Newton Cl. CV2: W'grve S 7B 52
CV10: Harts 1G 21
NEWTON HARCOURT 2D 141
Newton La. B79: Aus, Newt R 5E 6
B79: Newt R, Seck 5A 6
CV9: Aus 5E 6
Newton Mnr. La. CV23: Brow, Newt 7J 65
NEWTON REGIS 5D 6 (1D 139)
Newton Rd. CV23: Clift D, Newt 1C 76
NEWTON UNTHANK 1B 140
NEWTOWN 1A 138
NEW TOWN 7B 134
Newtown La. B46: Shu 5H 27
CV7: Fill 5H 27
NEWTOWN LINFORD 1C 141
Newtown Rd. CV11: Nun 6D 22
CV12: Bed 3F 41
(not continuous)
New Union St. CV1: Cov 5H 135 (5C 58)
Nicholls St. CV2: Cov 4F 59
Nicholson Cl. CV34: Warw 6H 97
Nickson Rd. CV4: Tile H 7C 56
Nicolas Everton Cl. CV8: Bran 3J 71
Nightingale Av. B36: Cas B 4A 24
Nightingale Cl. CV9: Ath 2D 16
Nightingale Ct. CV31: Lea S 7F 99
Nightingale Gdns. CV23: Brow 6J 65
Nightingale La. CV5: Cov 7H 57
(not continuous)
Nineacres Dr. B37: F'bri 3A 34
Nine Days La. B98: Redd 1A 92
Niton Rd. CV10: Nun 5E 22
Niven Cl. CV5: Alle 1E 56
Nobel Dr. CV22: Caw 1A 86
Noble Cl. CV34: Warw 3F 101
NOBOTTLE 2D 145
Node Hill B80: Stud 4C 92
Node Hill Cl. B80: Stud 4C 92
Nod Ri. CV5: E Grn 3E 56
Nolan Cl. CV6: Longf 2D 50
NO MAN'S HEATH 2F 7 (1D 139)
No Man's Heath La. CV9: Aus 5G 7
Nook, The CV11: Nun 2A 32
Nordic Drift CV2: W'grve S 1C 60
Norfolk Cres. CV10: Nun 1E 30
Norfolk St. CV1: Cov 4B 58
CV32: Lea S 6E 98
Norluck Ct. CV36: Ship S 4H 131
Norman Ashman Coppice CV3: Bin W 1E 70
Norman Av. CV2: W'grve S 5B 52
CV11: Nun 7C 22
Normanby Mdws. CV31: W'nsh 6E 102
Normandy Cl. CV35: H Mag 1C 100
Norman Pl. Rd. CV6: Cov 7J 49
Norman Rd. CV21: N'bld A 2F 75
NORMANTON LE HEATH 1A 140
NORTHAMPTON 2D 145
Northampton La. CV22: Dunc 5B 86
CV23: Dunc 5H 85
NORTH ASTON 3D 147
North Av. B40: Nat E C 1E 44
CV2: Cov 4G 59
CV12: Bed 3K 41
Northbourne Dr. CV11: Nun 5A 32
NORTHBROOK 3D 147
Northbrook Rd. CV6: Cov 6H 49
North Cl. CV32: Cubb 2J 99
Northcote Rd. CV22: Rugby 6F 75
Northcote St. CV31: Lea S 1F 103
Northcote Wlk. CV9: Ath 1C 16
North Dr. B95: Woot W 5H 93
NORTHEND 2D 120 (3A 144)
Northend Rd. CV47: Fen C 2F 121
NORTH EVINGTON 1D 141
Northey Rd. CV6: Cov 6D 50
NORTHFIELD 1B 142
Northfield Rd. CV1: Cov 5E 58
CV47: Sou 6G 107
Northfolk Ter. CV4: Canly 1G 67
Northgate CV34: Warw 1G 101
Northgate St. CV34: Warw 1G 101
NORTH KILWORTH 3D 141
NORTH LITTLETON 3B 142
NORTH NEWINGTON 2D 147
NORTH PIDDLE 3A 142
North Rd. CV23: Clift D 3B 76
North Solihull Sports Cen. 2A 34
North St. CV2: Cov 2G 59
CV9: Ath 3C 16
CV10: Nun 1F 31
CV21: Rugby 5G 75
CV23: Kils 6H 89
CV23: Mart 2D 104
Northumberland Av. CV10: Nun 7K 21
Northumberland Lodge *CV32: Lea S 4D 98*
(off Kenilworth Rd.)
Northumberland M. CV32: B'dwn 4C 98
Northumberland Rd. CV1: Cov 4A 58
CV32: Lea S 5C 98
Northvale Cl. CV8: Ken 3F 79
North Vw. CV2: W'grve S 5C 52
Nth. Villiers St. CV32: Lea S 5E 98
Northway B40: Nat E C 7F 35
CV21: Rugby 5G 75
(in Clock Towers Shop. Cen.)
CV31: Lea S 2E 102
Nth. Woodloes CV35: Leek W 3J 97
Nortoft La. CV23: Kils 4G 89
NORTON
Daventry 2D 145
Evesham 3B 142
Worcester 3A 142
NORTON CANES 1B 138
Norton Curlieu La. CV35: N Lin 1G 95
Norton Dr. CV34: Warw 5G 97
CV37: Lwr Q 5J 125
NORTON EAST 1B 138
Norton Grange CV5: Alle 1G 57
Norton Grange CV35: Lit K 6C 120
Norton Hill CV9: Aus 7H 7
Norton Hill Dr. CV2: Cov 1A 60
NORTON-JUXTA-TWYCROSS 1A 140
Norton Lea CV35: N Lin 2F 95
Norton Leys CV22: Rugby 2F 87
NORTON LINDSEY 2G 95 (2D 143)
Norton Rd. B46: Col 3F 25
Nortons Cl. CV47: N'end 2D 120
Norton's La. CV35: Rad 5B 128
Norton St. CV1: Cov 2J 135
Norwich Cl. CV11: Nun 3H 23
Norwich Cft. B37: Mars G 4A 34
Norwich Dr. CV3: Cov 3B 68
Norwood Gro. CV2: W'grve S 4A 52
NOSELEY 2D 141
NOTGROVE 3A 146
Nova Cft. CV5: E Grn 3A 56
Nuffield Ho. B36: Cas B 4A 24
Nuffield Rd. CV6: Cov 6G 51
NUNEATON 7D 22 (2A 140)
Nuneaton Arts Cen. 7C 22
Nuneaton Borough FC 7A 22
Nuneaton La. CV13: High H 1G 23
Nuneaton Mus. & Art Gallery 7D 22
Nuneaton RFC 7G 23
Nuneaton Rd. B46: Over W 1G 27
CV7: Fill 2C 38
CV9: Man 5F 17
CV10: Ansl 5A 20

Nuneaton Rd. CV10: Harts .1G 21
(Grange Rd.)
CV10: Harts .7H 17
(Woodford La.)
CV12: Bed .7H 31
CV12: Bulk .6D 32
Nuneaton Station (Rail) .6D 22
Nunts La. CV6: Cov .3B 50
Nunts Pk. Av. CV6: Cov .2B 50
Nunwood La. CV23: Prin .5B 82
Nursery La. CV31: Lea S .3E 102
(not continuous)
Nursery Rd. CV9: Ath .4E 16
CV10: Ans C .3D 20
Nutbrook Av. CV4: Tile H .5C 56
NUTHURST .1C 143
Nuthurst Cres. CV10: Ansl .1G 29
Nuthurst La. CV10: Asty .2G 29

O

OADBY .1D 141
Oak Av. CV7: Old A .2C 28
Oak Cl. CV8: Bag .6F 69
CV12: Bed .1J 41
Oak Ct. CV34: H'cte .6C 102
Oakdale Rd. CV3: Bin W .1E 70
Oakdene Cl. CV35: Clav .2D 94
Oakdene Ct. CV37: S Avon .3E 114
Oakdene Cres. CV10: Nun .4D 22
Oak Dr. CV10: Harts .3F 21
OAKEN .1A 138
Oakey Cl. CV6: Longf .2F 51
Oakfield Gdns. CV9: Ath .4D 16
Oakfield Ho. CV32: Lea S .5D 98
Oakfield Pk. *CV22: Rugby* .*6F 75*
(off Bilton Rd.)
Oakfield Rd. CV22: Rugby .6F 75
Oakford Dr. CV5: Alle .1D 56
Oakham Cres. CV12: Bulk .3F 43
Oakham Rd. GL56: Lit C .6C 134
Oaklands B76: Curd .5B 18
Oaklands, The B37: Mars G .6A 34
CV4: Tile H .5E 56
Oaklands Ct. CV8: Ken .7E 78
Oak La. CV5: Alle .6A 48
Oak La. Pk. Homes CV5: Alle .5B 48
Oakleigh CV33: L Hth .2K 119
Oakleigh Rd. CV37: S Avon .2D 114
Oakley Ct. *CV12: Bed* .*4D 40*
(off Newcomen Rd.)
Oakley Wood Rd. CV33: Bis T .7B 108 & 7D 102
(not continuous)
Oakmoor Rd. CV6: Longf .3G 51
Oakridge Rd. CV32: Lill .3G 99
Oak Ri. B46: Col .7F 25
Oak Rd. CV37: Tidd .4K 115
Oakroyd Cres. CV10: Nun .4J 21
Oaks, The CV4: W'wd H .2E 66
CV12: Bed .3F 41
CV32: Lea S .7B 98
Oak's Pl. CV6: Longf .3G 51
Oaks Pct. CV8: Ken .6C 78
Oaks Rd. CV8: Ken .7C 78
Oak St. CV22: Rugby .6G 75
OAKTHORPE .1A 140
Oakthorpe Dr. B37: K'hrst .7A 24
Oak Tree Av. CV3: Cov .2A 68
Oak Tree Cl. CV32: Lea S .5E 98
Oaktree Cl. B78: K'bry .5E 12
CV35: More M .4B 118
(not continuous)
CV37: Bear .6C 94
Oak Tree Ct. CV32: Lea S .5E 98
Oak Tree La. B96: Sam .5A 92
Oak Tree Rd. CV3: Bin .1C 70
Oak Way CV4: Tile H .5B 56
Oakwood Cl. CV9: Gren .2F 15
Oakwood Gro. CV34: Warw .6J 97
Oakworth Cl. CV2: W'grve S .6B 52
Oaston Rd. CV11: Nun .7E 22
Oatlands Cl. CV6: Cov .2C 50
Oban Dr. CV10: Nun .2G 31
Oban Rd. CV6: Longf .1F 51
Oberon Cl. CV11: Nun .3C 32
CV22: Bil .3D 86
CV34: H'cte .4C 102
Occupation Rd. CV2: Cov .4J 59
Oddicombe Cft. CV3: Cov .3D 68
ODDINGLEY .3A 142
Odeon Cinema
Coventry .3F 135 (5B 58)
Nuneaton .6G 31
Odingsel Dr. CV47: Long I .2B 106
ODSTONE .1A 140
Offa Dr. CV8: Ken .4E 78
Offa Rd. CV31: Lea S .2F 103
OFFCHURCH .2A 144
Offchurch La. CV31: Rad S .2K 103
Offchurch Rd. CV32: Cubb .2H 99
OFFENHAM .3B 142
OFFENHAM CROSS .1A 146
Ofield La. CV23: Kils .6H 89
Ogmore Rd. CV31: Lea S .2F 103
Okeford Way CV10: Nun .3G 31
Okehampton Rd. CV3: Cov .3E 68
Okement Gro. CV23: Long L .3B 74
Oken Ct. CV34: Warw .1F 101
Oken Rd. CV34: Warw .7F 97
Okens House and Doll Mus. .2G 101
Olaf Pl. CV2: W'grve S .7C 52
Oldany Way CV10: Nun .2F 31
OLD ARLEY .2C 28 (2D 139)
OLDBERROW .2C 143
Oldborough Dr. CV35: Lox .4B 116
Old Brewery Cl. CV36: Ship S .3J 131
Old Brickyard La. CV47: Nap .1F 111
Old Budbrooke Rd. CV35: H Mag .2A 100
OLDBURY
B69 .3A 138
CV10 .1D 20 (2A 140)
Oldbury Rd. CV10: Harts .2B 20
Oldbury Vw. CV10: Harts .2G 21
Oldbutt Rd. CV36: Ship S .5G 131
Old Cathedral .3J 135
Old Church Rd. B46: Wat O .1B 24
CV6: Cov .5F 51
Old Crown M. CV2: Ald G .2K 51
Old Damson La. B92: Sol .4A 44
OLD FALLINGS .1A 138
OLDFALLOW .1A 138
Old Farm Rd. CV9: Man .5E 16
OLDFIELD .2A 142
Oldfield Rd. CV5: Cov .4H 57
Old Ford Av. CV47: Sou .4G 107
Old Fosse Way CV36: Tred .5H 127
OLD GRIMSBURY .1D 147
Old Hall Ct. B79: Newt R .5D 6
Oldham Av. CV2: Cov .3K 59
Oldham Way CV23: Long L .4B 74
OLD HILL .3A 138
Old Hinckley Rd. CV10: Nun .6E 22
Old Holly La. CV9: Ath .1B 16
Old Ho. La. CV7: Cor .6E 38
Old Kingsbury Rd. B76: Mars .1G 19
Old Leicester Rd. CV21: Rugby .1G 75
(not continuous)
Old Meeting Yd. CV12: Bed .2H 41
Old Mill Av. CV4: Canly .3H 67
Old Mill Ct. B46: Col .5F 25
Old Mill Rd. B46: Col .5F 25
OLD MILVERTON .4A 98
Old Milverton La. CV32: B'dwn .4A 98
Old Milverton Rd. CV32: Lea S, Old M .4A 98
Old Orchard, The CV23: Bird .5A 104
Old Penns La. B46: Col .5F 25
Old Pound CV34: Warw .1G 101
Old Rectory Cl. CV23: C'over .1H 65
Old Rectory Gdn. B49: Alc .4B 112
Old Red Lion Ct. CV37: S Avon .4H 137 (5F 115)
Old Rd. CV7: Mer .5G 47
CV36: Long C .4C 134
CV36: Ship S .5H 131
CV47: Bis I .6C 110
CV47: Sou .6H 107
OX15: Ratl .6C 128
Old School La. CV35: H Hill .4A 100
CV35: Light .2H 119
CV37: Wilm .6J 113
Old School Mead B50: Bidf A .6F 123
Old School M. CV32: Lill .4F 99
Old Snitterfield Rd. CV37: Bear .6D 94
Old Sq. CV34: Warw .2G 101
Old Sq., The CV37: Shot .5C 114
Old Station Rd. B92: H Ard .4F 45
Old Stone Yd. CV32: Lea S .6C 98
OLD TOWN .7D 136 (5E 114)
Old Town CV37: S Avon .7E 136 (5E 114)
Old Town M. CV37: S Avon .6E 114
Old Tramway Wlk. CV37: S Avon .5E 124
(Shipston Rd.)
CV37: S Avon .5J 137 (5G 115)
(Swan Nest La., not continuous)
Old Tree La. CV35: Up Tys .7C 130
Old Vicarage Gdns. B80: Stud .3D 92
Old Warwick Rd. B94: Lapw .3F 91
CV31: Lea S .1C 102
CV35: Row .3F 91 & 4G 91
Old Watling St. *CV9: Ath* .*3B 16*
(off Long St.)
Old Winnings Rd. CV7: Ker E .7K 39
OLD WOODSTOCK .3D 147
Olive Av. CV2: Cov .2K 59
Oliver's Lock CV37: S Avon .2H 137
Oliver St. CV6: Cov .1F 59
CV21: Rugby .5F 75
Olivier Way CV2: W'grve S .6D 52
OLTON .3C 139
Olton Av. CV5: E Grn .3D 56
Olton Cl. CV11: Burt H .4J 33
Olton Pl. CV11: Nun .7A 22
Olympus Av. CV34: Warw .3B 102
Olympus Cl. CV5: Mil W .6K 47
Olympus Ct. CV34: Warw .3B 102
Omar Rd. CV2: Cov .5K 59
OMBERSLEY .2A 142
Ombersley Cl. B98: Redd .1A 92
Omega Pl. CV21: Rugby .4H 75
One O'Clock Ride CV3: Bin W .1G 71
Onley La. CV22: Rugby .3J 87
CV23: Barby .7D 88
Onley Ter. CV4: Canly .1G 67
Onslow Cft. CV32: Lea S .5D 98
Openfield Cft. B46: Wat O .2C 24
Ophelia Dr. CV34: H'cte .5C 102
Oratory Dr. CV3: W'hall .2J 69
Orchard, The B37: Mars G .5A 34
CV9: Bax .4F 15
(not continuous)
CV23: Mart .2D 104
CV34: Warw .3H 101
CV36: Whatc .3A 130
CV37: Lwr Q .5H 125
Orchard Blythe B46: Col .6G 25
Orchard Bus. Pk. CV21: Rugby .4G 75
Orchard Cl. B46: Col .5F 25
B50: Bidf A .6G 123
B76: Curd .5B 18
B78: Pole .6D 8
CV9: Aus .6G 7
CV9: Hurl .7K 13
CV9: With .3G 17
CV10: Harts .4F 21
CV36: Ship S .5H 131
CV37: Welf A .3B 124
CV47: Bis I .6C 110
LE10: Wlvy .2H 33
OX15: Lwr Bra .3H 133
Orchard Cotts. CV9: Ath .4D 16
Orchard Ct. CV3: Bin .6C 60
CV9: Ath .4C 16
CV32: Lea S .5D 98
CV37: Lwr Q .6H 125
Orchard Cres. CV3: Cov .7G 135 (7C 58)
Orchard Dr. B49: Alc .6B 112
CV5: E Grn .3A 56
Orchard Gro. CV47: S'ton .6C 106
Orchard La. CV8: Ken .6G 79
Orchard Pl. CV37: Cliff C .5B 124
Orchard Retail Pk. CV3: W'hall .3K 69
Orchard Ri. CV9: Gren .1F 15
Orchards, The CV37: Wilm .5K 113
Orchard St. CV11: Nun .7E 22
CV12: Bed .7H 31
Orchard Way B80: Stud .5D 92
CV8: Bubb .4J 81
CV10: Nun .5H 21
CV22: Bil .1D 86
CV23: Stret D .3H 83
CV37: S Avon .7A 136 (5D 114)
CV47: Long I .2B 106
CV47: Sou .4H 107
Orchid Cl. CV12: Bed .3E 40
Orchid Way CV23: Brow .7K 65
Ordnance Rd. CV6: Cov .2E 58
Orford Cl. CV35: Welle .3J 117
Orford Ri. CV10: Gall C .7D 20
Oriel Ho. B37: F'bri .2A 34
Orion Cres. CV2: W'grve S .4A 52
Orkney Cl. CV10: Nun .2F 31
Orkney Cft. B36: Cas B .5B 24
Orlando Cl. CV22: Bil .3D 86
Orlescote Rd. CV4: Canly .2H 67
Ormesby Cl. CV22: Bil .6E 74
Orpington Dr. CV6: Cov .2D 50
Orrian Cl. CV37: S Avon .2D 114
Orsino Cl. CV34: H'cte .6C 102
Orson Leys CV22: Rugby .2F 87
ORTON .2A 138
Orton Cl. B46: Wat O .1A 24
Orton La. CV9: Aus .7H 7
ORTON-ON-THE-HILL .1A 140
Orton Rd. B79: Wart .6G 9
CV6: Cov .3C 50
Orton Rd. CV9: Wart, Ort H .6G 9
Orwell Cl. CV10: Gall C .6F 21
CV23: Clift D .3C 76
Orwell Ct. CV1: Cov .1K 135 (3D 58)
Orwell Rd. CV1: Cov .6F 59
OSBASTON .1B 140
Osbaston Cl. CV5: E Grn .3C 56
Osborne Ct. CV31: W'nsh .4E 102
Osborne Rd. CV5: Cov .7A 58
Osbourne Ho. CV1: Cov .5F 135
Oslo Gdns. CV2: W'grve S .7C 52
Osprey Cl. CV2: W'grve S .7D 52
CV11: Nun .4D 32
Ossetts Hole La. CV35: Yarn C .1A 94
Oswald Rd. CV32: Lea S .7B 98
Oswald Way CV22: Rugby .5D 74
Oswin Gro. CV2: Cov .3J 59
Othello Av. CV34: H'cte .5D 102
Othello Cl. CV22: Bil .4D 86
Other Place, The .7G 137 (5F 115)
OTHERTON .1A 138
Otters Rest CV31: Lea S .3H 103
Ousterne La. CV7: Fill .2B 38
Outermarch Rd. CV6: Cov .7C 50
OUTWOOD .1A 142
OUTWOODS .7E 36
Outwoods Cl. CV9: Ath .4B 16
Oval Rd. CV22: Hillm .1K 87
Overbare Cl. B94: Tan A .4D 90
Overbecks Cl. CV22: Bil .6E 74
Overberry Cl. CV2: Cov .4K 51
Overberry Orchard CV33: Bis T .5B 108
Overbrook Grange CV11: Nun .2H 23
Overdale Rd. CV5: Cov .4G 57
Overell Gro. CV32: Lea S .5B 98
OVER GREEN .2A 18 (2C 139)
Over Grn. Dr. B37: K'hrst .6A 24
OVER KIDDINGTON .3D 147
OVER NORTON .3C 147
OVERSLADE .7E 74
Overslade Cres. CV6: Cov .7J 49
Overslade La. CV22: Rugby .2D 86
Overslade Mnr. Dr. CV22: Rugby .1F 87
OVERSLEY GREEN .6C 112
Oversley Ho. B49: Alc .4C 112
Oversley Mill Pk. B49: Ove G .6B 112
Overstone Rd. CV7: Withy .1C 54
Over St. CV6: Cov .6G 51
OVERTHORPE .1D 147
Overton Dr. B46: Wat O .1C 24
Overtons Cl. CV31: Rad S .3K 103
OVER WHITACRE .1G 27 (2D 139)
OVER WORTON .3D 147
Owenford Rd. CV6: Cov .6C 50

Owen Sq. *CV9: Ath* *3C 16*
(off Owen St.)
Owen St. CV9: Ath 3C 16
Owlets End B50: Bart 7J 123
Ox Cl. CV2: Cov 1G 59
Oxendon Way CV3: Bin 6A 60
Oxford Cl. CV11: Nun 3G 23
Oxford Pl. CV32: Lea S 6D 98
Oxford Rd. CV8: Rytn D 6A 70
CV23: Mart, Prin 5F 83 & 1C 104
Oxford Row CV32: Lea S 6D 98
Oxford St. CV1: Cov 4E 58
CV21: Rugby 5J 75
CV32: Lea S 6D 98
CV47: Sou 5H 107
Oxford Way CV35: Welle 5F 117
OXHILL 1E 130 (1C 147)
Oxhill Bridle Rd. CV35: Pill H 1D 128
Oxhill Rd. CV35: Mid T 7C 130
OXLEY 1A 138
Oxley Dr. CV3: Finh 5C 68
Oxstalls Cotts. CV37: S Avon 1J 115
Oxway Cl. CV36: Ship S 4H 131

P

Packhorse Rd. CV37: S Avon 3A 114
Packington Av. CV5: Alle 1F 57
Packington La. B46: Col 1G 35
B46: Max 3D 36
CV7: Lit P 1H 45
Packington Pl. CV31: Lea S 1E 102
PACKMORES 7G 97 (2D 143)
Packmore St. CV34: Warw 7H 97
PACKWOOD 1C 143
Packwood Av. B94: Lapw 1G 91
CV21: Hillm 1D 88
Packwood Cl. CV11: Nun 4B 32
CV31: Lea S 3G 103
Packwood Ct. CV37: S Avon 3G 137
Packwood Grn. CV5: E Grn 4E 56
PACKWOOD GULLETT 1C 143
Packwood House 1F 91
Packwood La. B94: Lapw 1F 91
Packwood M. CV34: Warw 7K 97
Packwood Rd. B94: Lapw 1F 91
Paddiford Pl. CV10: Nun 1C 30
Paddock Cvn. Pk., The B50: Bidf A 7G 123
Paddock Cl. B50: Bidf A 5F 123
CV47: Nap 2H 111
Paddock La. CV37: S Avon 6D 114
Paddock Pl. CV37: S Avon 7E 136 (6E 114)
Paddocks, The CV12: Bulk 2D 42
CV23: Stret D 3H 83
CV34: Warw 1H 101
Paddocks Cl. B78: Pole 1C 10
CV8: Wols 5J 71
Paddox Cl. CV22: Hillm 1B 88
Paddox Ct. CV23: Kils 6J 89
Padmore Ct. CV31: Lea S 2F 103
Padstow Cl. CV11: Nun 6G 23
Padstow Rd. CV4: Tile H 7C 56
Padua CV37: S Avon 1H 137
Page Rd. CV4: Tile H 1C 66
Paget Ct. CV2: Ald G 3H 51
Paget's La. CV8: Bubb 4K 81
(not continuous)
PAILTON 6K 55 (3B 140)
Pailton Cl. CV2: Cov 4J 51
Pailton Rd. CV23: Harb M 7K 55 & 1A 64
Pake's Cft. CV6: Cov 2A 58
Palermo Av. CV3: Cov 2E 68
Pallett Dr. CV11: Nun 4G 23
Palmer Ct. CV37: S Avon 5H 137
Palmer La. CV1: Cov 3H 135 (4C 58)
Palmer Rd. CV31: W'nsh 4F 103
Palmer's Cl. CV21: Hillm 1D 88
PALMERS CROSS 1A 138
Palmers Leys CV35: Kine 5D 120
Palmerston Rd. CV5: Cov 7K 57
Palm Tree Av. CV2: Cov 4J 51
Pampas Cl. CV37: S Avon 2D 114
Pancras Cl. CV2: W'grve S 5A 52
Pandora Rd. CV2: W'grve S 7A 52
Pangbourne Cl. CV11: Nun 3G 23
Pangbourne Rd. CV2: Cov 6J 51
Pangfield Pk. CV5: Cov 3G 57
Pantolf Pl. CV21: N'bld A 1E 74
Papenham Grn. CV4: Tile H 7E 56
Parade CV32: Lea S 6D 98
Parade, The B37: K'hrst 6A 24
CV11: Nun 1J 31
PARADISE 1F 59
Paradise St. CV1: Cov 6K 135 (6D 58)
CV21: Rugby 5J 75
CV34: Warw 7H 97
Paradise Way CV2: W'grve S 5C 52
Paradise Works CV6: Cov 7F 51
Paragon Pk. CV6: Cov 1D 58
Paragon Way CV7: Exh 5H 41
Parbrook Cl. CV4: Tile H 7C 56
Parish End CV31: Lea S 4G 103
Park & Ride
Austin Dr. 7G 51
Birmingham Rd. 3E 114
Canley 6J 57
Kenilworth Rd. 1A 68
Park Av. B46: Col 6F 25
B78: Pole 2D 10
B80: Stud 4D 92
CV6: Cov 3C 50
CV11: Nun 1A 32
Park Cl. CV8: Ken 4F 79
CV35: Clav 2D 94
CV37: Wilm 6J 113
Park Cotts. CV37: Snitt 5H 95
Park Ct. CV1: Cov 6G 135 (6C 58)
CV5: Alle 1F 57
CV21: Rugby *4H 75*
(off Park Rd.)
CV37: S Avon 3D 114
Park Dr. CV31: Lea S 1C 102
CV35: Clav 2D 94
Parkend CV21: Brow 1J 75
Parke Row CV35: Mid T 7C 130
Parkes Ct. CV34: Warw 1F 101
Parkes St. CV34: Warw 1F 101
Park Farm Cl. CV22: Bil 6D 74
Park Farm Ind. Est. B98: Redd 1C 92
PARK FARM SOUTH 1C 92
Parkfield Ct. B46: Col 5F 25
(Park Rd.)
B46: Col 6G 25
(Sumner Rd.)
Parkfield Dr. CV8: Ken 4F 79
Parkfield Rd. B46: Col 5F 25
CV7: Ker E 7A 40
CV21: N'bld A, Rugby 2D 74
Parkfields CV47: Sou 5H 107
PARK GATE 1A 142
Parkgate Rd. CV6: Cov 3B 50
Park Gro. B46: Wat O 1C 24
Park Hall WR11: Salf P 6A 122
Park Hall M. WR11: Salf P 6A 122
PARK HILL 4G 79
Park Hill CV8: Ken 4E 78
Parkhill Dr. CV5: Alle 3D 56
Pk. Hill La. CV5: Alle 1E 56
(High Beech)
CV5: Alle 2E 56
(Polperro Dr.)
Park Ho. CV37: Snitt 6H 95
Parkinson Dr. CV9: Ath 1D 16
Parkland Cl. CV6: Cov 3C 50
Parklands NN6: Crick 2K 89
Parklands Av. CV32: Lill 3G 99
PARK LANE 1A 138
Park La. B49: Gt Alne 1F 113
CV7: Fill 7E 28
CV10: Asty 7E 28
CV10: Gall C, Nun 7E 20
CV33: Har 6G 109
CV37: Lwr Q 5H 125
CV37: Snitt 5H 95
CV47: Sou 5H 107
Park La. Ter. CV33: Har 6H 109
Park Paling, The CV3: Cov 1E 68
Park Piece CV35: Kine 5C 120
Park Rd. B46: Col 6F 25
B78: Pole 2E 10
CV1: Cov 6H 135 (6C 58)
CV8: Ken 3E 78
CV9: Bad E 2E 14
CV12: Bed 3H 41
CV21: Rugby 4G 75
CV32: Lill 3E 98
CV34: Warw 7H 97
CV37: S Avon 3E 114
Parkside B37: Mars G 6D 34
CV1: Cov 5J 135 (5D 58)
Park Sq. B37: Mars G 5D 34
Parkstone Rd. CV6: Cov 4F 51
Park St. CV6: Cov 7E 50
CV11: Nun 1K 31
CV32: Lea S 6D 98
Park Vw. B49: Arr 6A 112
CV3: Cov 5G 59
Park Vw. Cl. CV7: Exh 5G 41
Park Vw. Ct. CV10: Nun 7J 21
Parkview Flats CV5: Cov 7B 58
Park Vw. La. CV37: N'bld S 1G 127
Parkville Cl. CV6: Cov 3C 50
Parkville Highway CV6: Cov 3B 50
Park Wlk. CV21: Rugby 4G 75
Parkway CV2: W'grve S 6D 52
Parkwood Ct. CV8: Ken 4F 79
Park Wood La. CV4: Tile H 1B 66
Parmiter Ho. CV32: Lea S 5D 98
Parnell Cl. CV21: Rugby 5F 75
Parolles Cl. CV34: H'cte 5C 102
Parr Cl. CV34: Warw 2B 102
Parrish Cl. CV47: Bis I 7B 110
Parrotts Gro. CV2: Ald G 1K 51
Parry Rd. CV2: Cov 7H 51
Parsonage Cl. CV33: Bis T 5C 108
Parsons Cl. CV36: Ship S 5H 131
Parsons Nook CV2: Cov 2G 59
Partridge Cl. B37: Chel W 2C 34
Partridge Cft. CV6: Cov 5G 51
Partridge Rd. CV37: B'ton 3B 114
Pastures Way CV34: Warw 4D 100
PATHLOW 3C 143
Patience Gro. CV34: H'cte 5D 102
Patricia Cl. CV4: Tile H 6A 56
Pattens Rd. CV34: Warw 6K 97
Patterdale CV21: Brow 1K 75
PATTISHALL 3D 145
Pauline Av. CV6: Cov 4H 51
Paul Stacey Ho. CV1: Cov 1K 135
Pavilion B40: Nat E C 2E 44
Pavilions, The B37: Mars G 5D 34
CV9: Ath 1B 16
Pavilion Way CV5: Cov 4K 57
PAXFORD 2A 146
Paxmead Cl. CV6: Cov 4A 50
Paxton Rd. CV6: Cov 3A 58
Payne Cl. CV32: Lea S 5E 98
Paynell Cl. CV6: Cov 4B 50
Paynes La. CV1: Cov 4F 59
CV21: Rugby 5D 74
Payton Ct. CV37: S Avon 2G 137
Payton St. CV37: S Avon 2G 137 (4F 115)
Peacehaven Cotts. CV10: Nun 2G 31
Peace Wlk. B37: Chel W 4B 34
Peacock Av. CV2: W'grve S 5B 52
Peacock Ct. CV35: Welle 3H 117
Peacock La. CV35: Mid T 6D 130
Peacocks, The CV34: Warw 6D 100
Peake Av. CV11: Nun 3F 23
Pearl Hyde Ho. CV1: Cov 1K 135
Pears Cl. CV8: Ken 4D 78
Pearson Av. CV6: Cov 5H 51
Peart Dr. B80: Stud 3B 92
Pear Tree Av. B78: K'bry 6E 12
CV10: Nun 5K 21
Pear Tree Cl. B79: Shut 2B 8
CV2: Cov 4H 51
CV37: Long M 2G 125
Peartrees CV47: N'end 2D 120
Pear Tree Way CV22: Bil 7B 74
Peat Cl. CV22: Bil 7E 74
PEATLING MAGNA 2C 141
PEATLING PARVA 3C 141
Pebblebrook Way CV12: Bed 4J 41
Pebble Island Way CV31: Lea S 3G 103
PEBWORTH 1A 146
Pebworth Cl. CV5: E Grn 4F 57
Pebworth Dr. CV35: Hatt 4A 96
PECKLETON 1B 140
Peckstone Cl. CV1: Cov 7K 135 (6D 58)
PEDMORE 3A 138
Pedmore Cl. B98: Redd 1A 92
Peel Cl. B92: H Ard 7H 45
CV6: Cov 1E 58
Peel La. CV6: Cov 2F 59
Peel Rd. CV34: Warw 7G 97
Peel St. CV6: Cov 1E 58
Pegmill Cl. CV3: Cov 7F 59
Pelham La. B49: Gt Alne 3F 113
PELSALL 1B 138
Pembroke Cl. CV12: Bed 4C 40
CV34: Warw 7H 97
Pembroke Ct. CV32: Lea S 5D 98
Pembroke Gdns. CV35: Welle 5G 117
Pembroke Ho. B36: Cas B 5A 24
Pembroke Way CV11: Nun 1K 31
Pembrook Rd. CV6: Cov 4C 50
Pembury Av. CV6: Longf 3G 51
Penarth Gro. CV3: Bin 1B 70
Pencraig Cl. CV8: Ken 4G 79
PENDEFORD 1A 138
Pendenis Cl. CV6: Cov 6G 51
Pendicke Ct. *CV47: Sou* *5H 107*
(off Pendicke St.)
Pendicke St. CV47: Sou 5H 107
Pendigo Way B40: Nat E C 2E 44
(not continuous)
Pendine Ct. CV32: Lea S 7B 98
Pendred Rd. CV22: Rugby 5E 74
Pendrell Cl. B37: F'bri 2A 34
Penelope Cl. CV33: Har 6H 109
Penfold Cl. CV33: Bis T 5C 108
Penmire Cl. CV9: Gren 7F 11
PENN 2A 138
Penn Ho. CV4: Tile H 6D 56
Pennine Way CV10: Nun 7G 21
Pennington M. CV21: Rugby 5F 75
Pennington St. CV21: Rugby 5F 75
Pennington Way CV6: Cov 6E 50
Penn La. B94: Tan A 1A 90
Penns Cl. CV32: Cubb 2J 99
Pennyford La. B95: Woot W 7G 93
Penny Hapenny Ct. CV9: Ath 3B 16
Pennyland La. CV8: Ken 2F 79
Penny Pk. La. CV6: Cov 3A 50
Pennystone Cl. CV31: Lea S 2H 103
Penrith Cl. CV6: Cov 4C 50
CV32: Lea S 5A 98
Penrith Gro. B37: Chel W 3C 34
Penrose Cl. CV4: Tile H 1E 66
Penryhn Cl. CV8: Ken 4G 79
Penryn Cl. CV11: Nun 7H 23
Penshurst Way CV11: Nun 4B 32
Pensilva Way CV1: Cov 3E 58
PENSNETT 3A 138
Pentire Cl. CV11: Nun 6G 23
Penzance Way CV11: Nun 6G 23
PEOPLETON 3A 142
Pepper La. CV1: Cov 4H 135 (5C 58)
Pepys Cnr. CV4: Tile H 4C 56
Perch Av. B37: F'bri 2A 34
Perchfoot Cl. CV1: Cov 7K 135 (6D 58)
Percival Dr. CV33: Har 6J 109
Percival Rd. CV22: Hillm 1K 87
Percy Cres. CV8: Ken 7C 78
Percy Rd. CV8: Ken 7C 78
CV34: Warw 7G 97
Percy St. CV1: Cov 4B 58
CV37: S Avon 3F 115
Percy Ter. CV32: Lea S 6B 98
Peregrine Dr. CV5: Alle 2E 56
Pericles Cl. CV34: H'cte 5C 102
Perimeter Rd. B40: Nat E C 2D 44
(not continuous)
Perkins Cl. WR11: Salf P 6A 122
Perkins Gro. CV21: Hillm 7B 76
Perkins St. CV1: Cov 2K 135 (4D 58)
Permian Cl. CV21: Rugby 2J 75

PERRY .2B 138
PERRY BARR .2B 138
PERRY CROFTS .1D 139
Perryman Dr. B78: Picc .3G **13**
Perry Mill La. B95: Ullen .4B **90**
Perrymill La. B96: Sam .6A **92**
PERSHORE .3A 142
Pershore Pl. CV4: Canly .2J **67**
Perth Ri. CV5: E Grn .3E **56**
PERTON .2A 138
Peter Ct. CV21: Rugby .5J **75**
Peter Hall La. CV2: W'grve S .1H **61**
Peter Lee Wlk. CV2: W'grve S .1C **60**
Peters Wlk. CV6: Longf .2G **51**
Petitor Cres. CV2: Cov .6J **51**
Peto Gro. CV34: H'cte .6D **102**
Pettiford La. B95: Pres B, Woot W .4K **93**
Pettiver Cres. CV21: Hillm .7B **76**
Petunia Cl. CV10: Nun .4G **31**
Peveril Dr. CV3: Cov .3A **68**
Peyto Cl. CV6: Cov .4C **50**
Pheasant Cl. CV12: Bed .4D **40**
CV37: B'ton .3B **114**
Pheasant Cft. B36: Cas B .4A **24**
Pheasant Oak CV4: Tile H .5A **56**
Phebe Cl. CV34: H'cte .5C **102**
Phillip Docker Ct. CV12: Bulk .3D **42**
Phillippes Rd. CV34: Warw .6H **97**
Phipps Av. CV21: Hillm .7B **76**
(not continuous)
Phoenix Ho. CV1: Cov .1K **135**
Phoenix Pk. CV7: Exh .6H **41**
Phoenix Vis. Cen. .3J 135
Phoenix Way CV2: Cov .4F **59**
CV6: Cov, Longf .3E **50**
CV6: Longf .2E **50**
PICCADILLY .2G 13 (2D 139)
Piccadilly B78: Picc .2G **13**
Piccadilly Cl. B37: Chel W .4C **34**
Piccadilly Cres. B78: Picc .3G **13**
Piccadilly Way B78: K'bry .7E **12**
Pickard Cl. CV21: Brow .1A **76**
Pickard St. CV34: Warw .1J **101**
Pickards Way CV7: Exh .7F **41**
PICKFORD .6B 48 (3D 139)
Pickford Cl. CV11: Nun .3C **32**
Pickford Grange La. CV5: Alle .7A **48**
PICKFORD GREEN .7A 48
Pickford Grn. La. CV5: Alle, E Grn .2A **56**
Pickford Way CV5: Alle, Cov .1E **56**
Picton Cft. B37: Chel W .3D **34**
Piers Cl. CV34: Warw .7H **97**
PIGEON GREEN .5H 95
Piggotts Cft. B37: F'bri .2A **34**
Pike Dr. B37: Chel W .2C **34**
Piker's La. CV7: Cor .3E **48**
Pilgrims Wlk. CV7: Ker E .1A **50**
Pilkington Rd. CV5: Cov .6H **57**
PILLATON .1A 138
PILLERTON HERSEY .1D 128 (1B 146)
PILLERTON PRIORS .3B 128 (1B 146)
Pilling Cl. CV2: W'grve S .6B **52**
Pill La. GL56: Lit C .6B **134**
Pimlico La. CV37: A'ton .4B **116**
Pinbury Cft. B37: Mars G .4B **34**
Pinders Ct. CV21: Rugby .5H **75**
Pinders La. CV21: Rugby .5H **75**
(not continuous)
Pine Cl. CV37: Shot .6C **114**
Pine Ct. CV32: Lill .4F **99**
Pine Gro. CV21: Hillm .7C **76**
Pineham Av. CV33: Har .6H **109**
Pinehurst CV32: Cubb .1J **99**
Pines, The CV4: Tile H .1B **66**
CV12: Bed .3E **40**
Pine Sq. B37: Chel W .3B **34**
Pine Tree Av. CV4: Tile H .5E **56**
Pine Tree Ct. CV12: Bed .1J **41**
Pine Tree Cres. CV47: Sou .4J **107**
Pine Tree Rd. CV12: Bed .1J **41**
Pinewood Av. CV9: Wood E .2K **13**
Pinewood Dr. CV3: Bin W .1E **70**
Pinewood Gro. CV5: Cov .7B **58**
Pinfold St. CV21: Rugby .5E **74**
Pingle Ct. CV11: Nun .2K **31**
Pingles Leisure Cen. .2K 31
Pingles Stadium, The .2J 31
PINKETT'S BOOTH .5A 48
PINLEY .1J 69 (1A 144)
Pinley Flds. CV3: Cov .7H **59**
PINLEY GREEN .2D 143
Pinner's Cft. CV2: Cov .2G **59**
Pinnock Pl. CV4: Tile H .6D **56**
PINVIN .3A 142
Pioneer Ho. CV1: Cov .1K **135**
CV1: Cov .2D 58
(off Leicester C'way.)
Pioneer Units CV11: Nun .1A **32**
PIPEHILL .1B 138
Pipers Ct. CV3: Finh .4K **67**
Piper's End LE10: Wlvy .2H **33**
Pipers La. CV8: Ken .4E **78**
CV10: Ans C .3B **20**
Pipers Rd. B98: Redd .1C **92**
Pipewell Cl. CV22: Bil .7C **74**
Pipit Wlk. CV23: Brow .6J **65**
Pipkin Ct. CV1: Cov .7K **135** (6D **58**)
Pippin Cl. B50: Bidf A .5G **123**
Pirie Cl. CV33: Har .6J **109**
PIRTON .3A 142
Pit Hill CV8: Bubb .4J **81**
PITSFORD .2D 145
Pittern Hill CV35: Kine .4A **120**
Pitt La. B92: Bick .4D **44**
Pittoms La. CV23: Barby .7E **88**
Pittway Av. CV36: Ship S .4G **131**
Plane Cl. *CV10: Nun .4K 21*
(off Spruce Rd.)
Plane Gro. B37: Chel W .4B **34**
Plank La. B46: Wat O .2A **24**
Plantagenet Dr. CV22: Bil .3E **86**
Plantagenet Pk. CV34: H'cte .5C **102**
Planter Cl. CV22: Caw .1A **86**
Plants Hill Cres. CV4: Tile H .7C **56**
Plato Cl. CV34: Warw .3B **102**
Playbox Theatre .4E 100
Pleasant Way CV32: Lea S .5E **98**
Pleck, The B50: Bidf A .6G **123**
Pleck Cl. B50: Bidf A .6G **123**
Plexfield Rd. CV22: Bil .7C **74**
Pleydell Cl. CV3: W'hall .3J **69**
Plomer Cl. CV22: Bil .1C **86**
Plott La. CV8: Rytn D .3G **83**
CV23: Stret D .3G **83**
Plough Hill Rd. CV10: Ans C, Gall C .6E **20**
Plough La. CV47: Bis I .6A **110**
Ploughmans Holt CV47: Sou .3H **107**
Plover Cl. B49: Alc .3B **112**
CV37: B'ton .2C **114**
Plowman St. CV21: Rugby .5F **75**
PLUMPTON .3C 145
Plymouth Cl. CV2: Cov .7J **51**
Plymouth Pl. CV31: Lea S .1E **102**
Poet's Arbour .5G 137
Poitiers Rd. CV3: Cov .2D **68**
Poland Av. CV37: Lwr Q .5H **125**
POLESWORTH .7D 8 (1D 139)
Polesworth Sports Cen. .2C 10
Polesworth Station (Rail) .6D 8
Polperro Dr. CV5: Alle .2E **56**
Pomeroy Cl. CV4: Tile H .1B **66**
Pond Farm M. CV5: E Grn .2C **56**
Pondthorpe CV3: W'hall .2A **70**
Pontypool Av. CV3: Bin .2B **70**
Pool Bank St. CV11: Nun .7C **22**
Pool Cl. CV22: Bil .1D **86**
CV37: Welf A .3B **124**
GL56: Lit C .6B **134**
Poole Rd. CV6: Cov .1K **57**
Pooley Fields Country Pk. .6D 8
Pooley Fields Heritage Cen. .6C 8
Pooley La. B78: Pole .1C **10**
Pooley Vw. B78: Pole .7D **8**
Poolgate CV35: Up Tys .7C **130**
Poolhead La. B94: Earls, Tan A .1B **90**
Pool Rd. B80: Stud .3D **92**
CV10: Nun .6A **22**
Pool Rd. Bus. Cen. CV10: Nun .6A **22**
Pool Rd. Ind. Est. CV10: Nun .6A **22**
Poolside Gdns. CV3: Finh .3A **68**
Poor's Piece Nature Reserve .4J 21
Pope St. CV22: Rugby .5E **74**
Poplar Av. B37: Chel W .5C **34**
CV12: Bed .3K **41**
Poplar Cl. B49: Ove G .5D **112**
Poplar Dr. B95: Woot W .4J **93**
Poplar Gro. CV8: Rytn D .7D **70**
CV21: Rugby .4G **75**
Poplar Ho. CV12: Bed .3K **41**
Poplar Nth. B95: Woot W .4J **93**
Poplar Rd. CV5: Cov .6K **57**
CV47: Bis I .6C **110**
CV47: Nap .3G **111**
Poplars, The B50: Bidf A .5G **123**
CV10: Nun .1D **30**
CV47: Nap .2G **111**
Poplars Trad. Est. B80: Stud .1C **92**
Poplar Ter. CV37: A'ton .1B **116**
Poplar Way CV10: Harts .4F **21**
Poppy Cl. CV10: Arb .4G **31**
Poppy Ct. CV3: W'hall .2K **69**
Poppy Dr. CV23: Brow .7K **65**
Poppyfield Ct. CV4: Canly .5H **67**
Porchester Cl. CV3: Bin .5C **60**
Porlock Cl. CV3: Cov .3E **68**
Porter Cl. CV4: Tile H .7C **56**
Portia Cl. CV11: Nun .3C **32**
Portia Way CV34: H'cte .5C **102**
Portland Ct. CV32: Lea S .6D **98**
Portland Dr. CV10: Nun .7G **21**
Portland M. CV32: Lea S .7D **98**
Portland Pl. CV21: Rugby .6K **75**
Portland Pl. E. CV32: Lea S .7C **98**
Portland Pl. W. CV32: Lea S .7C **98**
Portland Rd. CV21: Rugby .6K **75**
Portland Row CV32: Lea S .7C **98**
Portland St. CV32: Lea S .7D **98**
Portreath Dr. CV11: Nun .6H **23**
Portree Av. CV3: Bin .5B **60**
Portsea Cl. CV3: Cov .2D **68**
PORTWAY .1B 142
Portway Cl. CV4: Tile H .7C **56**
CV31: Lea S .2H **103**
Portwrinkle Av. CV6: Cov .1G **59**
Poseidon Way CV34: Warw .4D **102**
Postbridge Rd. CV3: Cov .3D **68**
POSTHILL .1D 139
Post Ho. Gdns. CV23: Pail .6K **55**
Postle Cl. CV23: Kils .7H **89**
Post Office La. CV9: With .4G **17**
CV35: Light .2G **119**
CV47: S'ton .6C **106**
Post Office Rd. CV9: Bad E .2F **15**
Post Office Row CV10: Asty .5J **29**
Post Office Yd. CV23: Brin .3D **62**
Potters Cl. CV23: Brin .4C **62**
POTTER'S GREEN .5A 52
Potter's Grn. Rd. CV2: W'grve S .5A **52**
Potters La. B78: Pole .2D **10**
Potters Rd. CV12: Bed .4E **40**
Potterton Works CV34: Warw .7A **98**
Potton Cl. CV3: W'hall .2A **70**
Potts Cl. CV8: Ken .5G **79**
Poultney Rd. CV6: Cov .1A **58**
Pound, The CV33: Har .5J **109**
Pound Cl. B94: Lapw .3G **91**
CV36: Ship S .4H **131**
Pound Fld. B95: Woot W .5G **93**
Pound La. B46: Col .1G **35**
CV32: Lill .4E **98**
Pound Way CV47: Sou .5J **107**
Powell Cl. CV33: Bis T .5C **108**
Powell Rd. CV2: Cov .3G **59**
Powell Way CV11: Nun .7D **22**
Powers Ct. CV32: Lea S .6D **98**
Powis Gro. CV8: Ken .4G **79**
Poyser Rd. CV10: Nun .4J **31**
Prebend, The CV47: N'end .1D **120**
Precinct, The CV1: Cov .4G **135** (5C **58**)
CV34: Warw .6J **97**
Precision Way B49: Alc .2C **112**
Prentice Cl. CV23: Long L .3B **74**
Prescelly Cl. CV10: Nun .1B **30**
PRESTON BAGOT .2C 143
PRESTON CAPES .3C 145
Preston Cl. CV4: Tile H .1D **66**
PRESTON GREEN .3K 93
PRESTON ON STOUR .3D 143
Pretorian Way CV21: Rugby .1G **75**
Priam Cir. CV34: H'cte .5D **102**
Price Cl. E. CV34: Warw .4D **100**
Price Cl. W. CV34: Warw .4D **100**
Price Rd. CV32: Cubb .3J **99**
Pridmore Rd. CV6: Cov .7D **50**
Primary Wlk. CV22: Caw .1A **86**
PRIMETHORPE .2C 141
Primrose Cl. CV23: Brow .7K **65**
Primrose Ct. CV23: Harb M .4B **64**
Primrose Dr. CV12: Bed .4E **40**
Primrose Hill CV34: Warw .6E **96**
Primrose Hill St. CV1: Cov .1K **135** (3D **58**)
Primrose La. B49: Ove G .6C **112**
Prince Harry Rd. B95: Hen A .2H **93**
Prince of Wales Rd. CV5: Cov .4J **57**
Prince Regent Ct. CV31: Lea S .2D **102**
Prince Rupert Cl. CV47: Temp H .3B **120**
Princes Av. CV11: Nun .1H **31**
Princes Cl. CV3: Cov .7H **59**
Princes Dr. CV8: Ken .2F **79**
CV31: Lea S .1B **102**
CV32: Lea S .7B **98**
Princes Dr. Ind. Est. CV8: Ken .1E **78**
Princes Rd. B78: Pole .7E **8**
CV9: Hurl .6K **13**
Princess Dr. CV6: Cov .5H **51**
Princess Rd. CV9: Ath .2D **16**
Princess St. CV6: Cov .7F **51**
Princes St. CV11: Nun .1H **31**
CV21: Rugby .4G **75**
CV32: Lea S .6F **99**
PRINCETHORPE .7G 83 (1B 144)
Prince Thorpe Ct. CV3: Bin .1A **70**
Princethorpe Way CV3: Bin .1K **69**
Prince William Cl. CV6: Cov .1J **57**
Printers Pl. CV37: S Avon .3D **136**
Prior Deram Wlk. CV4: Canly .7F **57**
Priors, The CV12: Bed .3J **41**
Priorsfield Rd. CV6: Cov .3A **58**
CV8: Ken .2B **78**
Priorsfield Rd. Nth. CV6: Cov .3A **58**
Priorsfield Rd. Sth. CV6: Cov .3A **58**
Priors Grange WR11: Salf P .6B **122**
PRIORS HARDWICK .3B 144
Priors Harnall CV1: Cov .3E **58**
PRIORS MARSTON .5G 111 (3B 144)
Priors Mdw. CV47: Sou .5J **107**
Priory Cl. B46: Col .7G **25**
B94: Lapw .1J **91**
Priory Ct. B80: Stud .2D **92**
CV11: Nun .7B **22**
(not continuous)
Priory Cft. CV8: Ken .5D **78**
Priory La. CV35: Pill P .3B **128**
Priory M. CV34: Warw .1G **101**
Priory Pk. Karting Circuit .7A 8
Priory Pl. CV1: Cov .3J **135** (4D **58**)
Priory Rd. B49: Alc .4B **112**
CV8: Ken .4D **78**
CV8: Wols .4K **71**
CV34: Warw .1G **101**
Priory Row CV1: Cov .3J **135** (4D **58**)
Priory Sq. B80: Stud .2D **92**
Priory St. CV1: Cov .4J **135** (4D **58**)
CV10: Nun .1C **30**
CV31: Lea S .2D **102**
Priory Ter. CV31: Lea S .1D **102**
Priory Tuery B49: Alc .5B **112**
Priory Wlk. CV9: Man .5E **16**
CV34: Warw .1H **101**
Private Rd. CV34: Warw .7D **96**
(not continuous)
Privet Rd. CV2: Cov .4H **51**
Proctor Way CV37: S Avon .3A **114**
Proffitt Av. CV6: Cov .5G **51**
Progress Cl. CV3: Bin .1C **70**
Progress Way CV3: Bin .7C **60**
Projects Dr. CV21: Rugby .2J **75**
Prologis Pk. CV7: Ker E .1A **50**
(not continuous)

Prospect Rd. CV31: Lea S . . . 3F 103
Prospect Way CV21: Rugby . . . 3J 75
Prospero Dr. CV34: H'cte . . . 5C 102
Prossers Wlk. B46: Col . . . 5F 25
Providence St. CV5: Cov . . . 7K 57
Ptarmigan Pl. CV11: Nun . . . 1B 32
Puckerings La. CV34: Warw . . . 2G 101
Pudding Bag La. CV23: Thurl . . . 7K 85
Puma Way CV1: Cov . . . 6J 135 (6D 58)
Pumphouse Cl. CV6: Longf . . . 7H 41
Pump La. CV7: Fill . . . 3K 37
Purcell Av. CV11: Nun . . . 5C 32
Purcell Cl. CV32: Lea S . . . 7E 98
Purcell Rd. CV6: Cov . . . 6H 51
Purefoy Rd. CV3: Cov . . . 7D 58
Purley Chase La. CV9: Man . . . 1A 20 & 7B 16
Purley Vw. CV9: Man . . . 5D 16
Purlieu La. CV8: Ken . . . 4B 78
Purser Dr. CV34: Warw . . . 4D 100
Purton Cl. B49: Alc . . . 3C 112
Purton M. CV31: Lea S . . . 2G 103
Putney Wlk. B37: F'bri . . . 2B 34
Pye Ct. CV23: W'hby . . . 2H 105
Pyree Sq. CV34: Warw . . . 4D 100
Pytchley Rd. CV22: Rugby . . . 7J 75
Pyt Pk. CV5: Cov . . . 3G 57

Q

Quadrant, The CV1: Cov . . . 5G 135 (5C 58)
CV11: Nun . . . 1A 32
Quail Cl. CV37: B'ton . . . 3B 114
Quantock Dr. CV10: Nun . . . 1B 30
QUARRY BANK . . . 3A 138
Quarry Cl. CV21: N'bld A . . . 1F 75
CV35: Leek W . . . 1H 97
Quarryfield La CV3: Cov . . . 6K 135 (6E 58)
Quarryfield La. CV1: Cov . . . 6K 135 (6E 58)
Quarry Flds. CV35: Leek W . . . 1H 97
Quarry La. CV9: Man . . . 6D 16
CV11: Nun . . . 3B 32
CV35: Row . . . 5K 91
Quarry Rd. CV8: Ken . . . 3C 78
Quarry St. CV32: Lea S . . . 7A 98
Quarrywood Gro. CV2: Cov . . . 3G 59
Quarry Yd. CV10: Nun . . . 7H 21
Queen Elizabeth Rd. CV10: Nun . . . 5H 21
Queen Isabel's Av. CV3: Cov . . . 7D 58
Queen Margaret's Rd. CV4: Canly . . . 7F 57
Queen Mary's Rd. CV6: Cov . . . 6D 50
CV12: Bed . . . 7J 31
Queen Philippa St. CV3: Cov . . . 2D 68
Queens Arc. CV11: Nun . . . 7D 22
Queens Av. CV36: Ship S . . . 4G 131
Queens Cl. CV8: Ken . . . 6D 78
CV33: Har . . . 6J 109
CV36: Ship S . . . 5G 131
Queens Ct. CV11: Nun . . . 7B 22
CV37: S Avon . . . 6E 114
Queen's Dr. CV35: Row . . . 5J 91
Queensferry Cl. CV22: Bil . . . 1C 86
Queensland Av. CV5: Cov . . . 5K 57
Queen's Pk. CV31: Lea S . . . 2C 102
Queens Rd. CV1: Cov . . . 5F 135 (5B 58)
CV8: Ken . . . 6D 78
CV9: Ath . . . 3D 16
CV11: Nun . . . 7B 22
CV23: Bret . . . 1C 72
CV36: Tred . . . 6J 127
Queens Sq. CV34: Warw . . . 2F 101
Queens St. CV36: Half . . . 2J 127
Queen St. CV1: Cov . . . 1K 135 (3D 58)
CV12: Bed . . . 3J 41
CV21: Rugby . . . 5G 75
CV32: Cubb . . . 2H 99
CV32: Lea S . . . 6E 98
Queens Way B78: Dord . . . 4C 10
Queensway B50: Bidf A . . . 5F 123
CV9: Hurl . . . 7K 13
CV10: Nun . . . 5E 22
CV31: Lea S . . . 2C 102
Queensway Trad. Est. CV34: Warw . . . 2C 102
Queenswood Ct. CV7: Ker E . . . 2H 49
Queen Victoria Rd. CV1: Cov . . . 5G 135 (5B 58)
(Ringway Queens)
CV1: Cov . . . 3F 135 (4B 58)
(Spon St.)
Queen Victoria St. CV21: Rugby . . . 5J 75
QUENIBOROUGH . . . 1D 141
Quilletts Cl. CV6: Cov . . . 5G 51
Quiney's Leys CV37: Welf A . . . 2A 124
Quiney's Rd. CV37: Shot . . . 5C 114
Quinn Cl. CV3: Cov . . . 1G 69
Quinneys Ct. B50: Bidf A . . . 6H 123
Quinneys La. B50: Bidf A . . . 6H 123
B98: Redd . . . 1A 92
QUINTON . . . 3A 138
Quinton Cl. CV35: Hatt . . . 4A 96
Quinton Lodge CV3: Cov . . . 1D 68
Quinton Pde. CV3: Cov . . . 1D 68
Quinton Pk. CV3: Cov . . . 1D 68
Quinton Rd. CV1: Cov . . . 7J 135 (6D 58)
CV3: Cov . . . 7J 135 (7D 58)
Quorn Way CV3: Bin . . . 7A 60

R

Rabbit La. CV12: Bed . . . 1C 40
Racemeadow Rd. CV9: Ath . . . 2D 16
Radbourne Cl. CV47: Sou . . . 6J 107
Radbourne La. CV47: Ladb . . . 3E 110
Radbrook Way CV31: Lea S . . . 2H 103
Radcliffe Gdns. CV31: Lea S . . . 2E 102
Radcliffe Ho. CV4: Canly . . . 4F 67
Radcliffe Rd. CV5: Cov . . . 7K 57
RADFORD
Coventry . . . 2B 58 (3A 140)
Worcester . . . 3B 142
Radford Circ. CV6: Cov . . . 3B 58
Radford Cl. CV9: Ath . . . 1D 16
Radford Hall CV31: Rad S . . . 2J 103
Radford Ho. CV6: Cov . . . 7A 50
Radford Rd. CV1: Cov . . . 1G 135 (1A 58)
CV6: Cov . . . 7A 50
CV31: Lea S . . . 1E 102
RADFORD SEMELE . . . 3J 103 (2A 144)
Radley Dr. CV10: Nun . . . 3G 31
Radlow Cres. B37: Mars G . . . 5B 34
Radnor Dr. CV10: Nun . . . 2D 30
Radnor Wlk. CV2: W'grve S . . . 6B 52
RADWAY . . . 5B 128 (1C 147)
Raglan Cl. CV11: Nun . . . 1K 31
Raglan Ct. CV1: Cov . . . 4E 58
Raglan Gro. CV8: Ken . . . 4F 79
Raglan St. CV1: Cov . . . 3K 135 (4E 58)
Raglan Way B37: Chel W . . . 3D 34
Ragley Hall . . . 3B 142
Ragley Mill La. B49: Alc . . . 3B 112
Ragley Way CV11: Nun . . . 2B 32
Railport App. NN6: Crick . . . 3K 89
Railway Cl. B80: Stud . . . 3C 92
Railway Cres. CV36: Ship S . . . 3H 131
Railway M. B49: Alc . . . 4B 112
Railway St. CV23: Long L . . . 4A 74
Railway Ter. CV12: Bed . . . 3J 41
CV21: Rugby . . . 5H 75
Rainbow Flds. CV36: Ship S . . . 4H 131
RAINSBROOK . . . 3J 87
Rainsbrook Av. CV22: Hillm . . . 1A 88
Rainsbrook Cl. CV47: Sou . . . 5K 107
Rainsbrook Dr. CV11: Nun . . . 3B 32
Rainsford Cl. CV37: Cliff C . . . 5C 124
Raison Av. CV11: Nun . . . 3G 23
Raleigh Rd. CV2: Cov . . . 4H 59
Ralph Cres. B78: K'bry . . . 5D 12
Ralph Rd. CV6: Cov . . . 2K 57
Rambures Cl. CV34: H'cte . . . 5D 102
Ramp Rd. B26: Birm A . . . 1C 44
Ramsay Cres. CV5: Alle . . . 7F 49
Ramsay Grn. CV35: Welle . . . 2H 117
RAMSDEN . . . 3A 142
Ramsden Av. CV10: Nun . . . 4H 21
Ramsden Rd. CV9: Man . . . 4F 17
Ramsey Rd. CV31: Lea S . . . 1F 103
Ramshill La. B95: Ullen . . . 4C 90
Ranby Rd. CV2: Cov . . . 3F 59
Randall Rd. CV8: Ken . . . 6D 78
Randle Rd. CV10: Nun . . . 7J 21
Randle St. CV6: Cov . . . 2A 58
Randolph Cl. CV31: Lea S . . . 2G 103
Ranelagh St. CV31: Lea S . . . 2E 102
Ranelagh Ter. CV31: Lea S . . . 2D 102
Range Mdw. Cl. CV32: Lea S . . . 4A 98
Rangemoor CV3: W'hall . . . 2K 69
Range Way B78: K'bry . . . 6E 12
Rankine Cl. CV21: N'bld A . . . 1D 74
Rannoch Dr. CV10: Nun . . . 6H 21
Rannock Cl. CV3: Bin . . . 5C 60
Ransome Rd. CV7: New A . . . 4E 28
Ransom Rd. CV6: Cov . . . 6E 50
Ranulf Cft. CV3: Cov . . . 1C 68
Ranulf St. CV3: Cov . . . 1C 68
Raphael Cl. CV5: Cov . . . 4G 57
RASHWOOD . . . 2A 142
RATBY . . . 1C 141
Ratcliffe Ct. CV10: Nun . . . 7H 21
RATCLIFFE CULEY . . . 2A 140
Ratcliffe Rd. CV9: Ath . . . 3D 16
Ratcliffe St. CV9: Ath . . . 3C 16
Rathbone Cl. CV7: Ker E . . . 7K 39
CV21: Hillm . . . 1C 88
Rathlin Cft. B36: Cas B . . . 6B 24
RATLEY . . . 7D 128 (1C 147)
Ratliffe Rd. CV22: Rugby . . . 2F 87
Raveloe Dr. CV11: Nun . . . 3K 31
Raven Cragg Rd. CV5: Cov . . . 7J 57
Ravenglass CV21: Brow . . . 1K 75
Ravensdale Av. CV32: Lea S . . . 5A 98
Ravensdale Rd. CV2: Cov . . . 4J 59
RAVENSTHORPE . . . 1D 145
Ravensthorpe Cl. CV3: Bin . . . 7A 60
Ravenswood Hill B46: Col . . . 5F 25
Raven Way CV11: Nun . . . 2B 32
Rawlinson Rd. CV32: Lill . . . 5F 99
RAWNSLEY . . . 1B 138
Rawnsley Dr. CV8: Ken . . . 3F 79
Rawn Vw. CV9: Man . . . 5E 16
Rayford Cvn. Pk. CV37: S Avon . . . 3H 115
Raymond Cl. CV6: Longf . . . 1F 51
Raynor Cres. CV12: Bed . . . 4D 40
Raynsford Wlk. CV34: Warw . . . 6F 97
Raywoods, The CV10: Nun . . . 1F 31
Reading Av. CV11: Nun . . . 3G 23
Reading Cl. CV2: Ald G . . . 3H 51
Reading Ct. CV37: S Avon . . . 3J 115
Readings, The CV47: Fen C . . . 2G 121
Read St. CV1: Cov . . . 4E 58
Reardon Ct. CV34: Warw . . . 6G 97
Recreation Rd. CV6: Cov . . . 3G 51
Rectory Cl. CV5: Alle . . . 1G 57
CV7: Exh . . . 4G 41
CV23: Barby . . . 7E 88
CV47: S'ton . . . 6C 106
OX17: Warm . . . 2J 129
Rectory Dr. CV7: Exh . . . 4G 41
Rectory La. CV5: Alle . . . 1G 57
CV23: Barby . . . 7E 88
CV36: Whatc . . . 3A 130
OX15: Lwr Bra . . . 3J 133
Rectory Rd. CV7: Old A . . . 3C 28
Redcap Cft. CV6: Cov . . . 2D 50
Redcar Cl. CV32: Lill . . . 3F 99
Redcar Rd. CV1: Cov . . . 2E 58
Red Deeps CV11: Nun . . . 4K 31
REDDITCH . . . 2B 142
Redditch Rd. B80: Stud . . . 2C 92
B95: Oldb, Ullen . . . 7A 90
Redditch Wlk. CV2: W'grve S . . . 7C 52
Redesdale Av. CV6: Cov . . . 3K 57
Redfern Av. CV8: Ken . . . 3E 78
Redgrave Cl. CV2: W'grve S . . . 6D 52
RED HILL
Alcester . . . 3C 143
Coventry . . . 4E 38
Red Hill CV35: Welle . . . 6H 117
Redhill Cl. CV35: Welle . . . 5G 117
Red Hill Furrows CV31: Lea S . . . 3G 103
Red Hill Gro. B80: Stud . . . 1D 92
Redland Cl. CV2: Ald G . . . 4A 52
Redland La. CV8: Rytn D . . . 6C 70
Redland Rd. CV31: Lea S . . . 3F 103
Redlands Cres. CV37: S Avon . . . 4B 114
Redlands Row GL56: Lit C . . . 6C 134
Red La. CV6: Cov . . . 2E 58
CV8: Burt G . . . 4A 66
CV10: Asty . . . 5J 29
Red La. Ind. Est. CV6: Cov . . . 1F 59
Red Lion Cl. CV47: Sou . . . 4H 107
Red Lion Ct. CV35: Kine . . . 5C 120
Red Lodge Dr. CV22: Bil . . . 1E 86
Red Rd. CV35: Lit K . . . 7C 120
Redruth Cl. CV6: Cov . . . 6G 51
CV11: Nun . . . 7H 23
Redthorne Gro. CV8: Ken . . . 1F 79
Redwing Cl. CV37: B'ton . . . 2B 114
Red Wing Wlk. B36: Cas B . . . 4A 24
Redwood Cft. CV10: Nun . . . 2G 31
Redwood Dr. B78: K'bry . . . 4E 12
Redwood Ho. B37: K'hrst . . . 7A 24
Redwood Pk. CV36: Ship S . . . 5H 131
Reeds Pk. CV33: Ufton . . . 2F 109
Rees Dr. CV3: Finh . . . 4C 68
Reeve Dr. CV8: Ken . . . 5E 78
REEVES GREEN . . . 7A 56
Regal Ct. CV9: Ath . . . 3D 16
Regal Rd. CV37: S Avon . . . 3E 114
Regency Arc. CV32: Lea S . . . 7D 98
Regency Cl. CV10: Nun . . . 5E 22
Regency Ct. CV5: Cov . . . 7K 57
Regency Dr. B49: K Cou . . . 2A 112
CV3: Finh . . . 3K 67
CV8: Ken . . . 6D 78
Regency Ho. CV32: Lea S . . . 7E 98
Regency M. CV32: Lea S . . . 7E 98
Regent Gro. CV32: Lea S . . . 7D 98
Regent Pl. CV21: Rugby . . . 4G 75
CV31: Lea S . . . 1E 102
Regent St. CV1: Cov . . . 5F 135 (6B 58)
CV11: Nun . . . 6D 22
CV12: Bed . . . 1J 41
CV21: Rugby . . . 5G 75
CV32: Lea S . . . 7C 98
Reg Hadden Ct. CV10: Nun . . . 5E 22
Regiment Ct. CV6: Cov . . . 5A 50
Regina Cres. CV2: W'grve S . . . 7C 52
Regis Wlk. CV2: W'grve S . . . 7B 52
Reigner Pl. CV34: H'cte . . . 6D 102
Relay Dr. B77: Wiln . . . 3A 10
Relton M. CV6: Cov . . . 1F 59
Rembrandt Cl. CV5: Cov . . . 4G 57
Remburn Gdns. CV34: Warw . . . 7H 97
Remembrance Rd. CV3: W'hall . . . 2K 69
Renfrew Wlk. CV4: Tile H . . . 7E 56
Renison Rd. CV12: Bed . . . 4E 40
Renolds Cl. CV4: Cov . . . 5G 57
Renown Av. CV5: Cov . . . 6H 57
Renshaw Ind. Est. B80: Stud . . . 3A 92
Repington Av. CV9: Ath . . . 1C 16
Repton Dr. CV6: Cov . . . 4H 51
Reservoir Dr. B46: Shu . . . 2B 26
Reservoir Rd. CV21: Rugby . . . 2J 75
Retreat, The B95: Woot W . . . 5H 93
Reuben Av. CV10: Nun . . . 5G 21
Rex Cl. CV4: Tile H . . . 7B 56
Reynolds Cl. CV21: Hillm . . . 1D 88
Reynolds Rd. CV12: Bed . . . 1G 41
Rhyl Rd. CV11: Bram . . . 6H 33
Ribble Cl. CV12: Bulk . . . 3D 42
Ribble Rd. CV3: Cov . . . 5F 59
Ribble Wlk. B36: Cas B . . . 4A 24
Ribbonbrook CV11: Nun . . . 1K 31
Ribbonfields CV11: Nun . . . 1K 31
Richard Joy Cl. CV6: Cov . . . 4C 50
Richards Cl. CV8: Ken . . . 4D 78
Richards Gro. CV31: Lea S . . . 3E 102
Richardson Cl. CV34: Warw . . . 6H 97
Richardson Way CV2: W'grve S . . . 6D 52
Rich Cl. CV34: Warw . . . 1J 101
Richmond Ho. B37: Chel W . . . 4C 34
Richmond Rd. CV9: Ath . . . 4C 16
CV11: Nun . . . 1G 31
CV21: Rugby . . . 6J 75
Richmond St. CV2: Cov . . . 4G 59
Richmond Way B37: Chel W . . . 2C 34
Rickyard, The CV23: Eas . . . 3J 63
Rickyard Cl. B78: Pole . . . 7D 8
Ricoh Arena . . . 2E 50

Riddell Cl. B49: Alc 4D **112**
Ridding Gdns. B78: Pole 2D **10**
Riddings, The CV5: Cov 1H **67**
CV9: Gren 1F **15**
Riddings La. CV9: Gren 7F **11**
Rideswell Gro. CV31: W'nsh 7E **102**
Ridge Ct. CV5: Alle 1E **56**
Ridge Dr. CV21: Rugby 4K **75**
RIDGE LANE 1A **20** (2D **139**)
Ridge La. CV10: Ridge L 1A **20**
Ridgeley Cl. CV34: Warw 5G **97**
Ridgethorpe CV3: W'hall 3A **70**
Ridgeway, The CV23: Barby, Kils 7J **89**
CV34: Warw 6J **97**
CV36: Gt Wol 7A **132**
Ridgeway Av. CV3: Cov 2C **68**
Ridgeway Cl. B80: Stud 5D **92**
Ridgewood Cl. CV32: Lea S 6A **98**
Ridgley Rd. CV4: Tile H 6C **56**
Ridgway, The CV37: Dray, S Avon, Wilm 7H **113** & 3A **114**
Ridsdale Cl. WR11: Salf P 6B **122**
Rigby Cl. CV34: H'cte 4B **102**
Rigdale Cl. CV2: Cov 5A **60**
Riley Cl. CV8: Ken 5G **79**
Riley Ct. CV21: Rugby 5J **75**
Riley Dr. B36: Cas B 3A **24**
Riley Ho. CV1: Cov 5H **135** (5C **58**)
Riley Sq. CV2: Cov 5H **51**
Rimell Cl. CV37: N'bld S 1G **127**
Ringway Hillcross CV1: Cov 3F **135** (4B **58**)
Ringway Queens CV1: Cov 5F **135** (5B **58**)
Ringway Rudge CV1: Cov 4F **135** (5B **58**)
Ringway St Johns CV1: Cov 5J **135** (5D **58**)
Ringway St Nicholas CV1: Cov 2G **135** (4C **58**)
Ringway St Patrick's CV1: Cov 6H **135** (6C **58**)
Ringway Swanswell CV1: Cov 2J **135** (4D **58**)
Ringway Whitefriars CV1: Cov 3K **135** (5D **58**)
Ringwood Highway CV2: W'grve S 4A **52**
Rinill Gro. CV31: Lea S 2H **103**
Riplingham CV32: Lea S 5D **98**
Ripon Cl. CV5: Alle 6E **48**
Risborough Cl. CV5: Cov 4G **57**
Risdale Cl. CV32: Lea S 5B **98**
Rise, The B37: Mars G 6A **34**
Rising La. B93: Bad C 2G **91**
B94: Lapw 2G **91**
River Cl. CV12: Bed 4F **41**
CV32: Lea S 7A **98**
River Ct. CV1: Cov 4B **58**
River Dr. CV9: Ath 1C **16**
Riverford Cft. CV4: Canly 4H **67**
Riverhead Ct. *B50: Bidf A* *6G 123*
(off Salford Rd.)
Rivermead CV11: Nun 7B **22**
Rivermead Dr. CV37: Tidd 3K **115**
Riversdale CV32: Lea S 7C **98**
Riversdale Rd. CV9: Ath 3E **16**
Riverside B49: Alc 4D **112**
B80: Stud 3D **92**
CV9: With 4G **17**
CV32: Lea S 7C **98**
CV37: S Avon 3H **115**
Riverside Cl. CV3: Cov 1F **69**
Riverside Ct. *B46: Col* *5G 25*
(off Prossers Wlk.)
Riverside Dr. B95: Woot W 5J **93**
Riverside Gdns. B95: Hen A 2H **93**
Riverside Wlk. CV31: Lea S 1A **102**
CV34: Warw 2H **101**
Riverslea Rd. CV3: Cov 6J **59**
Riversleigh Rd. CV32: Lea S 6A **98**
Riversley Rd. CV11: Nun 1J **31**
River Wlk. CV2: Cov 4J **51**
River Way CV36: Ship S 3J **131**
Rivington Glebe GL56: Lit C 6C **134**
Roach Cl. B37: Chel W 2C **34**
ROADE 3D **145**
Roadway Cl. CV12: Bed 3H **41**
ROAD WEEDON 3D **145**
Roanne Ringway CV11: Nun 7C **22**
Robbins Ct. CV22: Hillm 1B **88**
Robbins Way CV32: Lill 5F **99**
Robert Cl. CV3: W'hall 4J **69**
Robert Cramb Av. CV4: Tile H 7D **56**
Robert Hill Cl. CV21: Hillm 7C **76**
Robert Rd. CV7: Exh 5F **41**
Roberts Cl. CV23: Stret D 3H **83**
Robertson Cl. CV23: Clift D 3C **76**
Robey's La. B78: A'cte, B'moor 7A **8**
Robin Cl. B36: Cas B 4A **24**
Robin Hood Rd. CV3: W'hall 2J **69**
Robinia Cl. CV32: Lill 6F **99**
Robins Gro. CV34: Warw 4D **100**
Robinson Rd. CV12: Bed 5D **40**
ROBINSON'S END 1A **30**
Robins Way CV10: Nun 1A **30**
Robotham Cl. CV21: N'bld A 2F **75**
Rocheberie Way CV22: Rugby 1F **87**
Rochester Cl. CV11: Nun 1H **31**
Rochester Rd. CV5: Cov 7J **57**
Rochford Ct. CV31: Lea S 1C **102**
Rock Cl. CV6: Cov 5H **51**
CV10: Gall C 7E **20**
Rocken End CV6: Cov 6D **50**
Rock Farm La. CV8: Bag 1F **81**
Rockingham Dr. CV11: Nun 5B **32**
Rock La. CV7: Cor 6G **39**
Rock Mill La. CV32: Lea S 6A **98**
Rocky La. CV8: Ken 6G **79**
(not continuous)
Rodhouse Cl. CV4: Tile H 6B **56**
Rodney Cl. CV22: Bil 7C **74**
Rodway Dr. CV5: E Grn 3B **56**
Rodyard Way CV1: Cov 7K **135** (6D **58**)
Roebuck Pk. B49: Alc 3A **112**
Roe Cl. CV34: Warw 7H **97**
Roe Ho. La. CV9: App M, Aus 4J **7**
Rofs Cft. B78: Pole 7D **8**
Rogers La. CV37: Ett 3B **126**
Rogers Way CV34: Warw 4D **100**
Rokeby Ct. CV22: Rugby 2F **87**
Rokeby St. CV21: Rugby 5K **75**
Roland Av. CV6: Cov 3B **50**
Roland Mt. CV6: Cov 3C **50**
Rollason Cl. CV6: Cov 6C **50**
Rollason Rd. CV6: Cov 6B **50**
Rollasons Yd. CV6: Cov 3G **51**
ROLLESTON 1D **141**
Rollright Stones- King Stone Monolith 2B **146**
Romani Cl. CV34: Warw 1F **101**
Roman Pk. B46: Col 3F **25**
Roman Rd. CV2: Cov 4H **59**
Roman Way B46: Col 2E **24**
B49: Alc 5B **112**
B78: Dord 4D **10**
CV3: Finh 5D **68**
CV21: Rugby 1G **75**
CV36: Half 3J **127**
CV47: Sou 5J **107**
Romeo Arbour CV34: H'cte 5C **102**
Romford Rd. CV6: Cov 4B **50**
Romney Pl. CV22: Rugby 2F **87**
Romsey Av. CV10: Nun 3E **22**
ROMSLEY 1A **142**
Romsley Rd. CV6: Cov 1C **58**
Ro-Oak Rd. CV6: Cov 2K **57**
Rookery, The *B49: Alc* *5C 112*
(off Stratford Rd.)
CV10: Gall C 6D **20**
CV37: A'ton 1B **116**
Rookery La. CV6: Cov 2B **50**
CV37: Ett 2B **126**
CV37: N'bld S 1G **127**
Rookes Ct. CV37: S Avon 1E **136**
Rooks Nest CV23: Brin 4C **62**
Roosevelt Dr. CV4: Tile H 5C **56**
Rootes Halls CV4: Canly 4G **67**
Roper Cl. CV21: Hillm 1C **88**
Ropewalk B49: Alc 4B **112**
Rosaville Cres. CV5: Alle 1E **56**
Rose Av. B95: Hen A 1H **93**
CV6: Cov 2K **57**
Roseberry Av. CV2: Cov 5H **51**
Rose Cott. Flats CV5: E Grn 2B **56**
Rose Cft. CV8: Ken 3C **78**
Rosefield Pl. CV32: Lea S 7D **98**
Rosefield St. CV32: Lea S 7D **98**
Rosefield Wlk. *CV32: Lea S* *7D 98*
(off Rosefield St.)
Rosegreen Cl. CV3: Cov 2E **68**
Rosehill CV9: Ath 4E **16**
Rosehip Dr. CV2: Cov 1H **59**
Roseland Rd. CV8: Ken 6D **78**
Roselands Av. CV2: Cov 6K **51**
Rose La. CV11: Nun 1J **31**
CV47: Nap 3H **111**
Rosemary Cl. CV4: Tile H 4C **56**
Rosemary Hill CV8: Ken 4D **78**
Rosemary M. CV8: Ken 4D **78**
Rosemary Way CV10: Nun 4G **31**
Rosemount Cl. CV2: Cov 7A **52**
Rosemullion Cl. CV7: Exh 5H **41**
Rose Rd. B46: Col 4F **25**
Rosewood CV11: Nun 3B **32**
Rosewood Av. CV22: Rugby 1G **87**
Rosewood Cres. CV32: Lill 5F **99**
Ross Cl. CV5: E Grn 2E **56**
Ross Ct. CV21: Rugby 5K **75**
Rossendale Way CV10: Nun 2D **30**
Rosslyn Av. CV6: Cov 1J **57**
Ross Way CV11: Nun 5D **32**
Rotherby Gro. B37: Mars G 6B **34**
Rotherfield Cl. CV31: Lea S 1F **103**
Rotherham Cl. CV22: Caw 1K **85**
Rotherham Rd. CV6: Cov 4B **50**
Rotherhams Hill CV9: Bad E 3F **15**
ROTHERSTHORPE 3D **145**
Rother St. CV37: S Avon 6D **136** (5E **114**)
(not continuous)
Rothesay Av. CV4: Tile H 5F **57**
Rothesay Cl. CV10: Nun 2G **31**
ROTHLEY 1C **141**
Rothley Dr. CV21: Brow 1A **76**
Rothwell Rd. CV34: Warw 6E **96**
ROTTEN ROW 1C **143**
Roughknowles Rd. CV4: W'wd H 2B **66**
ROUGHLEY 2C **139**
Rouncil La. CV8: Ken 7C **78**
Round Av. CV23: Long L 3A **74**
Round Ho. Rd. CV3: Cov 7G **59**
Rounds Gdns. CV21: Rugby 5F **75**
Rounds Hill CV8: Ken 7C **78**
Round St. CV21: Rugby 5F **75**
ROUSHAM 3D **147**
ROUS LENCH 3B **142**
Rover Dr. B36: Cas B 3A **24**
Rover Rd. CV1: Cov 4G **135** (5C **58**)
Row, The CV7: Ansty 3F **53**
CV8: Bag 6F **69**
Rowan Cen., The CV9: Ath 3D **16**
Rowan Cl. B78: K'bry 5E **12**
CV3: Bin W 1F **71**
CV37: S Avon 2E **114**
Rowan Dr. CV22: Bil 6B **74**
CV34: Warw 7H **97**
Rowan Gdns. B78: Pole 2E **10**
Rowan Gro. CV2: W'grve S 4A **52**
Rowan Ho. CV4: W'wd H 2D **66**
Rowan Rd. CV10: Nun 5H **21**
Rowans, The CV12: Bed 3E **40**
CV23: Gran 6H **105**
Rowan Way B37: Chel W 4C **34**
CV10: Harts 3E **20**
Rowborough Cl. CV35: Hatt 5A **96**
Rowcroft Rd. CV2: W'grve S 1C **60**
Rowe Cl. CV21: Hillm 1E **88**
ROWINGTON 7J **91** (2D **143**)
Rowington Cl. CV6: Cov 2H **57**
ROWINGTON GREEN 5J **91**
Rowington Grn. CV35: Row 5H **91**
Rowland Av. B78: Pole 6D **8**
B80: Stud 4D **92**
Rowland Ct. CV7: Old A 3C **28**
Rowland St. CV21: Rugby 5F **75**
Rowlands Way CV9: Ath 1B **16**
CV36: Whatc 3B **130**
Rowley Cres. CV37: S Avon 3F **115**
Rowley Dr. CV3: W'hall 4H **69**
Rowley La. CV3: W'hall 5K **69**
ROWLEY REGIS 3A **138**
Rowley Rd. CV3: W'hall 5F **69**
CV8: Bag 5F **69**
CV31: W'nsh 5E **102**
ROWLEYS GREEN 2E **50**
Rowley's Grn. CV6: Longf 2E **50**
Rowleys Grn. Ind. Est. CV6: Longf 2E **50**
Rowley's Grn. La. CV6: Longf 2E **50**
ROWNEY GREEN 1B **142**
Rowse Cl. CV21: Brow 1J **75**
Roxburgh Cft. CV32: Cubb 2F **99**
Roxburgh Rd. CV11: Nun 3A **32**
Royal Ct. CV21: Rugby 5F **75**
Royal Cres. CV3: W'hall 3J **69**
ROYAL LEAMINGTON SPA 1D **102** (2A **144**)
Royal Mdw. Dr. CV9: Ath 1D **16**
Royal Oak La. CV7: Ash G 6C **40**
CV12: Bed 6C **40**
Royal Oak Yd. CV12: Bed 1H **41**
Royal Priors Shop. Cen. CV32: Lea S 7D **98**
Royal Pump Rooms, The *7D 98*
(off Parade)
Royal Shakespeare Theatre 5H **137** (5F **115**)
Royal Spa Cen., The 7E **98**
Royston Cl. CV3: Bin 4C **60**
Rubens Cl. CV5: Cov 4G **57**
RUBERY 1A **142**
Rudgard Rd. CV6: Longf 2G **51**
Rudge Rd. CV1: Cov 4F **135** (5B **58**)
Rufford Cl. B49: Alc 3C **112**
RUGBY 5G **75** (1C **145**)
Rugby La. CV23: Stret D 3J **83**
Rugby Library, Mus. & Art Gallery *5G 75*
(off Lit. Elborow St.)
Rugby Rd. CV3: Bin W 7D **60**
CV7: Withy 2C **54**
CV8: Bran 7D **60**
CV8: Wols 4A **72**
CV12: Bulk 3F **43**
CV22: Dunc 6D **86**
CV23: Barby 7E **88**
CV23: Brin 4D **62**
CV23: Chu L 3G **73**
CV23: Clift D 3B **76**
CV23: Clift D, Lilb 2G **77**
CV23: Eas 4K **63**
CV23: Harb M 4B **64**
CV23: Kils 3F **89**
CV23: Long L 4B **74**
CV23: Pail 7K **55**
CV23: Prin 7G **83**
(Burnthurst La.)
CV23: Prin 7C **82**
(Southam Rd.)
CV23: S Ash 4F **55**
CV32: Cubb, W Weth 2G **99**
CV32: Lea S 7A **98**
CV33: Wapp, W Weth 2G **99**
CV47: Sou, S'ton 3H **107**
Rugby RUFC 6E **74**
Rugby School Mus. 5G **75**
Rugby School Sports Cen. 6H **75**
Rugby Station (Rail) 4J **75**
Rugby Western Relief Rd. CV22: Long L 6B **74**
Rumer Cl. CV37: Long M 1G **125**
Runcorn Cl. B37: F'bri 1C **34**
Runcorn Wlk. CV2: W'grve S 7C **52**
Runnymede Gdns. CV10: Nun 1F **31**
Rupert Brooke Rd. CV22: Rugby 2E **86**
Rupert Brooke Statue *5G 75*
(off Regent St.)
Rupert Kettle Dr. CV47: Bis I 5C **110**
Rupert Rd. CV6: Cov 6B **50**
RUSHALL 1B **138**
Rushall Path CV4: Canly 1F **67**
RUSHBROOK 2A **90**
Rushbrook La. B94: Tan A 1A **90**
Rushbrook Rd. CV37: S Avon 7H **115**
Rush La. B50: Bidf A 5E **122**
B77: Dost 1E **12**
Rushmoor Dr. CV5: Cov 4K **57**
Rushmore Pl. CV31: Lea S 1F **103**
Rushmore St. CV31: Lea S 1F **103**
RUSHOCK 1A **142**
Rushock Cl. B98: Redd 1B **92**
Rusina Ct. CV31: Lea S 2D **102**
Ruskin Cl. CV6: Cov 1H **57**
CV10: Gall C 6F **21**
CV22: Rugby 3F **87**
Russell Av. CV22: Dunc 5D **86**

Russell Cl. CV47: Long I .2C 106
Russell St. CV1: Cov .1J 135 (3D 58)
CV32: Lea S .6D 98
Russell St. Nth. CV1: Cov .1J 135 (3D 58)
Russell Ter. CV31: Lea S .1E 102
Russelsheim Way CV22: Rugby .6G 75
Rutherford Glen CV11: Nun .3B 32
Rutherglen Av. CV3: Cov .2G 69
Rutland Av. CV10: Nun .7A 22
Rutland Cl. CV21: Hillm .6A 76
Rutland Cft. CV3: Bin .7B 60
Rydal Av. CV11: Nun .5H 23
Rydal Cl. CV5: Alle .6F 49
CV21: Brow .2K 75
Ryde Av. CV10: Nun .5E 22
Ryder Cl. CV35: H Mag .2B 100
Ryder Row CV7: New A .4E 28
Ryders Hill Cres. CV10: Nun .4H 21
Rye Cl. CV37: S Avon .2D 114
Ryeclose Cft. B37: Chel W .2D 34
Ryefield La. B76: Wis .2B 18
Rye Flds CV33: Bis T .5B 108
Rye Hill CV5: Alle .1E 56
Rye Hill Office Pk. CV5: Alle .7E 48
Ryelands, The CV23: Law H .2G 85
Rye Piece CV12: Bed .3J 41
Rye Piece Ringway CV12: Bed .2H 41
Ryhope Cl. CV12: Bed .4C 40
Ryland Cl. CV31: Lea S .2G 103
Ryland Rd. CV35: Barf .1C 108
Ryland St. CV37: S Avon .6E 114
Ryley St. CV1: Cov .3F 135 (4C 58)
Rylston Av. CV6: Cov .5A 50
Rylstone Way CV34: Warw .6G 97
Ryon Hill CV37: Ing .1K 115
RYTON .3F 43 (3A 140)
Ryton Cl. CV4: Canly .7F 57
RYTON-ON-DUNSMORE .7D 70 (1A 144)
Ryton Organic Gardens .7F 71
Ryton Rd. CV8: Bubb .5H 81

S

Sabin Cl. CV47: Long I .2B 106
Sackville Cl. CV37: S Avon .3B 114
Sackville Ho. *CV1: Cov* .3E 58
(off Adelaide St.)
SADDINGTON .2D 141
Saddington Rd. CV3: Bin .7A 60
Saddledon St. CV35: Mid T .6D 130
Sadler Cl. CV37: S Avon .1E 114
Sadler Gdns. CV12: Bed .3J 41
Sadler Rd. CV6: Cov .5A 50
Sadlers Av. CV36: Ship S .4G 131
Sadlers Cl. CV36: Ship S .4G 131
Sadlers Mdw. B46: Over W .2J 27
Saffron Cl. CV23: Brow .7K 65
Saffron Mdw. CV37: S Avon .6E 114
Saffron Wlk. CV37: S Avon .6E 114
St Agatha's Rd. CV2: Cov .4G 59
St Agnes Cl. B80: Stud .3B 92
St Agnes Way CV11: Nun .7F 23
St Albans Cl. CV32: Lea S .5A 98
St Andrews Ct. CV21: Rugby .4G 75
St Andrews Cres. CV22: Rugby .1G 87
CV37: S Avon .5A 136 (5D 114)
St Andrews Dr. CV11: Nun .3D 32
St Andrew's Rd. CV5: Cov .7K 57
CV32: Lill .2F 99
St Anne's Rd. CV22: Bil .7E 74
St Ann's Cl. CV31: Lea S .1G 103
St Ann's Rd. CV2: Cov .4G 59
St Asaphs Av. B80: Stud .3C 92
St Augustine's Wlk. CV6: Cov .7A 50
St Austell Cl. CV11: Nun .6H 23
St Austell Rd. CV2: Cov .4A 60
St Bartholomews Cl. CV3: Bin .5C 60
St Benedicts Cl. CV9: Ath .3C 16
St Bernards Wlk. CV3: W'hall .2K 69
St Blaise Av. B46: Wat O .2B 24
St Brides Cl. CV31: Lea S .2G 103
SAINTBURY .2A 146
St Buryan Cl. CV11: Nun .6H 23
Saintbury Cl. CV37: S Avon .6J 115
St Catherine's Cl. CV3: Cov .7H 59
St Catherine's Cres. CV31: W'nsh .5D 102
St Catherines Lodge CV6: Cov .3A 58
St Chads M. B94: Lapw .3J 91
St Chads Rd. B80: Stud .3B 92
CV33: Bis T .5B 108
St Christian's Cft. CV3: Cov. .7K 135 (7D 58)
St Christian's Rd. CV3: Cov .7E 58
St Christopher's Cl. CV34: Warw .7F 97
St Clements Ct. CV2: Cov .6K 51
St Columbas Cl. CV1: Cov .1G 135 (3C 58)
St Davids Cl. CV31: Lea S .1G 103
St Davids Orchard CV3: Bin .1B 70
St Davids Wlk. CV37: N'bld S .1G 127
St Davids Way CV10: Griff .6G 31
St Edithas Rd. B78: Pole .2D 10
St Ediths Cl. CV23: M Kirby .3J 55
St Ediths Grn. CV34: Warw .7K 97
St Edmonds Rd. CV9: Hurl .6K 13
St Elizabeth's Rd. CV6: Cov .2E 50
St Faith's Rd. B49: Alc .3B 112
St Fremund Way CV31: Lea S .3G 103
St Georges Av. CV22: Rugby .7G 75
St George's Cl. CV37: S Avon .3C 114
St Georges Rd. CV1: Cov .5F 59
CV9: Ath .1C 16
CV31: Lea S .2D 102
St Georges Way CV10: Nun .3H 31
St Giles Rd. CV7: Ash G .7D 40
CV35: Gay .7G 119
St Govans Cl. CV31: Lea S .2G 103
St Gregory's Rd. CV37: S Avon .1H 137 (4F 115)
ST HELENA .2D 10 (1D 139)
St Helena Rd. B78: Pole .2E 10
St Helens Rd. CV31: Lea S .3D 102
St Helen's Way CV5: Alle .6F 49
St Ives Rd. CV2: Cov .4K 59
St Ives Way CV11: Nun .6G 23
St James' Av. CV35: Welle .2H 117
St James Cl. CV37: A'ton .2C 116
St James Ct. CV3: W'hall .2A 70
CV47: Sou .5H 107
(off Market Hill)
St James Cres. CV47: Sou .4G 107
ST JAMES END .2D 145
St James Gdns. CV12: Bulk .3E 42
St James La. CV3: W'hall .3J 69
St James Mdw. Rd. CV32: Lea S .5A 98
St James Rd. CV47: Sou .4H 107
St Johns CV34: Warw .1H 101
St Johns Av. CV8: Ken .6D 78
CV22: Hillm .1A 88
St Johns Cl. B95: Hen A .2G 93
CV36: Cher .6G 133
CV37: S Avon .6E 114
St John's Ct. CV34: Warw .1H 101
CV37: S Avon .7B 136 (6E 114)
St Johns Flats CV8: Ken .6E 78
St John's Ho. CV34: Warw .1H 101
St John's La. CV23: Long L .3A 74
St Johns Rd. CV10: Ans C .3D 20
CV31: Lea S .2E 102
CV36: Cher .6G 133
St John's St. CV1: Cov .5J 135 (5D 58)
CV8: Ken .6E 78
St John St. CV21: Rugby .4G 75
St Judes Av. B80: Stud .3B 92
St Jude's Cres. CV3: W'hall .1K 69
St Just's Rd. CV2: Cov .3B 60
St Laurence Av. CV34: Warw .3F 101
St Laurence Cl. CV35: Row .7J 91
St Laurence Way B50: Bidf A .5G 123
St Lawrence Rd. CV10: Ansl .7A 20
St Lawrence's Rd. CV6: Cov .5F 51
St Leonards Cl. B37: Mars G .6A 34
B78: Dord .4D 10
CV47: P Mars .5G 111
St Leonards Vw. B78: Dord, Pole .2C 10
St Leonard's Wlk. CV8: Rytn D .7C 70
St Luke's Rd. CV6: Cov .3D 50
St Luke's Way CV10: Nun .7H 21
St Margaret Rd. CV1: Cov .5F 59
St Margarets Av. CV8: Wols .4J 71
St Margarets Ho. CV31: W'nsh .4F 103
St Margaret's Rd. CV31: Lea S .3F 103
St Mark's Av. CV22: Bil .2C 86
St Mark's Cl. B95: Ullen .5B 90
CV10: Nun .7H 21
CV35: Gay .7G 119
St Mark's Ct. CV22: Bil .1D 86
St Mark's La. CV32: Lea S .6C 98
St Mark's M. CV32: Lea S .6C 98
St Mark's Rd. CV32: Lea S .6B 98
St Martin's Av. B80: Stud .3C 92
St Martin's Cl. CV37: S Avon .5A 136 (5D 114)
St Martin's Rd. CV3: Finh .4C 68
(not continuous)
St Mary's Abbey .4C 78
St Marys Acre CV37: Bear .7D 94
St Marys Cl. B95: Ullen .6B 90
CV34: Warw .7F 97
CV47: Sou .4J 107
St Mary's Ct. CV8: Ken .6D 78
CV11: Nun .6C 22
(off Abbey Grn.)
St Mary's Cres. CV31: Lea S .1F 103
St Marys Gro. B79: Newt R .5D 6
St Mary's Rd. B49: Alc .4D 112
CV7: Fill .2C 38
CV9: Ath .3D 16
CV11: Nun .6C 22
CV31: Lea S .1F 103
CV37: S Avon .3F 115
St Mary's Ter. CV31: Lea S .1F 103
St Mary St. CV1: Cov .4J 135 (5D 58)
St Matthews Cl. CV10: Nun .7H 21
WR11: Salf P .6A 122
St Matthews St. CV22: Rugby .5G 75
St Michael's Av. *CV1: Cov* .3J 135
(off Bayley La.)
St Michaels Cl. CV7: Gun H .4D 28
CV9: Ath .2D 16
CV9: Wood E .2K 13
CV33: Ufton .2F 109
CV35: Clav .2D 94
CV47: Bis I .6B 110
St Michael's Cres. CV47: S'ton .6C 106
St Michaels Rd. CV2: Cov .4G 59
CV34: Warw .7E 96
CV35: Clav .2D 94
St Michael's Way CV10: Nun .7H 21
St Nicholas Av. CV8: Ken .6D 78
St Nicholas Chu. St. CV34: Warw .2H 101
St Nicholas Cl. B49: Alc .4C 112
CV1: Cov .2C 58
CV9: Aus .6H 7
St Nicholas Ct. CV6: Cov .7F 51
(Crabmill La.)
CV6: Cov .1B 58
(Dugdale Rd.)
St Nicholas Est. CV9: Gren .1F 15
St Nicholas Pk. CV34: Warw .2H 101
St Nicholas Pk. Leisure Cen. .1J 101
St Nicholas Rd. B95: Hen A .2H 93
CV31: Rad S .3K 103
St Nicholas St. CV1: Cov .1G 135 (2C 58)
St Nicholas Ter. CV31: Rad S .4J 103
St Nicholas Wlk. B76: Curd .5B 18
ST NICOLAS PARK .4G 23
St Nicolas Pk. Dr. CV11: Nun .4F 23
St Nicolas Rd. CV11: Nun .6E 22
St Osburg's Rd. CV2: Cov .4G 59
St Patricks Rd. CV1: Cov .6H 135 (5C 58)
St Paul's Cl. CV34: Warw .2F 101
St Pauls Ct. B46: Wat O .1B 24
St Paul's Cres. B46: Col .5F 25
St Paul's Rd. CV6: Cov .1E 58
CV10: Nun .1C 30
St Pauls Sq. CV32: Lea S .6E 98
St Paul's Ter. CV34: Warw .2F 101
St Peter's Av. CV9: With .4G 17
St Peters Cl. B46: Wat O .2B 24
CV9: With .4G 17
St Peter's Ct. *CV1: Cov* .1K 135
(off Vine St.)
CV35: Kine .5D 120
St Peter's Dr. CV10: Gall C .7E 20
St Peters La. B92: Bick .5D 44
St Peters Rd. CV9: Man .4F 17
CV21: Rugby .6J 75
CV32: Lea S .7D 98
CV35: Kine .5D 120
CV35: Welle .2H 117
St Peters Way CV37: B'ton, S Avon .2C 114
ST PETER THE GREAT .3A 142
St Phillips Ct. B46: Col .5G 25
Saints Way CV10: Nun .6E 22
St Thomas' Ct. CV1: Cov .5B 58
St Thomas Ho. *CV1: Cov* .5B 58
(off St Thomas' Ct.)
St Thomas Rd. CV6: Cov .3G 51
St Thomas's Cl. CV10: Nun .1C 30
St Wilfreds Cotts. CV7: Old A .2C 28
St Wulstan Ct. CV47: Sou .5J 107
St Wulstan Way CV47: Sou .4J 107
Salcombe Cl. CV3: W'hall .2K 69
CV11: Nun .6G 23
SALE GREEN .3A 142
Salemorton Ct. CV22: Dunc .3B 86
SALEWAY .3A 142
SALFORD .3B 146
Salford Cl. B98: Redd .1A 92
CV2: Cov .2G 59
SALFORD PRIORS .7C 122 (3B 142)
Salford Rd. B50: Bidf A .7D 122
Salisbury Av. CV3: Cov .2C 68
Salisbury Cl. CV8: Wols .5H 71
Salisbury Dr. B46: Wat O .1C 24
CV10: Nun .2G 21
SALPERTON .3A 146
Salters La. B95: Woot W .6A 94
Saltisford CV34: Warw .1F 101
Saltisford Gdns. CV34: Warw .7F 97
Salt La. CV1: Cov .4H 135 (5C 58)
Salt St. B79: App M, No Hth .2G 7
B79: No Hth .2G 7
CV9: App M .2G 7
Saltway La. OX15: Lwr Bra .3J 133
SALWARPE .2A 142
SAMBOURNE .6A 92 (2B 142)
Sambourne La. B96: Cou, Sam .7B 92
B96: Sam .6A 92
Sambourne Pk. B96: Sam .7A 92
Sam Gault Cl. CV3: Bin .1B 70
Sammons Way CV4: Tile H .6B 56
Sampson Cl. CV2: Cov .5J 51
Samuel Hayward Ho. *CV2: Cov* .5H 51
(off Roseberry Av.)
Samuel Va. Ho. CV1: Cov .1G 135 (3C 58)
Sanctus Ct. CV37: S Avon .6E 114
Sanctus Dr. CV37: S Avon .6E 114
Sanctus Rd. CV37: S Avon .6D 114
Sanctus St. CV37: S Avon .6E 114
Sanda Cft. B36: Cas B .6B 24
Sand Barn La. CV37: B Hill, Snitt .6K 95
Sandby Cl. CV12: Bed .1G 41
Sandel Cl. CV37: S Avon .4D 114
Sanders Cl. CV9: Ath .2D 16
Sanders Ct. CV34: Warw .7K 97
Sanders Rd. CV6: Longf .7H 41
WR11: Salf P .7C 122
Sandfield Ct. CV37: S Avon .6E 114
Sandfield La. CV37: N'bld S .1G 127
Sandfield Rd. CV37: S Avon .6E 114
Sandford Cl. CV2: Ald G .3K 51
SANDFORD ST MARTIN .3D 147
Sandford Way CV22: Dunc .6C 86
Sandgate Cres. CV2: Cov .5K 59
Sandhurst Gro. CV6: Cov .2B 58
Sandilands Cl. CV2: Cov .3A 60
Sandon Rd. CV11: Nun .6C 22
Sandown Av. CV6: Cov .4F 51
Sandown Cl. CV32: Lill .3G 99
CV37: S Avon .6C 114
Sandown Rd. CV21: Rugby .4J 75
Sandpiper Cl. CV23: Brow .6J 65
CV37: B'ton .2C 114
Sandpiper Rd. CV2: Ald G .3H 51
Sandpits, The CV12: Bulk .3E 42
Sandpits Cl. B76: Curd .5B 18
CV35: Mid T .6C 130
Sandpits La. CV6: Cov .4J 49
CV7: Ker E .4J 49
Sandpits Rd. CV35: Mid T .7C 130

Sandringham Cl. CV4: W'wd H 2D 66
Sandringham Ct. CV10: Nun 5A 22
Sandwick Cl. CV3: Bin 7B 60
Sandy La. B46: Over W 1G 27
B79: Newt R 1D 6
CV1: Cov 2C 58
CV6: Cov 2C 58
CV7: Fill 2D 38
CV21: Rugby 5E 74
CV23: M Kirby 2J 55
CV23: Mart 3E 104
CV32: B'dwn 1C 98
Sandy La. Bus. Pk. CV1: Cov 2C 58
Sandythorpe CV3: W'hall 2A 70
Sandy Way CV35: Barf 3C 108
Sandy Way La. B78: Dord 3F 11
Santos Cl. CV3: Bin 7B 60
SAPCOTE 2B 140
Sapcote Gro. CV6: Ald G 2H 51
Sapphire Ct. CV2: W'grve S 5D 52
Sapphire Dr. CV31: Lea S 3D 102
Sapphire Ga. CV2: Cov 5J 59
Sarawak Pl. CV22: Caw 1B 86
Sargeaunt St. CV31: Lea S 1D 102
Sark Dr. B36: Cas B 6B 24
SARSDEN 3B 146
Satchwell Ct. CV32: Lea S 7D 98
Satchwell Pl. CV31: Lea S 1E 102
Satchwell Wlk. *CV32: Lea S* *7D 98*
(in Royal Priors Shop. Cen.)
Saumur Way CV34: Warw 2A 102
Saunders Av. CV12: Bed 3H 41
Saunton Cl. CV5: Alle 5F 49
Saunton Rd. CV22: Bil 7F 75
Savages Cl. CV33: Bis T 5D 108
Saville Gro. CV8: Ken 3G 79
SAWBRIDGE 7K 105 (2C 145)
Sawbridge Rd. CV23: Gran 6H 105
Saxon Cl. B78: Pole 1C 10
B80: Stud 2D 92
CV3: Bin W 1F 71
CV22: Caw 1A 86
CV37: S Avon 5G 115
Saxon Ct. *B50: Bidf A* *6G 123*
(off High St.)
Saxonfields B50: Bidf A 6G 123
Saxon Mdws. CV32: Lea S 5A 98
Saxon Rd. CV2: Cov 3H 59
Saxon Way B37: K'hrst 2A 34
Scafell CV21: Brow 1K 75
Scafell Cl. CV5: E Grn 3E 56
Scar Bank CV34: Warw 6G 97
Scarborough Way CV4: Tile H 1D 66
Scarman Ho. CV4: Canly 3E 66
Scarman Rd. CV4: Canly 4E 66
Schofield Rd. B37: K'hrst 7A 24
Scholars Ct. CV37: S Avon. 4C 136 (5E 114)
Scholars Dr. CV22: Caw 1B 86
Scholars La. CV37: S Avon 5D 136 (5E 114)
Scholfield Rd. CV7: Ker E 7A 40
School Av. WR11: Salf P 6B 122
School Bell M. CV8: S'lgh 3B 80
School Cl. B37: K'hrst 6A 24
CV3: Cov 5F 59
CV36: Long C 2C 134
Schoolfield Gro. CV21: Rugby 5F 75
School Gdns. CV21: Hillm 7C 76
School Hill CV10: Harts 4F 21
CV47: Nap 2H 111
School Ho. La. CV2: W'grve S 1C 60
School La. B76: Lea M 4G 19
B79: Shut 2C 8
CV7: Exh 6E 40
CV8: Ken 4D 78
CV10: Gall C 5D 20
CV23: Stret D 3H 83
CV31: Rad S 3J 103
CV37: Bear 6D 94
CV37: Ett 2B 126
CV37: Tidd 2K 115
CV47: Ladb 3C 110
CV47: P Mars 5G 111
LE10: Wlvy 2J 33
OX15: Lwr Bra 3H 133
OX17: Warm 2H 129
School Rd. B49: Alc 4B 112
B95: Hen A 2G 93
CV12: Bulk 3D 42
CV35: Welle 3H 117
CV37: Snitt 6G 95
WR11: Salf P 5A 122
School St. CV8: Wols 5J 71
CV21: Hillm 7C 76
CV22: Dunc 6C 86
CV23: Chu L 3F 73
CV23: C'over 1J 65
CV23: Long L 4A 74
CV47: Sou 5J 107
CV47: S'ton 6C 106
School Wlk. CV11: Nun 1A 32
Scotchill, The CV6: Cov 5K 49
SCOTLAND END 2C 147
Scots Cl. CV22: Bil 2C 86
Scots La. CV6: Cov 1K 57
Scott Av. CV10: Nun 3E 22
Scott Cl. B50: Bidf A 5F 123
CV37: S Avon 6H 115
Scott Rd. CV8: Ken 7C 78
CV31: Lea S 2F 103
Scowcroft Dr. CV47: Bis I 7B 110
SCRAPTOFT 1D 141
Seabroke Av. CV22: Rugby 5F 75
Seaford Cl. CV6: Ald G 2H 51
Seagrave Rd. CV1: Cov 5E 58
Sealand Dr. CV12: Bed 2G 41
Seathwaite CV21: Brow 1J 75
Seaton Cl. CV11: Nun 6G 23
Sebastian Cl. CV3: W'hall 3H 69
SECKINGTON 5A 6 (1D 139)
Seckington La. B79: Newt R 5C 6
Second Av. CV3: Cov 6J 59
Second Exhibition Av. B40: Nat E C 2D 44
Sedgemoor Rd. CV3: W'hall 3H 69
SEDGLEY 2A 138
Sedlescombe Lodge CV22: Rugby 1F 87
Sedlescombe Pk. CV22: Rugby 1F 87
Seed Fld. Cft. CV3: Cov 1D 68
Seekings, The CV31: W'nsh 5F 103
Seekings Dr. CV8: Ken 5F 79
Seeney La. B76: Mars 1H 19
Seeswood Cl. CV10: Nun 2C 30
Sefton Rd. CV4: Canly 2J 67
Seggs La. B49: Alc 5B 112
Segrave Cl. CV35: Kine 5D 120
Selborne Rd. CV22: Bil 1D 86
Selby Way CV10: Nun 6G 21
Selina Dix Ho. CV1: Cov 1K 135
SELLY OAK 3B 138
Selsey Cl. CV3: W'hall 4J 69
Selside CV21: Brow 1K 75
Selworthy Rd. CV6: Cov 3D 50
Selwyn Cl. CV35: Welle 2H 117
Selwyn Ho. B37: Chel W 2D 34
Semele Cl. CV31: Rad S 3J 103
Senate Ho. CV4: Canly 4F 67
Seneschal Rd. CV3: Cov 1E 68
Sennen Cl. CV11: Nun 6H 23
Sephton Dr. CV6: Longf 7J 41
Servite Ho. CV8: Ken 6D 78
Sett, The CV35: Oxh 1D 130
Seven Acre Cl. CV33: Bis T 5B 108
Seven Mdws. Rd. CV37: S Avon 7C 136 (6E 114)
Seven Stars Ind. Est. CV3: Cov 1H 69
(Allard Way)
CV3: Cov 1G 69
(Wheler Rd.)
Severn Cl. B36: Cas B 5A 24
CV32: Lill 4G 99
Severn Rd. CV1: Cov 6F 59
CV12: Bulk 2C 42
Sevilla Cl. CV3: Bin 5C 60
Sevincott Cl. CV37: S Avon 3B 114
Sewall Highway CV2: Cov 1H 59
CV6: Cov 6G 51
Seymour Cl. CV3: W'hall 3J 69
CV35: H Mag 2B 100
Seymour Gro. CV34: Warw 2B 102
Seymour Homes B95: Woot W 5H 93
Seymour Pl. CV8: Ken 3C 78
Seymour Rd. B49: Alc 3C 112
CV11: Nun 1K 31
CV21: Rugby 2J 75
CV37: Shot 6C 114
SHACKERSTONE 1A 140
Shadowbrook La. B92: H Ard 6D 44
Shadowbrook Rd. CV6: Cov 2A 58
Shaftesbury Av. CV7: Ker E 6A 40
Shaftesbury Rd. CV5: Cov 7K 57
Shaft La. CV7: Mer 2H 47
Shakesfield Cl. CV36: Tred 6J 127
Shakespeare Av. CV12: Bed 3K 41
CV34: Warw 3E 100
Shakespeare Cen., The 2F 137
Shakespeare Ct. CV37: S Avon 2G 137
Shakespeare Dr. CV11: Nun 3C 32
Shakespeare Gdns.
CV22: Rugby 1E 86
Shakespeare Memorial Fountain 4E 136
Shakespeare's Birthplace 2F 137
Shakespeare St. CV2: Cov 2H 59
CV37: S Avon 2E 136 (4F 115)
Shakleton Rd. CV5: Cov 5A 58
Shamble, The *CV36: Ship S* *4H 131*
(off Market Pl.)
SHANGTON 2D 141
Shanklin Dr. CV10: Nun 5E 22
Shanklin Rd. CV3: W'hall 4H 69
Shapfell CV21: Brow 1K 75
SHARESHILL 1A 138
SHARNFORD 2B 140
Sharp Cl. CV6: Cov 4C 50
Sharpe Cl. CV34: Warw 7G 97
Sharpley Ct. CV2: W'grve S 6C 52
Sharratt Rd. CV12: Bed 3F 41
Shawbury La. B46: Shu 2E 26
CV7: Fill 6G 27
Shawbury Village B46: Shu 6G 27
Shawe Av. CV10: Nun 4D 22
SHAWELL 3C 141
SHEARSBY 2D 141
Shearwater Dr. CV23: Brow 6J 65
Sheepclose Dr. B37: F'bri 2A 34
Sheepcote Cl. CV32: Lea S 6E 98
Sheep Dip La. CV23: Prin 6G 83
Sheep St. CV21: Rugby 5G 75
CV36: Ship S 4H 131
CV37: S Avon 5G 137 (5F 115)
SHEEPY MAGNA 1A 140
SHEEPY PARVA 1A 140
Sheepy Rd. CV9: Ath 1C 16
Shelbourne Rd.
CV37: S Avon 3A 114
Shelby La. CV37: Snitt 5J 95
SHELDON 3C 139
Sheldon Gro. CV34: Warw 6H 97
Sheldrake Cl. CV3: Bin 6C 60
SHELFIELD
Alcester 2C 143
Walsall 1B 138
Shelfield Cl. CV5: E Grn 4F 57
SHELFORD 3B 140
SHELL 3A 142
Shelley Av. CV34: Warw 4E 100
Shelley Cl. CV12: Bed 4K 41
Shelley Ct. CV2: Cov 3J 59
Shelley Rd. CV2: Cov 4J 59
CV37: S Avon 6G 115
Shellon Cl. CV3: Bin 7B 60
Shelton Sq. CV1: Cov 4G 135 (5C 58)
SHENINGTON 1C 147
Shennington Rd. CV35: Up Tys 7D 130
SHENSTONE
Kidderminster 1A 142
Lichfield 1C 139
Shenstone Av. CV22: Hillm 7A 76
SHENSTONE WOODEND 1C 139
SHENTON 1A 140
Shenton Wlk. B37: K'hrst 7A 24
Shepherd Cl. CV4: Tile H 4D 56
CV47: Long I 2D 106
Shepherd Pl. CV35: Kine 6C 120
Shepherds Hill CV47: Sou 5J 107
Shepherds La. CV7: Mer 3C 46
Shepherd St. CV23: Mart 2D 104
Shepperton Bus. Pk. CV11: Nun 3J 31
Shepperton Ct. CV11: Nun 2J 31
Shepperton St. CV11: Nun 2J 31
Sheppey Dr. B36: Cas B 7B 24
Sherard Cft. B36: Cas B 6B 24
Sherborne Cl. B46: Col 1G 35
SHERBOURNE 1A 108 (2D 143)
Sherbourne Arc. CV1: Cov 4G 135 (5C 58)
Sherbourne Av. CV10: Nun 6G 21
Sherbourne Ct. CV1: Cov 6H 135 (6C 58)
CV35: Sher 7B 100
Sherbourne Cres. CV5: Cov 3J 57
Sherbourne Pl. CV32: Lea S 6E 98
Sherbourne St. CV1: Cov 5A 58
Sherbourne Ter. CV32: Lea S 5E 98
Sheridan Cl. CV22: Rugby 2F 87
Sheridan Dr. CV10: Gall C 6E 20
Sheriff Av. CV4: Canly 1F 67
Sheriff Rd. CV21: Rugby 5K 75
Sheriffs Orchard CV1: Cov 5G 135 (5C 58)
Sheringham Cl. CV11: Nun 2B 32
Sherington Av. CV5: Cov 3G 57
Sherlock Rd. CV5: Cov 4H 57
SHERNAL GREEN 2A 142
Sherwell Dr. B49: Alc 4B 112
Sherwood Cl. CV9: Wood E 2J 13
Sherwood Jones Cl. CV6: Cov 1B 58
Sherwood Wlk. CV32: Lill 3G 99
Shetland Cl. CV5: E Grn 3E 56
Shetland Dr. CV10: Nun 2F 31
Shetland Rd. CV3: W'hall 3H 69
Shetland Wlk. B36: Cas B 6B 24
Shevlock Way CV6: Cov 1G 59
Shillingstone Cl. CV2: W'grve S 3C 60
Shillingstone Dr. CV10: Nun 3F 31
SHILTON 1G 53 (3B 140)
Shilton La. CV2: W'grve S 4A 52
CV7: Shil 3B 52
CV12: Bulk 4F 43
Shilton La. Ind. Est. CV7: Shil 6G 43
Shilton Rd. CV7: Withy 2C 54
Shipston Ind. Est. CV36: Ship S 3G 131
SHIPSTON-ON-STOUR 4H 131 (1B 146)
Shipston Rd. CV2: Cov 1J 59
CV35: Up Tys 7A 130
CV36: Long C 1C 134
CV37: Ath S, S Avon 7G 115 & 4E 124
Shipston Swimming Pool 4G 131
SHIPTON-ON-CHERWELL 3D 147
SHIPTON-UNDER-WYCHWOOD 3B 146
Shirebrook Cl. CV2: Cov 4K 51
Shire Cl. CV6: Cov 5H 51
Shires Ga. Trad. Est. CV31: Lea S 2C 102
Shires Retail Pk., The CV34: Warw 2B 102
Shirland Rd. B37: Mars G 4A 34
Shirlett Cl. CV2: Ald G 2H 51
SHIRLEY 1C 143
Shirley Rd. CV2: W'grve S 7B 52
Shopping Cen., The CV31: Lea S 3F 103
Shorncliffe Rd. CV6: Cov 1H 57
Shortacre CV35: Kine 5D 120
Short Fishers Wlk. CV23: Brow 7K 65
SHORTHAMPTON 3C 147
SHORT HEATH
Birmingham 2B 138
Willenhall 1A 138
Shortlands CV7: Ash G 7D 40
Short La. CV47: Long I 2B 106
Shortley Rd. CV3: Cov 7E 58
Shortstones Wlk. CV23: Brow 7K 65
Short St. CV1: Cov 5K 135 (5D 58)
CV10: Nun 7H 21
Shortwheat Hill CV23: Brow 7K 65
Shortwood Ct. CV2: W'grve S 5B 52
Shortwoods, The B78: Dord 5D 10
SHOTTERY 5C 114 (3C 143)
Shottery CV37: Shot 5C 114
Shottery Cl. CV5: E Grn 4F 57
Shottery Rd. CV37: S Avon 7A 136 (5C 114)
SHOTTESWELL 6H 129 (1D 147)
Showcase Cinema 5D 52
Showell La. CV7: Mer 4J 47
Shreres Dyche CV34: Warw 4D 100
SHREWLEY 2D 143
Shrieve's Wlk. CV37: S Avon 5G 137 (5F 115)

Shrieve's Wlk. Shop. Cen. CV37: S Avon 4H **137**
Shrubberies, The CV4: Canly 4H **67**
Shrubland St. CV31: Lea S 2E **102**
(not continuous)
Shuckburgh Cres. CV22: Hillm 1K **87**
CV23: Bour D 7C **84**
Shuckburgh Gro. CV32: Lill 5F **99**
Shuckburgh Rd. CV47: Nap 1J **111**
CV47: P Mars 5G **111**
Shulmans Wlk. CV2: Cov 7K **51**
Shultern La. CV4: Canly 2G **67**
Shuna Cft. CV2: W'grve S 7C **52**
SHUSTOKE 2B **26** (2D **139**)
Shustoke Sailing Club 1B **26**
SHUTFORD 1C **147**
SHUTLANGER 3D **145**
SHUTT GREEN 1A **138**
SHUTTINGTON 2C **8** (1D **139**)
Shuttington Rd. B79: A'cte 3A **8**
Shuttle St. CV6: Cov 6H **51**
Shuttleworth Rd. CV23: Clift D 3B **76**
Shylock Gro. CV34: H'cte 6C **102**
SIBBERTOFT 3D **141**
SIBFORD FERRIS 2C **147**
SIBFORD GOWER 2C **147**
Sibree Rd. CV3: W'hall 4H **69**
SIBSON 1A **140**
Sibton Cl. CV2: Cov 5H **51**
Sidbury Rd. CV6: Cov 1C **58**
Siddaw Ho. *CV21: Brow* *1J* ***75***
(off Millers Dale Cl.)
Siddeley Av. CV3: Cov 6G **59**
CV8: Ken 6C **78**
Siddeley Wlk. B36: Cas B 3A **24**
Sidelands Rd. CV37: S Avon 4B **114**
Sidings, The CV21: Rugby 4H **75**
CV36: Ship S 3H **131**
Sidmouth Cl. CV2: Cov 7J **51**
CV11: Nun 6G **23**
Sidney Rd. CV22: Hillm 1K **87**
Signal Rd. CV36: Ship S 3H **131**
Silken Ct. CV11: Nun 1H **31**
Silksby St. CV3: Cov 7D **58**
Silver Birch Av. CV12: Bed 3E **40**
Silver Birch Cl. CV3: Bin W 1F **71**
Silverbirch Cl. CV10: Harts 4F **21**
Silver Birch Gro. CV31: Lea S 3D **102**
Silver Birch Rd. B37: K'hrst 6A **24**
Silverdale Cl. CV2: Ald G 2H **51**
SILVER END 3A **138**
Silverstone Dr. CV6: Longf 1E **50**
Silver St. CV1: Cov 2H **135** (4C **58**)
Silverton Rd. CV6: Cov 7F **51**
Silver Trees Dr. CV12: Bulk 1D **42**
Silver Wlk. CV10: Nun 1F **31**
Simmonds Way CV9: Ath 1C **16**
Simmons Ct. CV35: Welle 3H **117**
Simon Cl. CV11: Nun 2K **31**
Simon Ct. CV7: Exh 5G **41**
Simon Stone St. CV6: Cov 6F **51**
Simpson Gro. CV3: W'hall 2J **69**
Simpson Rd. CV36: Ship S 5H **131**
Sinclair Dr. CV6: Longf 7J **41**
Singer Cl. CV6: Cov 6G **51**
Sir Frank Whittle Bus. Cen. CV21: Rugby 3K **75**
Sir Henry Parkes Rd. CV4: Canly 1G **67**
CV5: Cov 1G **67**
Sir Thomas White's Rd. CV5: Cov 5K **57**
Sir Toby Belch Dr. CV34: H'cte 5D **102**
Sir William Lyons Rd. CV4: Canly 2G **67**
Sir Winston Churchill Pl. CV3: Bin W. 1E **70**
Siskin Cl. CV23: Brow 7J **65**
Siskin Dr. CV3: W'hall 4J **69**
Siskin Parkway E. CV3: W'hall 7J **69**
Siskin Parkway W. CV3: W'hall 7H **69**
Sissinghurst Cl. CV22: Bil 6E **74**
Sitwell Av. CV47: Long I 3D **106**
SKEFFINGTON 1D **141**
Skelwith Ri. CV11: Nun 5H **23**
SKETCHLEY 2B **140**
Skey Dr. CV10: Nun 5G **21**
Skiddaw CV21: Brow 1J **75**
Skipton Gdns. CV2: Cov 1H **59**
Skipton Lodge CV2: Cov 1H **59**
Skipwith Cl. CV23: Brin 4B **62**
Skipworth Rd. CV3: Bin 6C **60**
Sky Blue Way CV1: Cov 4E **58**
Skye Cl. B36: Cas B 6B **24**
CV10: Nun 2F **31**
Skywalk B40: Nat E C 2D **44**
Slack's Av. CV9: Ath 4C **16**
Slade, The CV47: Fen C 4G **121**
OX17: Farn 4H **121**
Slade Cl. CV11: Nun 4E **32**
SLADE HEATH 1A **138**
Slade Hill CV35: H Mag 1B **100**
Slade Mdw. CV31: Rad S 3J **103**
Slade Rd. CV21: Rugby 6J **75**
SLAPTON 3D **145**
Sleath's Yd. CV12: Bed 2H **41**
Sledmere Cl. CV2: Ald G 3H **51**
Sleets Yd. CV12: Bed 3H **41**
Slingates Rd. CV37: S Avon 3F **115**
Slingsby Cl. CV11: Nun 2A **32**
Slough, The B80: Stud 3A **92**
B97: Redd 3A **92**
Slowley Hill CV7: Old A 3J **27**
Small Brook Bus. Cen. B50: Bidf A 4H **123**
Smalley Pl. CV8: Ken 5D **78**
SMALL HEATH 3B **138**
Smallman Rd. CV10: Nun 4F **21**
Smarts Est. CV23: Kils 6J **89**
Smarts La. CV35: Up Tys 7C **130**
Smarts Rd. CV12: Bed 4F **41**
Smeaton La. CV23: Stret U 1A **62**
SMEETON WESTERBY 2D **141**
Smercote Cl. CV12: Bed 4D **40**
SMESTOW 2A **138**
SMETHWICK 3B **138**
Smite Cl. CV23: M Kirby 3K **55**
Smithford Way CV1: Cov 3G **135** (4C **58**)
Smithhill Pl. CV23: Brow 6K **65**
Smiths Cl. B50: Bidf A 5H **123**
Smith's La. CV37: Snitt 6G **95**
Smiths Orchard CV21: Rugby 5J **75**
Smith St. CV6: Cov 2F **59**
CV9: Wood E 2K **13**
CV12: Bed 4E **40**
CV31: Lea S 1D **102**
CV34: Warw 1G **101**
Smiths Way B46: Wat O 1A **24**
B49: Alc 3C **112**
SMITH'S WOOD 5A **24**
Smithy La. CV9: Bax 6F **15**
CV23: Chu L 3F **73**
SMOCKINGTON 3B **140**
Smorrall La. CV7: Cor 4H **39**
CV12: Bed 4A **40**
Smythe Gro. CV34: Warw 6G **97**
Snape Rd. CV2: Cov 2B **60**
SNARESTONE 1A **140**
SNEACHILL 3A **142**
Snellsdale Cl. CV23: Brow 6K **65**
SNIBSTON 1B **140**
SNITTERFIELD 6G **95** (3D **143**)
Snitterfield La. CV35: N Lin 4G **95**
CV37: Snitt 5J **95**
Snitterfield Rd. CV35: H Lucy 1A **118**
CV37: Bear 6B **94**
Snitterfield St. CV35: H Lucy 1A **118**
Snowdon Cl. CV10: Nun 1B **30**
Snowdrop Cl. CV12: Bed 4E **40**
SNOWSHILL 2A **146**
Snowshill Cl. CV11: Nun 4B **32**
Snuff La. OX17: Shotte 6G **129**
Soden Cl. CV3: W'hall 2K **69**
Soden's Av. CV8: Rytn D 7C **70**
Solent Dr. CV2: W'grve S 5B **52**
SOLIHULL 1C **143**
Solihull Parkway B37: Mars G 6D **34**
Solihull Rd. B92: H Ard 7G **45**
Solway Cl. CV31: Lea S 2G **103**
SOMERFORD 1A **138**
Somerly Cl. CV3: Bin 7B **60**
Somerset Dr. CV10: Nun 7K **21**
Somerset Pl. CV22: Caw 7B **74**
Somerset Rd. CV1: Cov 2C **58**
Somers Pl. CV32: Lea S 7C **98**
Somers Rd. CV7: Ker E 7K **39**
CV7: Mer 5B **46**
CV22: Rugby 5D **74**
Somers Wood Cvn. & Camping Pk. CV7: Mer 5B **46**
SOMERTON 3D **147**
Somerton Dr. B37: Mars G 6A **34**
Somerville Ho. B37: Chel W 2D **34**
Sommerville Rd. CV2: Cov 3J **59**
Soot La. OX17: Warm 2J **129**
Sordale Cft. CV3: Bin 6C **60**
Sorrel Cl. CV4: Tile H 7C **56**
Sorrel Dr. B78: K'bry 4E **12**
CV23: Brow 7K **65**
Sorrell Pl. CV10: Nun 4K **31**
Sorrell Rd. CV10: Nun 3K **31**
SOULDERN 2D **147**
SOUTHAM 5H **107** (2B **144**)
Southam Cl. CV4: Tile H 1C **66**
Southam Cres. CV33: L Hth 2K **119**
Southam Dr. CV47: Sou 7G **107**
Southam Leisure Cen. 4G **107**
Southam Rd. CV22: Dunc 7B **86**
CV23: Prin 7G **83**
CV31: Rad S 2J **103**
CV33: Ufton 2F **109**
CV35: Kine 5D **120**
CV47: Ladb 3C **110**
CV47: Long I, Sou 2H **107**
CV47: Nap 1G **111**
CV47: P Mars 5F **111**
Southam St. CV35: Kine 5D **120**
South Av. CV2: Cov 5G **59**
Southbank Ct. CV8: Ken 5D **78**
Southbank Rd. CV6: Cov 2J **57**
CV8: Ken 4D **78**
Southborough Ter. CV31: Lea S 2E **102**
Southbourne Ho. CV37: S Avon 2H **137**
Southbrook Rd. CV22: Rugby 7G **75**
Sth. Car Pk. Rd. B40: Nat E C 3E **44**
Southcott Way CV2: W'grve S 5B **52**
SOUTH CROXTON 1D **141**
South Dr. B46: Col 5D **24**
Southern La. CV37: S Avon 7F **137** (6F **115**)
Southey Rd. CV22: Rugby 2E **86**
Southfield Cl. CV10: Nun 6E **22**
Southfield Dr. CV8: Ken 3E **78**
Southfield Rd. CV22: Rugby 7J **75**
CV47: Sou 7G **107**
Southfields CV32: Lea S 4E **98**
Southfields Cl. B46: Col 1G **35**
South Grn. Dr. CV37: S Avon 5B **114**
SOUTH KILWORTH 3D **141**
Southlands CV9: Ath 4D **16**
Southlea Av. CV31: Lea S 2C **102**
Southlea Cl. CV31: Lea S 2C **102**
Southleigh Av. CV5: Cov 1K **67**
SOUTH LITTLETON 3B **142**
Sth. Lynn Gdns. CV36: Ship S 5H **131**
Southmead Gdns. B80: Stud 4D **92**
SOUTH NEWINGTON 2D **147**
Southorn Ct. CV32: Lill 4H **99**
South Pde. CV33: Har 6H **109**
Southport Cl. CV3: W'hall 3H **69**
South Ridge CV5: Cov 3F **57**
South Rd. CV23: Clift D 3B **76**
South St. CV1: Cov 4E **58**
CV9: Ath 3C **16**
CV21: Rugby 4K **75**
South Ter. CV31: W'nsh 5E **102**
South Vw. B78: K'bry 7E **12**
CV35: H Mag 2C **100**
South Vw. Rd. CV23: Long L 4K **73**
CV32: Lill 2G **99**
Sth. Warwickshire Bus. Pk. CV47: Sou 6G **107**
South Way B40: Nat E C 3F **45**
Southway CV31: Lea S 3E **102**
SOUTH WIGSTON 2C **141**
Sovereign Cl. CV8: Ken 7D **78**
Sovereign Ct. CV4: Canly 2G **67**
CV47: Sou 5H **107**
Sovereign Rd. CV5: Cov 5K **57**
(not continuous)
Sovereign Row CV1: Cov 5A **58**
CV5: Cov 5A **58**
SOWE COMMON 3B **52**
Sparkbrook St. CV1: Cov 4F **59**
Sparkbrook St. Ind. Est. CV1: Cov 4F **59**
Sparta Cl. CV21: Rugby 2G **75**
Spartan Cl. CV34: Warw 4C **102**
Spa Vw. CV31: W'nsh 4F **103**
Speedway La. CV8: Bran 1H **71**
Speedwell Cl. CV12: Bed 3D **40**
CV23: Brow 1A **76**
Speedwell La. CV9: Bad E 2E **14**
Spellow Cl. CV23: Brow 6K **65**
SPELSBURY 3C **147**
Spencer Av. CV5: Cov 6A **58**
Spencer Ct. CV37: S Avon 6D **114**
Spencer Rd. CV5: Cov 7F **135** (6B **58**)
Spencer St. CV31: Lea S 1D **102**
Spencer Yd. CV31: Lea S 1D **102**
Spernal Ash B80: Stud 6E **92**
SPERNALL 2B **142**
Spernal La. B80: Sper 6E **92**
SPETCHLEY 3A **142**
Sphinx Dr. CV3: Cov 6H **59**
Spicer Pl. CV22: Bil 7D **74**
Spiers Ct. B50: Bidf A 5G **123**
Spike La. CV23: Harb M 4B **64**
Spilsbury Cl. CV32: Lea S 5C **98**
Spindle St. CV1: Cov 1D **58**
Spinney, The CV4: Canly 5H **67**
CV9: Man 4F **17**
CV23: Long L 3A **74**
CV32: Lea S 6B **98**
CV47: Bis I 6C **110**
Spinney Cl. B78: B'moor 2C **10**
CV3: Bin W 1G **71**
CV7: Gun H 4C **28**
Spinney Hill CV34: Warw 6J **97**
SPINNEY HILLS 1D **141**
Spinney La. CV10: Nun 7H **21**
Spinney Path CV3: Finh 3K **67**
Spire Bank CV47: Sou 6H **107**
Spires, The CV10: Nun 7H **21**
Spitalfields CV12: Bed 3J **41**
SPON END 4A **58** (1A **144**)
Spon End CV1: Cov 4A **58**
Spon Ga. Ho. CV1: Cov 5A **58**
Spon La. CV9: Gren 7G **11**
Spon St. CV1: Cov 3F **135** (4B **58**)
Spottiswood Cl. CV22: Caw 1A **86**
SPRATTON 1D **145**
SPRING, THE 2D **78**
Spring Cl. CV1: Cov 4E **58**
CV23: Kils 7J **89**
CV37: Ett 2B **126**
Spring Ct. CV8: Bubb 4J **81**
Springdale Ct. CV11: Nun 1K **31**
SPRINGFIELD
Birmingham 3B **138**
Coventry 4H **41**
Springfield Bus. Pk. B49: Alc 3B **112**
Springfield Cl. CV36: Ship S 6H **131**
Springfield Cres. CV12: Bed 3H **41**
Springfield Gro. CV47: Sou 4H **107**
Springfield Pl. CV1: Cov 3D **58**
Springfield Rd. CV1: Cov 3D **58**
CV11: Nun 2A **32**
CV36: Ship S 6H **131**
Springfields B46: Col 7G **25**
Springfields Rd. B49: Alc 3B **112**
SPRINGHILL 1A **138**
Spring Hill CV7: Gun H 4C **28**
CV8: Bubb 4J **81**
Springhill CV10: Harts 3F **21**
Spring Hill Bus. Pk.
CV7: Gun H 4D **28**
Springhill Ho's. CV22: Rugby 1J **87**
Spring Hill Rd. CV10: Nun 5H **21**
Spring Ho. B37: K'hrst 7B **24**
Spring La. CV8: Ken 4E **78**
CV31: Rad S 3J **103**
Spring Pool CV34: Warw 1G **101**
Spring Rd. CV6: Cov 6F **51**
CV7: Barn 7D **42**
Springs Cres. CV47: Sou 4H **107**
Spring St. CV1: Cov 4E **58**
CV21: Rugby 5H **75**
Springwell Rd. CV31: Lea S 2H **103**
Spruce Gro. CV31: Lea S 3D **102**

Spruce Rd. CV2: Cov 4J 51
CV10: Nun 5K 21
Square, The CV8: Ken 5D 78
CV11: Nun 2A 32
CV22: Dunc 6C 86
CV35: Mid T 6C 130
CV37: Cliff C 5C 124
CV37: Ett 2B 126
CV47: Long I 2C 106
CV47: S'ton 6C 106
LE10: Wlvy 2H 33
Square La. CV7: Cor 4E 38
Square St. CV32: Lea S 6D 98
Squire Pl. CV47: Fen C 3G 121
Squires Cft. CV2: W'grve S 5B 52
Squires Rd. CV23: Stret D 3H 83
Squires Way CV4: Canly 2H 67
Squirhill Pl. CV31: Lea S 1F 103
Stable Wlk. CV11: Nun 2B 32
Stacey Ct. CV22: Bil 3D 86
Stadium Cl. CV6: Cov 4D 50
Stafford Cl. CV12: Bulk 3E 42
Stafford St. CV9: Ath 4C 16
Staines Cl. CV11: Nun 4G 23
Stainforth Cl. CV11: Nun 2B 32
Staircase La. CV5: Alle 1G 57
(not continuous)
Stamford Av. CV3: Cov 2C 68
Stamford Gdns. CV32: Lea S 6C 98
Standard Av. CV4: Tile H 6E 56
STANDEFORD 1A 138
Standish Cl. CV2: Cov 5A 60
Standlake M. CV31: Lea S 2G 103
Stand St. CV34: Warw 2F 101
STANFORD ON AVON 1C 145
Stanier Av. CV1: Cov 4A 58
Stanley Ct. CV31: Lea S 1G 103
Stanley Rd. CV5: Cov 7K 57
CV9: Ath 4C 16
CV11: Nun 6B 22
CV21: Hillm 7A 76
Stannells Cl. CV37: S Avon 7B 114
Stansfield Gro. CV8: Ken 5G 79
STANTON 2A 146
Stanton Rd. CV31: Lea S 2G 103
STANTON UNDER BARDON 1B 140
Stanton Wlk. CV34: Warw 6F 97
STANWAY 2A 146
Stanway Rd. CV5: Cov 7A 58
Stan Williams Ct. CV11: Nun 7E 22
Stapledon Grn. CV47: Temp H 2A 120
Staples Cl. CV12: Bulk 2E 42
STAPLETON 2B 140
Stapleton Cl. B80: Stud 4C 92
Stapleton Dr. B37: F'bri 2B 34
Stapleton Rd. B80: Stud 4C 92
Starbold Rd. CV47: Bis I 6B 110
Starcross Cl. CV2: Cov 7J 51
Stare Grn. CV4: Canly 2H 67
STARETON 5D 80 (1A 144)
Stareton Cl. CV4: Cov 2J 67
Star Ind. Est. CV2: Cov 2B 60
Starkey Cft. B37: Chel W 3C 34
Star La. CV35: Clav 1E 94
Starley Ct. CV3: Bin 1C 70
Starley Pk. CV7: Exh 5H 41
Starley Rd. CV1: Cov 5F 135 (5B 58)
Starley Way B37: Mars G 7C 34
Startin Cl. CV7: Exh 6F 41
Station App. CV31: Lea S 1D 102
Station Av. CV4: Tile H 7B 56
CV34: Warw 1H 101
Station Bldgs. B46: Wat O 1B 24
(off Minworth Rd.)
Station Dr. B46: Wat O 1B 24
Station Flds. CV47: Fen C 1J 121
Station Hill CV7: Old A 5A 28
Station La. B94: Lapw 3J 91
Station Link Rd. B26: Birm A 2D 44
B40: Nat E C 2D 44
Station Rd. B37: Mars G 5A 34
B46: Col 4F 25
B46: Neth W 5K 19
B49: Alc 4B 112
B78: Pole 7D 8
B79: Pole 7D 8
B80: Stud 3B 92
B92: H Ard 7H 45
B95: Hen A 1G 93
CV7: Old A 5B 28
CV8: Ken 5D 78
CV23: Clift D 3B 76
CV23: Kils 6J 89
CV23: Lilb 1J 77
CV33: Har 5J 109
CV34: Warw 1H 101
CV35: Clav 2D 94
CV36: Ship S 3H 131
CV37: Long M, Lwr Q 4G 125 & 4F 125
CV37: Path, Wilm 5J 113
CV37: S Avon 2B 136 (4E 114)
CV47: Bis I 6B 110
CV47: Dep B, Sou 1A 110 & 7F 107
CV47: Fen C 2G 121
CV47: Har 6K 109
CV47: S'ton 6D 106
WR11: Salf P 7C 122
Station Sq. CV1: Cov 6G 135 (6C 58)
Station St. CV9: Ath 3C 16
Station St. E. CV6: Cov 7E 50
Station St. W. CV6: Cov 6D 50
Station St. W. Bus. Pk. CV6: Cov 7D 50
Station Twr. CV1: Cov 6H 135 (6C 58)
Station Way B37: Mars G 3D 44
B40: Nat E C 2D 44
Staunton Rd. CV31: Lea S 3E 102
Staveley Way CV21: Brow 2K 75
STAVERTON 2C 145
Staverton Cl. CV5: E Grn 4D 56
Staverton Leys CV22: Rugby 2G 87
Steele St. CV22: Rugby 5E 74
Steels La. CV36: Cher 7F 133
Steeping Rd. CV23: Long L 3B 74
STEEPLE ASTON 3D 147
STEEPLE BARTON 3D 147
Steeplefield Rd. CV6: Cov 2A 58
Steeples, The CV23: Gran 6H 105
Stella Cft. B37: Chel W 3C 34
Stennels Cl. CV6: Cov 6K 49
Stephenson Cl. CV32: Lea S 6A 98
Stephenson Ct. CV23: Kils 7H 89
Stephenson Dr. B37: Chel W 2B 34
Stephenson Rd. CV7: Exh 6J 41
Stephen St. CV21: Rugby 5F 75
Stepney Rd. CV2: Cov 3G 59
Steppes Piece B50: Bidf A 5F 123
Steppey La. CV9: Man 7C 16
Stepping Stones B50: Bidf A 5F 123
Stepping Stones Rd. CV5: Cov 3K 57
Sterling Way CV11: Nun 4A 32
Stevenage Wlk. CV2: W'grve S 7C 52
Stevens Ho. CV1: Cov 1K 135 (3D 58)
Stevenson Rd. CV6: Cov 6A 50
Stewart Cl. CV4: Cov 5H 57
Stewart Ct. CV7: New A 4E 28
Stewart St. CV11: Nun 1H 31
Stidfall Gro. CV31: Lea S 2H 103
Stileman Cl. CV37: Lwr Q 5G 125
Stileman Cnr. CV37: Lwr Q 5G 125
Stiper's Hill B79: Wart 7E 8
STIRCHLEY 3B 138
Stirling Av. CV32: Cubb, Lill 2F 99
Stirling Cl. CV3: Bin 7B 60
STIVICHALL 2A 68 (1A 144)
Stivichall & Cheylesmore By-Pass CV3: Cov 4E 68
Stivichall Cft. CV3: Cov 2B 68
Stoat La. B49: Gt Alne 2F 113
STOCK GREEN 3A 142
STOCKINGFORD 1D 30 (2A 140)
Stocking Mdw. CV23: M Kirby 3K 55
Stockley Rd. CV6: Longf 7H 41
Stocks La. CV23: Thurl 6K 85
STOCKTON 6C 106 (2B 144)
Stockton Gro. CV32: Lea S 5E 98
Stockton Rd. CV1: Cov 3E 58
CV47: Long I, S'ton 3D 106 & 4A 106
STOCK WOOD 3B 142
STOKE 5K 59 (1A 144)
STOKE ALDERMOOR 7H 59
STOKE BRUERNE 3D 145
Stoke Floods Nature Reserve 4B 60
STOKE GOLDING 2A 140
Stoke Grn. CV3: Cov 5G 59
Stoke Grn. Cres. CV3: Cov 6H 59
STOKE HEATH 1H 59
Stoke Pk. M. CV2: Cov 4G 59
STOKE PRIOR 2A 142
Stoke Row CV2: Cov 3G 59
Stokesay Cl. CV11: Nun 1G 31
STONE 1A 142
STONEBRIDGE 4J 45
Stonebridge Cres. B37: K'hrst 1A 34
Stonebridge Highway CV3: Cov, W'hall 4C 68
Stonebridge Ind. Est. CV3: W'hall 5H 69
Stonebridge La. CV47: Bas 2A 106
Stonebridge Rd. B46: Col 5F 25
(not continuous)
CV33: L Hth 1K 119
Stonebridge Trad. Est. CV3: W'hall 4H 69
Stonebrook Way CV6: Longf 3F 51
Stonebury Av. CV5: E Grn 3B 56
Stonechat Rd. CV23: Brow 6K 65
Stonecross B46: Wat O 1B 24
Stonefield Cl. CV2: W'grve S 6C 52
STONEHALL 3A 142
Stonehall Rd. CV22: Caw 1A 86
Stonehaven Dr. CV3: Finh 5C 68
Stonehills CV21: Brow 1J 75
Stonehouse Cl. CV32: Cubb 2H 99
Stone Ho. Ct. CV23: Lilb 2J 77
Stonehouse La. CV3: W'hall 4J 69
CV7: Cor 7D 38
CV7: Gun H 5B 28
Stone Ho. M. CV35: Leek W 1H 97
STONELEIGH 3B 80 (1A 144)
Stoneleigh Abbey 6K 79
Stoneleigh Av. CV5: Cov 1K 67
CV8: Ken 3E 78
Stoneleigh Cl. CV8: S'lgh 3B 80
CV10: Harts 1G 21
Stoneleigh Ct. CV11: Nun 1J 31
Stoneleigh Deer Pk. CV8: Stare 5E 80
Stoneleigh Deer Pk. Bus. Village CV8: Stare 5D 80
Stoneleigh Rd. CV4: Canly 6H 67
CV8: Bag 2E 80
CV8: Bubb 4F 81
CV8: Ken 3E 78
CV8: S'lgh 7B 80
CV8: S'lgh P 7B 80
CV32: B'dwn, Cubb 2D 98
Stone Mdw. CV7: Ker E 7A 40
STONEPITS 3B 142
Stone Pits Mdw. CV37: Wilm 5H 113
STONESFIELD 3C 147
Stoneton Cl. CV47: Sou 6J 107
Stoneway Gro. CV31: Lea S 2H 103
Stonewell Cres. CV11: Nun 4D 32
Stoney Ct. CV3: Bin 1C 70
STONEYDELPH 1A 10
STONEYGATE 1D 141
Stoney Rd. CV1: Cov 7H 135 (6C 58)
CV3: Cov 7H 135 (6C 58)
CV10: Nun 5B 22
STONEY STANTON 2B 140
Stoney Stanton Rd. CV1: Cov 1J 135 (3D 58)
CV6: Cov 3D 58
Stoneywood Rd. CV2: W'grve S 6B 52
STONNALL 1B 138
STONTON WYVILLE 2D 141
Stoop, The CV3: Bin 6D 60
STOUGHTON 1D 141
STOULTON 3A 142
STOURBRIDGE 3A 138
Stour Ct. CV36: Ship S 5H 131
Stourhead Rd. CV22: Bil 6E 74
STOURTON
Shipston-on-Stour 6H 133 (2B 146)
Stourbridge 3A 138
Stour Vw. CV36: Half 3K 127
STOWE 1C 139
Stowe Dr. CV22: Bil 6E 74
CV47: Sou 6H 107
Stowe Pl. CV4: Tile H 6A 56
STOW-ON-THE-WOLD 3A 146
Strachey Av. CV32: Lea S 5C 98
Stradey Cl. CV3: Bin 6D 60
Straight Mile CV23: Bour D 6D 84
Stratford Av. CV9: Ath 4B 16
Stratford Boat Club 6J 137 (5F 115)
Stratford Brass Rubbing Cen. 7G 137 (5F 115)
Stratford Butterfly & Jungle Safari 6K 137 (5G 115)
Stratford Community Sports Cen. 4C 114
Stratford Ct. CV37: S Avon 3G 115
Stratford Leisure Cen. 2K 137 (4G 115)
Stratford Northern By-Pass CV37: B'ton, Dray 3A 114
Stratford Picture House 3E 136 (4E 114)
Stratford Rd. B49: Alc, Ove G 5B 112
B50: Bidf A 5J 123
B95: Hen A, Woot W 4G 93 & 4H 93
CV34: Warw 6D 100
CV35: H Lucy 2A 118
CV35: Lox 4B 116
CV35: Sher 7A 100
CV35: Welle 2F 117
CV36: Ilm 4C 126
CV36: Ship S 4H 131
CV37: Ett 1B 126
CV37: N'bld S 1G 127
Stratford Shire Horse Cen. 3D 143
Stratford St. CV2: Cov 3G 59
CV11: Nun 7D 22
STRATFORD-UPON-AVON 4G 137 (3D 143)
Stratford-upon-Avon Station (Rail) 1A 136 (4D 114)
Stratford-upon-Avon Steeplechase Course 7C 114
Strath Cl. CV21: Hillm 2C 88
Strathearn Rd. CV32: Lea S 6C 98
Strathmore Av. CV1: Cov 5E 58
Stratton St. CV9: Ath 3D 16
Strawberry Flds. CV7: Mer 5D 46
Strawberry Wlk. CV2: Cov 4K 51
Streamside Cl. CV5: Alle 6E 48
STREET ASHTON 5H 55
STREETHAY 1C 139
STREETLY 2B 138
STRETTON 1A 138
Stretton Av. CV3: W'hall 3J 69
Stretton Cl. GL56: Stret O 1A 132
Stretton Ct. CV21: Brow 1K 75
Stretton Cres. CV31: Lea S 3F 103
STRETTON EN LE FIELD 1A 140
Stretton Lodge CV3: W'hall 2J 69
STRETTON-ON-DUNSMORE 3H 83 (1B 144)
STRETTON-ON-FOSSE 2C 132 (2B 146)
Stretton Rd. CV8: Wols 2J 83
CV10: Nun 1G 31
STRETTON UNDER FOSSE 7F 55 (3B 140)
Stroma Way CV10: Nun 2F 31
Stuart Cl. CV34: Warw 3F 101
Stuart Ct. CV6: Cov 6G 51
CV32: Lea S 6C 98
Stuart Gdns. CV47: Temp H 2A 120
Stuart Ho. B46: Col 5G 25
Stubbs Cl. CV12: Bed 1G 41
Stubbs Gro. CV2: Cov 2H 59
Studland Av. CV21: Hillm 7B 76
Studland Grn. CV2: W'grve S 3C 60
STUDLEY 3D 92 (2B 142)
Studley Rd. B98: Redd 1B 92
Studley Swimming Pool 3D 92
Sturley Cl. CV8: Ken 3F 79
Sturminster Cl. CV2: W'grve S 3C 60
Stylers Way B95: Hen A 2H 93
Styles Cl. CV31: Lea S 1E 102
CV35: H Mag 1B 100
Styvechale Av. CV5: Cov 7K 57
SUCKLE GREEN 7F 11
Sudbury Cl. CV32: Lill 5G 99
Sudeley Rd. CV10: Nun 4J 31
Suffolk Cl. CV5: E Grn 4F 57
CV10: Nun 1E 30
CV12: Bed 2G 41
Suffolk St. CV32: Lea S 6E 98
SULGRAVE 1D 147
Sulgrave Cl. CV2: Cov 7A 52
Sullivan Ct. CV6: Cov 7H 51
Sullivan Rd. CV6: Cov 7H 51
Summer Ct. CV37: S Avon 1G 137
SUMMER HILL 2A 138
Summerton Rd. CV31: W'nsh 5E 102

Sumner Cl. CV35: H Mag 2B 100
Sumner Rd. B46: Col 6G 25
Sunart Way CV10: Nun 6H 21
Sunbeam Cl. B36: Cas B 3A 24
CV21: Rugby 5J 75
Sunbridge Ter. CV21: Rugby 5J 75
Sunbury Rd. CV3: W'hall 3J 69
Suncliffe Dr. CV8: Ken 7D 78
Sunderland Pl. CV35: Welle 5G 117
Sundew St. CV2: Cov 4K 51
Sundorne Cl. CV5: E Grn 3E 56
Sunfields Cl. B78: Pole 2E 10
Sunflower Dr. CV10: Nun 4G 31
Sunningdale Av. CV6: Cov 4D 50
CV8: Ken 5F 79
Sunningdale Cl. CV11: Nun 3C 32
Sunnybank Av. CV3: W'hall 3H 69
Sunnyside B95: Aston C 1K 113
Sunnyside Cl. CV5: Cov 4K 57
Sunnyside Ct. CV10: Nun 1F 31
Sunset Cl. B78: Pole 2D 10
Sunshine Cl. CV8: Ken 7E 78
Sunshine Cotts. CV37: Shot 5C 114
Sun St. CV21: Rugby 5J 75
Sunway Gro. CV3: Cov 2B 68
Surrey Cl. CV10: Nun 1E 30
Surrey Ct. CV34: Warw 7G 97
Sussex Cl. CV10: Nun 1E 30
Sussex Ct. CV34: Warw 7G 97
Sussex Rd. CV5: Cov 3K 57
Sutcliffe Dr. CV33: Har 6G 109
Sutherland Av. CV5: E Grn 3E 56
Sutherland Cl. CV34: Warw 6G 97
Sutherland Dr. CV12: Bed 1G 41
Sutton Av. CV5: E Grn 2A 56
SUTTON CHENEY 1B 140
SUTTON COLDFIELD 2C 139
Sutton Ho. CV22: Bil 7C 74
SUTTON IN THE ELMS 2C 141
Sutton La. OX15: Lwr Bra 4G 133
Sutton Pk. CV10: Nun 4G 21
Sutton Stop CV6: Longf 1H 51
SUTTON-UNDER-BRAILES 5H 133 (2C 147)
Swadling St. CV31: Lea S 2D 102
Swain Crofts CV31: Lea S 2F 103
SWALCLIFFE 2C 147
Swaledale CV4: Canly 2H 67
Swallow Av. B36: Cas B 4A 24
Swallow Cl. CV37: S Avon 2F 115
Swallow Ct. CV12: Bed 5C 40
Swallowdean Rd. CV6: Cov 6J 49
Swallowgate Bus. Pk. CV6: Cov 5C 50
Swallow Rd. CV6: Cov 5B 50
Swanage Grn. CV2: W'grve S 3C 60
Swan Bus. Pk., The CV37: S Avon 3D 114
Swan Ct. CV37: S Avon 5G 115
Swan Cft. Rd. CV2: Cov 2F 59
Swanfold CV37: Wilm 5J 113
Swan La. CV2: Cov 3F 59
Swans Cl. CV37: Wilm 5J 113
Swan's Nest La. CV37: S Avon 6K 137 (5G 115)
Swan St. B49: Alc 5B 112
CV32: Lea S 6E 98
CV34: Warw 2G 101
Swanswell St. CV1: Cov 1K 135 (3D 58)
Swanswood Gro. B37: Chel W 2C 34
Swan Theatre 6H 137
SWEPSTONE 1A 140
SWERFORD 2C 147
Swift Cl. B36: Cas B 4A 24
CV8: Ken 7E 78
Swift Pk. CV21: Rugby 1G 75
(not continuous)
Swift Point CV21: Rugby 6F 65
Swift Rd. CV37: S Avon 2F 115
Swift's Cnr. CV3: Cov 7E 58
Swift Valley Ind. Est. CV21: Rugby 7F 65
Swillington Rd. CV6: Cov 2B 58
Swinburne Av. CV2: Cov 5K 59
Swinburne Cl. CV10: Gall C 6F 21
Swindale Cft. CV3: Bin 7B 60
SWINDON 2A 138
SWINFORD 1C 145
Swithin's Dr. CV37: Lwr Q 5H 125
SWITHLAND 1C 141
Sycamore Av. B78: Pole 2D 10
Sycamore Cl. CV35: Welle 3J 117
CV37: S Avon 2E 114
CV47: S'ton 6B 106
Sycamore Ct. CV5: Alle 7D 48
CV35: Lit K 7C 120
Sycamore Cres. B37: Mars G 5A 34
CV7: New A 4F 29
Sycamore Gro. CV21: Rugby 4G 75
CV34: Warw 6J 97
CV47: Sou 3H 107
Sycamore Rd. B78: K'bry 4D 12
CV2: Cov 4H 51
CV10: Nun 5J 21
Sycamores, The CV12: Bed 3E 40
SYDENHAM 2G 103
Sydenham Dr. CV31: Lea S 2F 103
Sydenham Ind. Est. CV31: Lea S 2F 103
(Longfield Rd.)
CV31: Lea S 2F 103
(St Mary's Rd.)
Sydenham Sports Cen. 3G 103
Sydnall Flds. CV6: Longf 2F 51
Sydnall Rd. CV6: Longf 2F 51
Sydney Ct. CV12: Bed 3G 41
Sylan Ct. OX17: Farn 6J 121
Sylvan Dr. CV3: Cov 2K 67
Synkere Cl. CV7: Ker E 7A 40
SYSTON 1D 141
Sywell Leys CV22: Rugby 3F 87

T

Tachbrook Cl. CV2: Cov 4J 51
Tachbrook Ct. CV31: Lea S 2D 102
TACHBROOK MALLORY 7D 102 (2A 144)
Tachbrook Pk. Bus. Cen. CV34: Warw 3C 102
Tachbrook Pk. Dr. CV34: Warw 2B 102
Tachbrook Rd. CV31: Lea S, W'nsh 5D 102
Tachbrook St. CV31: Lea S 3D 102
(not continuous)
Tackford Rd. CV6: Cov 7G 51
TACKLEY 3D 147
TADDINGTON 2A 146
TADMARTON 2C 147
Tailor's La. CV37: Up Qui 7F 125
Tainters Hill CV8: Ken 3D 78
Talbot Ct. CV32: Lea S 6E 98
CV35: Welle 3J 117
Talbot Rd. CV37: S Avon 3F 115
Talisman Cl. CV8: Ken 6D 78
Talisman Sq. CV8: Ken 5D 78
Talisman Theatre 6D 78
Talland Av. CV6: Cov 1G 59
Tallants Cl. CV6: Cov 6G 51
Tallants Rd. CV6: Cov 6F 51
Tamar Cl. CV12: Bulk 2D 42
CV23: Long L 3B 74
Tamar Dr. B36: Cas B 4A 24
Tamar Rd. CV12: Bulk 3C 42
Tame Bank B78: K'bry 5D 12
Tamora Cl. CV34: H'cte 5B 102
TAMWORTH 1D 139
Tamworth Rd. B46: Neth W, Over W 1F 27
B46: Over W 3H 27
B76: Wis 1C 18
B77: Dost 2D 12
B78: Cliff, K'bry 2D 12
B78: Pole 1A 10
CV6: Cov 4E 38
CV7: Cor, Ker E 4E 38
(not continuous)
CV7: Fill, Old A 3H 27
CV9: Wood E 2K 13
Tamworth Sailing Club 7C 12
Tancred Cl. CV31: Lea S 3D 102
Tankards Hill GL56: Stret O 1A 132
TANNERS GREEN 1B 142
Tanners Gro. CV6: Longf 2D 50
Tanner's La. CV4: Tile H 6A 56
CV7: Berk, Tile H 6A 56
Tannery, The CV36: Ship S 4G 131
Tannery Cl. CV9: Ath 3D 16
Tannery Ct. CV8: Ken 5D 78
Tanser Ct. CV22: Dunc 6C 86
TANWORTH-IN-ARDEN 3D 90 (1C 143)
Tanyard, The B95: Hen A 1H 93
Tanyard Cl. CV4: Tile H 6B 56
Tapcon Way CV2: Cov 2B 60
Tappinger Gro. CV8: Ken 4G 79
TARDEBIGGE 2B 142
Tarlington Rd. CV6: Cov 1J 57
Tarn Cl. CV12: Bed 3G 41
Tarquin Cl. CV3: W'hall 1K 69
Tarragon Cl. CV2: Cov 5K 51
Tarrant Wlk. CV2: W'grve S 2C 60
Tasker's Way CV37: S Avon 4F 137 (5F 115)
TASTON 3C 147
Tatnall Gro. CV34: Warw 7G 97
TATTLE BANK 4B 94 (2C 143)
Tattle Bank CV47: Sou 6H 107
Taunton Way CV6: Cov 4A 50
Taverners La. CV9: Ath 4C 16
Tavern La. CV37: Shot 5C 114
Tavistock St. CV32: Lea S 6D 98
Tavistock Wlk. CV2: Cov 7J 51
Tavistock Way CV11: Nun 6F 23
Tay Cft. B37: F'bri 1C 34
Taylor Av. CV32: Lill 5F 99
Taylor Cl. CV8: Ken 3F 79
Taylor Ct. CV34: Warw 1F 101
Tay Rd. CV6: Cov 1B 58
Teachers Cl. CV6: Cov 2A 58
Tea Gdn., The CV12: Bed 5E 40
Teal Cl. CV37: B'ton 2B 114
Teal Rd. B80: Stud 3D 92
Teasel Cl. CV23: Brow 7K 65
Teddy Bear Mus., The 3D 136 (4E 114)
Ted Pitts La. CV5: Alle 4F 49
TEETON 1D 145
Telegraph St. CV36: Ship S 4H 131
Telephone Rd. CV3: Cov 5J 59
Telfer Rd. CV6: Cov 7B 50
Telford Av. CV32: Lill 2F 99
Telford Rd. CV7: Exh 5J 41
Templar Av. CV4: Tile H 6E 56
Templar Ind. Pk. CV4: Tile H 7F 57
Templars, The CV34: Warw 3H 101
Templars' Flds. CV4: Canly 1F 67
TEMPLE BALSALL 1D 143
Temple Ct. B46: Col 3F 25
Temple End CV33: Har 6F 109
TEMPLE GRAFTON 3C 143
Temple Gro. CV34: Warw 3F 101
TEMPLE GUITING 3A 146
TEMPLE HERDEWYKE 2A 120
Temple Hill LE10: Wlvy 1J 33
Templer Ct. CV11: Nun 1J 31
Temple St. CV21: Rugby 6J 75
Temple Way B46: Col 3E 24
Ten Acres B49: Alc 4C 112
Tenby Cl. CV12: Bed 4C 40
Teneriffe Rd. CV6: Cov 5F 51
Tenlons Rd. CV10: Nun 2F 31
Tenlons Rd. Ind. Est. CV10: Nun 2F 31
Tennant Cl. CV21: Hillm 7A 76
Tennant St. CV11: Nun 1A 32
Tennyson Av. CV22: Rugby 2E 86
CV34: Warw 4E 100
Tennyson Cl. CV8: Ken 5G 79
Tennyson Rd. CV2: Cov 4J 59
CV37: S Avon 7G 115
Ten Shilling Dr. CV4: W'wd H 2B 66
Tenter St. CV9: Ath 3C 16
Terrace, The CV35: More M 5C 118
CV37: Snitt 6G 95
CV37: Welf A 3B 124
Terrace Rd. CV9: Ath 3C 16
Terrett Ct. CV37: S Avon 4F 137 (5F 115)
Terry Av. CV32: Lea S 6A 98
Terry Rd. CV1: Cov 5F 59
TERRY'S GREEN 1C 143
TETTENHALL 2A 138
Tewkesbury Dr. CV12: Bed 2J 41
Thackeray Cl. CV10: Gall C 7F 21
CV22: Rugby 2F 87
CV37: Lwr Q 5G 125
Thackhall St. CV2: Cov 3F 59
Thames Cl. CV12: Bulk 2C 42
Thamley Rd. CV6: Cov 3A 58
Thane Cl. B80: Stud 3D 92
Thatchings, The CV22: Dunc 6C 86
Theatre St. CV34: Warw 2F 101
Thebes Cl. CV5: Mil W 6K 47
THEDDINGWORTH 3D 141
Theddingworth Cl. CV3: Bin 7A 60
THENFORD 1D 147
Thickthorn Cl. CV8: Ken 6F 79
Thickthorn M. CV8: Ken 7F 79
Thickthorn Orchards CV8: Ken 7F 79
Thimbler Rd. CV4: Canly 1G 67
Third Exhibition Av. B40: Nat E C 2D 44
Thirlestane Cl. CV8: Ken 3G 79
Thirlmere CV21: Brow 1J 75
Thirlmere Av. CV11: Nun 5G 23
Thirlmere Cl. CV4: Tile H 4C 56
Thirlmere Rd. CV12: Bed 3G 41
Thirsk Rd. CV3: Cov 3C 68
Thistle Way CV23: Brow 7K 65
Thistley Fld. E. CV6: Cov 1K 57
Thistley Fld. Nth. CV6: Cov 7A 50
Thistley Fld. Sth. CV6: Cov 1K 57
Thistley Fld. W. CV6: Cov 1K 57
Thomas King Ho. *CV1: Cov* *3E 58*
(off Wellington St.)
Thomas Landsdail St. CV3: Cov 7J 135 (6D 58)
Thomas La. St. CV6: Cov 5G 51
Thomas Naul Cft. CV4: Tile H 4D 56
Thomas Sharp St. CV4: Tile H 1E 66
Thomas St. CV12: Bed 3G 41
CV32: Lea S 6E 98
THOMAS TOWN 4D 92
Thomas Way CV23: Long L 3A 74
Thompsons Rd. CV7: Ker E 7J 39
Thomson Cl. CV21: Rugby 2H 75
Thoresby Pl. CV22: Caw 1K 85
THORNBY 1D 145
Thornby Av. CV8: Ken 6E 78
Thorncliffe Way CV10: Ans C 3D 20
Thorn Cl. CV21: Brow 2J 75
Thorney Rd. CV2: Cov 1H 59
Thornhill Dr. CV11: Nun 4D 32
Thornhill Rd. CV1: Cov 2D 58
Thornley Cl. CV31: Rad S 3K 103
Thorn Stile Cl. CV32: Cubb 1J 99
THORNTON 1B 140
Thornton Cl. CV5: E Grn 3A 56
CV34: Warw 6H 97
Thornton Ct. CV4: Tile H 5F 57
Thornton Ho. *CV32: Lea S* *5D 98*
(off Kenilworth Rd.)
Thorntons Lanes CV47: Nap 3H 111
Thorntons Way CV10: Nun 1A 30
Thorn Way CV47: Long I 2C 106
THORPE CONSTANTINE 1A 6 (1D 139)
THORPE LANGTON 2D 141
THORPE MANDEVILLE 1D 147
THORPE SATCHVILLE 1D 141
Threadneedle St. CV1: Cov 1D 58
Three Cornered Cl. CV32: Cubb 1J 99
Three Spires Av. CV6: Cov 2A 58
Three Spires Ind. Est. CV6: Longf 1G 51
Three Spires Junc. CV6: Cov 5E 50
THROCKMORTON 3A 142
Throckmorton Rd. B49: Alc 4D 112
Thruppence Cl. CV4: W'wd H, ... 2C 66
THURCASTON 1C 141
THURLASTON
Leicester 2C 141
Rugby 6K 85 (1B 144)
Thurlaston Dr. CV22: Dunc 3A 86
Thurlestone Rd. CV6: Cov 6K 49
Thurlow Cl. CV9: Ath 1C 16
THURMASTON 1D 141
Thurmaston Ct. CV32: Lea S 5D 98
THURNBY 1D 141
Thurnmill Rd. CV23: Long L 4C 74
Thursfield Rd. CV32: Lill 4F 99
TIBBERTON 3A 142
Tibbets Cl. B49: Alc 4C 112
Tibbits Ct. CV34: Warw 2G 101
Tiber Cl. CV5: E Grn 3D 56
Tiberius Cl. B46: Col 3F 25

Tiber Way CV21: Rugby 1F **75**
TIDBURY GREEN 1C 143
TIDDINGTON 3K 115 (3D 143)
Tiddington Ct. CV37: Tidd 3K **115**
Tiddington Rd. CV37: S Avon, Tidd 5G **115**
Tideswell Cl. CV3: Bin 6C **60**
Tidmarsh Rd. CV35: Leek W 1J **97**
TIDMINGTON 2B 146
Tidmington Cl. CV35: Hatt 5A **96**
TIFFIELD 3D 145
TILE CROSS 3C 139
Tile Gro. B37: K'hrst 7A **24**
TILE HILL 6B 56 (1D 143)
Tile Hill La. CV4: Cov 5G **57**
CV4: Tile H 6B **56**
Tile Hill Station (Rail) 7B 56
Tilehill Wood Nature Reserve 4B 56
Tilehurst Dr. CV4: Tile H 5B **56**
Tilemans La. CV36: Ship S 3G **131**
Tilewood Av. CV5: E Grn 3C **56**
TILTON ON THE HILL 1D 141
Timber Ct. CV22: Rugby 6J **75**
Timon Vw. CV34: H'cte 5C **102**
Timothy Gro. CV4: Tile H 6F **57**
Timothy's Bri. Rd. CV37: S Avon 2C **114**
Timothy's Bri. Rd. Ind. Est. CV37: S Avon 3C **114**
Tink a Tank CV35: Leek W 1H **97**
Tink-a-Tank CV34: Warw 2G **101**
Tintagel Cl. CV3: W'hall 3K **69**
Tintagel Gro. CV8: Ken 5F **79**
Tintagel Way CV11: Nun 6H **23**
Tintern Way CV12: Bed 3J **41**
TIPPER'S HILL 6D 28
Tipper's Hill La. CV7: Fill 6B **28**
Tippett Cl. CV11: Nun 5C **32**
TIPTON 2A 138
Tisdale Ri. CV8: Ken 3F **79**
Titan Bus. Cen. CV34: Warw 4C **102**
Tithe Barn Cl. CV35: H Mag 1B **100**
Tithe Barn La. B94: H'ley H 1E **90**
Tiverton Dr. CV11: Nun 6F **23**
Tiverton Gro. CV2: Cov 2K **59**
Tiverton Rd. CV2: Cov 2K **59**
Tiveycourt Rd. CV6: Cov 3G **51**
Tocil Cft. CV4: Canly 3H **67**
Tocil Wood Nature Reserve 5G 67
TODENHAM 5A 132 (2B 146)
Todenham Way CV35: Hatt 4A **96**
TOFT 7B 86
Toler Rd. CV11: Nun 6C **22**
TOLLADINE 3A 142
Tollard Cl. CV2: W'grve S 2B **60**
TOLLBAR END 4J 69
Toll Ga. Cl. CV37: S Avon 4A **114**
Toll Ga. Rd. CV47: Sou 4H **107**
Tom Brown St. CV21: Rugby 4H **75**
Tom Ellis Ct. CV7: Exh 5F **41**
Tom Henderson Cl. CV3: Bin 1B **70**
TOM HILL 1E 90
Tom Hill B94: Tan A 3D **90**
Tomkinson Rd. CV10: Nun 7K **21**
Tommy's Turn La. OX15: Up Bra 4G **133**
Tomson Av. CV6: Cov 2B **58**
Toms Town La. B80: Stud 4D **92**
Tom Ward Cl. CV3: Bin 1A **70**
Tomwell Cl. CV47: Sou 4H **107**
Tonbridge Rd. CV3: Cov 2G **69**
Topp's Dr. CV12: Bed 4E **40**
Topp's Heath CV12: Bed 4E **40**
Top Rd. CV7: Barn 5C **42**
Top St. CV47: N'end 1D **120**
Torbay Rd. CV5: Cov 3G **57**
Torcastle Cl. CV6: Cov 7F **51**
Torcross Av. CV2: Cov 2J **59**
Torpoint Cl. CV2: Cov 7J **51**
Torrance Rd. CV21: Rugby 5F **75**
Torres Cl. CV34: Warw 4D **100**
Torrington Av. CV4: Tile H 7B **56**
Torwood Cl. CV4: W'wd H 2D **66**
Totnes Cl. CV2: Cov 7J **51**
Touchstone Rd. CV34: H'cte 6C **102**
Tourist Info. Cen.
Birmingham International 2D 44
Coventry 4J 135 (5D 58)
Kenilworth 5D 78
Nuneaton 7D 22
Royal Leamington Spa 7D 98
Rugby 5G 75
Stratford-upon-Avon 4J 137 (4F 115)
Warwick 2G 101
Tove Ct. CV23: Long L 3B **74**
TOWCESTER 3D 145
Tower Cl. B50: Bidf A 6H **123**
CV37: S Avon 2F **115**
Tower Cft. B37: F'bri 1B **34**
B50: Bidf A 5H **123**
Tower Furlong CV23: Brow 6K **65**
Tower Hill B50: Bidf A 6G **123**
Tower Rd. CV12: Bed 3G **41**
CV22: Rugby 7J **75**
Towers Cl. CV8: Ken 7D **78**
Tower St. CV1: Cov 2H **135** (4C **58**)
CV31: Lea S 1E **102**
Tower Vw. Cres. CV10: Nun 1B **30**
Townesend Cl. CV34: Warw 6H **97**
Townfields Cl. CV5: Alle 7F **49**
Town Hill OX15: Ratl 7D **128**
Townsend Cl. B79: Newt R 4D **6**
CV23: Chu L 3F **73**
Townsend Cft. CV3: Cov 1C **68**
Townsend Dr. CV11: Nun 2B **32**
Townsend La. CV23: Long L 3A **74**
Townsend Rd. CV3: Cov 7C **58**
Townsend Rd. CV21: Rugby 5K **75**
CV37: Tidd 4K **115**
Townsends Cl. CV11: Burt H 3J **33**
Townshend Gro. B37: K'hrst 1A **34**
Town Sq. CV37: S Avon 4F **137**
Town Yd. CV23: Brin 3D **62**
Towpath Cl. CV6: Longf 7H **41**
Trafalgar Ct. B50: Bidf A 6G **123**
Trafalgar Ho. *CV1: Cov* *5B 58*
(off Windsor St.)
Trafford Cl. CV9: Ath 1C **16**
Trafford Dr. CV10: Nun 6H **21**
Trajan Hill B46: Col 3F **25**
Tramway Ct. CV37: S Avon 5G **115**
Travellers Way B37: Chel W 2D **34**
Tredford M. CV32: Lea S 6E **98**
TREDINGTON 6J 127 (1B 146)
Tredington Cl. B98: Redd 1A **92**
Tredington Pk. CV35: Hatt 5A **96**
Tredington Rd. CV5: E Grn 3D **56**
Treedale Cl. CV4: Tile H 7B **56**
Treforest Rd. CV3: Cov 7J **59**
Tregorrick Rd. CV7: Exh 6G **41**
Tregullan Rd. CV7: Exh 5H **41**
Treherne Rd. CV6: Cov 6B **50**
Trelawney Rd. CV7: Exh 6G **41**
Tremelling Way CV7: Gun H 4D **28**
Trenance Rd. CV7: Exh 6G **41**
Treneere Rd. CV7: Exh 5H **41**
Trensale Av. CV6: Cov 3K **57**
Trentham Cl. CV11: Nun 4B **32**
Trentham Gdns. CV8: Ken 4G **79**
Trentham Rd. CV1: Cov 3F **59**
CV10: Harts 1F **21**
Trent Rd. CV11: Nun 6E **22**
CV12: Bulk 3C **42**
TRESCOTT 2A 138
Tresillian Rd. CV7: Exh 5H **41**
Tressel Cft. CV34: H'cte 6C **102**
Trevelyan Cl. CV35: Clav 2D **94**
CV37: S Avon 3B **114**
(not continuous)
Trevelyan Cres. CV37: S Avon 3B **114**
Trevelyan Ho. B37: Chel W 4C **34**
Treviscoe Cl. CV7: Exh 6G **41**
Trevor Cl. CV4: Tile H 7B **56**
Trevor White Dr. CV22: Rugby 7H **75**
Trevose Av. CV7: Exh 6H **41**
Trewint Cl. CV7: Exh 5G **41**
TRIANGLE 1B 138
Triangle, The CV5: Cov 3F **57**
Tribune Trad. Est. CV21: Rugby 2G **75**
Trident Bus. Pk. CV11: Nun 1K **31**
Trident Ct. B37: Mars G 5E **34**
Trident Pk. CV34: Warw 4D **102**
Trident Rd. B26: Birm A 2C **44**
Trimpley Rd. CV6: Cov 1C **58**
Trinculo Gro. CV34: H'cte 6C **102**
Trinity Chyd. CV1: Cov 3H **135**
Trinity Cl. B79: Wart 5H **9**
CV37: S Avon 6F **115**
Trinity Coll. CV37: S Avon 6E **136**
Trinity Ct. CV21: Rugby 5H **75**
Trinity La. CV1: Cov 3H **135** (4C **58**)
Trinity M. CV34: Warw 1H **101**
Trinity Pk. B37: Mars G 3D **44**
Trinity Pl. CV37: S Avon 7E **136** (5E **114**)
Trinity Rd. B78: Frly, Picc 5A **10**
B78: K'bry, Picc 5E **12**
Trinity St. CV1: Cov 3H **135** (4C **58**)
CV32: Lea S 6D **98**
CV37: S Avon 6E **114**
Trinity Wlk. CV11: Nun 1A **32**
Trinity Way CV37: S Avon 7G **115**
Triton Pk. CV21: Rugby 7F **65**
Triton Way CV11: Nun 3J **31**
Triumph Cl. CV2: Cov 4A **60**
Triumph Ho. CV1: Cov 5H **135**
Triumph Wlk. B36: Cas B 3A **24**
Troilus Ct. CV34: H'cte 5D **102**
Trojan Bus. Cen. CV34: Warw 4C **102**
Trossachs Rd. CV5: E Grn 4D **56**
Troubridge Wlk. CV22: Bil 6C **74**
Troughton Cres. CV6: Cov 2A **58**
Troutbeck Av. CV32: Lea S 5A **98**
Troutbeck Rd. CV5: E Grn 3D **56**
Troy Bus. Pk. B96: Sam 4A **92**
Troyes Cl. CV3: Cov 1D **68**
Trueman Cl. CV34: Warw 7G **97**
Truro Cl. CV11: Nun 6G **23**
Truro Wlk. B37: Chel W 3A **34**
Trussell Way CV22: Caw 1A **86**
Trust Cotts. B96: Sam 7A **92**
Trusteel Ho's. CV23: C'over 2J **65**
Tryan Rd. CV10: Nun 7K **21**
TRYSULL 2A 138
Tuckwell Cl. CV47: S'ton 6B **106**
Tudor Av. CV5: E Grn 4D **56**
Tudor Ct. B95: Hen A 2H **93**
CV3: Cov 7G **135** (7C **58**)
CV7: Exh 6E **40**
CV34: Warw 3F **101**
Tudor Cres. CV9: Ath 2C **16**
Tudor Cft. B37: F'bri 4A **34**
Tudor La. CV47: Sou 6H **107**
Tudor Rd. CV10: Nun 5H **21**
Tulip Tree Av. CV8: Ken 4F **79**
Tulip Tree Ct. CV8: Ken 5F **79**
Tulip Wlk. B37: Chel W 5C **34**
Tulliver Cl. CV12: Bed 1H **41**
Tulliver Rd. CV10: Nun 4J **31**
Tulliver St. CV6: Cov 2B **58**
Tunnel Rd. CV10: Ansl 1G **29**
Turberville Pl. CV34: Warw 1F **101**
Turchil Rd. CV22: Caw 1A **86**
Turchil Wlk. CV22: Caw 1A **86**
TURKDEAN 3A 146
Turlands Cl. CV2: W'grve S 7C **52**
TUR LANGTON 2D 141
Turnberry Dr. CV11: Nun 4E **32**
Turner Cl. CV12: Bed 1G **41**
CV21: Hillm 1D **88**
CV34: Warw 4D **100**
Turner Rd. CV5: Cov 4H **57**
Turnpike Dr. B46: Wat O 1C **24**
CV37: Lwr Q 5H **125**
Turnstone Cl. CV23: Brow 7J **65**
Turpin Ct. CV31: Lea S 2D **102**
Turpin Ho. *CV21: Brow* *1J 75*
(off Dovedale Cl.)
Turton Way CV8: Ken 5G **79**
TURVES GREEN 1B 142
Tutbury Av. CV4: Canly 2J **67**
Tutbury La. CV23: Bret, Brin 1B **72**
Tuthill Furlong CV23: Brow 6K **65**
TUTNALL 1A 142
Tuttle Hill CV10: Nun 4K **21**
Tuttle Hill Ind. Est. CV10: Nun 4K **21**
Twelve O'Clock Ride CV3: Bin, Bin W 5G **61**
Twenty One Oaks CV9: Ath 5H **15**
Twickenham Way CV3: Bin 6D **60**
TWO GATES 1D 139
Two Pike Leys CV23: Brow 7K **65**
TWYCROSS 1A 140
Twycross Wlk. CV34: Warw 6F **97**
TWYFORD 1D 141
Tybalt Cl. CV3: W'hall 3J **69**
CV34: H'cte 4B **102**
TYBURN 2C 139
Tyler St. CV37: S Avon 2G **137** (4F **115**)
Tylney Cl. CV3: Bin 5D **60**
Tyne Cl. B37: F'bri 1B **34**
Tynemouth Cl. CV2: Ald G 1K **51**
Tynward Cl. CV3: Cov 3B **68**
Tysoe Cft. CV3: Bin 7B **60**
Tysoe Rd. CV35: Lit K 7C **120**
CV35: Oxh 2E **130** & 5A **130**
CV35: Rad 6A **128**
Tythbarn Leys CV23: Brow 7K **65**
Tything Rd. B49: Kinw 2C **112**

U

UFTON 2F 109 (2A 144)
Ufton Cft. CV5: E Grn 4E **56**
Ufton Fields Nature Reserve 3G 109
Ufton Hill CV33: Ufton 2F **109**
ULLENHALL 6B 90 (2C 143)
Ullenhall La. B95: Oldb, Ullen 5A **90**
Ullenhall St. B95: Ullen 5B **90**
ULLESTHORPE 3C 141
Ullswater Av. CV11: Nun 5G **23**
CV32: Lea S 5A **98**
Ullswater Rd. CV3: Bin 6A **60**
CV12: Bed 3G **41**
Ulverscroft Rd. CV3: Cov 1C **68**
Ulverston CV21: Brow 1K **75**
Umberslade Children's Farm 1C 143
Underhill Cl. CV3: Finh 5D **68**
Underpass, The B40: Nat E C 2D **44**
Unicorn Av. CV5: E Grn 3C **56**
Unicorn La. CV5: E Grn 3D **56**
(not continuous)
Union Bldgs. CV1: Cov 5H **135** (5C **58**)
Union Ct. *CV31: Lea S* *2E 102*
(off Ranelagh Ter.)
Union Pl. CV6: Longf 1F **51**
Union Rd. CV32: Lea S 6C **98**
Union St. CV22: Rugby 6G **75**
CV37: S Avon 3G **137** (4F **115**)
Union Wlk. CV31: Lea S 1E **102**
Unity Ho. CV1: Cov 1K **135**
University of Birmingham
Shakespeare Institute 6D 136
University of Warwick
Gibbet Hill Campus 4H 67
Kirby Cnr. Rd. 2F 67
University Rd. 3G 67
University of Warwick Science Pk. CV4: Canly 2F **67**
University Rd. CV4: Canly 3F **67**
Uplands CV2: Cov 2G **59**
Up. Abbey St. CV11: Nun 6C **22**
UPPER ASTROP 2D 147
UPPER BENTLEY 2A 142
UPPER BILLESLEY 7H 113
UPPER BODDINGTON 3B 144
UPPER BRAILES 1F 133 (2C 147)
Upper Cape CV34: Warw 7F **97**
UPPER CATESBY 3C 145
UPPER EASTERN GREEN 2B 56 (3D 139)
Up. Eastern Grn. La. CV5: E Grn 2A **56**
Up. Farm Gdns. CV35: Gay 6G **119**
Upperfield Way *CV3: Bin* *6C 60*
(off Middlefield Dr.)
Upper Gro. St. CV32: Lea S 6C **98**
UPPER HEYFORD
Bicester 3D 147
Northampton 3D 145
Up. Hill St. CV1: Cov 2F **135** (4B **58**)
CV32: Lea S 6E **98**
Up. Holly Wlk. CV32: Lea S 6E **98**
Up. Ladyes Hill CV8: Ken 3E **78**
UPPER LADYES HILLS 3E 78
Upper Mall *CV32: Lea S* *7D 98*
(in Royal Priors Shop. Cen.)

UPPER ODDINGTON 3B 146
Upper Pk. CV3: W'hall 3K 69
Upper Pct. CV1: Cov 3G 135 (4C 58)
UPPER QUINTON 7H 125 (1A 146)
Upper Ride CV3: W'hall 3K 69
Up. Rosemary Hill CV8: Ken 4D 78
UPPER SLAUGHTER 3A 146
Up. Spon St. CV1: Cov 4A 58
(not continuous)
Up. Spring La. CV8: Ken 2D 78
UPPER STOKE 3G 59
UPPER STOWE 3D 145
UPPER SWELL 3A 146
UPPER TYSOE 7C 130 (1C 147)
UPPER WARDINGTON 1D 147
UPPER WEEDON 3D 145
Up. Well St. CV1: Cov 2G 135 (4C 58)
Up. York St. CV1: Cov 6B 58
UPTON
Alcester 3C 143
Northampton 2D 145
Nuneaton 2A 140
Upton Dr. CV11: Nun 4B 32
Upton House 1C 147
Upton Rd. CV22: Rugby 5D 74
UPTON SNODSBURY 3A 142
UPTON WARREN 2A 142
Usk Way B36: Cas B 4A 24
Utrillo Cl. CV5: Cov 4G 57
Uxbridge Av. CV3: Cov 5J 59

V

Vale, The CV3: Cov 7H 59
Vale Cl. CV21: Hillm 1C 88
Valencia Rd. CV3: Bin 5C 60
Valenders La. CV36: Ilm 7C 126
Valentine Cl. CV37: S Avon 7D 114
Vale Vw. CV10: Nun 7K 21
Vallet Av. B49: Alc 3B 112
Valletta Way CV35: Welle 4G 117
Valley, The CV31: Rad S 4J 103
Valley Dr. CV21: Cosf 6F 65
CV21: Cosf, Rugby 7G 65
Valley Rd. CV2: Cov 1G 59
CV10: Gall C 7D 20
CV31: Rad S 4J 103
CV32: Lill 4F 99
Van Dyke Cl. CV5: Cov 4G 57
Vanguard Av. CV5: Cov 6G 57
Vanguard Cen. CV4: Canly 2G 67
Vanguard Rd. B26: Birm A 2C 44
Vardon Dr. CV3: Finh 4D 68
Vauxhall Cl. CV1: Cov 4E 58
Vauxhall Cres. B36: Cas B 3A 24
Vauxhall St. CV1: Cov 4E 58
Veasey Cl. CV11: Nun 1A 32
Vecqueray St. CV1: Cov 5E 58
Ventnor Cl. CV2: Cov 4A 60
Ventnor St. CV10: Nun 5E 22
Verbena Cl. CV2: Cov 5H 51
Verden Av. CV34: Warw 4D 100
Verdon Pl. CV35: Barf 2C 108
Verdun Cl. CV31: W'nsh 6F 103
Vere Rd. CV21: Hillm 7B 76
Vermont Gro. CV31: Lea S 2H 103
Verney Cl. CV35: Light 2G 119
Verney Dr. CV37: S Avon 2E 114
Verney Gdns. CV37: S Avon 2E 114
Verney Ho's. CV35: Lit K 7C 120
Verney Rd. CV33: L Hth 1K 119
Vernon Av. CV22: Hillm 1A 88
Vernon Cl. CV1: Cov 4E 58
CV32: Lea S 4C 98
Vernon Ct. CV1: Cov 4E 58
Vernons Ct. CV10: Nun 7K 21
Vernons La. CV10: Nun 7K 21
CV11: Nun 7K 21
Vernons M. CV10: Nun 7A 22
Verona Cl. CV11: Nun 3C 32
Vesey Cl. B46: Wat O 2B 24
Viaduct Cl. CV21: Rugby 4K 75
Vicarage Cl. B78: Dord 5C 10
CV9: Ath 4D 16
Vicarage Fld. CV34: Warw 7K 97
Vicarage Gdns. CV8: Ken 7E 78
Vicarage Hill B94: Tan A 2B 90
CV23: Clift D 4A 76
Vicarage La. B46: Wat O 2B 24
CV7: Ash G 6C 40
CV22: Dunc 6D 86
CV33: Har 6H 109
CV35: Sher 1A 108
CV36: Long C 2C 134
CV47: P Mars 5G 111
Vicarage Ri. CV33: Bis T 5C 108
Vicarage Rd. CV8: S'lgh 3B 80
CV22: Rugby 5F 75
CV32: Lill 4F 99
CV47: Nap 2J 111
Vicarage St. CV11: Nun 7E 22
Victor Hodges Ho. CV47: Sou 5H 107
Victoria Av. CV21: Rugby 4F 75
Victoria Bus. Cen. CV31: Lea S 1E 102
(off Neilston St.)
Victoria Bus. Pk. CV31: Lea S 1E 102
(off Neilston St.)
Victoria Cl. CV37: S Avon 1F 137 (4F 115)
Victoria Colonnade CV31: Lea S 1D 102
(off Victoria Ter.)
Victoria Ct. CV5: Cov 3H 57
Victoria M. CV3: Bin 5A 60
Victoria M. CV34: Warw 1F 101
Victoria Rd. B50: Bidf A 4F 123
CV9: Man 5E 16
CV10: Harts 3G 21
CV31: Lea S 7C 98
Victoria St. CV1: Cov 1K 135 (3E 58)
CV11: Nun 7D 22
CV21: Rugby 5E 74
CV31: Lea S 1C 102
CV34: Warw 1F 101
Victoria Ter. CV31: Lea S 1D 102
CV47: S'ton 6C 106
Victory Rd. CV6: Cov 6E 50
VIGO 1B 138
Villa Cl. CV12: Bulk 4D 42
Villa Cres. CV12: Bulk 4E 42
Village Hall Yd. CV47: Long I 2C 106
Village M. CV22: Bil 1D 86
Village Rd. OX17: Warm 2J 129
Villa Rd. CV6: Cov 1B 58
Villebon Way CV31: W'nsh 6E 102
Villiers Rd. CV8: Ken 4F 79
Villiers St. CV2: Cov 4G 59
CV11: Nun 1H 31
CV32: Lea S 6E 98
Vincent Av. CV37: S Avon 3E 114
Vincent Ct. CV37: S Avon 3F 115
Vincent St. CV1: Cov 5B 58
CV32: Lea S 6E 98
Vincent Wyles Ho. CV2: Cov 4A 60
Vinecote Rd. CV6: Longf 3F 51
Vine Cotts. CV35: H Lucy 2B 118
Vine La. CV34: Warw 7G 97
Vinery Ct. CV37: S Avon 5C 136 (5E 114)
Vine St. CV1: Cov 1K 135 (3E 58)
Violet Cl. CV2: Cov 3J 51
CV12: Bed 3E 40
CV23: Brow 7K 65
Virginia Pl. CV10: Nun 1E 30
Virginia Rd. CV1: Cov 4E 58
Viscount Cen. CV4: Canly 2G 67
Viscount Cl. CV31: Lea S 2D 102
Viscount Ho. B26: Birm A 2C 44
Vittle Dr. CV34: Warw 1F 101
Vogue Cl. CV1: Cov 2K 135 (4E 58)

W

Wackrill Dr. CV32: Lill 4G 99
WADBOROUGH 3A 142
Wade Av. CV3: Cov 3B 68
Wadebridge Dr. CV11: Nun 7F 23
Wade Gro. CV34: Warw 5G 97
Wade Ho. CV22: Bil 1C 86
Wade La. CV33: L Hth 2K 119
Wadham Ho. B37: Chel W 2C 34
Wadleys Cl. B50: Bidf A 5G 123
Waggoners Cl. CV8: Bubb 4J 81
WAGON OVERTHROW 6G 41
Wagstaff Dr. CV10: Nun 4F 21
Wagstaffe Cl. CV33: Har 6G 109
Wainbody Av. Nth. CV3: Cov 3A 68
Wainbody Av. Sth. CV3: Finh 4K 67
Wain Cl. B49: Alc 3D 112
Wakefield Cl. CV3: Bin 1B 70
CV9: Hurl 7J 13
Wakefield Gro. B46: Wat O 1B 24
Wakeford Cl. CV10: Ridge L 1A 20
Wake Gro. CV34: Warw 3D 100
Wakehurst Cl. CV11: Nun 4B 32
WALCOT 3C 143
WALCOTE 3C 141
Waldon Wlk. B36: Cas B 4A 24
Waldron Ct. CV37: S Avon 2F 137 (4F 115)
Walford Gro. CV34: Warw 6H 97
Walford Pl. CV22: Hillm 1B 88
Walkers Orchard CV8: S'lgh 3B 80
Walkers Rd. CV37: S Avon 2F 115
Walker's Ter. CV23: Brin 2B 62
Walkers Way B46: Col 6G 25
CV8: Ken 7D 78
CV12: Bed 4F 41
WALL 1C 139
Wallace Ct. CV34: Warw 1F 101
Wallace Rd. CV6: Cov 6A 50
Wall Av. B46: Col 7F 25
WALLBROOK 2A 138
Waller Cl. CV35: Leek W 1H 97
Waller St. CV32: Lea S 5E 98
WALL HEATH 3A 138
WALL HILL 2E 48
Wall Hill Rd. CV5: Alle 2F 49
CV7: Cor 6A 38
Wallingford Av. CV11: Nun 4G 23
Wallsgrove Cl. CV32: Lill 4F 99
Wallwin Ct. CV34: Warw 2F 101
Wallwin Pl. CV34: Warw 1F 101
Walmer Way B37: Chel W 2C 34
WALMLEY 2C 139
Walnut Cl. B37: Chel W 4B 34
CV10: Harts 3F 21
CV10: Nun 5K 21
Walnut Ct. CV31: W'nsh 4D 102
Walnut Cft. CV9: Bad E 3F 15
Walnut Dr. CV32: Lill 4F 99
Walnut St. CV2: Cov 4H 51
Walnut Tree Cl. CV8: Ken 6E 78
Walnut Way CV22: Bil 7B 74
WALSALL 2B 138
Walsall St. CV4: Canly 1E 66
WALSALL WOOD 1B 138
Walsgrave Gdns. CV2: W'grve S 7C 52
WALSGRAVE ON SOWE 7C 52 (3A 140)
Walsgrave Retail Pk. CV2: W'grve S 7D 52
Walsgrave Rd. CV1: Cov 4F 59
CV2: Cov 4F 59
Walsgrave Triangle Bus. Pk. CV2: W'grve S 5C 52
Walsh La. CV7: Mer 4G 47
Walsingham Dr. CV10: Griff 4G 31
Walter Scott Rd. CV12: Bed 4J 41
Waltham Cres. CV10: Nun 7G 21
WALTON
Lutterworth 3C 141
Warwick 7J 117 (3D 143)
Walton Cl. CV3: Bin 1A 70
CV11: Nun 5C 32
Walton Flds. CV35: Kine 6E 120
Walton La. CV35: Pill P 2B 128
Walton Rd. CV35: W'ton, Welle 4H 117
Walton Way CV35: Welle 4H 117
Wanley Rd. CV3: Cov 2D 68
WANLIP 1C 141
Wansfell Cl. CV4: Tile H 1E 66
Wantage Rd. B46: Col 3E 24
WAPPENBURY 2A 144
Wappenbury Cl. CV2: Cov 4J 51
Wappenbury Rd. CV2: Cov 4K 51
WAPPING 2D 92
WARD END 3C 139
Warden Rd. CV6: Cov 1B 58
Wardens, The CV8: Ken 4G 79
Wardens Av., The CV5: Alle 1F 57
Ward Gro. CV34: Warw 1A 102
WARDINGTON 1D 147
Wardour Dr. B37: Chel W 3C 34
Ward's Hill CV35: N Lin 2G 95
Wareham Grn. CV2: W'grve S 2C 60
Ware Orchard CV23: Barby 7E 88
Ware Rd. CV23: Barby 7E 88
WARESLEY 2A 142
Waring Way CV22: Dunc 5D 86
WARKWORTH 1D 147
WARMINGTON 2J 129 (1D 147)
Warmington Cl. CV3: Bin 7A 60
Warmington Gro. CV34: Warw 7D 96
Warmwell Cl. CV2: W'grve S 3B 60
WARNDON 3A 142
Warneford M. CV31: Lea S 1E 102
Warner Cl. CV34: Warw 6F 97
Warner Row CV6: Cov 7G 51
Warren Cl. CV8: Rytn D 7C 70
CV32: Lea S 4D 98
Warren Fld. CV8: Rytn D 7C 70
Warren Grn. CV4: Tile H 1D 66
Warren Rd. CV22: Hillm 7K 75
WARTON 5H 9 (1D 139)
Warton Cl. CV8: Ken 5G 79
Warton La. B79: Wart 7G 9
(Little Warton)
B79: Wart 4H 9
(Warton)
CV9: Aus 7F 7
CV9: Gren 1H 11
WARWICK 2G 101 (2D 143)
Warwick Arts Cen. 4F 67
Warwick Av. CV5: Cov 1A 68
Warwick By-Pass CV35: Barf 7H 101
CV35: Bud, Guys C, H Mag, H Hill 5D 100
Warwick Castle 2G 101
Warwick Cl. B80: Stud 4C 92
Warwick Ct. B37: Chel W 3D 34
CV3: Cov 7G 135
CV32: Lea S 6D 98
CV37: S Avon 1H 137 (4F 115)
Warwick Ct. (Verona) CV37: S Avon 2H 137
Warwick Cres. CV37: S Avon 1J 137 (4G 115)
Warwick Dr. CV9: Ath 1C 16
Warwick Gdns. CV10: Nun 1E 30
Warwick Grn. CV12: Bulk 4E 42
Warwick Ho. CV37: S Avon 1E 136
Warwick Ho. Ind. Pk. CV47: Sou 7H 107
Warwick La. CV1: Cov 4H 135 (5C 58)
Warwick M. CV37: S Avon 1J 137 (4G 115)
Warwick New Rd. CV32: Lea S 7A 98
Warwick Parkway Station (Rail) 1C 100
Warwick Pl. CV32: Lea S 7B 98
CV36: Ship S 4G 131
CV47: Sou 5H 107
Warwick Racecourse 2E 100
Warwick Rd. B95: Hen A 2H 93
CV1: Cov 5G 135 (5C 58)
CV3: Cov 7F 135 (7B 58)
CV8: Ken 5D 78
CV8: S'lgh 2B 80
CV8: Wols 5H 71
CV35: Kine 5C 120
CV35: Leek W 1H 97 & 7E 78
CV35: N Lin 2G 95
CV35: Welle 2H 117
CV37: B Hill, Ing, S Avon 3H 137 & 7K 95 (4F 115)
CV37: Ett 1B 126
CV47: Sou 6G 107
Warwick Row CV1: Cov 5G 135 (5C 58)
Warwicks, The CV35: H Mag 2B 100
Warwickshire Exhibition Cen. 2A 144
Warwickshire Mus. 2G 101
Warwickshire Yeomanry Mus. 2G 101
Warwick Station (Rail) 1H 101
Warwick St. CV5: Cov 7K 57
CV22: Rugby 5G 75
CV32: Lea S 6C 98
CV47: Sou 5H 107
Warwick Technology Pk. CV34: Warw 3K 101
Warwick Ter. CV32: Lea S 6C 98
Wasdale Cl. CV32: Lea S 6B 98

Washbourne Rd. CV31: W'nsh 5E 102
Washbrook La. CV5: Alle 4E 48
Washbrook Pl. CV36: Ilm 7C 126
Washford Dr. B98: Redd 1B 92
WASPERTON 3D 143
Wasperton Cl. CV3: Bin 7B 60
Wasperton La. CV35: Barf 3C 108
Waste La. CV6: Cov 5J 49
CV9: Ath, Gren 7H 11
Watch Cl. CV1: Cov 3F 135 (4B 58)
Watchmaker Ct. CV1: Cov 5B 58
Watcombe Rd. CV2: Cov 6A 52
Watercall Av. CV3: Cov 3C 68
Waterfall Cl. CV7: Mer 5E 46
Waterford Way CV3: Cov 6J 59
Watergall Cl. CV47: Sou 6J 107
Water Lily Way CV10: Nun 4G 31
Waterloo Av. B37: F'bri 1B 34
Waterloo Cl. CV35: Welle 4G 117
Waterloo Ct. CV34: Warw 7J 97
Waterloo Cres. B50: Bidf A 5H 123
Waterloo Dr. CV37: S Avon 6J 115
Waterloo Ind. Est. B37: F'bri 7B 24
B50: Bidf A 4H 123
Waterloo Pk. B50: Bidf A 4H 123
Waterloo Pl. CV32: Lea S 6D 98
Waterloo Ri. CV37: S Avon 7J 115
Waterloo Rd. B50: Bidf A 2F 123
Waterloo St. CV1: Cov 3E 58
CV31: Lea S 1F 103
Waterman Rd. CV6: Cov 2F 59
WATER ORTON 1B 24 (2C 139)
Water Orton La. B76: Min 7A 18
Water Orton Station (Rail) 1A 24
Watersbridge Gdns. CV10: Nun 3J 31
Watersfield Gdns. CV31: Lea S 1G 103
Waterside B78: Pole 1D 10
CV1: Cov 1H 135 (3C 58)
CV6: Longf 7J 41
CV37: S Avon 7G 137 (5F 115)
Waterside Ct. CV31: Lea S 2E 102
Waterside Dr. CV21: Rugby 2J 75
Watersmeet Gro. CV2: Cov 1H 59
Watersmeet Rd. CV2: Cov 1H 59
Waterson Cft. B37: Chel W 2D 34
Water Twr. La. CV8: Ken 3D 78
Watery La. B46: Neth W 2J 25
B95: Ullen 6B 90
CV6: Cov 2K 49
CV7: Cor 2C 48
CV7: Ker E 2K 49
CV8: Bubb 4G 81
CV9: Bad E 1D 14
CV35: Pill H 1D 128
CV35: Sher 7C 100
CV36: Ship S 4H 131
WATFORD 2D 145
Wathen Rd. CV32: Lea S 5E 98
CV34: Warw 7G 97
Watling Ct. CV11: Nun 1A 32
Watling Rd. CV8: Ken 3F 79
Watling St. B78: Dord 4A 10
CV9: Ath, Gren 7G 11
CV9: Man, With 4E 16
CV10: Cald, Harts 1D 22
CV11: Nun 1D 22
CV23: Clift D 1F 77
CV23: Kils 6J 89
Watson Cl. CV34: Warw 6G 97
Watson Rd. CV5: Cov 5H 57
Watton La. B46: Wat O 2C 24
Wattons La. CV47: Sou 5H 107
(not continuous)
Wattons Lodge CV47: Sou 5G 107
Watts La. CV21: Hillm 1D 88
Watts Rd. B80: Stud 5D 92
Waugh Cl. B37: Chel W 3B 34
Wavebeck Ct. CV23: Long L 3B 74
Waveley Rd. CV1: Cov 4A 58
Wavendon Cl. CV2: W'grve S 5B 52
Waveney Cft. B36: Cas B 4A 24
Wavere Ct. CV21: Brow 1K 75
Waverley Av. CV11: Nun 3A 32
Waverley Edge CV8: Bubb 5H 81
Waverley Rd. CV8: Ken 6E 78
CV21: Hillm 7C 76
CV31: Lea S 2E 102
Waverley Sq. CV11: Nun 4B 32
Waverton Av. B79: Wart 5H 9
Waverton M. CV31: Lea S 2G 103
Wavy Tree Cl. CV34: Warw 1F 101
Wawensmere Rd. B95: Woot W 5F 93
Wayside B37: Mars G 5A 34
Weale Gro. CV34: Warw 6H 97
Weatheroak Rd. B49: Alc 4D 112
Weaver Dr. CV23: Long L 4C 74
Weavers Cl. CV36: Ship S 4H 131
Weavers Cotts. CV36: Long C 3C 134
Weavers Wlk. CV6: Cov 6H 51
Webb Dr. CV23: Brow 7K 65
Webb Ellis Bus. Pk. CV21: Rugby 4H 75
Webb Ellis Road 6E 74
Webb Ellis Rd. CV22: Rugby 6E 74
Webb St. CV10: Nun 1C 30
WEBHEATH 2B 142
Webster Av. CV8: Ken 3F 79
Webster St. CV6: Cov 7E 50
WEDDINGTON 4D 22 (2A 140)
Weddington Ind. Est. CV10: Nun 6D 22
Weddington La. CV10: Cald, Nun 1C 22
Weddington Ter. CV10: Nun 6E 22
Wedgewood Cl. CV2: W'grve S 6A 52
Wedgewood Ho. B37: F'bri 1B 34
Wedge Woods CV5: Cov 7K 57
Wedgnock Grn. CV34: Warw 7F 97
Wedgnock Ind. Est. CV34: Warw 6D 96
Wedgnock La. CV34: Warw 7E 96
CV35: Beau, Leek W 1A 96
WEDNESBURY 2A 138
WEDNESFIELD 1A 138
Wedon Cl. CV4: Tile H 1C 66
WEEDON BEC 3D 145
WEEDON LOIS 3D 145
WEEFORD 1C 139
WEETHLY 3B 142
Weilerswist Dr. CV31: W'nsh 4D 102
Weland Cl. B46: Wat O 2B 24
Welchman Pl. CV35: Mid T 7D 130
Welcombe Cotts. CV37: S Avon 3F 115
Welcombe Ct. CV37: S Avon 3F 115
Welcombe Hills Obelisk 3D 143
Welcombe Rd. CV37: S Avon 1J 137 (4F 115)
Welcome St. CV9: Ath 3D 16
WELFORD 3D 141
Welford Gro. CV35: Hatt 4A 96
WELFORD-ON-AVON 2A 124 (3C 143)
Welford Pl. CV6: Cov 7D 50
Welford Rd. B50: Bart 7H 123
CV21: Rugby 4J 75
CV37: Long M 3G 125
Welgarth Av. CV6: Cov 1J 57
Welland Cl. CV23: Long L 3B 74
Welland Rd. CV1: Cov 6F 59
WELLESBOURNE 3H 117 (3D 143)
Wellesbourne Distribution Pk. CV35: Welle 4F 117
Wellesbourne Gro. CV37: S Avon 4C 136 (5E 114)
Wellesbourne Ho. CV35: Welle 4H 117
Wellesbourne Rd. CV5: E Grn 4E 56
CV35: Barf 2B 108
CV35: Char 2A 116
CV35: Light 4F 119
CV35: Lox, Welle 6D 116
CV37: A'ton 2A 116
Wellesbourne Water Mill 4J 117
Wellington Cl. CV35: Welle 5G 117
Wellington Dr. CV37: S Avon 6J 115
Wellington Gdns. CV1: Cov 5B 58
Wellington Rd. B50: Bidf A 4H 123
CV32: Lill 4F 99
Wellington St. CV1: Cov 3E 58
Well La. B94: Tan A 4D 90
Wellmeadow Gro. B92: H Ard 7G 45
WELLSBOROUGH 1A 140
Wells Cl. CV10: Gall C 7E 20
Wells Ct. CV3: Cov 1F 69
Well Spring Cl. CV9: Ath 3E 16
Wells St. CV21: Rugby 5H 75
Well St. CV1: Cov 2H 135 (4C 58)
Wells Wlk. B37: Mars G 4A 34
Welsh Cl. CV34: Warw 5G 97
Welsh Rd. CV2: Cov 3H 59
CV32: Cubb 3J 99
CV33: Cubb, Off 3J 99
CV47: Bas 1J 109
Welsh Rd. E. CV47: Sou 5J 107
Welsh Rd. W. CV47: Sou 3F 107
WELTON 2C 145
Welton Pl. CV22: Hillm 1K 87
Welton Rd. CV34: Warw 6F 97
Wembrook Cl. CV11: Nun 2K 31
Wembrook Ho. CV11: Nun 2A 32
Wendiburgh St. CV4: Canly 1E 66
Wendover Ri. CV5: Cov 3G 57
Wenlock Way CV10: Nun 7G 21
Wentworth Av. CV47: Temp H 3B 120
Wentworth Dr. CV6: Cov 2B 50
CV11: Nun 3C 32
Wentworth Rd. CV22: Bil 7E 74
CV31: Lea S 2H 103
WERGS 1A 138
Wesley Rd. CV21: Hillm 1C 88
Wessex Cl. CV12: Bed 1G 41
Wessex Ct. B79: Shut 2C 8
Wessons Rd. B50: Bidf A 5H 123
West Av. CV2: Cov 5G 59
CV7: Ker E 1A 50
CV12: Bed 3K 41
Westbourne Gro. CV22: Bil 7F 75
WEST BROMWICH 2A 138
Westbrook Ct. CV5: E Grn 3E 56
Westbury Ct. CV34: Warw 1J 101
Westbury Rd. CV5: Cov 2H 57
CV10: Nun 1D 30
Westcliff Dr. CV34: Warw 5G 97
Westcliffe Dr. CV3: Cov 3B 68
Westcotes CV4: Tile H 6F 57
WESTCOTT BARTON 3D 147
West Dr. B95: Woot W 4H 93
WEST END 2A 146
West End CV35: Rad 5A 128
West End Ct. CV34: Warw 2F 101
(off Crompton St.)
West End Cres. CV37: S Avon 6E 114
Western Rd. CV37: S Avon 1B 136 (4E 114)
Western Rd. Ind. Est. CV37: S Avon 1C 136 (4E 114)
WEST FARNDON 3C 145
Westfield Cl. CV10: Nun 6E 22
CV37: S Avon 2E 114
Westfield Cres. CV35: Welle 3G 117
Westfield Ho. B36: Cas B 5A 24
Westfield Rd. CV22: Rugby 6F 75
CV47: Sou 6G 107
Westfields B78: B'moor 2C 10
(Dexter Way)
B78: B'moor 2A 10
(Green La.)
Westgate Cl. CV34: Warw 2F 101
Westgate Ho. CV34: Warw 2G 101
(off Market St.)
Westgate Rd. CV21: Hillm 7A 76
West Grn. Dr. CV37: S Avon 4A 114
Westgrove Ter. CV32: Lea S 7B 98
WEST HADDON 1D 145
WEST HAGLEY 3A 138
Westham Ho. B37: F'bri 1B 34
Westham La. CV35: Barf 3A 108
Westhill Rd. CV6: Cov 1K 57
CV32: B'dwn 1E 98
Westholme Ct. B50: Bidf A 6G 123
(off Westholme Rd.)
Westholme Rd. B50: Bidf A 5F 123
WESTHORP 3C 145
Westlea Rd. CV31: Lea S 2C 102
Westleigh Av. CV5: Cov 1K 67
West Leyes CV21: Rugby 5G 75
Westmead Av. B80: Stud 3D 92
Westmede Cen. CV5: Cov 4G 57
Westminster Dr. CV10: Nun 5G 21
Westminster Rd. CV1: Cov 6F 135 (6B 58)
Westmorland Av. CV10: Nun 7K 21
Westmorland Rd. CV2: Cov 3B 60
West Oak Ho. CV4: W'wd H 2C 66
West of St Laurence CV35: Row 7J 91
WESTON 3C 145
Westonbirt Cl. CV8: Ken 3G 79
Weston Cl. CV22: Dunc 5C 86
CV31: Lea S 2G 103
CV34: Warw 1H 101
Weston Ct. CV21: Rugby 4J 75
CV36: Long C 2D 134
WESTON IN ARDEN 2D 42 (3A 140)
Weston La. CV8: Bubb 5H 81
CV12: Bulk 2D 42
WESTON-ON-AVON 3B 124 (3C 143)
WESTON-ON-THE-GREEN 3D 147
Weston St. CV1: Cov 1K 135 (3D 58)
WESTON SUBEDGE 1A 146
WESTON UNDER WETHERLEY 2A 144
W. Orchards Shop. Cen. CV1: Cov 3H 135 (4C 58)
West Pk. CV4: Tile H 7D 56
West Pk. Cl. CV37: S Avon 4A 114
West Ridge CV5: Cov 2E 56
West St. CV1: Cov 4E 58
CV23: Long L 3A 74
CV31: Lea S 1E 102
CV34: Warw 3F 101
CV36: Ship S 4H 131
CV37: S Avon 7D 136 (6E 114)
West Vw. CV10: Ans C 3D 20
West Vw. Rd. CV22: Rugby 6D 74
CV32: Cubb 2G 99
Westway CV21: Rugby 5G 75
Westwood Bus. Pk. CV4: W'wd H 2E 66
Westwood Cl. CV10: Nun 1E 30
Westwood Cres. CV9: Ath 4C 16
WESTWOOD HEATH 2D 66
Westwood Heath Rd. CV4: W'wd H 2A 66
Westwood Rd. CV5: Cov 6A 58
CV9: Ath 3C 16
CV22: Hillm 2B 88
Westwood Way CV4: W'wd H 2C 66
Wetherby Way CV37: S Avon 6D 114
Wetherell Way CV21: Brow 1J 75
Wexford Rd. CV2: Cov 5K 51
Weymouth Cl. CV3: W'hall 3K 69
Whaley's Cft. CV6: Cov 6B 50
Wharf, The CV36: Ship S 3H 131
CV37: Wilm 5K 113
Wharf Ind. Est., The CV23: Stret U 7E 54
Wharf Rd. CV6: Cov 2F 59
CV37: S Avon 3E 114
Wharf St. CV34: Warw 1J 101
Wharrage Rd. B49: Alc 4D 112
WHATCOTE 3A 130 (1B 146)
Whatcote Rd. CV35: Oxh 1D 130
WHATELEY 1G 13 (2D 139)
Whateley Ct. CV11: Nun 7C 22
Whateley La. B78: What 1G 13
Whateley's Dr. CV8: Ken 4E 78
Whateley Vs. B78: Picc 1H 13
Wheatcroft Dr. B37: Chel W 4C 34
Wheate Cft. CV4: Tile H 5D 56
Wheaten Cl. B37: Chel W 2D 34
Wheatfield Cl. B36: Cas B 5A 24
Wheatfield Rd. CV22: Bil 7C 74
Wheathill Cl. CV32: Lea S 5C 98
Wheatley Grange B46: Col 6F 25
Wheatley St. CV1: Cov 2K 135
(off White St.)
WHEATON ASTON 1A 138
WHEATSTONE PARK 1A 138
Wheat St. CV11: Nun 7D 22
Wheelbarrow La. CV35: Clav 2E 94
Wheeley Moor Rd. B37: K'hrst 7A 24
Wheelwright Ct. CV37: S Avon 2E 136
Wheelwright La. CV6: Cov 2C 50
CV7: Ash G 2C 50
Wheler Rd. CV3: Cov 7G 59
Whernside CV21: Brow 1J 75
WHETSTONE 2C 141
Whetstone Dr. CV21: Brow 1K 75
Whichcote Av. CV7: Mer 5E 46
WHICHFORD 2C 147
Whiley Cl. CV23: Clift D 3B 76
WHILTON 2D 145
Whimbrel Cl. CV23: Brow 7J 65
WHITACRE HEATH 5K 19 (2D 139)
Whitacre Heath Nature Reserve 5H 19
Whitacre Rd. CV11: Nun 7F 23

Whitacre Rd. CV32: Lill 5E 98
Whitacre Rd. Ind. Est. CV11: Nun 7F 23
Whitaker Rd. CV5: Cov 4G 57
Whitburn Rd. CV12: Bed 3C 40
Whitchurch Way CV4: Tile H 7D 56
Whitebeam Cl. CV4: Tile H 6B 56
Whitebeam Rd. B37: Chel W 5C 34
Whitebeam Way CV10: Nun 4K 21
Whitefield Cl. CV4: W'wd H 1B 66
Whitefields Flats CV4: Canly 4G 67
Whitefriars Dr. CV22: Caw 7A 74
White Friars La. CV1: Cov 5K 135 (5D 58)
Whitefriars Lodge Mus. 5K 135 (5E 58)
White Friars St. CV1: Cov 4K 135 (5D 58)
Whitehall Cl. CV10: Harts 1F 21
Whitehall Rd. CV21: Rugby 6H 75
White Hart La. CV33: Ufton 2F 109
Whitehead Dr. CV8: Ken 3G 79
CV35: Welle 2J 117
Whiteheads Ct. CV32: Lea S 6D 98
Whitehorse Cl. CV6: Longf 7H 41
White Horse Hill CV37: Snitt 6H 95
White Ho., The B95: Hen A 2H 93
Whitehouse Cres. CV10: Nun 1D 30
Whitehouse Rd. B78: Dord 3C 10
WHITE LADIES ASTON 3A 142
Whitelaw Cres. CV5: Alle 1F 57
WHITEMOOR 4F 79
Whitemoor La. B96: Sam 7A 92
Whitemoor Rd. CV8: Ken 4E 78
White Pump La. B95: Ullen 4C 90
Whiteside Cl. CV3: Bin 7B 60
Whites Row CV8: Ken 7E 78
WHITE STITCH 2E 46
Whitestitch La. CV7: Mer 3D 46
WHITESTONE 4B 32
Whitestone Rd. CV11: Nun 4C 32
White St. CV1: Cov 2J 135 (4D 58)
Whitethorn Dr. CV32: Lill 5F 99
Whitfield Cl. CV37: Tidd 3K 115
WHITLEY 2G 69
Whitley Ct. CV3: Cov 1F 69
Whitley Hill B95: Hen A 3K 93
Whitley Rd. B95: Hen A 2J 93
Whitley Village CV3: Cov 1F 69
WHITLOCK'S END 1C 143
WHITMORE PARK 5A 50
Whitmore Pk. Ind. Est. CV6: Cov 5C 50
Whitmore Pk. Rd. CV6: Cov 3C 50
Whitmore Rd. CV31: W'nsh 5E 102
WHITNASH 4E 102 (2A 144)
Whitnash Gro. CV2: Cov 2K 59
Whitnash Rd. CV31: W'nsh 4F 103
WHITTINGTON
Atherstone 1A 16 (2D 139)
Lichfield 1C 139
Stourbridge 3A 138
Worcester 3A 142
WHITTINGTON BARRACKS 1C 139
Whittington Cl. CV34: Warw 7K 97
Whittington La. CV9: Whitt 1K 15
Whittle Cl. CV3: Bin 7B 60
CV22: Bil 2D 86
Whittle Ct. CV32: Lea S 6F 99
WHITTLEFORD 6G 21 (2A 140)
Whittleford Rd. CV10: Nun 7H 21
Whitworth Av. CV3: Cov 6H 59
Whitworth Cl. CV35: Welle 4G 117
WHOBERLEY 5H 57 (1D 143)
Whoberley Av. CV5: Cov 4H 57
WIBTOFF 3B 140
Wickham Cl. CV6: Cov 4K 49
Wickham Ct. CV32: Lill 3F 99
WICKHAMFORD 1A 146
Wickham Rd. B80: Stud 3E 92
Wickmans Dr. CV4: Tile H 5A 56
Wiclif Way CV10: Nun 1B 30
Widdecombe Cl. CV2: Cov 6K 51
Widdrington Rd. CV1: Cov 2C 58
Wiggins Cl. CV21: Hillm 1D 88
Wiggins Hill Rd. B76: Min, Wis 5A 18
WIGGINTON
Banbury 2C 147
Tamworth 1D 139
Wight Cft. B36: Cas B 6B 24
WIGHTWICK 2A 138
WIGSTON 2D 141
Wigston Hill CV9: Bax 6F 15
Wigston Rd. CV2: W'grve S 5B 52
CV21: Hillm 1C 88
Wike La. B96: Sam 7B 92
Wilcox Cl. CV47: Bis I 7B 110
Wilcox Leys CV35: More M 5C 118
Wildcroft Rd. CV5: Cov 5G 57
Wilderness B95: Woot W 4J 93
Wildey Rd. CV12: Bed 3D 40
WILDMOOR 1A 142
Wildmoor Cl. CV2: Ald G 2H 51
Wilhelmina Cl. CV32: Lea S 7C 98
Wilkes Way B50: Bidf A 5G 123
Wilkins Cl. CV35: Barf 2B 108
Wilkinson Way B46: Shu 2C 26
Willans Pl. CV21: Rugby 4F 75
Willday Dr. CV9: Ath 1C 16
WILLENHALL
CV3 2K 69 (1A 144)
WV13 2A 138
Willenhall La. CV3: Bin 2A 70
WILLERSEY 2A 146
Willes Rd. CV31: Lea S 6E 98
CV32: Lea S 6E 98
Willes Ter. CV31: Lea S 7F 99
Willett Gdns. CV35: Welle 2H 117
Willett Ho. CV35: Welle 2H 117
(off Willett Gdns.)
WILLEY 3B 140
William Arnold Cl. CV2: Cov 3G 59
William Batchelor Ho. CV1: Cov 1H 135
William Beesley Cres. CV11: Bram 6G 33
William Bree Rd. CV5: E Grn 2A 56
William Bristow Rd. CV3: Cov 1E 68
William Cree Cl. CV8: Wols 5H 71
William Groubb Cl. CV3: Bin 1A 70
William Kirby Cl. CV4: Tile H 6E 56
William McCool Cl. CV3: Bin 7B 60
William McKee Cl. CV3: Bin 1A 70
William Malcolm Ho. CV2: Cov 4A 60
WILLIAMSCOT 1D 147
Williams Rd. CV31: Rad S 4J 103
William St. CV11: Nun 1A 32
CV12: Bed 3K 41
CV21: Rugby 5H 75
CV32: Lea S 7E 98
William Tarver Cl. CV34: Warw 1J 101
William Thomson Ho. CV1: Cov 3E 58
(off Clifton St.)
WILLINGTON 7K 131 (2B 146)
Willington St. CV11: Nun 6B 22
Willis Cft. B79: Wart 5H 9
Willis Gro. CV12: Bed 2J 41
WILLOUGHBY 3H 105 (2C 145)
Willoughby Av. CV8: Ken 6C 78
Willoughby Cl. B49: K Cou 1A 112
CV3: Bin 7A 60
Willoughby Ct. CV35: Lit K 6C 120
Willoughby Pl. CV22: Hillm 1K 87
WILLOUGHBY WATERLEYS 2C 141
Willow Bank CV37: Welf A 2A 124
Willowbrook Cotts. CV37: S Avon 5D 114
Willowbrook Rd. CV8: Wols 4J 71
Willow Cl. B49: Alc 6B 112
B78: K'bry 5E 12
CV10: Harts 4F 21
CV12: Bed 7G 31
CV31: W'nsh 6F 103
Willow Ct. CV34: H'cte 6C 102
Willow Courtyard CV2: Cov 7K 51
Willowdene Cvn. Site CV37: Wilm 4H 113
Willow Dr. CV35: Welle 3H 117
Willow End GL56: Lit C 6C 134
Willowfields Rd. CV11: Nun 3C 32
Willow Gdns. CV47: Sou 5H 107
Willow Gro. CV4: Tile H 5F 57
CV47: Long I 1C 106
Willowherb Cl. CV3: Bin 7B 60
Willow Ho. CV32: Lea S 7B 98
Willow La. CV22: Rugby 6J 75
Willow Meer CV8: Ken 4F 79
Willow Rd. CV10: Nun 6K 21
Willows, The CV9: Ath 1D 16
CV12: Bed 3E 40
CV37: S Avon 6A 136 (5D 114)
Willow Sheets Mdw. CV32: Cubb 1J 99
Willows Nth., The CV37: S Avon 4A 136 (4D 114)
Willow Tree Gdns. CV21: Hillm 7C 76
Willow Wlk. CV7: Old A 3C 28
Willow Way B37: Chel W 3B 34
B80: Stud 5D 92
WILMCOTE 5J 113 (3C 143)
Wilmcote Grn. CV5: E Grn 4E 56
Wilmcote La. B95: Aston C 2K 113 & 4F 113
Wilmcote Station (Rail) 5K 113
Wilmhurst Rd. CV34: Warw 7E 96
Wilmot Av. B46: Col 6F 25
WILNECOTE 1D 139
Wilnecote Gro. CV31: Lea S 3F 103
Wilson Cl. CV22: Bil 6C 74
Wilson Dr. CV37: S Avon 4D 114
Wilson Grn. CV3: Bin 6B 60
Wilson Gro. CV8: Ken 5G 79
Wilsons La. CV6: Longf 1F 51
CV7: Exh 7G 41
Wiltshire Cl. CV5: E Grn 4F 57
CV12: Bed 2G 41
WIMBLEBURY 1B 138
Wimbourne Cl. CV10: Nun 6G 21
Wimbourne Dr. CV2: W'grve S 3B 60
WIMPSTONE 1B 146
Winceby Pl. CV4: Tile H 6B 56
Winchat Cl. CV3: Bin 6B 60
Winchcombe Rd. B49: Alc 4D 112
Winchester Av. CV10: Nun 4D 22
Winchester Ct. CV22: Dunc 6C 86
Winchester Dr. B37: Chel W 3A 34
Winchester St. CV1: Cov 4E 58
Wincote Cl. CV8: Ken 5E 78
Wincott Cl. CV37: S Avon 6H 115
Windermere Av. CV3: Bin 6A 60
CV5: E Grn 3C 56
CV11: Nun 4G 23
Windermere Cl. CV21: Brow 1J 75
Windermere Dr. CV32: Lea S 5B 98
WINDERTON 1K 133 (1C 147)
Winderton Av. CV35: Hatt 5A 96
Winding Ho. La. CV6: Longf 2C 50
CV7: Ash G, Longf 2C 50
Windmill Av. B46: Col 5F 25
Windmill Cl. B79: Wart 6H 9
CV8: Ken 3E 78
CV36: Ilm 6C 126
(off Front St.)
Windmill Ct. CV6: Cov 3G 51
Windmill Cft. CV32: Cubb 2H 99
Windmill Hill CV32: Cubb 2H 99
Windmill Hill, The CV5: Alle 7E 48
Windmill Hill Community Nature Area 3K 21
Windmill Ind. Est. CV5: Alle 7D 48
Windmill La. CV7: Cor 7B 38
CV9: Aus 6G 7
CV9: Bax 5G 15
CV10: Asty 7J 29
CV22: Dunc 5A 86
CV47: Ladb, Sou 2C 110
Windmill Rd. CV6: Cov 3F 51
CV7: Exh 5G 41
CV9: Ath 2C 16
CV10: Nun 4J 21
CV31: Lea S 3D 102
Windmill Way CV35: Mid T 7C 130
Windridge Cl. CV3: W'hall 2K 69
Windrush Way CV23: Long L 3B 74
Windsor Ct. CV4: Tile H 5F 57
CV10: Nun 5K 21
CV21: Rugby 5G 75
CV32: Lea S 7D 98
CV37: S Avon 3E 136 (4E 114)
Windsor Gdns. CV10: Nun 7K 21
Windsor Pl. CV32: Lea S 7D 98
Windsor Rd. B36: Cas B 5A 24
B78: Pole 6D 8
Windsor St. CV1: Cov 5B 58
CV11: Nun 7C 22
CV21: Rugby 5J 75
CV32: Lea S 7D 98
CV37: S Avon 3E 136 (4E 114)
Windward Way B36: Cas B 5A 24
WINDY ARBOUR 6F 79
Windy Arbour CV8: Ken 4F 79
Winfield Rd. CV11: Nun 6C 22
Winfield St. CV21: Rugby 4K 75
Wingfield Ho. B37: K'hrst 7A 24
Wingfield Rd. B46: Col 7F 25
Wingfield Way CV6: Cov 4A 50
Wingrave Cl. CV5: Alle 1E 56
Winifred Av. CV5: Cov 6A 58
Winnallthorpe CV3: W'hall 2A 70
Winsford Av. CV5: Cov 3F 57
Winsford Ct. CV5: Cov 3G 57
Winsham Wlk. CV3: Finh 5C 68
Winslow Cl. CV5: Cov 4F 57
CV32: Lea S 6A 98
Winslow Ho. CV1: Cov 5B 58
(off Meadow St.)
WINSON GREEN 3B 138
Winspear Cl. CV7: Mer 5E 46
Winster Cl. CV7: Ker E 6A 40
Winston Av. CV2: Cov 6K 51
Winston Cl. CV2: Cov 6K 51
CV37: Shot 6C 114
Winston Cres. CV32: Lill 4G 99
Winterborne Gdns. CV10: Nun 2F 31
Winterton Rd. CV12: Bulk 4E 42
WINWICK 1D 145
Winwick Pl. CV22: Bil 1C 86
Winyates Rd. CV33: L Hth 2K 119
Wise Gro. CV21: Hillm 6B 76
CV34: Warw 5G 97
Wise St. CV31: Lea S 1D 102
Wise Ter. CV31: Lea S 1D 102
WISHAW 1B 18 (2C 139)
Wishaw La. B76: Curd 3A 18
Wisley Gro. CV8: Ken 4G 79
Wisteria Cl. CV2: Cov 4H 51
Wisteria Way CV10: Nun 4G 31
WITHERLEY 3G 17 (2A 140)
Witherley Rd. CV9: Ath 3D 16
WITHYBROOK 1D 54 (3B 140)
Withybrook Cl. CV2: Cov 4K 51
Withybrook La. CV7: Shil, Withy 1H 53
Withybrook Rd. CV12: Bulk 3F 43
Witnell Rd. CV6: Cov 1C 58
WITTON 2A 142
WIXFORD 1E 122 (3B 142)
Wixford Rd. B50: Ard G 2K 123
Woburn Cl. CV31: Lea S 2H 103
Woburn Dr. CV10: Nun 2G 31
Wolds La. LE10: Wlvy 2J 33
Wolfe Rd. CV4: Tile H 1D 66
Wolford Flds. CV36: Lit Wol 4E 132
WOLLASTON 3A 138
WOLLESCOTE 3A 138
Wolseley Cl. B36: Cas B 3A 24
Wolsey Rd. CV22: Bil 4D 86
WOLSTON 5J 71 (1B 144)
Wolston Ct. CV22: Dunc 3B 86
Wolston La. CV8: Rytn D, Wols 7E 70
Wolston Way CV3: W'hall 2J 69
WOLVERHAMPTON 2A 138
WOLVERTON 2D 143
Wolverton Flds. CV35: N Lin 2F 95
Wolverton Rd. B37: Mars G 6B 34
CV5: E Grn 4E 56
CV35: N Lin 2F 95
CV37: Snitt 4G 95
WOLVEY 2H 33 (3B 140)
WOLVEY HEATH 1K 33 (3B 140)
Wolvey Rd. CV12: Bulk 3F 43
WOMBOURNE 2A 138
Woodbine Cotts. CV32: Lea S 7C 98
Woodbine St. CV32: Lea S 7C 98
Woodbine Wlk. B37: Chel W 3D 34
Woodbridge Ct. CV21: Rugby 4H 75
Woodbrook Ho. B37: Chel W 3B 34
WOOD BURCOTE 3D 145
Woodburn Cl. CV5: Cov 3F 57
Wood Cl. B46: Col 5F 25
Woodclose Av. CV6: Cov 1K 57
Woodclose Rd. B37: F'bri 2A 34
Woodcock Cl. B94: Tan A 2B 90

Woodcote Av. CV8: Ken 2B 78
CV11: Nun 3G 23
Woodcote Dr. CV35: Leek W 1H 97
WOODCOTE GREEN 1A 142
Woodcote La. CV35: Leek W 1H 97
Woodcote Rd. CV32: Lea S 4C 98
CV34: Warw 7H 97
Woodcot Pk. Dr. CV37: Wilm 5H 113
Woodcot Pk. Homes Est. CV37: Wilm 5H 113
Wood Ct. CV2: Cov 7J 51
Woodcraft Cl. CV4: Tile H 5E 56
WOODEND 3D 145
WOOD END
B94 1C 90 (1C 143)
CV2 5J 51
CV7 7E 28 (3D 139)
CV9 2K 13 (2D 139)
Wood End Cft. CV4: Tile H 7C 56
Wood End La. B94: Tan A 1C 90
CV7: Fill 1E 38
Wood End Station (Rail) 1C 90
Woodfield Rd. CV5: Cov 7J 57
Woodford Cl. CV7: Ash G 1D 50
CV10: Nun 7H 21
WOODFORD HALSE 3C 145
Woodford La. CV10: Harts 7H 17
WOODGATE 2A 142
3A 138
Woodhall Cl. CV11: Nun 2C 32
Woodhams Rd. CV3: W'hall 5J 69
WOOD HAYES 1A 138
Wood Hill Ri. CV6: Cov 4D 50
Woodhouse Cl. CV3: Bin 7A 60
Woodhouse St. CV34: Warw 2F 101
Woodland Av. CV5: Cov 1K 67
Woodland Rd. CV8: Ken 2F 79
Woodlands, The CV9: Wood E 2K 13
CV10: Harts 2F 21
Woodlands Av. B46: Wat O 2B 24
Woodlands Cl. B78: Dord 5D 10
Woodlands Ct. CV3: Bin W 2F 71
CV5: Cov 7A 58
Woodlands Crematorium B46: Col 7D 24
Woodlands La. CV12: Bed 1E 40
Woodlands Pk. CV9: Hurl 7K 13
Woodlands Rd. CV3: Bin W 1F 71
CV12: Bed 2E 40
CV37: S Avon 2E 114
Woodlands Ter. B78: Dord 5D 10
Woodlands Way B37: Chel W 2D 34
Woodland Way B78: B'moor 2C 10
Wood La. B37: Mars G 5A 34
B95: Aston C 5F 113
CV7: Old A 2A 28
CV7: Shil 1E 52
CV10: Harts 3F 21
CV13: High H 1E 22
CV36: Cher 7G 133
Woodleigh Rd. CV4: W'wd H 2D 66
Woodloes Av. Nth. CV34: Warw 6G 97
Woodloes Av. Sth. CV34: Warw 6G 97
Woodloes La. CV34: Guys C 4G 97
CV35: Guys C 4G 97
WOODLOES PARK 5G 97
Woodman Ct. CV37: S Avon 3E 114
Woodmill Mdw. CV8: Ken 3E 78
Woodpecker Gro. B36: Cas B 5A 24
Woodridge Av. CV5: Alle 1D 56
Woodroffe Wlk. CV6: Longf 2G 51
Woodrow Dr. B98: Redd 1A 92
Woodrow Sth. B98: Redd 1A 92
Woodrow Wlk. B98: Redd 1A 92
Woodshires Rd. CV6: Longf 1F 51
Woodsia Cl. CV23: Brow 7K 65
Woodside CV7: Old A 3B 28
CV9: Gren 2G 15
Woodside Av. Nth. CV3: Cov 2K 67
Woodside Av. Sth. CV3: Finh 4K 67
Woodside Cl. CV9: Wood E 2K 13
Woodside Pk. CV8: Rytn D 3D 82
CV21: Rugby 3G 75
Woods Piece CV7: Ker E 7K 39
WOOD STANWAY 2A 146
WOODSTOCK 3D 147
Woodstock Rd. CV3: Cov 1D 68
CV11: Nun 3A 32
Wood St. CV9: Wood E 3J 13
CV10: Nun 7A 22
CV12: Bed 1G 41
CV21: Rugby 3G 75
CV32: Lea S 7E 98
CV37: S Avon 3E 136 (4E 114)
CV47: Sou 5H 107
Wood Ter. B96: Sam 6A 92
Woodview Rd. CV9: Ath 4D 16
Woodville Ct. CV34: Warw 1H 101
Woodville Rd. CV34: Warw 7G 97
Woodward Cl. CV31: W'nsh 6E 102
Woodward Ct. CV37: Snitt 6G 95
Woodway CV35: Bud, H Hill 7A 96
Woodway Av. CV35: H Mag 2B 100
Woodway Cl. CV2: W'grve S 6B 52
Woodway La. CV2: W'grve S 6B 52
WOODWAY PARK 5B 52
Woodway Wlk. CV2: W'grve S 6A 52
Woolgrove St. CV6: Cov 3G 51
Wooll St. CV21: Rugby 5G 75
WOOLMERE GREEN 2A 142
Woolpack, The CV34: Warw 2G 101
Woolpack Way CV9: Ath 3C 16
WOOLSCOTT 2B 144
Woolscott Rd. CV23: Gran 5H 105
CV23: W'hby 2F 105
Woolwich Rd. CV11: Bram 6H 33
WOOTTON 3D 147
Wootton Cl. CV37: S Avon 5J 115
Wootton Ct. CV32: Lea S 5D 98
Wootton Hall B95: Woot W 5J 93
Wootton Ri. B95: Woot W 5G 93
Wootton St. CV12: Bed 2J 41
WOOTTON WAWEN 5H 93 (2C 143)
Wootton Wawen Station (Rail) 5G 93
WORCESTER 3A 142
Worcester Cl. CV5: Alle 7E 48
Worcester Ct. CV6: Ald G 2H 51
Worcester Ho. B36: Cas B 4A 24
Worcester Pl. CV36: Ship S 4G 131
Worcester Rd. CV8: Ken 6F 79
Worcester St. CV21: Rugby 4G 75
Worcester Wlk. B37: Mars G 5A 34
WORDSLEY 3A 138
Wordsworth Av. CV34: Warw 3F 101
CV37: S Avon 6H 115
Wordsworth Dr. CV8: Ken 5G 79
Wordsworth Rd. CV2: Cov 3J 59
CV12: Bed 4K 41
CV22: Rugby 2E 86
Works Rd. B26: Birm A 3A 44
World of Shakespeare, The & Waterside Cinema 4H 137
WORLDS END 3C 139
WORMLEIGHTON 3B 144
Worsdell Cl. CV1: Cov 3B 58
Worsfold Cl. CV5: Alle 7E 48
Worths Way CV37: B'ton 2C 114
Wortley Cl. CV22: Caw 1A 86
Wrenbury Dr. CV6: Longf 2G 51
Wren St. CV2: Cov 4F 59
Wright Cl. B78: K'bry 6E 12
Wright St. CV1: Cov 2E 58
Wrigsham St. CV3: Cov 7J 135 (6D 58)
WROXALL 1D 143
Wroxall Dr. CV3: W'hall 3J 69
WROXTON 1D 147
Wulfstan Dr. CV47: Long I 3D 106
Wyatts Ct. CV12: Bed 2H 41
WYCHBOLD 2A 142
Wych-Elm Cl. CV22: Bil 7B 74
Wych Elm Dr. CV31: Lea S 3D 102
Wychwood Av. CV3: Finh 5C 68
Wychwood Cl. CV33: Bis T 5C 108
WYCK HILL 3A 146
WYCK RISSINGTON 3A 146
Wycliffe Gro. CV2: Cov 2H 59
Wycliffe Rd. W. CV2: Cov 2H 59
Wye Cl. CV12: Bulk 3D 42
CV32: Lill 4G 99
Wyegate Cl. B36: Cas B 4A 24
Wykeham Ho. *CV21: Brow 1J 75*
(off Millers Dale Cl.)
Wykeley Rd. CV2: Cov 3J 59
WYKEN 2K 59 (3A 140)
Wyken Av. CV2: Cov 2K 59
Wyken Cft. CV2: Cov 1K 59
Wyken Croft Nature Pk. 1K 59
Wyken Grange Rd. CV2: Cov 2J 59
WYKEN GREEN 7J 51
Wyken Lodge CV2: Cov 6K 51
Wyken Slough Nature Reserve 2J 51
Wyken Way CV2: Cov 2G 59
Wyke Rd. CV2: Cov 3J 59
WYKIN 2B 140
Wyld Ct. CV5: Cov 2F 57
WYLDE GREEN 2C 139
Wyley Rd. CV6: Cov 1A 58
Wyndshiels B46: Col 6G 25
Wynter Rd. CV22: Rugby 5D 74
Wyre La. CV37: Long M 2G 125
WYRE PIDDLE 3A 142
WYTHALL 1B 142
Wythburn Way CV21: Brow 1K 75
Wyver Cres. CV2: Cov 4J 59
Wyvern Cl. CV35: Welle 4G 117

Y

Yard, The CV37: Bear 7D 94
YARDLEY 3C 139
Yardley Cl. CV34: Warw 5H 97
Yardley St. CV1: Cov 3E 58
YARDLEY WOOD 3C 139
Yarmouth Grn. CV4: Tile H 7C 56
YARNINGALE COMMON 1B 94
Yarningale Rd. CV3: W'hall 3J 69
Yarranton Cl. CV37: S Avon 2D 114
Yarrow Cl. CV23: Brow 7K 65
Yates Av. CV21: N'bld A 2F 75
Yeats Cl. CV37: S Avon 7H 115
YELVERTOFT 1C 145
Yelvertoft Rd. CV23: Lilb 2J 77
Yelverton Rd. CV6: Cov 6C 50
Yeomanry Cl. CV34: Warw 1H 101
Yew Cl. CV3: Cov 7J 59
Yewdale Ct. CV2: W'grve S 5B 52
Yewdale Cres. CV2: W'grve S 5A 52
Yews, The CV12: Bed 3E 40
Yew Tree Cl. B94: Lapw 3J 91
Yew Tree Ct. CV9: Aus 6G 7
CV31: Lea S 3D 102
(off Tachbrook St.)
Yewtree Gdns. B95: Hen A 2G 93
Yew Tree Hill CV23: Brin 4C 62
Yew Trees, The B95: Hen A 2H 93
Yew Wlk. B37: Chel W 3B 34
York Av. CV9: Ath 2D 16
(not continuous)
CV12: Bed 3K 41
York Cl. B80: Stud 3B 92
CV3: W'hall 3J 69
Yorklea Cft. B37: F'bri 3A 34
Yorkminster Dr. B37: Chel W 3C 34
York Rd. CV31: Lea S 7D 98
York St. CV1: Cov 5B 58
CV11: Nun 7B 22
CV21: Rugby 5F 75
York Wlk. CV31: Lea S 7D 98
Youell Ct. CV3: Bin 6C 60
Young Cl. CV34: Warw 3D 100
Yule Rd. CV2: Cov 2K 59

Z

Zorrina Cl. CV10: Nun 6G 21

HOSPITALS and HOSPICES covered by this atlas.

N.B. Where Hospitals and Hospices are not named on the map, the reference given is for the road in which they are situated.

ALCESTER HOSPITAL 4C **112**
Kinwarton Road
ALCESTER
B49 6PX
Tel: 01789 762470

ALEXANDRA HOSPITAL, THE 1B **92**
Woodrow Drive
REDDITCH
B98 7UB
Tel: 01527 503030

BRAMCOTE HOSPITAL 5G **33**
Lutterworth Road
NUNEATON
CV11 6QL
Tel: 024 76388200

COVENTRY & WARWICKSHIRE HOSPITAL 3D **58** (1J **135**)
Stoney Stanton Road
COVENTRY
CV1 4FH
Tel: 024 76224055

GEORGE ELIOT HOSPITAL 2H **31**
College Street
NUNEATON
CV10 7DJ
Tel: 024 76351351

GULSON HOSPITAL 5E **58**
Gulson Road
COVENTRY
CV1 2HR
Tel: 024 76552225

HILLCREST HOSPITAL 1B **92**
Quinneys Lane
REDDITCH
B98 7WG
Tel: 01527 500575

HOSPITAL OF ST CROSS 7H **75**
Barby Road
RUGBY
CV22 5PX
Tel: 01788 572831

MARY ANN EVANS HOSPICE 2G **31**
George Eliot Hospital
College Street
NUNEATON
CV10 7DJ
Tel: 024 76865440

MERIDEN BMI HOSPITAL, THE 1C **60**
Walsgrave Hospital site
Clifford Bridge Road
COVENTRY
CV2 2DX

MIRAH HOUSE DAY HOSPITAL 6B **22**
Manor Court Avenue
NUNEATON
CV11 5HX
Tel: 024 76374434

MYTON HAMLET HOSPICE 1K **101**
Myton Lane
WARWICK
CV34 6PX
Tel: 01926 492518

NUNEATON PRIVATE BMI HOSPITAL 3J **31**
132 Coventry Road
NUNEATON
CV10 7AD
Tel: 024 76357500

ROYAL LEAMINGTON SPA REHABILITATION HOSPITAL 4C **102**
Heathcote Lane
WARWICK
CV34 6SR
Tel: 01926 317700

RUGBY MYTON DAY HOSPICE 7H **75**
Barby Road
RUGBY
CV22 5PY
Tel: 01788 550085

ST MICHAEL'S HOSPITAL (WARWICK) 7F **97**
St. Michael's Road
WARWICK
CV34 5QW
Tel: 01926 406789

SHAKESPEARE HOSPICE 4B **114**
Church Lane
Shottery
STRATFORD-UPON-AVON
CV37 9UL
Tel: 01789 266852

STRATFORD UPON AVON HOSPITAL 4E **114** (1C **136**)
Arden Street
STRATFORD-UPON-AVON
CV37 6NX
Tel: 01926 495321

UNIVERSITY HOSPITAL WALSGRAVE 1D **60**
Open Mid 2006
Clifford Bridge Road
COVENTRY
CV2 2DX
Tel: 024 76602020

WALSGRAVE HOSPITAL 1C **60**
Clifford Bridge Road
COVENTRY
CV2 2DX
Tel: 024 76602020

WARWICK HOSPITAL 7G **97**
Lakin Road
WARWICK
CV34 5BW
Tel: 01926 495321

WARWICKSHIRE NUFFIELD HOSPITAL, THE 2C **98**
Old Milverton Lane
LEAMINGTON SPA
CV32 6RW
Tel: 01926 427971

The representation on the maps of a road, track or footpath is no evidence of the existence of a right of way.

The Grid on this map is the National Grid taken from Ordnance Survey mapping with the permission of the Controller of Her Majesty's Stationery Office.